# Neurolinguistics

What biological factors make human communication possible? How do we process and understand language? How does brain damage affect these mechanisms, and what can this tell us about how language is organized in the brain? The field of neurolinguistics seeks to answer these questions, which are crucial to linguistics, psychology and speech pathology alike. Drawing on examples from everyday language, this textbook introduces the central topics in neurolinguistics: speech recognition, word and sentence structure, meaning, and discourse – in both 'normal' speakers and those with language disorders. It moves on to provide a balanced discussion of key areas of debate such as modularity and the 'language areas' of the brain, 'connectionist' versus 'symbolic' modelling of language processing, and the nature of linguistic and mental representations. Making accessible over half a century of scientific and linguistic research, and containing extensive study questions, it will be welcomed by all those interested in the relationship between language and the brain.

JOHN C. L. INGRAM is Senior Lecturer on the Linguistics Program at the University of Queensland. He has published widely on speech and language disorders, sound change in second language acquisition, phonetic variation in Australian English, connected speech processes, acoustic phonetics, foreign accent phenomena and forensic speaker identification.

CAMBRIDGE TEXTBOOKS IN LINGUISTICS

*General editors:* P. AUSTIN, J. BRESNAN, B. COMRIE, S. CRAIN,
W. DRESSLER, C. EWEN, R. LASS, D. LIGHTFOOT, K. RICE,
I. ROBERTS, S. ROMAINE, N. V. SMITH

# Neurolinguistics

An Introduction to Spoken Language Processing and its Disorders

# Neurolinguistics
## An Introduction to Spoken Language Processing and its Disorders

JOHN C. L. INGRAM

*University of Queensland, Australia*

CAMBRIDGE UNIVERSITY PRESS
Cambridge, New York, Melbourne, Madrid, Cape Town, Singapore, São Paulo, Delhi

Cambridge University Press
The Edinburgh Building, Cambridge CB2 8RU, UK

Published in the United States of America by Cambridge University Press, New York

www.cambridge.org
Information on this title: www.cambridge.org/9780521796408

First published 2007
Reprinted 2008

Printed in the United Kingdom at the University Press, Cambridge

*A catalogue record for this publication is available from the British Library*

ISBN 978-0-521-79190-8 hardback
ISBN 978-0-521-79640-8 paperback

For Carolyn

# Contents

# Figures

# Tables

# Preface and acknowledgements

This book is intended as a self-contained introduction to the study of the language–brain relationship for students of cognitive science, linguistics and speech pathology. The essentially interdisciplinary nature of the subject matter posed considerable difficulties for the author and will likely do so also for the reader. So please be warned. Despite my considerable efforts to keep the pathways open between the villages of the cognate disciplines concerned, the jungle is everywhere and its capacity for re-growth is relentless.

As appropriate for an introductory text, the book is accessible to a wide readership. Foundational concepts and issues on the nature of language, language processing and brain language disorders (aphasiology) are presented in the first four chapters. This section of the book should be complementary with many stand-alone introductory courses in linguistics, psychology or neuroanatomy. Subsequent sections deal with successively 'higher' levels of language processing and their respective manifestations in brain damage: speech perception (chapters 5–8); word structure and meaning (lexical processing and its disorders; chapters 9–11); syntax and syntactic disorder (agrammatism; chapters 12–14); discourse and the language of thought disorder (chapters 15–16), followed by a brief final chapter, speculating on unsolved problems and possible ways forward. Each major section of the book begins by posing the principal questions at an intuitive level which is hopefully accessible to all. The often quite specialized research methods by which answers to these questions have been sought are then introduced, in a selective review of the literature.

The field of relevant studies was broad to begin with and has grown vastly since the pioneering studies in psycholinguistics, neurolinguistics and computational models of language processing were undertaken in the 1970s and surveyed with such flair and scholarship in Caplan's *Neurolinguistics and linguistic aphasiology: An introduction* (1987). It would be an impossible task to update Caplan's seminal text in a single volume. Yet that was one of the quixotic goals that originally motivated the writing of this book. So, in each of the major topics that are taken up, the aim is to bring the reader to a view of the problems and issues that animate contemporary research. In this sense, the book is intended as an 'introduction' to the field and as such may serve as a resource for an advanced undergraduate or first-year graduate seminar.

It is difficult to date precisely the origins of this book and therefore to duly acknowledge the many people who have contributed towards it. But officially it began life as a collaboration with Helen Chenery, under the enthusiastic mentorship of Christine Bartels of Cambridge University Press. Helen's ghost-like presence can be detected in the persistence of the authorial 'we', a writing habit that I evidently found hard to break and a device that I may be guilty of deploying at times, to persuade the reluctant reader to my point of view on matters of deep uncertainty. I am grateful to both of them for their support and wise editorial counsel, especially through the difficult early stages, where something is taking shape, but God knows what the outcome will be and the enormity of the task ahead is beginning to sink in.

Neil Smith read the entire manuscript – not once, but twice – and offered many invaluable and always tactfully put suggestions. I am greatly indebted also to Lucy Carolan, whose impeccable stylistic judgement greatly improved the readability of the text. Max Coltheart and Stephen Crain read selected chapters and offered cogent feedback. Thanks particularly to the students who read drafts of these chapters and in some cases showed in their term essays how the story could be better told. Teaching can be a humbling experience and nothing motivates hard thinking like the blank stares that can accompany the presentation of one's latest pearls of wisdom. Most importantly, I would like to thank my wife, whose name appears in the dedication, for putting up with a distracted fool for several years of late nights and the squeaking chair in the wee hours.

# Note on the text

Words in bold type are explained in the Glossary (pp. 380–6 below).

PART I

# Foundational concepts and issues

# 1 Introduction and overview

## Introduction

This book is about language processing in the human brain and, more specifically, what happens to spoken language when certain areas of the brain are damaged. Language processing is what takes place whenever we understand or produce speech; a mundane task, but one of extraordinary complexity, whose mysteries have baffled some of the greatest minds across the centuries.

Neurolinguistics is the technical term for this field, introduced into academic usage by Harry Whitaker (1971), who founded the leading journal that bears this title. As Whitaker noted at the time, it is a key assumption of neurolinguistics that 'a proper and adequate understanding of language depends upon correlating information from a variety of fields concerned with the structure and function of both language and brain, minimally neurology and linguistics'. Today, some thirty years later, it seems necessary to add 'cognition' or cognitive science to the list of minimally necessary disciplines. A well-articulated cognitive science is needed to provide the hoped for integration of two otherwise very different fields of study: language and neurobiology.

Considerable progress and a vast body of research have accumulated since then. Yet leading advocates of the cognitive science perspective on language as a biologically grounded human ability (such as Chomsky, Pinker and Deacon, to mention just three) disagree on some fundamental questions. To what extent are our language learning capabilities 'hard-wired' into the human brain and unique to the species? How is 'innate linguistic competence' actually deployed in language learning? Is it closely bound to specific stages of neurological maturation or can it be re-invoked in maturity for second language acquisition or recovery of language competence after neurological damage? To what extent are the component skills activated in language processing separable from one another in function or in actual locus of operation in the brain? To what extent are language abilities separable from thinking or other mental activities?

Assuming at least some 'modularity' of language and its supporting cognitive, perceptual and motor competencies, a number of highly practical questions arise. Can recovery of language following brain injury be facilitated by therapy intervention strategies targeted at specific retained abilities in order to work around lost competencies, or can those lost competencies themselves be recovered?

3

Despite the controversies and profound uncertainties concerning the best way forward, there are good reasons for believing that a special relationship exists between human language on the one hand, and what makes human brains different from those of other mammals or our close primate relatives on the other. In this chapter we offer some arguments intended to establish a direct link between the brain and language, through an appeal to the concept of co-evolution of brain and language (Deacon, 1997a): the idea that language abilities arose as both a consequence and a cause of recent and rapid evolutionary brain changes, resulting in the emergence of homo sapiens. In chapters 2 and 3 we invite you to evaluate the language–brain relationship for yourself, as we describe the language faculty in broad outline from the separate perspectives of the linguist (chapter 2) and the aphasiologist (chapter 3). Linguists are trained to analyse patterns of language production and usage, with the aim of unravelling the complex code which enables speakers and listeners to map between sound and meaning. Aphasiologists observe the great variety of communication disorders that can arise as a consequence of damage to the language areas of the brain by strokes, tumours or traumatic injury. By and large, the classical studies of aphasia were conducted by neurologists and neuropsychologists who had no specialized linguistic training. Similarly, linguists formulated their theories of human language independently of any serious considerations of language loss in aphasia. Thus, Whitaker's (1971) assertion that progress in the study of language depends on some successful synergy between linguistics and neurology has always been controversial, and so the introductory chapters of this book should be regarded as a first approximation at defining a 'problem space' – the language–brain interface. In subsequent chapters, we explore in detail the various stages of language processing, from the decoding of phonological targets in the perception of speech, to word recognition, morphological analysis, syntactic parsing, semantic interpretation and understanding discourse. We consider the production of language and production disorders in aphasia only insofar as they throw light upon the nature of the brain's language processing mechanisms. At the 'higher' levels of language processing, a clear distinction between the mechanisms underlying language comprehension and language production is difficult to maintain, despite the fact that the task demands imposed upon listeners and speakers are very different. Speakers and listeners clearly must share a common linguistic knowledge base – a grammar in the broadest sense of the term – but just how that tacit knowledge is deployed in comprehending and speaking is a moot point.

Our concern is primarily with language comprehension and its disorders. However, the neural mechanisms that the brain has evolved for language processing are based, at least in part, upon novel synergies that have evolved between the motor control and the auditory perceptual systems. These synergies are needed for imitation learning of rapid gestural sequences for speech production and perception. Consider, for example, the utility of a vocal communication system that required 20-plus seconds to say: '*Look out, you are about to step on a snake!*'

We shall consider the evidence for the neural synergy between speech production and perception in subsequent chapters.

Language is used not only to convey our thoughts and feelings to others, but also to represent them to ourselves. But thinking is not equivalent to talking to oneself, and the linguistic expressions with which we clothe our thoughts are merely signposts to meaning, not explicit representations of those meanings. Linguistic expressions are under-determined with respect to the message the speaker intends to convey.

Trying to understand how the brain processes language may always lie just beyond the realm of scientific feasibility. But for the sake of thousands of people every year who suffer the traumatic effects of language loss through aphasia we are obliged to make our best effort. Cognitive neurolinguistics has its origins about as far back as one chooses to trace them, from Aristotelean speculations in the third century BC on the nature of words and ideas, or from Broca's (1861) famous observation that 'the seat of articulate language lies in the left posterior frontal convolution', or from Chomsky's programmatic reformulation of the goals of linguistics as a branch of cognitive science in the 1960s. But the most significant developments in the field have occurred in only the past three decades. Psycholinguists and neuroscientists have devised behavioural and neuroimaging techniques to fractionate the different stages of language processing: from the instant the auditory system reacts to the acoustic signal of speech, to the few hundred milliseconds that it takes to complete linguistic decoding of the speaker's message. Most recently, powerful neuroimaging techniques have potentially greatly enhanced our powers of observing 'real-time' language processing. The extent to which this potential will be realized in the near future largely depends upon how well the new imaging techniques can be harnessed to the 'on-line'[1] methods and theories of language processing developed by psycholinguistics over the preceding three decades. There is cause for cautious optimism that we may be on the threshold of new insights into language and the human brain–language relationship, which enables us to communicate with one another a range of ideas, worries, conjectures, desires or demands, unknown to other species, regardless of whether we believe them capable of entertaining such things.

## Co-evolution of language and the brain

It is uncontroversial, in scientific circles at least, that the human brain has undergone very rapid growth in recent evolution. The brain has doubled in size in less than one million years. The cause of this 'runaway' growth (Wills, 1993)

---

[1] 'On-line' refers to observational methods that are intended to capture sentence processing as it takes place in 'real time', as distinct from 'off-line' observational methods, which are not time-sensitive, that tap into comprehension or production processes after the fact, or after they have taken place. Grammaticality judgements or judgements of semantic well-formedness are examples of 'off-line' tasks.

is a matter of conjecture and endless debate. A strong case can be made that the expansion of the brain was a consequence of the development of spoken language and the survival advantage that possessing a language confers. The areas of the brain that underwent greatest development appear to be specifically associated with language: the frontal lobes and the junction of the parietal, occipital and temporal lobes (the POT junction – more of this later).

It is easy, perhaps all too easy, to reconstruct plausible scenarios illustrating the survival advantages that possession of a hands-free auditory/vocal means of communication with the symbolic power to represent almost any imaginable situation would confer on a social group. Perhaps it was the superior linguistic abilities of homo sapiens, with brains and vocal tracts better adapted for speech and language, that led to the rapid displacement and extinction of the Neanderthals in Europe, some 40,000 years ago (Mellars, 1996). Language is of such importance in our daily lives and culture that it is almost impossible to imagine how our species could survive without it.

But perhaps the most surprising thing about the evolution of language and the brain structures required to support it is – as indicated earlier – how rapidly they were acquired by our species. It is well known that quite dramatic phenotypical changes can take place under adaptation pressures in relatively short periods of evolutionary time. However, there appears to be no parallel in other species to the rapid increase in cranial capacity accompanied by the signs of an evolving material culture that one finds in the human archaeological record. What drove this massive yet selective increase in brain tissue, confined mainly to the cerebral cortex and to some regions more than others? According to the co-evolution hypothesis, it was the voracious computational requirements of a symbolic representational system, i.e. of a language. It is not difficult to appreciate this point. Just look up from the book and cast an eye around the myriad of recognizably distinct objects in your immediate field of view. A large proportion of them have names. All the others can effectively be provided with names by verbal constructions such as: 'low radiation energy sticker' for the object fixed to the screen monitor casing of my PC. Language, as every language user knows, involves a kind of doubling of our perceptual universe. For every object of experience, there is at least a name or a naming construction to represent that object. Once the germ of a representational system has implanted itself in the mind/brain, there is no quarantining its spread to the whole realm of imaginable experience. This is evident from the period of explosive vocabulary growth that occurs in normal human infants around two to three years of age, for which there is no parallel in even the most loquacious of the signing chimps that have been studied (Savage-Rumbaugh and Levin, 1994). The voracious growth of a representational system is also movingly illustrated in the diary of Helen Keller, the remarkable woman, rendered blind and deaf in infancy, who suddenly discovered the representational function of tactile signs at an age when she was old enough to consciously appreciate their communicative significance. Everything suddenly required a name.

While the origins of language remain obscure, the co-evolution hypothesis claims that once the seeds of a symbolic representational system were sown, the brain responded with a vigorous and unprecedented increase in its processing and storage capacity. According to the co-evolution hypothesis, the brain as a system which supports representational computation cannot remain 'a little bit pregnant' with language. 'Representational computation' is perhaps an awkward way of saying 'thinking with language'. Representational computation conveys the idea that thinking supported by linguistic expressions involves a second-order level of manipulation, not just of objects, events or states of affairs, as perceived or imagined in 'the mind's eye', but also the manipulation of *symbolic representations* of those objects, events or states of affairs. Thus, perception and episodic memory provide a first-order 'internal' representation of the 'external' world. But language users have access to a second-order and publicly shareable level of symbolic representation, whereby objects of perception are coded as linguistic expressions.

In addition to linking the evolution of language to symbolic reasoning – an idea which has a respectable philosophical pedigree in European philosophy (von Humboldt, 1999 (1836); Cassirer, 1953, 1962; Werner and Caplan, 1963) though not widespread acceptance in contemporary cognitive science – the co-evolution hypothesis asserts that a quantal increase in the brain's processing capacity was required to accommodate this second-order representational system. Also, that although the evolutionary adaptation of the brain took place in incremental steps, the pace of change was such as to produce a qualitative new step in speciation. Furthermore, the co-evolution hypothesis asserts, controversially, that thinking-with-language is a unique facility of human brains. Deacon's (1997a) book-length exposition of the co-evolution hypothesis is a bold and controversial idea. It has met with a very mixed reception from linguists, depending on their theoretical orientation (Hudson, 2001; Hurford, 1998; Poeppel, 1997). As a scientific hypothesis, it is rather too difficult to prove or to refute. We offer it here primarily to set you thinking along the paths we wish to explore in this book. Norman Geschwind in the 1960s (see chapter 3) was the first to offer a clear account of how recently evolved cortical structures that distinguish humans from primates enabled the formation of extensive networks of cross-modal associations, which in his view provided the neural-computational basis for vocabulary formation, and hence the evolution of a natural system of symbolic representation.

## An alternative view of co-evolution

Another reason for believing that the joint study of brain–language relationships will be productive derives from the study of language itself and how it is acquired. Language, as we shall presently discover (if you have not done so already), is the most complex of human artefacts,[2] re-invented by each successive generation of language learners, who are quite unaware of the enormity

---

[2] artefact: tool or human construction. Language is a cognitive rather than a physical artefact; a vessel for containing or carrying meanings.

of their accomplishment. Linguists like Noam Chomsky have long argued that young children can only accomplish the remarkable feat of learning their native language by virtue of inheriting some specialized neural machinery specifically designed for that task. The reference here is to Chomsky's *principles and parameters* (P&P) model of grammar (Haegeman, 1991; Radford, 1997). The principles are structural properties to which all languages supposedly conform, constituting a *universal grammar* (UG). The parameters define the ways languages can vary from one another. The idea is that if a large part of the structural complexity of human language is pre-programmed into structural principles, then language learners have only to discover the parameter settings appropriate for their language community. Thus, the 'principles' set limits on how human languages may vary, confining natural languages to a restrictive set of possible types, thereby narrowing the 'search space' of the language learner. Furthermore, if a special 'parameter setting' mechanism for language learning can be invoked, then it is easier to see how first language acquisition could be under the control of 'instinctive' maturational mechanisms, by analogy to such behaviours as nest building in birds or 'learning to walk' in mammals. In this way, a language faculty can be conceived as a special-purpose module of the mind/brain, dedicated to the demands of spoken language communication and acquired through special learning mechanisms linked to the maturation of perceptual, motor and cognitive systems of the infant brain.

Clearly a great deal of investigative groundwork is needed to isolate the principles and parameters that underlie natural languages and to then show how such principles and parameters may be incorporated into a model of first language acquisition.[3] But this is precisely what linguists and psycholinguists in the Chomskian paradigm seek to do. We cannot evaluate the P&P theory until we have elaborated at least a first approximation model of language structure, which we will begin to do in chapter 3, and elaborate with respect to a specific theory of agrammatism in chapter 14. The P&P theory of language is in fundamental respects antithetical to the idea, advanced in the previous section, that language is an undifferentiated 'symbolic system'. Nevertheless, P&P theory also provides an alternative formulation of the co-evolution hypothesis that the emergence of natural language drove the most recent 'runaway' stage of evolution of the human brain, albeit a formulation with a very different conceptual foundation as a modular 'faculty of language'.

We briefly sketch here in somewhat stark terms some differences in perspective between language as a symbolic system (as expounded by Deacon, 1997a) and the P&P theory of language, which represents, if any one position can, the textbook orthodoxy of linguistic theory. We will elaborate the major theoretical issues currently in dispute in chapter 4, in the attempt to build a biologically grounded theory of language processing. Deacon's model of language has been

---

[3] Second language learning appears to be different in fundamental respects from first language acquisition. Parameter setting may only be available as a window of opportunity during the critical period of first language learning; or once set, parameters may not be re-set.

described as linguistically naive. This may be true, but in adopting positions opposed to the prevailing orthodoxy in linguistic theory, he finds allies in alternative models of language and language learning which have psycholinguistic credibility.

By enumerating the differences between the two perspectives we will generate some clear expectations as to where to look for significant theoretical alternatives, for contending hypotheses about how the brain might organize itself for language. Firstly, there is the issue of **modularity** which expresses itself at the level of both broad and fine-grained mental architecture. At the level of broad mental architecture, Deacon's view of language as a symbolic system draws no clear distinction between cognition and language processing. By contrast, while the P&P model is not very explicit on how the distinction should be drawn, it is recognized that there is a necessity to do so, if language is to be consistently viewed as a modular component in an integrated cognitive system. The existence of mental disorders specific to language processing (aphasia and aphasic disorders) would seem to argue in favour of modularity in the broad. But as we shall see, the history of aphasia is a battlefield littered with fallen standards of both houses in this unresolved dispute.

At the fine-grained level, within language itself, Deacon's 'symbolic system' of language also draws no hard and fast distinctions between components of linguistic competence, such as the computational aspects (syntax) and the encyclopaedic (lexical) aspects of the speaker's internal grammar. But in the P&P model, as indicated previously, the principles that govern structure building operations in the syntactic component of the grammar are quite distinct from the constraints that apply in the lexicon in word formation. We might expect, therefore, that language disorders in aphasia might fractionate along fault lines between modular components of the language faculty as described by P&P theory. Again, the modular view appears to be supported on superficial inspection of the syndrome of 'agrammatism' in Broca's aphasia compared with the pattern of lexico-semantic impairment observed in Wernicke's aphasia. But on closer inspection the association between the linguistic competence model and patterns of aphasic performance turn out to be deeply problematical, as we shall see. The P&P theory has been productive of a great deal of research into aphasia in recent years, but so too have non-modular language processing theories based on neural network models explicitly framed in opposition to the perceived prevailing linguistic orthodoxy.

Related but distinct from the question of modularity are issues of *learnability* and how language abilities are embedded in the biological makeup of brain's capacity for language. Deacon's theory postulates a somewhat elusive propensity for 'symbolic processing' underlying our unique linguistic capabilities. He is at pains to demonstrate that some apes, like the celebrated Kanzi (Savage-Rumbaugh and Levin, 1994), have this capacity also, to a limited extent. But this is quite a different standard of proof from showing that human infants (or the infants of some other species) have the capacity to spontaneously acquire languages whose syntax conforms to specific properties specified by a theory of UG, and, equally critically, an *inability* to learn the grammars of artificial languages whose syntactic rules violate principles of UG (Smith, Tsimpli and Ouhalla, 1993).

Or to consider an example much closer to the themes of this book: a theory of UG might be expected to predict that at least some acquired language disorders in aphasia should reflect specific patterns of language impairment that are more or less isomorphic with the specific components of a grammar competence model. Grodzinsky's (2000) trace deletion (or chain disruption) hypothesis of agrammatism is such a case in point, which we will consider in detail in chapter 14.

Chomsky and the generative grammarians may be correct. On the other hand, we should also consider the possibility that human languages are just too complex, too diverse, or too contrary, to be reducible to a core set of principles and parameters. However, if the co-evolution hypothesis (in either of its competing versions) is correct, then we might hope to find independent confirmation of its validity by studying what Eric Lenneberg (1967), another pioneer in the field, called the *biological foundations of language*. This involves examining neurological structures that underpin language comprehension and production, correlating language acquisition with brain maturation in infancy, investigating loss of language caused by damage to various brain regions, and correlating the evolution of different brain structures across the species with the evolution of language. Some progress has been made in these endeavours. In this book we will focus primarily on two sources of evidence: (a) what can be learned about language and the brain from psycholinguistic and neurolinguistic studies of language processing in 'normal' language users (such as, dear reader, you and I), and (b) from clinical and experimental studies of those who have suffered neurological disorders or diseases which have impaired some or all aspects of their spoken language.

## Language areas in the brain

Language is predominantly lateralized to the left hemisphere in the vast majority of people, even the majority of left-handers. While the functional asymmetries of the left and right hemispheres are well known and have been much debated in the popular and technical literature (Hellige, 1993; Chiarello, 1998), anatomically, the structures of the brain appear to be quite symmetrical. But the one known region where a structural asymmetry has been found occurs in the *planum temporale*, which is part of *Wernicke's* area, the second language area, known after its discoverer Karl Wernicke in 1874. The planum temporale of the left temporal lobe was found to be larger than its right hemisphere counterpart in 84 per cent of cases (Galaburda, Lemay, Kemper and Geschwind, 1978). The reason why this rather unique asymmetry was not observed by previous generations of anatomists, though it is quite visible to the naked eye, is that the planum temporale is located within the fold of the sylvian fissure, out of sight from surface inspection of the temporal lobe.

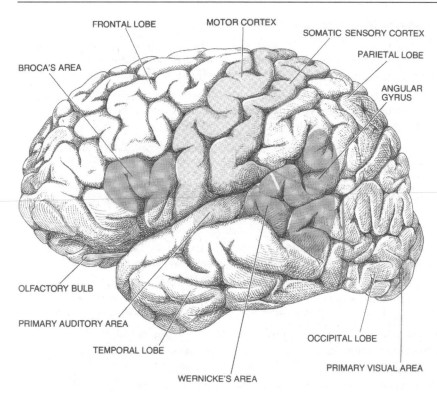

FRONTAL LOBE          MOTOR CORTEX

SOMATIC SENSORY CORTEX

PARIETAL LOBE

BROCA'S AREA

ANGULAR
GYRUS

OLFACTORY BULB

PRIMARY AUDITORY AREA

OCCIPITAL LOBE

TEMPORAL LOBE

PRIMARY VISUAL AREA

WERNICKE'S AREA

Figure 1.1  *The cerebral cortex: the language areas and major anatomical landmarks*

The functional significance of this long-overlooked cerebral asymmetry is no doubt related to the fact that the planum temporale overlaps with Wernicke's area.

## Aphasia as evidence of the brain's representation of language

The study of aphasia, or the loss of language functions caused by damage to the 'language areas' of the brain, has been our major historical source of evidence for the study of brain–language relationships. We can trace the clinical study of brain–language relationships to Paul Broca's (1861) famous discovery of the language area that bears his name, located in the posterior region of the left frontal lobe of the cerebral cortex. The precise role of Broca's area in normal language functioning remains controversial to this day (see chapter 9).

Disease or injury to the recently evolved regions of the cerebral cortex may be revealing of how language is organized in the brain. We can have various types of injury. Focal damage to a limited region may occur as a consequence of a 'stroke', when a blood vessel bursts or an artery is blocked and there is oxygen deprivation to some local region of the brain. Alternatively, damage may be more diffuse, such as occurs in Alzheimer's disease. Here the disease process affects the inter-connectivity of nerve cells over a wide area of the cortex, usually starting in the medial regions of the temporal lobe (affecting word retrieval) and later spreading to other areas of the cortex and affecting language more profoundly (particularly semantic processing). Focal brain damage is more likely to affect specific language functions. The classical nineteenth-century discoveries of the language centres were made as a result of observing the effects of focal brain lesions.

## The language faculty (localization and modularity)

Are different aspects of language located in different regions of the brain (the **localization** hypothesis) or are language abilities distributed throughout the whole brain (the holistic view)? The localization hypothesis, you may know, goes back to the pre-scientific theories of *phrenology* (Gall, 1809), the study of skull shapes, which tried to associate mental abilities with bumps on the skull.

Phrenology has long been discredited. Bumps on the outer surface of the skull are not a reliable guide to the relative size or shape of the underlying brain regions. Nor is there solid evidence that local variations in size and shape of the cerebral cortex can be associated with mental abilities or psychological traits.[4] This is a *neurolinguistic* question. It bears upon the relationship between the brain and language functions. Can different components of linguistic competence be separated out from one another and be seen to function more or less autonomously (the modularity hypothesis)? Or is it the case that different aspects of language and language-related cognitive functions interact with one another to such an extent that they cannot be separated (the interactionist position)? This is a *psycholinguistic* question. It bears on the relationship between language and mind (or language and cognition).

We shall explore both of these issues in some depth in subsequent chapters as we investigate different aspects of the complex chain of events that underlie spoken communication and the disruptions to it that can occur when the brain machinery is damaged. There are many unsolved mysteries involving the relationship between physiological processes of the brain and psychological processes of the mind which constantly threaten to derail our inquiry. Most of what we call *language processing* takes place beyond the accessibility of conscious awareness. We fancy that we are aware of what we are trying to say as we speak, and we are at least partially aware of what others are saying to us, because we can frequently

---

[4] On the other hand, convolutions of cerebral tissue and blood vessels may leave indentations on the *inside* of the skull that may be used as archaeological evidence of brain evolution (Jerison, 1990). Also, the search to correlate regional brain size with mental abilities continues, illustrated by the widely publicized recent report that Einstein's brain, while unremarkable in other respects, was found to be unusually convoluted and 15 per cent larger than 100 control cases in both left and right inferior parietal lobes, an area 'associated with spatial and mathematical reasoning ability' (Witelson, Kigar and Harvey, 1999).

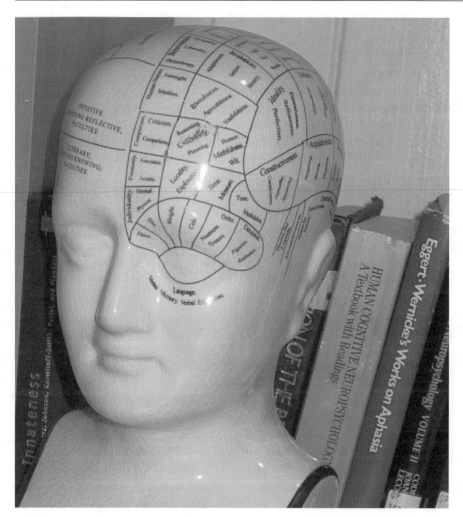

Figure 1.2  *Phrenology model, according to L. N. Fowler. (1811–1896)*

anticipate what they will say next. But for reasons of time-pressure if no other, we cannot possibly consciously monitor more than a small fraction of the highest levels of decision making and control that are involved in spoken communication. For a start, consider that something of the order of a hundred individual muscles must be coordinated, within an order of hundredths of a second precision, when we speak; or consider that individual words from a mental lexicon of tens of thousands of items must be accessible *in real time* when we listen to speech, and that complex syntactic structures must be constructed on the fly as words are put together – again, in real time, as sentence meanings are extracted from word strings.

It is not hard to establish convincing links between the evolution of the brain and language. Classical studies of aphasia have provided suggestive models of how language abilities may be organized in the brain, though the evidence is by no means conclusive or internally consistent. It is very hard to declare with any degree of confidence that such and such a theory has been shown to be correct or incorrect about how the brain processes language. Faced with the complexity of spoken language processing and the more tangible and therefore more astonishing complexity of the brain, and given the still feeble investigative tools at our disposal (though great strides seem to have been made in the last two decades), any theory of language processing that we can currently envisage is almost certain to be demonstrably wrong beyond the very short horizons of the foreseeable future. If current trends of technical and scientific advances continue, all currently competitive theories of language processing will probably seem ridiculously simplistic from a vantage point not far into the new millennium. Faced with this dilemma, we have not tried too hard to present the reader with a theoretically coherent account of language processing, or to resolve conflicts and contradictions between contending theories. We will be well satisfied simply to expose them clearly for your scrutiny.

## Study questions for chapter 1

1.    What is 'language processing' about? What does *on-line* language processing entail?

2.    What does it mean to say that language (or language processing) is a 'modular' ability? How would you establish that a given ability is modular?

3.    What does the 'co-evolution of brain and language' hypothesis claim?

4.    Explain what is meant by a 'second-order' representation of experience and how it relates to the co-evolution hypothesis.

5.    How could one test the coevolution of brain and language hypothesis?

6.    Is the co-evolution hypothesis falsifiable?

7.    Is falsifiability a good or a bad thing in a scientific theory? Justify your position.

8.    How does the linguistic concept of 'universal grammar' speak to the concept of a 'modular' faculty of language?

# 2 Aspects of linguistic competence

## Introduction

In the previous chapter, we described language as 'the most complex of human artefacts'. In this chapter we shall flesh out this claim with an overview of the major components of the linguistic system from the perspective of the linguist. Broadly speaking, any language may be viewed from three complementary perspectives: (a) as an internalized body of 'tacit' knowledge, (b) as a social construction or set of conventions shared by a language community or (c) as a natural object 'out there' in the external world (the '**E-language**'). The internal view of language (or '**I-language**', as it is sometimes referred to by Chomskian linguistics) is clearly the most relevant perspective for the concerns of this book. The I-language consists of the personal knowledge base that each speaker of the language carries around in his/her head as to how meanings or intentions may be encoded in linguistic expressions. Language users rely on their I-language to interpret or decode other speakers' linguistic expressions and to encode their own meanings in the expressions that they produce. The I-language is usually thought of as a personal dictionary of word meanings and rules for utterance construction; an internal grammar, which we know how to use but cannot easily describe.

Because each speaker acquires language under unique circumstances, I-language grammars may vary somewhat from one speaker to another, in ways that are probably mostly inconsequential for communication between members of a speech community. It is held almost as an article of faith by many linguists that humans share a universal capacity for language learning which ensures equality of outcome in terms of acquisition of an I-language grammar. However, there is typically a range of linguistic diversity in any community of speakers. The success or failure of any given communicative encounter may be affected not only by the degree to which the I-language grammars of the interlocutors match one another but also by a host of extra-linguistic performance factors: lapses in attention, memory block, momentary distractions, the lingering fog of last night's celebration, etc. Trying to decide whether some singular lapse or habitual pattern of impaired language comprehension or production is caused by some I-language idiosyncrasy or deficiency, or whether it is better explained by other accompanying mental processes is a familiar diagnostic dilemma for speech and language pathologists and for psycholinguists attempting to construct theories of 'language performance'. This will also be a recurrent theme throughout this book. In recent years, psycholinguistics and neurocognitive scientists have developed an arsenal of techniques intended to monitor on-line language processing. However, in this chapter we are concerned less with questions of process and more with questions of content. We shall try to characterize the contents of I-language grammar – what are linguistic expressions made from (how many levels of organization are needed to describe human languages, the nature of word classes, the recursive nature of grammatical rules that underlie the generative power of human languages, etc.)? – and we shall offer a preliminary answer to the vexed question of how linguistic forms map onto meanings.

To achieve this goal, we need to take on board a fundamental lesson that forms the basis of modern linguistics' legitimate, if not entirely uncontroversial claim to status as an independent science (see Sampson, 1998). Language may be treated as an external phenomenon: as a set of arbitrary but shared conventions, or as an object 'out there' in the world with an existence independent of particular speakers or utterances, capable of being observed, classified and analysed. It was not until the nineteenth and early twentieth centuries that European linguistics freed itself from the subjectivity encouraged by I-language introspectionism and developed descriptive analytical tools that enabled languages to be objectively studied and compared with one another.[1]

The structures that linguists discover are revealed in patterns of language usage: habitual collocations of phrases, words and sounds that form nested patterns of sequential statistical dependencies, as utterances are inevitably generated and processed in time (Bybee, 2001). Language structures are intangible, but none the less real. They exist in statistical word patterns created by the myriad of well-formed sentences generated in accordance with the rules of grammar, to which speaker-hearers are exposed through years of language acquisition and subsequent usage. Our brains are voracious and highly sensitive analysers of these sequential patterns of language input and output. We typically react quickly very to any departures from the expected sequences that we may encounter in the stream of spoken or written language – just as you no doubt reacted to the transposition of *very* and *quickly* in the present sentence. We may refer to this phenomenon as grammatical anomaly detection, and use it as one of many indicators of the 'mental computations' that take place when we listen to and comprehend spoken language.

The 'external forms' that linguists discover in patterns of language use are obviously selected in specific instances by the communicative intentions of speakers in conformity with the constraints of the speaker's grammar. However, the mapping between form and meaning is often complex, indirect and not fully explicit. Comprehending spoken language requires a great deal by way of inference on the part of the listener and shared understanding of the utterance context on the part of both speaker and listener, which we shall refer to as 'pragmatics'. For example,

---

[1] In this, European linguistics was merely rediscovering what the Sanskrit grammarians, led by Panini, had practised two millennia earlier.

compare the way that you assign reference to the pronoun *he* in the following sentences, which are identical except for the final adjective:

(1)      *The teacher refused the pupil's request because **he** was naughty.*
(2)      *The teacher refused the pupil's request because **he** was busy.*

Reference assignment is a key aspect of semantic interpretation, and is heavily influenced by 'real world knowledge'. Notice, however, that pragmatic knowledge does not mandate a particular reading of the sentence, but merely biases the listener's interpretation of the utterance one way or the other. It is quite possible, though unusual, to construc *he* as referring to the teacher in (1) above – a point whose significance we shall discuss later (chapter 12, sentence processing and syntactic parsing).

Linguistics emphasizes the study of external forms, because these are the structures that are accessible to objective scrutiny from the primary linguistic data – the set of possible well-formed sentences of a language, or a linguistic corpus of observed linguistic expressions. Conversely, the meanings of sentences are not directly observable, despite what our naive intuitions as language users may seem to tell us to the contrary. This point is not generally well appreciated by those unacquainted with linguistics. But consider for a moment the word *telephone*, which for most people invokes a mental image of an object that sits on a desk, has a touch-pad dial, a liftable receiver, etc. Words typically invoke concepts or mental representations of objects. That is the whole point of having words. However, words as external forms are typically embedded in larger linguistic expressions – phrases or sentences – and take their linguistic significance from their position within the larger expression. Thus, *telephone* is usually a noun, or head of a noun phrase, but may readily be pressed into service as a verb:

(3)      [[The [telephone]$_N$]$_{NP}$ [rang]$_{VP}$]]$_S$.
(4)      [[I]$_{NP}$ [[telephoned]$_V$ [her]$_{NP}$]$_{VP}$]$_S$.

A noun is defined linguistically by its distributional properties. Nouns may be inflected for number, gender, or case.[2] Nouns are typically flanked by characteristic closed-class words, such as determiners. They may be pre-modified (in English) or post-modified (as in French) by open-class words, typically labelled 'adjectives'. Similarly, verbs and other open-class words are defined by their distributional properties.

## Forms and meanings

It is tempting, in the interests of trying to map external forms onto meaning in a direct and economical manner, to define word classes in terms of

[2] In English, gender and case inflections are confined to the pronoun system. Other languages make much more extensive use of these two nominal inflectional categories. See later sections of this chapter for further discussion.

Table 2.1 *Distributional properties of nouns and verbs (in English)*

| Nouns | Verbs |
|---|---|
| inflect for number: e.g. *books* | inflect for tense: e.g. *book**ed*** |
| take article: e.g. ***the*** book | inflect for subject agreement: e.g. *he books* vs. *they book* |
| pre-modified by adjectives: e.g. *a **good** book* | pre-modified by auxiliary verbs: e.g. ***have** booked* |
| pronominalize: e.g. *he, they, it*, etc. | 'pronominalize' with *do*: e.g. *he **did** X* |

'semantic roles' that they typically play in sentences. Thus, nouns may be said to stand for 'things' which may act as 'agents' or 'recipients' of the 'actions' of verbs, which are 'doing-words', etc. But notional definitions of word classes, like noun, verb, adjective or adverb, only describe prototypical word usages and fail in many instances. On the other hand, the major word classes may be defined formally in terms of their distributional properties. Some distributional properties of nouns and verbs, the two most basic word classes, are illustrated for English in Table 2.1.

The distributional properties of word classes (known as 'parts of speech' in traditional grammar) provide reliable structural cues for recognizing the various functional roles of words in sentences. At the same time, they provide a viable alternative to unworkable notional definitions of word classes. The great advantage of a distributional approach to the definition of word classes from the twin perspectives of linguistic analysis and language acquisition is that it provides a secure foundation for discovering or inductively learning the syntactic structures of any given language. The significance of this finding, which was a key achievement of 'American' structural linguistics of the mid twentieth century, will become apparent in later chapters when we discuss 'connectionist' models of sentence processing. The downside of the distributional over the notional approach to defining word classes is that it complicates the mapping from sounds and words to sentence meanings in linguistic expressions. But in the final analysis, this complication is probably more apparent than real. It is probably a consequence of having a syntax.

However, there are two qualifications that need to be made about the indirect and complex relationship between form and meaning in linguistic expressions. The first concerns language users who might be described as 'not fully competent', such as very young children, second language learners, or aphasics who have lost access to part of their language competence. Such language users may resort to simplified strategies or heuristics for sentence processing.

An example of a sentence processing heuristic is the 'agent first' strategy, which says: 'assume that the first noun phrase (NP) you encounter in a sentence is the "agent" of the "action" of the verb'. The strategy works for simple transitive sentences like (5):

(5)      *John kissed Mary.*

The 'agent first' strategy expresses an important word-order cue in this case because if the nouns are reversed, so are the roles of agent and recipient and consequently our semantic reading of 'who-did-what-to-whom'. Such sentences are termed 'semantically reversible' because either the subject or the object NP could equally plausibly play the role of agent or recipient. Reversible constructions therefore provide good test cases of whether listeners can make effective use of word-order cues in extracting an important aspect of sentential meaning:

(6)      *Mary kissed John.*

But, of course, the 'agent first' strategy fails for simple passive sentence constructions, where the first mentioned NP is the recipient or experiencer, not the agent:

(7)      *John was kissed by Mary.*

Also, the 'agent first' strategy is simply not relevant for the vast majority of verbal constructions that one is likely to encounter, as the following passage chosen at random from some 'pulp' fiction readily to hand amply illustrates:

> Lady Winwood *being denied*, the morning caller *inquired* with some anxiety for Miss Winwood, or in fact, for any of the young ladies. In face of the rumour which *had come* to her ears it *would be* too *provoking* if all the Winwood ladies *were to withhold* themselves. But the porter *held* the door fully open and *said* that Miss Winwood *was* at home.      (G. Heyer, *The convenient marriage*)

Not one of the italicized verbal expressions in the passage above is applicable to the 'agent first' strategy. The application of heuristics in sentence processing is a complex matter of on-going research, as is the related question of whether heuristics should be actively taught as part of a language remediation program. It is a defining characteristic of heuristics as sentence processing 'rules of thumb' that they will fail a certain proportion of the time and tend to fail on all but the most basic linguistic expressions. We discuss heuristics in language processing further in chapter 12.

The second qualification that is needed to the statement that the mapping between linguistic form and meaning is indirect and complicated is that non-compositional form–meaning relationships must be set aside. The meanings of sentences (5) to (7) above are clearly compositional. That is to say, the meaning of the sentence is composed or computed from the meanings of the words or constituent lexical expressions, in accordance with structural cues (morpho-syntactic or phonological) that may be encoded in the utterance. Thus, the lexical items *John, Mary* and *kiss* are combined with the morpho-syntactic cues, such as word order and grammatical inflection (e.g., *-ed*, past tense), together with whatever prosodic cues may be present – an aspect of the phonological form of the utterance – to construct a *sentence meaning*.

However, idiomatic expressions such as '*kicked the bucket*' in (8) below constitute classical examples of non-compositional form–meaning mappings. Idioms of various kinds abound in natural language (Jackendoff, 1997). Their importance in normal language usage has probably been seriously underestimated by linguists, who focus upon the rule-governed aspects of language. Actually sentence (8) is ambiguous, having both a partially non-compositional semantic reading (the idiomatic) and a fully compositional 'literal' interpretation:

(8)     *John kicked the bucket.*     <John died.>[3]
                                      <John kicked the bucket.>

The idiomatic reading of (8) is partly compositional because the sentential meaning is a compositional function of the lexical item *John* and the idiom '*kicked-the-bucket*', which is also a lexical item, or more precisely, a lexicalized syntactic form.

The non-compositional mapping will also be referred to as the 'lexical route' to meaning in this book. All that is required for non-compositional meaning is to recognize the phonological form of a linguistic expression and to retrieve its meaning directly from its lexical entry. The lexicon may be thought of, at first approximation, as an encyclopaedic store of form–meaning pairings. We typically think of lexical entries as comprising 'words' in a mental dictionary. But idioms may constitute phrases or even whole sentences:

(9)     . . . *break the ice*
        . . . *let the cat out of the bag*
        *That's the way the cookie crumbles.*

On the other end of the continuum, a lexical entry may be a word fragment, such as a single suffix or prefix:

(10)     . . . ***unwanted*** . . .

Another qualification is in order here. Idiomatic expressions such as (8–9) above do have internal compositional morpho-syntactic structure. They are probably processed in the same way as 'normal' phrases. It is just that their meanings are non-compositionally derived. Thus, it needs to be recognized that the form and the meaning of linguistic expressions may be independently compositional or not. Idioms as syntactic phrases are compositional in form but non-compositional in the way they assign meaning. The distinction here can also be illustrated at the word level with two English verbs that have overlapping meanings. In its past tense form *go* is non-compositional in linguistic form, whereas *depart* clearly is morphologically compositional. However, semantically, both expressions are clearly compositional (see Table 2.2).

The independence of form and meaning with respect to compositionality points to a fundamental distinction, which is commonplace in linguistic descriptions of languages (competence models), but controversial in models of language

---

[3] We shall adopt the convention of representing the meanings of expressions by paraphrases placed inside angle brackets (<. . .>). This provides a convenient way of sparing the reader a formal semantics for representing the meanings of linguistic expressions. We postpone discussion of the nature of lexical meaning and semantic disorders to chapters 10 and 11.

Table 2.2 *Compositionality of form and meaning*

| Expression | Form | Meaning |
|---|---|---|
| *went* | suppletive: non-compositional | <leave + past>: compositional |
| *departed* | stem + affix: compositional | <leave + past>: compositional |

processing (performance models): a distinction between the derivation or recognition of the structures or forms in linguistic expressions on the one hand, and the derivation or extraction of meanings on the other. Most would agree on the need to distinguish between parsing the structure of a linguistic expression and interpreting its meaning or semantic content. But do these two activities represent distinct tasks or stages in sentence processing? Can the ability to extract forms and meanings be separately impaired in aphasia? Can different levels of form and meaning processing operate in partial or complete independence of one another? If so, precisely how are the component processes organized or orchestrated in language processing? These are fundamental questions to do with the modularity of language processing, with which we shall be occupied throughout this book. We shall have more to say on modularity at the end of this chapter, but first let us lay down what might be regarded as a minimal specification of the components of a human language code, or model of linguistic competence. Our model comes (as indicated previously) from linguistic research, from the study of the external forms of language, where 'a language' is viewed as a natural object of scientific investigation, whose properties may be observed by the application of appropriate analytical methodology.

## Minimal design features of a language

The bare minimum requirements for any language (natural or artificial) appear to be a vocabulary (a lexicon) and a set of combinatory rules for combining 'words' into well-formed expressions (sentences). We may wish to draw a distinction between the compositional rules or constraints that make a sentence grammatically well formed and those that are responsible for semantic well-formedness, or for assigning meaning to expressions. However, the structure of natural (human) languages requires us to recognize multiple levels of units.

How many levels? The linguist Charles Hockett (1960), discussing ways in which human languages differ from other known communication systems in the natural kingdom, pointed out a property he called 'double articulation'[4] to

---

[4] The notion derives from the French structural linguist André Martinet (1957), who in turn seems to have borrowed the idea from Aristotle who 'wrote in *The Poetics* (section 20) that "The Letter is an indivisible sound of a particular kind, one that may become a factor in an intelligible sound"' (Mannheim, 1991).

describe the two-tier relationship of form to meaning that is created by having a structural distinction between morphemes and phonemes. Morphemes are the minimal linguistic units which carry specific meanings or grammatical functions (such as tense, aspect, number, negation, possession, etc.). **Phonemes** are minimal units that serve to distinguish or signal differences in meaning, but carry no specific meaning of their own. This 'double articulation' in the sound-to-meaning mapping enables human languages to construct distinctive phonological forms for large vocabularies of words, using a relatively small inventory of sound units (phonemes or **distinctive features**). No other known animal communication system possesses this dual-level code for the phonological forms of words. Indeed, the vast majority of non-human communication systems seem to map 'utterances' to meanings in a simple one-to-one fashion (e.g. [low growl][5] means <back off!>).

Hockett's distinction obliges us to postulate at least three levels of structure in human language: the segmental (phonemic), the word (morphemic), and the sentence levels. However, this is still too few. Syntactic structures, as illustrated in (1) and (2) above, have hierarchical constituent or phrase structure. Hierarchical structure is also observed in the morphological structure of words.

Furthermore, in order to account for the structural properties of complex (multi-clause) sentences and for deictic (referring) expressions, even in simple sentences, it is necessary to make reference to an overarching level of discourse structure. Compare, for example:

(11)     *The old man died.*
(12)     *An old man died.*

The use of the definite article in (10) implies that the speaker is referring to a particular person, assumed to exist already as a referable entity in discourse structure. Table 2.3 below summarizes the four basic levels of organization structure found in any human language and their corresponding form- and meaning-based subsystems.

The highest level of linguistic representation, known as *discourse*, has somewhat different properties from the lower levels of linguistic structure – sentences, phrases, words, etc. Discourse structure is not so directly reflected in objective properties of linguistic expressions. Rather, it represents a conceptual framework which explains the functional significance of certain words or structural properties of linguistic expressions. Discourse structure is cooperatively created by speaker and listener in the course of a conversational exchange (assuming we are dealing with a sequence of successful communicative speech acts). It consists of a mutual understanding of what makes up the topic or topics under discussion, what

---

[5] We shall use square brackets ([. . .]) to indicate sounds or phonetic sequences, which will usually be expressed using the symbols of the International Phonetic Alphabet (IPA). See any respectable linguistics textbook for details.

Table 2.3 *Basic levels and components of linguistic representation in human languages*

| | Components of a linguistic expression | | |
| --- | --- | --- | --- |
| | Form | | Meaning |
| Level | Phonology | Syntax | Semantics |
| Discourse | Discourse prosody | Information structure | |
| Sentence | Sentence prosody | Phrase structure | Sentence semantics |
| Word | Word prosody | Morphology | Word semantics |
| Segment | Phonemes, distinctive features | | |

constitutes 'old' (shared) information, what needs to be signalled as 'new' information, and what needs to be done to distinguish between potentially ambiguous referents or 'players' in the scenario created by the discourse. Discourse structure also explains the use of turn-taking devices and certain prosodic features of utterances. In other words, discourse is a conceptual level of linguistic representation, rather than something which is directly reflected in the distributional properties of elements of linguistic expressions.

## Phonology and syntax as aspects of form

Because speech[6] is the primary medium of natural language, some of the structural properties of language can only be adequately described by reference to properties of speech. These are the phonological aspects of linguistic form. However, many of the structural aspects of language (thanks to the 'double articulation' of form and meaning at the level of the word, mentioned previously) can be expressed without any need to make reference to phonological form. Thus, syntactic structures arise from the combinatorial possibilities of words and morphemes.[7] But words and morphemes have their independent phonological specification, such that the syntax can be expressed largely without reference to properties of speech: largely, but not entirely.

In many linguistics textbooks, it is conventional to portray syntax as belonging to the sentential level and phonology to the sound structure of words. But this is really only a convenient oversimplification of the relationship between

---

[6] However, manual signs or gestures take over as the primary medium in deaf linguistic communities, and quite a few language communities employ secondary signing systems, particularly in contexts where speaking is taboo – see Kendon (1988) on Australian aboriginal sign language usage.

[7] Classical expositions in the tradition of American structural linguistics are: Harris (1951, reprinted 1960) *Structural linguistics* and Fries (1952) *The structure of English*.

phonological and morpho-syntactic structures. Phonological form clearly pene-trates to the level of sentence and discourse structure in the form of *prosody* (or the systems of stress and intonation, in the case of English prosody). There is a good deal of controversy in linguistics over the relationship between syntax and prosody. The majority view amongst contemporary phonologists appears to be that prosody and syntax represent independent hierarchies or parallel structures with somewhat different formal properties (Selkirk, 1984). Thus, phonologists refer to 'the prosodic hierarchy' of 'phonological words', 'clitic phrases', 'minor and major phonological phrases', etc. (see Beckman, 1996; Shattuck-Hufnagel and Turk, 1996) where each level of prosodic constituency is defined exclu-sively in terms of prosodic features (pitch accents and temporal phrase boundary markers). In fluent speech, there is a close but flexible alignment between such phonologically defined constituents and syntactically defined entities, such as clause boundaries (Crystal, 1975). However, it remains an open question as to whether prosodic constituency is best seen as a direct phonetic exponent of sen-tential and discourse structure (Steedman, 1990), or whether there are separate and distinct 'prosodic' and 'morpho-syntactic' hierarchies. We favour the former view on grounds of parsimony, but leave it as an open question, as one of the more difficult and as yet unsolved questions of modularity in the language faculty.

## Phonology: the sound patterns of spoken language

We recognize words by their phonological forms. This may seem an innocent and obvious truism, but it glosses over several thorny problems of speech perception, which we consider in chapters 3–5. Ever since Edward Sapir (1933, reprinted in English, 1947), one of the pioneers of modern linguistics, made the observation that Tony, his native speaker informant, was selectively sensitive to certain phonetic features of words in his native language (Southern Paiute), linguists have regarded it as almost self-evident that the sounds which form the phonological shapes of words are somewhat 'abstract' properties. Listeners seem to pay selective attention to the 'distinctive' phonetic features of words (i.e. those that signal potential contrasts of meaning) while ignoring accompanying 'non-distinctive' phonetic features.

Thus, English listeners typically hear the 'same' vowel, /æ/,[8] in the words *cat, tack, cad* and *can*, overlooking substantial differences in vowel duration in the normal pronunciation of the first two words compared with the second two. Listeners also tend to ignore the nasalized quality of the vowel that phonetically distinguishes the /æ/ in *can* from the other three words. These non-distinctive

---

[8] To avoid ambiguity, when referring to sounds as phonemes (abstract phonological segments) in some particular language, we shall enclose them in forward slashes (e.g.: the /æ/ sound in *can*). When we wish to refer to sounds as they are pronounced, or as phonetic variants of a phoneme, we shall enclose them in square brackets.

phonetic features are captured in a phonetic transcription, but deliberately omitted from the phonological (phonemic) representation:

(13)    cat      tack     cad      can       Orthographic form
        /kæt/    /tæk/    /kæd/    /kæn/      Phonological form (phonemic)
        [kʰætˀ]  [tʰækˀ]  [kʰæːd]  [kʰæ̃ːn]    Phonetic form

Similarly, listeners overlook obvious phonetic differences between the aspirated [kʰ] word initially in *cat* and the glottalized and unreleased [kˀ] which is typically found word finally, in order to arrive at the perceptual impression that these are two instances of the 'same sound'. In view of the fact that native listeners tend to ignore them, one might be tempted to conclude that non-distinctive phonetic properties of spoken words might be inconsequential in speech perception. But clearly this is not the case. Listeners rely in critical cases on non-distinctive features for such things as word segmentation. Compare:

(14)    cats can          cat scan
        [kʰætskʰæ̃ːn]       [kʰætskæ̃ːn]

The distinction between distinctive and non-distinctive phonetic features is commonplace in linguistics and in the phonological descriptions of languages. But the distinction is problematic in models of speech perception and language processing. Does the phonetic level of description represent the input to the perceptual apparatus and the phonological description, a specification of how phonological forms are stored in the internal lexicon of the language user? How are non-distinctive phonetic features exploited by the perceptual system? (These are questions we need to answer but must defer for the present; we take them up in chapter 5.)

Quite independent of the distinction between phonetic and phonological levels of representation, there is the problem of the dual identity of phonetic/phonological features as specifications for both the speech production and perceptual systems. The speaker's task of controlling the articulatory mechanism to produce phonological targets is so different from that of the listener in recognizing such targets in the acoustic signal that many have suggested independent 'memory' storages for the the perception and production of words. On the other hand, the regularities of sound pattern which are captured in the phonological rules of languages are neutral with respect to the production–perception distinction. Furthermore, speech production and perception are intimately associated through the feedback loop that operates as we self-monitor whenever we speak. The question of separate perception and production storage systems for the phonological forms of words may be resolved by clinical evidence of modularity. If it could be shown that one could be separately impaired while the other remains intact (and vice-versa) in different forms of speech or language pathology, then we might conclude that separate perception and production memories exist for the phonological forms of words. We take up this issue in chapters 5–9.

## Prosody: the phonology of supra-segmental features

*Prosody* may be informally defined as the 'music' of a language, its characteristic melody and rhythm. We do not wish to suggest, however, that the prosody of a language is mere decoration. Prosody refers to the supra-segmental features of the sound pattern of the language, i.e. those features which extend over a span of speech which is greater than a single segment. Syllables, for example, are supra-segmental units.

English prosody is made up of three inter-related systems:

–    Stress: prominence relationships amongst syllables
–    Rhythm: patterns of stress in time
–    Intonation: linguistic use of voice pitch

Prosody in English and related European languages can be analysed under these three main headings. However, tone languages (Chinese, Vietnamese and many others) or languages like Japanese that employ pitch-accents on words have rather different word prosodies. Such differences in prosodic systems produce significant prosodic interference effects (interference of L1 prosody on L2) for second language learners, reducing intelligibility for English listeners and inducing considerable 'foreign accent' colouring of the learner's speech. Altered prosody is a prominent characteristic of the rare neurological speech disorder known as 'foreign language syndrome' (Ingram, McCormack and Kennedy, 1992). Dysfluency in speech production, such as found in speech apraxia,[9] impairs prosody.

Prosody plays an important role in speech perception as well as production. Recent developmental studies of speech perception, discussed in chapter 6, indicate that adaptation to the prosodic patterns of one's native language aids language learners and mature listeners in the difficult task of word segmentation in the continuous acoustic stream of speech.

*Stress*: Phonetically speaking, stress refers to the level of prominence that falls on a syllable in relation to other syllables in the utterance. Stressed syllables in English are usually of greater duration, spoken on a contrastively higher (or sometimes lower) level of voice pitch, or spoken more loudly, than unstressed syllables. Some linguists identify stress with the relative amount of articulatory and phonatory effort that goes into the production of a syllable. Stress is a relative property, not an absolute value. For example, a syllable may contain an inherently long or short vowel. Under stress, its duration may increase, but its status as a long or short vowel will be preserved.

Stress in English is an important aspect of the sound pattern of words. One syllable takes primary stress, the highest level of prominence in the word. There

---

[9] Speech apraxia, a neurological speech disorder chiefly characterized by difficulties in voluntary initiation of speech, is widely considered to be a problem of 'speech motor programming', rather than a language impairment per se (Rosenbek, McNeil and Aronson, 1984).

are (at least) two lower levels of prominence: secondary stress and tertiary stress. Compare stress levels in:

(15)        *elec*tric      elec*tric*ity      elec*tric*ian      elec*tric*ality (?)

Stress in English words is said to be culminative. That is, one syllable acts like a linchpin, giving an overall organization to the pronunciation of the word. In a language which allows for polysyllabic words, the culminative function of word stress helps speakers recall the sound pattern of the word. The mechanism involved is called chunking by psychologists. We demonstrate its role in speech perception in chapter 6.

It is debatable whether tone languages like Standard Chinese or Vietnamese possess a system of word stress. In some languages, the stress pattern of a word is regular and predictable. In English, word stress appears to be predictable also, because native speakers can intuitively assign stress patterns to nonce words:

(16)        *florosure    experiate    andosal    entole*

However, the rules for word stress assignment in English are very complex. They reflect the historical division between the Germanic and Latinate parts of English vocabulary.

Some words are typically spoken without stress:

(17)        *The **man** in the **wind** and the **west  moon**.*

Articles, prepositions, conjunctions, auxiliary verbs – in short, the closed class items of the vocabulary – are usually pronounced unstressed in connected speech. Note, however, each of these 'little words' has a citation form in which the vowel takes on full vowel quality instead of a *schwa* (*the* /ði/, /ðə/, etc.). The alternation of stressed and unstressed syllables which is set up by function words and major lexical items in spoken sentences gives rise to linguistic rhythm in English. This shows that stress operates above the level of the word. When it does so, stress is often referred to as accent.

Probably all languages employ emphatic stress or accent, where a particular word in the phrase is given prominence over other items, for example:

(18)        *I **love** that hat.*

There is a special type of phrase-level stress, often referred to as contrastive stress or accent. It occurs in utterances such as:

(19)        *My mum lives in **Mel** bourne.*

Here, the speaker is countermanding an assumption on the part of the listener that his/her mother lives somewhere else. What in effect the contrastive stress is doing here is saying:

(20)        ***No**, she lives in **Mel** bourne.*

**Compounds**: Stress also operates between the level of the word and the phrase in English and many other languages. English has a very productive way of forming new words by compounding, which we shall examine in the context of morphology (word-building). Consider the following forms:

(21)     *hot-dog*     *look-in*     *friendly-society*
         *hot dog*     *look in*     *friendly society*

Note how the stress pattern distinguishes the compound from the phrasal construction. It is not just a matter of prominence. There are timing or foot structure considerations as well (see below).

**Rhythm**: English is said to be a stress-timed language. That is, it obtains rhythmic regularity by a tendency to alternate stressed and unstressed syllables. With a little exaggeration of the normal spoken form, it is possible to tap out the rhythm of many ordinary English utterances such as:

(22)     *Stressed syllables tend to occur at regular intervals of time*.

There has been much debate among phoneticians as to whether English as a stress-timed language differs from languages like French or Italian, which are said to be syllable-timed. It does seem that there is a tendency towards isochrony (even timing) of stressed syllables in fluent English speech. Evidence can be adduced for a timing unit above the syllable in English, which is called the foot. A foot comprises a stressed syllable, followed (optionally) by one or more unstressed syllables:

(23)     Foot Foot
         S W S W          S = strong, stress bearing
         *Woolongabba*[10]   W= weak, unstressed.
         [wʊləngæbə]

**The foot**: The foot is a familiar unit in discussions of poetic metre. But does it belong in a description of the sound pattern of English or in the sound patterns of other languages? Do native English speakers have a tacit knowledge of feet as units in their spoken language? It can be argued that they do. Some have proposed the expletive infixation test. The expletive in question for Australian English is, of course, *bloody*.

In Australian English *bloody* can be fairly freely inserted into spoken utterances. However, there are restrictions on *bloody* insertion. You can say:

(24)          Woolon[bloody]gabba           but not:   *Wool[bloody]ongabba
              [bloody]Woolongabba                      *Woolonga[bloody]bba
         even: [bloody]Woolon[bloody]gabba

---

[10] A suburb of Brisbane, Australia.

The rule is that *bloody* can be inserted only at foot boundaries. English speakers could only have clear intuitions about expletive infixation if they have tacit knowledge of foot boundaries.

**Intonation**: Intonation operates exclusively at the level of the phrase and above. It is possible, of course, to illustrate intonational effects with one word utterances. Compare your intuitions with the annotated meanings of the following intonational 'tunes':

(25)

| *yes* | *yes* | *yes* | *yes* | *yes* |
|---|---|---|---|---|
| fall | low rise | level | high rise | rise fall |
| <plain assent> | <continue> | <bored> | <surprise> | <strong assertion> |
| <declaration> | <go on> | <impatient> | <pleading> | <command> |

A single word here is as a phrase. The analysis of intonation is a complex subject. However, we may say that intonation contours have three basic functions in the language:

– Illocutionary: marking speaker's attitude and intended purpose of the utterance (e.g. asking [a question], declaring [a proposition], etc.).
– Demarcative: marking phrase boundaries.
– Highlighting: marking 'new' or 'important' information, focusing attention on some word or constituent.

The illocutionary function of intonation is probably the one which is most familiar to you. It is illustrated in the examples of *yes* cited above. Illocutionary force in speech is largely carried by the voice pitch inflection, which falls on a lexical item, often at the end of the utterance. How many distinct 'tunes', each with a distinct illocutionary force, are there? This is a vexing question. However, you can appreciate the phenomenon under discussion by considering the examples cited above.

The demarcative function of intonation can be seen as actually part of the syntax of the language, though most linguists would argue that prosodic structure and syntactic structure are independent of each other. The demarcative function of intonation helps the listener 'chunk' utterances at the phrasal level. It has been suggested that the intonational phrase is a basic unit of utterance planning in speech production. To illustrate the demarcative function:

(26)    *When we go to the **movies**, we always buy **popcorn**.*
    *We always buy popcorn when we go to the **movies**.*

In the first sentence, there is an obligatory intonation break after movies (indicated orthographically by the comma). The voice pitch executes a low-rise on *movies*, often followed by a brief pause. In the second sentence, there may be an intonation break after popcorn, but as likely as not, the whole sentence will be a single intonational phrase.

What is the reason for this difference between the two sentences? Notice that in the first sentence, the dependent clause comes before the *main* clause. The intonation break with the low-rise terminal could be seen as letting the listener know that 'there is more to come' (you have not yet heard the main clause). When the main clause comes first, as in the second sentence, this intonational marking is not required.

The highlighting function of intonation can be seen in the tendency to mark new information with intonational effects. When a topic is first introduced into discourse, it is likely to be accented as the intonational centre of the phrase, to be thus highlighted and draw the listener's attention. On subsequent mention, the item shifts out of intonational focus. It is now old information. You may have noted some overlap here with what was said about phrasal stress earlier. This is no coincidence. Linguists have argued over the demarcation between stress and intonation systems in the prosody of the language.

## Semantics: the representation of meaning

The semantic properties of linguistic expressions are the most prob- lematical to deal with, because we have no really satisfactory way of representing meanings. Meanings tend to be differently represented by logicians, philoso- phers, psychologists and linguists. Various meta-languages have been proposed for different aspects of meaning: frame theory for conceptual representation at the discourse level (Minsky, 1975); (first-order) predicate calculus for represent- ing propositional relationships; conceptual dependency theory (Schank, 1975) or conceptual structure theory (Jackendoff, 1983) for aspects of intra-sentential meaning representation; semantic feature theory (Lyons, 1995) or prototype the- ory (Lakoff, 1987) for the semantics of words, etc. The main difficulty is that the various meta-languages do not cohere. Each tends to handle more or less well some restricted range of phenomena, and make conflicting assumptions about the nature of meanings and how they are manipulated.

However, based on comparative grammars of natural languages, it is possible to see that the major components of sentence meaning have reflexes in aspects of grammatical structure. We summarize these in Table 2.4 below. At the dis- course level, we draw no distinction between semantic components and syntactic exponents of meaning (see Table 2.3), because as indicated previously, we regard discourse structure as fundamentally a conceptual object that is co-operatively constructed in the course of a dialogue, or by the speaker, but with an 'eye' on the listener, in the case of a monologue or narrative. The information structure of discourse (made up of topics and comments about objects of reference) and the communicative intentions of speakers clearly drive the choice of linguistic expressions in speech production. They are also the basic 'objects of inference' in speech perception and language comprehension.

It is important to emphasize that the syntactic categories referred to in Table 2.4 are usually not direct expressions of the semantic properties from which

Table 2.4 *Semantic components and syntactic exponents*

| Semantic property | Syntactic category |
|---|---|
| <Assertion/presupposition> | Main/subordinate clause |
| <Specificity, and reference> | Deixis |
| <Thematic roles> | Case |
| <Time reference> | Tense, aspect |
| <Intention, possibility, obligation> | Modality |

they ultimately derive. These categories merely reflect their prototypical seman-tic functions. Syntactic features have a life of their own in the language, their meanings/functions change over time, as languages inevitably change. We illus-trate this point several times in the brief thumbnail sketches of these categories summarized in Table 2.4.

## Assertion/presupposition and clause structure

Simple, one-clause sentences convey a single proposition. In semantic terms, a proposition consists of a single predicate – usually expressed as the head of a verb phrase – associated with one or more arguments that fill *thematic roles* required by the predicate. Predicates are indicated by capital letters in the following examples. We define thematic roles shortly.

**Linguistic expression**     **Semantic predicate/argument structure**

(27)  $[_S [_{NP}$ *Nurse Betty][$_{VP}$ adores [$_{NP}$ Dr Revell]]]*.     <ADORE ($_{Ag}$ Nurse Betty) ($_{Ex}$ Dr Revell)>

(28)  *This relationship sucks.*     <SUCK ($_{Th}$ This relationship)>

(29)  *It's hot today.*     <HOT ($_{Loc}$ Today)>

The predicate <ADORES> takes two arguments, an <Agent> and an <Experiencer>, whereas the predicate <SUCK>, expressed by the colloquial intransitive usage of *suck*, roughly meaning <merits contempt>, takes a single <Theme> as its argument.

Complex, multi-clause sentences contain two or more propositions, semanti-cally connected in ways that are suggested by the syntax of subordination. Main or tensed clauses assert the principal proposition of the sentence, while subordi-nate clauses, which are often signalled by a bare infinitive and lacking full, overt, thematic role specification, carry propositions, the truth of which is not so much asserted as presumed or presupposed. Compare:

(30)  *John $_i$ liked[0 $_i$ to learn statistics].*    LIKE ($_{Ex}$ John $_i$) ($_{Th}$ LEARN ($_{Ag}$ John $_i$) ($_{Go}$ Statistics))

(31)  *John $_i$ learned[0 $_i$ to like statistics].*    LEARN ($_{Ag}$ John $_i$) ($_{Go}$ LIKE ($_{Ex}$ John $_i$) ($_{Th}$ Statistics))

In (30) above it is presupposed that John learned some statistics but it is asserted that he enjoyed doing so, whereas in (31), John's (eventual) liking of statistics is presupposed, and it is the fact that it was learned which is asserted. The gram-matical subject (or the Agent role) of the verb in the subordinate clause is not overtly marked in the dependent clause, but it is covertly present, in the form of what linguists call a 'null anaphor' (represented by a zero (0) in the syntactic description).

As indicated in the semantic representations in (30–1), it is assumed that in deriving a semantic interpretation of the sentence, all verbs or predicates will be assigned their appropriate arguments, whether or not they appear explicitly in the linguistic expression. Typically, the null subject NP of a non-finite verb (such as *to learn* in (30) above) can be found 'upstairs' in the main clause, where it explicitly appears as the subject NP argument of the main verb (*John* in '*John liked . . .*' in (30) above). Native speakers expect this kind of ellipsis of functional constituents in subordinate clauses. They learned it as part of the syntax of complex sentences. However, knowing or being able to infer that *learn* and *liked* take the 'same subject' and refer to the same object of discourse is a necessary part of the semantic interpretation of the sentence. For this reason, null anaphors are part of the machinery of grammatical description in linguistic theories that seek to show how syntactic structures map onto meanings.

As we shall see later, one of the more startling achievements of psycholinguistics in recent years has been to demonstrate that such 'invisible constituents' as null anaphors are detectable in experiments on real-time (on-line) sentence processing and by implication have psychological reality for language users.

## Specificity, reference and deixis

Syntactic structures have an important role to play in the assignment of reference to referring expressions, such as nouns and pronouns. The reference of a pronoun is constrained by its location in the syntactic structure of the sentence. Consider a standard example:

(32)    *Bill thought he was a goner.*

The first interpretation of this sentence for most people could probably be paraphrased as <*Bill thought that he, himself, was a goner.*> However, the sentence is ambiguous and could also mean that <*Bill thought that he (someone else) was a goner.*> The ambiguity would usually be resolved by discourse context. But consider the sentence

(33)    *He thought Bill was a goner.*

Sentence (33) can only mean < *He (someone else) thought Bill was a goner.*> It cannot be construed in such a way that *he* and *Bill* are co-referential.

Why is it that *he* and *Bill* may or may not be co-referential in (32), but must be non co-referential in (33)? The answer depends upon the respective positions of the two NPs in the syntactic structure of the sentence. A pronoun may not be co-referential with a noun phrase that it **c-commands**. C-command is a form of relationship of domination between nodes in a syntactic tree. A relationship of C-command holds between nodes X and Y if the first branching node that dominates X also dominates Y. The pronoun *he* in (33) c-commands the noun phrase *Bill* and consequently the two expressions cannot be co-referential. But *he* does not c-command *Bill* in (32) and hence co-reference is allowed. Thus it can be seen that the syntactic structure of the sentence constrains the reference of referring expressions by filtering out some of the pragmatically possible alternative interpretations. This is one useful way to think of how syntactic structures constrain semantic interpretation.

Reference and the negotiation of exactly what is being referred to is a huge theoretical problem for natural language-processing, not to mention a practical one in many conversational exchanges, particularly when one of the parties is language-impaired. Virtually any lexically headed constituent in a linguistic expression is capable of carrying reference. Whole sentences may make reference to events or states of affairs and then be indexed by a pronoun in subsequent discourse. For example, the sentence sequence (27–9) may be construed as a 'mini-discourse'. The NP in (28) *'This relationship'* can be readily construed as referring to the situation described in (27) *'Nurse Betty adores Dr Revell'*. Even the pronoun *It* (in 29) which would normally be interpreted as non-referential in *'It's hot today'*, can be read in context, as referring to Nurse Betty's relationship with her doctor.

However, linguistically speaking, reference-marking properties are the province of nominal expressions: nouns, noun phrases and their specifiers (articles, demonstratives, etc.), and pronouns. Thus, if we wish to mark the reference of some action or event that might normally be expressed by a verb or verb phrase, it is common to nominalize the expression:

(34)     *destroy (the city)* → ***the*** *destruction (of the city)*

*Deixis* is the term used to refer to the set of reference-marking expressions, some examples of which are:

|        | Expression | Category | Common meaning/function |
|--------|-----------|----------|-------------------------|
| (35) | ***the*** *boy* | definite article | specific reference |
| (36) | ***a/some*** *boy* | indefinite article | non-specific reference |
| (37) | *the boy* ***with glasses*** | prepositional phrase | restrictive reference |
| (38) | *the boy* ***that I told you about*** | relative clause | restrictive reference |

The relative clause in (38) is an example of the recursive power of sentence embedding used for a particular semantic function, in this case, to narrow the range of possible discourse referents of the expression *the boy*.

Recursion is a powerful property of natural language that enables language users to construct utterances of indefinite complexity by permitting structures to be embedded inside each other. Thus the syntactic patterns that define the structures of a simple sentence apply to main clauses and, with certain qualifications regarding ellipsis (mentioned previously), to subordinate clauses in complex sentences. Languages that possess recursive rules not only permit the generation of sentences which are indefinitely long (e.g. of the *'This is the dog that. . . . that lived in the house that Jack built*' variety), but also make it possible to parse such sentences with a small set of rules or syntactic patterns, recursively applied to input strings of words. Only human and no other animal languages appear to show evidence of recursive structures. But artificial languages such as algebra or C (human inventions) are recursive. Recursive structure appears to be a prerequisite property for any language that supports a compositional syntax and semantics of any substantial expressive power. However, not all would agree with this position (Christiansen, 1992). We shall return to the issue in discussing competing models of sentence processing (chapters 12 and 13).

## Thematic roles and case

The verb is the pivotal element in the syntax of the clause and in the semantics of the single proposition, as is evident from the examples previously cited. There have been numerous attempts to categorize the predicate–argument relations used to characterize propositional semantics in terms of a small number of 'thematic role' types. None have proved entirely satisfactory, but the following serves as an example:

| | |
|---|---|
| Agent | Performer of action; must be capable of volitional activity |
| Experiencer | Sentient being affected by action or process of the predicate |
| Theme | Non-sentient entity undergoing action or process |
| Goal | Object created, result attained, or end point of action or process |
| Source | Origin in time or space of action, process or event |
| Location | Placement in time or space of action, process, or event |

You may judge for yourself how well the above thematic roles describe the predicate–argument relations in the propositional semantics of sentences (27–31) above. For example, is the meaning of *like* enough of a passive experience to warrant the label of 'experiencer' being applied to the subject of this verb, and is *adore* sufficiently active to justify differently labelling the subject of this verb as an 'Agent'? While 'Dr Revell' as a sentient being could be called an 'Experiencer' of Nurse Betty's adoration, does it matter that he is only a delusional projection of a TV soap opera hero (Richards and Flamberg, 1993)? Probably not. However, how far should one go in licensing anthropomorphic thematic role assignments in expressions such as '*Cars love Shell*'? Here we venture into the murky waters of semantic theory.

Thematic roles gain syntactic expression to a greater or lesser extent in languages as case inflections on nouns or pronouns. Languages with relatively free word order, such as Latin, employ extensive case inflection, whereas languages like English with relatively fixed word order tend to restrict case marking to the pronoun system, and only minimally there. While it is possible to match (semantic) thematic roles with (syntactic) case categories, in prototypical instances, the two should not be conflated. Table 2.5 attempts to demonstrate this by illustrating

Table 2.5 *Grammatical case, thematic role and grammatical function*

| Case category | Thematic role (prototype) | Grammatical function | Pronoun form (English) | Prepositional expression |
|---|---|---|---|---|
| Nominative | Agent (theme) | Subject | I, we, he, she, they | by — (in passives) |
| Accusative | Experiencer | Object | me, us, him, her, them | |
| Genitive | Possessive | | my, mine, your, yours, his, her, etc. | of — |
| Dative | Recipient | Indirect object | | to —, for — |
| Ablative | Instrument | | | with — |
| Locative | Location | | | at —, near — |

how the major case inflections map into grammatical functions, English pronoun inflections, and prepositional phrases.

Just as prepositions in English are polysemous (e.g., *by* has an agentive meaning in passive constructions, but also can have a locative meaning *<next to>*), so case inflections may take various meanings in case-inflected languages.

## Time reference: tense, aspect and modality

Time reference, which signals to the listener when the event spoken of transpired, often specifically in relation to the time of speaking, is clearly important information that is usually linked to the main verb. The grammatical reflexes of time reference are tense and aspect. Mood is another important semantic category of verbal expressions, carrying information about the speaker's attitude towards the event spoken about. We have previously seen that illocutionary force is one of three key functions of intonation, a component of prosody. But illocutionary meanings conveying speaker's attitude, particularly attitudinal meanings related to the time of the event, such as *<promising>* or *<predicting>*, are part of the mood-marking system of the language.

English employs a small set of modal auxiliary verbs, placed just before the main verb and any other auxiliary verbs, to mark these *<speaker's perspective>* types of meaning. English modal auxiliary verbs come in present–past tense pairs (can, could; will, would; may, might; shall, should, etc.). Notice that the 'past' tense forms of each of these modal auxiliaries usually carry a meaning, not of *<past time reference>*, but one that adds an element of *<the hypothetical>* to core meanings of the modal verbs *can*, *will*, *may*, etc. This is a complication of the form–meaning mapping between time reference (a semantic notion) and tense (a grammatical inflection of a verb), but one that is restricted to modal verb constructions:

(39)   *He **comes** today.*          present tense   &lt;current time reference&gt;
       *He **came** today.*           past tense      &lt;past time reference&gt;[11]
       *He **can** come today.*       present tense   &lt;possibility or permission&gt;
       *He **could** come today.*     past tense      &lt;remote possibility&gt;
       *He **will** come today.*      present tense   &lt;prediction, future time reference&gt;
       *He **would** come today.*     past tense      &lt;hypothetical&gt;

Tense marking on verbs in complex sentences also serves as a cue to the structure of subordination. The main clause is always marked for tense, but verbs in subordinate clauses often appear as bare infinitives (lacking tense marking – see (30–1) above). Thus, tense also functions, along with other structural cues such as subordinators (*because*, *which*, *who*, etc.) and complementizers (*that, for*), to signal the hierarchy of subordination in complex sentences, so that the listener can distinguish the main assertion of the sentence from any other accompanying propositions, the truth of which is merely presupposed. In all likelihood, this role for tense in the information structure of complex sentences derives from the fact that time reference is something that only needs to be explicitly marked on the major asserted proposition of the utterance. But the fact that a feature like tense marking is regularly associated with a structural position renders that feature likely to become 'grammaticalized' as a marker of that position and to take up any meanings associated with it.

## Concluding remarks

Though necessarily brief and sketchy, this chapter has broadly outlined the major components of a language competence model. We have focused upon the formal properties of linguistic expressions and how they relate to aspects of meaning. What gives human language its expressive power is its multi-layered organization of units and their combinatory possibilities. Specifically, the capacity for recursion in structure building operations makes it possible to contemplate a compositional semantics. However, it must be acknowledged that precisely how a compositional semantics works, and just what its representations might look like, lies beyond our present understanding.

Although human language has evolved structural complexities which are clearly beyond those of other communication systems yet discovered, it has not abandoned the most primitive and direct way of mapping form to meaning – the lexical route, as we noted in our discussion of idiomatic expressions. The potential for a picturesque construction to lexicalize into a meaning that could not be compositionally derived from its constituents is always present. Idioms are being invented and extinguished all the time.

---

[11] As a reviewer points out, even the association of past tense with past time reference in lexical verbs is an oversimplification in certain contexts. Compare the meanings of: '*If he comes today . . .*' and '*If he came today . . .*' The past tense here signals consequences that are more *remote* from the current context of speaking.

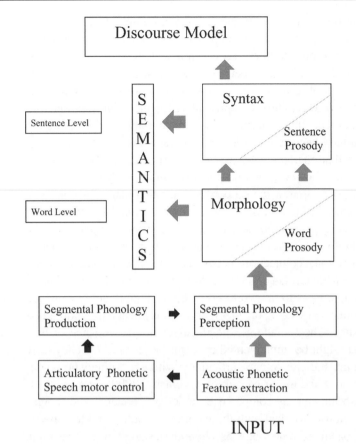

Figure 2.1  *Components of the linguistic model*

   The picture of a competence model which we have drawn and summarized in Figure 2.1 is one that would be recognized by any linguist, though elements of it may be controversial. One possibly controversial feature follows Jackendoff (1997) in declining to identify lexical items with any specifically definable level of linguistic representation, such as the word or the morpheme. Any structural unit above the morpheme may be lexicalized.

   An omission from the diagram of our competence model in Figure 2.1 is the apparent failure to separately represent the lexical and compositional mappings between form and meaning. However, this is due simply to the topographic limitations of a flat two-dimensional plane. If we contemplate a curved surface, such as the wrapper around a soup can, and locate the aspects of form and meaning on opposite surfaces of the can wrapper, then we may naturally represent the two routes to meaning by going left or right around the surface of the can. We might even contemplate implementing the mapping between form and meaning in a 'performance model' of language processing as a 'race around the can'. But we must defer such considerations to later chapters.

In a box-and-arrow diagram such as Figure 2.1. the boxes are intended to represent modular components of the system and the arrows, channels of information flow, showing how the various modules may communicate with one another. The connecting arrows in Figure 2.1 have been selectively restricted to represent the basically bottom-up flow of information in language comprehension. Language production would involve a set of arrows representing top-down information flow. Also, in the interests of reducing diagram clutter, some possible feedback loops in language processing have been suppressed, save for depicting peripheral aspects of the feedback loop that operates when we hear ourselves talk. This is shown in the dark arrows. Note, however, that the feedback loop in Figure 2.1 depicts the processing of external input in speech perception, rather than self-monitored speech. The dark arrows in Figure 2.1 represent a controversial hypothesis, the 'motor theory' of speech perception, which claims that speech signals activate motoric aspects of production at a basic level of perceptual processing. We depict these hypothetical functional connections between the perception and production mechanisms at the phonetic level in order to illustrate the point that arrows linking boxes represent hypotheses as to the workings of the system; hypotheses which may be tested in various ways, using the methods of experimental psycholinguistics or neurolinguistics. These matters concern linguistic performance or how a competence model might be implemented in language processing. They raise questions of how linguistic competence articulates with extra-linguistic cognitive, perceptual, memory and motor capacities. Chomsky (2000) refers to these extra-linguistic constraints on the competence model as 'phonetic' and 'cognitive' 'interface conditions'. We deal with these complex matters and the diverse questions that they spawn, as to how one tests hypotheses about what goes on in people's heads during language processing, in subsequent chapters, as the story unfolds.

## Study questions for chapter 2

1.     Compare and contrast the three ways of defining 'a language' (social construct, I-language and E-language). Which of these ways of viewing language is most useful for characterizing an individual's 'linguistic competence'?

2.     Where do grammatical categories like 'noun', 'verb', 'article', 'preposition', etc. (parts of speech) come from? Are they I-language constructs, E-language constructs, or perhaps both?

3.     Give an example of a 'sentence processing heuristic' and the kind of language user one might expect to employ such a sentence interpretation strategy. How might one detect the use of sentence processing heuristics?

4.     Distinguish, with appropriate examples, between 'compositional' and 'non-compositional' routes to meaning.

5.      How would you show that 'compositionality' can apply independently to form and meaning in human languages? What does this tell us about the mappings between forms and meanings in human language? What implications might it have for 'modularity' of language processing?

6.      Charles Hocket identified 'double articulation' as a unique design feature of human language(s). Explain what he means by this feature. Is it really unique to human language, or may it be found in some other animal communication systems?

7.      Can you identify any other plausible candidates as 'unique design features' of human languages?

8.      How about 'recursion'? What does it designate? Is it unique to human language? What is its significance for the expressive power of language?

9.      How many distinct levels of structure (form) and meaning need to be recognized in the description of any human language? How do they differ from one another (e.g. how might one distinguish between the levels of 'discourse' and 'sentence structure', or between the 'morphemic' and the 'phonemic')?

10.     Distinguish between 'distinctive' (phonological) and non-distinctive (phonetic) features in the sound structure of words (with appropriate examples). Although listeners are generally more aware of phonological than mere phonetic contrasts, show (with a well-chosen example) that the latter can be critical for word recognition.

11.     Although the mapping between form (syntactic category) and meaning is often complex or obscure in specific examples, some broad generalizations can be made between syntactic categories and their typical 'semantic functions'. Review examples of these form–meaning pairings in Table 2.4. (Given one, be able to identify the other.)

# 3    The neuroanatomy of language

## Introduction

This chapter seeks to 'let the brain do the talking' about how it organizes itself for language. Our approach is consistent with the co-evolution hypothesis of chapter 1, and a long-established principle that biological systems evolve new capabilities by reconfiguring or adding an emergent layer of control upon systems already evolved to serve more basic and often quite unrelated biological functions. Thus, three functionally distinct systems for breathing, coughing (expelling foreign bodies from the windpipe) and deglutition (chewing and swallowing food) were harnessed into a single co-ordinated system for controlling the airstream, voicing and articulation mechanisms for the emergent function of speech production. Similarly, human language capabilities most likely emerged as a reconfiguration of pre-linguistic (or pre-symbolic) systems of perceptual representation, memory and response planning, which in turn evolved from more primitive sensory-motor (stimulus–response) control systems.

Of course, the brain cannot speak for itself, so we are obliged to adopt the next best course and view our subject matter from the perspective of those whose principal concern was/is the understanding of the brain and who were bold (or foolish) enough to extend their inquiries to the question of how the brain represents language. We begin by reviewing the classical clinical findings from the history of aphasiology to acquaint the reader with the major symptom clusters of speech and language disorder and to provide a first-approximation model of how language may be represented in the brain.

With the benefit of hindsight and a little historical licence to keep the narrative clear, we sketch a pre-psycholinguistic understanding of how language is represented in the brain, dubbed the BWL (Broca-Wernicke-Lichtheim) model. Although the BWL model was formulated around the turn of the previous century, it continues to provide a useful organizing framework for contemporary cognitive neurolinguistics. The continued utility of the BWL model derives from its basis in notions of functional neurology that were new at the time, but are now regarded as foundational: notions involving (a) functional relations between primary, sensory and motor areas of the cerebral cortex, (b) secondary association areas, and (c) the structural and functional connections of both of these to other 'higher' cortical regions and to the subcortical structures of the brain.

The BWL model and the later functional neuropsychological theories which succeeded it (most notably that of Luria, 1970, 1973) are based on a 'pre-theoretical' understanding of language and its structure (Grodzinsky, 1990). But, contrary to the position of some contemporary neurolinguists, this does not detract from the interest of the BWL model from the perspective of language processing in the brain. There are many arguments, but no compelling reasons, why the organization of communication capabilities in the brain should be isomorphic with any particular linguistic theory of language structure, unless, of course, the theory in question were specifically formulated to take account of human brain structure and function.[1]

It is generally agreed that the period of scientific study of brain and language relations began with the identification of 'the language centres' of the cerebral cortex in the latter half of the nineteenth century, when disciplinary boundaries for the study of brain, mind and language remained fluid. It was not until around the middle of the nineteenth century that some neurologists began to realize that close clinical observations of patterns of aphasic symptoms might have profound implications for how the mind or brain is organized for higher mental functions. Goodglass (1993) makes the observation that although perceptive case descriptions and self reports of various aphasic symptoms can be found scattered in the medical literature of previous centuries, it is not until the nineteenth century that appropriate clinical terminology evolved, which was capable of labelling distinctions that observers were capturing in their behavioural descriptions. Thus, Rommel (1683) (cited in Goodglass, 1993, p. 14) reported a case of 'a rare *aphonia*' (a term which means literally loss of voice), which involved a woman who was unable to utter words spontaneously or by repetition, but who 'was able to recite her prayers by rote, provided that she performed them in the order in which she had learned them'. The term 'aphasia' specifically denoting a loss or disorder of language, as distinct from one of voice, articulation or cognitive function, did not come into general use until some years after Paul Broca's seminal paper had appeared in 1861.

As aphasiology emerged as a sub-field of clinical neurology, terminological difficulties persisted. Writers borrowed terms from related fields such as linguistics and used them in idiosyncratic ways, or coined new terms, which quickly assumed the status of diagnostic categories or even sub-faculties of mind, before their usage was widely understood or accepted by the field. Nevertheless, during the mid nineteenth and early twentieth centuries, the major types of aphasic disorder were mapped, and although dispute remains over how well their categories can be localized in the brain or modularized in the machinery of mind, clinically based descriptions of aphasia and their associated cortical regions provide a departure point for contemporary neurolinguistic models of language.

---

[1] But that is the goal of our enterprise: a theory of language that is jointly constrained by what linguistic investigations can tell us about the nature of language structure and what neuropathology and neurolinguistic investigations can tell us about how the brain represents and processes spoken language.

The BWL model provided not only a framework for the classification of aphasic symptoms but also a first approximation towards a theory of how language is organized in the brain. The model was refined in the mid 1960s by Norman Geschwind (1974), who used it to provide perspicacious accounts of somewhat rare, but theoretically important **disconnection syndromes**. The BWL model is the direct forebear of contemporary neuropsychological models of language, all of which are highly modular, but tend to divide on questions of localization (see Coltheart, 2002). As a theory of language processing in the brain, the BWL model is severely constrained by the kind of evidence available at the time: informal clinical observations of language performance correlated with neuropathology. These limitations were partly overcome with the introduction of experimental psycholinguistic techniques for the study of aphasia, initially using 'off-line' tests of *meta-linguistic* abilities (syntactic comprehension, grammaticality judgements, etc.), in the 1960s and 1970s (Caplan, 1987; Lesser, 1989). These are topics for subsequent chapters, too complex to consider here, and tangential to our aim for this chapter of 'letting the brain speak for itself'.

However, in the last two decades, little short of spectacular developments in functional neural imaging techniques have provided a new window on 'on-line' language processing and how language is represented in the brain. The chapter concludes with an introduction to these powerful new observational techniques. It is too early yet to say what impact this technological revolution will have upon our understanding of how language is represented in the human brain. But as of the present time of writing, it seems fair to say that our notions of the biological foundations of language and the localization of supporting perceptual and motor skills, derived from clinical observation and the BWL framework, have been augmented but not fundamentally changed by functional imaging data derived from on-line language processing by normal language users.

## An orientation to the structures of the cerebral cortex

Before we embark upon our description of language from the perspective of the brain, we offer a brief anatomical orientation, no substitute for a text book on neuroanatomy, but a guide to key structures. Although the neuroanatomy of the human brain is bewilderingly complex, a surprising purchase on understanding what is known about the neural representation of language can be gained by reference to a relatively small number of landmarks readily observable from inspection of the surface of the brain. The most important structure for understanding the neural basis of language is that part of the brain which evolved most recently, the *cerebral cortex*. This paired, 6-cellular, thin mantle of neural tissue, much folded in upon itself so as to pack inside the cranium, encapsulates the older evolutionary structures of the brain that basically regulate vital functions and provide the foundations of sensory processing and motor control: the

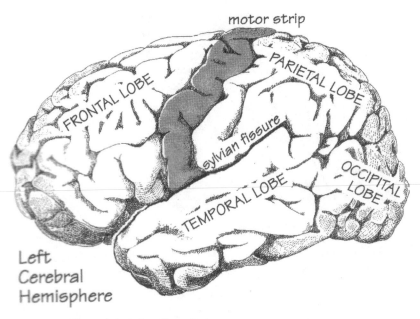

Figure 3.1  *Lobes of cerebral cortex*

*mid-brain* (comprising the basal ganglia, thalamus and putamen); the *brainstem*; and the *cerebellum*.

The left and right hemisphere of the cerebral cortex are roughly symmetrical in appearance and each is anatomically divided into four major lobes: *frontal*, *parietal*, *occipital* and *temporal*. All four are clearly discernible from landmarks on the surface, formed from the major *sulci* (Latin: 'furrows, fissures') and *gyri* (Latin: 'convolutions'). These border crossings between the cortical lobes also mark the location of the *primary sensory* and *motor regions* of the cerebral cortex. Thus, the temporal lobe on the lower lateral surface of the cerebral cortex is separated from the frontal and parietal lobes (above) by the *sylvian fissure*. At approximately halfway along the sylvian fissure, along the inward folding margin on the top surface of the *superior temporal gyrus*, we find the *primary auditory cortex*, which is the cortical receiving area for sensory input from the auditory system.

The frontal lobe is separated from the parietal lobe by the *central sulcus*, which divides the *precentral gyrus* (the anterior-most region of the parietal lobe) from the *postcentral gyrus*. The precentral gyrus, also known as the *somatosensory cortex*, contains arrayed along its length a 'sensory strip', a neural map of the body, known as the sensory *homunculus*, distorted in proportion to the density of tactile receptors on different areas of the skin and position sense receptors embedded in joints and muscle fibres. The postcentral gyrus (of the frontal lobe) contains a homologous neural map of the body to that of the precentral gyrus, but with the critical functional difference in that it directs *efferent* neural impulses or 'motor commands' to corresponding muscles on the opposite side of the body.

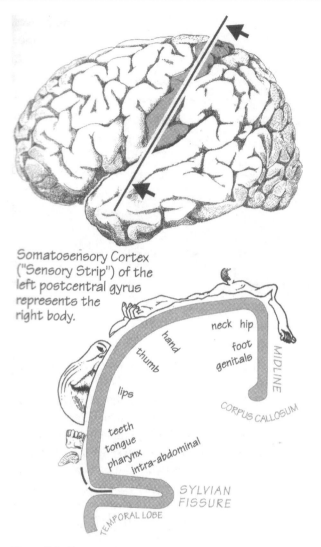

Figure 3.2  *Somatosensory cortex*

Stimulation of a specific area of the postcentral gyrus by a small locally applied electrical current induces involuntary movements in muscles innervated by that particular region of the primary motor cortex. Similarly, electrical stimulation of a corresponding region of the somatosensory cortex produces local tactile sensations.

Mapping of the human somatosensory and motor cortex in wide-awake neurosurgery patients was pioneered by Wilder Penfield in the late 1940s, but the procedure – though greatly aided by modern imaging techniques – is still used today, as the following snippet from the neurosurgery operating table indicates:

Probing the left somatosensory cortex:
[The neurosurgeon] lowers the two silver wires [of the handheld stimulator] until they gently touch the exposed cortical surface and then lifts them again. 'Feel anything?' 'No, nothing', replies Neil . . . 'Hey! Someone touched my hand!' Neil volunteers . . . 'Which hand?' asks [the neurosurgeon]. 'My right one, sort of like someone brushed the backside of it. It's still tingling a little' . . . [The neurosurgeon] has located the hand area of somatosensory cortex with the stimulator. 'Turn down the current a little' . . . a voice comes down the intercom saying that the stimulator is now set at two milliamperes, down from three. 'Felt it again', Neil reports. 'Same place as before, but it isn't continuing to tingle.' Neil is picking up on our strategy . . . 'That's on the side of my face', Neil says. 'The right side. Cheek sort of.' 'Did it tingle afterward?' [the neurosurgeon] asks. 'No. Didn't feel normal though. Funny kind of feeling.'        (Calvin and Ojemann, 1994, p. 11)

At the back of the brain, in the posterior extremities of the occipital lobe, lies the *primary visual cortex*, which is the best understood of the primary sensory-motor regions in terms of its functional architecture. An additional sensory region, the olfactory centre, which is actually sited sub-cortically in phylogenetically old brain tissue, deserves mention for sake of completeness: the four senses (sight, touch, hearing, smell) and the primary motor cortex.

Yoke the four primary sensory regions and the motor cortex together and you have the building blocks of an adaptive control system, which a mobile organism needs for survival in this uncertain world. Of course the cerebral cortex does not act alone, but in concert with the cerebellum and the lower brain centres. There is a kind of duplication of the sensory-motor maps of the cerebral cortex to be found in the cerebellum. In relation to the cerebral cortex, the cerebellum may be said to function as a kind of auxiliary control system for fine tuning the coordination of complex motor sequences, by receiving and mapping the same sensory information that flows to the cerebral cortex, integrating it with 'motor commands' flowing from the cortex, and relaying it back to higher cortical centres as well as to the motor periphery, 'corrective feedback' ensuring a smooth and accurate execution of 'the motor plan'.[2]

There is not just a single map on the cerebral cortex for each of the four primary sensory areas and the one motor region of the cerebral cortex. Multiple neural maps of the sensory and motor periphery have been discovered, mainly from single-cell recordings in mammals and from neuroimaging studies on humans in recent years. For example, there appear to be several **tonotopic** (frequency organized) maps of sounds in the region of the primary auditory cortex. Penefield and colleagues identified a 'supplementary motor area' in the late 1940s. This renders the concept of a primary centre somewhat problematical. However, the

---

[2] I have placed elements of this thumbnail sketch of the function of the cerebellum in quotation marks to indicate hypothetical components of a complex task that is not well understood and which is beyond the scope of this text.

classical concept of the organization of the cerebral cortex, developed through the nineteenth and twentieth centuries, still remains cogent today. The classical model holds (a) that the cerebral cortex is organized around dedicated, modality-specific, sensory and motor areas that represent projections of spatially distributed sensory receptors and (b) that surrounding these primary sensory-motor areas are regions of *association cortex*, whose basic function is to 'make connections' among patterns of co-activation across different sensory modalities and/or patterns of neural co-activation in time.

As the size of the cerebral cortex grew with the evolution of homo sapiens, the proportion of neural tissue given over to primary projection of sensory and motor information to and from the peripheral sensory organs shrank and the proportion of associative cortex increased. Figure 3.3 below shows a flat projection of the cerebral cortex of the Visible Man and the macaque monkey to give an indication of where the recent evolutionary growth of the cerebral cortex has taken place.

Apart from the absolute difference in surface area (the human cerebral cortex is five times larger, only part of which can be attributed to differences in body size), there are substantial differences in relative size of different lobes of the cerebral cortex and the relative space given over to modality-specific projection of sensory information (not shown in the diagram). The frontal lobes are relatively larger in the human brain (36 per cent of cortical area, compared with 26 per cent in the macaque) and the occipital lobe is proportionately smaller (19 per cent of cortical area in the human brain, 36 per cent in the macaque). Since the time when humans and macaque monkeys shared a common ancestor, there has been a relative increase in the size of the frontal cortex compared with the posterior cortical regions, where our most sophisticated perceptual machinery lies in the association areas that surround the primary sensory areas for touch, hearing and vision.

The flat map projection of the cerebral cortex inevitably involves some local distortion of distances (as does any two-dimensional projection of a curved surface). However, it enables representation of cortical tissue which is normally hidden from view in the cerebral convolutions but which comprises 70 per cent of the total surface area in humans and about 60 per cent in the macaque monkey. The problem of establishing homologous cortical regions (brain structures that share a common ancestry) across species is a major problem – especially where some functions, such as language, may be far more developed in one of the species. However, we shall endeavour to do just that later when we have examined the classical aphasic data on language localization in the human brain.

Before recounting the familiar story of the discovery of the language areas, a word about cerebral localization of perceptual and higher cognitive functions in general is in order.

Simple perceptual features (sensory properties) show more consistency of localization across subjects (brains) than complex perceptual features that are linked to some specific knowledge domain and occupy a higher place on the

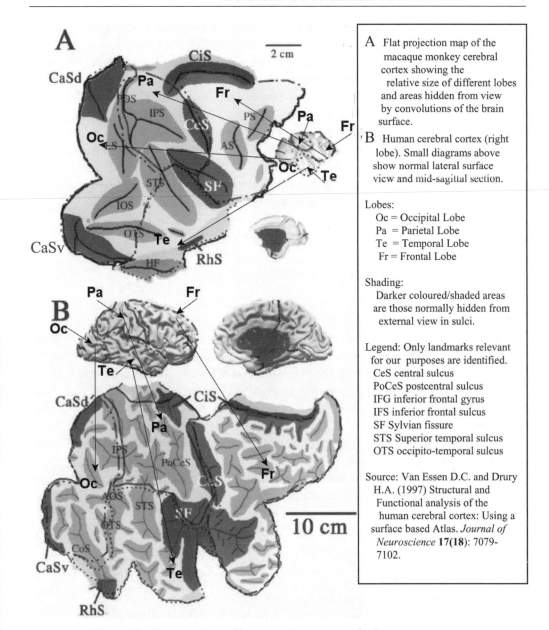

Figure 3.3  *Flat projections of human and macaque cerebral cortex*

'onto-phylogenetic' task hierarchy.[3] Thus, low-level feature detectors for vision and hearing will show more consistency and less inter-brain variability than grapheme (letter) or phoneme detectors, or similar knowledge-domain-linked property detectors. The reason for this is fairly obvious on reflection.

---

[3] Apologies for this terminological mouthful, but it usefully expresses two fundamental principles of evolutionary development and acquisition sequence in neurocognitive development. See p. 55.

Opportunities for individual differences in experience with the feature in question, differential exposure to the knowledge domain in which the feature gains expression, and other factors that can impinge on the course of acquisition[4] have a greater chance to affect the course of acquisition of complex perceptual property detectors and how they are encoded within episodic and semantic memory.

## Discovery of the language areas

The announcement of the discovery of a language area in the brain by the ambitious young anatomist and polymath Paul Broca has assumed almost legendary status in the history of aphasiology. Broca startled the Anthropological Society of Paris with an autopsy demonstration that 'the seat of articulate language' lies in the inferior frontal gyrus of the left frontal lobe. Broca's subject, Lebourge, a long-term resident of Bicêtre hospital, nicknamed 'Tan' because that was the single syllable he was capable of uttering, had died several days previously, after his language (or lack thereof) had been assessed by Aubertin, a well-known proponent of the popular but controversial doctrine of phrenology. Lebourge's aphasia was of long standing, caused by a cyst on the brain. Although virtually inarticulate, he apparently understood what was said to him and could take care of himself and communicate to a limited extent with those around him.

Broca characterized Lebourge's mutism as an inability to 'mobilize the organs of articulation to produce the spoken form of words'. Broca recognized that his patient presented with a motor deficit which was specific to the production of spoken language. Execution of non-linguistic movements by the same muscles of the face, lips, tongue and jaw were unimpaired. Broca was describing a condition that would probably nowadays be labelled *speech dyspraxia*, an inability to initiate voluntary movements for purposes of speech production. Broca originally called this condition *aphemia*. He recognized it as distinct from another form of language disorder that he referred to as *verbal amnesia*, in which motor speech production was intact but words could not be recalled or were inappropriately used – a condition that would probably nowadays be termed *anomia*.

In view of his profound speech production deficit, it is difficult to assess the extent of Lebourge's linguistic impairments. 'Broca's aphasia', as the term has come to be used, encompasses a broader range of language impairments than Broca himself described. People with extensive damage to Broca's area, in addition to profound speech production difficulties, also often manifest signs of **agrammatism**, an apparent selective loss or impairment of grammatical words and inflectional morphemes. Overt signs of agrammatism can be observed in the speech of Broca's aphasics whose production difficulties are not so profound as

---

[4] For example, Lisa Menn (1983) and others have found that individual preferences and avoidance strategies play a significant role in shaping the course of early lexical acquisition and phonological development.

to prevent them from producing multi-word utterances. Below are three typical examples drawn from free narrative transcripts of the patients' speech:

### Sample 1

What brought you to hospital?

Yes . . . ah . . . Monday . . . ah . . . Dad . . . Peter Hogan, and Dad . . . ah . . . hospital . . . and ah . . . Wednesday . . . Wednesday nine o'clock and ah Thursday . . . ten o'clock ah doctors . . . two . . . two . . . an doctors and . . . ah . . . teeth . . . yah . . . And a doctor an girl . . . and gums, an I.

### Sample 2

Describe your job.

Lower Falls . . . Maine . . . Paper. Four hundred tons a day! and ah . . . sulphur machines, and ah . . . wood . . . Two weeks and eight hours. Eight hours . . . no! Twelve hours, fifteen hours . . . workin . . . workin . . . workin! Yes, and ah . . . sulphur and . . . Ah wood. Ah . . . handlin! And ah sick, four years ago.

### Sample 3

Telling about a recent movie:

Odessa! A swindler! down there . . . to study . . . the sea . . . (gesture of diving) . . . into . . . a diver! Armenia . . . a ship . . . went . . . oh! Batum! a girl . . . ah! Policeman . . . ah . . . I know! . . . cashier . . . money . . . ah! cigarettes . . . I know . . . this guy . . .

As many have noted before, though nowadays the comparison has less meaning, agrammatic speech has a *telegraphic* quality, as if motivated by the need to conserve cost or effort. This observation, originally made by Pick (1931 [translated 1973]), has spawned countless controversies over the nature of agrammatism: does it arise from pressure to simplify linguistic expressions to their bare-bones information-bearing elements, to economize on articulatory effort or to circumvent other performance restrictions (such as a limited sequential storage capacity for utterance planning)? Or does the absence of function words and grammatical inflections signify a selective impairment of grammatical or morphological competence? These are issues we shall explore later.

In 1874 another milestone in the history of aphasiology was laid by Karl Wernicke with the publication of a monograph that identified a second language area, damage to which produced symptoms that were complementary to those of Broca's aphasia. The complementary nature of the language disorder in Wernicke's aphasia is evident from their strikingly different language productions:

### Speech sample: Wernicke's aphasia

What brings you to hospital?

Boy, I'm sweating, I'm awful nervous, you know, once in a while I get caught up, I can't mention the tarripoi, a month ago, quite a little, I've done a lot well, I impose a lot, while, on the other hand, you know what I mean, I have to run around, look it over, trebbin and all that sort of stuff.

Thank you Mr X. I want to ask you a few –

Oh sure, go ahead, any old think you want. If I could I would. Oh, I'm taking the word the wrong way to say, all of the barbers here whenever they stop you its going around and around, if you know what I mean, that is tying and tying for repucer, repuceration, well, we were trying the best that we could while another time it was with the beds over there the same thing . . .

The speech of a Wernicke's patient is quite fluent: no *ums* and *ers* or painful, groping and prolonged pauses. Speech rate and intonation sound normal. There are no obvious difficulties with articulation, unlike the Broca's patient. But the Wernicke's aphasic does have problems with the phonological form of some words, making numerous sound substitutions (*paraphasias*) and occasional *neologisms* (see Table 3.1).

Table 3.1 *Typical phonological errors in Wernicke's aphasic speech*

| Spoken form | Target word | Error type | Error label |
|---|---|---|---|
| tarripoi, trebbin | not known | substitution(?) | neologism |
| tying | *trying* | omission | paraphasia |
| repuceration | *recuperation* | transposition | paraphasia |

Wernicke's enduring contribution to the field was to draw some deceptively simple but quite powerful inferences about the functional significance of direct and indirect neural pathways connecting the two primary language areas. Wernicke's theory is traditionally dubbed both *connectionist* and *localizationist*. It is not 'connectionist' in the contemporary computational sense, but in fact articulates the logic of the **double dissociation**,[5] which underlies all subsequent proposals for modular neuropsychological theories of language. Nor is it particularly localizationist, in that Wernicke's model can accommodate the kinds of insights into aphasic language performance that are usually attributed to such anti-localizationists as Hughlings Jackson (1866), Henry Head (1926) and Kurt Goldstein (1948).

## The classical account: the Broca-Wernicke-Lichtheim (BWL) model

Wernicke's language area is located on the left superior temporal gyrus, in the auditory association area surrounding the primary auditory cortex,

---

[5] Double dissociation is a methodological requirement for localizing some particular mental function to a brain area. It is required to demonstrate not only that loss or damage to the brain area in question is associated with loss or impairment of the mental function in question, but also that preservation of the area in question, in the face of possibly extensive damage elsewhere in the brain, is associated with normal maintenance of the mental function in question. See discussion below on the role of the arcuate fasciculus in conduction and transcortical aphasias.

Table 3.2 *Complementary symptoms of Broca's and Wernicke's aphasia*

| Broca type | Wernicke type |
| --- | --- |
| – dysfluent effortful speech | – fluent but empty speech, normal prosody |
| – absence of function words and inflectional morphology | – function words and grammatical inflections present |
| – short utterances | – utterances of normal length |
| – relatively intact comprehension | – poor comprehension |
| – awareness of deficit | – unaware of deficit |

though it is sometimes taken, incorrectly, to extend to the posterior region of the supra-marginal gyrus of the temporal lobe and even to the *angular gyrus* at the junction of the parietal, temporal and occipital lobes (see Figure 1.1, p. 11).

The proximity of Wernicke's area to the primary auditory cortex is paralleled by the proximity of Broca's area to that of the primary motor cortex, which directly controls the muscles of articulation and vocalization. The auditory/acoustic analysis routines for speech perception and the articulatory engrams (memory traces) for speech production are traditionally considered to be stored in these two anatomically separate regions,[6] which are directly connected via a subcortical fibre tract known as the *arcuate fasciculus*.

The complementary symptom patterns of Broca's and Wernicke's aphasia are summarized in Table 3.2. To a degree, this complementarity follows from the proximity of the respective language areas to their respective adjacent motor and sensory regions. But the contrasting pattern of deficits project from speech into language itself: Broca's aphasia into the grammatical impairments of language production and perception; Wernicke's aphasia into symptoms of lexical deficits.

As was appreciated in Wernicke's time, everything in the cerebral cortex is interconnected. However, more complex mental tasks are likely to involve distributed neural networks invoking transient connections between localized nuclei of cells which are functionally more specialized for particular components of the task at hand. Localized networks in close spatial proximity to primary sensory and motor projection areas of the cortex are more likely to be functionally specific, serving 'simpler' or more 'basic' operations on sensory input or motor output. From such considerations, it may be inferred what the consequences of a disconnection in the direct pathways between the anterior and the posterior language centres might be: a breakdown in those kinds of language processing tasks that require close co-operation between speech perception and production at a relatively elementary level. The ability to repeat or 'parrot back' a short phrase is an example of such a task, whereas to maintain an interlocutor role in a conversational exchange of any substance would be an example of a complex verbal exchange, engaging the full cognitive resources of speaker and listener. Thus,

---

[6] This is an oversimplification. See Blumstein, Burton *et al.* (1994) and chapter 8 for further discussion.

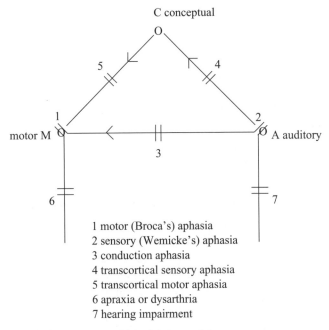

1 motor (Broca's) aphasia
2 sensory (Wemicke's) aphasia
3 conduction aphasia
4 transcortical sensory aphasia
5 transcortical motor aphasia
6 apraxia or dysarthria
7 hearing impairment

Figure 3.4   *The Wernicke-Lichtheim model*

disconnection of the direct connections between the sensory and motor speech areas through a lesion of the arcuate fasciculus should impair simple repetition more than it should conversational language use. This is precisely the predicted symptom pattern of **conduction aphasia**.

Lichtheim (1884), Wernicke's disciple and the third contributor to the classical BWL model, refined the 'connectionist' model further, expressing the indirect pathway between the sensory and motor language areas which is utilized in all 'conceptual' uses of language, as a link in a famous schematic diagram (Figure 3.4).

The 'C' node in the diagram does not represent a neural 'centre' in the sense that the 'M'and 'A' nodes in the diagram stand for the speech motor and auditory centres respectively, but rather, an abstract locus for *afferent* or incoming information from auditory perception to the conceptual level of speech processing, and a locus for conceptual formulation of speech acts that are ultimately assembled in the speech motor area as 'instructions' or motor commands to the articulators. The seven numerically labelled inequality signs stand for different types of disconnection between 'centres' that could arise from localized brain lesions. For example, $\neq 3$ represents disconnection of the arcuate fasciculus. Damage to the speech centres themselves ($\neq 1$, $\neq 2$) represent Broca's and Wernicke's aphasia respectively. The 'disconnections' $\neq 4$ and $\neq 5$ were labelled 'transcortical sensory aphasia' and 'transcortical motor aphasia'.

It is hard to imagine what kind of brain lesion might selectively cut the flow of information from the speech perception system to the conceptual processor

whilst preserving the information flow from the conceptualizer to the speech production centre, to produce what is known as *transcortical sensory aphasia* in
the BWL schema (and vice-versa in the case of *transcortical motor aphasia*)[7].
This distinction was subsequently abandoned by many aphasiologists. However,
it is possible to have widespread brain damage to peripheral regions of the cortex
whilst preserving intact the more medial cortical tissue that encompasses the primary language areas. Such a pattern of damage to cortical tissue can arise from
anoxia due to carbon monoxide poisoning. Norman Geshwind described such a
case of a woman who suffered massive cortical damage by carbon monoxide poisoning (Geschwind, Quadfasel and Segarra, 1968). Although blind and severely
intellectually impaired, she was capable of primitive verbal interaction with her
environment. She could repeat phrases and even complete stock, over-learned
sayings, such as 'Ask me no questions and I'll . . . [tell you no lies].' She learned
to sing along with advertising jingles that she heard repeated over the radio that
was constantly left playing by the bed. In short, thanks to the preservation of the
sensory and motor speech centres and their direct interconnections, this patient
was capable of the type of language performance which is disrupted in conduction aphasia. Geschwind referred to this rare syndrome as 'disconnection of the
speech areas'. In the classical BWL model it would be a particularly severe case of
'transcortical sensory-motor aphasia'. Notice the complementarity of the symptoms of 'conduction' aphasia and 'transcortical' aphasia, linked to the disruption
or preservation of the direct or indirect anatomical pathways between the receptive and motor language areas. This constitutes a 'double dissociation' between
two distinct symptom patterns and two distinct sites of lesion.

Lichtheim also elaborated the classical model further to provide a disconnection account of acquired reading and writing disorders. Reading and writing may
be described as secondary or derived language competencies. Writing systems
(orthographies) are parasitic upon, or iconic representations of, spoken language.
Thus, it is only possible to decipher ancient scripts if one knows or simultaneously
reconstructs the spoken language in which the text was written. Also, reading and
writing can only be taught to children who have substantially completed primary
language acquisition. In a literate individual, reading and writing skills provide
alternative sensory and motor access channels (other than listening and speaking) to acquired linguistic competencies. Thus, auditory perceptual impairments
which may disrupt spoken language comprehension do not necessarily mean that
the individual concerned will be reading-impaired. Similarly, the cortical speech
area which controls articulation and vocalization is distinct from that which inner-
vates the muscles of the dominant hand, so a patient may be quite dysfluent yet
be able to communicate through writing. Reading and writing are to a degree
functionally independent of speaking and listening – precisely to what degree,
and exactly how literacy skills interact with primary linguistic competencies,

---

[7] This criticism was originally made by Freud (1891 [English translation 1953]) in a brilliant but
   overlooked monograph, and later more influentially by Goldstein (1948).

is of course a matter of ongoing research and debate. Lichtheim's proposal for the neuroanatomical basis of reading and writing skills and how they connect to the neuroanatomy of language has been largely adopted with refinements by contemporary neuropsychology.

Lichtheim proposed that decoding of written symbols took place in the left angular gyrus at the junction of the occipital, temporal and parietal lobes, also adding a visual input pathway to Wernicke's language flow diagram. He also proposed a motor-control centre to support writing, similar to Broca's area for speech, connected through both direct and indirect pathways to the other language centres and the (somewhat mysterious) 'C node' or conceptual centre. Without going into details, you can appreciate how the addition of these secondary nodes and pathways resulted in a range of possible new symptom patterns of differential receptive or productive, speech or language, reading or writing impairments, depending upon what 'centres' sustained damage or what connecting 'pathways' between centres were disrupted. You can appreciate also that one could take the BWL model and weaken its anatomical claims by denying the strict localization of 'centres' to specific brain regions. One would then have a 'functional' neuropsychological model, the empirical validity of which would rest entirely upon observed patterns of language performance deficit. This is why it was argued previously that the BWL model, although localizationist, can accommodate non-localizationist theories, if it is interpreted as a modular functionalism, essentially the theoretical position espoused by contemporary cognitive neuropsychologists such as Coltheart (2002).

Norman Geschwind (1974) gives one of the most compelling defences of the classical BWL model in the modern era. His account of anomia is an appropriate way to conclude this brief description of the traditional neuroanatomical model of language organization. Pure cases of naming disorder (anomia), uncontaminated by any other signs of language disorder, are rare. However, naming difficulties are present, to some degree, in most forms of aphasia and can be traced to a host of possible causes: semantic memory loss, sensory perceptual disorder, failures of phonological retrieval, etc., which are variously expressed in 'naming' tasks: confrontation naming (object or picture naming), word-finding in connected speech, or greeting an acquaintance.

As Geschwind (1974) observes, the anatomical basis of anomic disorder has been a traditional battleground between localizationists who implicate the left parieto-temporal region and those who assert no specific site of lesion but a correlation with overall cortical damage affecting processes critical to various aspects of naming behaviour. Geschwind argues, as much on grounds of comparative neuroanatomy as regional brain–symptom correlations, for the special status of the parietal-occipital-temporal junction (POT), an area encompassing the supra-marginal angular gyrus. This was one of the cortical regions identified as having undergone most rapid expansion in the recent evolution of the human brain (referred to in chapter 1). The POT, centred as it is at the junction of three lobes and the secondary association areas of the somaesthetic (tactile and body orientation), the visual and the auditory senses, is strategically located for the formation of *cross-modal* sensory connections. Geschwind points out that a large proportion of words[8] or the concepts that they denote may be thought of as complexes of cross-modal associations. There are problems with the notion that lexical items are literally stored in the POT (see the 'postscript' to this chapter) and Geschwind did not formulate his theory in these terms. As David Caplan (1987) points out, Geschwind's analysis of the neuroanatomical basis of naming and anomia is clearly in the spirit of classical localizationism. But it is also consistent with the non-localizationist emphasis on phylogenetically and ontogenetically late-developing cortical structures in the service of language and symbolic representation.

## Non-localizationist views

The British neurologist Hughlings Jackson is usually credited with elaborating a key distinction between impairments of automatic and volitional behaviour, and linking it to brain evolution and the hierarchy of mental functions: from simple reflexes to logical reasoning, and the kind of language use which supports inference, plans, and the evaluation of options for action and communication about such things. He observed that 'propositional speech' is often impaired while the more automatic uses of language, such as expletives, emotional expressions, greetings or conversational routines, may be preserved intact. The notion that linguistic expressions serve a range of communicative functions linked to mental processes that may be arranged on a hierarchy of increasing evolutionary sophistication may be found in nineteenth-century Darwinian psychology (Spencer, 1867 [reprinted 1977]). However, it is a theme which is elaborated in the writings of subsequent non-localizationist theorists of aphasia such as Henry Head and Kurt Goldstein. And, as we shall see, the distinction between *strategic*, consciously mediated language processing and *automatic*, sub-conscious processing has been a critical consideration in experimental psycholinguistic investigations of aphasia dating from the early 1980s (Milberg and Blumstein, 1981) to the present day.

Roman Jakobson (1941 [English translation 1968]) revived the idea that 'ontogeny recapitulates phylogeny' with his notion that in the course of language acquisition, the child retraces the evolution of language in the species, drawing the additional inference that language breakdown in aphasia represents a retreat to a more primitive or infantile level of language function. Jakobson's notion that aphasics retreat to immature strategies in language processing has influenced psycholinguistic investigations of aphasia, through the application of *heuristics* or processing strategies used by less than fully competent language users (young children, aphasics, second language learners) when presented with

---

[8] With the notable exclusion of function words and connectives.

complex constructions, beyond the structures of simple sentences, issues that we shall take up in chapter 12.

## Site of lesion studies

World Wars I and II were a boon to the study of aphasia, providing neurologists with thousands of opportunities to observe the effects upon language of traumatic brain lesions of all shapes, sizes and locations. A. R. Luria was the most energetic collector of these 'experiments of nature' and one of the most skilful pioneers and practitioners of the art of overlaying sites of lesions and correlating them with acutely observed behavioural and subjective descriptions of language and cognitive impairment (e.g. Luria, 1947 [English translation 1970]). Clinical correlations of this kind are fraught with methodological difficulties, and while many detailed and fascinating case studies can be found in the literature, only a very coarse-grained resolution on the question of localization of language functions can be expected when groups of patients with similar lesion sites are compared.

An example from Luria (1973) (Figure 3.5), showing the relationship between the incidence of disorders of phonemic identification (the primary symptom of what he called *acoustic aphasia*) and different lesion sites, serves to illustrate the kind of correlation that can be expected between a narrowly defined perceptual deficit and the focal point of a localized cortical lesion, typically produced by bullet or shrapnel wound to the head. Patients with phoneme identification disorder have difficulty discriminating words like *pat*, *bat*, *bet*, *bad*, *bird*, . . . etc.

As you see, when the lesion is centred in the auditory association cortex or Wernicke's area, the incidence of phonemic perception disorder is high (94.7 per cent – but, significantly perhaps, not 100 per cent, as strict localization would require). As the primary lesion site is located further away from the auditory association zone, the incidence of phonemic perception disorder declines, but it still remains a detectable symptom in a significant minority of patients whose primary site of lesion may be at some distance removed from the auditory association cortex. Does this sort of data argue for or against the localization hypothesis? We leave you to ponder this question.

The association of damage to the anterior language areas with the symptom pattern of Broca's aphasia and damage to the posterior language areas with those of Wernicke's aphasia has been well established in carefully conducted surveys of the literature (Benson and Ardila, 1996). But beyond this gross statistical correlation, the resolving power of these kinds of studies is inherently low. No two brain lesions are likely to be precisely identical and small differences observable at a gross neuroanatomical level may be crucially significant. Furthermore, individuals may differ significantly in how they accommodate to brain injury, depending on the configuration of the original impairments they experience, and the compensatory strategies that they adopt for circumventing their difficulties. It needs to be borne

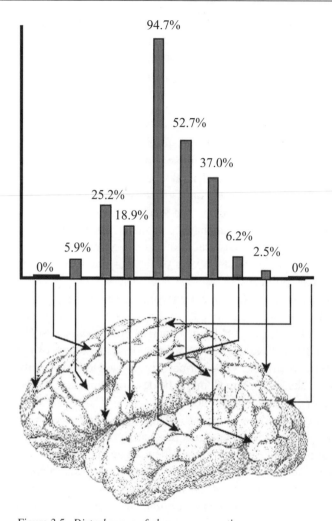

Figure 3.5  *Disturbances of phoneme perception*

in mind that drawing inferences about functional localization on the basis of focal brain damage is reasoning from a *loss* of function caused by removal of brain tissue and that this is a different thing from making observations about the active role that the same site may play in language or cognitive processing under normal operating conditions.

## The neuropsychological perspective

The classical BWL neural model of language postulated a degree of modularity of language processing, founded on the twin notions of (1) localized sensory and motor peripheral skills to support speaking, listening, writing and reading, and (2) a hierarchy of language functions, ranging from autonomous, reflex-like processes involving the primary speech sensory and motor areas and their direct pathways, to 'higher' language functions that involve complex cognitive processes that are neither localized nor autonomous, but dependent upon the functional integrity of the cerebral cortex as a whole. The hierarchy of functions is implicit but not clearly spelled out in the classical BWL model.

Subsequent to the 'classical period' of the articulation of the BWL model, two divergent paths can be discerned in the history of aphasia research, one of which lapsed, the other of which flourished into what has become the dominant approach, at least in clinical circles, of cognitive neuropsychology. The path which was abandoned pursued a rational, analytical taxonomy of aphasic symptoms, supported by argument and introspection. Goldstein's (1948) attempt to elucidate the distinction between symbolic and sub-symbolic processing and its implications for the neuropathology of language is a still visible relic of this approach. Its weaknesses are those of analytical introspective psychology, which disappeared from the intellectual horizon following World War II with the ascendancy of Anglo-American empiricism.

The second approach can be seen in contemporary neuropsychological approaches to aphasia (Howard and Franklin, 1988; Kay, Lesser and Coltheart, 1992). The pioneering work of Luria (1947) encompasses both approaches. On the empirical side, Luria devised clinical tests, partly as demonstrations, of his patients' striking deficits, involving tasks that normal subjects would find trivially easy. A 'battery' of such tasks, it was hoped, might be developed to characterize the spectrum of aphasic language deficits/abilities.

A difficulty of this approach is that a collection of language tests is never more than a collection of tests; performance indices that resist analysis into underlying processes. Proponents of neuropsychological assessment argue that by considering a patient's performance across a range of tests, such as *phoneme discrimination, letter recognition, word and non-word repetition, lexical decision* in aural and visual modalities (reading), *sentence comprehension*, etc., one obtains a map of a patient's perceptual, cognitive or linguistic abilities/deficits. But a neuropsychological test battery is not a street directory to the city of the mind. Whilst it may be useful to chart a patient's performance on a range of tests because they yield scores that correlate with various real-life communicative and literacy skills, such tests do not provide a window on or a natural taxonomy of the skills or competencies involved in normal or disordered language processing. If only the workings of the mind or the brain were so readily observable.

However, it is worthwhile to reflect upon one such neuropsychological model which has been very influential in clinical circles, the *single word processing model* (Howard and Franklin, 1988) and ask: how much does it owe to the classical BWL model that we have sketched above? The model appears quite complicated, but on closer inspection, one finds that apart from the postulation of several buffers – temporary storage bins or 'scratch-pads' for holding interim results of various postulated mental computations – the single word processing model is, in fact, a close literal translation of the BWL model (as augmented by Lichtheim).

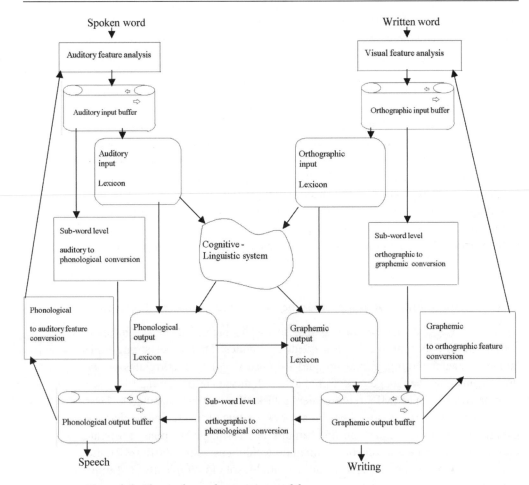

Figure 3.6 *The single word processing model*

The model postulates separate sensory and motor 'lexicons' for listening, speaking, reading and writing; direct and indirect links between modality specific language centres and a central cognitive system for the representation of word meaning. The added computational machinery, of postulating different kinds of temporary storage buffers, constitutes an architectural hypothesis that was inspired by artificial intelligence models of lexical representation and language processing developed in the 1960s (Quillian, 1968; Collins and Quillian, 1969). The validity of this modular architecture of modality-specific storage buffers remains an open question as a psycholinguistic hypothesis.

## Neural imaging

The last three decades have witnessed an exponential growth in the technology of brain imaging. Neural imaging techniques may be broadly classified as structural or functional. Structural imaging techniques, like the familiar x-ray, provide an anatomical picture of brain tissue structures. Computerized axial tomography (CAT scan) and magnetic resonance imaging (MRI) fall into this category.

Functional imaging techniques provide a means of monitoring the activity or functional integrity of different brain regions, by imaging localized metabolic or electrical activity in neural tissue. Metabolic imaging techniques exploit the fact that brain regions of higher local activity – so called 'hot spots' – have higher rates of glucose uptake and demand higher rates of cerebral blood flow. Estimates of regional cerebral blood flow (rCBF) may be obtained by radiographic techniques, such as positron emission tomography (PET scan), or by the detection of minute magnetic field changes induced by increased blood flow and changes in the proportion of oxyhaemoglobin in local blood vessels, using an adaptation of the standard MRI technique to produce functional magnetic resonance images (fMRI).

## Metabolic functional imaging

Vascular changes in response to locally increased metabolic brain activity occur over time frames of seconds to minutes. This places strong limitations on metabolic imaging techniques for observing neural correlates of on-line cognitive and language processing, as we shall see (Jaeger *et al.*, 1996; see chapter 10). PET and fMRI require mental tasks that can be sustained at least over several seconds and do not permit any observation of fine temporal changes in brain states that accompany on-line stimulus processing and response formulation. However, metabolic functional imaging techniques, particularly fMRI, are providing good and increasingly accurate spatial resolution (typically, 3–4 mm$^2$ at the time of writing). fMRI is supplanting the older PET imaging technology because it is non-invasive, provides superior spatial resolution and has a better signal to noise ratio, enabling single-subject data to be gathered over multiple stimulus presentations. The signal-to-noise ratio in PET imaging is usually sufficient only for comparisons between groups of subjects, a limitation that also applies to most behavioural measures of on-line processing (such as the semantic priming technique, discussed later). Techniques with sufficient discriminating power for single-subject studies are needed for investigating higher cognitive functions, particularly in cases of brain damage, where individual compensatory strategies may play an important role.

## Encephalographic functional imaging

Encephalographic functional imaging techniques such as event-related potential recording (ERP) or magnetoencephalography (MEG) measure moment-by-moment changes in brain electrical activity and thus potentially provide sufficiently fine time resolution to enable inferences to be drawn about neural

Table 3.3 *Components of the ERP response*

| Name | Locus | Possible interpretation |
| --- | --- | --- |
| ELAN (N150) | left anterior | Early syntactic processing, phrase structure violation detection |
| N400 | left central | Semantic processing, semantic anomaly detection or 'surprise' reaction |
| P700 | left central | Late syntactic processing, re-analysis or late anomaly detection |

events in on-line processing. ERP evolved from electroencephalography (EEG), in which scalp electrodes record voltage fluctuations arising from the summed action potentials of large populations of cortical neurons beneath the skull. When the EEG signal is time-locked to the presentation of a stimulus event, we obtain an event-related potential recording. The components of an EEG signal which are time-locked to the presentation of some sensory stimulus are weak in relation to the asynchronous components of the signal (background noise of ongoing neural activity). Multiple samples of the same stimulus event with time-locked signal averaging are used to extract the time-varying components of the event-related potential which are reflected in peaks and troughs (positive and negative summations of voltage) in the time-averaged EEG signal.

Early components of the ERP signal (approximately 150 ms or less post-stimulus) have been linked to early sensory processing. Thus, 'early', 'middle' and 'late' components are detectable in an auditory evoked potential (AEP) in response to an auditory stimulus. The earliest component (1.5–15 ms post-stimulus) reflects processing in lower brainstem nuclei. The next component (25–50 ms) reflects an upper brainstem – auditory cortex response, which is followed by a negative polarity at approximately 100 ms, possibly indicative of auditory perceptual processing. There is an important ERP component known as the 'mismatch negativity' (MMN) which occurs 100–200 ms post-onset, in response to a stimulus which stands out as a mismatch in a sequence of otherwise identical stimuli. The MMN can be used to investigate discrimination capabilities for various kinds of auditory stimuli.

The later emerging components of the ERP (200–700 ms) are thought to be associated with higher-level perceptual or cognitive processes. These components are typically labelled by the direction and timing of their peak amplitude. Thus, the N400 designates a negative polarity voltage peak at approximately 400 ms post-stimulus. The identification, labelling and interpretation of ERP components has grown from a small cottage industry to a very large enterprise in recent years, as ERP has become the instrument of choice for observing on-line language processing in psycholinguistic laboratories. Three components of the ERP that have been the focus of much attention in the language processing literature are summarized in Table 3.3.

Taken at face value, the three ERP components suggest a modular account of language processing, whereby a fast-acting, dedicated parser assigns an initial syntactic interpretation to the input word stream. At the same time, lexical access is taking place, driven in the first instance by auditory word recognition algorithms triggered by activation of the receptive language area of the left temporal lobe. At roughly 400 ms post-stimulus, a sentential semantic representation is formed as syntactic information from the parser is integrated with lexico-semantic information from word retrieval. At 700 ms post-stimulus, integrative processes of a different order may be invoked when the language processor encounters a discrepancy in the language input that forces a major revision or re-analysis of the utterance, such as occurs in processing a 'garden path' sentence (see chapter 12). The account just sketched derives from Friederici's (1995) neurolinguistic model of sentence processing, which in turn is closely based on Lynn Frazier's (1978) influential model of syntactic parsing in sentence processing.

The interpretation of temporal components of ERP signals is highly controversial. This example is simply intended to illustrate the potential for decomposing the ERP signal into temporal components that may be related to stages of on-line processing. Encephalographic imaging has good time resolution, potentially in the order of milliseconds. Its spatial resolution is relatively poor, though much improved in recent years by the use of larger electrode arrays and enhanced signal processing capabilities.

## Magnetoencephalography

Magnetoencephalography (MEG) is the measurement of the weak magnetic fields generated by neuronal activity in the human brain. The time resolution of MEG is comparable to that of ERP, but its spatial resolution is superior, because the weak magnetic fields which are detected by the sensor array (of SQUIDS:) in MEG are less affected by the conductivity profile of the brain, skull and scalp. MEG is said to have a spatial resolution of a few millimetres on the surface of the brain, which degrades to a few centimetres for deep structures such as the thalamus. It might therefore appear that MEG has the fine temporal resolution needed to study on-line processing combined with the spatial resolution of fMRI. But the spatial aspect of the equation would be misleading.

The electro-magnetic field fluctuations measured by encephalographic recordings represent the massed action of thousands of neurons recorded over a curved surface (the skull). It is a major and only partially solved problem to locate the principal sources of electrical activity within the brain that are responsible for generating these fields. Known as the 'inverse problem', the problem of calculating the generating current distribution within the brain from the magnetic field at the surface has no unique solution unless some simplifying assumptions are made, such as assuming a specific number of dipole generators. In practice, the assumption of a principal source generator is not unreasonable for sensory experiments where activity in a particular brain region may be expected to be time-locked to the presentation of the stimulus.[9] But for more complex processing tasks, where the number of generator loci is an open question, the inverse problem is more serious.

## Combined imaging methods

It is possible to project functional images of brain activity (or source generators derived from them) onto static structural images of the brain. This is standard practice in fMRI, where the 'hot spots' are superimposed on the static MR scan images. Dynamically changing source generators derived from MEG or ERP may also be projected onto MR images. Hybrid systems that combine the spatial resolution of structural brain imaging with the fine temporal resolution of functional encephalographic imaging provide exciting new windows on brain activity. However, having more precise information on where the generators of brain activity lie also raises more sharply the problem of locus mapping across the brains of different individuals. Methods exist for plotting individual brain maps into a common reference frame. But the more precisely we locate a reference point on a brain map, the more likely it is that individual differences in brain morphology will render its identification problematical across individuals.

## The subtraction method

A serious problem for isolating regional brain metabolic or electrical activity associated with language processing is that of separating activity specific to the language function of interest from other perceptual, motor or cognitive processes that accompany the experimental task and often threaten to mask the process one is trying to observe. The standard approach researchers adopt is to compare brain activation patterns on two closely related tasks, one of which entails more of, and the other of which entails less of, the process of interest. The activation patterns of the two tasks are obtained and one is subtracted from the other, on the assumption that the difference image which results reflects only the effects of the target process. Thus, Caplan *et al.* (2000) used PET imaging to assess whether Broca's area is specifically implicated in the processing of more complex syntactic structures. Sentences matched for lexical content and plausibility but differing on syntactic complexity were presented for subjects to read, while their rCBFs were measured. Reading sentences is, of course, a complex task, involving multiple component skills. By subtracting the activation patterns of the more from the less complex sentence sets, the investigators sought to isolate just the effects of syntactic complexity. The results supported the BWL model, yielding greater activation in the subtracted image over Broca's area in the left hemisphere.

---

[9] The MEG sensors are most responsive to relatively large neurons close to the surface of the cortex and aligned at right angles to the surface of the brain (e.g. the primary receptor cells of the auditory cortex located in the fold of the superior temporal gyrus).

But suppose that the subjects engaged in more sub-vocal rehearsal of sentences in the syntactically more complex stimulus set; a plausible reaction, and one that could differentially engage the speech motor areas, but may have nothing to do with syntactic processing *per se*. The authors anticipated this objection and sought to inhibit any motor rehearsal of stimulus sentences by having the subjects repeatedly pronounce the word 'double' while engaged in the reading task. It is not our intention to debate the effectiveness of this control, but simply to draw the reader's attention to the potential hazards of 'task subtraction' as a method of isolating component processes in a complex mental task. This is part of the problem of modularity of mental functions. It could yet prove a major stumbling block to progress in the area.

## Summary: functional neural imaging

In summary, imaging methods have breathed new life into old questions of localization and modularity of language functions. However, the respective technologies are still very new; experimental artefacts and methodological pitfalls abound. We shall consider evidence from imaging studies in the context of on-line mechanisms in language processing in subsequent chapters. But it would be fair to conclude that at the time of writing, these techniques have not yet resulted in a need to re-draw the picture derived from the classical BWL model of the neurological basis of language functions.

## Postscript: linguistic structures and the neuroanatomy of language

How do the neuroanatomical models of language outlined in this chapter relate to the functional 'anatomy of language' presented in the previous chapter? This, dear reader, is a homework exercise that we hope you keep working on long after you have set aside this text. We shall take up this basic question in ensuing chapters, but to start you off, ask yourself where in the BWL model you would locate *the lexicon*. Do any of the classical aphasic syndromes present themselves as a 'lexical deficit'? Is anomia perhaps a candidate? We have seen that pure anomia is a very rare condition, but anomic symptoms (word finding difficulties) usually accompany most varieties of aphasia. A case can be made for associating pure anomia with damage to the POT junction (Geschwind, 1974). But the commonness of anomic deficits in a broad range of other aphasic disorders suggests that the lexicon is located in no one area, but depends for its operation on the functional integrity of all neural systems that serve language.

Furthermore, lexical items in chapter 2 are described as complexes of phonological, morphosyntactic and semantic features. The BWL model suggests that various bits of a word may be stored in different areas of the brain: the 'how-to-pronounce-me' bits in Broca's area, the 'sound-pattern bits' for auditory recognition in Wernicke's area, and the semantic features – depending on whether the concept that the word represents is comprised of predominantly 'picture-able' or 'functional' properties – just about anywhere!

In the mid 1970s it was popular to argue that the major division between lexical and rule-governed aspects of linguistic competence (a fundamental division in the linguist's 'anatomy of language') is reflected in the major symptom clusters of Broca's and Wernicke's aphasia. Certainly agrammatism is a prominent feature of Broca's aphasia and the fluent speech of Wernicke's aphasics is conspicuous for its lack of lexical content. At the time, psycholinguistic experimenters had just discovered what they took to be hard evidence for a specific deficit in syntactic processing in Broca's aphasia, which blocked the comprehension of *semantically reversible* sentences containing critical syntactic cues (see chapter 12). But this neat direct mapping between the structure of the language code and the neuro-anatomical organization of language in the brain did not remain uncontested for long.

# 4    On modularity and method

## Introduction

In the two preceding chapters, we have explored in a preliminary way two different paths to understanding the human 'language faculty' (Chomsky, 1965; Jackendoff, 1997) or our capacity for spoken language communication. The linguistic approach seeks to isolate and describe the elements of a system of spoken communication by studying varieties of linguistic expressions in the world's languages and human language in general. The neuropathological approach examines types of language breakdown in response to brain damage of various kinds. It is hoped that the search for parallels or correspondences in these two very different domains will yield empirical constraints on a theory of language that could not otherwise be discovered if these two strands of inquiry were conducted in isolation from one another. For example, a fundamental distinction that grammarians draw between lexis and rule in the architecture of the language faculty may turn out to have a correspondence – or not – in the classification of language pathologies, reflecting the organization of language capacities in the human brain. We have already provided you with some classical findings from these two domains, which provides at least a foundation for speculation and further inquiry.

However, it is time to draw some critical methodological distinctions in the interests of making our search for correspondences and a cross-disciplinary theory of language more precise. The distinctions that we draw here will anticipate issues discussed more fully in subsequent chapters. In that sense, they will provide useful guideposts through the thicket of current controversy in neurolinguistics. But though they should prove useful in separating competing theories, the ultimate validity and utility of many of these distinctions is contested, and the initial effect of drawing them may induce as much confusion as shed light on the object of our inquiry. So be warned, methodological distinctions are used as moats to protect academic fortresses as often as they serve as canals for the free commerce of ideas.

Foremost among the useful/invidious distinctions to be drawn is Chomsky's celebrated distinction between linguistic *competence* and *performance*: the extent to which a theory of linguistic *knowledge* can and should be separated from a theory of language *use*, i.e. a model of language comprehension or production. Not unrelated is the question of *modularity* versus *integration* of linguistic with higher cognitive abilities in general. The modularity debate can, if one accepts the competence–performance distinction, be directed towards the issue as to whether linguistic knowledge is made up of discrete components (phonology: knowledge of sound patterns; morphology: knowledge of word structure; syntax: sentence structure knowledge, etc.) or whether a performance model of language use is modular in its construction (e.g. are separate modular processing components responsible for recognition of phonological forms of words, the parsing of syntactic structures, the assignment of word and sentence meanings, etc.?). From our perspective, questions of modularity of processing are clearly of central concern. Modular theories of language performance generally assume modularity of linguistic knowledge (competence), but may in addition invoke additional specialized processing machinery, such as rapidly decaying specialized sensory information storage (SIS) or long-term memory and retrieval mechanisms (LTM), required to implement a language processor that utilizes a modular linguistic knowledge base.

Jerry Fodor's (1983) monograph *The modularity of mind* has become the classical exposition of modularity from the perspective of language processing, in which he identifies nine characteristic or defining properties (depending on your viewpoint) of modular processing systems. In retrospect, it can be seen that Fodor's account of modularity encapsulates a number of seismic theoretical divisions, of which modularity is only one. In particular, he links modularity with the existence of specialized innate, or hard-wired, processing capacities, which is strictly speaking a quite separate issue. Recently the cognitive psychologist Max Coltheart (2002) has uncoupled the notion of modularity in processing from its nativist Fodorian assumptions and elevated it to a methodological precept, by linking it to the concept of a **double dissociation**, a way of identifying mental modules through careful clinical study of patterns of functional impairment caused by brain injury. He likens mental processing to a manufacturing operation, developing the more palatable analogy of 'a chocolate factory' to illustrate the logic of discovery of modular mental abilities. Because of its central relevance to our quest, we shall subject Coltheart's concept of modularity to close scrutiny in this chapter. We shall also raise some of the more imponderable quasi-philosophical issues that beset any extended discussion of modularity: *learnability* – the role of nature versus nurture in the acquisition of modular mental (specifically linguistic) skills and abilities; and *reductionism* – the extent to which modular mental processes can and ought to be reduced to physical brain processes, via neurophysiological concepts such as the establishment and activation of *cell assemblies* and the like (Hebb, 1949; Pulvermüller, 2002). We raise these theoretical issues in this chapter, but will explore them further in subsequent chapters as they emerge as recurrent themes in different aspects of language processing and language breakdown.

## Chomskian modularity

For Chomsky, like the scholastics of an earlier pre-scientific era, the mind is a kind of repository of human knowledge – containing not only propositional knowledge (*knowing that*), but 'tacit' knowledge (*knowing how*) of various kinds, such as 'how-to-walk' or 'how-to-talk', i.e. how to map between sound (speech) and meaning. Chomsky's particular concern as a cognitive scientist has always been with the 'knowing how' of language: what that knowledge consists of and how it is acquired. In the early days of generative grammar Chomsky saw that this knowledge, or at least a significant component of it, the grammar of a language, could be rigorously captured in a system of re-write rules (known as 'phrase-structure' rules: S → NP VP; NP → D N; . . . etc.), augmented by structure-changing 'transformations' that establish derivational relationships between basic or *kernel* sentences and non-kernel sentence types. Kernel sentences were originally intended to capture the core syntactic structures of the simple sentence in the language (Harris, 1958; reprinted in Harris, 1970). Non-kernel sentences, though often equivalent in propositional meaning, were derived from kernel sentences by transformational rules (e.g. *The cat sat on the mat* →$^T$ *The mat was sat on by the cat.* or →$^T$ *It was the cat that sat on the mat.*).

The specific tenets of Chomsky's theory have evolved almost unrecognizably since transformational grammar was first propounded (Chomsky, 1955, 1957), but the idea that the grammar of a language may be expressed as a logico-mathematical system, with precisely definable formal properties, remains a key insight and distinctive contribution of Chomsky's theory of language. The other key, unchanged tenet of his theory is that the particular properties (or *parameters* in one of the later formulations) of the formal model restrict the range of possible natural language grammars, and these restrictions, if incorporated *a priori* (before experience), constitute an innate module in the mind of the language learner.

It was recognized early on by Chomsky and Miller (1963) that unrestricted recursive rule application is required of a production system that has the capacity to generate syntactic structures of unbounded complexity, while making use of a restricted set of core sentence types and the phrase structure rules that generate them.[1] But obviously there are practical restrictions on the length of sentences that

---

[1] An important parenthetical note is required here. A phrase structure grammar is technically a 'production system', which generates structural descriptions for sentences which are well-formed grammatical expressions according to the set of re-write rules that the grammar employs. However, there is no implication that such a production system should be construed as a performance model of sentence production. It is simply a formal mechanism for enumerating grammatically well-formed expressions and for assigning structural descriptions to sentences that accord with native speakers' grammatical intuitions. Nothing more. Much confusion arose in the early years of psycholinguistics, for which Chomsky himself must be held responsible, when the 'grammar' in this narrow technical sense was confused with the broader and never precisely defined sense of grammar as a device for 'mapping sound to meaning'.

language users can employ, and certain forms of recursion must be highly constrained, in ways that cannot be naturally accounted for by the properties of recursive re-write rules (e.g. *The cat meowed. The cat the dog chased meowed. ??The cat the dog the car ran over, chased, meowed.*). Chomsky and Miller's solution was to impose extrinsic *performance* restrictions on the operation of recursion in centre-embedded constructions. But can a limitation on the comprehension or production of syntactic structures, such as restricting centre embedding to a depth of one or two cycles, be legitimately regarded as a restriction which lies *outside* the domain of the grammatical module? Many would argue that it cannot. Although these concerns may seem somewhat 'academic', they make their appearance in numerous ways and various guises in the psycholinguistic and aphasic literature, as we shall see.

Does agrammatism in Broca's aphasia represent a deficit of grammatical competence or one of performance? Those such as Grodzinsky (1990) who argue for a competence deficit seek a quite specific correspondence between a pattern of aphasic language impairment in comprehension or production and a property or mechanism of a formal competence model. Thus, case assignment (see chapter 2) depends, according to the principles and parameters model (Chomsky, 1981), upon the correct assignment of case roles to null constituents – traces – such as the 'underlying' object of the verb *chased* in the object relative clause: *The cat the dog chased . . .* The reason why agrammatic patients have difficulties with constructions such as these is that their competence grammars lack this specific mechanism of trace assignment, according to Grodzinsky's 'trace deletion hypothesis' (see chapter 9 for discussion). On the other hand, Stephen Crain (Crain, Ni and Shankweiler, 2004), an otherwise staunch advocate of Chomskian modularity in language acquisition, argues that grammatical competence remains intact in acquired agrammatism. We defer consideration of this issue to contrast modularity of knowledge with modularity of process; the sense in which the term has been most influential in psycholinguistics.

## Fodorian modularity

Jerry Fodor's celebrated account of modularity may be seen as an apologia for the Chomskian enterprise applied to the domain of language performance. It cuts directly to the chase by viewing modules as processing devices or transducers that mediate between 'peripheral' sensory information and 'higher' or 'central' levels of language processing. *The modularity of mind* is not about knowledge representation *per se*, though Fodor does have his own distinctive position on this question (see Fodor 1975, 1987; Fodor and Pylyshyn, 1988). Rather, modularity for Fodor concerns the language processing mechanisms which enable speakers and listeners to share knowledge representations about states of the world. The leading idea for the monograph is conveyed by a quote from Merrill Garrett in the dedication:

'*What you have to remember about parsing*', Merrill said, '*is that basically it's a reflex...*'

Modular systems are higher-level perceptual and mental processes that have some of the defining properties of the humble reflex arc. They are fast-acting, triggered by highly specific input conditions, mandatory in their operation, inflexible and hard-wired. While most of the examples of modular systems that Fodor discusses come from research in speech perception (which we discuss in chapters 5–7), others represent 'core' language processes, such as syntactic parsing and semantic interpretation. A module, in Fodor's terms, is a functionally specific processing device, which has evolved through evolutionary pressure to provide reflex-like speed of processing in some critically time-dependent task. Fodor argued that language processing, a hugely complicated task, which we manage to accomplish in real time,[2] must be supported by modular processing systems operating in parallel.

Fodor identifies nine properties of modular systems. We shall briefly explain each of these properties, with an example. It is no coincidence that six of the nine examples come from speech perception and involve peripheral input processing systems. But modularity is not confined to peripheral systems (i.e. systems based around the primary senses of vision, hearing, touch, etc.). Language processes are 'central' (cross-modal, or multi-modal); and they are modular, according to Fodor.[3] Although it is not explicitly mentioned below, modular processes are taken to be substantially hard-wired into the brain and genetic make-up of members of the species.

Modular systems are dedicated computational devices, designed (by nature) for some specific information processing task. They tend to be *domain-specific*, i.e. they apply in some restricted domain of information and no other. Fodor cites the example of phonetic feature detectors, sensory devices for detecting the presence of particular phonetic features in speech signals (features such as *voicing*, *aspiration*, *nasality*: the building blocks of speech sounds). These are dedicated feature detectors, good for speech recognition, but nothing else. Fodor is referring to evidence, which we shall take up later, bearing on the existence of such dedicated devices in the human auditory system.

Modular processing systems are *mandatory* in their operation. We have no choice in their application. They are automatic, simply triggered off by the appropriate stimuli. When we are exposed to speech-like stimuli, for example, we cannot choose but to process them under the 'speech listening mode'. Again, we shall look into evidence for such a specialized processing mode later.

---

[2] *Real time* is used in a relative sense here to mean sufficiently fast that we are unaware that the process in question took any time at all.

[3] We use 'central' here, in the neurological sense of the term, meaning not dependent on a particular sensory modality or motor control system. In Fodor's restrictive use of the term, language functions are always 'peripheral' because they always involve input-output mappings between sound and meaning (language comprehension) or meaning and sound (language production). Furthermore and controversially, according to Fodor, central processes – thinking, inference, abduction – lie beyond the pale of cognitive science.

Table 4.1 *Fodor's criteria for modularity*

| Properties of modular systems | Examples |
| --- | --- |
| 1. Domain-specific | phonetic feature detectors |
| 2. Mandatory operation | the speech listening mode |
| 3. Limited central access | awareness of sub-phonemic properties of speech |
| 4. Fast-acting | on-line word recognition |
| 5. Informationally encapsulated | phoneme restoration |
| 6. 'Shallow' analysis | extraction of surface forms, not deep structure |
| 7. Fixed neural architecture | motor control circuits in the cerebellum |
| 8. Specific patterns of breakdown | aphasic syndromes |
| 9. Maturational sequencing | language acquisition |

We have only *limited central access* to modular processes. By this Fodor means that modular processes are largely beyond conscious awareness. We are not capable of monitoring them or reflecting upon them. They are opaque to introspection. Our example from Table 4.1 above, that listeners are unaware of sub-phonemic properties of speech, needs more explanation than can be given right now. Essentially what Fodor means here is that most of the fine phonetic detail of speech is responded to and is utilized by the perceptual system in speech recognition, even though most of this detailed information is not consciously accessible to the perceiver. One reason why such information is not available to conscious experience is explained by Fodor's next property of modular systems.

Modular systems are *fast-acting*. Modular systems probably evolved because of the need to process stimuli in real time. Speed is of the essence when danger signals are encountered. Reflexes are good protection against some noxious stimuli, because they are fast-acting. The trouble with reflexive responses however is that they are inflexible, or just plain dumb. Modular mental processes can be a bit dumb too, but they are quick, and they can be part of a system that behaves quite intelligently. As an example of a fast-acting modular process, Fodor cites lexical retrieval, the process of contacting words in the mental dictionary. Lexical access is almost instantaneous. We recognize a word almost as soon as we hear it, despite the fact that we carry around in our heads a recognition vocabulary of on average 60,000 words. How do we do it? More on this later.

Modular systems tend to be *informationally encapsulated*. This is similar to the first property of modular systems. What Fodor means is that a modular system responds only to input of a given type and yields output of a given type. An informationally encapsulated processor is oblivious to all other information passing around it, no matter how relevant that information might subsequently turn out to be. For example, a modular word recognizer cares only about phonological features. All other accompanying acoustic information in the speech signal is simply ignored. What happens, for example if we block out or mask part of a word with a piece of extraneous noise or a 'cough'? One effect that has been observed is called 'phoneme restoration'. The masked sound is reinstated by the listener who 'hears' it as if it were really there. Many perceptual illusions are like this. We shall look at evidence for information encapsulation when we look at how listeners syntactically process sentences (called parsing). The idea is that the parser charges ahead, constructing syntactic structures on the basis of word strings that it encounters. Sometimes it builds what turn out to be wrong structures and the parser is forced to back-track.

Because modular systems tend to be fast-acting and informationally encapsulated, they can only perform *shallow analysis* on the input to which they are exposed. We will try to be more precise about what Fodor means by a 'shallow' analysis when we come to discuss syntactic parsing and sentence processing. For those with some linguistic background, Fodor is here referring to 'surface structure' representations. A modular syntactic processor will assign surface structure syntactic representations, not deep structures or semantic representations.

Modular processes employ a *fixed neural architecture*. The most convincing examples of fixed neural architectures which are dedicated to the performance of certain processing tasks are all rather low on the information processing hierarchy. One might cite the specialized neural architecture of the cerebellum, which it has been argued is well adapted to the task of error correction or fine adjustment to the timing of pre-planned motor gestures from incoming sensory information, in order to produce smooth sequencing of complex motor behaviour (Eccles, 1973). Phonetic feature detectors in speech perception could be cited as examples of fixed neural architecture for 'high-level' perceptual processing, though the physiological evidence for this specialized circuitry is lacking.

One clinical manifestation of a modular process is that, according to Fodor, it will be subject to a distinctive pattern of disintegration as a result of brain damage. Suppose, for example, that as a result of evolutionary adaptation motorists were to evolve a specialized 'zebra crossing detector'. Damage to this module would result in an **agnosia** (perceptual blindness) for zebra crossings while all other aspects of the motorist's visual perception would remain intact. Of course we have no direct evidence yet for zebra crossing detectors, but the neuropsychological literature is replete with clinical accounts of strange modular deficits, many of them not very well documented.

Developmental signs of modular mental processes are familiar to psycholinguists from Chomskian accounts of language acquisition. Chomsky regards language acquisition as a biologically controlled maturational sequencing, akin to learning to walk; something that unfolds according to a genetically programmed timetable, absorbing critical 'parameter settings' from the linguistic environment at particular stages in the child's language development.

## Summary: Fodor's concept of modularity

Mental modules according to Fodor are specialized processing facilities, dependent upon triggering conditions, mainly instantiated by peripheral sensory motor processes, but found also in those central processes that support rapid on-line language processing. Modular mental processing in Fodor's scheme constitutes a layer of reflex-like processing operations that support the elaborate computational operations needed to construct linguistic representations on the basis of a rapidly changing and transitory speech signal. Fodor's account of modular mental processes has a strong *a priori* flavour, as though the necessity of their existence ought to be self-evident once their properties have been clearly stated. However, there is sufficient exemplification in Fodor's account, particularly drawn from experimental work in speech perception and on-line studies of language comprehension, to bring empirical evidence to bear on some key claims for modular language processing.

Fodor's (1983) monograph acted as something of a lightning rod for the subsequent two decades of psycholinguistic research. It provided a plausible neuropsychological framework within which modular theories of language processing, derived from linguistic competence models, could be evaluated using evolving specialized experimental paradigms and newly emerging methods of computational modelling. It was the new computational modelling techniques based on connectionist learning models (Rumelhart and McClelland, 1986) that provided the most direct challenge to Fodorian accounts of language processing and modularity.

## Modularity uncoupled: Max's chocolate factory

While Fodor's nine characteristic properties of a modular processing system define a coherent nativist perspective on language processing, they do not, as Coltheart (2002) correctly points out, specify the *only* logically or empirically possible concept of modularity. Modularity of mental processing could arise as a result of learning or experience as much as from 'innate knowledge' or 'hard-wiring' of specialized perceptual or motor capabilities. In other words, we may uncouple the defining properties of modular processing ('domain specificity', 'information encapsulation') from the merely accompanying properties that characterize a particular *kind* of modularity ('mandatory operation', 'fast-acting', 'limited central access', etc.). Coltheart's major concern lies with the methodology of establishing functional modularity through observation of patterns of neurocognitive impairment. How can we establish what modules make up the 'cognitive architecture' of the mind? Contrast this with Fodor, who is concerned to identify the properties which identify a mental process as 'modular'. Fodor's exemplifications of modular functions turn out to be, with the notable exception of core language processing capabilities (sentence parsing or production and the like), specialized *peripheral* perceptual and motor control systems, that just happen in many instances to serve primary language processing in one way or another. Coltheart considerably widens the scope of possible modular functions to include virtually the whole domain of acquired cognitive abilities – reading, recognizing faces, picture naming, etc.

The questions then become: what constitutes a module? how can mental modules be identified and their functional relationships between one another established? Coltheart (2002) argues that the neuropsychological method provides a way of establishing the modular architecture of cognition in general. This may be achieved, it is claimed, by careful observation and inference of possibly quite rare patterns of modular functional impairment, usually but not necessarily associated with brain damage, and by showing how such deficits can be *dissociated* from other skills or functions that remain intact. Hence, the case for a perceptual module for 'face recognition' may be advanced if one can find neuropsychological patients whose ability to recognize familiar faces is lost, and has become dissociated from visual object recognition in general (which remains unimpaired). Cases of *prosopagnosia* (or 'face blindness', a selective impairment of the ability to recognize familiar faces) are rare. Such a disorder suggests, but by no means demonstrates, that some 'extra' or 'special' processing module, over and above the abilities called upon for recognizing depictions of visual objects in general, may be required for recognizing faces. The case for modularity of face recognition is strengthened if the complementary clinical pattern of impaired visual object recognition (visual agnosia) *without* prosopagnosia can be found, thereby establishing a double dissociation of the two abilities.

Coltheart (2002) is careful to point out that a double dissociation of two distinct mental capabilities does not provide an overwhelming case for their modularity. Their dissociation could stem from the fact that while they may share some or many common processing resources, each is critically dependent upon the integrity of at least one processing capability that the other is not dependent on.

Mental processes are difficult and dry abstractions to contemplate. So let us consider chocolate factories and what we can learn of their operation by merely observing their inputs and outputs over a prolonged period of time, sufficient to observe the variety of ways that their manufacturing operations can break down. Let us further assume, crucially, that all chocolate factories employ the same manufacturing process. Chocolate factories take, among other things, as their raw input, whole cocoa beans, and yield, among other things, as their output, cocoa powder and chocolate bars. We may take it on Max's authority that there are a number of common manufacturing processes, a breakdown in any one of which can halt the production of both cocoa powder and chocolate bars: some fault of roasting, grinding, refining or pressing of the raw beans. A breakdown in the chain of manufacturing operations that halts production of both cocoa powder and chocolate bars is less informative than a breakdown which halts one but not the other product(s). Suppose we observe many more instances of disrupted output in the production of chocolate bars than cocoa powder and that every instance of disruption of cocoa powder production is invariably accompanied by a shutdown in the output of chocolate bars. What would you conclude? That cocoa powder production is a necessary step in the manufacture of chocolate bars? A reasonable inference perhaps, but one which would have to be abandoned if we were to observe a single, reliably attested, incidence of double dissociation,

Table 4.2 *Production plant states of operation*

| State of plant operation | Cocoa powder | Chocolate bars |
| --- | --- | --- |
| 1. Fully functional | + | + |
| 2. Plant shutdown | − | − |
| 3. Chocolate bar production down | + | − |
| 4. Cocoa powder production down | − | + |

i.e. where *both* single patterns of dissociation are attested – however rare one of those single patterns of dissociation may be. The various scenarios are illustrated in Table 4.2.

Over time, a range of operational scenarios may be observed, some more frequent than others. Because cocoa powder and chocolate bar production share many production processes, the most likely breakdown scenario will be disrupted output of both products. But if we observe occasional instances of chocolate bar production breakdown without impaired cocoa powder production we might reasonably infer that some 'extra step' is required for the production of chocolate bars, over and beyond what is required for cocoa powder production. Alternatively, it might be the case that chocolate bar production is simply more sensitive to the overall operational efficiency of the plant, or is critically dependent on the timely supply of a greater number of raw materials (such as dairy products). The single dissociation scenario involves observation over time of plant states of operation (1. and 2. and 3.) *or* (1. and 2. and 4). A double dissociation scenario involves observing over time each of the four possible states of plant operation (1. and 2. and 3. and 4.), and in particular (3. and 4.).

In general, a host of factors can underlie patterns of production disruption in chocolate factories. Single dissociations (selective impairments) of product outputs are usually open to a range of interpretations, one of which is that the dissociated product (e.g. chocolate bars) is critically dependent on the integrity of some specialized processing step in production (e.g. 'conching' or slow blending of ingredients within a critical temperature range). In practice, many interpretations are compatible with single dissociation scenarios. Observed patterns of double dissociation more clearly establish functional separation – at some stage of production – between two distinct product outputs. But here too, multiple hypotheses about what has happened to produce the various patterns of disrupted output may be entertained. Double dissociations of product lines merely provide stronger evidence of processing modularity than single dissociations.

Given the generally reliable operation of chocolate factories, the multiple possible mechanical and human causes of production failure, and the assumption that chocolate factory management are not prone to advertise their accidents, one may have to wait some time before all potential patterns of production failure can be observed. Moreover, the inferential payoff of studying patterns of production failure may seem decidedly limited. At this point, most serious students of chocolate production will want to take the guided factory tour (samples included), to see the layout of the plant machinery and get a 'hands on' view of the production processes. But our host (Max) counsels against this rash move. The modern choco-late factory is a very complicated plant, and – here the analogy between brains and chocolate factories becomes a little understated – observing the machinery in operation is liable to confuse as much as it aids our functional understand-ing of how its various products (process outcomes) relate one to another. Given our presently very primitive understanding of chocolate factory plants, our host advises methodological caution. Understand the inter-relationships among the product lines before you venture onto the shop floor.

What wc confront here is the question of *reductionism* and levels of expla-nation. Can a satisfactory functional understanding of the relationships among perceptual and cognitive capabilities be offered in the absence of understanding their neurophysiological (and neurochemical) substratum? Let us defer dealing with this fundamental question for a moment, save to observe that, from a clini-cal perspective, a functional mapping of a patient's neuropsychological abilities provides a logical starting point for planning therapeutic intervention strategies. But whether such a 'functional mapping' constitutes an appropriate starting point for understanding language and language-related real-time cognitive processing is a moot point.

## Modularity and real-time processing

Coltheart's (2002) uncoupling of the defining and characteristic fea-tures of modular processing has both fortunate and unfortunate consequences. Modular impairments are most clearly demonstrated in the mature brain, often as a result of focal brain injury, which can often yield surprisingly specific deficits in complex cognitive behaviours that were performed as highly automated skills prior to the pathology. In this sense, uncoupling modularity of function from 'innately wired' competencies and recognizing the importance of learning in the establishment of functional automatons is a step in the direction of empirical ade-quacy. Specialization of cognitive function is typically acquired in human beings through the joint influences of neural maturation and sensory-motor experience (learning).

However, it also needs to be emphasized that the objects of our inquiry are *real-time* processing capabilities. Consequently, it seems to be a mistake to uncouple the defining properties of 'domain specificity' and 'encapsulation of function' from Fodor's other characteristic properties of modularity: 'fast-acting', 'manda-tory operation', 'limited central access', which lend modular processes their reflex-like character and speed of action. Just as important as their contribution to increasing the behavioural repertoire of the organism that possesses them is the fact that modular capabilities operate in real time, without imposing a significant additional load on limited attentional resources. Our ability to automate complex cognitive functions by consigning them to modular processing 'frees up' scarce attention-directed problem-solving resources for other complex tasks that cannot normally be accomplished in real time. The loss of a modular ability, due to stroke or other brain damage, typically drives the victim to use compensatory strategies to retrieve at least some lost automaticity of function. Recovery may be seen as partial or full restoration of automaticity of the original function.

Hence, modularity should be confined to real-time or **on-line** mental processes and capabilities. Thus, a loss of scrabble or chess playing ability would not qualify as a modular deficit, but an acquired loss of capability to understand speech, or to recognize printed words or familiar faces, would do so, provided that the deficits themselves can be shown to be sufficiently discrete and dissociated from normal performance in clearly related on-line tasks. As pointed out in chapter 1, a certain modularity of language from other higher cognitive functions is uncontroversially apparent from the fact that aphasia – a selective loss of language or communicative skills – is observed, and not infrequently in human populations. At issue is the question of granularity: how fine-grained and specific are the patterns of functional dissociation that can be observed, and, perhaps more fundamentally, the question of temporal processing: how can we understand mental capabilities as the outcomes of real-time computational processes? We will defer the question of granularity of language processing for the present, but must take up the issue of modularity and real-time processing because it raises a fault-line disagreement that continues to divide the field, concerning the type of computations involved in the act of language processing.

## Real-time processing

It is not so much what our brains can do but what they can do in real time that matters, and how that is accomplished. We are accustomed to perceive a coherent world of perceptual objects. What we apprehend when someone speaks to us (assuming we are not aphasic and they address us in our native language) is the *meaning* of what we understand them to have said. But if psychology and neuroscience have taught us anything at all over the past two centuries or so, it is that our immediate apprehension of a coherent world of objects and meanings is (contrary to naive experience) not something which is simply given to us 'on a platter', but rather, something that is constructed by the mind/brain from the primary datum of sensory experience. Our experience of a perceptually coherent world is utterly dependent upon the delicately orchestrated light show of a couple of billion well-trained and harmoniously wired neurons.[4] The notion that a world of stable objects, or the meaning of a spoken utterance, is the product of a host of complicated neural computations that take place in close to real

---

[4] Readers who doubt the truth of this non-obvious proposition should read some of the numerous excellent personal accounts of what can happen to the coherence of one's perception of the world when the brain experiences traumatic insult, such as A. R. Luria (1987).

time is a fundamental assumption of modern neuroscience, though it is also universally acknowledged that we remain profoundly ignorant as to the nature of these computations.

It is agreed that at least a proportion of these computational processes are hierarchically organized. At lower levels of the processing chain, modality-specific sensory detectors located in the primary sensory-receptive areas of the cerebral cortex will respond to stimulation of a specific type that falls within the cells' receptive field, corresponding to an area of the somatic surface served by one or a small population of sensory receptors (for touch, hearing or vision). At the next level, more complex perceptual property detectors may receive input primarily from same-modality cortical sensory property detectors, but also from inter-neurons linked to distantly located sensory detectors from a different sensory modality, to yield a property detector which is sensitive to cross-modal sensory stimulus contingencies. At a still higher level of perceptual processing – and here the circuitry is more difficult to establish with any degree of certainty – a highly specialized property detector for particular speech sounds or phonetic features may respond, when a whole assembly of cells distributed across speech motor and auditory cortical regions becomes activated, usually as a result of producing speech gestures or viewing others articulating. We are referring here to a quite recently discovered neural circuit of 'mirror neurons' and its possible role in activating phonetic feature detectors for speech recognition; a topic taken up in more detail in chapters 7–9.

Neural circuits, or more precisely artificial neural networks (ANNs) designed to simulate the kind of computations thought to take place in the brain, have also been proposed for higher levels of language processing such as syntactic parsing (Pulvermüller, 2002). Pulvermüller (2002) sketches an outline of a strongly reductionist view of language processing, partly substantiated by neurophysiological findings at the sensory level, but highly speculative beyond that; a view that is only partially compatible with Fodorian notions of language processing, and one that Coltheart, with his anti-reductionist stance on psychological processes, would regard as premature at best.

Two styles of computational modelling, one characterized as *symbolic* and the other as *connectionist*, have vied for ascendancy in the language processing literature in the past three decades over the nature of the computations involved in language processing. We review in broad brush strokes the issues in this debate, which has tended to generate more heat than light, in the following section. Yet proponents in both camps would agree that *levels of processing* need to be distinguished, and that there is a natural logical dependency of higher-order cognitive processes upon lower-order sensory/perceptual processes, however much they may disagree as to how such processes should be modelled.

To advance the scientific study of real-time language processing, we obviously require observational techniques that provide a window on the various stages of processing and reveal the functional dependencies of higher-order processes upon lower-order processes. Such techniques include behavioural, reaction-time-based measures, and phenomena such as **priming effects** that may be interpreted as manifestations of automatic sub-conscious processing. In recent years, high temporal resolution functional imaging techniques such as EEG (electroencephalography), ERP (event-related potential recording) and MEG (magnetoencephalography) have allowed researchers to fractionate a complex process such as reading aloud a single word into sequenced phases of neural processing: decoding the visual array on the primary occipital cortex, associating orthographic form with phonological features required for word recognition in the region of the angular gyrus, semantic activation of word meanings in the dominant temporo-parietal cortex, followed by activation of the prefrontal cortex and Broca's area as the articulatory programs for saying the word are activated. The precise timing, sequencing, coordination and indeed detailed characterization of all of the above-named processes remain questions of open debate (see Poeppel and Hickok, 2004, and the contributions therein, for a summary of the current state of play).

As the temporal and spatial resolution of functional neuroimaging improves – perhaps by the joint application of haemodynamic and electromagnetic techniques – we can expect a more precise picture to emerge, of how specific task demands shape spatio-temporal patterns of neural activity in different aspects of language understanding and production. However, it remains a huge step to explicitly model how the various sources of tacit linguistic knowledge, from the auditory-acoustic consequences of combining certain speech gestures (at the phonetic level) to collocational restrictions on word classes (at the syntactic level), are effectively exploited in language processing, and when it becomes appropriate, given the current state of knowledge, to attempt to characterize these operations in terms of their neural substrate. This is the unsolved reductionist problem of the language–brain relationship.

## The connectionist challenge

Modular theories of language processing have their origins in linguistic theory, cognitive psychology and the traditional 'expert systems' approach to artificial intelligence (AI). In fact, linguistic theory is the ultimate source of most modular theories, given that cognitive psychology and classical AI models of natural language processing took their inspiration largely from Chomsky's (1957, 1965, 1981) theory of linguistic competence.

Connectionist models of language have their historical antecedents in learning theory in psychology and in a much older philosophical tradition of empiricism and associationist views of mind. But what sets contemporary connectionist models of language apart from their behaviourist and empiricist forebears is that they take the form of computational simulations, rather than being purely 'paper and pencil' models. A computational simulation can be evaluated by measuring the performance of the model against the 'real thing' – in this case, some aspect of human language performance: word recognition, lexical retrieval, assigning syntactic descriptions to sentences, responding 'appropriately' to verbal input, etc.

A modular (symbolic) theory of language processing can, of course, also be expressed or implemented as a computer program. Many such simulations were developed in classical AI, some as early as the 1960s. Connectionist simulations of language processing date from the 1980s (see Rumelhart and McClelland, 1986). Connectionist models have the capacity to *learn*, or at least to simulate learning. They are adaptive. It is this property that makes connectionist models interesting to psycholinguists.

## Connectionist architectures

There is a great variety of connectionist or artificial neural network (ANN) architectures, each with different learning properties and capabilities. Networks differ in the number, type and arrangement of connections between units in the net; whether or not they require a specific training regime, what sort of learning rule they may use to modify connection weights; whether they are localist or distributed networks. For a good non-technical introduction to neural networks, which covers the types of models that we will deal with in this book, read 'Why connectionism?', chapter 2 of Elman *et al.* (1996).

We shall examine some influential connectionist models of different aspects of language processing in subsequent chapters. But to give you a feel for what a connectionist model looks like, consider the word perception model of Rumelhart and McClelland (1981) shown as Figure 4.1. This network can be trained to recognize visually presented words.

It consists of three hierarchically arranged sets of units. At the lowest level we have feature detector units. Each of these units responds to a visual property (a line at some specific angle) that could be part of a stimulus array. Various combinations of these features activate different letter detectors. The letter detector units when activated transmit excitation to word detectors, which 'recognize' or are excited by various combinations of letters.

This network requires supervised training. This is done by adjusting connection weights on the connections between units. Initially, these connection weights are randomly assigned, but after training, there should, for example, be high weighting values for the connection between the two left-most feature units and the 'T' letter detector. On the other hand, the connection weights between these two feature detectors and the 'A' letter detector should be close to zero after training. Training a neural network is conducted by an algorithm for weight adjustment, known as a learning rule. There are many varieties of learning rule; one well-known type is known as 'back propagation'. The details of the back propagation algorithm need not concern us.

You may wonder why there are connections between units at the word level. What are these connections doing? They are inhibitory connections. The effect of an inhibitory connection is to dampen down activity in the unit that receives

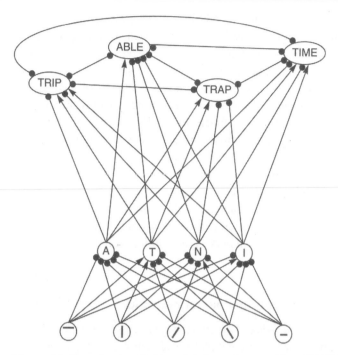

Figure 4.1 *Neural network for printed word recognition (McClelland and Rumelhart, 1981)*

an inhibitory connection. This has the effect of setting up a competition between units that have inhibitory connections between them. Thus, the most excited unit in the pool sends out the most inhibition to its competitors. This is called a 'winner take all' architecture. It is appropriate for our word recognition model, because when you are presented with a letter sequence, that sequence signifies one and only one word. This is a mechanism to help ensure that the word unit with the most appropriate feature and letter level input will emerge as the winner, with the highest level of activation.

One other notable property of this network is that excitation and inhibition can flow top-down from higher- to lower-order units as well as bottom-up. Top-down information flow can simulate the effects of expectancies based on previous experience or domain-specific knowledge. Whether or not such top-down effects are appropriate depends upon the behaviour or processing that one is trying to model.

Is this a faithful model of how the brain is wired for visual word recognition? Most probably not, but it was a sufficiently close analogy to interest cognitive scientists in the 1980s. The model is easy to understand from a functional point of view and it did simulate some aspects of human reading behaviour. The major criterion for evaluating a connectionist model like this is not so much 'Is it a good analogue of how the brain is wired?' but, rather, 'Can it simulate interesting and non-obvious aspects of the process under study?'

This model has very limited learning capabilities. It has its functional architecture hard-wired, where each unit has a designated task. It is incapable, for example, of learning to recognize *new* words. One would have to 'rewire' the system to introduce each new word. Such a network is known as 'localist', because every node in the network refers to a functionally significant element (in this case, a particular feature, letter or word). Nowadays we have more flexible and powerful neural network architectures, where the functional entities in the object domain are not instantiated in particular nodes, but distributed across activation patterns of whole populations of 'hidden' units. These are known as 'distributed' networks, an example of which, the 'simple recurrent' or 'Jordan-Elman' network, we shall examine in some detail in chapter 7.

Connectionist models employ statistical algorithms similar to those that engineers have used in pattern recognition for a number of years. Automatic speech recognition is one area where statistical pattern recognition techniques have been extensively used.

## Connectionist models and neural networks

Connectionist models are often referred to as neural networks because they have some of the basic properties of a biological neural network. A connectionist model consists of a number of simple processing units (artificial neurons) that are highly interconnected through their inputs and their outputs. Connections between units may be excitatory or inhibitory. In 'deciding' whether or not to 'fire' a processing unit integrates all of the excitatory and inhibitory influences that are operating upon it at a given time. Hence we have a rough analogy with the way neurons in a biological network behave.

Learning is a matter of modifying the connection weights on 'synapses' – the points of contact between processing units. This simulates one long-standing theory of how learning is thought to modify synaptic pathways in the brain – facilitating some connections, inhibiting others. Connectionist models have proved attractive to some because they seem to directly model neural activity in the brain. Others, however, eschew these neurological analogies and argue that it is premature to make claims about how the brain works.

## Symbolic algorithms versus statistical processors

We can pursue analogies between ANNs and biological neural networks at the more abstract level of functional computational similarities. Here ANNs have some attractive properties recommending them over 'symbol manipulation' algorithms of the kind exemplified in classical AI natural language processing programs or 'expert systems' approaches to speech recognition.

Symbolic algorithms are deterministic in their control structure (e.g. 'Do $x$; If $y$ then do $z$; Else . . .'). A sequence of operations is under the control of a program that specifies a series of steps leading to a terminal state or a solution, assuming that the algorithm does not crash or fall into a loop. Whether the algorithm is simple or complex, involving a single sequence of steps or multiple processes running in parallel, the steps to the solution are fully determined by the program, supported by a knowledge base. It is possible to write programs that can dynamically alter or build their knowledge base as a result of interaction with a data stream, and thus in a sense acquire new knowledge (see discussion of Quillian's (1968) program for acquiring word semantics, chapter 10). Such programs are very demanding on programming time and effort and are progressively more difficult to debug as the knowledge database grows in size and complexity. Symbolic algorithms for speech and language processing typically require large amounts of detailed information about the domain of application that may well be beyond the ken of even leading experts in speech and language.

Connectionist algorithms, of course, also have initial and terminal states, but the steps in between are under the control of an error correction algorithm rather than a pre-specified set of operations and a knowledge base. A connectionist machine learns to map inputs onto outputs according to some criterion of optimal fit. At the start of training, the input-output (I-O) mapping may be arbitrary, certainly non-optimal, and as training or exposure to the data stream progresses, the I-O mapping improves until it usually reaches some asymptotic level of performance, at which point the training phase is terminated. Following training, our connectionist algorithm can be deployed, making use of the 'knowledge' it has acquired during training, which is stored in its network weights.

Connectionist models have the useful property that they usually respond with 'graceful degradation' to the introduction of noise or error into the system. That is to say, performance declines but does not crash, and partial learning can result in system responses that are better than responses elicited on the basis of no training. On the other hand, expert systems based on deterministic symbolic algorithms have been described as 'brittle'. When a problem is encountered, they tend to fall in a heap. The property of graceful degradation has been exploited to advantage in some notable connectionist simulations of aphasia and acquired reading disorders (see Plaut and Shallice, 1993).

Even at this cursory and highly abstracted level of discussion, it should be apparent that the symbolic modelling approach to computational simulation will be more congenial to a 'rationalist' model of language processing, composed of discrete modules of *a priori* specified knowledge. On the other hand, the *tabula rasa*, learning-through-experience approach of ANN modelling will have more appeal for empiricist approaches to language learning and language processing.

## Hybrid models

The distinction between symbolic algorithms and connectionist models is not as clear-cut as the preceding discussion might suggest. In recent years, we see the appearance of hybrid models of language processing, which seek to

Table 4.3 *Competing approaches to language modelling*

| The modularity hypothesis | Connectionist modelling |
|---|---|
| 1. Modular architecture | Uniform architecture |
| 2. Specialized computational routines | Non-specialized learning mechanisms |
| 3. Discrete symbol manipulation | Non-symbolic algorithms |
| 4. Nativist assumptions | Empiricist assumptions |

achieve some optimal division of labour between symbolic algorithms and connectionist models in an architecture that incorporates both elements.

There are some aspects of spoken language processing that lend themselves more readily to connectionist models. Advances in speech technology strongly suggest that the intricate mapping between acoustic properties of speech signals and the phonetic or phonological specifications of words in a speech recognition lexicon are best modelled by some kind of ANN, especially if effects of speaker characteristics and speaking style are to be accommodated, along with the effects of phonological environment on the expression of particular speech sounds.

On the other hand, it is by no means clear at the present time that connectionist models have the requisite representational power for levels of language processing that have traditionally been the province of symbolic parsers. This is a question which we will take up in the final chapter, where we seek to evaluate the contribution of connectionist models to sentence processing.

The current state of computational modelling in psycholinguistics is very fluid. Perhaps the differences between symbolic and connectionist approaches which are summarized in Table 4.3 above should not be overstated. We have examples of modular theories that have metamorphosed into connectionist models, such as Marslen-Wilson's influential 'cohort' theory of lexical access, discussed in chapter 7. The theory began life as a model of how words are retrieved from the lexicon by serial search procedure.

Originally cast as a deterministic search algorithm, following the appearance of the TRACE model, a localist connectionist model of speech perception (McClelland and Elman, 1986; Elman and McClelland, 1986), the cohort theory was recast as a connectionist model, based upon a concept of spreading activation, with little violence to the basic theory but with an enhanced potential for computational modelling.

## Summarizing

We have discussed three conceptions of modularity: Chomsky's modularity of linguistic competence, Fodor's modularity of language processing, and Coltheart's more general notion of modularity and how modular mental processes may be identified through patterns of dissociation due to acquired or developmental disorders of one kind or another. Each of these views raises theoretical and methodological issues that have yet to be resolved. Let us summarize them briefly.

## Modularity of linguistic competence

In Chomsky's view, it is innate knowledge of the limits on language variation which makes language acquisition possible. Those who advocate this position usually argue from the 'poverty of the stimulus', attempting to show that young infants know a lot more about the structure of language than could reasonably be attributed to them via known inductive learning processes. Human languages are restricted in quite specific and arbitrary ways. (Well, perhaps not in strictly arbitrary ways, but ways that interface, in some ill-defined sense, 'optimally', with human sensory-motor and cognitive systems: of phonetic form and logical form, in the terminology of Chomsky's 1995 'minimalist program'.) For example, innate knowledge or appreciation of the relationship of 'c-command' between constituents may explain why it is that infants, from as early an age as can be reliably tested, show adult-like restrictions on how they interpret the reference of pronominal expressions such as 'he, him, her, herself, himself, . . .' (Crain and Pietroski, 2001).

The strong *a priori* stance of Chomsky's competence model should not be regarded as anti-empirical in principle. On the one hand, it lays down a strong challenge to opponents, to offer a plausible account of how significant aspects of linguistic behaviour can be acquired without any reliance on innate linguistic competence. That was precisely the challenge which Rumelhart and McClelland thought they had met, when in 1986 they proposed a simple neural network for modelling the acquisition of English inflectional morphology (regular and irregular tense marking in particular), without reliance on a rule-based module (see chapter 9). The dust from that debate has still not settled, though it does not address any specific property that generative theory has ever claimed for universal grammar. On the deeper question of how human infants acquire syntactic constraints on pronominal reference, there have been *no* connectionist proposals, to this author's knowledge.

On the other hand, a strong competence model should predict the occurrence of quite specific modular aphasic deficits, such as Grodzinsky's trace deletion hypothesis (TDH) mentioned earlier or others yet to be discussed. A strong theory of linguistic competence should also predict, though this is not a central theme of this book, that while the language learner has an innate facility to acquire any of the possible structural generalizations found in human languages on the basis of very little positive and practically no negative evidence,[5] there are many

---

[5] Negative evidence is evidence that a rule or generalization that a learner may have come up with is, in fact, wrong. Instance-based learning algorithms such as employed by many neural networks rely heavily on corrective feedback. It is claimed that in naturalistic settings, a first language is acquired almost in the absence of negative evidence.

conceivable artificial grammars and rules – even quite simple ones – that should defeat human language learners, because they lie outside the 'visible spectrum' of structural possibilities that the language acquisition device is predisposed to consider.

An interesting case study is provided by Neil Smith and associates (Smith, Tsimpli and Ouhalla, 1993) of a 'polyglot savant': a young man, Christopher, otherwise mentally impaired and requiring institutional care, who possessed a remarkable facility for learning languages. Like most savants, he delighted in demonstrating his prowess on tasks that most of us would find onerously difficult or tedious, such as performing sight translations from Danish, Finnish, Dutch, Hindi, Norwegian, Polish and up to a dozen other languages, into English or vice versa. Christopher presented a highly unusual case of someone with an exceptional specialized language learning ability combined with a reduced general-purpose problem-solving capacity. Christopher's unusual appetite for learning new languages afforded the possibility of testing the modularity of the LAD (language acquisition device), by observing his progressive mastery of a real language that he had not previously encountered (Berber), and an invented language (Epun – named after Nupe, a west African language, spelled backwards), the rules of which were specifically designed to violate some principles of universal grammar, according to Chomsky's principles and parameters model.

Thus it was predicted that Christopher should be able to acquire the rules of Berber with his unusual facility for natural language learning, but stumble badly over learning those rules of an artificial language which violated structural principles of universal grammar, even though the rules themselves might not be inherently complicated and might be sufficiently transparent to someone with normal cognitive or general problem-solving capabilities. A small group of control subjects of normal intelligence and linguistic abilities also undertook to learn Berber and Epun. It was anticipated that comparison of Christopher's performance with that of the control subjects should amplify the effects of any differences between learning attributable to the specialized LAD and that which can be sourced to general learning ability. However, the test was not entirely straightforward, because neither Berber nor the artificial language Epun was being acquired as a *first* language, during the 'critical period' of infancy when children have a sponge-like capacity for absorbing language data and when 'parameter setting' presumably takes place.

Rather, the subjects were learning a second language (real or artificial), in a situation where inference and general problem-solving capacities might be expected to be brought into play, as well as any specialized language acquisition skills. By manipulating the naturalness of certain rules to be learned in Epun, the artificial language, the investigators hoped to expose a dissociation between Christopher's remarkable facility for language learning and his poor inferential capacities. For example, where 'normal' subjects might be expected to struggle but eventually succeed in acquiring an artificial rule of negation that violated universal constraints of negative sentence formation in natural languages, Christopher would be expected to fail. On the other hand, Christopher's savant ability for absorbing new vocabulary and morphological patterns in natural languages should reveal themselves in rapid mastery of the intricacies of Berber inflectional morphology.

The expected dissociation between Christopher's linguistic and general inferential abilities was found. But the control group also failed to master an unnatural rule of negation based on departures from unmarked constituent ordering (e.g. SVO [prevailing unmarked pattern] → OVS [to signal the negation of a simple proposition]), though they succeeded in recognizing similar patterns in 'puzzles' presented outside the context of language learning. Thus, both the control group and Christopher evidenced a degree of 'dissociation' between linguistic and general-purpose inferential capabilities, in support of the modularity hypothesis.

However, Christopher's savant linguistic abilities can certainly not be regarded as a case of sustained linguistic plasticity beyond the normal critical period, or the product of a hyperactive LAD. His extraordinary facility for recognizing and recalling patterns of inflectional morphology did not extend to core aspects of syntax which are the objects of parameter setting in Chomsky's GB model. For example, he characteristically failed to show sensitivity for the 'null subject' parameter and its consequences in his learning of any new languages, uncritically applying the native English parameter setting, and making typical syntactic transfer errors as a consequence. The *null subject* parameter allows some languages, such as Greek, Spanish and Italian, but not others, like English, to omit subject pronouns in contexts where they are easily recoverable from context. The setting of this parameter is correlated with the acceptability of the complementizer 'that' appearing in expressions such as:

(1)          * Who do you think **that** arrived?

Sentences such as (1) are unacceptable in English, but acceptable in Greek, a language where the null subjects are allowed. Christopher, who was described as 'fluent in Greek, after several years of exposure to a wide variety of data', was still prone to incorrectly reject the Greek equivalent of sentence (1) as ungrammatical, though it is well formed to a native speaker of Greek.

More revealing perhaps of the limited nature of his savant linguistic abilities was Christopher's uncritical acceptance of incoherent texts in a translation task, where for example, a sequence of *n* consecutive words of a text are accepted and then the next *n* words are deleted, then the next *n* accepted . . . etc., to produce a discourse like the following (*n* = 7th) order approximation from what was formerly a perfectly coherent text:

> *The pharaohs had enough stone to build enough papyrus, too, so there was nothing as large as floating islands. The papyrus a modest fifth of the Sphinx's length. Of the underworld of mummies and stood it made us realize what giant structures.*

Christopher happily translated this and other such passages into French and back into English without apparent difficulty or protest at their lack of overall coherence.

What can we conclude from this unusual case, of a linguistic savant? The modularity of Christopher's linguistic abilities is clearly not that of a Chomskian LAD, with its capacity for fully flexible parameter setting in adapting to language particular syntactic constructions. Despite his formidable lexical and morphological pattern recognition capabilities, Christopher shows evidence of being more bound than most second language learners by the syntactic parameter settings established during primary language acquisition.

Like other savants who evidence prodigious but encapsulated talents in specific areas, such as drawing, calculation or musical ability, Christopher's case seems to exemplify the potential of the human brain, under unusual circumstances which are not well understood, to dedicate its computational resources within a restricted task domain, to the possible detriment of development of other skills and capabilities. Such cases of aberrant modularity might be seen as pathologies of developmental scheduling in the allocation of computational resources. A lifelong investment of substantial computational resources into learning patterns of inflectional morphology could be seen as an expression of a developmental language disorder, just as a *failure* to acquire such patterns at a particular stage of language development could also be seen to underlie the symptoms of **specific language impairment** (SLI).

We know little about the computational resource allocation required to coordinate the construction of an elaborated world of perceptual experience. But research into early speech perception by infants is providing some insights into this process. In the domain of language acquisition, which closely follows a complex schedule of attunement of the perceptual system to the communicative signals of speech and gesture, a similar scheduled allocation of dedicated computational resources may be required for the task of syntactic parameter setting. That this scheduling is substantially, but not entirely, under genetic control is strongly suggested by the uniform manner in which core features of the computational component of language (functional categories and grammatical inflections) emerge at about the same time regardless of the background of the language learner (Smith, 2004).

## Fodor's modularity of processing

There are obviously close similarities between Chomsky's and Fodor's positions on modularity. Both are strongly nativist in stance. But whereas Chomsky locates modularity firmly in the language faculty, Fodor locates it in the mechanisms that support language processing: the performance mechanisms that support decoding of linguistic expressions from speech signals, or their encoding into spoken utterances (though the latter processes were not explicitly discussed in his 1983 monograph).

At the time Fodor's monograph was written, findings of species-specific neural mechanisms for speech perception in the form of 'phonetic feature detectors' (Eimas, Siqueland, Jusczyk and Vigorito, 1971) were hot news in the scientific literature, together with a range of convergent experimental evidence that speech perception required specialized 'hard-wired' mechanisms (see chapters 5–7). Today, the picture is both more elaborated and less clear-cut respecting the roles that genetics and learning mechanisms play in the acquisition of speech perception skills. Hence, Fodor's strongly nativistic model of language performance is less compelling than when it first appeared. However, Fodor's emphasis on real-time processing was prescient. Behavioural and neural imaging techniques for observing on-line processing have continued to grow in importance.

## Coltheart's functional modularity

We have seen that Coltheart's uncoupling of the issue of modularity of processing from Fodor's nativist assumptions about modular processing mechanisms enabled us to see modularity of various mental functions as an outcome of maturational and learning mechanisms, and, through the concept of functional dissociation, to link patterns of modular impairment to questions of the architecture of normal mental processes. Modularity clearly extends not only to spoken language processing, which many would agree is substantially under the control of species-specific maturational mechanisms, but also to secondary language-based skills, such as reading and writing, which are clearly modular in operation in mature literate individuals, and can also be subject to modular deficits in brain injury or developmental disorder.

However, we suggested that Coltheart (2002) went too far in uncoupling modularity of mental functions from their real-time operation, for two reasons. Firstly, real-time operation provides both the evolutionary motivation and the explanatory challenge for modular mental processes. Secondly, the development of methods of observation of real-time or on-line mental processing, which has been the major methodological focus of psycholinguistics over recent decades, is necessary, because the observation of clinical patterns of dissociation of cognitive abilities, while suggestive, is not up to the task of yielding a taxonomy of mental processes.

We would draw a similar conclusion, though on less certain grounds, regarding the uncoupling of modular mechanisms from their neural substrate. While it is true that, beyond the neural circuitry of only the most the most elementary of sensory-motor processes, ignorance still reigns supreme in cognitive neuroscience, there are sufficient new hypotheses being generated into the nature of cell assemblies, functional pathways, and loci of operations by the new generation of macro-cellular imaging techniques, to suggest that substantial progress is being made on the reductionist enterprise. For the extended argument on this point, see the rest of the book.

## Study questions for chapter 4

1.    Distinguish between linguistic *competence* and *performance*. Explain why a theory of language processing involves both competence and performance considerations. (Be as explicit as you can here, to the extent of sketching your own box-and-arrow model (flow chart) of spoken language processing, identifying those components of your model that you would identify as 'competence' and those that you would consign to 'performance'.)

2.    Explain, briefly and in very general terms, how Chomsky links modularity of linguistic knowledge to language acquisition.

3.    Explain why Chomsky and Miller (1963) considered that the processing difficulty of multiply centre-embedded sentences such as '*The cat the dog the car ran over, chased, meowed*' constitutes a good argument for the need of a competence–performance distinction.

4.    The existence of aphasia can itself be taken as *prima facie* evidence of the modularity of linguistic competence. Explain why. Or perhaps not? Justify your answer.

5.    If you were asked to wield Occam's razor on Fodor's nine properties of modular systems, reducing the list to three or four, which would you retain as most fundamental? Why?

6.    What criteria does clinical neuropsychology use for identifying functional modularity?

7.    If real-time operation is a criterion for identifying mental modules, then should there be a module for 'chess playing' or 'scrabble' and another for 'music making'?

8.    Connectionist and 'expert systems' (symbolic) models of language processing are usually regarded as occupying opposing positions on the question of modularity. But is this really justified? Consider as a case in point the localist connectionist model of reading discussed in chapter 4.

9.    Review Neil Smith's case of Christopher, a 'linguistic savant'. Does this case constitute special evidence for modularity of linguistic competence?

# PART II

# Speech perception and auditory processing

# 5    The problem of speech recognition

## Introduction

The ability to perceive and comprehend speech is, as we argued in the previous chapter, one of the human brain's more astonishing evolutionary accomplishments. Engineers and computer scientists have sought to emulate human speech recognition for about four decades, but it may be as many more before the best automatic speech recognition device can perform as well as the average five-year-old, though great strides have been made in recent years. Recognizing speech and the identity of the speaker is an ability that we normally take for granted, unless we are unfortunate enough to lose this vital skill temporarily or permanently as the result of 'a stroke' (cerebrovascular accident) or some other form of damage to language-critical areas of the brain.

In this and the following two chapters we will be concerned with the early or peripheral stages of spoken language comprehension: with auditory signal processing; with the extraction of phonetic features that make up the 'sound shapes' of words; with how the phonological forms of words are retrieved from lexical memory and how these 'sound traces' of words may be represented in the recognition lexicon. We will leave to later chapters questions of how words are put together to form phrases or sentences, which belong to later stages[1] of the spoken language comprehension process.

## Three aspects of word recognition

There are three aspects to the problem of spoken word recognition that need to be considered:

1.      The input signal: the acoustic structure of speech and how speech signals are processed by the human auditory system.

---

[1] We do not wish to commit to any particular model of speech recognition at this point, by reference to 'early' vs. 'later' stages of spoken language processing, although use of these terms may suggest a sequential bottom-up model of speech recognition, in which speech sounds are extracted first, followed by words, then phrases, etc. We want to keep open the possibility of massively parallel processing in spoken language comprehension, as well as possible *interactions* between processing levels.

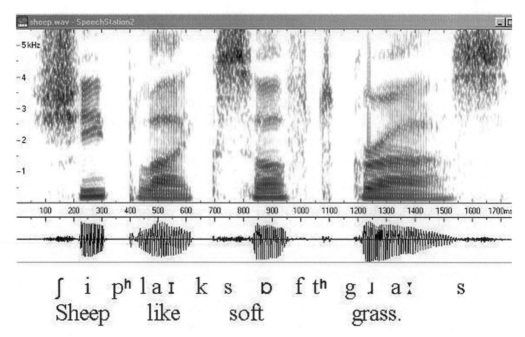

ʃ  i  pʰ laɪ  k  s  ɒ  f tʰ  g ɹ  aː      s

Sheep    like    soft        grass.

Figure 5.1 *Spectrogram:* sheep like soft grass

2.    The internal phonological representation: the way that words or phonological targets are stored in the speech recognition lexicon.

3.    The interface between (1) and (2) above: how the auditory input makes contact with the internal forms in the recognition lexicon. This process has been called 'lexical information retrieval'. But we are concerned here with only one aspect of lexical retrieval, retrieving the phonological forms of words from the lexicon, so that they can be pattern matched with the auditory input.

## Speech signals, spectrograms and speech recognition

A most revealing representation of the acoustic structure of human speech and the communicative calls of many other species is provided by 'the spectrogram',[2] a continuous display, at some specified bandwidth (or time and frequency resolution), of the acoustic energy which is present in the signal. An example is shown in Figure 5.1, a spectrogram of the phrase *'Sheep like soft grass'*.

When they were first invented, researchers were impressed by the information-rich nature of speech spectrograms. Even with minimal experience in 'reading'

---

[2] Spectrograms used to be produced by a specialized analogue instrument, 'the sound spectrograph'. Nowadays, we use digital means to analyse speech on inexpensive desktop or laptop computers.

spectrograms it is possible to discern clear acoustic boundaries between (**obstruent**) consonants and vowels. Note, for example, where the turbulent noise energy of the **fricative** 'sh' [ʃ] in *sheep* suddenly changes to the structured energy of the vowel 'ee' [i], with its three main energy bands, located at approximately 200, 2000 and 2500 Hz on the vertical axis of the spectrogram. These energy bands in the spectrogram, which are technically known as **formants**, represent the first three resonant frequencies of the vocal tract. Speech sounds made with a relatively open vocal tract and vibrating vocal folds (vowels, liquids [l, r], and glides [w, y]) have distinctive formant patterns on the spectrogram, reflecting the particular resonating frequencies associated with the oral cavity shape used for their production. One class of sounds, the stop consonants, like the [k] in '*like*' involve a brief blockage of all energy flow and are signalled by a short silent period of zero energy on the spectrogram (located at time 620–690 in Figure 5.1 above). Other acoustic–articulatory mappings take more training in 'spectrogram reading' to spot, such as the distinctive formant frequency change in the diphthong [aɪ] of '*like*', or the difference between the spectral energy concentrations for the fricatives [s] (4–6 kHz) and [ʃ] (3–5 kHz). For a condensed but comprehensive introduction to speech spectrography see Ladefoged (2001), chapter 7.

When they were first invented, towards the end of World War II, it was hoped that spectrograms, or 'voice prints' as they became known in the popular press, could be 'read', like we scan text, to provide 'visible speech' as an alternative sensory channel for word recognition by the deaf. Alternatively, it was thought that one could scan spectrographic displays into a computer to provide automatic dictation. These hopes proved illusory. Although the study of spectrograms has yielded much valuable knowledge about the acoustic structure of speech and the mapping between articulation and sound, it has not resulted in 'visible speech aids' for the hearing-impaired, and computers have all kinds of difficulties converting speech spectrograms into sensible letter sequences. Early expectations that the study of spectrograms would yield a quick solution to the problem of speech perception foundered on some overly simplistic assumptions that early investigators made as to how acoustic properties of speech map onto the phonological targets which are the objects of speech recognition.

### A simple model of speech recognition: phoneme to sound matching

One initially plausible but simplistic model would be to identify each phoneme target with a spectral energy pattern (a time-slice of the spectrogram), then to store a prototype energy pattern for each phoneme in the recognition lexicon. Speech, or more precisely phoneme recognition, would then simply involve comparison and matching of spectral energy slices from an input signal against a store of phoneme templates, assuming that some method of slicing up the spectrogram into phoneme-sized chunks can be accomplished.[3] In a model of word recognition such as this, which is phoneme-based, words would be recognized as phoneme strings. Clearly, one would have to correctly recognize the phonemes in order to retrieve the word (e.g. Did you say *glass* or *grass*?). But this phoneme matching model of word recognition fails, both with human spectrogram readers and with not-so-clever computers. Readers with background knowledge of phonetics or phonology can probably appreciate why. But before taking up the question of why the phoneme matching model is inadequate, let us consider an even simpler model, found in some early automatic speech recognition (ASR) systems.

### An alternative model: word to sound pattern-matching

An alternative to the spectrogram–phoneme matching model of word recognition is the spectrogram–word matching model. For each word in the lexicon, there is a spectrogram template. Such a model cannot, of course, account for our ability to recognize the sounds that comprise individual words (e.g., *cat* [k æ t]), much less our ability to correctly identify *non-word* tokens (such as *glick* [glɪk]). However, for many speech recognition applications, it is the words that matter, not the sounds that comprise them. Nor is the storage cost of matching input patterns against the several thousand templates that may be needed for a working vocabulary much of a consideration nowadays. Besides, it has been argued by some psycholinguists that our ability to hear phonemes in speech is derivative of our learning to read and familiarity with an alphabetic script. Phoneme perception, some have argued, is not a prerequisite for word recognition. But even if these arguments have some validity (which we doubt) the spectrogram–word matching model fares no better than the spectrogram–phoneme matching model. In fact, it fares worse, because it leads to a theoretical dead end in terms of research strategies.

## Why speech recognition is difficult

There are several reasons why speech recognition has proved to be such a daunting skill for speech scientists to explain or for engineers to emulate, though as normal language users we do it with such apparent ease that we tend to assume there is nothing to explain.

### The segmentation problem

As a native speaker you have no difficulty discerning the boundaries of words and phrases, or of breaking words down to their constituent syllables

---

[3] In many cases, it is possible to acoustically segment the speech signal at points of discrete transition between consonants and vowels (see Stevens, 1998). But such an acoustic segmentation does not correspond one for one with the phonological segmentation of a phonemic transcription. Nevertheless, a segmentation of the speech signal at points of maximal acoustic change can provide a useful first stage for a more sophisticated speech recognition algorithm.

and sounds. But what happens when you listen to speech in a language that is completely unfamiliar to you? One of the first things you notice is that you have no idea where words or phrases begin and end. Words and phrases in connected speech are just that, *connected*, not separated by convenient little spaces like the printed words on this page. Word boundary detection poses a non-trivial problem for first and second language learners and we discuss various strategies available to the perceptual system for dealing with it below. Problems of segmentation extend also to linguistic units above and below the level of the word. Above the word level, phrase boundaries are not always reliably signalled by prosodic cues, such as pausing, intonation or final segment lengthening. Below the word, phoneme boundaries are often not clearly marked by discontinuities in the speech signal.

## The variability problem

Recognizing speech is more akin to reading handwriting than printed text. The factors which make the legibility of individual letters more problematic in handwriting also operate in speech. That is because both represent complex connected sequences of motor gestures that express the individuality, state and circumstances of their author. The first of these factors to be considered is the immediate phonological environment, or the context of other sounds surrounding the sound in question, commonly referred to as '**coarticulation effects**' by phoneticians, or as 'connected speech processes' by phonologists.

Pronounce quietly to yourself the initial sounds of the words *shoe* [ʃu] and *sheep* [ʃip] or *keep* [kip] and *cool* [kul]. Notice how the *sound* of the initial consonant varies, sounding higher in 'pitch' before the vowel [i] than the vowel [u]. This is because the initial consonant is coarticulated with the following vowel. Rounding of the lips in anticipation of an upcoming [u] vowel lowers the centre frequency of the noise burst of the consonant. Similarly, spreading of the lips in anticipation of an upcoming [i] vowel elevates the frequency of the noise burst in the preceding consonant.[4] Anticipatory coarticulation effects, where the expression of a sound is affected by one that has yet to be fully pronounced, are more prominent in English than carry-over effects of a previously articulated sound, but these local sound interactions in speech are mutual. For example, the acoustic feature which enables American English listeners to distinguish between /r/ and /l/ in contrastive phrase pairs like '*or gone – all* gone' or '*or done – all*

---

[4] These frequency shifts are brought about acoustically by changes to the shape and hence the resonating characteristics of the vocal tract 'downstream' from the point of constriction where fricative noise is generated. Lip rounding effectively lengthens the acoustic tube anterior to the point of oral constriction, thereby lowering its resonant frequencies. Lip spreading effectively shortens the tube, raising the resonant frequencies. See Stevens (1998) for further discussion. In the case of the stop consonant [k], there are concomitant shifts in the place of articulation of the stop, with the constriction further to the back of the mouth before the back vowel [u], and further forward towards the hard palate in the case of [i], reinforcing the acoustic effects of the lip rounding and spreading gestures associated with these vowels.

*done*' also affects the expression of the following stop consonants /d/ and /g/. A preceding /r/ shifts the perceptual boundary between /d/ and /g/ closer to /g/. We shall consider how local effects of coarticulation between speech sounds may be accounted for in a model of speech perception in more detail later. Let us first consider the more global influences which make the mapping between speech and the linguistic message problematical.

***The speaking environment*:** is rarely noise-free. We spontaneously adapt our manner of speaking, often in ways that we are quite unaware of, in order to accommodate the listener, or to make our speech more intelligible. For example, most people raise their voice pitch about 5–10 per cent when they speak over the phone, though the precise reason for this is a matter of conjecture.

***Speakers' vocal tracts*:** differ in size, shape and behaviour. Smaller vocal tracts produce higher frequency resonances than those of larger vocal tracts. Consequently, a child's vowels may sound very similar to those of their elder siblings or parents, while appearing different on the spectrogram, which faithfully reflects the acoustic differences due to vocal tract size. Yet our ear manages to ignore the irrelevant acoustic differences and focuses automatically on the phonetic qualities of speech sounds. This ability of the ear to distinguish phonetically relevant from irrelevant acoustic variation is something we acquire early in speech and language development.

***Speech rate and style*:** Suppose I suddenly increase my rate of speech (perhaps in anticipation of being interrupted), or slow my delivery (as I plan what to say next, or try to retrieve a word that is on the tip of my tongue). Native listeners will automatically compensate for the acoustic changes that such manoeuvres on the part of the speaker induce in the speech signal. But machine speech recognizers typically have great difficulty making these accommodations – as do second language learners who are not fluent in the target language, or aphasics, who have impaired speech processing.

Similarly, we automatically adjust our speech style to the social context of speaking. This obliges the listener to do the same in processing speech. Consider, for example, how different levels of formality in speaking style affect the expression of connected speech processes in how you might say the phrase '*I'm going to leave*' in Australian English, as captured in a phonetic transcription (Figure 5.2).[5]

Where a person's speech habitually falls on the continuum of formal–casual stylistic variation will depend to some extent on their reference dialect or sociolect.

---

[5] We use *phonetic transcription* in accordance with the conventions of the *International Phonetic Alphabet* (IPA) to indicate the pronunciation in the figure. If you have access to the Web, you may listen to the differences between formal and casual speech style that are captured in these transcriptions from resources located at http://www.cambridge.org/9780521791908.

Phonetic transcription    Speaking style

[aɪmgoʊɪŋtəliv]          very careful, formal
[aɪm goʊəntəliv]         careful, formal
[aɪm goʊnəliv]
[aɪm gənəliv]            conversational
[aɪŋgənəliv]             casual
[aɪŋənəliv]
[aŋənəliv]               quite casual
[aŋŋəliv]
[aŋəliv]                 super-casual

Figure 5.2 *Speaking style and alternative pronunciations of* I'm going to leave

For my teenage son, 'super-casual' seems to be the habitual target, rendering many of his utterances unintelligible outside the exclusive sociolect of his 'mates'.

But encounters of the adolescent kind notwithstanding, as listeners, we accommodate automatically and effortlessly to a wide range of phonetic variation caused by shifts in speech rate, style and regional accent, which quite profoundly affect the acoustics of the speech signal. It is this flexibility on the part of the human speech perception system that we seek to explain or to simulate in automatic speech recognition. As a further illustration of the effects of connected speech processes on the acoustic structure of the speech signal, consider the following spectrogram of the phonetician Peter Ladefoged saying:

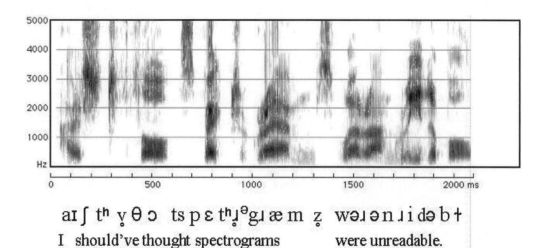

aɪʃ tʰ ɣθɔ tsp ɛ tʰɹᵊgɹæ m z̥ wəɹənɹidəbɫ
I  should've thought spectrograms        were unreadable.

Figure 5.3 *Spectrogram:* I should have thought spectrograms were unreadable

You may like to try your hand at segmenting this spectrogram, by assigning a phonetic transcription aligned to the acoustic segments in the spectrogram. You will find that there have been some striking transformations. The vowels [ʊ] and [æ] that you may have expected to hear in the auxiliary verbs '*should have*' seem to be missing, through the combined effects of *vowel reduction* and *devoicing*, two very common connected speech processes in this variety of English, even though the speaking style is not particularly informal.

The sources of acoustic variability which render individual sounds difficult to distinguish in connected speech tend to be correlated with one another. Coarticulation effects are more prevalent in casual and fast speech styles than in formal and slow speech. Hence, rate and style are correlated dimensions of speech variation, but not completely so, because under certain circumstances it is possible to speak quickly, while suppressing some of the coarticulation effects that might interfere unduly with the intelligibility of speech. Most connected speech processes are motivated by the need to simplify articulation. As such, we might expect to find that casual and fast speech styles share common characteristics, regardless of the speaker's language or dialect. While this is true, it is also the case that connected speech processes themselves vary considerably across languages and dialects (Nolan and Kerswill, 1990). Connected speech processes have a learned component, which is language- and dialect-specific, as well as a universal basis, common to speakers of all languages, by virtue of the fact that we all share a common articulatory apparatus.

It has been suggested that if the speech perception system had an 'inbuilt' knowledge of the acoustics of the human speech production mechanism, then the task of mapping the acoustic signal of speech onto articulatory targets would be greatly facilitated. This view, known as the 'motor theory of speech perception' (Liberman, Cooper, Shankweiler and Studdert-Kennedy, 1967), has been much debated. We will consider some of the evidence for and against it later. However, even if it turns out to be the case that there is some knowledge of articulatory–acoustic mapping 'hard-wired' into the human speech perception apparatus, there still remains considerable scope for language-specific expression of these articulatory constraints; considerable scope, in other words, for the operation of general-purpose learning mechanisms to acquire the relevant acoustic–articulatory mappings needed to 'perceive speech gestures'.

### The rate of information transmission in speech perception ▪

The articulators move very quickly in fluent speech, resulting in transmission rates of 8–10 phonemes per second (3–4 syllables or 2–3 words per second). It is known that one of the effects of damage to the left temporal lobe as a result of stroke or similar injury is to impair temporal processing abilities. Slowing down the rate of speech is a technique that helps aphasics with speech comprehension deficits. Interestingly, it also seems to help second language learners.

Perhaps the human auditory system or, more particularly, neural resources in the language dominant left hemisphere have evolved refined temporal processing capabilities for handling the rapid sequential changes in speech. One thought-provoking finding arose from early research attempts to build a reading machine for the blind, based on an 'auditory cipher' (recounted in Mattingly and Studdert-Kennedy, 1991). The idea was to convert printed letters into sound sequences, using a scanner and a device that produced a discriminably different sound for each letter of the alphabet and punctuation mark. The only and intractable problem was that even highly trained and motivated subjects could not learn to use the device, at least not at rates of scanning text which approached those of normal reading. Researchers found that if sounds were presented at rates of more than 2–3 per second, listeners were incapable of perceiving the order and identity of the sounds. So how then, researchers asked themselves, do we manage to perceive speech sounds when they are presented to us at 3–4 times this rate in normal conversation? (We shall return to this problem later.)

The rate of speech transmission does not affect the complexity of the mapping between the speech signal and the perceptual targets, like the sources of variability in the speech signal considered previously. However, it is relevant for considering the speed with which the perceptual mechanism has to operate. Models of speech perception often postulate a temporary sensory storage *buffer* to hold sensory information while it is being identified. When you consider the size of the average working vocabulary (several tens of thousand items) and the short time that it takes to identify words, the speed with which the auditory system operates in speech recognition is truly impressive. If phoneme buffers exist, then they are filled, emptied and refilled very rapidly in the course of speech perception.

## Lexical retrieval in speech perception

Lexical retrieval refers to the mechanism whereby information is accessed from the mental lexicon. How does this process operate? We will consider several competing theories, but before doing so, let us ask what *role* lexical retrieval plays in speech perception. Some might argue that if you possess a lexicon, then the problem of word segmentation in speech perception will take care of itself. Assuming that the listener's attention is directed to a single talker,[6] the speech signal at any point in time will carry information about only one word at a time, though from the perspective of the listener there may be a number of candidates for that target. But the listener having decided on a target word, then

---

[6] The tracking of a single channel of speech in a noisy environment, where there may be several competing signals, constitutes a serious practical difficulty for speech perception under normal operating conditions. This has been labelled *the cocktail party problem* (Cherry, 1978). More generally, it is the problem of auditory scene analysis (Bregman, 1990), the ability to separate and selectively attend to different perceptual objects in the auditory field of the listener: a fundamental problem, but one that is beyond the scope of our discussion.

the word boundaries will take care of themselves, in the sense that what comes before or after the word boundary must belong to the end or the start of some other word.

While it is no doubt the case that having a lexicon greatly facilitates the task of word segmentation, we also know that word boundaries can be (imperfectly) predicted from statistical dependencies among sequences of sounds that arise from the **phonotactic rules** of the language (e.g. given a consonant sequence such as [...ndk...] in English, where may a word boundary fall?). Simply on the basis of exposure to the speech of a foreign language, but without being given information about the words of the language, listeners can, after a while, guess with better-than-chance accuracy where the word boundaries lie. By approximately six months of age pre-linguistic infants also show sensitivities to the phonotactics of the ambient language (Jusczyk, Luce and Charles-Luce, 1994). Thus, phonotactic constraints provide an alternative source of information about word boundary segmentation to that provided by lexical knowledge.[7] Word boundary detection is also facilitated by prosodic cues, which may be quite language-specific, as we shall see.

When you consider the matter, it is clear that we must be able to do quite a bit of phonological processing of speech without recourse to lexical access. Evidence for this will be presented later, when phonological representations are examined in more detail. But first, consider the following short arguments. We have all occasionally experienced the phenomenon of hearing a word but not actually recognizing it until after some short delay (Oh *that* is what she said!) – delayed lexical access. To accomplish delayed lexical access, the phonological form of a word must be held for a time awaiting identification. To be able to do this, it must be the case that phonological forms can exist, at least for a short time, independently of particular lexical entries.

Secondly, we would have great difficulty acquiring new words if we could not extract phonological forms as independent entities from the speech signal. There are any number of *possible or potential words* not previously encountered that could serve as new lexical items. Learning new words involves assigning semantic and syntactic features to phonological forms. But we need to be able to extract phonological forms from the speech signal in the first instance. In other words, speech perception involves *phonological parsing* as a precondition of lexical access and learning new words and names.

### Phonological parsing prior to lexical access

Phonological parsing is the process of extracting the phonological features that identify words from the speech signal. We may perform a little

---

[7] But in order to take advantage of phonotactic constraints, don't you need to be able to recognize the sounds in the first place? This is typical of the chicken-or-egg problems that bedevil theories of speech perception. However, it is not an insoluble dilemma, as we shall see.

experiment which has the dual purpose of (a) demonstrating that a good deal of phonological processing of speech can take place without lexical access and (b) indicating the nature of the **phonological representations** that English listeners construct from speech.

For those with web access, you may listen to a *nonce phrase*, a meaningless but speech-like utterance that is repeated once (http://www.cambridge.org/9780521791908). You will be asked to write down what you hear.

Subjects in our experiment (Ingram, Park and Mylne, 1997) were fairly successful at transcribing most of the sounds in this particular nonce phrase. It sounds kind-of English, because the sounds that comprise the phrase are all legitimate English phonotactic sequences and the phrase is spoken with English *prosody*.[8] This is quite a hard test if English is not your native language, particularly if the latter is one with very different phonotactics or prosody. When this experiment was originally conducted, another group of listeners was given a parallel sentence to transcribe with exactly the same instructions as the first group.

This spoken 'phrase' has the same segmental content (the same phoneme string) as the first nonce phrase, but it lacks the *prosodic features* of stress and intonation of the first utterance.[9] This explains why it sounds 'weird'. Subjects did not do as well at transcribing the second nonce phrase. A comparison of the accuracy of the subjects' transcriptions of the two nonce phrases, plus the results based on a nine-syllable nonce phrase transcription, with and without prosodic structure, is shown in Figure 5.4.

The results of this experiment show that having prosodic structure facilitates the retention of segmental information, possibly by helping to bind the constituent syllables together into a coherent whole. This is essentially what we do when we *chunk* numerals into groups to retain telephone numbers, at least long enough to complete dialling. The first and the last parts of the nonce phrases are better retained than the middle portions, but it is the main effect of prosody or its absence which is of interest.

This simple experiment has its limitations. We cannot be sure that it is *prosody alone* which caused the first nonce phrase to be better perceived/recalled than the second one. Coarticulation effects across syllable boundaries may have provided some additional redundant cues for listeners that would not have been present

---

[8] The nonce phrase was spoken using a stress and intonation contour appropriate for the phrase *French-language teaching instructions*, a compound phrasal construction which provided a coherent prosodic contour for the nonce phrase.

[9] The second nonce phrase was constructed by digitally splicing syllables using a speech editing program in the following manner. Each syllable from the original nonce phrase was spoken as a separate word in a carrier phrase: '*Please say —— again*' (e.g. *Please say flant again. Please say nem again* . . . etc.) The syllables were then spliced out of the carrier phrase and combined to form the second nonce phrase, which then had identical segmental content to the first, but lacked the prosodic features of the first nonce phrase. Care was taken to ensure that the first and second nonce phrases were of roughly equal duration.

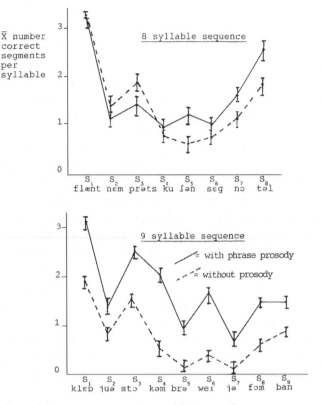

Figure 5.4 *Transcription accuracy of the nonce phrases.*

in the prosody-free version.[10] However, the point of the demonstration is that prosody (stress, rhythm and intonation) is part of the phonological structure of the utterance and that when phonological parsing cannot be completed because crucial phonetic cues are lacking in the stimulus, then the ability of the perceptual apparatus to retain the segmental components of the phonological representation is impaired.

Was lexical access engaged in any way in this experiment? Well, yes and no. On the one hand, it is probably impossible *not* to engage the lexicon whenever speech or speech-like stimuli are presented. So no doubt lexical access was attempted, though interestingly nobody reported hearing the words *ant* [ænt], *its* [əts], *coo (or coup)* [ku], *nor* [nɔ(r)], all of which are embedded in the nonce phrase:

*fl**ant** nempr**its** **ku**shen* **sig***nortle*

We refer to this phenomenon as 'the problem of embedded words'. How does the speech recognizer manage to avoid false word boundary segmentation? Consider

---

[10] On the other hand, the individual syllables in the spliced version may have been more distinctly articulated and hence be marginally more perceptible than in the original utterance, so this argument cuts both ways.

the phrase '*recognize speech*', spoken casually in the author's dialect, as indicated in the phonetic transcription given below. The phrase contains within it quite a large number of phoneme sequences that match items in the lexicon, but the speech recognizer apparently manages to avoid making any of these 'false positive' word identifications.

| Pronunciation: | [r ɛ k ə n aɪ z: p i t ʃ] | phonetic transcription |
|---|---|---|
| embedded words: | *a    I* | false word segmentations |
| | *an ice* | |
| | *wreck    nice beach* | |
| target phrase. | *recognize    speech* | correct word segmentation |

Problems of word segmentation would be highly prevalent and much more obvious to native listeners than they are, were it not for the fact that we have a highly efficient mechanism for rejecting false positive identifications. How this is accomplished in the lexical retrieval of phonological forms in speech perception is discussed later (chapter 7).

Also, there were no pause breaks (spoken equivalents of 'blank spaces' in printed text) present in the spoken nonce phrase '*flant nemprits kushen signortle*' that the subjects heard, to indicate to them that the phrase was made up of just four nonce words. When subjects were asked, after completing their transcriptions, to indicate how many 'words' they heard in the nonce utterance and where those word boundaries might lie, the most frequent response for the number of words was four and the most popular sites for the word boundaries were those indicated by the blank spaces in the orthographic transcription given above.

Why did nobody report hearing the words in the bold portions of the utterance that correspond to the phonological strings of items present in their lexicon? And how was it that listeners were so successful at detecting word boundaries in the absence of lexical retrieval? These are questions we address later. For the moment, let us simply conclude that phonological forms are parsable from the speech signal, without the need for successful lexical retrieval (word identification). We will use the term *phonological form* to refer to the 'sound shape' of words as they are stored in the listener's **recognition lexicon**. Let us now try to be more specific about the nature of these phonological forms, which constitute the targets of the speech perception mechanism.

## Phonetic forms and phonological representations

The **phonetic representation** of a word is usually taken to mean a detailed specification of how that word was pronounced. However, as we have argued, the phonetic properties of words and the sounds that comprise them vary with speaker, speaking style, speech rate and phonological context (position in a word). This phonetic variation constitutes a major problem for a speech recognizer. Researchers in automatic speech recognition have traditionally referred to this as the problem of speech or speaker **normalization**, the idea being that some set of properties that are invariant over speakers and tokens, or some means of normalizing the speech signal to a common timescale in the case of rate variation, should be sought and incorporated into the speech recognition procedure (see Perkell and Klatt, 1986). But there is also a sense in which the sound properties of words of our language remain invariant over tokens (speakers, contexts and occasions), as perceptual targets of word recognition. Speech perception is concerned with how the mapping between the variable phonetic forms and the invariant phonological targets of words is achieved through processing speech signals. In this section we are concerned to characterize differences between the phonetic forms and phonological representations of words, in preparation for tackling the central questions of speech perception: how are invariant phonological features extracted from the highly variable phonetic properties of speech?

Linguists like to distinguish between **distinctive** and non-distinctive phonetic features of spoken words. This distinction is well motivated. Native listeners are robustly sensitive to the presence of distinctive features in speech. They are much less aware, in fact it usually requires a course in phonetics to make them aware, of the presence of non-distinctive phonetic features in speech. Consider, for example, the quality of the vowel in the word *ban* [bæ̃n] compared to the vowel in the word *bad* [bæd].[11] Once their attention is drawn to it, most English speakers can hear the difference in vowel quality between the vowels in these two words, despite the fact that they will also assert that it is 'the same' vowel. Vowels nasalize before a nasal consonant in English and many other languages. This nasal quality of the vowel is entirely predictable in English. We cannot signal a lexical contrast using vowel nasal resonance alone, compared with e.g., Bengali, Hindi, Tamil, French, to name a few; all languages for which vowel nasality is a distinctive feature:

Hindi minimal pairs

| | |
|---|---|
| *bad smell* | *bamboo* |
| /bas/ | /bãs/ |
| *mother-in-law* | *breath* |
| /sas/ | /sãs/ |

How will a native speaker of Hindi who has just started to learn English respond to the vowel quality difference in the English words *bad* and *ban*? The chances are that s/he will think these words contain different vowels. The take-home message here is that phonological representations (and hence the phonological content of lexical items) consist entirely of distinctive features, with no redundant or non-distinctive phonetic features. This conclusion is somewhat controversial, so we will need to justify it in more detail later.

While distinctive features have a privileged status as the building-blocks of phonological representations, they are not necessarily better preserved or more

---

[11] The wavy line over the vowel in the phonetic transcription of *ban* indicates that the vowel is *nasalized*.

Table 5.1 *Properties distinguishing phonetic and phonological representations*

| Phonetic | Phonological |
|---|---|
| 1. fully specified or 'concrete' | under-specified or 'abstract' |
| 2. continuous or quasi-continuous | discrete or 'all-or-nothing' |
| 3. entrained or temporally co-ordinated | nested or hierarchically structured |

prominent as attributes of the speech signal. As we saw in the illustrations above, whole segment-sized bundles of distinctive features may be obliterated at the whim of connected speech processes. But, under clear speech conditions, speakers will try to preserve distinctive feature contrasts. However, this can often be achieved more effectively by preserving a non-distinctive than a distinctive feature contrast. Compare the ways that you say *bag* and *back*. What aspects of pronunciation or properties of the signal best support the *voicing* contrast between the *g* and the *k* here? Phonetic observations show that it is the length (duration) of the preceding vowel rather than the voicing (or voicelessness) of the stop which is the more important cue.

Here we have an apparent paradox (not a real one): it is the voicing feature which distinguishes *bag* and *back* phonologically (and this is the feature that will be apparent to native speakers), but the critical phonetic cue for the perception of this distinction lies in the (non-distinctive) length of the preceding vowel. It is worth pondering this apparent paradox. The distinction being made here between the phonetic and the phonological levels of description is crucial and also a little tricky, because the terms 'phonetic' and 'phonological' are used in various ways in the literature. We will use phonetic to mean the sounds actually produced by speakers or the auditory and acoustic correlates of these articulations. Phonological features are descriptions of speech sounds which are somewhat abstract or **phonetically under-specified**, in ways that will be made clear later. Phonological representations define the relevant level of speech sound description to account for processes of lexical retrieval in spoken language processing.[12]

We have already claimed that the distinction between the phonetic and the phonological levels of speech processing is important for a model of normal speech perception. It should be possible to find evidence of such a distinction in disorders of speech perception or production in aphasia. This is a controversial question, which we take up in chapter 8. In the meantime, let us simply be clear on the properties that supposedly distinguish phonetic from phonological representations of speech. There are three important ones (see Table 5.1).

---

[12] We have made this claim, but not yet considered all the relevant evidence, and not everyone agrees with our conclusion.

## Under-specified (abstract) versus fully specified (concrete) forms

The first property, that phonological representations are under-specified in relation to phonetic representations which contain all the properties of words or sounds relevant for a complete articulatory or acoustic description, has already been mentioned. The distinctive features of a word may be thought of as a sub-set that remains when the non-distinctive or redundant features have been accounted for by phonological rule. Distinctive features enable us to define minimal pairs, useful for illustrating the phonemes of a language:

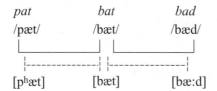

| *pat* | *bat* | *bad* | orthographic |
|---|---|---|---|
| /pæt/ | /bæt/ | /bæd/ | phonological |
| | | | distinctive features |
| | | | non-distinctive features |
| [pʰæt] | [bæt] | [bæ:d] | phonetic |

## Discrete (categorical) versus graded (continuous) properties

Phonological features are necessarily discrete, though the properties which comprise their phonetic substance are continuous or quasi-continuous[13] articulatory or acoustic variables. For example, voicing is a graded phonetic property of stop consonants, but phonologically a stop consonant is either voiced or voiceless, assuming the language in question has this distinction.

The discrete nature of phonological features derives from their function of being used to distinguish lexical items. To convince yourself of this, imagine a language that has only four words (your own language at an early stage of acquisition, if you like). Suppose you formed these words by whistling different notes. Although you can produce a whole range of notes, for purposes of word recognition a note would have to fall into one of four discrete categories: low,

---

[13] Stevens (1972, 1998) makes the important point that some phonetic features' dimensions make for quasi-continuous or *quantal* phonetic contrasts. These are features for which continuous artic-ulatory variation yields sharp or 'quantal' category distinctions in the acoustic domain. What this means is that for certain articulatory gestures, there may be considerable tolerance for error or sloppy approximation to some articulatory target, without the acoustic signal changing sub-stantially, but just outside these tolerance boundaries small articulatory changes produce a large acoustic change. Languages will tend to favour building their phonological contrasts from such quantal phonetic features, because they allow a certain 'slack' in the articulatory mechanism, without threatening loss of the perceptual contrast. The vowels /i/ /a/ /u/ are said to have this quantal property, whereas vowels such as [ɛ] *bet* and [æ] *bat* do not. The vowels /i/ /a/ /u/ are very common phonemic targets in the world's languages. The vowels /ɛ/ and /æ/ and the /æ–ɛ/ contrast are comparatively rare. The opposite consideration also applies. Some sound contrasts rely on delicate *timing perception*, such as involved in the /ta–da/ voicing contrast. Suppose there were regions of temporal continuum where the ear was less sensitive to timing contrasts. It would make sense for languages to locate their **voice onset time** contrasts across, rather than within, these regions of relative acoustic insensitivity. See chapter 6 for further discussion.

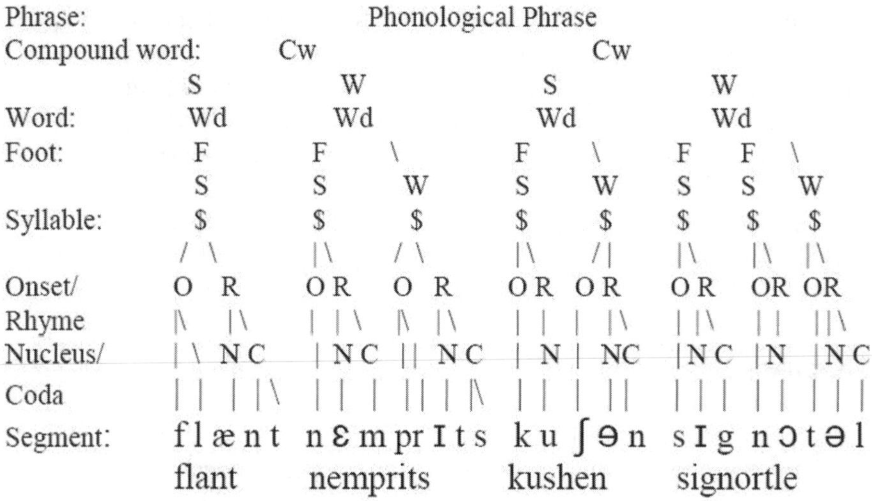

| Phrase: | Phonological Phrase | | | | | | | |
|---|---|---|---|---|---|---|---|---|
| Compound word: | Cw | | | | Cw | | | |
| | S | W | | | S | | W | |
| Word: | Wd | Wd | | | Wd | | Wd | |
| Foot: | F | F | \ | | F | \ | F | F \ |
| | S | S | W | | S | W | S | S | W |
| Syllable: | $ | $ | $ | | $ | $ | $ | $ | $ |
| | / \ | \|\ | / \ | | \|\ | / \| | \|\ | \|\ | \|\ |
| Onset/ | O R | O R | O R | | O R | O R | O R | O R | O R |
| Rhyme | \|\ \|\ | \| \|\ | \|\ \|\ | | \| \| \| \|\ | \| \|\ | \|\ | \| \| | \|\|\ |
| Nucleus/ | \|\ N C | \| N C | \|\| N C | | \| N \| N C | \| N C | \| N | \|\| N C |
| Coda | \| \| \| \|\ | \| \| \| | \| \|\| \| \|\ | | \| \| \| \|\| | \| \| \| \| \| \| \| | \| \| \| \| \| |
| Segment: | f l æ n t | n ɛ m pr I t s | k u ʃ ə n | | s I g n ɔ t ə l | | | |
| | flant | nemprits | kushen | | signortle | | | |

Figure 5.5 *Levels of prosodic structure*

low-mid, mid-high, and high, for purposes of phonological contrast. Alternatively, you could use sequences of notes to signal words, in which case you would need only 'low' and 'high' to make the four sequences: LL, LH, HL, HH. Or, you might introduce a temporal feature such as 'long' or 'short' notes. But no matter how many features you use, or how large the vocabulary of items to be distinguished, the phonological coding of the sound contrasts will always be discrete.[14]

## Hierarchical organization versus entrainment

Speech is composed of gestures that must be co-ordinated in time, like the instruments of an orchestra. The phonological plan, which can be likened to an orchestral *score*, is hierarchically organized and *a-temporal* until it is actually implemented in speech. Following Cummins and Port (1998), we will use the term 'entrainment' for the operation of implementing the phonological plan into a gestural performance that takes place in real time. How entrainment takes place in speech production is a mystery that is fortunately outside the scope of this book. Interested readers are directed to Levelt (1989) and Levelt, Roelofs and Meyer (1999).

The hierarchical nature of phonological representations was indicated earlier, in the discussion of prosody in chapter 2, where some linguistic justification was given for recognizing four basic levels of constituency in the prosodic hierarchy: the spoken phrase, the word, the foot and the syllable, with its sub-constituents, the onset, rhyme, nucleus and coda. We illustrate the prosodic structure of the nonce phrase '*flant nemprits kushen signortle*' in Figure 5.5. This nonce phrase

---

[14] There has been considerable debate over the origins of the discrete phonological features in speech perception, under the heading of *categorical perception*. See chapter 6.

was modelled on the prosodic structure of an actual utterance: *'French language teaching instructions'*. This phrase, as written, is actually ambiguous. Perhaps the most natural reading of it is something equivalent to 'instructions for teaching French language', i.e. where 'language-teaching' is a compound noun. However, if you listen to the phrase again, you will hear that the model is actually made up of two compounds 'French-language' and 'teaching-instructions'.[15] There was no particular reason for saying the nonce utterance this way. That just happens to be the way the phrase came out.[16]

## Summary

A theory of speech recognition seeks to account for how we extract phonological information from the highly variable acoustic speech signal. The sound spectrogram provides a useful representation of the changing energy components of the speech signal, but to extract phonological information from speech signals has proven to be a challenging task.

While clearly we need to be able to associate properties in the speech signal with the phonological targets of words in the recognition lexicon, a good deal of phonological parsing of the speech signal can take place without relying on successful lexical access (being able to identify particular words stored in our mental dictionary). Indeed, it is a requirement of any speech recognizer that it be able to parse phonetic input into possible word forms which the listener may never have heard before.

The phonetic features that comprise the auditory and articulatory properties of words are not all equal from the perspective of a native speaker/listener. Distinctive features have a privileged status in phonological representations (the sound structures of words given in the *recognition lexicon*). Phonological representations have the properties of being phonetically under-specified, discrete and hierarchically organized, whereas speech itself is made up of phonetic features that are fully specified, continuously variable, and entrained (overlaid on one another in time).

Speech perception and language processing are complementary constructive activities, in which a listener seeks to build a linguistic representation of what was said in conformity with the intended meaning of the speaker. Hence, both are

---

[15] You can tell this because of the extra prominence that occurs on the first word of each compound: '**French** language', '**teach**ing instructions'. This is the stress pattern of English compounds. It is indicated on the tree diagram, by the S versus W notation above the words.

[16] Perhaps the SW SW pattern was generated in the interests of rhythmic harmony. Hayes (1980) has discussed the tendency of spoken languages to prefer regular alternations of strong and weak syllables, in order to avoid *stress clash*. There is quite a literature on this topic (Shattuck-Hufnagel, Ostendorf and Ross, 1994). For a discussion of rhythm in speech disorders, see Grela and Gandour (1999) and McCormack (1994).

parsing operations. In this chapter we have been concerned to convey an idea of the kinds of objects that listeners construct when they parse speech signals. We have yet to tackle questions of what kind of processing mechanisms are required for speech recognition. This will be the concern of the following chapters, where we put flesh on the bones and start to consider competing models of speech perception and the experimental findings that bear on their validity.

# 6    Speech perception: paradigms and findings

## Introduction

In the previous chapter, we drew some tentative conclusions and made some quite strong claims about speech perception: that it is a 'bottom-up', highly modular process; that the objects of speech perception are abstract, hierarchically structured phonological targets; that speech differs in important respects from other kinds of auditory perception; that special, species-specific neural machinery may be required to support speech perception. It is time to consider more closely the experimental evidence to see if these claims can be substantiated, to examine the tools that have been developed for studying speech perception, and to approach the controversies that currently animate the field. We will not attempt a comprehensive review, but simply explore some long-standing themes and introduce the specialized experimental paradigms with which one needs to be familiar to understand current research.

One of the guiding themes of speech perception research has been the question of whether 'speech is special': whether specific adaptation of the perceptual system has occurred with the evolution of human language to support the demands of spoken communication. Several key concepts and experimental paradigms have been developed in an attempt to answer this question. Two early paradigms, **dichotic listening** and **categorical perception**, provide the foundational concepts for understanding contemporary issues. Specifically, the dichotic listening paradigm raises questions of hemispheric specialization and cortical mechanisms for speech perception that remain central to contemporary neuroimaging studies. Experiments on categorical perception bear on questions of levels of perceptual processing and the way in which language-specific learning and neurological maturation interact to shape the perception of speech sounds.

Consideration of these 'classical studies' enables us, in the later sections of this chapter, to make a foray into some leading questions of contemporary interest: **perceptual magnet** effects and the role of early language experience; **prosodic bootstrapping** as a solution to the problem of speech segmentation, which has been alluded to earlier; the **gating paradigm** and whether it can provide us with insight into the nature of phonological representations in speech perception (also raised previously).

## The speech mode hypothesis

In the previous chapter, we made reference to a paradoxical finding. Native listeners are capable of identifying phoneme sequences in speech at rates that would be impossible to achieve with a simple auditory cipher that scans text and presents each letter as a distinct sound, in order that blind people might 'read with their ears'. There are a number of approaches to making sense of this apparent paradox, which emerged in the early days of speech perception research (Liberman *et al.*, 1967).

One response, which has directed a whole program of research and has yielded a rich armoury of experimental paradigms, if not a great deal of consensus about the interpretation of the findings, is to argue that speech perception is fundamentally different from other forms of auditory perception. One way that speech is special in relation to other forms of auditory perception is that the perceptual targets of speech are intimately linked with a highly specialized system for their production. For the vast majority of speech sounds that we hear, we know exactly how they were produced, because either we generated them ourselves, or they were produced by speakers who talk very much like we do. This does not apply to the thousand-and-one other everyday sounds that we recognize on a habitual basis. In fact, when we listen to speech, we may automatically engage our neural apparatus for speech production. Recent evidence that may be interpreted as support for this *motor theory* of speech perception comes from neuroimaging studies, suggesting that a specialized perceptual-motor system of 'mirror neurons', located in the prefrontal cortex (Broca's area), but with intimate connections to the superior temporal gyrus, lies at the basis of imitative capabilities for speech and gestural communication in primates and human beings (Fadiga *et al.*, 1995; Rizzolatti *et al.*, 1996; Rizzolatti and Arbib, 1998; Hari *et al.*, 2000; Nishitani and Hari, 2000; Sundara, 2001; Avikainen *et al.*, 2002; Fadiga *et al.*, 2002).

The motor theory of speech perception predates modern brain imaging techniques and has excited long-standing controversy (Liberman, 1957; Lane, 1965; Liberman *et al.*, 1967). In its strong form, the motor theory of speech perception makes the claim that neural control mechanisms for speech production are activated in the course of speech perception. A less controversial form of the 'speech is special' view holds that speech perception requires specialized signal processing capabilities, which have presumably evolved to support our unique language faculty.

Researchers at Haskins Laboratories[1] first formulated the idea that speech perception involves the engagement of a special speech listening mode. This is referred to as the speech mode hypothesis (SMH). The experimental paradigms developed to test the SMH are perhaps more important than the hypothesis itself, which has proved rather elusive. Before considering the evidence, let us be clear

[1] Haskins Laboratories, Connecticut, USA, pre-eminent for speech research in the twentieth century, remains a leading centre to this day: http://www.haskins.yale.edu/

on what is meant by 'processing sounds in a speech listening mode'. A personal anecdote serves our purpose here. You may well have had a similar experience[2] to the following: I was killing time in a bookstore, back in the days when students spent as much time in street protests as in classroom-related activities, when I heard distant shouting. I listened, trying to make out what all the shouting was about. Then it dawned upon me, some two or three seconds later, that this was not another street protest getting underway, but simply the sound of the coffee urn doing its thing right next to me, inside the bookstore. Clearly, my auditory system had badly misread the input and switched into 'speech processing mode' for an extended period before disengaging (a couple of seconds is a long time in the world of speech processing).

For those with ready access to the web, a more vivid demonstration of what it means to process auditory signals in the speech listening mode may be given (courtesy of Robert Remez of Haskins Laboratories). Click on http://www.cambridge.org/9780521791908. Navigate to 'Online resources . . . 6.1 Remez' and make a brief note of what you hear.

Having just read the foregoing anecdote, you were probably primed to hear the auditory stimulus as 'weird speech'. Maybe you even managed to identify what was said.[3]

However, most people initially hear this stimulus simply as a 'funny noise', definitely *not* speech. For those who hear this signal in the speech listening mode, most can identify what was said on repeated presentation. Listening to **sine wave speech** is one way to induce the perceptual system flip-flop between what are usually quite separate auditory processing modes. Clearly it takes special stimuli to induce this chronic indecision in the perceptual apparatus. That is one reason why a speech synthesizer is a basic item in the speech researcher's tool kit.[4]

## Strong and weak versions of the speech mode hypothesis

Now that you have a feel for what it means to process sound in the speech listening mode, we can sharpen our ideas on the *speech mode hypothesis*

---

[2] I hasten to assure the reader that occasional auditory illusions of the type described here are perfectly 'normal'; clearly distinguishable from 'voices in the head' (auditory hallucinations) that are a clinical sign of schizophrenia.

[3] This is *sine wave speech*, a stimulus that has been synthesized from the spectrogram of a natural utterance, by replacing the acoustic energy in the original signal with *sinusoids* that track the frequencies of the major spectral peaks in the original speech signal. This operation preserves information about the changing resonances of the vocal tract and the major *manner of articulation* cues, but replaces the *voice source*, generated by vocal fold vibration in the larynx, with a decidedly non-human source signal. For those with web access, the original signal used to synthesize the above example of sine-wave speech is available from http://www.cambridge.org/9780521791908.

[4] The geeks among you may wish to play around substituting various source signals as excitations of the vocal tract filter. I once heard the first couple of bars of Beethoven's Fifth Symphony, used as the excitation source for a time-varying vocal tract function of a spoken phrase. It is remarkable to hear the full Boston Symphony Orchestra *saying* 'We were away a year ago.'

(SMH). There are two main forms that the SMH can take. The *weak* version, which is uncontroversial and accepted by everyone who really thinks about the matter, says that when we listen to speech or speech-like sounds, we cannot help but engage in linguistic processing, which involves accessing a vast store of specialized tacit knowledge about speech acquired in the course of language acquisition. But there is a *strong* version of the SMH, which is advocated by those who claim that *speech is special*: namely, that specialized perceptual mechanisms dedicated to the task of speech recognition, and in some sense hard-wired into the brain, are required (the auditory association cortex in the superior temporal gyrus being the favoured site, with possible linkages to Broca's area), at least for certain aspects of speech recognition. What evidence is there for this *strong* version of the SMH?

We will selectively consider evidence from three experimental paradigms, dichotic listening, categorical perception and duplex perception. The first two of these paradigms have in their time spawned cottage industries, first in studies with normal adults, then with adaptations, to studies of speech perception in special populations: infants, speech and language disordered listeners, second language learners.

## Dichotic listening

Doreen Kimura (1961) was one of the first to present competing auditory stimuli simultaneously to the left and right ears of listeners over headphones, asking them to identify both stimuli. Although she was not the first to use the technique (Broadbent (1956) had employed it a few years earlier in studies of *attentional* mechanisms), she was the first to find a small but statistically significant advantage for the perception of spoken numerals presented to the *right* ear. This right-ear advantage she attributed to the localization of speech and language processing in the so-called dominant left hemisphere of the cerebral cortex. The right-ear advantage was found only for speech sounds. Non-speech sounds either showed no ear advantage (in the majority of right-handed individuals) or, for some classes of sounds, a slight left-ear advantage.

Researchers at Haskins Laboratories (and subsequently many others), who were predisposed to the 'speech is special' view of speech perception, conducted a series of investigations involving the perception of synthesized speech, using the **pattern playback**[5] speech synthesizer. They found that some speech sounds showed consistently stronger tendencies to yield right-ear advantages than others.

The findings on the relative strength of the right-ear advantage for different phonetic classes of speech sounds converged nicely with independent findings from an unrelated experimental paradigm designed for the study of **categorical perception**. Why should stop consonants elicit stronger right-ear advantages than other speech sounds, and vowels show no ear advantage?

---

[5] For those with web access the Pattern Playback speech synthesizer is illustrated at http://www.cambridge.org/9780521791908, courtesy of Phillip Rubin, Haskins Laboratories.

Table 6.1 *Tendencies towards right-ear advantage in dichotic listening*

| No consistent ear advantage | Weak right-ear advantage | Strong right-ear advantage |
|---|---|---|
| Vowels | Liquids ([l],[r]) Glides ([j], [w]) Fricatives | Stop consonants |

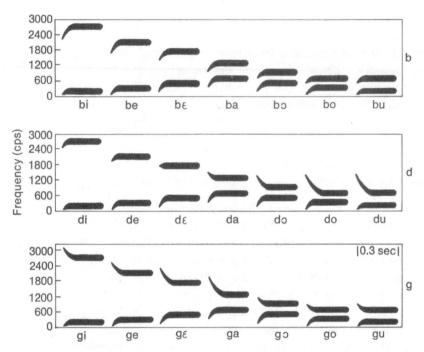

Figure 6.1 *Stop consonant + vowel syllables produced by the pattern playback synthesizer*

Examination of typical test stimuli used in these experiments, shown in Figure 6.1, suggests why. These are various CV (stop consonant + vowel) syllables produced by the pattern playback synthesizer.

Information about the stop consonant's place of articulation (whether it is a [b], [d] or [g]) is carried by the dynamically changing **formant transitions**, which represent changing vocal tract resonances as the articulators move from their point of closure into position for the following vowel. Then follows the steady-state formant targets for the vowel [i], [a] or [u]. Note that each vowel has a characteristic pattern of formant frequencies, which is stable for that vowel across different stimuli. But the formant transitions to the vowel, which serve to identify particular stop consonants, vary depending on the vowel that follows. In other words, the acoustic cues for consonants vary with context, whereas the cues for the vowels are context-invariant. Acoustic cues which are context-dependent will be more difficult for the auditory system to process than those which do not vary with context. The perceptual system will be required to abstract away from the context in order to make use of context-variable cues. It was argued that special neural-perceptual machinery might be required for this task.

Inspired by auditory neurophysiological experiments, involving micro-electrode recordings from individual nerves in the auditory cortex of various species, some speech researchers suggested that the specialized neural machinery for speech recognition might take the form of phonetic feature detectors (Eimas and Corbit, 1973), i.e. sensory detector neurons dedicated to extracting phonetic features from speech signals. For obvious reasons, no one proposed probing the human brain with small electrodes in search of phonetic feature detectors, though the bullfrog's auditory cortex had been extensively explored for neurons that emit highly selective responses – say, just to the mating calls of other bullfrogs, who have 'the right stuff'.[6]

However, Eimas and others thought they had *indirect* evidence for phonetic feature detectors from experiments with infant speech perception, involving cat-egorical perception of just those kinds of phonetic features (place of articulation, or voicing discrimination in stop consonants) which typically showed strongest right-ear effects in the dichotic listening paradigm. We consider this evidence in the next section.

## Categorical perception

Categorical perception is also a phenomenon with quite a long history of study. It too was thought at one time to be unique to human speech perception and the detection of certain phonetic features. Controversy over the status of categorical perception (Lane, 1965; Liberman *et al.*, 1967) goes back to the early studies, which found that vowels did not usually behave categorically, whereas stop consonants did, and other sound classes took an intermediate role. The debate has since been resolved in favour of the doubters. Categorical perception is not unique to speech perception, but is a general perceptual phenomenon that emerges under certain conditions where categorical distinctions are imposed on sensory continua for purposes of object recognition.

Nevertheless, categorical perception remains of considerable interest, for its value as a diagnostic of perceptual learning. Categorical perception can be loosely defined as a tendency to perceive contrasts on sensory continua more sharply at

---

[6] Caution must be exercised here. Just because we find that certain neurons in the frog's brain respond in a highly selective way to biologically significant sounds, this does not imply that such cells are responsible for *detecting* the signal properties that characterize that sound. Even if they could be shown to be part of the perceptual mechanism (and not, say, some ancillary arousal mechanism), their exact role in processing sensory signals would remain to be specified. Extending the analogy from bullfrog-call detectors to human-language phonetic-feature detectors involves a further speculative leap of inference.

category boundaries that distinguish discrete objects of perception. Thus, there is a transition region in the vowel formant space where an /ɛ/ (bed) will change its identity to an /æ/ (bad) for English listeners. Similarly, there is a point on the **voice onset time** (VOT) continuum where a /p/ will suddenly switch identity to a /b/. (Or to use a more familiar example, from the domain of colour perception: imagine a 'green' which gradually changes hue and at some point becomes a 'blue'.) Suppose you could discriminate hue more sharply at the blue-green boundary than within the blue or green regions of the colour spectrum. That would indicate a *tendency* towards categorical colour perception.

However, we need to define categorical perception more precisely than this for purposes of assessing whether it is a special property of speech or some other domain of perception. Categorical perception can be defined operationally in terms of our ability to discriminate between stimuli in relation to our ability to identify those same stimuli. Where our ability to discriminate between tokens is no better than our ability to label them (place them in categories), then we have a case of pure categorical perception. For those with web access, the easiest way to appreciate the distinction between categorical and non-categorical perception is to listen to the following series of stop consonants, generated on the old pattern playback speech synthesizer from http://www.cambridge.org/9780521791908.

Having listened to the series, do you agree that it runs from a stop sounding like [ba] through [da] to [ga]? Imagine being presented with sounds one at a time, drawn at random from this stimulus continuum and being asked to *identify* each stimulus as a 'b', 'd' or 'g'. Suppose a record of your identifications of the stimuli at each point along the b-d-g continuum were kept and then plotted on a graph showing the proportion of /b/ /d/ and /g/ responses at each point on the continuum. The result would be an *identification function*, like the ones shown in Figure 6.2.

Now suppose you are asked to discriminate pair-wise among the stimuli on this continuum. There would be little point in asking you to discriminate between, say stimulus (1) and stimulus (9). That would be too easy. So let us take the hardest case, seeing if you can discriminate between pairs of stimuli that are *adjacent* to one another on the continuum (1–2, 2–3, 3–4, . . . 8–9). Suppose we present several repetitions of all of these pair-wise discriminations and plot your success rate as a function of each of the single-step contrasts across the continuum. We would obtain a graph known as a discrimination function, shown in Figure 6.2. One interesting feature of this graph is that at certain points on the continuum, discrimination is markedly better than at other points. The positions on the continuum where discrimination is best correspond precisely to cross-over points on the identification function. In other words, discrimination is best at category boundaries (between /b-d/ and /d-g/).

The 'sharpening' of discrimination sensitivity at category boundaries constitutes a tendency towards categorical perception. But for strict categorical perception it should be the case that we can only discriminate between stimuli

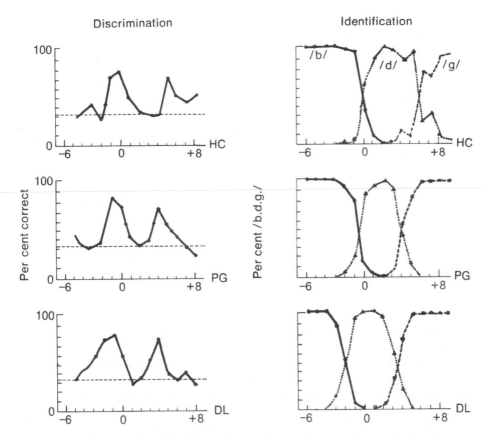

Figure 6.2 *Discrimination and identification functions for /b-d-g/ for three listeners*

that fall at category boundaries. For the stop consonants illustrated in Figure 6.2, strict categorical perception does apply, because performance falls to *chance level* on one-step discriminations that fall *within* phoneme boundaries.

The importance of the distinction between strict categorical perception and a mere tendency towards categorical perception loomed large in earlier theoretical debates, when categorical perception was thought to be unique to the speech listening mode and confined to a restricted class of phonetic contrasts. Vowel sounds typically manifest only a slight tendency towards categorical perception. Phonemic contrasts on stop consonants typically met the criterion for strict categorical perception, and the sonorant consonants and fricatives typically ranged between, in a result that paralleled the findings on the strength of the right-ear advantage in dichotic listening, reported earlier. Thus, categorical perception of certain phonemic contrasts appeared to provide independent corroboration of a specialized speech processing facility.

The case for a strong version of the speech listening mode hypothesis appeared to be further strengthened when Eimas *et al.* (1971) reported categorical perception of the voicing contrast among stop consonants in infants as young as one month of age, using a behavioural test of novel stimulus detection, known as the non-nutritive sucking paradigm. A variant of the 'odd-ball' technique: infants sucking on a teat are habituated to a series of identical sounds (e.g. [ta ta ta ta . . .]). An odd-ball is then introduced at random into the series. (e.g. [ta ta ta da ta . . .]). If the infant's sucking rate momentarily increases following presentation of the odd-ball, then we infer that it has been detected as a novel stimulus. Eimas *et al.* manipulated voice onset time, known to be a powerful cue to the voicing contrast of initial stop consonants in adult speech. Eimas *et al.* found that infants could detect a VOT contrast, provided that the difference in VOT between the habituating stimulus and the odd-ball spanned a critical point on the VOT continuum: the point which separated voiced from voiceless stops in the ambient language. A VOT contrast of the same magnitude but which did not span a phoneme boundary was not detected by the infants. The suggestion was that infants have their auditory systems tuned to at least some of the phonetic features of their language, at an age when they are clearly too young to have learned the linguistic significance of such contrasts. This study pioneered an active field of research into the speech perception capabilities of infants.

Eimas *et al.*'s strong nativist interpretation of the original findings was undermined by subsequent research on several grounds. Kuhl and Miller (1975) found categorical tendencies in VOT perception in chinchillas and other non-human species, for whom phonetic feature detectors would clearly serve no communicative function. While this finding was a clear blow to the hypothesis of an innate phonetic feature detector for 'voicing', it raised another puzzle: was it entirely coincidental that chinchillas should show heightened discrimination sensitivity at a region of the VOT auditory continuum that English and many other languages (see Lisker and Abramson, 1964, 1971) use for making phonemic voicing contrasts among stop consonants? Rather than argue that human beings have evolved some special neural machinery to enhance a specific phonetic contrast, it makes better sense to suggest that languages have simply taken advantage of a natural discontinuity that exists on a temporal dimension of auditory contrast that is common to mammalian auditory systems in general – a case of taking advantage of a naturally occurring non-linearity in a sensory continuum.

Further undermining the 'speech is special' hypothesis, categorical perception (or at least categorical tendencies) were found for the perception of auditory contrasts other than speech, such as the contrast between a plucked versus a bowed note on a stringed instrument. Indeed, Beale and Keil (1993), among others, using a graphical distortion technique known as 'morphing', have constructed complex visual continua and demonstrated categorical tendencies for *face recognition*, when the faces to be identified are highly familiar, as illustrated in Figure 6.3.

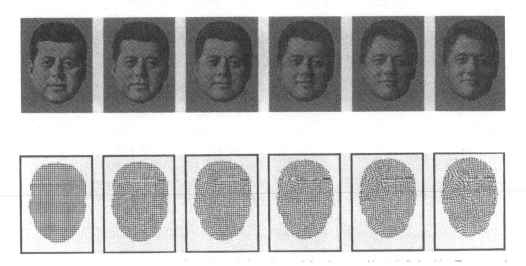

Figure 6.3 *Morphing visual images to create a 'Clinton-Kennedy' continuum*

The strength of the categorical effect in the perception of these complex and unique perceptual dimensions created by morphing between two images was directly related to the familiarity of the faces. Clearly, we are not dealing here with non-linear response tendencies or natural discontinuities on some well defined sensory continuum, as appears to be the case with categorical perception on the VOT continuum. Also, unlike the case of neonate discrimination of VOT contrasts, learning and object recognition obviously play a key role in the categorical discrimination of these morphed images. In all probability, therefore, the perceptual mechanisms underlying categorical perceptual response tendencies are quite different in the two cases.

But we are left with a dilemma. Are the categorical effects we observe in adults' perceptual responses to phonetic contrasts in speech qualitatively changed by exposure to the ambient linguistic environment compared with those of infants to the same stimuli? And if learning plays a significant role in the establishment of these response categories, precisely what mechanism is involved, and – a question of paramount significance to speech pathologists and second language teachers – how plastic (modifiable) is this learning mechanism beyond the critical formative age of first language learning? We consider the role of linguistic experience further below, and a possible learning mechanism for modifying neural maps for speech sound identification and discrimination in chapter 7 (Guenther and Gjaja, 1996; Guenther *et al.*, 1999). In the meantime, we consider an important property that distinguishes phonetic feature continua from auditory properties in general, namely, the sensitivity of the former to modification by phonological context.

## Coarticulation effects and category boundary shifts ▨▨▨▨▨▨

As indicated in chapter 5, phoneme category boundaries may be shifted by coarticulation effects. Thus, the strongest category boundary cue for the place of articulation contrast between (alveolar) /t/ and (velar) /k/ stops, which is the second formant transition, is systematically shifted closer to the velar end of the continuum when the preceding sound is a palatal fricative /ʃ/ rather than an alveolar fricative /s/ (e.g. *Foolish* tapes/capes; *Christmas* tapes/capes; Mann and Repp, 1981). A similar category shift in the alveolar–velar place of articulation boundary for stop consonants is also observed when an /r/ precedes the target stop compared with an /l/ (*or* done/gone; *all* done/gone; Mann and Liberman, 1983).

There remains some uncertainty whether there is a common articulatory basis for the above alveolar–velar category boundary shift, in the spreading of lip protrusion associated with both /ʃ/ and /r/, or possibly a more palatal point of articulation for a following alveolar stop, or some combination of both these factors.[7] However, if there are such things as 'phonetic feature detectors' mediating perception of stop consonant place of articulation, then their acoustic triggering conditions must be dynamically tunable to phonological context. In other words, these detectors would be highly complex and specialized perceptual analysers, if not 'hard-wired', then at least 'programmed' for the kinds of acoustic–articulatory mappings encountered in speech and probably only in speech stimuli. Such detectors would clearly satisfy Fodor's (1983) criteria for modular processors.

Mann (1986) presented some provocative findings on category boundary shifts for /d-g/ contrasts in Japanese learners of English. She tested native English listeners and adult Japanese learners of English with short and long exposure to L2, for /d-g/ category boundary shifts following /ʃ/ or /s/ and, crucially, following /l/ or /r/. As everyone knows, the English /l-r/ contrast is very difficult for Japanese learners of English. Not even the advanced learners in Mann's study could consistently label the English /l/ and /r/ tokens on an identification task. However, both Japanese groups showed perceptual boundary adaptations identical in form to those of the English controls in their responses to stimuli on the /d-g/ continuum as a function of a preceding /l/ or /r/ sound.

Mann concluded that these results favour a strong version of the speech mode hypothesis: that context effects in speech perception express themselves in automatic compensation for coarticulation, even when the context involves a foreign phonological contrast that the listener cannot reliably identify. It is as though listeners tacitly know *how* speech sounds are generated and can therefore adapt perceptually to contextually altered acoustic cues, even though they may be unsure of *what* the context signifies phonologically. The requisite knowledge of articulatory–acoustic mapping is presumably acquired early in first language acquisition and generalizes to an extent to non-native speech perception.

---

[7] In the authors' dialect /ʃ/ and /r/ are both pronounced with somewhat pursed lips and an alveopalatal point of constriction involving the body-blade of the tongue. The pronunciation of /r/, however, varies considerably with regional and social dialect in English.

Consistent with this notion, Fowler, Best and McRoberts (1990) found evidence of coarticulatory influences of preceding liquids (/l/ and /r/ sounds) in young infants' perception of the /d-g/ contrast.

However, additional experiments with animal subjects and using non-speech stimuli have challenged the strong motor-theory of context-induced perceptual boundary shifting. Lotto, Kluender and Holt (1997) reported context effects with Japanese quail. One group of quail were trained to peck upon hearing a synthesized /ga/ while not to peck on hearing /da/, and another group were trained with the opposite response pattern. Both groups were then tested under conditions of a preceding synthesized syllable (/ar/, /al/ or /a/) or no context. Quail trained to peck to /ga/ pecked more when stimuli were preceded by /al/ than when preceded by /ar/. Thus, Japanese quails exhibited shifts in pecking behaviour contingent upon preceding context and their shifts were analogous to human shifts in consonant identification.

Lotto and Kluender (1998) found that a context effect similar to that of a preceding liquid could also be induced in human listeners with a non-speech-contextual stimulus – one that matched the frequency characteristics of a preceding /r/ or /l/ third formant transition. Similarly, Stephens and Holt (2003) found that a preceding /ar/ or /al/ could shift the perceptual boundary for discriminating non-speech sounds that match the frequency characteristics of the principal acoustic cue for differentiating synthetic /d/ and /g/ sounds.

Clearly quail – Japanese or otherwise – have little need of a phonetic processor, and an articulatory compensation mechanism cannot account for context-induced perceptual boundary shifting with non-speech stimuli. The debate over whether these findings can be accounted for by a single perceptual mechanism, whether of a general auditory nature or specialized for speech, whether peripheral or central to the auditory system, continues (Fowler, Brown and Mann, 2000; Holt and Lotto, 2002).

We turn next to an experimental paradigm that combines the techniques of dichotic listening and categorical perception, known as **duplex perception**. Although difficult to work with, this is a potentially powerful experimental tool because it enables construction of experiments where the effects of perceptual processing in the speech or the non-speech listening mode can be investigated using identical sets of input acoustic stimuli.

## Duplex perception

Duplex perception is a striking phenomenon that involves the dichotic presentation of the acoustic elements of a phonetic stimulus, separately to each ear – the invariant portions of a [ba], [da] or [ga] stimulus (called the *base*) to the right ear, and the variable portions of the formant transitions to the left ear (see Figure 6.4).

If the third formant transition is set loud enough in relation to the base stimulus, the listener experiences the unusual sensation of hearing the unintegrated formant

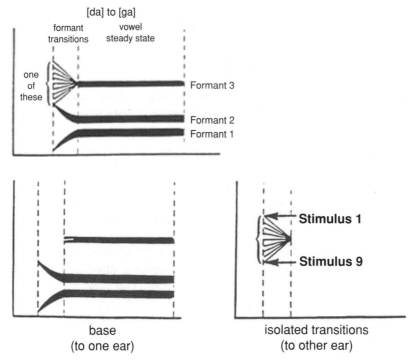

Figure 6.4 *Duplex stimulus construction*

transition, which sounds like a brief pitch glide or 'chirp', in the left ear and, *simultaneously*, the integrated phonetic stimulus – the syllable [ba], [da] or [ga] – in the right ear. (Hence the term duplex, to describe this dual-level perceptual experience.) The listener's attention may then be directed either to the linguistic target (the identity of the syllable) or to the perception of the unintegrated acoustic cue that carries the place-of-articulation information for the stop.

Some would argue that the experiential fact of duplex perception of itself constitutes evidence for the existence of a modular level of phonetic processing in speech perception (Xu, Liberman and Whalen, 1997). Duplex perception provides a unique opportunity to assess the strong version of the speech mode hypothesis. By directing listeners' attention to the phonetic percept (the syllable *ba*, *da* or *ga*) or to the third formant transition (chirp), one can investigate the effect of the processing task upon the response characteristics of the auditory system. It has, for example, been found that while perception of the stop's place of articulation is categorical, perception of the chirps is non-categorical (Liberman, Isenberg and Rakerd, 1981). In other words, when formant transitions are integrated with the base components presented in the opposite ear, they are treated categorically by the perceptual system, but when processed as non-speech auditory stimuli their perception is non-categorical.

Gokcen and Fox (2001) reasoned that duplex stimuli processed under the speech listening mode (by requiring listeners to make a phonetic judgement about the stimulus) should show a distinctive pattern of neural response compared with those same stimuli processed under a non-speech listening mode, when subjects' attention is drawn to non-linguistic aspects of the stimulus: the chirps. They used event-related potentials (ERPs) as the index of neural response pattern and duplex and non-duplex stimuli (synthetic [da]-[ga] syllables) to present listeners with phonetic and non-linguistic perceptual judgements. The presence or absence of the duplex component (the overlaid impression of a chirp) was controlled by adjusting the amplitude of the synthetic third formant transition. There was little consistency of pattern in the relative amplitude of positive and negative components of the ERPs, which was highly variable among subjects. However, differences in the latencies of the ERP components were found, with consistently longer latencies for duplex stimuli over plain synthetic syllables and tone glides (chirp only stimuli). The authors argue that their results are compatible with a modular account in which the additional ERP latency is caused by an additive effect of linguistic and non-linguistic processing in the case of the duplex stimuli.

### Sine wave speech

**Sine wave speech**, as we saw earlier in this chapter, provides another way of manipulating the task of the listener to process sounds in the speech or non-speech listening modes, similar to duplex perception. Recently, Dehaene-Lambertz *et al.* (2005) reported an investigation into the neural correlates of listening in the speech or non-speech mode to sine-wave synthetic [ba]-[da] sounds, using ERP and fMRI functional imaging techniques. The use of two quite different imaging techniques with the same stimuli and task enables us to obtain better insights into possible underlying neural mechanisms and the conditions that trigger speech or non-speech listening modes.

The listening mode was manipulated through the experimental instructions. In the non-speech listening mode condition, subjects were not told of the 'speech-like' nature of the synthetic stimuli, which were presented as a discrimination task, where three identical stimuli on each trial were followed by a fourth, which was either the same or different from the preceding three. Discrimination was tested under two conditions: (a) where the final stimulus in a trial consisted of a formant transition (F$\Delta$) expected to induce a category boundary shift (say, from *ba* to *da*; called the *phonemic* change condition), or (b) an F$\Delta$ transition of equal acoustic magnitude but not expected to be perceived as a phonemic change (called the *acoustic* change condition). Under the speech listening mode condition, subjects were told how sine wave speech stimuli were made and practised hearing them until they could clearly distinguish tokens of *ba* and *da* drawn from extremes of the *ba-da* phonetic continuum, before undertaking the discrimination test. Our expectation, based on the SMH, would be that subjects would show categorical perception of sine wave speech perceived under the speech listening mode, with

enhanced discrimination of differences that cross phoneme boundaries, but continuous or non-categorical perception under the non-speech listening mode, with
diminished within-phoneme boundary discrimination.

However, subjects' behavioural responses to the stimuli differed under the two
brain imaging conditions. Under the ERP recording, the manipulation of the listening condition was effective. None of the subjects reported hearing sine-wave
stimuli as speech sounds, until they were exposed to training for the speech listening mode condition. On the other hand, under fMRI recording, during the
initial 'non-speech' listening condition, most subjects reported hearing the sine
wave stimuli as speech sounds within the first block of trials. The noisy conditions of the fMRI scanner, compared with the quiet ERP recording, apparently favoured processing these ambiguous stimuli in the speech listening mode.
Just as in the bookshop anecdote (earlier this chapter, p. 114 above) and in the
discussion of 'top-down' processing effects in speech perception (next chapter,
pp. 145–7 below) high-level linguistic effects intrude on speech processing more
prominently under marginal listening conditions.

However, not all subjects responded to the stimuli as 'speech sounds' under
fMRI recording, and by careful use of self report it was possible to separately
analyse responses gathered under speech and non-speech listening modes for both
imaging techniques. ERP responses to difference detection (mismatch responses
or MMRs) were faster to stimuli perceived under the speech listening mode
under ERP recording and more asymmetrical (strongly lateralized to the left
hemisphere) under both imaging techniques.[8] Switching to the speech mode significantly enhanced activation in the posterior parts of the left superior gyrus
and sulcus relative to the non-speech mode. The authors conclude, and you may
judge for yourself, that 'these results demonstrate that phoneme perception in
adults relies on a specific and highly efficient left-hemispheric network, which
can be activated in top-down fashion when processing ambiguous speech/non-
speech stimuli' (Dehaene-Lambertz *et al.*, 2005: 21).

### Conclusions: is speech perception special?

We have examined four paradigms: dichotic listening, categorical perception, duplex perception and sine wave speech, each originally advanced as
support for the strong version of the speech mode hypothesis, that the human
auditory system is specially adapted for speech perception, possibly in the form
of phonetic feature detectors located in the auditory association cortex. Initially,
dichotic listening and categorical perception studies found converging evidence
for the specialized nature of the perceptual machinery required for recognizing certain context-dependent phonetic features, such as place of articulation or
voicing in stop consonants. But as research in these two paradigms matured, it

---

[8] fMRI does not have sufficient temporal resolution to compare with response time for evoked
potentials elicited by ERP.

became evident that certain non-speech auditory perceptual tasks also showed evidence of the 'specialized processing' that these paradigms were designed to detect, thereby raising the possibility that it was not speech *per se* which is special, but perhaps the *level* or *type* of perceptual processing involved. For example, Halperin, Nachson and Carmon (1971) were able to show right-ear advantages for dichotic non-speech stimuli consisting of tonal sequences, beyond a basic level of complexity. Papçun *et al.* (1974) found that experienced morse code operators showed a right-ear advantage for dichotically presented morse code letters, but novice operators did not, leading the authors to conclude that the right-ear advantages under the dichotic listening paradigm require complex temporal processing in combination with a well-learned internal code, but not specifically a speech code.

Categorical perception also turned out not to be specific to the perception of speech, though some phonetic features are more prone than others to categorical effects. Nor did the categorical tendencies in newborn infants' discrimination of phonetic features turn out to provide evidence of innate modular speech processing devices. Rather, the evidence from developmental studies seems to be that modularity is an acquired property of perceptual systems in which learning and maturation interact in ways that are not yet well understood.

## Linguistic experience and phonological parsing

Practically from birth, the human auditory system has been shown to be capable of discriminating any phonetic contrast that speech researchers present it with, gauging neonates' sound discrimination abilities by various autonomic nervous system responses to novel stimuli. It is also true that in the ensuing weeks and months, infants evince selective listening preferences for their caretaker's voice; for sound contrasts in the ambient linguistic environment – as distinct from those of languages not experienced (Polka and Werker, 1994); preferences for rhythmically structured stimuli – both for speech rhythms in general (Mehler *et al.*, 1988; Nazzi, Bertoncini and Mehler, 1998) and for those that are specific to the native language (Cutler *et al.*, 1986; Cutler and Otake, 1994). In other words, long before children utter their first recognizable words, the perceptual system is being attuned to the phonological structure of its linguistic environment.

In this section we review three strands of evidence. We consider perceptual magnet effects as an example of attunement to segmental contrasts of the native language. Next, we review recent evidence on *prosody* or the supra-segmental features of language, and the role that they may play in *bootstrapping* our abilities for segmenting speech into words (the segmentation problem discussed earlier). Finally, under this heading of the effects of linguistic experience, we consider some controversial psycholinguistic evidence, making use of the gating paradigm, designed to address the question, also raised previously, of phonetic under-specification of items in the **recognition lexicon**. We shall argue that while

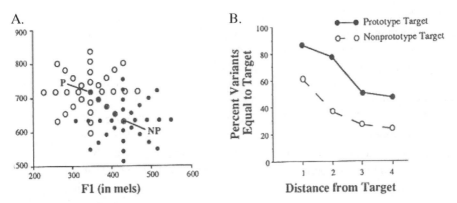

Figure 6.5 *Prototype (P) and non-prototype (NP) [i] vowels and perceptual magnet effects*

the gating experiments fail to provide unequivocal evidence as to the nature of phonological representations in the recognition lexicon, they provide insight, and testable hypotheses about *phonological parsing mechanisms* that operate at the level of extracting segmental features from the speech signal.

## Tuning the auditory system: perceptual magnet effects

Categorical perception involves enhanced discrimination at the boundaries between phonological categories on some phonetic feature/dimension. In 1991 Patricia Kuhl found evidence of what looks, at first appearances, to be a complementary effect: *reduced* sensitivity for discrimination contrasts with stimuli that fall at or around the *centre* of a perceptual category, i.e. reduced discrimination in the region of good exemplars or *prototypes* of a perceptual target. She dubbed this a **perceptual magnet** effect because prototypes appear to act as *attractors*, shrinking perceptual distances in their immediate vicinity. Consider, as a case in point, the 'best' or most '[i]-like' token of the vowel [i] (*heed*) from a set of synthetic candidates created with slightly different F1 and F2 formant frequencies.

Now, suppose we were to test your discrimination sensitivity in the region of a prototype [i] and compare it with your discrimination sensitivity in the region of a non-prototypical [i] (a bad exemplar of the vowel). This could be done by constructing a series of comparison stimuli at equal physical 'distances' from the prototype and the non-prototype in the F1–F2 vowel formant space (see Figure 6.5) and then testing for discrimination sensitivity using the comparison stimuli about their respective prototype and non-prototype stimuli. If the perceptual magnet effect holds, discrimination will be poorer in the region of the perceptual prototype. It is as though the good exemplar of the perceptual category acts as an attractor or a magnet that draws the comparison stimuli closer.

Perceptual magnet effects thus appear to be the complement of categorical boundary effects, and both may eventually turn out to be variant expressions of a single discrimination learning mechanism. However, they behave sufficiently differently to warrant separate treatment at the present time. Unlike categorical perception, magnet effects have not (yet) been demonstrated in non-human species such as monkeys (Kuhl, 1991). Perceptual magnet effects have been demonstrated in vowel as well as consonant discrimination, unlike categorical perception, which is usually found only for consonants. Also, magnet effects seem to be language-specific and dependent upon extended exposure to the ambient sound contrasts of a particular language. They are not found before six months of age, whereas category boundary effects on discrimination sensitivity appear to be present from the outset, or at least from the earliest age at which testing has been carried out.

Willerman and Kuhl (1996) found differences between Swedish, English and Spanish listeners' vowel discrimination sensitivity among mid to high front vowels; but not in ways that are entirely accountable from the distribution of target vowels in the vowel spaces of the respective languages, where Swedish has five vowel contrasts ([i], [y], [ʉ], [e], [ø]), English has three ([i], [ɪ], [e]) and Spanish only two ([i], [e]). Taken in context with other recent studies of cross-language vowel perception (Polka and Bohn, 1996; Ingram and Park, 1997), it is clear that the once widely held position that 'listeners' linguistic experience has essentially no effect on their ability to discriminate small differences in vowel formant frequencies' (Stevens *et al.*, 1969) stands in need of modification. But the nature of this perceptual learning is a matter of much current interest and debate. Some have questioned the replicability of perceptual magnet effects (Lively and Pisoni, 1997; Sussman and Lauckner-Morano, 1995). Aaltonen *et al.* (1997) found that only listeners who display sensitivity to prototype–non-prototype distinctions produce magnet effects in vowel discrimination. Others (Guenther and Gjaja, 1996; Lotto, Kluender and Holt, 1998) have shown that magnet effects can be modelled simply on the basis of exposure to tokens, using a self-organizing neural network.

The relationship between perceptual magnet effects and categorical perception is unclear at present (Iverson and Kuhl, 2000). However, magnet effects appear to be an expression of the shaping of auditory perception by exposure to spoken language during infancy. If perceptual magnet effects can be successfully modelled with a self-organizing neural network, then they can no longer be taken as evidence for modularity and the strong version of the speech mode hypothesis.

## Prosodic bootstrapping

We also know that sensitivity to the prosody of the ambient language develops progressively though the pre-linguistic period of infancy. **Prosodic bootstrapping** refers to the hypothesis that language learners may employ prosodic features of their language to help solve the word and phrase boundary segmentation problem discussed in the previous chapter. Anne Cutler and colleagues (Cutler *et al.*, 1986; Cutler, 1990, 1994) have argued that pre-lexical processing of speech is highly language-specific, and, by implication, learned. They find that prosodic parsing strategies, for assigning word boundaries prior to actual word recognition, operate in speech perception, and that these parsing strategies vary across languages. English listeners use a metrical segmentation strategy based on the regularity of stressed syllables. French listeners employ a more strictly syllable-based segmentation strategy. Japanese speakers use a timing unit known as the *mora* (haku, or onsetsu), which is reflected in the *kana* writing system.

The evidence for language-specific prosodic parsing strategies comes mainly from experiments involving listeners' *reaction times* to sounds embedded in different types of prosodic constituent. We can illustrate this most easily with a comparison between French and English. French has a clear and simple syllable structure. Syllable boundaries provide French listeners with reliable cues to segmentation of the speech signal. English syllable structure is more complex and often less clear. Compare, for example, the syllabification of the following French and English words:

|          | CVC/CVC   | CV/CVC    |
|----------|-----------|-----------|
| French:  | balcon    | balance   |
|          | CVC/CV/CV | CV-C-VCC  |
| English: | balcony   | balance   |

In the case of the two French words *balcon* and *balance*, the syllabification is clear and unambiguous, as it is also in the English word *balcony*. However, native speakers often disagree on the syllable boundary placement for words like English *balance*. Linguists often hedge their bets here, by saying that the /l/ in this word is **ambisyllabic**, straddling two syllables, and belonging no more to one than to the other. English syllables do not provide the listener with clear segmentation of the speech signal.

It has been found that if we present French listeners with words of varying phonetic content and ask them to respond as quickly as possible whenever they hear the sequence /ba/, they will react more quickly in the affirmative to words like *balance*, where /ba/ matches the first syllable, than to words like *balcon* where the /ba/ does not match a syllable in the target word. But English listeners do not show this sensitivity to the syllable structure of the target word. They respond with roughly equal speed, regardless of whether the monitored-for-sound sequence matches or does not match a syllable boundary in the target word.

However, English listeners are sensitive to prosodic units defined in terms of sequences of stressed syllables, technically called *feet* (or foot structure). English listeners are faster to recognize the embedded word 'mint' in the non-word [mɪntəf], which is made up of a strong (S) and a weak (W) syllable, than they are the same target in the non-word [mɪntaɪf], which comprises two strong syllables. The foot structure of the two words is:

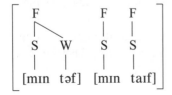

Notice, that the target '*mint*' falls within the same foot in the first case, but is spread over two feet in the second case (the '*t*' in [mɪntaɪf]' forms the onset of the second foot). According to Cutler's metrical segmentation strategy, English listeners provisionally assign a word boundary whenever they encounter the leading edge of a new foot. More specifically, English listeners employ a metrical parsing strategy which tells them to begin a lexical search each time that they encounter a strong syllable. This segmentation strategy will not always work of course, because there are words in English that begin with weak syllables (e.g. *convince*, *reverse*). However, a search of actual dictionaries and some large corpora of spoken English show that this parsing strategy works for the majority of cases (Cutler and Carter, 1987).

Subsequently, metrical parsing strategies were tested with Japanese listeners (Cutler and Otake, 1994). They found sensitivity for moraic structure, as shown by the following words ('.' indicates a syllable boundary, 'm' = mora):

| Japanese: | *tanishi* | *tanshi* |
|---|---|---|
| | ta.ni.shi | ta.n.shi |
| | m m m | m m m |

When asked to listen for the 'n' (Romanized script), Japanese listeners detected the moraic nasal in *tanshi* more quickly than the non-moraic one in *tanishi*.

It is important to qualify the results of these studies by noting that the method of reaction time measurement in a monitoring task, where the target matches or fails to match a prosodic unit that may be used in lexical access, is an indirect one, susceptible to unintended influences. For instance, we cannot be sure that the influence of mora structure in the Japanese experiment does not simply reflect the learning of Japanese *kana* orthography. Disentangling familiarity with written forms from the direct phonological influences of the spoken language is a difficult issue and a good reason for regarding these results as interesting, but provisional.

Another obvious potential criticism of the foregoing cross-language studies of prosodic parsing strategies is that they rely upon adult responses in experimental paradigms which are quite far removed from the context of 'prosodic bootstrapping' in which pre-verbal infants are attempting to segment speech into words or word-like chunks. But in recent years corroboration has been forthcoming, that infants between six and twelve months of age show progressive acquisition of word segmentation strategies based in part on language-specific prosodic parsing strategies, as well as an emerging sensitivity to phonotactic (sound sequencing) constraints and to allophonic variation which carries positional cues (recall our '*cats can*' vs. '*cat scan*' example, p. 25). Jusczyk *et al.* (1999) reports evidence that English infants at 7.5 months can segment words that conform to the predominant SW stress pattern (e.g. *kingdom*) but fail to segment words with the less frequent WS stress pattern (e.g. *surprise*) until about 10.5 months of age.

There is also evidence using **low-pass** filtered speech with newborns, that the capacity to discriminate broadly among speech rhythm types may be present from birth. Nazzi *et al.* (1998) reported that French infants discriminated between stress-timed English and mora-timed Japanese, but failed to discriminate between stress-timed English and stress-timed Dutch. In a further experiment, infants heard different combinations of sentences from English, Dutch, Spanish and Italian. Discrimination was observed only when English and Dutch sentences were contrasted with Spanish and Italian sentences. These results suggest that newborns can use prosodic and, more specifically, rhythmic information to classify utterances into broad language classes defined according to global rhythmic properties.

## Phonetic and phonological levels of processing in speech recognition

It was argued in the previous chapter that in the course of perceiving speech, the listener constructs a **phonetically under-specified** phonological representation of the sound input, and that this provides a *phonological access code* for retrieving information from the lexicon, which is required for word recognition. It was further claimed that non-distinctive (redundant) phonetic features are not part of phonological representations, though it was implied that such features, e.g. the lengthening of a vowel before a voiced obstruent (*bag* [bæːg]), may nonetheless, in some sense, be perceptually important. We offered 'hearsay' evidence that native listeners attend only to distinctive features in attempting to recognize speech. But can we do better? Can experimental procedures be devised for getting at these issues? We consider one promising technique below, known as the **gating paradigm**.

The issues at stake are (a) the nature of phonological representations in the recognition lexicon and (b) the mechanism – we refer to it as a parsing operation – whereby listeners extract phonological features from speech, prior to, or in order to facilitate, lexical retrieval. Phonologists have long held the view that phonological representations of items in the mental lexicon are phonetically under-specified, i.e. represented in a form in which sounds are stripped of contextually predictable phonetic features (see Archangeli, 1988 for discussion). On the other hand, studies of speech perception have tended to support the view that listeners exploit redundant phonetic features as soon as they become available in the stimulus. Thus, English listeners can detect an upcoming nasal consonant from nasal resonance in the preceding vowel, before the appearance of the nasal consonant (Ali, 1971), as in examples such as *can* [kæ̃ːn] (nasal resonance on vowel) versus *cad* [kæːd]. This can be demonstrated using the gating paradigm, whereby listeners are presented with stimuli from which the final consonant has been electronically excised or gated (see Figure 6.6)[9] and are asked to try to identify or guess the missing final consonant. Typically, English listeners can identify an up-coming nasal consonant on the basis of the (predictable) nasal resonance

---

[9] You can easily do this on your PC using a sound capture and editing facility.

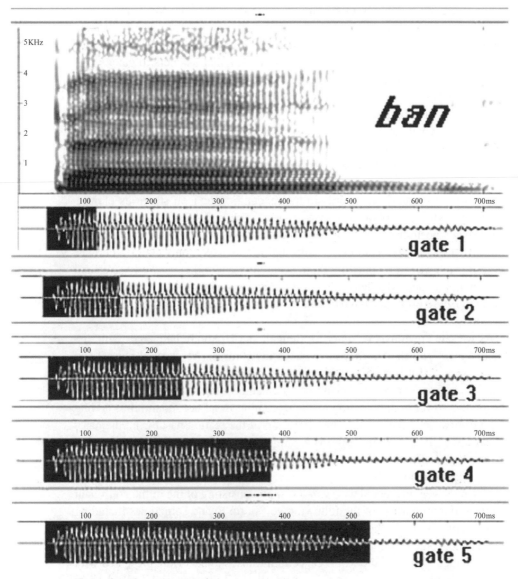

5KHz

4

3

2

1

100    200    300    400    500    600    700ms

gate 1

gate 2

100    200    300    400    500    600    700ms

gate 3

100    200    300    400    500    600    700ms

gate 4

100    200    300    400    500    600    700ms

gate 5

*ban*

Figure 6.6 *The gating paradigm*

on the vowel, quite some time (say, 50–100 ms) before they are presented with the acoustic cues that the nasal consonant is being articulated.[10]

If word recognition involves matching acoustic signals of speech to stored representations of words in the lexicon, then these findings would seem to indicate that nasal resonance (a redundant phonetic feature of the vowel) is present in

[10] These cues, which are reliable acoustic *landmarks*, involve major spectral changes in the signal caused by the sudden blockage of oral airflow and channelling of the airstream through the nasal cavity when the blade of the tongue makes contact with the roof of the mouth to start the nasal consonant.

the phonetic representation of *ban* in the recognition lexicon. Most speech perception researchers would probably subscribe to this view. However, Lahiri and Marslen-Wilson (1991) drew precisely the opposite conclusion, from an experiment comparing the responses of Bengali and English listeners to gated CVC stimuli, where the final consonant could be either a nasal consonant or an oral (non-nasal) consonant. They concluded that phonological forms in the recognition lexicon must be phonetically under-specified, or made up of only distinctive features. Ohala and Ohala (1995) conducted a similar study with Hindi and English listeners, obtained similar results to those of Lahiri and Marslen-Wilson and arrived at more or less the opposite conclusion, finding strong support for *fully specified* phonetic representations in the recognition lexicon.

So, who is correct? Are words in the recognition lexicon stored as phonetically fully specified phonetic forms (replete with redundant features – Ohala and Ohala's position) or as under-specified phonological representations (made up only of distinctive features – Lahiri and Marslen-Wilson's claim)? Perhaps there is some way of reconciling these apparently contradictory views. We shall present Lahiri and Marslen-Wilson's findings, supplemented with Ohala and Ohala's (1995) results and our own data using French listeners (Ingram and Mylne, 1994).

As we saw previously (chapter 5), Bengali and Hindi are languages with distinctive nasal vowels (i.e. they have phonemic contrasts between non-nasal and nasal vowels). But Bengali and Hindi, like English, also *nasalize* a vowel when it occurs before a nasal consonant. In articulatory terms, the **velum** is lowered during the vowel in anticipation of the upcoming nasal consonant, thus adding nasal resonance to the vowel. This spreading of the feature nasal from the nasal consonant to the preceding vowel is a natural process found in many languages. In resisting nasalization of vowels before nasal consonants, French is exceptional to the general trend.[11]

Listeners were presented with *gated* stimuli consisting of the initial consonant and a (variable) portion of the following vowel, up to and sometimes including the point of closure for the following consonant. The listener's task was to predict the final consonant from the truncated (gated) [CV. .] portion of the stimulus, by trying to identify the whole word. On certain trials, subjects were presented with a gated stimulus containing significant vowel nasal resonance ([Cṽ.]), derived either from a word containing a distinctively nasal vowel (e.g. *bãs* 'bamboo') or from a word containing a nasal consonant (e.g. *ban* 'flood'). You might expect that listeners would find such stimuli ambiguous, because the nasal resonance

---

[11] The situation is complicated by alternative phonological analyses of French nasal vowels. In traditional generative treatments, nasal vowels are sourced to underlying nasal consonants, a *morpho-phonemic* rule of vowel nasalization, followed by deletion of the nasal consonant – as suggested by the orthography. This analysis has historical merit, but it does not alter, and cannot easily account for, the fact that contemporary French has a phonemic contrast between nasal and oral vowels, supported by a phonetic process of suppressing nasalization of vowels before nasal consonants.

on the vowel could signal either a word with an inherently (distinctively) nasal vowel (CṽC), or a word ending in a nasal consonant (CVN).[12]

In fact, Bengali listeners (and Hindi ones as well) did not behave in this way, as you can see from the graph of their responses to the gated CVN and CṽC stimuli, which plots the proportion of responses of each type (CVC, CVN or CṽC). They responded to gated CVN (Figure 6.7[i]) and gated CṽC stimuli (Figure 6.7[ii]) in exactly the same way, up to the gating point when the acoustic landmark for the final consonant becomes apparent in CVN stimuli. In other words, Bengali listeners responded to perceived vowel nasal resonance as though it signalled a distinctive nasal vowel. Only when the final consonant of a gated CVN stimulus appeared at a late gating point in the stimulus sequence did listeners revise their analysis (see the response pattern in Figure 6.7[i] for the last two gating points). In effect, listeners were perceptually 'garden pathed' by gated CVN stimuli up until the disambiguation point, when the final nasal consonant is detected.

Lahiri and Marslen-Wilson (hereafter L&MW) interpret this behaviour of listeners as evidence that only distinctive features of words are represented in the recognition lexicon. This they term the *underlying representation hypothesis*, which states that lexical items contain only distinctive (non-redundant) phonetic information. They argue that for a gated [Cṽ. .] stimulus the only candidates available from the recognition lexicon for matching against the auditory signal are items containing *distinctively nasal* vowels. Non-distinctive nasal resonance is, they claim, not part of the lexical representation of words like *ban*. That is why there are no competing CVN candidates available for matching against a [Cṽ. .] stimulus and why no ambiguity is evident in subjects' responses to such stimuli. To fully appreciate L&MW's argument, it is necessary to see the results in the context of Marslen-Wilson's *cohort theory* of lexical access which we deal with more fully in chapter 7.

Ohala and Ohala (1995) sought to replicate the L&MW study, using Hindi and English listeners. Hindi parallels Bengali with respect to distinctive vowel nasality and anticipatory vowel nasalization. Ohala and Ohala (hereafter O&O) introduced some methodological 'refinements' and obtained somewhat but not substantially different results. Also prompted by the findings of the L&MW study, we conducted our own replication experiment, closely following the original methodology of L&MW, using French listeners and French stimuli. The reason for looking at French is that although the language has a set of distinctively nasal vowels, and vowels may also occur before nasal consonants, the process of nasal feature spreading (anticipatory nasalization) is suppressed in French:[13]

---

[12] There is an assumption here that the phonetically minded may have spotted. Nasal resonance on the vowel derived from nasal spreading is assumed to be indistinguishable perceptually from nasal resonance that is inherent to a nasal vowel. Although not specifically tested by L&MW or by O&O, this does appear to be the case in both languages.

[13] It may be, though this is only conjecture, that only languages with distinctive vowel nasalization block anticipatory nasalization and that this is done in the interests of facilitating phonological parsing of nasal resonance.

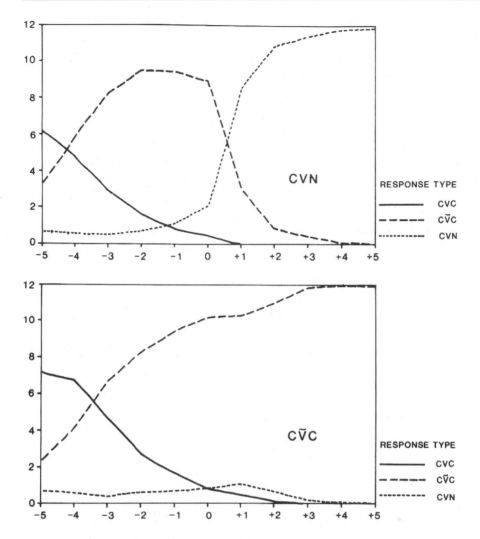

Figure 6.7 *Gating experiment: Bengali listeners' response to nasalized vowels*

|  |  | phonemic | phonetic |
|---|---|---|---|
| *bon* | 'good' (masc.) | /bõ/ | [bõ] |
| *bonne* | 'good' (fem.) | /bon/ | [bon] |

Results from the three studies are shown in Table 6.2 for the three languages that have distinctive nasal vowels: Bengali, Hindi and French. Results for the English subjects in both the L&MW and the O&O experiments showed that as soon as they detected nasal resonance in the vowel, listeners predicted an up-coming nasal consonant. English listeners' responses to vowel nasalization may or may not be a problem for the L&MW account. Ohala argues that these results are a problem for a theory of under-specified phonological representations. L&MW disagree. (What do you think?)

Table 6.2 *Results of three gating experiments:*
*percentage of responses up to vowel offset*

| Stimulus | | Response type | | |
|---|---|---|---|---|
| | | CVC | CṼC | CVN |
| CV(C) | Bengali | 85 | 1 | 14 |
| | Hindi | 72 | 19 | 9 |
| | French | 93 | 4 | 3 |
| CṼ(C) | Bengali | 35 | 60 | 5 |
| | Hindi | 14 | 72 | 14 |
| | French | 49 | 48 | 3 |
| CV(N) | Bengali | 25 | 67 | 8 |
| | Hindi | 21 | 53 | 26 |
| | French | 86 | 8 | 6 |

There are some differences in the response patterns of the Bengali and Hindi subjects, which can probably be attributed to methodological differences between the two experiments, but the basic finding, that listeners' default response to vowel nasalization is to treat it as a distinctive feature of the vowel, regardless of its actual source, was replicated.

The French listeners did not perceive gated CVNs as instances of CṼCs because our French speaker's vowels in these stimuli did not contain nasal resonance, thanks to the suppression of nasal spreading which is characteristic of French.[14] For French listeners, the potential ambiguity of gated [Cṽ. .]s simply does not arise.

## Conclusions from the gating experiments

What is the take-home message from these gating experiments? Do they tell us whether representations in the recognition lexicon are fully specified or under-specified (the underlying representation hypothesis)? Our answer, which we invite you to critically consider, is that L&MW are basically correct. Phonological representations in the recognition lexicon *are* constituted from distinctive features. But to give a coherent account of the findings – in particular, (a) the fact that English listeners respond appropriately to non-distinctive vowel nasalization, and (b) that Hindi and Bengali listeners treat vowel nasal resonance as indicative of a distinctively nasal vowel – we need to draw some explicit inferences as to the *processing mechanism* that is involved in *parsing* the phonetic input.

Clearly there is something wrong with L&MW's claim that in recognizing words listeners 'match' a phonetic input against (phonetically under-specified)

---

[14] This was confirmed by acoustic analysis of the vowels (Ingram, Park and Mylne, 1997).

representations in the recognition lexicon. Template-matching models of word recognition have long been abandoned in automatic speech recognition, as overly simplistic. In this context, the model is actually incoherent. It does not make sense to talk about matching a fully specified phonetic representation to an under-specified phonological target. A more constructive notion of perceptual processing is required if L&MW's claim about the nature of representation in the recognition lexicon is to be interpreted as a workable hypothesis about auditory word recognition.

Let us assume that listeners build perceptual representations on the basis of phonetic features detected in the speech input stream. Let us further assume that the targets that they construct have some kind of segmental structure, so that it makes sense to refer to the phonological features of the current segment or some upcoming segment. When English listeners encounter vowel nasal resonance as an input phonetic feature, it can only signal a forthcoming nasal consonant. For Bengali and Hindi listeners there is potential ambiguity here, but the gating studies indicate that they resolve the ambiguity on the fly by assigning nasal resonance to the current phonological segment. In the case of CVN words, this parsing strategy fails, and 20–60 milliseconds later they are obliged to re-analyse the phonological content of the input and assign the feature of nasality to the subsequent consonant.

A parsing strategy or heuristic which says, in effect, 'Assume the phonetic feature (cue) that I have just detected signals a phonological property of the segment that is currently under consideration' should be quite efficient. But it will occasionally lead to temporary mis-parsing of the speech signal. It is tempting to speculate that French acquired the low-level phonetic process of suppression of nasal spreading (at some cost in terms of increased articulatory effort) precisely to avoid these perceptual garden paths. It should be possible in principle to observe behavioural manifestations of phonological backtracking, using methods similar to those for observing syntactic repairs (see chapter 10), but given that the time constraints on phonological segment parsing will probably be an order of magnitude shorter than syntactic parsing, it may not be experimentally feasible to do so.

On a more general plane, these gating experiments lead us to a model of speech perception as one of active feature extraction and structure building, analogous to parsing mechanisms that have been proposed for higher levels of language processing. They raise the possibility that a common architecture, from the processing of speech signals to the construction of semantic representations, may be found that will make it possible to provide an integrated account of speech and language processing – fields that have hitherto tended to go their separate ways, despite the fact that they are obviously one seamless stream of information processing from the perspective of native speakers and listeners.

But two major problems remain to be tackled before the claims of our model can be assessed against competitors in the field. As we indicated in the previous chapter, any model of speech perception must provide mechanisms for accommodating to *phonetic variation* caused by speaker differences and such things as variation in vocal tract morphology, speech accent, dialect and speaking style. Any theory of speech and language processing must also deal explicitly with the role of the lexicon and the nature of the *procedural memory access* mechanism employed in speech and language processing. The type of active construal mechanisms which we have assumed to operate in our account of speech perception thus far have powerful competitors in various *connectionist* or neural network models, which have strongly impacted on the field in recent years. Connectionist models employ radically different models of lexical memory and an approach to handling phonetic variation that is coincidental with the phonological content of the speaker's message. Connectionist models also play a prominent role in contemporary accounts of speech and language processing disorders. We shall defer consideration of these issues until we deal with theories of lexical access in chapter 7. Perhaps what will be ultimately required is a hybrid model that combines the benefits of trainability found in neural network models with the potential explanatory power of analytical parsing models. But such a synthesis remains to be demonstrated. At the present time, what we have is an abundance of seemingly conflicting conceptions of what the basic mechanisms supporting speech and language processing might look like.

# 7    The speech recognition lexicon

## Introduction

Thus far, we have not entirely neglected but certainly down-played the role of the lexicon in speech perception. In chapters 5 and 6 we sought to make a case that speech recognizers must be able to build phonological representations of possible word forms, purely on the basis of acoustic phonetic input. Otherwise, it is difficult to account for the robustness and flexibility of our 'bottom-up' speech recognition capabilities. But it is also true that the goal of speech recognition is to identify words in the service of understanding whole utterances, and that there are a host of 'top-down' lexical, semantic and discourse effects that arise as a consequence of lexical retrieval mechanisms. Such effects express themselves in (a) the different ways that we respond perceptually to words (e.g. *kelp*) versus non-words (whether pronounceable like *klep* – a possible word – or phonotactically illegal, like *tlep*), (b) **neighbourhood effects**, arising from the fact that particular words vary in the number of phonologically near neighbours that compete for matching to the acoustic signal, and (c) other effects, such as **phoneme restoration** (see below), which may or may not be lexical in origin, but nevertheless require explanation.

The account given in previous chapters has characterized speech perception as an active process whereby phonological forms are constructed from speech-specific (phonetic) features in the acoustic signal, via the application of specialized perceptual analysers that exploit tacit knowledge of the sound pattern of the language and the sound production constraints of the human vocal tract. But we have not been sufficiently explicit about how contact is made with the stored inventory of phonological forms of words that make up the speech recognition lexicon, and what consequences such contact may have for how speech is perceived. This is the task of the present chapter. We shall see that the task of developing an explicit model of storage and retrieval of phonological forms raises strong challenges for the 'bottom-up' and modular theory that has been implicit in our account of speech perception thus far. The two most influential models of lexical access in spoken language processing in recent years, the **cohort** (Marslen-Wilson, 1984) and **TRACE** models (McClelland and Elman, 1986, Elman and McClelland, 1986), are interactive in their architecture, with 'top-down' information flow from activated lexical entries competing at the earliest opportunity with 'bottom-up' information flow from phonetic analysers. In addition, *instance-based* associative models of memory applied to the domain of speech recognition challenge the traditional linguistic conception, argued for in the previous chapter, that phonological forms in the recognition lexicon are constituted out of phonetically abstract distinctive features, and that, on the contrary, individual qualities of a speaker's voice and the episodic memory traces of recently encountered tokens of particular words are registered in word memory traces (Goldinger, 1997, 1998).

Early psycholinguistic models (Forster, 1976; Marslen-Wilson and Welsh, 1978) viewed lexical retrieval as an active search and match procedure. Dedicated perceptual processors would first identify phonological targets, usually conceived of as phonemes or distinctive features in the speech signal. The lexicon would then be searched for a match to the sensory input. In seeking to match the input, it was suggested that frequently used lexical items should be examined first, in order to account for the well-known frequency effect that the naming latency for a word is strongly related to its frequency of usage (Oldfield and Wingfield, 1965).[1]

Considering that perceptual targets must be encountered sequentially in speech, and that there are severe time constraints operating in speech processing, Marslen-Wilson suggested that a maximally efficient search procedure would be one that reduced the search space as successive phonological targets became available. He proposed this as a design feature of the lexical retrieval mechanism and dubbed it the cohort model. With the wisdom of hindsight, the logic of the cohort model now seems to be less of a design feature of the lexical retrieval mechanism than something which is mandated by the sequential nature of the speech signal. Cohort structure and frequency effects have been incorporated into all subsequent theories of form-based lexical retrieval.

But what has substantially changed since the early days of psycholinguistic research are our views on the mechanism of lexical access. Symbolic search algorithms have been superseded by connectionist models based on notions of spreading activation, inhibition and competition among neuron-like processing units. While there is still much debate about the architecture of lexical retrieval and in particular the problem of how to interface recognition (perception) and retrieval (memory) processes, a consensus has emerged that a great deal of parallel processing takes place at all levels of perception, which the serial architecture of the older search models is ill-equipped to accommodate. Connectionist models systematically blur the boundaries between perception and recall. Perception is simply stimulus-driven recall. To illustrate the advantages of connectionist models, it is useful to appreciate the limitations of a conventional symbol-processing search model. So this is where we shall take up the discussion.

---

[1] Interestingly, the effect of word frequency on *recognition* latency (time to recognize a word that has been presented previously) is just the opposite to what it is in a word-naming task. Episodic memory traces are stronger for previously encountered low-frequency words than high-frequency words, just as they are for recognition recall of unusual rather than frequently occurring incidents. For a recent fMRI study and discussion of theories see de Zubicaray *et al.* (2004).

After demonstrating the advantages of connectionist over symbolic search models of lexical retrieval of phonological forms, we next consider the evidence of top-down or lexical effects in speech perception and whether an interactive architecture such as the TRACE model is required to account for them. Following the leads of Cairns *et al.* (1995) and Norris, McQueen and Cutler (1999), we find that what appear at first inspection to be top-down or lexical effects can be re-analysed as bottom-up or pre-lexical effects that may be modelled by alternative neural network architectures designed to capture statistical dependencies in temporal sequences, such as those found in phonotactic constraints and coarticulation effects. We are thus not obliged to abandon the modularity that we argued for in previous chapters on the basis of non-lexical considerations.

However, there is little doubt that major advances in the field of speech perception in recent years have come with the development of connectionist models of lexical access. As a result of the introduction of these powerful computational models, there is every prospect of bridging the gulf which had grown up between the fields of automatic speech recognition (ASR) and speech perception. There may be less consensus amongst researchers on the basic issues of modularity and learning mechanisms in speech perception than there was twenty years ago. But there are many more tools available for modelling experimental findings. When evaluating competing models of lexical access and spoken word recognition, it is well to constantly bear in mind the great adaptive capacity of the human perceptual processor to accommodate to particular task demands of any given experimental paradigm. It is this adaptability that provides a major challenge to current theories.

In this chapter we are concerned with only one aspect of lexical structure and functioning: the retrieval of lexical items by their phonological forms from speech signals. There are 'deeper' levels of lexical structure: morpho-syntactic and semantic, and even a level of sound structure that linguists have dubbed the **morpho-phonemic**, which are not considered here. These deeper levels of lexical representation come into play in tasks that involve central or cross-modal linguistic processing, such as reading, speaking and processing for meaning in general. They will be taken up in subsequent chapters.

## Search models of lexical retrieval

The humble filing card system is not an unfair characterization of first-generation models of lexical retrieval, where each card in the file represents a distinct lexical item. Entries in the mental card file are ordered, alphabetically (like any dictionary or filing card system) and by frequency of usage (unlike conventional dictionaries). The way that items are arranged in the file – what Forster (1976) called the *lexical access code* – is crucial for determining lexical access times. Reaction times in word naming or lexical decision tasks have been the major means of testing different models of lexical retrieval. In random access memory of the type found in your hard disk, items are written wherever space is found for them. Retrieval times in a random access device vary from one seek operation to another, depending on where the read-heads begin to scan the disk, and it is only meaningful to talk of average seek times. On the other hand, if all seek operations begin from the same point and follow a predetermined sequence, then the time required to retrieve an item will depend upon the structure of the search path.

Here, metaphorically speaking, is how a typical search model might retrieve the lexical item *cat* from the acoustic signal. First, the perceptual analysers (the phoneme detector department, PDD) register that a word initial /k/ has been detected. An automaton, known as a 'comparator', whose task in life is to compare messages from the PDD against phonological forms in the mental card file, starts flipping through all the lexical items beginning /k/, arranged in order of frequency of occurrence. Our diligent drudge is interrupted in his search by the appearance of another piece of intelligence from the PDD: 'The next phoneme is [æ].' All the [k] initial words that do not have [æ] as their phoneme in second position drop out of the cohort of possible candidates and the search resumes, starting with the most frequent /kæ. . ./ beginning words. It is an open bet as to whether the word *cat* would be retrieved from the lexicon before or after the detection of [t].

This simple caricature of a lexical search model in operation is sufficient to illustrate the principal strengths and weaknesses of such models. On the positive ledger, it is possible to make quite strong predictions about how the model will behave with respect to reaction time data. But this is also a weakness, because the model does not accommodate to varying task demands like the human lexical retrieval system. For example, frequency effects have been found to be stronger in lexical decision tasks than word naming (Forster, 1990). Also, if a word has been recently presented it will be recognized more quickly. But recency effects, which are quite distinct from frequency effects, are difficult to incorporate into a search model. The only means a search model has at its disposal to accommodate to newly discovered factors that affect the speed of lexical retrieval is to propose an additional access code which promotes some items on the order of retrieval and demotes others. As the inventory of such factors grows, search models tend to become unworkable.

Perhaps more seriously, search models may be found wanting on grounds of parsimony. Parallel processing is employed for phoneme or phonological feature detection, but serial processing is used to explain lexical access times. Aside from the question of how perceptual and retrieval processes are synchronized – for which purpose hypothetical sensory buffers are usually invoked – there is also the question of precisely what purpose the comparator serves and how it might be implemented. You may have wondered from our '*cat*' retrieval example just what useful function, in terms of identifying the word, the comparator serves. Is it possible to dispense with the retrieval component of the model and the awkward problem of synchronizing the parallel with the serial components of the recognition/retrieval task, whilst retaining an account of lexical effects in speech perception? Activation models solve the problem of co-ordinating the lexical retrieval of phonological forms of words with feature recognition in the speech input stream by incorporating both operations into a single process of TRACE activation and de-activation. Changing objects of perception are conceived of as traces (patterns of neural activation) that wax and wane as attention restlessly shifts from one object to another under the joint influences of sensory input and internal mental processes.

## The TRACE model

TRACE (McClelland and Elman, 1986) was the first connectionist model of word recognition/lexical retrieval to demonstrate the feasibility of dispensing with a separate retrieval mechanism, within the simple and integrated architecture of a localist neural network. TRACE was in turn a development of an earlier neural network model of written word recognition (McClelland and Rumelhart, 1981), which we illustrated briefly in chapter 4. Although other lexical activation models pre-date TRACE – in particular Morton's (1970) Logogen model, an early competitor to search models of lexical retrieval – the TRACE model was the first to take the form of a computer simulation that successfully modelled a range of pre-lexical and lexical effects. Although its *localist* network architecture has been superseded by *distributed* networks with more powerful learning capabilities, TRACE remains one of the most comprehensive and successful simulations of a broad range of known perceptual effects (e.g. categorical perception, coarticulation effects, phoneme restoration, lexical biasing of phonetic targets), some of which are considered below. Otherwise, see McClelland and Elman (1986), or Protopapas (1999) for a more recent review.

### Architecture of TRACE

The TRACE model of spoken word recognition is an elaboration of the localist network of word reading (McClelland and Rumelhart, 1981) introduced in chapter 4. It differs from its predecessor in two respects. Firstly, the feature detector nodes have been re-designed for TRACE to extract phonetically relevant acoustic parameters from the speech signal. Secondly, to accommodate the temporal sequential nature of speech signals a major complication was introduced. Words are represented as patterns of activation on feature, phoneme and word nodes – 'traces' – that build and decay over time. Time in TRACE is modelled as a sequence of time frames, in which each frame replicates the entire set of network nodes and interconnections. The need to reproduce the whole hierarchy of units for each temporal slice of speech input imposed heavy restrictions on the size of simulations that could be implemented with the TRACE model. Although it provided some temporal animation, this architecture was cumbersome and too inflexible to accommodate speech rate changes and other temporal effects found in real speech. The model could however simulate basic coarticulation effects in terms of modifications of feature parameter values by adjacent speech segments.

Two versions of TRACE were developed. TRACE I (Elman and McClelland, 1986) was used to simulate phonetic processing and pre-lexical effects in speech perception. It operated on spoken word input, extracting in parallel from the speech signal eleven acoustic phonetic features, each coded for eight distinct levels of activation. Each 'distinctive' feature comprised a mini-network of 'level' nodes; one for each of the eight activation levels of a feature. The 'level' nodes in a feature network were each connected in an excitatory manner to a transducer tuned to respond to a particular level of the acoustic property that the feature was designed to detect. The level nodes within a feature network were mutually inhibitory, in a 'winner-take-all' configuration, so as to ensure that on any one time frame the feature network yielded a single activation level value to present to the phoneme detector units. Because feature values change more rapidly (with new readings from the speech signal every 5 ms) than phoneme values, phoneme nodes were represented on every third time frame (one per 15 ms).

Units decay at a rate that is commensurate with the time-window of their excitation. For example, phonemes may be expected to change state 5–8 times per second, whereas word units have a slower rate of excitation/decay and feature units have rapid decay functions. Phoneme units were detected and distinguished from each other by feature-level activation patterns gathered over a variable number of adjacent time frames, depending on the inherent duration of the target phoneme. The connections between feature and phoneme units were all (mutually) excitatory but those between different phonemes within a time slice were all inhibitory. (Why was this required?[2]) As feature node activation patterns change and feed their information upward to phoneme units that compete for possession of a time slice, patterns of unique phoneme sequences emerge on successive time frames of the phoneme unit layer. These sequential patterns of phoneme activation then feed the word level units for word recognition.

But before turning to lexical effects, let us ask how coarticulation effects, or the mutual phonetic modification of adjacent speech sounds, are handled by TRACE. These are dealt with in a top-down fashion, by allowing phoneme nodes to modulate the connection strengths (weights) between phonemes and feature values in adjacent or near-neighbour time frames, as shown in Figure 7.1. This kind of adjustment of the feature values of a phoneme in the context of another phoneme will generally take effect earlier when the context phoneme precedes, rather than follows, the feature-to-phoneme connections that it is modifying. (Can you see why this is so?[3]) Unlike the motor theory of speech perception,

---

[2] Because only one phoneme would be activated at any given point in time. However, down at the phonetic level, phonemes may gather activation from feature nodes in overlapping time frames.

[3] Because a phoneme must be already activated in order to be able to modulate the activation of a nearby feature-to-phoneme connection weight, and the sequential activation of segments necessarily occurs in a left-to-right order. Interestingly, anticipatory (right-to-left) coarticulation effects are generally stronger than 'carry-over' (left-to-right) effects in English.

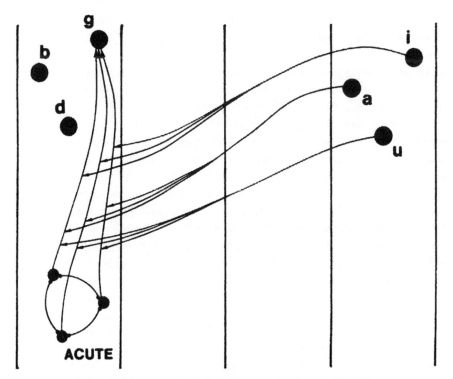

Figure 7.1 *How coarticulation effects are simulated in TRACE*

TRACE simulates the acoustic effects of coarticulation rather than the articulatory mechanisms responsible for their generation.

## Lexical effects in TRACE

TRACE II (McClelland and Elman, 1986) was used primarily to simulate word recognition and lexical influences on phoneme recognition. For these simulations, the phoneme units were fed predetermined patterns of appropriate feature-level activation, in order to reduce computational overhead so that interactions between the word and phoneme levels could be more fully explored using test vocabularies of reasonable size. Replicating the functional architecture of lower levels in the network, connections between word nodes are mutually inhibitory, so that the most highly activated word node exerts the strongest damping on the excitation of other competitors. A 'winner-take-all' scenario results, which is appropriate, so each word unit competes with every other for the perceptual identity of the sequence of time frames that they occupy. This design feature, known as *lateral inhibition*, is extensively used in localist networks to speed selection among competitors.

Lateral inhibition at the word level provides TRACE with a mechanism for solving the problem of false word segmentation raised in chapter 5 (recall the '*recognize speech*' example, p. 105). The idea is that longer words, which gather their activation over a larger number of time frames, will inevitably inhibit activation of shorter 'false positive' words that are contained within them. Thus *recognize* will (eventually)[4] suppress its embedded lexical competitors *wreck, a, an, ice* and *nice*, because, with its larger footprint on the speech signal, it will continue to gather bottom-up activation when its embedded competitors have ceased to.

Word frequency effects in TRACE may be accounted for by adjusting unit activation thresholds, such that higher frequency words have lower thresholds of activation than lower frequency words. These thresholds can be established on the basis of training the network with a realistic corpus of speech such as the London-Lund corpus of conversational speech (Svartvik and Quirk, 1980) or may be set *a priori* on the basis of word frequency counts.

It is probably clear by now that TRACE has the capability to model the cohort effects that motivated Marslen-Wilson's cohort theory, which was originally cast as a search model of lexical access. Bottom-up activation of the first one or two phonemes in a word will weakly activate a large cohort of candidates. As subsequent phonemes become activated, some will rapidly gain and others just as rapidly decline in activation and the cohort will be winnowed by increasingly tight constraints on phonological form. You can probably also appreciate that the size of the test lexicon and the representativeness of the phonological forms it contains will critically influence how faithfully TRACE will reflect patterns of activation that might be expected in human lexical access. The strength of top-down activation from the lexicon upon any given phoneme or feature-level node will be summed across all the currently active lexical nodes. Patterns of summation of lexical activation in the sample lexicon may only be expected to faithfully model those in the human recognition lexicon if the relative frequencies of word usage and the statistical structure of phoneme occurrences and phoneme sequences are faithfully represented in the test lexicon.

The transitory effects of lexical competition should, in principle, be observable behaviourally in human subjects, by 'on-line' experimental techniques such as the cross-modal semantic priming paradigm or other reaction-time-based probes of lexical activation. These behavioural indices can then be compared with TRACE simulations of lexical activation patterns. We review a couple of notable studies that have followed this methodology to show how TRACE accounts for some well-known phenomena, usually (but possibly mistakenly) attributed to top-down lexical effects in speech perception.

## Empirical tests of the TRACE model

The finding that phoneme detection times are faster in spoken words than in pronounceable non-words (e.g. detection times for /d/ in *medal* vs. '*ledam*'; Cutler *et al.*, 1987) has been taken as evidence of top-down lexical influences on

---

[4] Longer words will usually be lower in frequency of usage than their embedded word competitors; initially, therefore, embedded words may attain higher activation levels than their competitors, but eventually be suppressed.

phoneme perception and can be modelled as such in TRACE. Similarly, faster detection times for phonemes in near-words that share many phonological features with actual words, compared with non-words that lack near lexical neighbours (e.g. response times for /k/ in '*mekal*' (close to *metal* and *medal*) vs. '*lekam*') can also be interpreted as a lexical effect, consistent with an interactive activation model. However, lexical effects in phoneme monitoring tasks have proven to be quite susceptible to strategic processing influences (Wurm and Samuel, 1997) and experimental factors that can direct listeners' attention either to pre-lexical or to lexical attributes of the stimuli used in the experiment (Cutler *et al.*, 1987). TRACE mandates lexical influences in phoneme monitoring and cannot explain the variability of listeners' behaviour under different conditions of phoneme monitoring.

Two other effects, 'phoneme restoration' and the '**Ganong**' effect, are also often cited as lexical effects on phoneme perception. They too can be modelled by TRACE, but not with sufficient flexibility to account for the range of human perceptual performance observed under different experimental conditions. Phoneme restoration refers to a listener's ability to restore a phoneme target that has been removed from a spoken word or masked by a brief burst of noise strategically placed over a phonetic segment within a word. The Ganong effect is a related phenomenon, named after its discoverer (Ganong, 1980). A perceptually ambiguous segment, such as a fricative [s/ʃ] which has had its noise energy shaped so as to produce a sound intermediate between [s] and [ʃ], may be spliced into the last segment position of words ending in 's' or 'sh' (e.g. *Christmas* vs. *foolish*). If the Ganong effect is operating, the perceptual identity of the final segment /s/ or /ʃ/ will be determined by its lexical context. On the other hand, if the 'oddness' of the final segment is evident to the listener, it is an indication that lexical effects have failed to override the slight phonetic anomaly of the final fricative. In TRACE simulations, as you might expect, /s/ or /ʃ/ is activated depending on lexical context. Furthermore, examination of the feature node values will also show that the effects of modification by lexical context extend down to the phonetic level. However, for human listeners, the Ganong effect is only found under listening conditions where the stimuli are significantly degraded, such as by low-pass filtering at 3 kHz (McQueen, 1991).

Observant readers may have noted that we originally cited 'phoneme restoration' as an effect of modular processing in chapter 4; a case of perceptual closure where the only features relevant for the perceptual identity of an object are specific to the class (speech sounds) to which the object belongs. Yet in the present context, phoneme restoration is being cited as a phenomenon supporting a top-down interactive model. We shall allow this apparent inconsistency to stand as an object lesson for how tricky it can be to bring empirical arguments to bear on questions of architecture in a model of speech perception. In fact, phoneme restoration, as well as the other two effects on phoneme perception discussed above (the Ganong effect and phoneme monitoring in words/non-words), can be accounted for by bottom-up modular processing mechanisms, as we shall presently see. But before doing so, it is well to consider some of the apparently strongest evidence for top-down influences on phonetic processing in speech perception, TRACE's ability to perceptually compensate for coarticulation effects.

## Modelling coarticulation effects and other sequential dependencies

We have seen how TRACE implements coarticulation effects, by 'hard wiring' modifications to the feature specifications of a phoneme by other phoneme units that may be active in adjacent time frames. Using an initially ambiguous [s/ʃ] feature specification, Elman and McClelland (1988) showed that a bias quickly developed towards an /s/ or /ʃ/ phoneme target depending on the lexical context, as in the final segment in words like *Christmas* vs. *foolish*, thus successfully modelling the Ganong effect. But they were also able to extend the demonstration of top-down effects to show that TRACE was capable of generating category boundary shifts for a following /k-t/ discrimination in cross-matched word pairs such as

Christmas   tapes
Foolish     capes

Even /s/ and /ʃ/ units initially fed with ambiguous [s/ʃ] feature input, whose phonemic identity was determined by lexical bias, were found to shift the phonetic boundaries for a following /k-t/ contrast in the contextually appropriate direction.

However, simply because lexical effects are capable of modifying phonetic input to phoneme units in ways appropriate to simulate coarticulation effects, this does not necessarily demonstrate the correctness or appropriateness of a top-down interactive model if an alternative bottom-up model can be shown to exist. Furthermore, a model such as TRACE, which allows lexical influences to override or modify phonetic input, risks compromising the system's ability to detect discrepancies or respond effectively to unexpected features at the perceptual level.

There is also the downside, mentioned earlier, which TRACE shares with all localist networks, that while its behaviour is quite transparent in terms of the domain that it seeks to model, its learning capability is severely limited. Too much is required to be stipulated. Given a representative inventory of word nodes, each with a stipulated phoneme structure, and with activation thresholds set to mirror frequency effects in lexical retrieval, TRACE manages to accurately model aggregated activation patterns in the human recognition lexicon, both within a given time frame and across adjacent time frames. However, the network has not *learned* the relevant sequential dependencies that will determine the connection strengths between phonemes in a string. They arise through aggregation of unit activations over a pre-designed network of nodes.

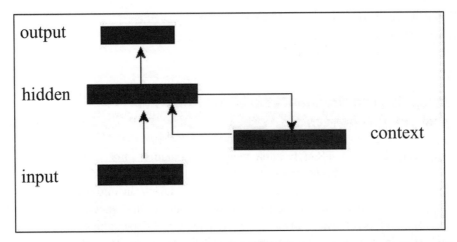

Figure 7.2 *Simple recurrent network (SRN). Each rectangle represents a layer of network nodes*

What we really want is a learning architecture that can extract sequential dependencies and recurrent patterns in the data stream, so that such things as word boundaries can be detected as emergent properties of the data, without having to stipulate *a priori* the structure of the lexicon. In other words, what we seek is a bottom-up learning device with the capability to assign word-level boundaries by exploiting sequential dependencies between units at the phonemic and phonetic levels. We require, in effect, a network that can solve the word boundary bootstrapping problem which confronts the pre-lingual infant. Jeffrey Elman (1990a) demonstrated just such a device in a seminal paper suggestively titled 'Finding structure in time'. Cairns *et al.* (1995) showed that this network, known as a *simple recurrent network* (SRN), could successfully model the Ganong effect, phoneme restoration and other phenomena previously treated as 'top-down' effects by TRACE.

The architecture of a simple recurrent network is illustrated in Figure 7.2 (reproduced from Elman *et al.*, 1996). The network is made up of a layer of input units, a layer of output units, a layer of 'hidden' units and a layer of 'context' units. Context units simply copy the hidden unit activations on the previous machine cycle, and are then fed back to the hidden unit layer, combined with activation from the input units, on the next machine cycle. By this recurrent loop, units in the hidden layer continually receive a diminishing 'echo' of their previous state in addition to updated activation patterns from the input layer on the next time frame. The recurrent loop provides the network with a kind of 'memory' of its previous states. The network's task is to predict the activation pattern on the output units.

Let us consider how the SRN may be applied to account for phoneme restoration or to capture other sequential regularities which may be present in the speech stream. We may pose the following problem for the network: given the current state of the input nodes (phonetic feature activations at time $= t_1$), how well can the output units, which we may conceive as phoneme units, predict the next phoneme in the sequence (at time $= t_{1+1}$)? The problem of predicting the next upcoming phoneme given the current state of phonetic input is not, of course, the primary task of phoneme recognition, but it is a task that is relevant for exploiting sequential regularities, such as phonotactic constraints. The error of prediction will fluctuate with position in the word. There are quite strong constraints on consonant sequencing in syllable onsets and codas in English and all natural languages. Entropy (unpredictability in sequencing) will typically peak at word boundaries.

Cairns *et al.* (1995) trained an SRN of the type described above on a representative corpus of spoken conversational English (the London-Lund corpus, Svartvik and Quirk, 1980). The corpus is transcribed in a 'broad phonetic transcription', which corresponds to a phonemic transcription. To render the transcription closer to a narrow phonetic transcription more typical of coarticulated connected speech, the investigators pre-processed the corpus with a set of connected speech rules as illustrated by the following example:

> *I won't be*        was pre-processed to: *I wom be*
> /aɪ woʊnt bi/            →            [ə woʊmbi]

The phonetic segments were then converted to a phonetic feature representation to serve as the input data stream for the SRN. Cairns *et al.* were able to show that the SRN could simulate the same range of contextual effects as Elman and McClelland (1988) demonstrated with TRACE. For example, an input segment with an ambiguous phonetic specification [s / ʃ] was successfully disambiguated as /s/ in words like *Christmas*, and as / ʃ / in words like *foolish* by the trained network. Yet this network has no lexicon! It must have learned that the transitional probability of an /s/ is higher than that of a / ʃ / following a [ə] and that / ʃ / is more likely than /s/ after an [ɪ]. The fact is that top-down lexical effects and bottom-up effects of sequential dependency can be hard to distinguish.

Why then favour a bottom-up processing account of their exploitation? We would reiterate two points made previously: an argument on grounds of parsimony, and another on grounds of relevance to the critical issue of learnability. The SRN model makes fewer assumptions or requires less stipulation about the model parameters. But more importantly, the bottom-up model points in the direction of a solution to a general problem of language acquisition: how higher-level linguistic units may be parsed from sequential dependencies formed over lower-strata units. This approach is by no means new in linguistics. Structural linguists such as Zellig Harris in the late 1940s sought just such algorithms as 'discovery procedures' for grammar construction. Although subsequently repudiated under the influence of Chomsky's critique of structural linguistics, the search for 'discovery procedures' was never completely abandoned because of its obvious relevance for language learning. The SRN has proven to be a simple but quite powerful learning algorithm. We shall consider it further later in the context of syntactic parsing.

## Modelling variability: a challenge for connectionist models?

Another consequence of connectionist modelling has been to offer a new approach to the problem of accounting for various sources of phonetic variability that make speech recognition 'difficult' (chapter 5). Neural network models have encouraged exemplar- or instance-based models of memory which challenge the traditional distinction between procedural and episodic memory and the concept, which we advocated on the basis of the gating experiments in chapter 6, that the recognition lexicon is made up of phonetically under-specified phonological targets. Or to put it in more technical-jargon-free terms: connectionist models favour a view that the memory traces by which words are recognized are rich in auditory details that evoke not only the phonological form of the word, but the speaker who uttered it, and indeed at least the most recent episodic contexts in which the utterance occurred.

As Elman and McClelland (1986) noted, the conventional approach has been to regard signal variability in speech recognition as 'noise' to be removed by 'signal normalization' operations of various kinds in order to retrieve some reified form of the input signal that could then be compared against abstract forms in the recognition lexicon. The approach is best illustrated by the various normalization schemes that have been proposed for accommodating the effects of differing vocal tract sizes on formant frequencies for vowel perception. However, the problem with this approach of treating non-linguistic sources of signal variability as 'noise' is that it fails to exploit powerful constraints that come into play when the various sources of signal variability are *jointly* considered.

Thus, being able to identify the speaker and being familiar with their speaking characteristics will facilitate the task of identifying the phonological content of their speech, as was demonstrated by Pisoni (1997) in a series of experiments. Listeners were trained on spoken word lists to recognize the voices of an initially unfamiliar group of speakers. Half of the listeners were then tested for word recognition on items that were not included in the training sessions but which were produced by the speakers on whose voices the listeners had been trained. A second control group of listeners were also tested for word recognition on the same set of words, but produced by a different group of speakers from those used in the speaker-identification training sessions. Under various levels of masking noise (signal to noise ratios: $+5$ to $-5$dB), word recognition scores were higher for the experimental group who had been familiarized with the speaker voices. The results were even stronger for key words in sentences, when whole sentences were used as the basis for training in the speaker identification phase. These results are not surprising. To revive an analogy made early in our discussion of speech perception, it is easier to read the handwriting of someone with whom we correspond frequently than the handwriting of someone we do not know.

For a signal like speech that is potentially informative on a multitude of categories (phonological content, speaker identity, gender, etc.), the more categories simultaneously opened or activated by the input, the tighter appear to be the constraints on recognition for any one of the component categories. To be simultaneously identifiable in terms of a range of perceptual/cognitive categories (who said what and how), a 'rich' auditory featural representation of the stimulus would seem to be needed.

When we combine this consideration with experimental findings that subjects engaged in memory tasks[5] have a high capacity for episodic recall of incidental detail, it can be seen why many researchers have suggested that an instance-based or 'exemplar' model of speech sound/word representation is required. Taken quite literally, such a model claims that every encountered token of a stimulus is stored (e.g. as a vector of auditory feature weights, plus a vector of category weights) as an instance in a large associative memory. Following some unspecified training period in which the network weights for a large (but finite) set of exemplars are established, the network can be used to select (identify) category labels for auditory feature vectors associated with new exemplars, based on some metric of similarity.

The foregoing account of an exemplar model of word recognition is rather too vague and programmatic. Johnson (1997) offers a more detailed but still programmatic suggestion as to how an exemplar-based model of speech recognition might be implemented. However, a central tenet of exemplar models, that a multiple category speech recognition system (one that supports the simultaneous extraction of speech and speaker information) requires a rich auditory representation, appears to be undeniable. But does this invalidate the contention that speech recognition involves the selection/construction of *abstract* phonological targets, which we have argued for previously? Not at all. As speech and language users, we can focus attention on the auditory-phonetic properties of speech signals for a variety of purposes. When we do so for purposes of processing the linguistic content of the message it is the phonological identity of the speech signal which is of paramount interest. If we focus upon the speaker's identity, emotional state or whatever, other auditory properties come into prominence. When we consider the full range of auditory properties of speech which may potentially be brought to conscious awareness, we are referring to an enriched phonetic[6] level of perceptual representation. But it is the phonological representation which is perceptually relevant for spoken language processing.

---

[5] Such as recognizing whether a particular word in a list has occurred previously.

[6] The term 'enriched phonetic level' is appropriate here because such an awareness of the properties of speech extends beyond what is captured in a narrow phonetic transcription (as for example represented in the symbols and diacritics of the IPA). The IPA, although it can be used to capture non-distinctive phonetic properties that may capture allophonic, stylistic and to some extent individual differences in voice and speech quality, was basically developed for purposes of linguistic transcription. It is ill equipped to capture many quite audible features that distinguish individual speakers (see Rose, 2002).

## Auditory-phonetic and phonological levels of representation

Auditory-phonetic and phonological representations can be distinguished by their temporal persistence. Auditory-phonetic representations are held for a brief period of time (a few tenths of a second) in a rapidly decaying sensory storage buffer. Phonological representations, on the other hand, are held in short-term memory where their 'half life' depends in part upon how long they are held as objects of the listener's attention. Phonological representations can be kept alive through rehearsal via the 'articulatory loop' (Baddeley, 1986). To a degree, we can gain access to differences between the auditory-phonetic and the phonological levels of processing speech by manipulating report latencies in speech perception experiments. The longer the delay between presentation of a stimulus and our experimental subjects' report of what they heard, the more likely we are to tap the phonological representation rather than details of the phonetic representation of the signal. This is because material captured in the sensory storage buffer decays quickly, and subsequently only phonological features, which are employed in lexical access, are available for report by listeners.

Different techniques used to assess speech perception capabilities impose different working memory and processing demands upon the listener and thereby affect the level and kind of representations that are reported. Discrimination tasks usually require less processing and elicit shorter reaction times than identification judgements. Hence, they usually tap somewhat lower and more 'enriched' levels of auditory processing than an identification task. (See Ingram and Park (1997) in relation to Japanese and Korean learners' discrimination identification of the English 'r-l' contrast.) Furthermore, different ways that discrimination judgements may be elicited can also variously tax processing demands and therefore differentially affect the level of speech processing that listeners report. Werker and colleagues (1984) have explicitly manipulated report latencies to tap different levels of processing in speech perception.

Clinical and experimental studies of types of auditory comprehension deficit provide another potential source of information on functional levels of speech processing. We take up this topic in the next chapter when we consider disorders of auditory processing, speech perception and lexical access.

# 8    Disorders of auditory processing

## Introduction

It is abundantly clear from the foregoing three chapters that there are
many unresolved questions on processes underlying spoken word recognition:
the extent to which speech perception relies upon special mechanisms, distinct
from the processing of auditory signals in general; the delineation of distinct
levels of signal processing in the auditory system and how they interact (e.g.
'bottom-up' or feed-forward processing versus 'top-down' or feed-back controlled processing); whether mechanisms employed in speech production play
an active role in speech perception (the 'motor' theory of speech perception);
the concrete or abstract nature of stored representations of speech sounds in the
recognition lexicon. An important source of evidence on all of these questions,
as with the broader question of language processing, comes from the study of
auditory processing disorders. Yet as Polster and Rose (1998) point out in their
review of the field, a clear taxonomy of disorders of auditory processing has yet to
emerge. This they attribute to a range of factors: (a) the comparative rarity of discrete disorders of auditory processing, (b) difficulties of differential diagnosis of
auditory processing disorders from aphasia and other forms of auditory agnosia,
(c) the inconsistent use of terminology by pioneers in the field, and, perhaps most
importantly, (d) our ignorance about the underlying neural mechanisms at higher
levels of auditory processing in the brain.

The purpose of the present chapter is to provide a framework for the clinical
evaluation of auditory processing disorders underlying the perception of single
words. Such a framework should provide clinicians with a means of mapping a
particular patient's auditory processing difficulties within the spectrum of tasks
required for reliable single-word recognition, assuming an intact hearing mechanism, and ignoring – because we shall deal with them later – higher levels of
language processing. Our previous discussion of speech perception has provided
a host of diagnostic possibilities, not all of them mutually compatible, and many
dependent upon theoretical assumptions about 'normal' speech perception which
are actively contested in the literature. Nevertheless, if you can find convincing
clinical evidence that a patient's performance fits a particular pattern of theoretically possible disability, then not only may you have a better handle on possible

remediation strategies, but also interesting evidence in support of one theory over another.

We will outline a classification of auditory processing disorders, which is compatible with the clinical literature and which embodies the major stages of auditory processing that have been proposed in the speech perception literature. Our classification of symptoms may err a little on the side of excessive modularity, with a proliferation of rare subcategories of auditory processing disability. Such a bias may be inherent in the single-case-study literature. To counteract it, we ask you to bear in mind a lesson drawn in the previous chapter from recent studies of cross-modal and cross-talker speech perception (Goldinger, 1997; Pisoni, 1997): that the brain, damaged or not, takes maximum advantage of multiple sources of variability (or constraint satisfaction) in speech recognition. Thus, the additional variability in the mapping from speech signals onto phonological targets which is introduced by different speakers does not impair but *enhances* speech recognition, provided the speaker's voice is familiar to the listener. And multiple channels of sensory information (say, being able to view as well as hear the speaker) invariably enhance recognition performance, despite the fact that multimodal stimuli, such as 'talking heads', might seem to add to the complexity of the perceptual **binding problem**.[1] Our brains seem to be designed for perceptual multi-tasking, for extracting multiple sources of information from multiple channels of sensory information at the same time, and for integrating these features into a stable and coherent world of apprehended objects. The perceptual objects that particularly interest us in this chapter happen to be single spoken words. But perception of any kind of complex perceptual object is normally supported by a host of lower-level feature detection and integration mechanisms. If the mechanisms themselves are impaired, this could have flow-on consequences for higher-order object recognition. Impairments of object recognition are traditionally referred to in the neurological literature as **agnosias** of one kind or another. A major concern of this chapter, therefore, is how to differentially diagnose between a high-level disorder of word perception and the contributory or flow-on effects of damage to some more basic or distinct but functionally related perceptual process, such as perceiving the identity of the speaker.

After having described the major types of agnosia that could contribute to disorders of single-word perception, we take up the question of their neurological substrates. In recent years, neuroimaging studies have begun to contribute to our understanding of the various levels and types of processes that have been proposed, both on theoretical grounds and on the behavioural evidence in the speech perception literature. For example, the discovery of a mirror neuron system in primates and humans provides suggestive evidence for the kind of sensory-motor

---

[1] The problem of how to integrate information from separate sensory modalities in order to perceive a unitary cross-modal percept. Kuhl and Meltzoff (1984) have presented evidence that infants 3–4 months of age achieve cross-modal integration of facial gesture and auditory perception from their gaze preferences in the **head-turning paradigm**. They can associate the vowels [i] and [u] with the appropriate visual displays for the lip spreading or rounding gesture.

loop that is implied in the motor theory of speech perception. Impairment to a specialized feedback loop of this kind offers the possibility of modular phonological impairments, specific to the decoding of speech signals. On the other hand, lower-order disruptions to auditory feature detection may express themselves in a range of speech and non-speech discrimination tasks that may have flow-on consequences for single-word perception.

One of the major sources of controversy in the clinical literature concerns these flow-on effects and the extent to which they support various reductionist theories of receptive language impairment. For this reason, we preface our presentation of a clinical taxonomy of disorders of auditory processing with a discussion of the role of temporal order processing in receptive language disorders.

### Flow-on effects of temporal sequencing deficit

Some four decades ago, Robert Efron (1963) proposed a bold but still cogent hypothesis, that receptive aphasic language disorder could be explained in terms of an acquired deficit of temporal order judgement; a general perceptual ability crucial for processing the rapidly changing speech signal. Efron supported his hypothesis with experimental findings from aphasics with either a dominant anterior temporal lobe damage focus (Broca type) or a posterior focus (Wernicke type). He determined that thresholds for reliable reporting of the correct sequencing of non-speech auditory stimuli (such as a noise burst followed by a complex tone, followed by another noise) were approximately ten times slower for Broca's aphasics than for normal controls. Wernicke-type aphasics, on the other hand, were more impaired in the perception of visual temporal order judgement, a finding consistent, Efron argued, with the more posterior locus of their cerebral damage. He drew attention to the well-known clinical phenomenon that aphasic comprehension is often aided by slowing down the rate of speech. A range of other phenomena implicate the dominant left hemisphere, and the temporal lobe in particular (aside from its name!), in time-critical sequential signal processing. (Recall previous discussion of dichotic listening and categorical perception experiments in chapter 6.)

Tallal and colleagues (1973, 1978) subsequently offered essentially the same hypothesis, that a deficit in perception of rapid temporal sequences, though presumably of a congenital rather than an acquired nature, underlies developmental aphasia, which is nowadays often referred to as specific language impairment (SLI) (Bishop, 1992; Gopnik, 1999). Tallal hypothesized that, rather than being a primary causal factor, any language deficit in acquired aphasia, or language learning delay in developmental aphasia, may be seen as a 'flow-on effect': that is, a consequence of impairment to a perceptual capability upon which language processing depends but which is not specific to the language faculty or to language learning capabilities. This hypothesis carried the implication that treatment strategies should be directed at enhancing the perception of temporal sequencing rather than language therapy *per se*. Supporting evidence was enlisted from reports that an intensive treatment program using computer-assisted training in temporal order discrimination resulted in significant improvement of receptive language skills (Tallal *et al.*, 1996).

The strongest – and therefore, from a scientific point of view, the most useful – form of Efron and Tallal's temporal processing deficit hypothesis predicts that every case of acquired or congenital aphasic comprehension deficit will be accompanied by impaired rapid temporal order judgement (TOJ). A single well-documented case of receptive language impairment accompanied by normal TOJ would be sufficient to falsify the strong version of the temporal processing deficit hypothesis. A weaker version of the hypothesis predicts that TOJ or some related time-sensitive perceptual processing disorder will invariably accompany certain kinds of receptive aphasic language impairment. Though more 'reasonable', such a hedged hypothesis is clearly more difficult to disprove and requires more elaboration before it can be tested. There is sufficient uncertainty in the field for us to advise you to keep an open mind on all but the strongest versions of the TOJ hypothesis for SLI. For a recent critical review of the role of auditory temporal processing deficits in SLI and dyslexia, see Rosen (2003). But whichever variant of the temporal processing deficit hypothesis of developmental language disorder turns out to be empirically correct (or indeed if neither proves correct), there will be implications for a general model of language processing in 'normal' as well as aphasic language users.

Also, it seems appropriate to conclude this brief discussion of possible 'flow-on' effects of a deficit in temporal processing upon language processing with a word of caution. The perceptual ability to report the order of occurrence of state changes in an auditory stimulus (TOJ) cannot be synonymous with the ability to extract linguistic information rapidly in time from speech signals. Recall from chapter 5 the early attempts to construct an auditory cipher for the blind and the finding that phoneme transmission rates in speech typically exceed maximum TOJ rates for non-speech sound sequences by a factor of 2 or 3. Rates of phoneme transmission in speech comprehension reflect information-processing efficiency in a specific cognitive domain. The relevance of TOJ measurements for perceptual processing of speech is therefore questionable.

## Levels and types of auditory processing disorder

As we move up the perceptual processing hierarchy, the responses required of the perceptual system (the types of features to be detected) are increasingly domain-specific and dependent upon information retrieval from long-term memory. Thus, 'higher level' perceptual deficits are seen to involve cognitive and memory components and are traditionally labelled as agnosias of one kind or another. Auditory agnosias refer to failures to recognize various kinds of auditory objects, such as the identity of a voice which should be familiar, or common environmental sounds (e.g. the sound of a car door opening, or coffee percolating).

The stimulus itself does not go undetected; *something* is heard, but the sensory components of the stimulus are either misinterpreted or remain uninterpreted. On the other hand, disorders at lower levels of auditory perceptual processing are traditionally regarded as forms of *deafness*. It does not help matters that clinical usage is not very precise here, so that what one author calls **verbal agnosia** another may term **pure word deafness**. (Similarly, an inability to recognize word letter shapes could be termed either 'orthographic agnosia' or 'letter blindness'.)

In attempting to delineate levels and types of auditory processing deficits more precisely, researchers have been guided, at the auditory-acoustic level, by neurophysiological studies of signal processing in the auditory system of higher mammals, particularly primates. To investigate higher-level auditory processing disorders in aphasia, researchers have also been guided by methods developed for the study of normal speech perception (discussed in chapter 6) and lexical access (chapter 7). In general, we might expect that evidence for (or against) modular mechanisms in speech perception would find similar confirming (or disconfirming) evidence in disorders of speech comprehension. Thus, if a special speech listening mode can be demonstrated in normal listeners, through studies of categorical perception or dichotic listening, analogous modular deficits in phonetic processing – distinct from general auditory-acoustic processing deficits – might also be expected to occur, however infrequently, as a result of certain types of injury to the linguistically mature brain. Behavioural methods developed for the study of normal speech perception and lexical access represent our best currently available tools for investigating higher-level language comprehension disorders. But increasingly, neuroimaging studies with human subjects, both normal and language-impaired, employing careful control of the acoustic stimuli and the listener's task are helping to delineate levels and types of auditory processing disorder (Näätänen, 1999; Pettigrew *et al.*, 2004).

## Clinical classification of auditory processing disorders

Since the emergence of aphasiology as a specialized branch of neurology, several distinct syndromes of central auditory processing disorder have been recognized (see Table 8.1 below). In the vast majority of cases, these syndromes do not present in pure form but as some mixture of symptom types and for this reason their independent existence as modular disorders has often been questioned, and their underlying mechanisms and localization have remained matters of conjecture. At one end of this clinical continuum we have auditory processing disorders that can be difficult to distinguish from hearing impairment as assessed by standard **pure tone audiometry**. At the other end of the continuum are disorders of spoken word recognition, where it is hard to distinguish between difficulties in extracting phonological targets from the speech signal (sound recognition) and processes of retrieval of phonological forms from the recognition lexicon (lexical

Table 8.1 *Disorders of auditory processing and word recognition*

| Disorder | Definition/symptoms | Proposed mechanisms/ lesion site |
|---|---|---|
| Cortical deafness | Diminished awareness or 'deafness' to auditory stimuli with intact sub-cortical auditory system | Bilateral lesions to primary auditory cortex |
| Auditory agnosia and general auditory-acoustic impairment | Impaired recognition of auditory objects of various kinds | Damage to complex auditory feature detectors in auditory association cortex |
| Speech agnosia or 'pure word deafness' phonemic aphasia | Impaired auditory recognition of speech sounds or spoken words, but otherwise intact hearing and language functions | Impaired phonetic feature detectors, or damage to specialized speech sensory-motor cell assemblies |
| Phonological retrieval disorder | Impaired lexical retrieval from phonological form | Impaired temporal-parietal cell assemblies serving lexical retrieval and word meaning |

access). As indicated in the previous chapter, activation models of lexical retrieval (such as the TRACE model) solve this problem by doing away with the distinction between recognition and retrieval entirely, amalgamating the two processes into one that involves competitive activation and decay of hierarchically organized units, from simple sensory detectors to complex perceptual objects.

## Disturbances of auditory-acoustic processing

Disturbances of auditory-acoustic processing refer to central nervous system hearing impairments and impairments to perceptual mechanisms that enable listeners to construct a coherent 'auditory scene' or identify sound objects in response to auditory stimulation. At this level of auditory perceptual awareness, we are not talking about the comprehension of spoken language or even the processing of speech sounds, but rather our awareness of sounds and general sound-analysing capabilities, which may be differentially distributed between the left and right hemispheres. Although disturbances at this level of auditory processing are rightly termed 'pre-linguistic', they may impact upon spoken language comprehension. The relevance of disturbances of auditory-acoustic processing for language comprehension disorders in aphasia remain a subject of some controversy, as we saw with our earlier discussion of the 'flow-on effects' of auditory deficits for SLI. We begin by drawing a distinction between central hearing loss, exemplified in the rare condition of *cortical deafness*, and the also rare disorder of general *auditory agnosia*, where central hearing is intact but the *identity* of the sound eludes the listener.

## Cortical deafness

Cortical deafness is a rare form of hearing loss that occurs when there is damage to the primary auditory receiving areas in the superior temporal lobes of the cerebral cortex (Heschl's gyri). Bilateral damage seems to be necessary to produce cortical deafness, which presents itself as a lack of awareness of all kinds of auditory stimuli, including speech. Persons with cortical deafness show a greatly diminished awareness of sound objects in their auditory environment, presumably because many of the specialized acoustic feature analysers which are the building blocks of auditory object discrimination are non-functional. Paradoxically, such persons may show certain behavioural responses to auditory stimuli that they cannot consciously report hearing, and even present with a normal pure tone audiogram, because the sub-cortical auditory system is intact. Unilateral damage to the auditory cortex is unlikely to cause central hearing loss because each ear projects auditory fibres to the ipsi-lateral as well as the contra-lateral auditory cortex, unlike the visual system, where there is separation of the right and left visual fields of each eye.

Recent studies (e.g. Bilecen *et al.*, 1998) using high spatial resolution neuroimaging methods have confirmed earlier findings, obtained with micro-electrode studies, that the primary auditory cortex, located on the superior temporal gyrus (Heschl's gyrus), contains multiple functional mappings of the cochlea. In each of these cortical 'maps', neurons are spatially distributed such that adjacent cells mirror the frequency responses of auditory nerve fibres along the basilar membrane, i.e. each cortical cell is tuned to respond most vigorously to a particular frequency. The fact that this **tonotopic organization** is multiply represented in the primary auditory cortex (and elsewhere in the brain) strongly suggests multiple parallel processing of basic auditory features.

## Auditory agnosia

Auditory agnosia refers to an inability to recognize familiar everyday sounds, such as water dripping from a tap, a door closing or the ring of a telephone. Unlike cases of cortical deafness, persons with auditory agnosia are consciously aware of auditory stimuli, but unable to identify what they are hearing. The ability to discriminate between similar sounds may be relatively intact, but sound identification is severely compromised. Auditory agnosia is usually accompanied by difficulties in speech sound identification, but in rare cases, a selective impairment in the recognition of non-speech auditory objects may occur, possibly as a consequence of hemispheric specialization and asymmetrical damage to the right and left auditory cortical regions (Spreen, Benton and Fincham, 1965; Schnider *et al.*, 1994).

General auditory agnosia impairs the identification of all types of sounds, but specific agnosias for particular classes of auditory stimuli are sometimes observed, such as **amusia**, a selective impairment of the ability to identify components of musical stimuli, such as melody and rhythm, or a diminished affective response to or appreciation of music. Amusia may be congenital (Peretz and Hyde, 2003) or acquired as a result of brain injury (Peretz and Coltheart, 2003). Any natural taxonomy of specific auditory agnosias might be expected to correspond quite closely to that observed for categories of specific semantic impairment in word recognition (discussed in chapter 11), given that object identification and naming are likely to be organized in a common system of semantic memory in the brain. Thus, encountering specific deficits of naming for artefacts or living things, we might expect also to find selective auditory agnosias occurring along similar lines. But this parallelism between specific auditory agnosias and naming disorders is currently no more than a plausible hypothesis requiring further testing. Speech agnosia (word blindness) constitutes a special case of specific auditory agnosia, which we discuss below. But first, let us inquire into the probable neural substrate for generalized auditory agnosia.

Auditory object recognition relies, in the first instance, upon the integrity of complex feature analysers that respond to aspects of the spectral and temporal composition of complex acoustic signals (i.e. sounds with more than one frequency component). We have seen that bilateral damage to primary auditory feature analysers in Heschl's gyri can produce cortical deafness. A secondary level of auditory processing in response to complex auditory signals seems to be served by neurons that form a 'belt' around the primary auditory cortex, from which they receive the majority of their input (Rauschecker, 1998). Neurons in the auditory belt are more responsive to multiple-frequency or frequency-varying sounds than to simple 'pure tone' stimuli. Such feature analysers may be seen as the auditory equivalent of 'edge' detectors in the visual system – not strictly simple, but not particularly complex feature detectors, which in turn may serve as input for still more complex feature detection, based on temporal sequencing of auditory-acoustic features or combinations of spectral components. The complex auditory feature detectors referred to here presumably do not have the functional specificity of phonetic feature detectors, 'grandma's voice' recognizers, or specific auditory memory triggers, but rather, constitute a pool of property detectors that distinguish many different kinds of auditory objects.

However, impairment of complex auditory feature detectors in the auditory association area of the superior temporal gyrus is not the only cause of general auditory agnosia. Bilateral damage to the *insula*, a deep region of the temporal lobe that lies beneath the opercula (the fronto-temporal cortical language areas, encompassing Broca's and Wernicke's areas), has been found to induce total auditory agnosia (Bamiou, Musiek and Luxon, 2003). The insula appears to act as a gateway for multiple sensory information channels, similar to the thalamus, to which it is intimately connected. The reviewers assert that recent 'functional imaging studies demonstrate that the (left and right) insulae participate in several key auditory processes, such as allocating auditory attention and tuning in to novel auditory stimuli, temporal processing, phonological processing and visual–auditory integration' (Bamiou *et al.*, 2003: 433). Thus, damage to an area which projects fibres directly to complex auditory feature detectors and appears to regulate attention to auditory stimuli can also induce general auditory agnosia, as well as damage to the analysers themselves.

## Auditory-acoustic processing deficits and aphasia

Divenyi and Robinson (1989) investigated the non-linguistic auditory capabilities of eleven aphasic subjects and compared their performances with a group of right hemisphere damaged non-aphasic subjects and a non-brain damaged control group. The aphasic group was not preselected according to any predetermined criteria. Various non-linguistic auditory assessments were given which included frequency discrimination, gap detection, gap discrimination, discrimination of frequency transitions, temporal order discrimination, detection of tones in noise with and without frequency uncertainty, and frequency selectivity.

The left hemisphere damaged group evidenced clear deficits in functions dependent upon spectral analysis (such as frequency discrimination), but also in auditory functions necessary to 'rapidly re-adjust the spectral focus of listening' (such as discrimination of frequency transitions and temporal order). These disturbances were not specific to the left hemisphere damaged group, however, with the performances of the right hemisphere damaged group differing on four of the seven tests. All four of these tests were pitch-related, with the pattern of differential performance related to an increased severity of dysfunction in the right hemisphere damaged group.

Of greater interest however was their analysis of the relationship between performance on the non-speech auditory discrimination tests and spoken language comprehension abilities in their subjects, particularly the left hemisphere damaged group, who showed a range of comprehension scores. Using a combined index of auditory comprehension derived from scores obtained on standardized language assessments, Divenyi and Robinson (1989) found 'an orderly deterioration' on four of the seven auditory function measures as the level of language comprehension decreased. The tests which best distinguished levels of language comprehension performance were as follows: frequency discrimination, frequency change discrimination, a tone-in-noise detection task, and a measure of internal consistency in subjects' level of auditory discrimination performance. Interestingly, temporal order discrimination did not significantly discriminate among levels of language comprehension in the left hemisphere damaged group.

In summary, the majority of the studies reported in the literature have concluded that patients with disturbances of general auditory-acoustic processing usually also evidence an auditory comprehension disorder (Albert and Bear, 1974; Divenyi and Robinson, 1989). In addition, whilst a variety of pre-linguistic auditory disturbances may arise as the result of both left and right hemisphere cerebral damage, a disruption of certain auditory processing functions that are necessary for analysis of rapidly changing spectral characteristics appear to be associated with disturbances in spoken word comprehension.

## Effects of brain damage on phonetic feature extraction

The literature contains numerous case studies of patients who present with an inability to understand speech but who are able to recognize other common (non-speech) signals presented auditorily (such as a telephone ringing or a dog barking). For example, Luria describes a thirty-year-old patient named Burs who received a penetrating shrapnel wound of the posterior portion of the left temporal lobe and who from the time of injury was unable to understand the speech of others: 'when more than one person spoke at a time or someone spoke to him from a distance, the words seemed to blend into one another and what he heard was undifferentiable noise' (Luria, 1970: 131).

Another patient aged eighteen with a head trauma similar to that of patient Burs was described by Luria as being unable to comprehend the speech of others; sometimes common words sounded unfamiliar to him, as though they were not spoken in Russian (his native language). In severe cases, Luria described the effects of lesions to the temporal lobe as resulting in speech sounding 'as unarticulated noise (the babbling of a brook, the rustling of leaves)' (Luria, 1973: 135). In less severe cases, the patient may have difficulty in comprehending similar sounds that differ only by one distinctive feature (e.g. pointing to the picture of the *bin* when related phonological foils are included such as pictures of a *pin* and a *fin*). This disorder has been given various labels – e.g. phonemic imperception (Luria, 1970, 1973; Varney, 1984), disturbances of acoustic-phonetic processing (Caplan, 1992), and word-sound deafness (Kohn and Friedman, 1986; Franklin, 1989) – and is most often reported in patients with posterior brain lesions, usually to the left temporal lobe.

### Pure word deafness

Pure word deafness refers to a rare modular disorder in which perception of speech sounds and word recognition is severely compromised, but hearing and non-speech auditory object recognition is intact, together with central language functions and language-dependent skills such as reading and writing. Speech is usually fluent, with occasional or moderate sound substitutions (phonemic paraphasias). The patient's singular, conspicuous deficit is an inability to recognize the sound shapes of words. Subjectively, speech is experienced as 'meaningless noise, garbled sound, or a foreign language' (Mendez and Rosenberg, 1991). Auditory comprehension in general is obviously impaired, but patients will typically perform better in conversational speech where they can exploit contextual cues than on tests of isolated word recognition.

The syndrome of pure word deafness may be seen as an argument for the existence of speech-specific neural processing routines, possibly taking the form of 'phonetic feature detectors'. Although it is a rare condition, Poeppel (2001) reports that sufficient data are available to assess the lesion site in at least fifty-nine cases, forty-two of which involved bilateral temporal lobe lesions to the primary and secondary auditory cortex. In the remaining cases, lesions were reported to be left unilateral, but of a kind that resulted in isolation of the posterior superior temporal gyrus from both hemispheres.

However, in most cases where there is a prominent deficit in phoneme identification and word recognition other accompanying auditory perceptual deficits are also found. We will reserve the term 'pure word deafness' for the rare situation where an acoustic-phonetic mapping disorder is the singular perceptual deficit and employ the more neutral term 'word-sound deafness' where word and phoneme identification simply present as prominent symptoms of the patient's perceptual disorder.

### Studies of prevalence of word-sound deafness

Whilst patients with acoustic-phonetic processing disorders are most often reported to have impaired auditory comprehension, the reverse need not be the case. That is, patients who show poor performance on assessments of auditory comprehension may not always evidence disturbances in phonetic feature extraction, the implication being that the locus of their poor auditory comprehension may lie elsewhere in the language processing system. Varney (1984) found that of a sample of eighty patients with left hemisphere lesions, forty-four (55 per cent) were impaired in auditory comprehension, but only fourteen (18 per cent) showed defective phoneme discrimination test performances. All the patients who failed in phoneme discrimination were also impaired on the test of auditory comprehension, but a number of patients with severely impaired auditory comprehension performed normally in phoneme discrimination. Varney (1984) also found that deficits in phoneme discrimination were typically seen in the acute stage of aphasia, with most patients having recovered normal phoneme discrimination at four months post onset of aphasia.

This view of the transitory nature of acoustic-phonetic processing disorders is not upheld by a more recent study by Gow and Caplan (1996) whose subject group, selected on the basis of impaired performance on a phoneme discrimination task, were between 4 months and 282 months post onset of their cerebro-vascular accident. It would appear that the impaired acoustic-phonetic processing can remain a significant feature of a patient's aphasia profile for quite some time and remain stable over time and between tests (Gow and Caplan, 1996).

### The nature of word-sound deafness

Variations in nomenclature have caused considerable confusion in the literature on word-sound deafness. Some authors refer to a condition called pure word deafness or auditory verbal agnosia, which is defined by Praamstra *et al.* (1991) as being characterized by a selective impairment of auditory verbal comprehension with preservation of other language functions. The condition in its pure form is very rare, so most authors agree that where there is a disparity between auditory verbal comprehension and other linguistic functions, the cases are best referred to as word-sound deafness or word deafness. Franklin *et al.* (1995) use the term word-sound deafness to signal that although comprehension of spoken words is impaired, the deficit typically occurs in patients with other impairments such as with lexical access or reading impairments. Thus word-sound deafness is considered to describe a symptom that may appear with other aphasic symptoms. In its pure form, affecting only the recognition of words in the auditory modality, it is rightly referred to as the syndrome of pure word deafness. Because it has been generally supposed that the underlying mechanisms responsible for both pure word deafness and word-sound deafness are similar, the literature investigating the nature of the disturbances in pure word deafness is also of interest to us.

The underlying problem for a patient with word-sound deafness is at the stage of extracting the phonetic features from the speech input such that the patient has problems discriminating between widely variant words (the severe form) or between similar-sounding words (a milder impairment). In the early literature (Oscar-Berman, Zurif and Blumstein, 1975; Auerbach, Allard, Naeser, Alexander and Albert, 1982), an emphasis was placed on differentiating two levels of processing deficit in pure word deafness; a pre-phonemic (or auditory) impairment and a disorder in phonemic discrimination (a deficit at the phonetic level of processing). It seems quite apparent now that what was referred to then as the pre-phonemic form of pure word deafness is similar to the non-specific auditory processing deficits we have described in the previous section. For example, Auerbach *et al.* (1982) describe a patient with a disorder of 'pre-phonemic auditory acuity' with deficits observable on tasks such as the assessment of temporal auditory skills, as well as with consonant-vowel (CV) identification. We would suggest that the patient reported by Auerbach *et al.* (1982) has deficits with both acoustic-phonetic processing and a non-linguistic auditory processing disorder (as described in the previous section).

More recently, most authors reserve the term word-sound deafness for those cases where the patient has a deficit in linguistic discrimination that is independent of a temporal order acuity problem. Whether word-sound deafness can exist independently of deficits to non-specific auditory processing remains open to debate. For example, Praamstra *et al.* (1991) suggest that word-sound deafness is caused by both phonemic deficits and more general non-linguistic processing deficits.

Much of the research investigating the nature of the acoustic-phonetic processing deficit in aphasia has used two experimental paradigms: phoneme discrimination and phoneme identification tasks. In the former, a subject is presented with two auditory stimuli (e.g. /pa/ /pa/) and must respond as to whether they are the same or different. In the phoneme identification task, however, the subject is asked to label the phoneme and therefore must first classify the stimuli into a known phonemic category and then attach a label to that category. It is presumed that these two tasks tap into different aspects of acoustic-phonetic processing. Blumstein, Cooper, Zurif and Caramazza (1977) investigated aphasics' abilities to discriminate and identify the distinctive feature of voicing in stop consonants by using the synthetically produced consonants /t/ and /d/. The authors found that one group of patients performed well on both tasks, and another group of patients performed poorly on both tasks. Of interest, however, is that a third group of patients could discriminate between the stop consonants but could not attach the appropriate label. The reverse pattern, however, did not occur. That is, no patient performed well on the labelling tasks but poorly on the discrimination task.

These results indicate that acoustic-phonetic processing disorders can affect an early linguistically relevant processing ability such as the discrimination of voice onset time, as well as another linguistic processing ability such as labelling of speech sounds. Thus, there are two levels of processing: one based upon the function of a set of property detectors (that underpins patient performance on phoneme discrimination) and another level that makes use of these properties for linguistic processing (and allows for correct phoneme identification). Blumstein *et al.* (1977) emphasized the interaction between lower-level acoustic-phonetic abilities and higher-level phonological abilities in the latter task, where they argued that a subject must 'assign a stable category label to a speech stimulus, i.e., to use phonological information in a linguistically relevant way' (p. 381). Thus phonemic discrimination abilities are a prerequisite for intact labelling, but the reverse is clearly not the case.

Whilst Blumstein *et al.*'s (1977) study investigated only the synthetic stop consonants /t/ and /d/, a more comprehensive examination of aphasic subjects' acoustic-phonetic processing using several types of phonetic features in both natural and synthetic speech tokens was undertaken by Gow and Caplan (1996). Gow and Caplan were particularly interested in two issues. Firstly, are the acoustic-phonetic deficits of aphasic subjects limited to a specific subset of phonetic contrasts, such as 'place of articulation' or 'voicing' discrimination? Secondly, does the use of synthetic speech stimuli (typically isolated CV or CVC syllables), employed in previous studies, unduly simplify the listener's task by removing ambiguities as to the location of syllable boundaries that would be present in natural speech stimuli? In a typical speech signal, patients must be able to segment or localize critical spectral features that vary rapidly in time.

Twenty-two aphasic subjects selected for inclusion in the study on the basis of impaired acoustic-phonetic processing on a pretest were asked to discriminate between spoken one-syllable, synthetic one-syllable and synthetic two-syllable stimuli. Their phoneme discrimination abilities were compared with identification performance using the same types of synthetic and spoken syllable stimuli. The complete tests were administered on two further occasions; at one year after initial testing and then again one week after that.

Overall, Gow and Caplan (1996) found that phoneme discrimination and phoneme identification tasks may be reliable measures of acoustic-phonetic processing in aphasic individuals, although spoken rather than synthetic stimuli may enhance reliability of the assessments. The nature of the acoustic-phonetic processing difficulties appeared to be related to the computational complexity of the judgement and to the degree with which the phonemic processing depended upon the rapid appreciation of temporal structure in the speech signal. Aphasic subjects were found to have higher scores for vowel rather than consonant discriminations, suggesting that aphasics are primarily impaired in their ability to process time-varying spectral cues. Vowel identity, which is encoded primarily by frequency values of the first three formants, can be made without recourse to temporal information. Temporal processing impairments were also postulated as the source of subjects' greater difficulties with discriminating consonants in syllable coda (i.e. VC) as opposed to syllable onset position (CV), and for an advantage of articulator-free (manner and sonorance) feature discrimination over articulator-bound (place and voicing) feature discrimination. Articulator-bound feature contrasts depend on or vary with the target configuration of the articulators at the time the sound contrast is produced, whereas articulator-free features are less context- and time-dependent for their effective acoustic cues.

The data from the aphasic subjects showed that certain types of feature discriminations were more vulnerable to the effects of brain damage. The pattern of performance, however, across consonant versus vowel, place versus voice, articulator-free versus articulator-bound and CV versus VC discriminations was quite similar for both aphasic and control subjects, suggesting that processing difficulty and/or complexity may be related to task performance. Like Blumstein *et al.* (1977), Gow and Caplan (1996) found that phoneme identification was more severely impaired in the aphasic subjects than phoneme discrimination, suggesting that phoneme identification involves several other processes that are vulnerable to brain damage (e.g. having identified the phonetic features, subjects must then integrate them into a stable phonemic representation).

### The neural basis for speech agnosia or pure word deafness ▪

Disturbances in acoustic-phonetic processing are found in single left hemisphere lesions (Studdert-Kennedy, Shankweiler and Pisoni, 1973) but bilateral temporal cortico-subcortical lesions appear to be far more common (Poeppel, 2001). The lack of consensus as to cerebral hemisphere localization is extended to controversy surrounding the relationship between specific aphasia subtypes and disorders of acoustic-phonetic processing. It seems that neither the traditional aphasic subtypes nor lesion sites are related in any clearly systematic way to disturbances of acoustic-phonetic processing, although a tendency exists for temporal lobe lesions to be more closely linked with word-sound deafness. Blumstein (1994) concluded that 'speech perception impairments emerge in nearly all aphasic patients, suggesting that the neural basis for speech perception is broadly distributed in the language hemisphere' (p. 29).

There is little direct evidence from aphasic studies to support the existence of modular specialized feature detectors. However, this might simply reflect a lack of sufficiently detailed studies incorporating repeated observations over time to establish that well-attested patterns of dissociation between specific features can exist in impairments of phonemic perception. Interestingly, Gow and Caplan (1996) observed that while there were strong overall similarities in the aphasics' performance, several patients did show 'reliable reversals of the general pattern of results observed in the group' for particular phonetic features. Thus, one subject showed an advantage for voicing discriminations over place of articulation discriminations across three separate testing sessions, while another showed 'an advantage for discriminations of articulator-bound [place] features over articulator-free [manner] ones'.

If specialized phonetic feature detectors exist, then they probably do so not as single cell units but as distributed neural circuits that span both the sensory and motor language areas. The patient group most likely to provide evidence of disruption of such specialized phonetic circuits would be conduction aphasics rather than the Broca's or Wernicke's aphasics who have been the subject of most studies.

Neuroimaging studies of subjects engaged in active or passive listening to speech have yielded mixed findings, with many studies showing a pattern of bilateral activation in the regions of the left and right superior temporal gyrus (Norris and Wise, 2000), but with others showing, in addition, activation of Broca's area, predominantly in the left hemisphere. Hickok and Poeppel (2004) suggest that a critical determinant in the variability of these activation patterns is task-related, depending on whether the goal of listening is predominantly semantic (meaning-directed) or phonetic (interpreting the gestural structure of the word).

They propose an initial acoustic-phonetic decoding system centred around the primary auditory cortex bilaterally. This cortical processing system 'then diverges into two processing streams, a ventral stream, which is involved in mapping sound onto meaning, and a dorsal stream, which is involved in mapping sound onto articulatory-based representations' (Hickok and Poeppel, 2004: 72). A task such as phoneme identification or discrimination, which is very commonly used in speech perception experiments, activates the speech-motor control loop as the subject engages in detailed analysis-by-synthesis to determine precisely how the signal was produced. On the other hand, word recognition or listening for meaning would be expected to more fully engage the ventral processing stream,[2] which articulates with the parieto-temporal semantic storage system.

This neurological model of word processing has a number of features to recommend it. It readily accounts for some otherwise difficult to explain clinical dissociations between auditory comprehension and 'sub-lexical' phoneme perception in aphasia. Broca's aphasics typically have intact lexical comprehension

---

[2] The terms 'dorsal' and 'ventral' are adopted by way of analogy with a similar functional anatomical pathway distinction in the visual system (Milner and Goodale, 1993). They do not very accurately convey the direction of pathways in this context.

A

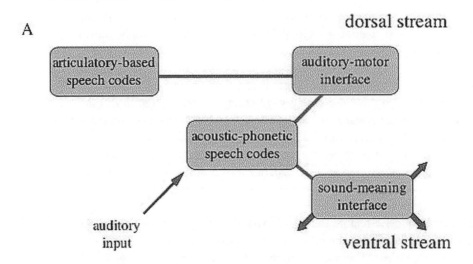

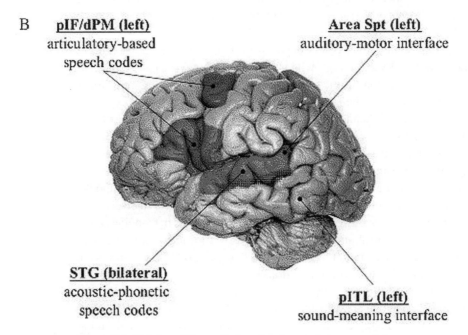

Figure 8.1 *Hickok and Poeppel's dorsal and ventral stream model*

yet, as we have seen, often perform poorly on tests of phoneme identification or discrimination (Miceli *et al.*, 1980; Gow and Caplan, 1996). Wernicke's aphasics often manifest the opposite pattern. This double dissociation is predicted by Hickok and Poeppel's model (Figure 8.1). The 'ventral' processing stream serves lexical access, which we discuss in the following section. Support for the dorsal processing stream, involving the speech sensory-motor loop, derives from neurophysiological evidence for a 'mirror neuron' system for the imitation of goal-directed manual gestures (grasping, holding, manipulating objects) in monkeys and its homologous system for speech motor control in humans.

## Mirror neurons and the speech-motor loop

A few years ago, Rizzolatti *et al.* (1996) caused a stir with a report that

> In area F5 of the monkey premotor cortex there are neurons that discharge both when the monkey performs an action and when he observes a similar action made by another monkey or by the experimenter. We report here some of the properties of these 'mirror' neurons and we propose that their activity 'represents' the observed action. We posit, then, that this motor representation is at the basis of the understanding of motor events. Finally, on the basis of some recent data showing that, in man, the observation of motor actions activates the posterior part of inferior frontal gyrus, we suggest that the development of the lateral verbal communication system in man derives from a more ancient communication system based on recognition of hand and face gestures.     (Rizzolatti *et al.*, 1996: 131)

It was undoubtedly the extrapolation from a manual gestural system in monkeys to a proposed vocal and articulatory imitation system in humans, along with the suggestion that manual signing and facial gesture may provide an evolutionary bridge to spoken language, that provoked widespread interest in the mirror neuron system. Many previous studies using single neuron recordings had observed cells that are selectively activated by biologically significant visual or auditory stimuli. But what was of particular interest were those 'mirror' cells, which were selectively activated by the observation of quite specific gestures performed by other actors and hence, it could be argued, were part of a *representational system* for purposive activity, the precise neural mechanisms for which are, of course, not understood.

Since then, there have been a number of neuroimaging studies which have further substantiated the case for a speech-motor control loop operative in speech perception. No human study has provided direct evidence of mirror neurons, simply because of ethical restrictions on inserting micro-electrodes into cells in human cortices (and subsequently 'sacrificing' the subject to find out precisely where they were placed). But among the population explosion of papers bearing reference to mirror neurons in the last few years, evidence for activation of the speech-motor system in the course of speech perception has been obtained.

Two studies used the technique of *transcranial magnetic stimulation* (TMS) to reveal subliminal levels of motor activity in relevant speech muscles while subjects listened for particular phonemes in spoken words, pseudo-words and non-word auditory stimuli. TMS is a noninvasive technique for electrical stimulation of the nervous system. When a magnetic field of appropriate intensity is applied to a specific area of the motor cortex, motor-evoked potentials (MEPs) can be recorded from specific muscles on the contra-lateral side of the body. The amplitude of these potentials may be modulated by the behavioural context. The modulation of MEPs' amplitude can be used to assess the central effects of various experimental conditions.

Fadiga *et al.* (2002) recorded MEPs from tongue muscles in subjects instructed to listen carefully to acoustically presented spoken words,[3] pseudo-words and non-speech stimuli (tone sequences). The words contained either a medial geminate (double) '*rr*' (e.g. *carro* 'float – in a parade': Italian), requiring an active tongue gesture, or a geminate '*ff*', a labial sound with no active tongue gesture. During the stimulus presentation the participants' left motor cortices were stimulated. The results showed that listening to words and pseudo-words containing the geminate '*rr*' produced a significant increase of MEPs recorded from tongue muscles as compared to listening to words and pseudo-words containing the geminate '*ff*' and listening to non-speech sounds. Furthermore, the facilitation due to listening to the '*rr*' consonant was stronger for words than for pseudo-words.

Similar results were obtained by Watkins *et al.* (2003), also using the TMS technique. They recorded MEPs from the major lip muscle (orbicularis oris) to monitor labial gestures while subjects listened to continuous speech, non-speech sounds, viewed speech related lip movements or eyebrow (non-labial, non-speech-related) movements. Again, listening to speech enhanced MEP activity in the lip muscle under TMS stimulation of the left, but not the right motor cortex. These two studies provide only indirect evidence for the existence of a mirror neuron system, but they support the motor theory of speech perception and the notion that listening to speech promotes activation in speech-related motor centres. Other TMS studies (Meistera *et al.*, 2003; Seyal *et al.*, 1999) have linked speech activity to heightened MEP activity in the right hand (dominant left motor cortex) but not the left hand, thereby substantiating a connection between manual gesture for communicative purposes and speech, consistent with the gestural theory of speech origins.

In summary, there is suggestive but not conclusive evidence from investigations of the mirror neuron system to support Poeppel's hypothesis of a 'dorsal-stream' speech-motor loop operating in speech perception when task requirements emphasize accuracy of phonetic decoding of the speech signal. But speech perception under normal listening conditions may not depend upon active use of the sensory-motor feedback loop. Processing words for meaning under favourable listening conditions may shift the focus of mental activity onto lexical retrieval and semantic analysis. The depth of phonetic analysis required may not involve more than what can be extracted by complex acoustic property detectors situated bilaterally in the region of the superior temporal sulcus (STS). In other words, the speech-motor loop augments a 'first pass' acoustic/phonetic analysis, conducted within the STS, by offering a supplementary, 'in depth', articulatory

---

[3] To hold subjects' attention to the task they were intermittently asked to say whether the previous stimulus that they heard had been a real word of Italian or not. No explicit phoneme monitoring was required.

analysis-by-synthesis facility, which is invoked whenever the listening conditions get tough, or the task is demanding of greater phonetic precision.

As we have attempted to demonstrate in previous chapters, the goal of phonetic analysis of the acoustic signal of speech is to deliver an under-specified, somewhat abstract, phonological representation to the next stage above perceptual processing of the speech signal; this representation then functions as the 'access code' for lexical retrieval.[4] Phonological representations comprise categorical perceptual targets made up of distinctive (meaning-bearing) sound contrasts, part articulatory, part auditory in their feature specification.

We have no clear idea how perceptual targets such as 'words' are represented in the brain in the form of their access code for lexical retrieval (Phillips, 2001), nor of the computational mechanisms underlying lexical retrieval, but we can distinguish clinically between groups of aphasics that differ in terms of whether their deficit lies primarily with the perception of phonetic features or with the manipulation or retrieval of phonological features. Broadly speaking, patients with anterior damage might be expected to lack the supplementary perceptual skills conferred by an intact speech-motor loop. Posterior aphasics, on the other hand, would be expected to demonstrate impairment of phonological feature manipulation and retrieval.[5]

## Disturbances in accessing the recognition lexicon

Is it possible that brain damage can lead to a selective deficit in the ability to access the phonological form of a word correctly in the recognition lexicon? Franklin (1989) described three patients (EC, AH and MK), who were unimpaired in phoneme discrimination (and so presumably had intact acoustic-phonetic processing), but who all showed poorer performance on a test of auditory lexical decision. The ability of a patient to judge whether spoken stimuli such as *table* or *ludge* are words or non-words is a useful means of assessing the functioning of the access mechanisms of the recognition lexicon. The three patients were significantly better at the written lexical decision task than when the stimuli were presented auditorily.

If a patient had difficulty at the level of access to the recognition lexicon, then a deficit here should lead to the patient hearing a word as another word which is phonologically related to the correct word (e.g. the patient is asked to point

---

[4] Do not feel obliged to agree with the model expounded here. It contradicts aspects of other models of speech perception expounded earlier, such as the connectionist model 'TRACE', which draws no hard and fast distinction between the process of recognition (perception) and retrieval from long-term memory.

[5] Although we stand by this distinction between phonetic and phonological types of breakdown it is difficult to assess from the standpoint of perception. It is easier to demonstrate in production, where fluent aphasics generate many more categorical errors (slips of the tongue) and dysfluent aphasics make graded errors of timing and gestural control, though even this distinction has not gone unchallenged (Mowrey and MacKay, 1990).

to the picture of the *coat*, but problems of lexical retrieval lead to him hearing the target as *goat*). The three patients described by Franklin (1989) with word-form deafness who made errors on a lexical decision task (where they were asked to indicate whether they recognized a word spoken by the examiner as a real word or a made-up word) also made substantial numbers of errors on a word–picture matching task using phonologically related foils. The results from these two tasks (lexical decision and word–picture matching with phonological foils) provide strong evidence that patients can evidence a selective disruption of lexical access via the phonological access code. None of these patients, however, showed difficulty in discriminating minimal pairs (e.g. indicating whether /pin/ or /bin/ were the same or different).

The results reported by Franklin (1989) confirmed an earlier study which explored the relationship between on-line processing of phonological information and lexical access in aphasic patients. Milberg, Blumstein and Dworetzky (1988a) used a lexical decision paradigm in which they asked subjects to listen to two words and respond 'Yes' or 'No' as to whether the second word (the target) was a real word or a non-word. In normal subjects there is a decreasing amount of facilitation as a function of phonological distortion. Real word primes (e.g. *cat*) yielded the strongest priming effects for a related target such as *dog*, followed by primes that differed by one feature (e.g. *gat*) and then more than one phonetic feature (e.g. *wat*). Milberg *et al.* (1988b) interpreted these results as showing that 'even a non word stimulus receives a lexical interpretation if it shares a sufficient number of phonetic features with an actual word in the listener's lexicon' (Milberg *et al.*, 1988b: 279) and subsequently primes a related target.

It is worthwhile spending a little time on understanding the statement that even non-words receive a lexical interpretation. Are the authors proposing that a non-word such as *gat* receives temporary status as a real word that is able to prime the related target *dog*? This seems unlikely. Connectionist models of spoken word recognition that we reviewed in Chapter 6 (e.g. the 'TRACE' model, Elman and McClelland, 1986), which proposed localist representation of phoneme detectors in the internal lexicon, may offer an alternative explanation. On this view, a non-word (*gat*)[6] would activate some shared feature detectors in closely phonetically related words (such as *cat*). This partial activation of *cat* would then lead to excitation of semantic information, some of which is shared by the target word *dog*. Presentation of the target word would then require less processing for it to be accessed because it has already been 'primed' by the shared semantic features of *cat*.

Non-brain damaged listeners show diminished lexical priming for non-word primes that are phonetically similar to a real-word related prime. The priming effect of the non-word is proportional to its phonetic similarity to the real-word

[6] The full edition of the Oxford English Dictionary has three entries for *gat*, the concise Oxford dictionary lists one (a colloquial usage, *gat*, a firearm, contraction of *gatling gun*), and the Pocket Oxford, no entry. We feel it is safe to assume that *gat* is not an item in the mental lexicon of most English speakers.

prime (e.g. priming for *cat* [kæt] > *gat* [gæt], > *wat* [wæt]). However, Milberg *et al.* (1998a) found that for fluent (Wernicke-type) aphasics, the non-word primes (*gat* and *wat*) were just as effective as the real word *cat* for priming a semantically related word (*dog*). The result suggests a diminished sensitivity for distinctive feature contrasts in these patients. The fluent aphasics may have a decreased threshold of sensitivity for lexical access and therefore access more words in the lexicon than do normal listeners. It is impossible to say whether these deficits reflect difficulties in accessing the lexicon or disorganization to the lexicon itself. The pattern of performance for non-fluent aphasics was quite different. This group of patients showed priming only for the phonologically correct word leading to accurate but slowed lexical access whereby a smaller subset of lexical entries was activated upon presentation of the prime word. Both fluent and non-fluent aphasics, however, showed similar phonological feature sensitivity when the non-words were presented singly for identification as either a real word or nonsense word. This contrasting pattern of performance between impaired on-line processing and spared off-line judgement seems best interpreted by supposing that the deficits arise either in the various processes contributing to automatic lexical access or with deficits in the activation thresholds of lexical items.

To what extent disturbances in lexical access lead to impaired auditory comprehension is still open to debate, although the cases reported by Franklin (1989) all had an auditory comprehension impairment. Taking an interactive view of language comprehension, one could argue that disturbed acoustic-phonetic processing may be compensated for by input from semantic, syntactic and discourse levels of processing. However, we have not yet considered these higher-level 'top-down' influences on word processing and auditory (language) comprehension more generally. They are the subject of later chapters.

## Summary

Disorders of auditory comprehension can arise from impairments at various levels of perceptual processing, from the basic extraction of acoustic features employed in the analysis of all kinds of auditory signals, to specialized phonetic feature analysis capabilities for speech recognition. We have argued for a model of single word processing in which the specialized neural resources for speech perception are linked to a speech-motor control loop that provides supplementary power to primary acoustic-phonetic recognition capabilities located bilaterally in the superior temporal gyrus. Following suggestions from Hickok and Poeppel (2004), we distinguish perceptual processing of speech from phonological access and retrieval mechanisms, which interface with the system of extracting word meanings and morpho-syntactic parsing.

# PART III

# Lexical semantics

# 9    Morphology and the mental lexicon

## Introduction

Our discussion thus far has been confined to problems of word recognition and the retrieval of phonological forms from the speech signal. But we have yet to address three core issues of language processing at the lexical level: (1) how word meanings are represented in the mental lexicon; (2) how lexical meanings are assigned to words in the context of sentence processing; and (3) the precise nature of the items which make up the mental lexicon, which we have thus far identified as 'words', but have not attempted to define with any precision.

We shall tackle the third of these questions first, the nature of items in the mental lexicon. Perhaps the fundamental issue here is: to what extent do language users decompose words into their constituent morphemes, or minimal units of meaning, as discussed in chapter 2?[1] It is almost universally acknowledged, by linguists and psycholinguists alike, that the units of lexical representation are smaller than words, the units conventionally separated by white space in printed text. Few would argue, for example, that *cat* and *cats*, although they are clearly different words, constitute separate entries in the *mental lexicon*. Rather, *cats* is a morphological construction, made up of the **lexeme** *cat* plus the plural inflectional suffix: i.e. *cat* + *s*. The assumption here is that in the course of processing words for meaning, listeners 'strip' inflectional affixes off word forms to access lexical meanings (Taft and Forster, 1976). But how far does this affix stripping extend?

Consistent with the 'dual route' model argued for in chapter 2, we recognize that mapping from the sound structure of a word to its meaning may be achieved compositionally (by rule) or by directly matching a word-form in the mental lexicon (the lexical route). The compositional route is more likely in the case

---

[1] Another key issue concerning the organization of the mental lexicon concerns how the syntactic, semantic, morphological and phonological properties of words are accessed in speech production and perception. Levelt and colleagues (Roelofs, Meyer and Levelt, 1998) argue that the syntactic and semantic properties of lexical items are bundled together into abstract lexical units known as **lemmas**, which are separately represented from a lexical item's morphological and phonological properties, which are bundled together as **lexemes**. Others dispute this dual-level model of lexical representation (Caramazza and Miozzo, 1998). Predictably, we will adopt an agnostic stance on this issue, save to make the uncontroversial point that lexical items must be independently accessible either from their spoken (or written) forms (the dominant route for the listener) or from their semantic and syntactic features (the dominant route for the speaker).

of a verb like *departed*, which is transparently compositional in morphological structure. However, the lexical route is the only option for a suppletive (completely irregular) form like *went*, though, as is well known, young children may go through a stage when they over-generalize to '*goed*' on the basis of regular verbs. There has been much controversy in psycholinguistic circles over how morphological inflections (such as past tense for verbs and plurals of nouns) are acquired and to what extent regular and irregular forms are processed by the same or different mechanisms in language comprehension.

There has also been disagreement among linguists and psycholinguists over the units that comprise lexical representations and how far the morphological decomposition of words should be pursued. In general, linguists favour maximal decomposition into root morphemes, to reveal the complex network of regularities that exist in the lexicon of any natural language, particularly those, like English, whose writing system reflects a rich history of language contact. Psycholinguists, on the other hand, are usually reluctant to pursue lexical decomposition any further than recognizing **inflectional** morphemes and the most productive of the **derivational** morphemes. Language users, they argue, are not etymologists.

Classical psycholinguistic investigations of the extent of morphological decomposition in the mental lexicon (Berko, 1958; Derwing, 1976) used elicitation techniques to test the productivity of morphological and morpho-phonemic rules; the assumption being that morphological decomposition of word forms is justified in so far as it can be shown that language users have access to productive rules of morphological composition for building novel word forms. Although the very notion of symbolic linguistic rules later came under strong challenge by connectionist models (Rumelhart and McClelland, 1986), we argue, consistent with the position taken in chapter 2, that the test of productivity which Berko originally proposed was well motivated. More recently, repetition priming effects have provided another source of evidence that a psychologically real level of morphological decomposition of word forms can be established, which yields a set of lexical formatives that support phrase and sentence level processing (Marslen-Wilson *et al.*, 1994). In addition to compositionality, the notion of semantic transparency of morphological constructions turns out to be critical for identifying lexemes of the mental lexicon.

Linked to the issue of what constitute the building blocks of the mental lexicon is the controversy over single route versus dual route models of lexical access. We hinted at our position on this question in chapter 2 when we asserted that language provides two routes to mapping sound to meaning: the compositional and the non-compositional. However we have yet to examine the question in depth. It is appropriate to do so in the second part of the current chapter, because a major controversy has raged over the regular and irregular inflectional morphology of English tense and number. Although the debate began and still remains largely focused on the best way to represent the kind of tacit linguistic knowledge implicit in performance on productive tests of morphology, in recent years it has been extended to the underlying neurological mechanisms, as revealed by neuroimaging studies of normal language users, and by behavioural tests and neuroimaging with fluent (Wernicke type) and dysfluent (Broca type) aphasics (Marslen-Wilson and Tyler, 1998).

Observant readers may have noticed a shift in terminology, from reference to the 'recognition lexicon' of previous chapters, to the 'mental lexicon' that has occurred in the current chapter. Modular neurocognitive theories of language posit a central, modality-non-specific lexicon that functions as a unitary resource for language comprehension and production, but which is supported by possibly several, modality-specific recognition and production lexicons (e.g. one for auditory processing, another for reading; one for speaking, another for writing). The existence of modular aphasic deficits linked to language input and output modalities provides *prima facie* support for such a modular theory, though a more integrated architecture is certainly not ruled out by the available clinical evidence. It may well be, then, that the lexicon we access in the initial stages of speech processing is rather different from the one invoked once words have been identified and morpho-syntactic processing is underway.

Morphemes may ultimately be best regarded as 'emergent' constituents of words, whose 'outward' phonological forms may be retrieved by parsing words into substrings (possibly by neural networks, such as the simple recurrent network (SRN) discussed in chapter 7), but whose 'inner' semantic properties we have not yet considered. We tackle this difficult issue in the next chapter (chapter 10), where we discuss lexical semantics. The major concern of the present chapter lies with the morphological structure of words and the grammar or 'syntax' of word formation, rather than with the semantics of words, although admittedly the distinction is a fuzzy one.

## Morphological decomposition in the mental lexicon

Okay, so what is a word? In some respects this is a silly question, given that, as we have seen previously, all native speakers tacitly know how to divide the speech stream up into words with great reliability, speed and precision, despite the potential ambiguities of words-within-words (recall the '*recognize speech*' example, chapter 5). Even a humble neural network, trained to minimize errors in predicting the next phoneme in a sequence generated from a large corpus of text, can form an internal representation of where the word boundaries occur (see chapter 17). From a statistical perspective, a word boundary may be viewed as a spike in the level of uncertainty as to what the next sound will be.

But this addresses only one side of the coin. From the perspective of extracting *meanings* from words, we want to know what the basic units of analysis are and how much of a word's meaning is compositionally assigned versus how much is assigned by direct lexical look-up. Setting aside the special case of idiomatic expressions, the meaning of a phrase or a sentence is compositionally assigned, as are syntactic structures in general. But the assignment of meaning to morphologically complex words is only partially compositional. The **inflectional morphology** of a word – those affixes which fall at the outermost edges of words (all of them suffixes or word endings in English: *cats*, *stronger*, *rained*, . . .) and which mark a word's grammatical class – are clearly compositional with respect to meaning, if not compositional in form.

We argued in chapter 2 that phrasal idioms like '*kick the bucket*' are more common than is generally supposed, suggesting that we make extensive use of 'the lexical route' to meaning assignment beyond the level of the word. At or below the level of the word, morphology provides for compositional meaning assignment, as forms like *cats* [noun+plural], *chases* [verb+agreement], *chased* [verb+tense], *chasing* [verb+progressive aspect], *smaller* [adjective+comparative], *uncool* [negative+adjective], etc. attest.

But how far does morphological decomposition extend to words in the mental lexicon? Almost everyone would agree that affix-stripping should be extended to all inflectional suffixes (*-s*, *-ed*, *-ing*, etc.), which, after all, are as much part of the syntax of the sentence as they are the morphology of the word. There is much less agreement as to how far decomposition extends to the **derivational morphology** of words.[2] For example, *government* is readily decomposable into *govern* <rule> + *ment* <noun-maker> and it partakes in a fairly productive morphological process for creating abstract nouns from transitive verbs (*argument*, *discernment*, *refinement*, *amazement*, *arrangement* . . .). But can the paradigm be extended to *detriment* or *department*? And surely not to *apartment*? It may be reasonably argued that not all language users will perceive even some of the more 'transparent' morphological relationships involved in these Latinate words, which were probably 'borrowed whole' into English. In any event, what implications does their compositional status hold for on-line language processing?

Early investigators took the young child's ability to produce appropriate inflections of novel word forms on cue as conclusive evidence of morphological rule learning (e.g. '*This is a wug. Now there are two of them. There are two. . . .*' Berko, 1958). Over-generalization of irregular forms was taken to be diagnostic of rule learning, at a stage when the child, having just discovered a regularity, has not yet learned the exceptions to the rule. Rumelhart and McClelland (1986) set the connectionist cat among the psycholinguistic pigeons by showing how an associative network, whose learning mechanism makes no distinction between 'rule-based' and 'irregular' forms, could be trained to produce both, and moreover, simulate an immature stage of 'over-generalization' in the course of doing so. However, some of the pigeons held their ground, demonstrating that in many respects the connectionist simulations inadequately modelled the natural course of morphology acquisition (Pinker and Prince, 1988). The connectionists responded by building more sophisticated simulations (MacWhinney *et al.*, 1989). Again, the

---

[2] The distinction between derivational (word building) and inflectional (word class defining) affixes is not entirely clear cut. Derivational affixes form new stems by attaching to other stem or root morphemes. Inflectional affixes are 'stem completing' in that they attach to the outermost margins of words and cannot be further built upon.

Table 9.1  *Form–frequency relations in English past tense*

| Basic or non-tensed form | Past tense form | Occurrence in speech | Morphological type |
|---|---|---|---|
| *go* | *went* | very high frequency | suppletive |
| *leave* | *le<u>f</u>t* | mid range frequency | partial regularity |
| *depart* | *depart**ed*** | low frequency | fully regular |

pigeons scattered, but mostly just temporarily (Pinker and Prince, 1994; Pinker, 2000). Today both cats and pigeons occupy the square in an unstable misalliance, which we shall describe in some detail shortly. But before attempting to evaluate the current state of skirmish in the square, let us return to some paradigmatic examples cited in chapter 2 and recapitulated in Table 9.1.

Words that have a high *token frequency* of occurrence in speech are much easier to retrieve than low-frequency words.[3] However, the low-frequency words which take regular inflections – of which there are hundreds – are much more numerous than the high-frequency irregular verbs, of which there may be a couple of dozen. As such, the class of regularly inflected words can be said to have a high *type frequency*.

If the language supplies a regular phonological form (such as *ed*) to mark a class of words that have a low token but a high type frequency (most verbs in their past tense), then a compositional alternative to lexical retrieval of past-tense forms for the majority of verbs in the language is available. To wit: 'attach the suffix -*ed*'.[4] This explains why low (token) frequency nouns and verbs get regular inflections and why very high (token) frequency verbs like *be*, *go*, *get* etc. resist regularization. But what are we to make of partially regularly inflected forms like the past tense of *leave*?

The past tense of *leave* is regular in that it appears to take a regular /t/ suffix. But it is irregular insofar as it also changes the stem verb: the /i:/ vowel (spelled 'ea') is shortened and lowered to /e/ and the final /v/ is devoiced to /f/. There are not many verbs of this intermediate type (e.g. *keep* [/ki:p/ – /kept/], *leap*, *creep*, *sleep*). They are of intermediate token frequency and low type frequency. As a class, they bear strong 'family resemblances' of phonological similarity with one another. In this respect they are quite different from the fully regular verbs that take the -*ed* ending. There are no phonological restrictions on what verbs may be subject to regular inflection. In fact, that is the whole point of having a regular inflection. It should be applicable to any novel form, so long as it

---

[3] This is the well-known word frequency effect on lexical access times mentioned earlier (p. 141).
[4] The rule for regular past-tense endings on English verbs is a little more complicated than orthography indicates. The past-tense form is /əd/ if the verb ends in /t/ or /d/. Otherwise it is /t/ if the word ends in a voiceless obstruent. Otherwise the form is /d/.

meets the criterion of being 'inflectable' – in this case, a verb, capable of carrying the past-tense inflection. It is also worth noting that these partially regular verbs tend to be unstable (is the past tense of *leap*, '*leaped*' or '*leapt*'?).

This tripartite classification of English past-tense forms into very high token frequency irregulars, mid-frequency range partially regular forms, and low-frequency regulars applies to the inflectional morphology of English nouns – and not only to English nouns and verbs, but to the inflectional morphology of other languages as well. With respect to English nouns, the regular plural inflection -*s* (/s/ ~ /z/ ~ /əz/) is overwhelmingly the dominant pattern, but a few irregularly pluralized nouns persist amongst the core high-frequency vocabulary items (*child*, *man*, *foot*, . . .), and there are some partially regular noun classes, whose members are linked by phonological family resemblances of their stems (*knife* [naɪf – naɪvz], *wife*, *life* . . . *house*, [haʊs – haʊzəz] . . . *path*, *oath*) and whose plural forms tend to be unstable. For example, how likely might you be to regularize pronunciation of the somewhat 'old-fashioned' and infrequently used plural of *oath* to *[oʊθs], rather than [oʊðz]? On the other hand, you would be much *less* likely to regularize the pronunciation of the much more frequent *path* to *[paθs] rather than [paðz].

Our challenge is to formulate a theory of word representation and word processing which can take account of the three (graded) types of morphological construction shown in Table 9.1 above, from the transparently compositional (regular) forms (*dined*, *approached*, etc.) to the non-compositional (irregular) forms (*ate*, *came*, etc.) and the partially regular forms in between. Moreover, any theory of word representation and processing also needs to account for the way in which these three types of morphological inflection are related to token and type frequencies as indicated above. Can a single learning mechanism and representational system accommodate all three types? Or do we require a dual-route theory, perhaps incorporating a race model, as suggested previously (chapter 2)? Or possibly, three different learning mechanisms may be needed, one for each type: a kind of 'rote learning' of exceptional forms in the case of suppletives, a rule-based learning mechanism for the fully regular compositional forms, and perhaps an exemplar or prototype matching model to handle the intermediate case of partially irregular forms. While the three-mechanism model may seem closest to the descriptive facts, it is the least attractive of the three options from the perspective of theoretical parsimony.

## Psycholinguistic studies of word structure

One fruitful approach to the question of the extent to which native speakers decompose words into their morphological constituents exploits the phenomenon of **priming**, which we shall make extensive use of in the next three chapters. Priming refers to the facilitatory or sometimes inhibitory effect that presentation of an item, usually a word, can have on the lexical retrieval or

Table 9.2 *Test conditions and morphological priming effects*

| Conditions | Example: prime – probe | Priming effect |
|---|---|---|
| 1. [+Morph. + Phon] | *friendly – friend* | Yes |
| 2. [+Morph. −Phon] | *elusive – elude* | Yes |
| 3. [+Morph. −Phon] | *serenity – serene* | Yes |
| 4. [−Morph. + Phon] | *tinsel – tin* | None |

*Source:* Marslen-Wilson *et al.* (1994)

identification of a subsequent lexical item. In a priming experiment, words are usually presented to subjects in pairs. The first word, called the **prime**, is typically presented shortly before some target or **probe** word, which may be related to the prime in some way – phonologically, semantically or morphologically. **Priming effects** are usually assessed by measuring reaction time to the probe word, comparing the speed of lexical access to that of a probe word which is unrelated to the prime, but is otherwise comparable on all other factors likely to affect its speed of retrieval or identification. Thus in a semantic priming experiment, lexical access time for the probe word *author* should be shorter, by a few tens of milliseconds, when preceded by the related prime *book*, compared with an unrelated control probe word such as *flower*.

There are many variations on this basic priming paradigm and a good deal of care must be taken with the design of stimulus materials, such as the elapsed time between presentation of the prime and the probe word, known as the inter-stimulus interval (ISI), or matching word frequencies for related and unrelated probe words. We shall discuss these control conditions as the need arises. For present purposes, it is sufficient to note that using a **cross-modal** lexical priming paradigm (CMLP), where subjects heard spoken prime words and responded with a lexical decision task[5] to visually presented probes flashed onto a computer screen, it was the morphological relation between the prime and the probe word, not any phonological similarity between prime and probe, that was found to matter (Marslen-Wilson *et al.*, 1994). For example, when subjects heard the word *friendly* spoken at the same time as they made a lexical decision to the visual probe *friend*, their responses were faster by 40–60 milliseconds than to an unrelated probe, but when *tinsel* was the auditory prime for the probe word *tin*, no priming effect was obtained.

These two priming conditions are contrasted analytically in terms of the presence or absence of phonological and morphological similarity relations between prime and probe in Table 9.2 (conditions 1 and 4). Note that the two probe words *friend* and *tin* bear identical phonological relationships with their respective primes *friendly* and *tinsel*, but differ in terms of morphological relatedness.

---

[5] The lexical decision task was simply deciding whether or not the letter sequence flashed on the screen was a real word or a non-word. (In approximately half of the experimental trials the probe letter sequence was a phonotactically legal non-word letter sequence, e.g. '*glark*'.)

The *'tin'* in *tinsel* is clearly not a stem morpheme. This contrast is crucial for demonstrating that the cross-modal priming effect derives from the morphological relations between prime and probe and not their shared phonological similarity. Two other conditions of morphological and phonological relatedness were included in the first of a series of experiments reported in Marslen-Wilson *et al.* (1994) (conditions 2 and 3 in Table 9.2). Conditions 2 and 3 involve clear relationships of morphological constituency between prime and probe words, but phonological relationships that are less transparent than in conditions 1 and 4 and are hence tagged [-Phon.]. Only condition 4, where there is a phonological identity between the probe and the first few phonemes of the prime, failed to yield a priming effect.

Although it might initially seem a little surprising, this absence of a phonological priming effect is precisely what we might expect, given the phenomenon of suppression of 'false word' segmentation that we noted in our earlier discussion of word perception and the TRACE model (chapters 5–7).

These results, which show the dominance of morphological over phonological relationships in priming, may well be conditional on the use of the cross-modal priming paradigm, where the prime is presented in auditory modality and where probe word lexical access is tested in the visual mode. In the cross-modal paradigm, prime–probe word interactions must be triggered at a level of lexical processing where the items share common linguistic features, irrespective of differences in their mode of sensory apprehension. Also, the task – lexical decision, rather than word identification (naming) – probably helps to promote a 'deeper' level of lexical processing in the cross-modal priming paradigm than in uni-modal priming (e.g. visual prime – visual probe).

## Semantic and morphological relatedness

At this point, you probably should also be wondering about the effects of latent **semantic similarities** amongst the prime–probe pairs in this experiment, and whether such effects can be separated from those of morphological relatedness *per se*. Marslen-Wilson *et al.* (1994) attempted to achieve just this analytical separation in subsequent experiments in the series. You be the judge of their success in this endeavour. They leave it to linguistic and etymological authority (such as the Oxford Dictionary) to say whether a morphological relationship exists between e.g. *authority* and *author* (Yes, I knew that.), *casualty* and *casual* (Huh? – Yes, Virginia – via the French connection, from Latin: *cāsuāl-is* <depending on chance>).

On the other hand, semantic relatedness was determined by native-speaker judgements of perceived 'relatedness of meaning', on a nine-point rating scale from 'very unrelated' to 'very related'. A preliminary rating experiment was conducted (n = 15 subjects) to enable the experimenters to set up some **factorial contrasts** between prime–probe pairs, in order to separate the effects of morphological relatedness, semantic relatedness and phonological similarity. These are illustrated, along with the results of the priming experiment, in Table 9.3.

Table 9.3 *Morphological and semantic relatedness priming effects*

| Condition | Example: prime – probe | Priming effect |
|---|---|---|
| 1. [−Sem. +Morph.] | *casualty – casual* | None |
| 2. [+Sem. +Morph.] | *punishment – punish* | Yes |
| 3. [+Sem −Morph. −Phon] | *idea – notion* | Yes |
| 4. [−Sem. −Morph. +Phon] | *bulletin – bullet* | None |

*Source:* Marslen-Wilson *et al.* (1994)

Table 9.4 *Morphological type and priming effect*

| Condition | Morphological type | Example | Priming effect |
|---|---|---|---|
| **Suffixes:** | | **prime – probe** | |
| 1. [−Sem. +Morph.] | derived – stem | *casualty – casual* | none |
| 2. [+Sem. +Morph.] | derived – stem | *punishment – punish* | yes |
| 3. [−Sem. +Morph.] | derived – derived | *successful – successor* | none |
| 4. [+Sem. +Morph.] | derived – derived | *confession – confessor* | **none** |
| **Prefixes:** | | | |
| 5. [−Sem. +Morph.] | derived – stem | *restrain – strain* | none |
| 6. [+Sem. +Morph.] | derived – stem | *insincere – sincere* | yes |
| 7. [−Sem. +Morph.] | derived – derived | *depress – express* | none |
| 8. [+Sem. +Morph.] | derived – derived | *unfasten – refasten* | **yes** |

Adapted from Marslen-Wilson *et al.* (1994)

The results shown in Table 9.3 indicate that insofar as the prime and the probe stimuli are perceived to be semantically related, a priming effect is obtained. There is no evidence here for an independent effect of priming by virtue of a morphological relationship between the prime and probe stimuli. However, Marslen-Wilson *et al.* (1994) do not describe their results this way. They say that only morphologically related pairs which are 'semantically transparent', or perceived to be semantically related, yield priming effects. This is quite a way short of demonstrating an independent role for morphological structure – apart from semantic relatedness – in word processing. But, there is more . . . as there usually is in a Marslen-Wilson experiment.

## Priming effects of prefixes and suffixes

Evidence for an independent role for morphological structure comes from the way that semantic transparency was found to interact with prefixed versus suffix-derived morphological constructions shown (in bold) in Table 9.4. If semantic transparency were the only relevant consideration, then we should expect to obtain a priming effect under condition 4, similar to that obtained under condition 8 and all other [+Sem] conditions in this and the preceding two tables of results. But we do not. *Confession* fails to prime *confessor*. Yet *unfasten* primes *refasten*. What is going on here?

The words *confession* and *confessor* are semantically related by virtue of their common stem (verb) and this semantic similarity should yield a priming effect, but none was evident in the subjects' responses to this priming pair or others of its type, made up of two semantically related, derived words, involving suffixation. The investigators inferred that some countervailing inhibitory effect to semantic or identity priming by the shared stem must be at work. This, they argue, can only come from competition or mutual inhibition between the two derivational suffixes *-ion* and *-or*. Note that this analysis's assumes that derivational morphemes (both noun-making suffixes in the present case) have some kind of independent lexical status. But why should these two morphemes be in competition with one another?

An answer to this question can be gleaned from a phenomenon that we discussed previously under lexical retrieval in speech perception (chapter 7). The suffixes *-ion* and *-or* will always be competitors as perceptual targets in word recognition when they seek to attach to some verbal stem to form a derived noun. The target word must be *confession*, or *confessor*, or conceivably some other alternative. But the point is that it must be one of these alternatives. Lateral inhibition between lexical competitors was the mechanism invoked in the 'TRACE' model and in the revised activation version of the cohort model, to resolve competing perceptual hypotheses about the identity of an input string. Why not invoke it here also and at the same time grant independent lexical status to those productive (and semantically transparent) morphemes that enter into complex word formation?

We need also to explain at the same time why prefixes do not mutually inhibit one another, thereby allowing for priming effects in condition 8 in Table 9.4. An answer to this question would seem to lie in the right-to-left nature of language processing. In a left-to-right model, the stem will be recognized before the suffix. A particular stem may therefore activate a limited number of competing suffixes (e.g. *govern-*: *-or*, *-ment*, *-ance*, . . .). But a prefix typically allows numerous and unpredictable stem attachments (*un-*: *-do*, *-kind*, . . . etc.). Although the stems that can enter into construction with a particular prefix may form cohorts of competitors, those cohort sets will typically be much larger and resolved later in word processing than the small cohort of suffixes that may attach to a particular stem. Marslen-Wilson *et al.* postulate a mental lexicon made up of free stems (stem morphemes that can stand as free forms or words), and affixes which can combine to yield 'semantically transparent' complex morphological constructions. Affixes which attach to the right of a stem are functional competitors in the cohort model of language processing. Marslen-Wilson *et al.* conceptualize this competition as inhibitory connections between suffixes in a localist connectionist model.

## Conclusions from the Marslen-Wilson *et al.* study

Marslen-Wilson *et al.*'s way of modelling the differential behaviour of stems and suffixes in terms of inhibitory connections between suffixes which are absent in the case of prefixes may be too literal-minded a metaphor, but it is a good starting point for an explanation of why suffixes inhibit one another but prefixes fail to do so. Also, the differential priming effects for prefixes and suffixes demonstrated in this experiment provide some solid evidence for an independent role for morphological structure in word processing; an indication that morphemes have functional significance and are not merely emergent statistical patterns in language data, a possibility suggested earlier.

We have spent some space on this well-designed series of experiments because it illustrates how an on-line psycholinguistic technique (cross-modal semantic or identity priming) may be brought to bear on questions of linguistic representation and processing, which otherwise seem intractable by introspection or conventional linguistic analysis. The question in this case was: what are the minimal meaningful units into which native speakers decompose words and how do these units interact in word processing? The tentative answer revealed by analysis of the results – and here the reader is strongly recommended to go to the original source and check our conclusions for her/himself – is that native listeners decompose words into morphemes, which have independent lexical status, insofar as the morphological relations are semantically transparent. On questions of process, much uncertainty remains, but the findings are consistent with a left-to-right dual route model of lexical access, consistent with the findings from speech perception discussed in previous chapters.

## Cross-linguistic generalizations on morphological processing

Because left-to-right processing is a ubiquitous feature of spoken language, one might expect the differential behaviour of prefixes and suffixes in cross-modal lexical priming that Marslen-Wilson *et al.* observed in English to hold across all languages. This question has yet to be investigated.

Languages differ greatly in terms of the kinds and complexity of morphological structures that they employ.[6] However, the basic distinction between rule-based or regular inflectional/derivational processes and irregular ones is probably universal. That being so, it seems likely that systematic differences in the processing of regular and irregular inflections as revealed by on-line techniques such as the cross-modal priming paradigm will be found across languages. However, languages may vary in terms of how easy or difficult it is to show such differences. In English, which has a somewhat impoverished inflectional morphology, consistent differences in the degree of morphological priming for regular and irregular inflections has been hard to demonstrate reliably. In Marslen-Wilson *et al.*'s (1994) study, which we have examined in some detail, the degree of morphological priming was just as strong for the partially regular alternations (*elusive* – *elude*, *serenity* – *serene*) as it was for fully regular alternations

---

[6] Arabic with its 'templatic' morphology provides a particular challenge for psycholinguistic models of word decomposition. See Boudelaa and Marslen-Wilson (2004).

(*friendly – friend*). However, other investigators have found reduced morphological priming for the irregular alternations (Stanners *et al.*, 1979). Kempley and Morton (1982) found no facilitation at all for irregular inflectional priming.

It may be that differences in the processing of regular and irregular inflections, as reflected in morphological priming, emerge more clearly in languages with a richer inflectional morphology, as has been suggested by Sonnenstuhl, Eisenbeiss and Clahsen (1999) in a study of German inflectional morphology. Or morphological priming (independent of semantic priming) may be more easily demonstrated in a highly inflectional language like Hebrew (Plaut and Gonnerman, 2000). The investigation of such cross-linguistic differences in morphological processing is currently an active topic of psycholinguistic research.

## Neuroimaging studies of normal and aphasic morphological processes

There is also a growing body of functional neuroimaging data bearing upon possible differences in the neural representation and processing of regular and irregular morphology. We first discuss studies of fully competent language users and then turn to consider cases of aphasia where there is a differential pattern of impairment to regular and irregular morphological constructions; potential cases of 'double dissociation' that are traditionally considered to provide strong evidence for a dual-path model.

### PET and MEG studies of morphological processing

One early study in this rapidly developing field (Jaeger *et al.*, 1996) used positron emission tomography (PET, introduced in chapter 3) to assess the foci of neural activity during the production of regular and irregular inflections, and to test predictions made in accordance with what we have called the traditional BWL model of language representation in the brain: rule-based processing in the left posterior frontal region (Broca's area) and lexical retrieval in the superior temporal region and the angular gyrus (Wernicke's area).

Subjects were nine right-handed male native English speakers. Their task was to either simply read aloud word lists of verbs in their uninflected base form (forty-six items per list) or to generate the past-tense equivalents appropriate for each stimulus word. There were five types of list: (a) regular past-tense inflected forms (e.g. *pull, place, love*, . . .), (b) irregular past-tense inflected forms (e.g. *fall, build, shoot*, . . .), (c) a nonce list of forms to be produced in the past tense (e.g. *mab, gruck, prane*, . . .), and two additional lists to act as 'baseline' conditions: (d) a mixed list of real verbs to be simply read out in their uninflected form (e.g. *hit, clean, change*, . . .), and (e) a nonce word list, also to be simply read out loud.

The items were presented in blocks of forty-six trials in order to allow approximately one minute for a distinctive regional haemodynamic response of the brain to develop to a level recordable by the PET scanner for each of the five experimental conditions. In order to compare brain activity levels and patterns specifically attributable to the task of generating past-tense inflections under the three experimental conditions of interest (past-tense formation for regular, irregular and nonce verb forms) it was necessary to 'parcel out' the neural activation associated with lower-level visual processing of the input stimulus and the common motor activity involved in producing the spoken response. Hence the 'method of subtraction' was used (see chapter 3, p. 63), performing a pixel-by-pixel subtraction of the cumulative regional brain activation levels associated with one of the three past-tense formation conditions and one of the two corresponding 'passive reading' conditions ((c) or (f) above). Thus it was hoped to remove the neural activation that was common to the three tasks – effectively background noise – to reveal distinctive differences in brain activity associated with generating regular, irregular and nonce-word past-tense forms.

The results are summarized graphically in Figure 9.1, where various cross-sectional (sagittal, coronal, transverse) diagrams and cortical maps of left and right hemisphere *subtracted* activation levels are shown on a grey scale for each of the three conditions. There is quite a lot of information in these three sets of pictures. Take your time in comparing them. Begin by comparing projected patterns of cortical activity on the surface views of the left hemisphere (bottom right-hand picture in each of the three diagrams). But before you do so, it may be instructive to make three small hand sketches of the cerebral cortex and shade in the patterns of activation that you are *expecting* to find for each of the three experimental conditions, in accordance with the BWL model.

According to the BWL model, rule-based, combinatorial aspects of language processing should have a focal area of activity in the inferior frontal gyrus of the left hemisphere (Broca's area) and lexical retrieval operations should maximally activate association cortex in the parieto-temporal region (the angular gyrus, and regions encompassed by Wernicke's area, broadly defined). In any event, we would expect different patterns of regional cerebral activation for regular and irregularly inflected verbs, and the pattern activation for nonce-verb past-tense formation should closely resemble that of regular verbs, because nonce verbs can only be inflected by rule, having by definition no lexical entry.

However, the observed pattern of regional cortical activation for the nonce past-tense forms *(baff – baffed)* is no closer to that of the regular past-tense forms *(pull – pulled)* than it is to that of the irregular plural forms *(sweep – swept)*. In fact, the nonce past-tense formation condition shared more common areas of heightened neural activity with the irregular past-tense condition than it did with the regular past-tense condition, contrary to what might be expected if regular past-tense and nonce past-tense production shared a common rule-based processing mode. Furthermore the locus of activation in the left frontal region for the nonce production condition was not over Broca's region, but prefrontal cortex that has been implicated in working memory loaded tasks.

While there was heightened activity in the posterior language areas of the left hemisphere under irregular past-tense formation, activation was by no means confined to this region. Nor was posterior language area activation more prominent

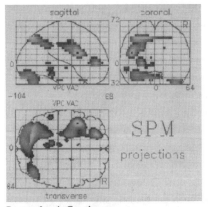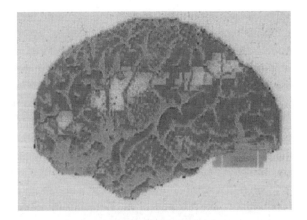

**Irregular inflections**:

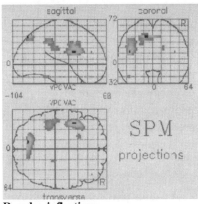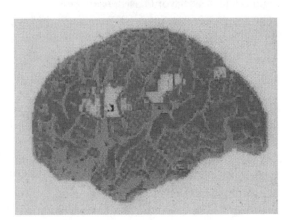

**Regular inflections**

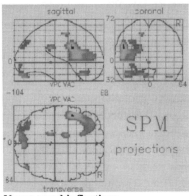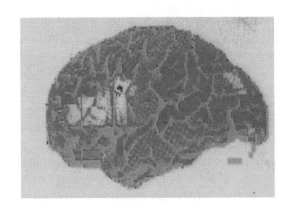

**Nonce word inflections**

Figure 9.1   *PET activation for regular, irregular and nonce past-tense forms*

under irregular past-tense production. In sum, there is little support for the differential predicted patterns of neural activation for regular vs. irregular past-tense formation.

But perhaps the most telling finding concerns the levels of activation and the task demands on the listener, which were as much a product of the blocked trial condition under which subjects' responses were elicited, as they were to any differences in regular vs. irregular morphological processing. Blocking of items was necessitated by the low time resolution of PET imaging. There was highest overall activation for the irregular past-tense forms, less for the nonce forms, and least in the case of regular past-tense words. As Seidenberg and Hoeffner (1998) point out in their critical review of Jaeger *et al.* (1996), presenting items in blocks of trials imposes different task demands on subjects under the three conditions, which the reader can readily verify subjectively. Consider a blocked sequence of irregular verbs (*fall, build, shoot, dig, sit, spend, wear, blow, . . .*). Each item in the list has to be processed on its own terms (*fell, built, shot, dug, . . .*). No expectations as to the correct past-tense form can be formed from one trial to the next. Compare the situation to a blocked series of regular verbs (*flip, shock, sip, spell, fear, want, heat, . . .*). Pretty soon an expectation is established that one needs only to 'add *-ed*' (or more accurately, produce one of the three regular allomorph suffixes, /d, t, əd/), paying minimal attention to the stimulus. Similar considerations apply to the (regular) nonce forms. The choice of correct responses is quickly narrowed as a block of trials is delivered, permitting subjects to devote fewer mental resources to the task at hand, encouraging 'shallow processing'. The novelty of nonce forms may add a phonetic working memory component to the task of nonce past-tense production. This could account for the added prefrontal activity noted above under the nonce-word condition. In summary, the need to arrange item types into trial blocks, necessitated by the poor temporal resolution of PET imaging, introduced task-specific performance considerations that confounded possible processing differences between regular and irregular morphological processing.

Recent developments in magnetoencephalography (MEG) have provided researchers with the necessary temporal and spatial resolution to capture changes of regional activation spreading across the cerebral cortex as the brain responds to the task of generating the past-tense inflection of a verb, over a single stimulus trial (Dhond *et al.*, 2003). Some technical documentation of the recording apparatus and procedure are noted to reference the current state of the art.

An array of 204 electromagnetic sensors covering the whole scalp continuously monitored changes in the brain's regional magnetic field, as the subject silently formulated the past tense of a regular or irregular verb, presented in infinitival (uninflected) form on a screen in the centre of the subject's visual field. Signals obtained from single novel presentations of regular or irregular verbs were separately averaged over eighty trials for each of the twelve participating subjects (neurologically normal, right-handed males, aged 18–30). Not the raw signal averages for each of the 204 recording channels, but the estimated loci and strength of 1700 dipole electromagnetic current generators (approximately one generator every 10 mm) assumed to lie at uniform depth under the cortical surface, were calculated across the sensor array, over a 5 ms time frame. The sensor array locations were mapped into a 3D representation of the cortical surface using high resolution MRI images of each subject's brain, which were then fitted into a common or averaged reference map of the cortical sulci and gyri, generated from a population of thirty-five subjects.

A composite frame-by-frame moving image of the pattern of spreading neural activation[7] on each trial was obtained as the subject successively decoded the visual stimulus, recognized the verb, retrieved its past-tense inflection and assembled its phonological target in order to formulate the 'silent response'.[8] The activation pattern may be viewed from the perspective of the whole task, examining the combined activation produced by regular and irregular verb inflection, or we may focus on differences in neural activity associated with irregular vs. regular past-tense formation by subtracting the composite activity gathered under one condition from that of the other. If there are no, or only minor, distinguishing features between the two composite activation patterns, we may infer very similar neural processing operations underlying regular and irregular past-tense inflection.

Focusing first on the combined response to the task of past-tense inflection, the following activation pattern was obtained:

> Cortical activity begins in bilateral primary visual areas at ~100 ms and quickly spreads to specialized form processing areas in the anteroventral occipital cortex. This response peaks at ~165 ms and is strongly lateralized to the left (language dominant) hemisphere. By ~240 ms, activity has advanced further anteriorly to encompass Wernicke's area and the surrounding cortex in the left superior temporal lobe associated with lexicophonemic representations, as well as ventral occipitotemporal [angular gyrus] areas associated with lexicoiconic processing. By ~340 ms, activity is predominantly in the anterior temporal lobe including areas thought to contain multimodal semantic representations. Activity then shifts by ~470 ms to become more bilateral and frontal (including Broca's area), with a reactivation of the occipitotemporal areas. At ~570 ms activity is especially prominent in right dorsolateral prefrontal cortex.

This pattern of activation, once established over the first quarter of a second post-stimulus, was sustained and widespread, particularly over the language-dominant hemisphere. In contrast to this widespread and powerful overall response, significant changes related to verb regularity are relatively brief, small and local.

---

[7] Actually, images were constructed from statistical measures of the probability of chance variation from background signal noise levels, rather than direct measures of MEG field strengths *per se*. See Dhond *et al.* (2003) for details.

[8] Silent rehearsal rather than spoken responses were elicited to avoid movement artefacts. Additionally, subjects raised their right index finger to indicate when a regular -*ed* past-tense verb was encountered, so that a record of correct processing of the stimuli could be obtained.

Figure 9.2 shows the significant differences in brain response patterns to irregular vs. regular verbs that were observed at different epochs of the brain's response. Dhond *et al.* observe:

> At ∼340 ms irregular verbs evoke greater activity in the left ventral occipitotemporal cortex (vOT), an area where lexico-iconic representations are thought to be stored or accessed. At ∼470 ms, regular verbs evoke greater activity in Broca's area (Ba), a location classically associated with rule-based grammatical transformations. At ∼570 ms response modulation again increases to irregular verbs, this time in the right anterior dorsolateral pre-frontal cortex (dlpF), an area associated with controlled retrieval and other strategic processes.

How well do the findings support the BWL model of localized language processing and what bearing do they have upon the dual-route vs. single-mechanism debate over regular vs. irregular morphological inflection? Support for the traditional BWL model comes from the pattern of neural activation observed over the combined trials of regular and irregular inflections. The sequential involvement of primary then specialized visual association cortex, followed by activation of cross-modal occipito-temporal association cortex, leading to activation of the language production area, all predominantly in the left hemisphere, is precisely what the BWL model would predict for the task of past-tense inflection as a whole. Also, the more localized and fleeting differences observed when the activation patterns of regular and irregular inflection tasks are subtracted from one another are broadly in line with predictions of the dual-route model, but with some provisos.

Increased activation for irregular past-tense verbs at ∼340 ms might be expected on the basis that greater depth of lexical retrieval is required for irregular past-tense forms which have idiosyncratic phonological properties related specifically to the lexical stem. Greater activation in Broca's area at ∼470 ms for the regular past-tense items is consistent with clinical and psycholinguistic findings about the role of Broca's aphasia in rule-governed linguistic behaviour. Increased activity in the right (non-dominant) pre-frontal cortex is perhaps not a predicted finding of the dual-route model, but could simply be an effect of requiring subjects to raise a finger of their left hand after each verb that took an *-ed* ending, elicited to ensure that subjects kept on-task.

However, the authors are appropriately cautious in their conclusions in support of the dual-route model of past-tense inflection. The vast bulk of MEG activation observed on the inflection task was shared in common by the regular and irregular items, which is what a single-process model would predict. Regular and irregular inflection probably represent minor variations on a theme in the task of orchestrating the language processing symphony. Nevertheless, it is encouraging and exciting to see that such fine details of language performance can now be detected by MEG imaging.

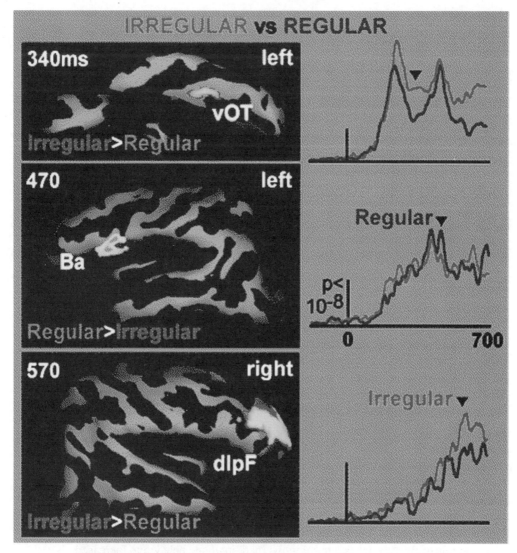

Figure 9.2 *MEG differences to regular and irregular verbs*

## Summary

We began this chapter by addressing the problem of morphological decomposition in the mental lexicon: whether a word such as *antidisestablish-ment* is broken down into its constituent morphemes *anti- dis- establish -ment* in the course of language processing. On the basis of some experiments with the cross-modal lexical priming paradigm, we tentatively concluded that seman-tic transparency, combined with a degree of phonological transparency (***permit – permiss+ion***), constituted the criterion that language users employ in these matters, unless perhaps they happen to be philologists or generative phonologists of the 'old school'. This implies, but does not precisely define, strict limits to 'affix stripping' in natural language processing. Some may be content to pursue the problem no further, but most psycholinguists would like to draw implications from these findings for underlying mechanisms of language processing, in particular to find in such results implications for or against the dual-route or single-route model of lexical access.

But such inferences are problematical. We also identified three superficial subtypes of morphological relation found in English tense and number inflections: (1) fully productive, regular forms of high type but low token frequency (-s and -ed), (2) partially productive and partially regular forms of intermediate type and token frequency, members of which bore strong phonological 'family resemblances' (e.g. *leave – left, dream – dreamt, sleep – slept*), and (3) suppletive or completely irregular forms of high token but very low type frequency (e.g: *children, went*). It is quite conceivable, though not particularly parsimonious an explanation, that three distinct learning mechanisms – rule-based learning, analogical learning and 'rote' lexical learning – could underlie the acquisition of morphology, but debate has focused on two broadly competing positions: (a) a 'dual-route' model that distinguishes categorically between rule-based learning and an 'associative' learning mechanism (Pinker, 2000), and (b) various unitary connectionist models that claim to be able to handle the behavioural, developmental and neuro-processing differences observable among the three superficial types of morphological relation.

We have not been able to properly address questions of underlying mechanism here, particularly the case for connectionism, which offers the potentially most parsimonious theory. Questions of modelling learning mechanisms in language processing raise fundamental unsolved issues of 'representation' for psycholinguistics, which will be discussed in the final chapter. Suffice it to say that the issues are intricate both empirically and conceptually and are unlikely to be resolved any time soon. In this chapter, we have also introduced evidence for a double dissociation between rule and lexically based aspects of morphological processing in some aphasic patients (Marslen-Wilson *et al.*) and evidence from neuroimaging studies of English past-tense formation, which seem to favour a dual-route localizationist theory, broadly compatible with the BWL model, for a division of labour between lexical (posterior) and rule-based (anterior) language processes. But as we have seen, the commonalities in neural processes involved in tasks of irregular versus regular inflection assignment – what might derisively be called 'wuggery' – quite outweigh the slight, but potentially critical differences between them. Observations of any such differences push current imaging techniques to the limits of their temporal and spatial resolution of brain activity. So it is unsurprising that findings in this area too are contested.

A final point concerns the question of whether morphological structure plays an *independent* role in word processing, aside from phonological and semantic relatedness among lexical items. In the priming experiments of Marslen-Wilson *et al.* (1994) discussed earlier, morphological structure appeared to play no independent role. But English is well recognized to be 'inflectionally challenged' in relation to languages like German, Italian, Hebrew, Turkish, Latin or – right out there – Warlpiri (Laughren, 2002). Plaut and Gonnerman (2000) have suggested that the extent to which morphological structure plays a role independent from phonological and semantic transparency in accounting for morphological priming effects depends upon the complexity of a language's inflectional morphology. The researchers trained a neural network on a common set of morphologically related words varying in semantic transparency. The training set of words was embedded in either a morphologically rich or an impoverished artificial language. They found that 'morphological priming increased with degree of semantic transparency in both languages. Critically, priming extended to semantically opaque items in the morphologically rich language but not in the morphologically impoverished language' (Plaut and Gonnerman, 2000: 445). It is beyond the scope of current discussion to evaluate the significance of Plaut and Gonnerman's findings. Readers are encouraged to consult the primary source; but be warned, the relevance of studies using machine learning algorithms and simulated language data for natural language processing can be hard to evaluate, as we shall see in chapter 17.

In conclusion – though it is really a prefatory comment – the notion of 'semantic transparency' has been invoked in this chapter as though it were a conceptual primitive, as though we knew intuitively what it means for two words to be clearly related semantically. This is true at a pre-theoretical level. Semantic relatedness between words can be judged by human raters and thus 'operationally defined'. But to explain how word meanings are represented in the mental lexicon and assigned in the course of word recognition is another matter entirely. This is the big problem that we tackle in the next two chapters. It serves the salutary purpose of making some of the trickier, perhaps intractable, problems of morphological parsing that we have discussed in the present chapter seem simple and superficial by comparison.

# 10 Lexical semantics

## Introduction

In the previous chapter we inquired into the structure of words and the extent to which they can be decomposed into smaller constituents, morphemes. Morphological decomposition was seen to be justified, up to a point, on evidence from cross-modal semantic priming studies. The evidence suggested that morphological decomposition may be justified insofar as the morphological components of a word are semantically transparent, i.e. to the extent that the meaning of the whole word can be clearly related to the meanings of its component morphemes (e.g. *indefensible* = <not>(<defend>(<able>))). However, we did not provide an explicit account of 'semantic transparency', other than to appeal to language users' intuitions about the meanings of words. A theory of lexical semantics should provide an explicit account of word meaning; of how similarities and differences in word meaning are established, how various word meaning relations, such as synonymy (*violin – fiddle*), antonymy (*long – short*), hyponymy (*horse – animal*) etc., are established.

We defined morphology as the syntax of the word. This chapter concerns the semantics of words or word meanings. A useful theory of lexical semantics needs to account not only for the meaning of individual words but for how word meanings change in context with other words. Consider the meaning of *good* in the phrase *good friend* (<loyal, reliable>). Now consider the meaning of the same word in the phrase *good lover* or *good meal*. Clearly, there is a chameleon-like quality to the meaning of some words, which needs to be accounted for. The meanings of words are said to be stored in the mental dictionary, along with their phonological and morpho-syntactic features. Lexical knowledge clearly varies from speaker to speaker. Languages also vary from one another in how they lexicalize our knowledge and perception of the world. Hence, lexical semantics though intimately connected with pragmatics (knowledge of the world) is distinct from it. Lexical knowledge is confined to knowledge of word meanings and word usage.

Depending on the size of the dictionary that you consult, you will almost invariably find multiple meanings listed for any given word, and the more common the word, the more meanings it will typically have listed against it. Consider, for example, the number of distinct meanings of *show* that are found in the Pocket

Table 10.1 *Some meanings of* show *and (scrambled) contexts of usage*

| Context | Meaning |
| --- | --- |
| ...***show*** *it is true* ... | <cause to be visible> |
| ...***show*** *your tickets* ... | <a display> |
| ...*a* ***show*** ... | <indicate one's feelings> |
| ...*white* ***shows*** *the dirt* ... | <demonstrate, explain> |
| ...***show*** *your anger* ... | <offer for scrutiny> |

Oxford, or some similar dictionary. Table 10.1 lists some of the nuances of meaning of *show* against some typical contexts in which the word may be used. The contexts have been scrambled. A native speaker will have no difficulty unscrambling the context list to match the appropriate meaning. But how is this accomplished? This is one of the major unsolved tasks for a theory of lexical semantics; to be able to represent the basic meaning of a word and *show* (<explain>) how it varies in the context of other words.

Polysemy is a major problem for lexical semantics. How does a speaker/hearer retrieve or assign the appropriate word meaning for a given context? As George Miller (1999) eloquently argues, native speakers are extraordinarily good at finessing word meanings in context in the course of interpreting sentences. This is a problem for language learners and for artificial natural language understanding systems.

Another way that we might seek to evaluate a theory of lexical semantics would be to ascertain how well the model can detect semantic anomalies such as:

| | Anomalous expression | Intended expression |
| --- | --- | --- |
| (1) | *? club for married bachelors* | ?? |
| (2) | *? a vase of whiskey* | *a **flask** of whiskey* |
| (3) | *? colourless green ideas* | ?? |
| (4) | *? your heart's dissent* | *your heart's **content*** |
| (5) | *? deep freeze structure* | *deep **phrase** structure* |
| (6) | *? bang my hammer with a finger* | *bang my **finger** with a **hammer*** |

Expressions (1–3) above are made-up examples and are clearly semantically anomalous to varying degrees. Examples (4–6) are drawn from a corpus of actual speech errors (Fromkin, 1971) produced by normal language users, where we can be fairly sure of the intended expression, which in each case is clearly non-anomalous. It is the detection of anomaly in the actual expression which is of interest to us here, rather than *how* the anomalous utterance was produced. The vast majority of semantic anomalies generated by normal or aphasic speakers are errors of word selection or word sequencing, where the error and the target word (indicated in bold italics above) share common semantic and phonological properties. We shall explore the possible sources of the semantic anomalies in

(1–6) above in more detail presently. But note that these anomalies are different in kind from syntactic anomalies and syntactic anomaly detection mentioned in chapter 2.

Yet another task by which one might evaluate a model of lexical semantics turns on the ability of the system to generate acceptable paraphrases for individual words or phrasal expressions such as *a jug of whiskey*, or to express commonalities and differences of meaning between verbal expressions that are semantically related (*a bottle of wine* vs. *a jug of whiskey*). Again, native speakers are adept at this task, but we are still a long way from constructing an explicit model which performs at, say, the level of an average five year old on any of the above tasks.

There remain fundamental unresolved problems on how to approach the analysis of word and phrase meanings. One such problem, which is beyond the scope of our discussion and is unlikely to be resolved any time soon, is whether semantic theory should be grounded in logic or in psychology; in some formalized propositional calculus of truth conditions for possible worlds, or in perceptual experience and its internal cognitive representation. To some extent, the answer to this longstanding controversy may lie in the level of analysis adopted. A propositional calculus approach is clearly more applicable to sentence-level semantic analysis, and the way we perceive objects in the world is clearly of critical interest for the semantic properties of words.

Although the focus of our discussion will be on lexical rather than sentential semantics (the semantics of words rather than sentences), we cannot afford to ignore the combinatorial semantics of phrases, as words take much of their meaning from their immediate context.

## Semantic networks

One of the earliest attempts to construct a computational model of lexical semantics was undertaken by Ross Quillian (1969) in a system ambitiously dubbed 'The teachable language comprehender' (TLC), a program designed to be capable of being taught to 'comprehend' English text. Quillian began, as we have done, by asking what a model of lexical semantics should be able to do: to produce semantic paraphrases, to detect points of overlap and contrast in word meanings, to apply knowledge of word meanings stored in the mental lexicon to the interpretation of 'text' or linguistic expressions, and to perform these tasks in a human-like manner.

Like many pre-computational models and all subsequent computational models of the lexicon, the TLC envisaged the lexicon as a **semantic network** encoding both world knowledge and the meanings of words.[1] Quillian's semantic network is a symbolic, not a connectionist network. The **nodes** of the network represent

[1] Most theorists would recognize the need to distinguish lexical semantics (knowledge of word meanings) from conceptual semantics (world knowledge). Quillian's model understandably ignores this distinction and the complications that arise from it.

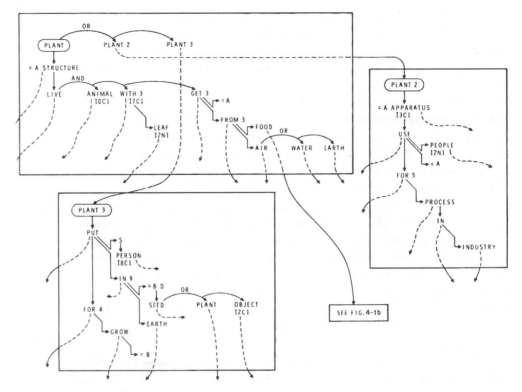

Figure 10.1  *Three planes representing the meaning of* Plant *in Quillian's TLC model*

concepts or words, which are linked by **arcs**, which in turn represent a small number of relational types. The meaning of a word may be more or less fully expressed first by accessing its root node in the network and traversing the network elements to which this node is linked in a series of steps. In Quillian's model, like a conventional dictionary, a word's meaning is defined by other words, whose meanings are defined, in turn, by other words. Thus, defining the meaning of a word is a somewhat open-ended exercise.

After two years of work, Quillian came to realize that his original goal of constructing a self-extending semantic network, which was capable of learning new word meanings by building on the existing network, was too ambitious. He modified his aim to that of formulating a coding scheme that a trained user could employ to extend the functional vocabulary of the system and enhance its performance. In recent years, connectionist models of semantic memory have come closer to the ideal of a self-teaching system. But these systems are typically more restricted in the tasks that they perform, such as semantic processing for document retrieval.

To illustrate Quillian's model and gain an appreciation of its strengths and weaknesses, consider how the TLC represents the polysemous word *plant* (refer to Figure 10.1). The word plant in its *basic meaning*, which is the sense that would be acquired first in language acquisition or be accessed most readily in word meaning recognition, might be paraphrased in something like the following way.

PLANT 1:    \<living structure, not an animal, frequently has leaves, gets its food from air, water, earth>

*Plant* has two other meanings, PLANT 2 and PLANT 3:

PLANT 2:    \<apparatus used for any process in industry>
PLANT 3:    \<put (seed, plant, etc.) in earth for growth>

These three meanings of *plant* are *disjunctive* in their usage, expressed by the exclusive OR arc in Figure 10.1. The basic meaning of *plant* (PLANT 1) and pointers to its alternative meanings (PLANT 2 and PLANT 3) are expressed in a 'plane of word memory'. Quillian's notion of a 'plane' is not very clearly defined. We may think of it as comprising a head-word-concept and its immediate dependent word-concepts and their linkages (relations). A plane is intended to capture the first approximation specification of the meaning of a word, which may be elaborated through arcs that point to word-concepts outside the plane. Note the use of the conjunction arc (AND) to bind together the properties that define the basic meaning of *plant* (i.e. PLANT 1: living, not animal, with leaves, GET (food, FROM (air, water, earth))).

Quillian identified four basic types of arc linking nodes in a semantic network. In addition to the basic logical relations of disjunction (OR) and conjunction (AND), which we have just illustrated, his system recognized a subordinate–superordinate relation, which others have labelled 'the ISA relation' and which defines a relationship of class membership (e.g. *dog – animal*). Quillian expresses instances of the ISA relation with the notation '= A' in Figure 10.1 (PLANT = A STRUCTURE). This is the kind of hierarchical relationship that is basic to a thesaurus and any taxonomy of objects in the natural world. A third type of linkage, which may simply be thought of as 'property attribution', links one node directly to another, declaring in effect that the node to which an arrow points is a property of the node from which that arrow points (e.g. STRUCTURE → LIVE). A fourth type of complex linkage between three nodes is used to capture what would nowadays be termed 'thematic roles': the three-way relationship that a verb or a preposition typically contracts with nouns that they head (e.g. FROM 3 (*food*$_{goal}$, *air*$_{source}$)).

Quillian's classification of arc types is somewhat idiosyncratic. He overlooks certain kinds of semantic relation that are nowadays quite widely recognized in lexical semantic analysis and are used in the comprehensive lexical semantic database WordNet (Fellbaum, 1998). For example, a part–whole relationship, 'the HAS relation', is useful for representing functional components of many objects (e.g. *cat*: HAS (AND (*fur*, *whiskers*, *eyes*, etc.))). Another semantic relation, confined to verbs, but useful for relating basic verb meanings to synonyms that elaborate a manner of executing the basic verb, is referred to as **troponymy**

Table 10.2 *Searching semantic space for commonalities of word meaning*

| Word pair | Possible relationships of meaning |
|---|---|
| plant – live | |
| cry – comfort | |

in WordNet (e.g., *walk*: *stroll*, *wander*, *march*, etc.). Quillian's model does not explicitly distinguish this type of relational meaning between a basic verb and its various 'manner of doing' elaborations. However, the elaborations themselves can be expressed by particular concept-mediated attribution linkages (e.g. HASA (*plant*, *leaves*) is represented in Figure 10.1 by traversing the arcs from: '= A STRUCTURE → WITH 3 → LEAF').[2]

Comparison of Quillian's TLC with other symbolic models of semantic decomposition of word meaning raises the vexing question of what relational meanings (set of arc types) should be regarded as primitive and on what criteria a set of semantic primitives might be established. Quillian's approach to this difficult theoretical problem is pragmatic. How well does the system achieve its task of simulating human lexical semantic processing in relation to the effort required to build the network?

### Testing Quillian's model

Having constructed a TLC network of quite modest size by today's memory capacities (holding up to 850 words, but usually tested on networks of only 50–60 words), Quillian then tested his model by getting it to compare and contrast pairs of different word meanings. For example, consult your own semantic memory to find the semantic linkages between each of the word pairs in Table 10.2. For each pair of words provide one or more sentences which show the different relationships of meaning that can pertain between the two words of a given word pair.

Reflect on how you achieved the task of linking the senses of the words in each pair. You may have searched memory for contexts in which both words in the pair could co-occur. You may have consulted the first meanings that came to mind for each word, matched them for meaning and then moved on to consider secondary senses in which each word is used. (In all probability, you can't say clearly what you did to obtain your answers.)

The answers that Quillian's TLC generated to this task of word meaning comparison are shown below in Table 10.3. The responses, whose quality you may judge for yourself, were obtained by (a) going to the root node of each word in a given pair and then (b) traversing the arcs of its memory plane, looking for

---

[2] Certain notational details, expressing the strength or likelihood of the attribution, which are idiosyncratic to the TLC model have been suppressed. See Quillian (1968) for details.

Table 10.3 *TLC's responses to word-pair meaning comparisons*

| Word pair | Retrieved relationships of meaning |
|---|---|
| plant – live | 1. Plant is live structure.<br>2. Plant is structure which get3 food from air. This food is thing which being2 has to take into itself to7 keep live. |
| cry – comfort | 1. Cry2 is among other things to make a sad sound.<br>2. To comfort3 can be to make2 something less2 sad. |

nodes that match the other member of the pair (e.g. Go to PLANT 1; search plane of PLANT 1 for instances of LIVE. Do the same for LIVE 1, looking for instances of PLANT, keeping a record of any 'intersections' that are found). The search for intersections is then extended from the primary meaning plane of each word to planes at one arc removed, again alternating between each member of the word pair and keeping a record of the search path for any linkages that were encountered. This search of semantic space Quillian characterized as a form of 'spreading activation' from the respective root nodes for the target words, through the semantic network. The path associated with each identified 'intersection' would be saved in temporary memory until the search had run its course, or been terminated. Finally, a separate program was deployed to 'translate' each intersection path into a kind of 'Me Tarzan. You Jane' verbal expression, as appears in Table 10.3.

### Evaluation of TLC

It is worthwhile reflecting a little on the achievements, real or merely apparent, of TLC as a model of verbal semantic memory. It is capable of verbalizing information relevant to the intersection of word meanings (or usages may be a better term) for pairs of words that are 'known' to the system. We may well protest that the TLC really has no 'understanding' of word meanings, though it does seem to meet, more or less, one kind of Turing test[3] of word meaning comprehension. Could the TLC's model of semantic word memory be adapted to meet more challenging tests of word meaning comprehension? This is an empirical question which does not seem to have been pursued in the subsequent literature.

### From word to sentence meanings

We have already seen in Quillian's attempt to address the problem of polysemy in individual words (e.g. the multiple meanings of *plant* or *show*

---

[3] Alan Turing (1950) proposed that if a computer's behaviour on a given task is indistinguishable from that of a human being then we are justified in attributing to the computer whatever attributes the human uses to accomplish that task.

triggered by immediate context) that it is necessary to construct networks of semantic relations between word-concepts, which can provide a basis for computing relationships of semantic paraphrase and performing other such tests that may aid in evaluating a model of word meaning. But in order to explain the effects of immediate context upon word meaning, it proved necessary to postulate the essential conceptual machinery that is required for expressing sentence meanings. Many lexical formatives can operate as nouns or verbs (predicates or arguments in the semantic structure of a proposition). Hence, *plant,* a noun, may be pressed into service as a verb (predicate) and *show,* which is basically a verb, may also serve as an argument in the predicate argument structure of a simple proposition.

When attention turns to the semantics of the clause (or single proposition in semantic terms), the pivotal role of the verb becomes apparent. In chapter 3 we examined part of the problem of semantically binding the nominal and verbal elements of clause structure in terms of a theory of thematic role assignment, intended to capture the range of senses that a verb contracts with its arguments. For example, *give* requires an <agent> or <source> as subject, a direct object as <theme> and (optionally) an indirect object as <goal> or <recipient>, expressible either as a double object construction (7), or as noun phrase plus prepositional phrase (8), which may in certain contexts be optional (9):

(7)    John gave the library a book.    <GIVE (*Ag* John)(*Th* book)(*Go* library)>
(8)    John gave a book to the library.[4]
(9)    John gave a book.

In many studies of aphasia and language acquisition, the ability to assign thematic roles correctly has been taken as an operational criterion of sentence comprehension. However, by any stricter test of meaning extraction, it is clear that much more is required. Consider the problem of semantic paraphrase posed by examples (10) and (11) below. How are we to demonstrate/compute their meaning equivalence? In addition to assigning thematic roles to the nominal expressions (*They, John, the room*) some way of decomposing verbal expressions (predicates) is needed.

(10)    They didn't let John go out of the room.
(11)    They prevented John from leaving the room.

The approach to this problem, which was implicit in Quillian's TLC model, but pursued more systematically in the sentence-level semantic theories of Lakoff (1971), Jackendoff (1972, 1997), Schank (1975) and Pustejovsky (1995), is to postulate (a) a small set of semantic primitives – basic elements of verb

---

[4] Sentences (7) and (8) are truth-conditionally equivalent, but not, strictly speaking, identical in meaning. *The library* has higher topicality than *a book* in (7) above. The reverse is true for sentence (8). This is a consideration of information structure rather than propositional meaning (see chapter 15). But notice that the close synonym *donate* does not allow the double object construction: *\*John donated the library a book.*

meanings – and (b) a parsing mechanism or set of inferential rules that can represent the complex meanings of lexical items when they function as verbs. To take George Lakoff's (1971) well-known example:

(12)     *kill* = <CAUSE ($_\text{Ag}$ —, BECOME (NOT (ALIVE ($_\text{Th}$ —))))>

Thus, the meaning of transitive *kill* may be expressed in a compositional function that shows a systematic relationship to the meaning of intransitive *die* <BECOME (NOT (ALIVE ($_\text{Th}$ —)))>, through the addition of a causative semantic function, which also adds an element of <agency> or intentionality. The change of state involved in the meaning of *die* can be systematically related to the meaning of the stative expression *'be dead'*, which in turn may be derived from 'not alive'. Similarly, the meaning of *murder* could be derived by augmenting the causative element of meaning in *kill* by an element of 'malicious intention'.

There is of course a problem of justifying any taxonomy of verb meanings, just as there is with semantic feature theory in general (Katz and Fodor, 1963). We may approach this problem via comparative lexical analysis (Wierzbicka, 2004) across languages (and cultures), or by seeking a common grounding in universal perceptual and cognitive categories, as in cognitive linguistics (Miller and Johnson-Laird, 1976; Lakoff, 1987; Langacker, 1987). Either approach is fraught with difficulties. But the various taxonomies of verb meaning which have been offered tend to have some common features, which are potentially investigable by psycholinguistic and neurolinguistic methods and which may throw light on, and in turn obtain confirmatory evidence from, patterns of lexical semantic deficit in aphasia.

## Conceptual dependency theory

Roger Schank (1975) offered the radical hypothesis that all verb meanings are expressible as compositional functions of just eleven semantic primitives or types of ACT, [5] supported by an indefinite number of STATE conditions, which may change as a result of actions or processes. To give a flavour of Schank-style semantic decomposition, consider his 'conceptual dependency' representation for the sense meaning of '*John ate a frog*':

The conceptual dependency graph in Figure 10.2 is derived partly from semantic information written into lexical items and partly from some highly general rules of conceptual structure formation. The two nominal elements *John* and *frog*, which Schank quaintly labels 'picture producers' (PPs) so as to avoid any suggestion of reference to the formal category 'noun', are linked to the category of ACT words by a highly general rule of inference: PP → ACT, which states in effect that 'PPs can perform actions'. Other general rules of 'conceptual dependency syntax' which are invoked in Fig. 10.2 are:

---

[5] These are: PROPEL, MOVE, INGEST, EXPEL, GRASP, PTRANS, ATRANS, MTRANS, MBUILD, SPEAK, INTEND.

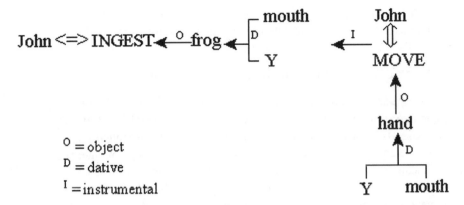

$$^O = object$$
$$^D = dative$$
$$^I = instrumental$$

Figure 10.2  *Conceptual dependency diagram for* John ate a frog

$ACT^O \leftarrow PP$      ACTs can have objects of PPs, which further elaborate the meaning of the ACT.

$ACT^D \begin{bmatrix} PP_2 \\[2ex] \rightarrow PP_1 \end{bmatrix}$      ACTs can have directions that are locations of PPs.
$PP_1$ indicates the final location
and $PP_2$ the initial location of the object.

ACT I ⇕      ACTs have instruments that are themselves entire conceptualizations. The actor of the main conceptualization and the subordinate conceptualization must be the same.

Written into the lexical representation of *eat* is the semantic information that it is an ACT of type INGEST, which involves the ACT of MOVing some object Y via one's *hand* to one's *mouth*.

The conceptual representation in Figure 10.2 above can be augmented by further general inferential rules of the kind: 'a PP can be described by a specified state and a value for that state can be assigned' by world knowledge, to the effect that 'eating frogs can make one ill'. Schank imposes no limits on the number and kind of different states and makes liberal use of numerical scales to represent degrees of a state (e.g. *sick – well*: HEALTH $_{(1-9)}$).[6] He also defines state relations for knowledge representation of part–whole relationships (e.g. *hand* is part of *arm*) and relationships of containment (e.g. *hands* may CONTAIN PPs). Thus, the conceptual dependency diagram may be elaborated to show (Figure 10.3) the additional information that *eating* the *frog* caused *John* to be ill and that the *hand* used for eating was part of *John* and contained a *frog* during the course of eating. This additional information, which may seem quite tangential to the original sentence (*John ate a frog*), is needed to support enriched lexical inferencing, which, in turn, is required for all but the most direct forms of semantic paraphrase.

Stepping back from the details of Schank's proposal and attending to features that it has in common with other psychologically inspired models of lexical

---

[6] This lack of restriction on the number of states is one reason why Schank can get away with a small number of verb primitives (e.g. to *hurt* Y is to cause a state change in Y's level of well-being).

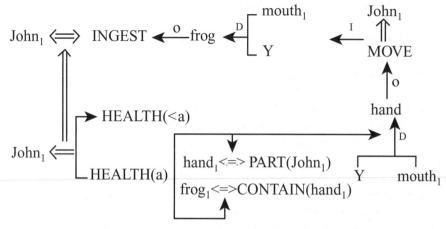

Figure 10.3 *Augmented conceptual dependency diagram for* John ate a frog

semantics, there are some notable characteristics. The semantic primitives of verb meaning are grounded in a concrete spatio-temporal world in which physical objects collide with one another or are actively propelled through changes of state or location by wilful beings. The first six of Schank's verbal semantic primitives make reference to concrete movement: PROPEL, MOVE, INGEST, EXPEL, GRASP, PTRANS. The meanings of the first five of these primitives is conveyed by their ordinary language usage. PTRANS refers to a change in physical spatio-temporal location of some object. Three additional primitives, ATRANS, MTRANS and MBUILD, are mental projections or metaphorical extensions from the physical to the mental world of concepts otherwise applicable to a tangible world of concrete objects. Thus, ATRANS is transference of some abstract property (e.g. ownership) that often has a concrete or literal reading (PTRANS) that accompanies the act of giving and functions as a synonym of it (e.g., *John gave Mary a book* = <physically transferred to her *a book*>, <consigned to her possession *a book*>). MTRANS means 'to transfer information'. Hence to tell X about Y is to transfer knowledge from one metaphorical location in X's domain to that of Y. MBUILD means 'to create or combine thoughts'. Cognitive grammar has greatly elaborated these notions of mind-as-body-projection, through the concept of *image schemas* and their role in explaining patterns of polysemy (see Lee, 2002).

## Evaluation of symbolic models of lexical semantics

We have gone to some pains (hopefully not too much) to specify what a performance model of word meaning should be able to accomplish. It should be able to handle polysemy (variation of word meaning with phrasal context). It should be able to compute obvious and non-obvious relationships of meaning between words and phrases. It should be able to perform semantic paraphrase. These goals were more explicitly and comprehensively addressed by the previous generation of symbolic expert system style models (Quillian, 1968; Schank, 1975). Symbolic networks provide a data structure to support lexical inference, which enables the construction of Turing tests for models of word comprehension.

An important practical difficulty posed by such models is their fragility of performance as they grow more complex; their inflexibility. Symbolic semantic networks have no capacity to learn from language experience but must be coded by an expert. They therefore fail to effectively exploit contextual information available from processing large corpora: the collocation statistics of word usage. In recent years, non-symbolic network models of semantic memory, utilizing neural networks have become prominent in the computational and psycholinguistic literature (McClelland and Rogers, 2003; McRae, 2004).

Experience with expert system models of semantic memory also demonstrated that a fully fledged model of word-to-sentence level semantic processing is infeasible at the present time. The required depth and detail of world knowledge and inference is too great. Nevertheless, the pioneering investigations we have reviewed here were instructive in clarifying the goals of a semantic theory from the perspective of language processing. Symbolic semantic networks have found application in domain-limited information retrieval systems, such as the Unified Medical Language System (UMLS), designed to enhance access to medical literature by facilitating the development of computer systems that understand biomedical language (Verspoor, 2005), and in domain-general but processing-limited applications such as WordNet, a program that generates synonym sets.

## Investigating semantic structures

Knowing when and how to lower one's explanatory goals to the realm of currently feasible inquiry is an essential part of the art of scientific investigation. We cannot explicitly model the extraction of word meaning in context, but we may be able to ask limited questions about the organization and retrieval of semantic information in on-line sentence processing. We may be able to answer questions such as: When does phrasal context start to exercise an influence on the sense-meaning of a word? Are some semantic relations that we have previously identified as important for explicating the meaning of words more accessible or more rapidly computed on-line than others? Is semantic memory organized into relatively discrete modules or is it distributed in a homogeneous system? To what extent are there relatively independent, modality-specific, semantic systems that serve different domains of word meaning, or regions of the mental thesaurus? Does the fact that some lexical items represent clusters of highly correlated properties or features render their retrieval more robust than other items whose distinguishing semantic features are more sparse and essentially uncorrelated? These are some of the questions that have been actively pursued by psycholinguistics in recent years. They may not be the core questions to ask, and the answers that they may yield will not constitute a theory of word meaning, but they may narrow the range of viable alternative theories. Convergent evidence may also be sought from neuropsychological studies of symptom clusters in lexical semantic disorders in aphasia and in neuroimaging studies of lexical semantic processing in normal and language-impaired speaker/hearers.

## The role of context in word-sense disambiguation

Context-dependent word meaning processing takes place in stages. This is clear from behavioural studies of on-line lexical retrieval. In a pioneering study using the cross-modal semantic priming paradigm (introduced in chapter 9), Swinney (1979) found that both meanings of an ambiguous word such as *bug* (<insect> or <covert listening device>) are initially activated, regardless of a strongly biasing discourse context (such as '*Rumour had it that for years the building had been plagued with problems. The man was not surprised when he found several spiders, roaches, and other bugs in the corner of his room.*') Subjects responded more quickly on a lexical decision task to a visual probe word related in meaning to either sense of the prime *bugs*, when the probe was flashed on a computer screen at the same time they heard *bugs* spoken in the context sentence. Thus, a lexical decision to the contextually inappropriate but related word *spy* was facilitated just as much as the contextually appropriate related word *ant*. But when a delay was introduced by presenting the probe word three syllables after subjects heard the ambiguous prime word, only the contextually appropriate probe (*ant* in this case) received a significant priming effect.

What do these results signify? They indicate that an ambiguous prime word initially activates both of its meanings, the contextually appropriate and the inappropriate, but that after a delay of about .25 s, presumably the time it takes for context to be assimilated, only the contextually appropriate meaning of the prime word survives to facilitate lexical decision to the probe. Thus, lexical meaning retrieval is a process which is initially autonomous of context effects. This finding was historically important as one of the first solid empirical arguments for modularity, at least in the initial stages, of word meaning assignment.

## Semantic priming and the activation/retrieval of word meaning

The semantic priming paradigm enables us to investigate other aspects of the time course of word meaning activation/retrieval. At what point in the course of word recognition do the semantic properties of a word become active? Early 'search' models of lexical access (see chapter 6) assumed that a word's meaning is not available until its phonological form has been fully determined. However, activation models such as TRACE and the cohort model (Marslen-Wilson, 1987) allow for partial and parallel activation of multiple word meanings before competition reduces the cohort to just one or two candidates. Are some semantic properties of words activated earlier than others? Various kinds of semantic relation may be established between prime and probe words (such as (1) category coordinates: *dog – cat*, (2) antonyms: *hot – cold*, (3) functional relations: *hammer – nail*). Establishing which kinds of semantic relations most effectively prime a probe word in a lexical decision or a word-naming task may provide insight into the structure of semantic memory.

However, there are three methodological caveats that must be considered before attempting to use experimental findings from the semantic priming paradigm as a window to on-line word meaning retrieval. These are (i) the specific type of priming paradigm used, including the modality of the prime and probe words, (ii) the potential impact of non-automatic or strategic influences upon priming effects, and (iii) the distinction between associative and semantic effects in priming. The three caveats are related to one another.

Although it may be argued that the same mechanism of spreading semantic activation should operate regardless of auditory or visual mode of presentation, semantic priming effects have been found to vary substantially with the type of stimulus used (Moss, Ostrin, Tyler and Marslen-Wilson, 1995). Our concern is with spoken language processing, where automatic priming effects seem to be more robust at short inter-stimulus intervals. The speech signal unfolds and decays rapidly in time. Auditory lexical processing may be singularly sensitive to temporal stimulus contingencies.

The priming paradigm is informative about rapid, unconscious and automatic processes involved in spoken language processing only insofar as it is uncontaminated by expectancies or strategies that subjects may develop in response to specific conditions or task demands of the priming experiment itself. Measures that can be taken to minimize strategic processing include the use of short inter-stimulus intervals between prime and probe stimuli (less than 250 ms), the use of distractor items and an appropriate range and mixture of related and unrelated prime–probe pairs.

The third caveat is not universally acknowledged by researchers who employ the priming paradigm, but is nevertheless quite crucial for the question of how directly the priming paradigm reflects processes of lexical retrieval and semantic composition that we infer must take place in sentence processing and which the computational models of Quillian and Schank, discussed earlier, sought to emulate. Is the priming paradigm selectively sensitive to **semantic relations** of specific kinds, as distinct from generalized associative linkages that may be established from normative word association tests? If automatic priming effects could be accounted for simply in terms of normative word associations, as some have argued (Lupker, 1984; Shelton and Martin, 1992), then there would be no need to postulate an underlying network of well-articulated semantic relations to account for priming effects. Or to put it more directly, semantic priming effects might be successfully modelled by associative networks that are simply responsive to the statistics of word collocation.

Table 10.4 *Prime–probe relations used by Moss* et al. *(1995)*

|  | Category coordinate | | Functional | |
|---|---|---|---|---|
|  | Natural | Artefact | Instrumental | Scripted |
| Associated | cat – dog | boat – ship | bow – arrow | theatre – play |
|  | brother – sister | coat – hat | umbrella – rain | beach – sand |
| Non-associated | aunt – nephew | aeroplane – train | knife – bread | party – music |
|  | pig – horse | blouse – dress | string – parcel | zoo – penguin |

However, evidence suggests that semantic priming may still be obtained when prime and probe words are semantically related but associatively unrelated (Fischler, 1977; Ostrin and Tyler, 1993).[7] The interaction between semantic relation types and associative strength between prime and probe words has been most thoroughly explored in a series of studies by Moss *et al.* (1995); Moss, McCormick and Tyler (1997). In the first series of experiments, Moss *et al.* (1995) considered four kinds of semantic relation that may obtain between prime and probe: two types of category coordination, between 'natural objects' or 'artefacts', and two types of functional relation, where prime and probe words were related either by some activity expressible by a verbal predicate (e.g. *bow* **shoot** *arrow*) or by conventional situational knowledge, referred to as a 'script'. The four kinds of semantic relation were crossed with a two-level factor of associative linkage (associated vs. non-associated). The eight conditions that resulted are illustrated in Table 10.4.

Category coordinate relations are the most frequently used in studies of semantic priming. Here the prime and probe words are both basic members of some superordinate category (e.g. *cat – dog*: <domestic animal>). There has been considerable discussion in the neuropsychological literature over whether natural objects (animals, plants, objects in the natural world) are semantically organized differently in some respects from artefacts (man-made objects). Category coordination may be a more readily identifiable semantic relation for pairs of natural objects than artefact pairs, because taxonomic relations based on perceptual properties are more applicable to natural objects than to artefacts. On the other hand, functional properties may be more salient for artefacts, which tend to be identified by their usages. Category-specific semantic deficits for subclasses of natural objects (such as fruit and vegetables) have been found in some aphasics (Warrington, 1975), which it has been argued reflect modularity of semantic categories for natural objects (see chapter 12).

Within the domain of functional relations Moss *et al.* (1995) distinguished between quite specific functional relations that can be generally captured in a frame 'x VERB y' (e.g. *bow* SHOOT *arrow*) and more generalized script or scenario-based knowledge that 'x IS-USUALLY-FOUND-WITH y' (e.g. *play*

---

[7] By 'associated' we mean that a large percentage of people give the probe word as the first word they think of in response to the prime in a free association test.

IS-FOUND-WITH *theatre*). Script knowledge lies more clearly in the domain of pragmatics than lexical knowledge. Moss *et al.* speculated that evidence of differential behaviour between these two kinds of functional relation in semantic priming may be informative about the vexed distinction between the domains of lexical semantic and pragmatic knowledge.

### Results: associative and semantic priming and the effect of prime type

For the four types of prime–probe relation tested (see Table 10.4) there was an appreciable 'boost' to the priming effect if prime and probe words were associatively linked. However, in all but the case of the 'functional script' type of semantic relation, there was a significant independent effect for semantically related primes, compared with unrelated primes (the control condition). Moss *et al.* (1995) thus confirmed earlier findings that semantic priming cannot be attributed solely to normative association strength; an important result for arguing the case that semantic priming effects, being sensitive to specific semantic relations, are indicative of semantic activation in lexical retrieval in general. Also, the boost in priming for associated over non-associated semantically related items was found to be diminished when prime and target words were presented in different modalities (as in the cross-modal priming paradigm).

However, the strength of priming effects associated with different kinds of prime–probe semantic relationship also varied with the mode of stimulus presentation, rendering it difficult to argue that any hierarchy of accessibility or rapidity of activation for different types of semantic relation exists. The authors concluded that further research involving varying of inter-stimulus intervals of both primes and targets in visual and auditory modality will be needed to determine whether differences in the time course of activation for particular types of semantic relation can account for the complex pattern of results across different priming paradigms.

In a subsequent study, Moss, McCormick and Tyler (1997) went some way to providing empirical data on the differential activation of semantic relations over time. Using cross-modal priming in which the visual probes were presented at the 'isolation point'[8] of the auditory prime word, they confirmed earlier evidence for the activation of multiple word meanings before the point at which a word can be recognized. Specifically with respect to differential semantic priming, they found that for words referring to man-made objects, information about their function and design is activated more quickly than information about their physical form.

In summary, semantic priming remains the principal behavioural indicator that psycholinguists possess for the study of on-line retrieval/activation of lexical semantic information in word and sentence processing. The majority of studies using this paradigm have employed visual primes and probes, in visual word

---

[8] The isolation point is the point in the phonological sequence at which a word becomes uniquely identifiable. See discussion of the gating paradigm, chapter 6.

recognition or lexical decision tasks, which are subject to strategic (post-lexical) processing effects and are only indirectly relevant to spoken language processing. The importance of semantic over form-based (phonological or orthographic similarity) priming effects appears to be promoted by use of the cross-modal priming paradigm. Despite the relative maturity of this methodology, we still lack a solid body of consensual findings on the critical issue of the time course of differential activation of a hierarchy of semantic properties which would give us confidence that the paradigm really constitutes a window on lexical semantic processing. We can however be assured that when properly conducted, semantic priming effects represent more than activation on the basis of normative associative strength between prime and probe.

## Brain imaging studies of lexical semantic activation

In recent years, functional neuroimaging studies have provided an additional source of evidence on the topography and time course of lexical semantic processing in the brain. The questions posed in these investigations understandably have a more localizationist flavour, given that the various imaging methods are designed specifically to indicate regional variation in brain metabolic or bioelectrical activity. Also, many studies of normal brain activity in lexical processing have been influenced by some rare but striking case reports of category-specific semantic deficits in aphasia, such as the patient who could readily identify and name animals and living things, but experienced difficulty with inanimate objects (particularly tools and artefacts), or another patient who had the opposite differential semantic deficit for animate objects (Warrington and McCarthy, 1983; Warrington and Shallice, 1984). Well-documented cases of 'double dissociation', where one patient manifests a specific pattern of impaired and preserved semantic processing and another patient manifests the complementary pattern, are suggestive of modular semantic organization in the normal brain. We shall discuss these issues in the next chapter, which deals specifically with disorders of lexical semantic processing.

Neuroimaging studies of semantic organization in the normal brain are also informed by neurological models of the division of mental or computational labour in the brain between sensory and motor functions, episodic vs. non-episodic memory, or declarative vs. procedural knowledge (Ullman, 2001). In other words, modular or localist notions of brain organization for perception, action and memory are taken as the starting point for neurolinguistic models of lexical semantic organization. Hence, nouns of high imageability ('picture producers') may be expected to have more of a posterior (temporal-occipital) locus of representation in the brain, and verbs ('action words'), more of an anterior (frontal) representation. However, conflicting findings have been reported in the imaging literature on the question of cerebral localization for different semantic and grammatical categories of words.

Tyler, Stamatakis *et al.* (2003) used fMRI to examine the neural activation associated with conceptual processing of nouns referring to animals and tools and for verbs referring to tool-associated actions (e.g. drilling, painting) and biological actions (e.g. walking, jumping). They found that object names and their associated actions activated the same areas of the temporal lobe, suggesting that names for objects and actions activate a single distributed semantic network. There was no evidence of category specificity for either objects or actions, and the same pattern of activation was evoked for the appearance and motion attributes of both living and non-living categories.

Essentially the same team of researchers (Tyler, Bright *et al.*, 2003) carried out a PET study to determine whether there is any regional specialization for the processing of concepts from different semantic categories, using picture stimuli and a semantic categorization task. They found robust activation of a large semantic network extending from the left inferior frontal cortex through the inferior temporal lobe and posteriorly into the occipital cortex. The only category-specific effect observed was additional activation for animals in the right occipital cortex, which was interpreted as being due to the extra visual processing demands required to differentiate one animal from another. They interpreted the findings of this and the previous study as converging evidence (across imaging techniques as well as experimental tasks) for a non-differentiated, distributed network for conceptual knowledge representation.

Two recent studies suggest that it may be necessary to qualify the conclusion of an undifferentiated semantic storage, when attention is paid to previously overlooked semantic and morpho-syntactic attributes of the stimuli and the subject's task. The first of these studies takes up a distinction between simple or coarse-grained feature analysis and complex or fine-grained analysis for differential object recognition, drawn from neurocognitive research with non-human primates. The distinguishing perceptual semantic features of objects may be structured in a hierarchical system, with posterior neurons in the inferior temporal cortex representing simple features and anterior neurons in the perirhinal cortex representing complex conjunctions of features (Bussey and Saksida, 2002). The perirhinal cortex lies on the ventral (inner side) of the inferior temporal gyrus. In macaque monkeys it is a small (20 mm) strip of anatomically distinct cortical tissue. The perirhinal cortex is thought to play a key role in object identification and recognition by binding together sensory attributes from different modalities into a multi-modal reified percept (Murray and Bussey, 1999).

Tyler, Stamatakis, Bright, Acres, Abdallah, Rodd and Moss (2004) tested the implications of these claims for object naming in an event-related fMRI Study. Coloured pictures of common objects were presented to subjects for naming at two levels of specificity – basic and domain-specific. The researchers reasoned that domain-level naming requires access to a coarser-grained representation of objects, involving only posterior regions of the inferior temporal gyrus. In contrast, basic-level naming requires finer-grained discrimination to differentiate between similar objects, and thus should involve anterior temporal regions, including the perirhinal cortex. They found that object processing always activated the fusiform gyrus (lateral occipito-temporal gyrus) bilaterally, irrespective of the task, whereas the perirhinal cortex was only activated when the task required finer-grained discriminations. These results are open to the interpretation that the same kind of hierarchical structure, which has been proposed for object processing in the monkey temporal cortex, operates similarly in humans. Should this hypothesis withstand further scrutiny, it may point to an interesting insight, of a common, across-species foundation for conceptual categories, upon which the lexical semantics of human languages are projected.

Another perspective on and argument for a certain modularity and localization of lexical processing comes from a recent fMRI study of semantic judgements with inflected nouns and verbs (Tyler, Bright, Fletcher and Stamatakis, 2004). We shall explore this study in more detail as an object lesson in the importance of careful attention to stimulus properties and the nature of task demands. Previous studies have yielded inconsistent findings on the question of distinct patterns of activation for nouns and verbs, some finding a differential pattern (Damasio and Tranel, 1993; Perani *et al.*, 1999) and others none (Warburton *et al.*, 1996; Tyler *et al.*, 2001; Tyler, Stamatakis *et al.*, 2003). Tyler, Bright *et al.* (2004) speculated that the inconsistent findings may have been caused by varying use of noun and verb morphological inflection in the test stimuli. As we have indicated previously, English verbs and nouns often appear without specific inflectional marking and may serve either part of speech in different contexts. But in a more highly inflected language, like Italian, overt inflectional marking is required.

Tyler, Bright *et al.* (2004) presented subjects with a semantic judgement task involving nouns and verbs, where there was minimal ambiguity in basic lexical class membership (selecting nouns and verbs strongly biased in their usage towards one or the other inflectional category) and where all items were explicitly inflected for that category (with regular plural -*s* or progressive -*ing* marking). The semantic judgement task involved deciding whether the third member of a triplet belonged or did not belong to a semantic class determined by the preceding pair. The triplet stimuli were either regularly inflected nouns or verbs, matched as closely as possible for word length and frequency. A baseline condition was included in which subjects judged whether a target letter sequence (in capitals) matched or did not match the preceding letter pair (see Table 10.5). The baseline task fMRI activation patterns were subtracted from the activation patterns obtained from the noun and verb judgements, in order to isolate the semantic processing component of the judgement task from the orthographic processing components.

Areas of heightened activation level associated with semantic judgements were statistically identified by subtraction of the fMRI activation patterns for words (nouns + verbs) from those obtained from judgements of the baseline stimuli. Several peak activation areas were identified. They clustered into three or four regions, predominantly in the temporal lobe and the left frontal gyrus, but with some located sub-cortically. The pattern of activation was consistent with a widely

Table 10.5 *Triplet stimuli used in semantic judgement task (Tyler* et al., *2004)*

|  | Related | Unrelated |
|---|---|---|
| NOUN | *sparrows, thrushes, WRENS* | *ravens, canaries, WEAZELS* |
| VERB | *eating, grazing, DINING* | *talking, speaking, LEAPING* |
| BASE LINE | kkk, kkkkkk, KKKKK | ttt, tttt, MMMM |

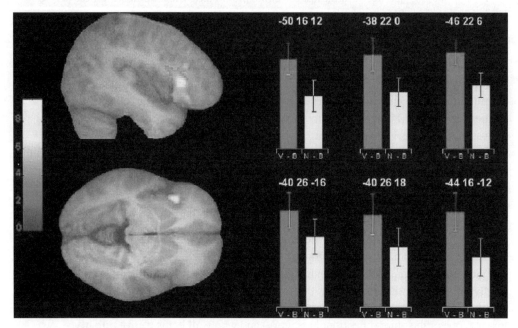

Figure 10.4  *The areas activated in the verbs–nouns contrast. Bars show signal levels within the verb-noun activation area (grey = verbs, white = nouns)*

distributed network for conceptual knowledge representation and semantic judgement.

However, the critical comparison involved the subtraction of noun and verb activation patterns which resulted in a single well-defined cluster of activation peaks (small white patches) in the left inferior frontal gyrus (Figure 10.4).

The noun-verb activation area was confined to Broca's area and an adjacent region. Why did the noun-verb subtraction yield a more restrictive and well-defined activation pattern than the word-baseline subtraction, and what are the implications of these findings? Undoubtedly the noun-verb subtraction is a functionally highly restrictive comparison – of activation patterns for a semantic judgement task that is identical, except that in one case the stimuli are inflected verbs and in the other case inflected nouns (matched for word length and frequency). The noun-inflected items also resulted in activation above baseline in Broca's area, but there was a significant boost in the case of verbs which was specifically restricted to Broca's area. By contrast, the word-baseline subtraction involves a contrast that is functionally much less well defined. We can only surmise as to what extent the subtraction operation removes or 'controls' for activation associated with 'orthographic' or perceptual components of the word comparison task. In fact, the two tasks (comparing meanings of read words and of checking letter sequences for orthographic identity) may be largely incommensurate, so that the word-baseline subtraction is hardly a reflection of a residual 'semantic processing' component of the task, and the resulting activation pattern may be uninterpretable as such (a methodological problem with the subtraction method that we flagged earlier in chapter 2).

The results of this study may say little about the locus of lexical semantic processing in the brain, but they do provide useful corroborative evidence from aphasia of the crucial role of Broca's area in morpho-syntactic processing, a topic that we take up in chapter 14. In the second part of their paper, Tyler, Bright *et al.* (2004) show that there is substantial overlap between the area of verb activation in the left inferior frontal gyrus (Broca's area) and the lesion site of patients who have difficulties with regular verbal inflection.

In conclusion, brain imaging studies of lexical semantic activation have not yet yielded definitive evidence of localized or modular semantic organization. But that may be because the behavioural probes that have been used have not employed the right tasks or made the right comparisons. The techniques of neural imaging have continued to develop to the point where they now approach the limits of spatial resolution, beyond which individual differences in brain anatomy begin to pose serious restrictions on cross-brain comparisons. Similarly, temporal resolution is now approaching the point where some imaging techniques may be taken as measures of on-line processing. The challenge is now to bring greater sophistication to bear on the design of relevant psycholinguistic tasks to be used in conjunction with these powerful observational tools.

## Summary

We began this chapter by asking what a model of word meaning should be able to accomplish, and we focused upon polysemy – how words change their meaning according to the immediate linguistic context in which they are 'embedded' – as the fundamental property and problem to be accounted for. We then asked what kind of computational mechanism might be required to account for this rapid adaptation of a word to its surroundings in the course of on-line sentence comprehension, and explored the potential of symbolic networks of the kind developed in first-generation AI models of lexical processing. Although such networks have the unfortunate property of rapidly growing to unmanageable size and complexity before they model even a fraction of the terrain of language use, they have proved useful in providing an explicit characterization of what is deemed to constitute critical tests of lexical semantic competency: the ability to paraphrase a particular verbal expression in a variety of ways, to retrieve commonalities or intersections of meaning between related words or phrases, etc. These investigations stimulated psycholinguistic and neurolinguistic inquiries into the nature of lexical semantic organization, yielding in some cases quite specific suggestions, such as Schank's proposal to ground verb meaning representations in a set of concrete primitives for motion and interaction between tangible entities, which may be metaphorically extended to a 'mental' plane to represent relations and impacts between people and other sentient beings. AI investigations of semantic space have subsequently taken a quite different turn, using statistical networks empirically driven by huge language corpora and the exigencies of information search and retrieval.

Psycholinguistic and neurolinguistic research on lexical semantic processing has been dominated by the problem of finding ways to unpack stages from initial contact with lexical entries, to the elaboration of context-constrained word meaning. A host of reaction-time-based semantic priming paradigms have been tried but with limited success. There are many specific reasons for this, some of which we have discussed previously, and probably one overarching difficulty, namely that reaction time measures are too slow and too subject to contamination by strategic considerations that fall outside the relevant time window of on-line processing. In recent years, advances in the temporal and spatial resolution of neuroimaging techniques are beginning to yield insights into the organization and retrieval of lexical semantic information. We explore this topic further in the next chapter.

# 11   Lexical semantic disorders in aphasia

## Introduction

The previous chapter's discussion of lexical semantics sought to address the fundamental problem of how word meanings are modified by context in sentence processing. These considerations are central to the goal of developing a combinatorial semantics of natural language processing – a task that is beyond the grasp of current theory or computation. However, it is important not to lose sight of the fact that words and idioms (phrase-like chunks of the *kick-the-bucket* variety) are also discrete linguistic entities, and that isolated word recognition, retrieval and production constitute a quasi-modular component of linguistic competence in its own right. Severe word-finding difficulties constitute a criterial symptom for a diagnosis of **anomic aphasia** or serve as a sign of incipient Alzheimer's disease. Phonemic or semantic paraphasias are characteristic features of fluent speech production in Wernicke's aphasia and may be accompanied by an agnosia (perceptual deficit) for the phonological form or the meanings of isolated words.

Indeed it has been argued that an initial stage of context-independent word recognition is required, in which all of the possible roles that a given word may play in different linguistic contexts are activated (perhaps in proportion to their likelihood of use), prior to the selective inhibitory or excitatory effects of context which rapidly constrain the system to settle on a dominant interpretation. This in fact was the conclusion to which Swinney (1979) was led in his celebrated 'bug' study of CMLP reported previously (chapter 10). Assuming that a context-independent level of lexical recognition/retrieval exists, we then require a framework or a model that enables us to predict patterns of word errors likely to occur in isolated word production or perception in aphasia. In the case of phonological errors, **distinctive feature** theory has provided a useful metric (Blumstein, 1973) for predicting the likelihood of particular sound substitutions, transpositions and omissions that occur frequently in aphasia and much less frequently in normal speech production. It does not seem to matter precisely which of several competing distinctive feature systems is used, provided that it adequately encodes the distinctive sound contrasts of the language. Also, the pattern of phonological errors found in aphasia does not differ qualitatively from that which is found in 'slips of the ear and tongue' observed to occur occasionally in normal listeners and speakers (see chapter 7).

Table 11.1 *Semantic feature specification*

|         | man | woman | boy | girl | mare | colt |
|---------|-----|-------|-----|------|------|------|
| **human** | + | + | + | + | − | − |
|         |     |       |     |      |      |      |
|         |     |       |     |      |      |      |

When it comes to meaning-based errors of single word perception or production, the common practice has been to propose some scheme of **semantic features**, although it is widely recognized that linguistic analysis can provide no comparable grounding for a set of semantic primitives as in the case of phonological similarity. However, native speakers' intuitions about word meaning are sufficiently stable and reliable to permit *a posteriori* attribute classes to be defined across collections of (well-chosen) words.

As a demonstration, we invite you to supply the missing semantic features and their values to specify the meaning contrasts among the six words given above, using the first line of Table 11.1 as a guide. Do this before you turn the page or read further.

English speakers readily infer the semantic relations of gender and maturity that are encoded in this small set of words. This method of *componential semantic feature analysis* (Lyons, 1995), based on native speakers' semantic intuitions, works quite well for carefully defined subsets of words and can provide a basis for computing relations of semantic similarity between words. However, it is clearly impractical for large or arbitrarily generated sets of lexical items, as you will no doubt discover if you substitute each of the words in Table 11.1 with the next item that appears alphabetically in the dictionary, i.e. *manacle, womb, boycott, girth, margarine, column* (Australian Pocket Oxford, 3rd edn), and attempt to repeat the feature assignment exercise.

But for well-defined word sets involving semantically transparent relations among the lexical items, componential feature analysis can provide a means of computing relations of semantic similarity, which in turn can be readily converted to a metric of distances in semantic space. Semantic distance metrics can then be used to construct and test models of lexical semantic organization and semantic breakdown in aphasia, dementia, or other scenarios involving impaired lexical access or degraded lexical semantic representations, as we shall illustrate.

It is trivially easy to convert a fully specified feature table into a half matrix of similarity scores (Table 11.3) among the words in the test set, by simply counting the number of feature values that all word pairs have in common. These similarity scores may then be converted to dissimilarity scores, which have the useful property that a word's semantic dissimilarity with itself is zero and all other dissimilarity scores may be treated as monotonically related[1] to distances

---

[1] A monotonic relation is one that makes no stronger assumption about the relationship between one variable (dissimilarity scores in this case) and another (distances in semantic space) than that they share the same rank ordering. See Kruskal and Wish (1977).

Table 11.2 *Semantic feature assignment*

|         | man | woman | boy | girl | mare | colt |
|---------|-----|-------|-----|------|------|------|
| **human**  | + | + | + | + | − | − |
| **female** | − | + | − | + | + | − |
| **mature** | + | + | − | − | + | − |

Table 11.3 *Semantic similarity scores*

|       | man | woman | boy | girl | mare | colt |
|-------|-----|-------|-----|------|------|------|
| man   | 3 | 2 | 2 | 1 | 1 | 1 |
| woman |   | 3 | 1 | 2 | 1 | 0 |
| boy   |   |   | 3 | 2 | 0 | 2 |
| girl  |   |   |   | 3 | 1 | 1 |
| mare  |   |   |   |   | 3 | 1 |
| foal  |   |   |   |   |   | 3 |

in a semantic space, whose properties may subsequently be explored by a variety of mathematical techniques, such as **multidimensional scaling** (MDS).

The take-home message here is that providing one has a method of coding native speakers' reliable intuitions about meaning contrasts among a set of test words, using semantic properties that language users find appropriate, it may not matter that we do not have access to a definitive *a priori* inventory of semantic features. With these methodological preliminaries, we now turn to consider the major issues which have animated research into lexical semantic disorders in aphasia, with an eye to what they can tell us about the nature of the semantic organization of the lexicon in the brain. Most of this work addresses the semantic processing of isolated words, though we shall subsequently consider some recent research on the integration of words with linguistic context in aphasia.

## Early work

According to the classical BWL model and consistent with more recent neurolinguistic models (Pulvermüller, 2002) informed by neuroimaging findings, the principal site for the storage of isolated word forms and their meanings lies in and around Wernicke's area in the left posterior temporal lobe. Early psycholinguistic experiments established that fluent but moderately comprehension impaired aphasic patients[2] performed poorly on a variety of tests of semantic relatedness judgement (Zurif, Caramazza, Myerson and Calvin, 1974; Goodglass and Baker, 1976; Cohen, Kelter and Woll, 1980; Caramazza and Berndt, 1982). For example, Goodglass and Baker (1976) showed that aphasic patients with

[2] Patients who, though comprehension-impaired, were capable of being instructed on the experimental tasks.

Table 11.4 *Types of semantic relation between word pairs*

| Associative type | Example |
| --- | --- |
| identity | *sheep – sheep* |
| superordinate | *sheep – animal* |
| attribute | *sheep – wool* |
| contrast coordinate | *sheep – cow* |
| function associate | *sheep – shear* |
| functional context | *sheep – farm* |

lesions to the posterior language area and comprehension deficits performed poorly on an associative judgement task that required them to perceive different relations of semantic similarity between word pairs such as those illustrated in Table 11.4.

At issue was the question of whether the poor performance of the aphasic group was caused by difficulties accessing and manipulating information from lexical storage, or whether there was actual loss or degradation of the semantic network itself (i.e. a performance or a competence deficit – a familiar theme in aphasia research). Goodglass and Baker opted for the impaired competence hypothesis, inferring that 'qualitative changes in the associational structure of the semantic field' occurred, at least in the case of the more comprehension impaired group. They offered two pieces of evidence in support of their position.

Firstly, there was a qualitative, not just a quantitative performance difference between the more severely comprehension impaired subjects on the one hand, and mildly impaired and non-impaired control subjects on the other. For the control and mildly comprehension impaired subjects the contrast coordinate (CC) associative type was more difficult to judge than the other five types (see Table 11.4), as assessed by error rate and response times. But the CC relation was *no more* difficult than the other relations for the more severely comprehension impaired group. These findings were replicated in an independent study (Chenery, Ingram and Murdoch, 1990). They suggest a different response mechanism may be operative in the low comprehension group. We discuss the ramifications of this in more detail presently.

Secondly, and this finding was also replicated (Chenery *et al.*, 1990), the low comprehension group demonstrated an association between their ability to name a target word (e.g. *sheep* in Table 11.4) and their performance on the semantic judgement task. That is, items that were successfully named were also more accurately judged on the semantic relatedness test. This pattern of performance was only found in the low comprehension group. It suggests a model of localized semantic impairment that may be specific to particular lexical nodes or be differentially distributed to regions of lexical semantic space, in line with (a) a competence deficit hypothesis and (b) a functionally differentiated lexical storage.

Both of these conclusions were controversial at the time and remain so to some extent today. We shall address the question of a competence or performance deficit of lexical-semantic impairments in fluent aphasia first, and then turn to the question of modularity of lexical semantic impairments – expressed in the whimsical analogy of the mental lexicon as a kind of supermarket, with a 'tools and artefacts' section, a 'living things' section, an 'activities area', a 'produce department', etc. (Pinker, 1994).

## Competence or performance deficit in lexical semantic disorder?

Let us return to consider in more detail what implications follow from the finding that the recognition of CC (contrast coordinate) relations is more difficult than other types of semantic relation in a paired associate judgement task for normal language users, but not apparently for moderately comprehension impaired patients. The CC was the only category in which our normal control subjects did not perform at ceiling level on judgements of semantic relatedness made under time pressure. CC was also the most difficult category for the mildly comprehension impaired aphasic group and the brain damaged non-aphasic group of controls (Chenery *et al.*, 1990). The differential pattern of performance suggests the low comprehension group was employing a different response strategy to detect relations of semantic similarity.

Now consider the nature of the task and what makes the recognition of a CC relation different from the other semantic relation types. Note firstly that detection of the identity relation (*sheep – sheep*) requires no semantic judgement. This relation was correctly identified by all subjects, regardless of their level of comprehension impairment. For four of the remaining five associative categories, detection of a two-term association is required to spot the semantic relatedness of the word pair (e.g. *sheep – animal*: ISA (x, y), where x = <sheep>, y = <animal>; *sheep – wool*: HAS (x, y), where x = <sheep>, y = <wool>; etc.). However, the CC relation requires the identification of a nested two-function argument structure, a conjunction of two functions, in which the conjunction itself is the superordinate function and there are three terms (x, y and z): e.g. *sheep – cow*: AND (ISA (x, z), ISA (y, z)), where x = *sheep*, y = *cow*, z = *farm animal*. Arguably, it is the added complexity of the three-term relation which makes the CC judgement more difficult for normal language users.

But to explain why the CC is *not* more difficult for the low comprehension aphasic patients, an appeal to some alternative strategy for spotting the semantic relatedness is needed. Suppose that instead of identifying the specific semantic relationship, we set a lower goal for the task, one of simply recognizing whether or not the two elements of a pair are 'somehow connected in some way'.[3] An

---

[3] This strategy is quite compatible with the instructions given to the subjects for the task.

algorithm that is sensitive to collocational word associations could provide a probabilistic estimate of the likelihood that any two words constitute a 'related pair'. It would not be necessary to identify precisely the nature of the semantic relation. If this strategy is used then instances of the CC category are no more difficult to detect than instances of the other associative categories. We hypothesized that the low comprehension aphasic group were responding to the task using a pre-conceptual strategy of this kind.

In summary, two principal findings from the off-line study of semantic relatedness judgement by Goodglass and Baker (1976), replicated by Chenery *et al.* (1990) – namely (a) the differential performance of the low comprehension aphasic group, which was consistent with a 'pre-conceptual' processing strategy, and (b) the correlation between the ability to name specific items and to make relatedness judgements on those same items – both pointed to structural, substantive damage to underlying semantic networks or to deficits of lexical semantic processing in the low comprehension aphasics. However, as you may by now have come to expect, a complication emerged with the introduction of on-line behavioural testing paradigms such as CMLP. Findings from automatic lexical priming led many to argue – contrary to the traditional BWL model, and in the face of accepted clinical wisdom – that underlying semantic networks and basic processes of lexical semantic retrieval were *intact* in Wernicke's aphasia. Rather, it was suggested, if there are disruptions to core processes of lexical semantic retrieval in aphasia, then they are to be found not in the so-called 'receptive' aphasias but in aphasias of the Broca's type.

It will take the remainder of this chapter and the two subsequent chapters on syntactic processing and agrammatism to sort out these issues and (hopefully) to restore some coherence to the current picture of the field. So, reader, please bear with us.

## Behavioural on-line measures of lexical access and organization in aphasia

About the same time as off-line experimental evidence of compromised semantic networks in Wernicke's aphasia emerged, other investigators were finding evidence of 'normal' semantic priming in Wernicke's aphasics and other comprehension impaired patients, suggesting, paradoxically, that lexical activation, which was considered the main mechanism of early and automatic lexical retrieval, was intact in these patients (Milberg and Blumstein, 1981; Blumstein, Milberg and Schrier, 1982). Blumstein *et al.* (1982) examined priming or facilitation effects on lexical decisions to auditorally presented words or non-words, preceded by a related/unrelated prime. Their subjects consisted of a mixed diagnostic grouping of aphasic patients (Wernicke, Broca, transcortical, conduction and global) at various levels of auditory comprehension deficit, as assessed by the Boston Diagnostic Aphasia Examination. The subjects were split into high and low comprehension groups for the purpose of assessing the impact of comprehension level upon semantic priming.

There was a significant facilitation effect of a preceding related lexical prime (compared with an unrelated word), which appeared to be present in the responses of both the high and the low comprehension groups, supporting the results of a previous study in which visual stimuli were used (Milberg and Blumstein, 1981). The authors concluded:

> the fact that semantic facilitation occurs in the auditory as well as the visual modality is evidence that the performance of the aphasic subjects reflects the characteristics of the lexical access system independently of modality of word presentation . . . this system of organization seems to be relatively spared, and semantic information appears to be available to the aphasic patient *as long as* no overt semantic manipulation or judgement is required.        (Blumstein *et al.*, 1982: 313)

Thus, a distinction was drawn between volitional (strategic) and automatic mechanisms of semantic processing, which is also close to one of Fodor's (1983) distinguishing properties of a modular processing system, discussed in chapter 3. To wit: automatic activation is fast-acting, occurs without the allocation of attention, and is not under strategic control. In contrast, controlled processing is slow-acting, requires attention and is under the strategic control of the subject.

The claim, then, is that automatic processes of lexical semantic retrieval remain intact in fluent, comprehension impaired aphasia, but the ability to manipulate semantic properties of words is impaired in 'meta-linguistic' tasks which are sensitive to attentional resource allocation and strategic processing. This hypothesis is not simply a modification of the traditional BWL model of comprehension impairment, in order to accommodate findings derived from the on-line lexical decision paradigm, but is in direct conflict with the traditional view, because 'off-line' assessment tasks come to be regarded as tapping into *post-lexical* processing, which lies outside the domain of primary linguistic competence.

Milberg, Blumstein and Dworetzky (1987) and Milberg, Blumstein, Katz, Gershberg and Brown (1995) extended the above hypothesis to claim a **double dissociation** in the lexical comprehension of Wernicke's and Broca's aphasics. Wernicke's aphasics, it was claimed, have preserved automatic lexical semantic processing but impaired strategic processing, whereas Broca's aphasics evince the opposite pattern of impaired automatic but intact strategic processing. Both arms of this double dissociation hypothesis need to be subjected to critical scrutiny. Neither is particularly well supported by available experimental evidence.

## On-line lexical processing in Wernicke's aphasia

Subsequent priming experiments have been generally supportive of Blumstein *et al.*'s (1982) original finding that automatic semantic priming occurs in fluent, comprehension impaired aphasics, when a related prime word is presented before a semantically related probe, at an inter-stimulus interval which is probably too short for strategic effects to operate in brain damaged subjects (ISI < 500 ms). But priming effects in Wernicke's aphasics do not precisely mimic those of normal control subjects. Some investigators report evidence of '**hyper-priming**' in Wernicke's aphasia. For example, Milberg *et al.* (1988a) found that a 'phonetically distorted prime' (differing only on a single distinctive feature of the initial consonant, e.g. *gat* [gæt]) elicited just as strong a semantic priming effect as its 'undistorted' counterpart *cat* [kæt] for a related probe word (*dog*). In the case of normal listeners, such semantic priming effects are either weak (Milberg *et al.*, 1988b) or not found at all (Marslen-Wilson and Zwitserlood, 1989; see also chapter 7). Milberg *et al.* (1988a) ascribed this 'phonetically mediated' hyper-priming in Wernicke's aphasia to impaired phonological discrimination combined with 'normal' spreading semantic activation. However, Gordon and Baum (1994) and Baum (1997) failed to replicate this finding. Baum (1997) also found that her more severely comprehension impaired subjects (classified as clear cases of Wernicke's aphasia rather than anomia) showed *weaker* semantic priming effects than normal controls or a group of Broca's aphasics.

## On-line lexical processing in Broca's aphasia

The experimental evidence on automatic semantic priming in Broca's aphasia is even more equivocal than is the case for Wernicke's aphasia, though for some reason the hypothesis of an impaired mechanism of automatic lexical activation seems to have taken firmer hold in the literature. There are at least three competing theories for a supposed lexical access impairment in Broca's aphasia: the 'slowed activation' model (Prather, Zurif, Stern and Rosen, 1992; Prather, Zurif, Love and Bronwell, 1997), the 'reduced activation' model of Milberg *et al.* (1995), and the 'failed-integration' model of Hagoort (1997), which identifies a failure of post-lexical semantic integration of word meaning with phrasal context.

Direct evidence for the slowed activation model is claimed on the basis of just three single case studies (Swinney *et al.*, 1989; Prather *et al.*, 1992, 1997). Swinney *et al.* (1989) first suggested the idea that lexical access is pathologically slowed in Broca's aphasia as one possible explanation why their Broca's patient showed facilitation only for the dominant and not for the non-dominant meaning of ambiguous words in biasing sentential contexts (e.g. *bug – insect*, but not *bug – spy*). Prather *et al.* (1997) used a *list priming* paradigm in which subjects make lexical decisions to every probe presented in a list of equi-temporally spaced items. Successive items in the list may or may not be semantically related. The idea is to prevent subjects forming expectancies that are much more likely to arise when stimuli are presented as prime–probe pairs. Prather *et al.* (1997) varied the list presentation rate over several steps between ISI 300 and 1500 ms. Normal controls obtained a significant priming effect only at 500 ms. The Broca's aphasic primed at a single ISI of 1500 ms. In a subsequent study also using the list priming paradigm, another Broca's patient showed significant priming at ISI = 1500 and

2100 ms, but not at shorter ISIs, nor at an ISI = 1800 ms (Prather *et al.*, 1997). The single Wernicke's patient included in the second study showed significant priming at ISI = 300, 500, 800, and 1100 ms, but not at ISI 1500+ ms. The authors attempt to draw conclusions about a delayed rise time in 'automatic' priming in Broca's aphasia from these findings. But there is insufficient information about the time course of 'automatic' priming in the normal controls with which to compare the performance of the aphasics.

Also, it is necessary to set against the two list priming experiments the findings from other studies which have obtained lexical facilitation effects at ISIs compatible with automatic semantic priming (Milberg *et al.*, 1995; Tyler *et al.*, 1995; Baum, 1997; Hagoort, 1997). As we cautioned in the previous chapter, it is difficult to separate automatic from strategic (expectation-driven) processing in the standard semantic priming paradigm. However, varying the duration of the ISI and the proportion of related to unrelated primes are two well-established ways of manipulating the influence of strategic processing upon lexical decisions. Milberg *et al.* (1995) used both of these manipulations to assess semantic priming in two groups of aphasics (Broca's and Wernicke's) and two groups of young and older control subjects. The pattern of results was quite complex, but for our purposes it is sufficient to note (a) that the Broca's group (as well as the Wernicke's) showed semantic priming at both the *short* and the long ISI (150 and 2000 ms respectively), and (b) that the Broca's aphasics (along with the normal controls) were influenced by prime–probe predictability, whereas the Wernicke's aphasics were not. The authors argue, though not very convincingly in the face of their significant short ISI priming effect, that Broca's aphasics showed a greater reliance on 'heuristic' strategies than did the young or the old normal controls.

We conclude this review of on-line lexical semantic activation in Broca's aphasia by considering some recent studies that put the case for normal automatic activation of lexical meanings in the first instance, followed by a failure of integrative processes whereby lexical meanings are modified in linguistic context, as discussed in the previous chapter. In short, Hagoort's (1990, 1997) hypothesis that the 'functional locus of [Broca's aphasic] comprehension deficit is at the level of post-lexical integration processes' seems to provide the best fit with currently available on-line and off-line evidence. We can also circumvent some of the limitations of the priming paradigm by making use of developments in functional neuroimaging techniques.

Swaab, Brown and Hagoort (1997) employed ERP and the well-known N400 effect as an index of semantic incongruity processing. They constructed contrasting sets of sentences, in which the last lexical item was congruous or incongruous with sentential context (e.g. '*The little girl dropped her ice-cream on the floor/sky.*') An N400 incongruity effect is to be expected where the last word is semantically or pragmatically incompatible with sentence context. The experimental subjects comprised Broca's and Wernicke's aphasics, divided into high comprehension (mildly impaired, n = 7) and low comprehension (moderately–severely impaired, n = 7) groups, a group of right hemisphere damaged but non-aphasic patients (n = 6), plus a group of normal elderly age-matched controls (n = 12). Subjects were asked to listen carefully to sentences presented over headphones. Their N400 responses to final words in congruous and semantically anomalous contexts were recorded for later comparison. The non-brain damaged control subjects showed the expected N400 effect of incongruity, which had a centro-parietal distribution. Similarly for the right hemisphere damaged patients, a significant N400 effect was observed, though of smaller magnitude than that observed for the non-brain damaged controls. The high comprehension aphasic group also showed a significant N400 effect, which was statistically no different from the normal controls. In the case of the low comprehension group, there was also an evident N400 effect, but it was weaker over the early (300–500 ms) epoch of the N400 response, but rose to comparable strength with that of the high comprehension patient group in the late (500–700 ms) epoch of the N400.

Thus, a delayed onset of the N400 response is what sets the low comprehension aphasic group apart from the high comprehension aphasics, the right hemisphere damaged patients, and the age-matched normal controls. Swaab *et al.* (1997) argue that this result could be due to a delay in integrating the lexical item with its linguistic context, or in other words to a delayed detection and late response to the contextual incongruity. Five of the seven low comprehension subjects in this study were clinically classified as Broca's aphasics. There were only three Wernicke's aphasia patients in the study and site of lesion data were not reported in any detail. So it is not possible to make cross-comparisons between diagnostic category or site of lesion and severity of comprehension impairment from the data of this study.

## Lexical integration in aphasia

We saw that the early psycholinguistic work based on off-line assessment yielded support for the traditional BWL model of preserved lexico-semantic function in anterior (Broca type) aphasics and lexical semantic disorder in posterior (Wernicke type) aphasia. On-line behavioural studies seemed to turn conventional wisdom on its head for a period, but it now appears to be the case that reports of 'normal' lexical activation/access in Wernicke's aphasia and delayed, diminished or disrupted lexical activation in Broca's aphasia were premature. On balance, experimental evidence suggests that a form of relatively 'unlicensed' spreading activation occurs in Wernicke's aphasia in response to lexical stimulation, but that evidence of 'post-lexical' integrative selection and control is absent. Broca's aphasics yield inconsistent evidence of automatic semantic activation, possibly depending on their level of preserved language comprehension. Evidence of delayed lexical integration in Broca's aphasia is suggested by relative strength and time-course of the N400 incongruity effect. So far, only comparatively gross lexical integration effects have been detected by the ERP. Nor has the effect of diagnostic category (Wernicke's vs. Broca's aphasia) been systematically crossed with the severity of comprehension impairment. We might predict an absence of N400 incongruity effects in the case of Wernicke's aphasia.

It is also worth noting that the semantic incongruities registered by the N400 response in Swaab *et al.* (1997) represent rather gross pragmatic/semantic violations that are an order of delicacy removed from some of the subtle contextual modifications of lexical meaning required by a compositional theory of lexical semantics, such as **aspectual coercion**, which we shall now turn to consider.

One of the problems faced by a theory of compositional lexical semantics is that often when words are required to be combined into phrasal meanings, some necessary lexical elements seem to be missing, or need to be inferred. A sentence such as *'John read the book.'* provides no difficulty in this respect, because the verb *read* is standardly assumed to have as part of its lexical representation the semantic selectional information that *read* takes as an object something that is <capable-of-being-read>. The noun *book* clearly meets this requirement, so the two items can be readily merged into a single compositional entity: <read (x), where x = book>. But consider the sentence

(1)        *John began the book.*

The verb *began* requires as its semantic complement some activity and *book* is clearly not an activity. Fully competent language users have no difficulties with sentences such as (1). They readily draw the correct lexical inference that *began* is an elliptical form for *'began to read'* (or possibly *'began to write'*). It is said that they 'coerce' the correct lexical inference. A related form of 'aspectual coercion' can be seen in the contrasting sentences

(2)        *John slept. – John slept for hours.* (non-enriched interpretation)
(3)        *John jumped. – John jumped for hours.* (enriched interpretation)

Notice that the meaning of *sleep* undergoes no change when it is merged with the durative prepositional phrase *'for hours'*. However, *jumped* as a 'point action' verb has no inherent duration, and when it is combined with a durative adverbial expression its meaning must be coerced into an interpretation of 'repeated activity'(Jackendoff, 1997) or, alternatively, 'enriched' with the notion repetition so that the verb is compatible with the on-going nature of the activity implied by the adverbial phrase. Again, competent native speakers perform this inferred change of meaning effortlessly. However, on tests of on-line transient working memory load detection, Piñango, Zurif and Jackendoff (1999) observed a computational cost for the enriched composition operation required for aspectual coercion in normal subjects. This raises the question of whether lexical semantic coercion effects are observed in Broca's and Wernicke's aphasics.

Piñango and Zurif (2001) assessed Broca's and Wernicke's aphasics' interpretation of coerced (enriched composition) sentences and their non-coerced counterparts using a picture-matching task. As would be predicted by the traditional BWL model, the Broca's aphasics performed better overall on the task than the Wernicke's patients. More importantly, the Broca's group performed just as well on the coerced (enriched interpretation) items as the non-enriched interpretation items, indicating that they were capable of performing the contextually triggered lexical inference. However, the Wernicke's subjects performed significantly more poorly on the coerced items, indicating that their fine contextual integration of lexical meaning was impaired. Control subjects performed 'flawlessly' on both types of items.

It may be objected that the experiment did not measure 'on-line' comprehension. On the other hand, on-line behavioural or physiological measures (such as ERP) are probably not yet capable of detecting semantic effects of this delicacy in brain damaged subjects. Further work is clearly called for. In particular, it would be useful to obtain more information on how the factors of severity of comprehension impairment interact with locus of lesion or aphasia type in the assessment of these fine-grained lexical integration effects in sentence processing.

## Category-specific semantic impairment

We turn next to the topic of category-specific semantic impairments in aphasia, which have been the subject of much interest and controversy for the prospective light that they shed on the neural basis of lexical semantic organization. Warrington and McCarthy (1983) reported a case of a patient with a curiously circumscribed semantic disorder, who could name and recognize the relevant semantic attributes of animals, foods and flowers, but not of inanimate objects. This report was followed a year later by another (Warrington and Shallice, 1984), of four patients, all in partial recovery from simplex encephalitis, who had a complementary specific semantic impairment of *retained* knowledge for inanimate objects but an inability to identify living things and foods. Since these two seminal papers, over 100 reports of similar, modular-like lexical semantic disorders have appeared, and a new discipline known as *cognitive neuropsychology* has emerged, with its own distinctive single-case study methodology and perspective of functional modularity on the study of mind (Coltheart, 2002; see also chapter 3). Almost the whole collection of published studies up to 2002 – those that met certain tests of methodological rigour and informativeness – are comprehensively reviewed by Capitani, Laiacona, Mahon and Caramazza (2003).

Before discussing these cases, a brief comment is needed to situate them within the concerns of the present chapter and this book as a whole. Nearly all cases of specific semantic impairment will involve some form of anomia (word finding difficulties), which are a prominent feature of most forms of aphasia. However, the neuropsychological tests used to identify specific semantic impairment are typically off-line, meta-linguistic tasks, aimed at assessing patients' awareness of conceptual relations among everyday objects and concepts, which just happen to be typically instantiated with single words (*boy, telegraph, grasp, hammer,* etc. . . .). They are not tests of language function *per se*. Patients diagnosed with specific semantic impairment are not necessarily aphasic; or rather, they are

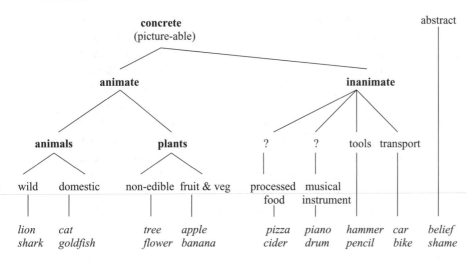

Figure 11.1 *Types and relative incidence of category-specific semantic disorders*

necessarily aphasic only insofar as they suffer from a particular kind of semantic impairment, which may, depending upon other symptoms that they present with, be seen as part of a larger picture of dementia, memory loss or agnosia, of one kind or another.

The starting point for any inquiry into category-specific semantic impairment is, of course, the range and type of different impairments that have been found. How do they cluster with respect to one another and how clearly may various types be distinguished? Descriptors for the various categories of deficit gain mention in the literature with very uneven frequency. From Capitani *et al.*'s (2003) review, we constructed a taxonomy of terms frequently used to describe different semantic impairments (Figure 11.1). The terms are arranged hierarchically into superordinate–subordinate categories with their likely affiliations indicated, . where there is clear guidance from the literature. More frequently mentioned categories are indicated in bold. Care must be exercised when interpreting categories of semantic deficit so identified. The categories of semantic deficit that have been investigated have undoubtedly been influenced by the availability of test material and the categories of deficit previously identified in the literature. Items from the various semantic domains need to be controlled for difficulty level in the target population, who are usually elderly, with a range of educational and occupational backgrounds. Individual interests, and patterns of habitual exposure to particular knowledge domains, are clearly relevant for interpreting profiles of test performance. For example, in the few cases where preservation for abstract objects but impaired recognition for concrete objects has been found, subjects are typically well-educated professionals, accustomed to exercising a high level of abstract verbal expression in their daily employment (Crutch and Warrington, 2003).

A number of theories have been offered to explain category-specific deficits. The *sensory/functional theory* (S/FT) (Warrington and Shallice, 1984) proposes that knowledge of objects is organized by sensory features (e.g. form, motion, colour, taste, etc.) and functional properties (how, when, where the object is typically used). Categories differ as to the importance or weight assigned to each of these properties. Category-specific semantic disorders arise when a brain lesion affects a particular set of properties upon which a given category of objects is particularly dependent for distinguishing among its members. Thus, the topography of where the brain stores different kinds of sensory and functional information about objects and their properties is thought to be responsible for the specific types of semantic deficit which are observed. Although the relevant circuits or 'cell assemblies' (to use a Hebbian expression – see p. 67 above) may be quite widely distributed in the cortex (with conceivable involvement of sub-cortical structures), the S/FT is clearly a localizationist theory of specific category semantic impairment. According to the S/FT the double dissociation that has been observed in the literature between selective semantic deficits for living things or for artefacts (with the incidence running at a ratio of approximately 3:1 in favour of the former type) is attributed to topographically differentiated cortical regions responsible for sensory-feature-based object storage and recognition versus functional-feature-based object storage and recognition.

Opposing the S/FT is the *correlated feature* theory (CFT), a non-localizationist model in which word meanings are stored in a distributed semantic network, the topography of which is determined by the way in which properties of objects are statistically related to one another in the world, rather than by how they are organized in the brain's systems for representing objects of perception or action schema. This theory is also referred to as the organized unitary content hypothesis (OUCH: Caramazza, Hillis, Rapp and Romani, 1990; Capitani *et al.*, 2003). It is closely related to a computational model of semantic memory proposed by McRae, de Sa and Seidenberg (1997), which employs a Hopfield neural network, and which was primarily developed to model automatic semantic priming effects in normal listeners, but which may also be used to model semantic impairments in Alzheimer's patients, including cases of category-specific semantic disorder (Devlin, Gonnerman, Anderson and Seidenberg, 1998). According to the CFT, the greater likelihood of category-specific impairment for animate objects over artefacts (tools, etc.) follows from the fact that animals and other living things are typically dependent for their recognition and discrimination on properties that tend to be highly correlated, whereas tools are identified by functional features that are more sparsely distributed in semantic space and less correlated with one another. While the CFT provides an explanation for the dominant pattern of impaired identification for animate objects, it would seem to have a hard time accounting for the less frequent but attested pattern, where artefacts are more poorly identified than living things – the other arm of the double dissociation in category-specific semantic impairment.

A third type of model for category-specific semantic impairment combines a prototype theory of semantic structure with an evolutionary perspective on brain organization. On this view, the brain has evolved dedicated neural machinery for recognizing and responding rapidly to certain categories of objects that have high survival significance for the individual (e.g. systems for face recognition, predator detection, food identification). These objects are recognized on the basis of prototypes (exemplar matching) rather than feature matching. Category-specific semantic deficits, such as an impairment for fruit and vegetables, would be linked to prototype identification systems that serve specific biological functions (e.g. recognition of edible natural plants). What distinguishes this third class of model from the other two is that it predicts patterns of performance which are knowledge-domain-dependent, in the sense discussed earlier in this chapter with reference to the Goodglass and Baker (1975) study and its replication (Chenery *et al.*, 1990). The domain-dependent (DD) hypothesis of category-specific semantic impairment asserts modularity but not necessarily neural localization of semantic impairments. Support for the DD hypothesis could come in a number of ways. For example, by showing that judgement of an attribute which may apply in different semantic domains can be selectively impaired in one domain but judged accurately in another (e.g. impaired judgements for relative size of animals: *donkey, cow, elephant*; but unimpaired for artefacts: *cup, mug, bowl*). Alternatively, the DD hypothesis may gain support from observing domain-specific impairments that cut across assessment methods and stimulus modalities (such as confrontation naming, attribute judgement, visual or auditory recognition) – see Caramazza and Shelton (1998).

These three theories of category-specific semantic impairment are by no means totally incompatible with one another. They constitute an area of active on-going research. The three models of semantic impairment involve some common issues and may be usefully compared with competing theories of speech perception (phonological form recognition) which we discussed previously in chapters 5–7. Issues in speech perception, such as modularity of processing and the evolution of specialized phonetic detectors for categorical perception of speech sounds (strong version of the 'speech mode hypothesis') vs. learned sensitivity to graded auditory features as the basis of speech sound identification (auditory learning model), have parallels in competing theories of category-specific semantic impairment. Feature-based vs. prototype-based models of object recognition are another obvious parallel question.

## A case study of domain-specific semantic impairment ▬▬▬

To help focus the explanatory issues at stake and to do some justice to the systematic case study approach advocated by cognitive neuropsychologists, we summarize the case of FAV, who presented with an unusual fine-grained selective semantic deficit for the category of fruit and vegetables, embedded within a less severe broad category impairment for living things (Crutch and Warrington, 2003). FAV, a 78-year-old retired businessman, suffered a stroke which left him with an acute episodic memory loss, a visual field deficit (right homonymous hemianopia) and a residual language impairment involving a severe deficit in confrontation naming. The stroke caused extensive damage to the left inferior temporal lobe, extending back into the left primary visual cortex, but sparing the medial and superior gyri and the frontal portion of the left temporal lobe.

On initial neuropsychological assessment, after his condition had stabilized, it was found that FAV's visual object recognition, spatial perception and literacy skills were intact. His 'propositional' speech was 'fluent and the content well expressed, with only occasional episodes of word finding difficulty' (Crutch and Warrington, 2003: 358). He suffered a severe deficit for picture naming in general, most pronounced in the area of colour names and animal names. But, remarkably, he retained a facility for naming verbs. On frequency-matched sets, he was able to name 39/40 verbs but only 24/40 picturable nouns.

One year later, FAV was still described as 'gravely anomic' on tests of confrontation naming. His comprehension at the sentence level was 'entirely satisfactory'. In sharp contrast with his poor naming skills, he 'performed at a very high level on a graded two-choice synonym test for both concrete and abstract nouns'. The selective preservation of certain lexical semantic domains was still apparent. 'He obtained a very satisfactory score on a word-picture matching test that probed abstract and emotional words in addition to concrete words' (Crutch and Warrington, 2003: 360).[4]

The authors conducted a test to see if FAV's confrontation naming deficit was modality-specific, by comparing his ability to name pictures with his ability to name items from spoken 'dictionary definitions' (e.g. *'What do we call the heavy lockable metal box used for keeping valuable goods?': safe*). FAV scored approximately 50 per cent correct, regardless of whether the names were elicited from definitions or picture presentation. Hence, we appear to be dealing with an amodal semantic deficit, rather than some kind of visual perceptual impairment, consistent with earlier testing indicating intact visual-spatial perception.

Next, Crutch and Warrington (2003) focused on FAV's category-specific semantic impairment, testing with items matched for difficulty from three distinct domains: artefacts, flora and fauna. The items were tested through picture naming, and a semantic probe task, which was delivered in two modes: visually (via depiction of the object) and aurally (spoken presentation). The probe task involved either attribute or associative knowledge (e.g. ***apple*** *:* _pips_, *stone, segments*; ***ostrich*** *:* _walk_, *swim, fly*). Naming was poor for flora and fauna (18 per cent correct) but only mildly impaired for artefacts (73 per cent correct). On the semantic probe test of comprehension FAV scored close to ceiling for artefacts and fauna (95–98 per cent correct) but was significantly impaired on flora (63–70 per cent correct). Pictorial or spoken mode of item presentation yielded the same pattern of performance. Thus, the domain of FAV's naming impairment appeared

---

[4] The apparent asymmetry of intact performance going from (read) 'concrete words' to picture identification on the one hand but impaired naming of depicted concrete objects on the other is interesting, but not commented on by the authors.

to be more extensive than his performance deficit on the semantic probe task, which was more narrowly confined to plants.

Further semantic probe testing was undertaken with three new sets of items matched for word frequency and familiarity: animals, fruits and vegetables, and foods. The aim was to explore the subcategories of plant life more closely by introducing a distinction between edible plants and processed (non-living) food. A more elaborate probe test with items at three levels of difficulty was constructed, delivered in written mode. The new items were also tested via picture naming. For this set of items, FAV's confrontation naming was very poor across the board, with scores of no more than 1/20 in each category. Performance on the semantic probe task was equally high for animals and (non-living) food items (average = 87 per cent correct for both categories), but poor for fruit and vegetable items (58 per cent correct; chance performance = 33 per cent).

To summarize the findings from the test series: FAV has severe global anomia for naming from pictures, except in the case of verbs. This is combined with an amodal semantic deficit for plants in general and edible plants (fruit and vegetables) in particular. The semantic deficit for edible plants did not apparently extend to processed foods. What are we to make of this rather unusual but not unprecedented case of fine-grained semantic impairment for the category of fruit and vegetables? None of the three theories advanced earlier seems to provide an entirely satisfactory account of the semantic impairment.

## Explaining patterns of category-specific semantic impairment

A semantic deficit for fruit and vegetables, which does not extend to other foodstuffs, is interesting from the evolutionary perspective of the DD (domain-dependent) theory. The 'MacDonald's era' has hardly been with us long enough to register an evolutionary adaptation upon our food-foraging conceptual categories. But it is interesting to note that many languages in hunter-gatherer societies have separate lexical categories to distinguish plant food from flesh food. The distinction is ubiquitous among the aboriginal languages of Australia (Dixon, 1980).

However, turning to the S/FT model, fruit and vegetables as a perceptual/conceptual category may share a critically sufficient number of common sensory properties (taste, texture and appearance – as the supermarket ads promote) to form a natural semantic grouping. Selective damage to the neural substrate that serves fruit and vegetable recognition could lie at the basis of the category impairment. If such a basis could be convincingly demonstrated – say through neural imaging investigations of active areas of normal shoppers' brains as they browse a virtual supermarket – then we might obtain confirmation for the S/FT model of this highly specific semantic category impairment.

But if your semantic memory for consumable objects really *is* organized in a distributed (Hopfield) neural network on the basis of correlated features (according to the CFT), then it is quite conceivable that a low level of corruption in the network might create some local chaos in the fruit and vegetable department, while the canned peas and pickled onions remain undisturbed on their respective shelves some aisles away. The point is that a well-trained neural network will organize its basins of attraction so that they reproduce the topographic organization of products in the supermarket.[5] Localized product mix-ups (category-specific semantic disorders) are not strange phenomena in such a model. But what is unusual, or requires special consideration, is why the disruption should consistently occur around a particular basin of attraction. The answer would appear to lie in the impaired operation of particular features, or the selective scrambling of one feature or a small number of features that are critically important for distinguishing a category of objects. These effects can be simulated. But to explain why certain category-specific semantic disorders occur and why others are not observed probably requires an appeal to factors that are extrinsic to the network, such as the neural substructure of the brain's sensory and memory systems.

## Summary

Until quite recently the majority of studies of lexical semantic disorder in aphasia have attended to the properties of single words, their activation and retrieval. Little attention has been paid to the integration of primary word meanings into linguistic context, which is a central issue for a compositional semantics and a model of sentence processing. The early off-line investigations of lexical semantic function in aphasia provided initial experimental support for the traditional BWL model associating impaired lexical semantic operations with Wernicke's aphasia and essentially intact lexical semantic function in patients that presented with an anterior speech and language pathology. On-line investigations, primarily based on automatic semantic priming, have been widely interpreted as providing evidence that undermines the traditional picture, some even claiming that 'double dissociation' between on-line (automatic) and off-line (judgement-mediated, strategy-based) is to be found in Broca's and Wernicke's aphasia. We have argued that a critical scrutiny of the on-line evidence does not support overturning the traditional model.

Studies of category-specific semantic impairment continue to be the area where language pathology can make its most distinctive contribution towards the development of a neurolinguistic model of lexical semantics of the single word. However, the sometimes strikingly domain-limited nature of lexical semantic

---

[5] Setting aside considerations such as the location of refrigeration plant, ease of restocking, and theft protection, supermarket product layout is undoubtedly highly influenced by considerations of semantic similarities among its products and the need to locate competitors near to one another.

impairments does not lead us to a highly modular or localizationist model of lexical semantic organization. This is most clearly demonstrated by the ability of distributed artificial networks to model both levels of overall function and domain specificity in lexical semantic disorders. However, the full range of attested categories of disorder cannot be easily accounted for by a distributed model of semantic representation based solely on feature correlations. Some appeal to the neural substrate of perceptual and conceptual categories is needed.

# PART IV

# Sentence comprehension

# 12    Sentence comprehension and syntactic parsing

## Introduction

In this chapter we discuss the role of syntactic processing in sentence comprehension. As elsewhere in this book, we will approach this question from a dual perspective. Firstly, we shall examine the sentence comprehension strategies of people who, as a result of brain injury, appear to have lost their facility to utilize the grammatical rules of their language, and suffer a condition known as **agrammatism**. This is roughly equivalent to posing the (perhaps somewhat naive) question: if one loses one's syntax, what are the consequences for sentence comprehension? In exploring this question, we shall review the first generation of psycholinguistic investigations into a core topic of aphasia research and set the stage for contemporary inquiries employing sophisticated on-line behavioural and neuroimaging techniques.

The second major theme of the present chapter concerns the processing of syntactically ambiguous and 'garden path' sentences by perfectly fluent native listeners. Sentences which can be syntactically read or 'parsed' more than one way, or which initially lead us 'up the garden path' towards a misconstrual that we are subsequently forced to re-analyse, have the potential to tell us much about how the human parser works. We shall introduce both of these major themes of the aphasic and psycholinguistic literature informally in this chapter, through appeal to your linguistic intuitions as native speakers of English, leaving it to the subsequent chapter to deal with methodological issues of 'on-line' processing and how we might infer the mental and neural operations that take place in apparent real time when we understand spoken language.

But before either of these themes can be taken up, some preliminary clarification is required, regarding the relationship between a *linguist's* formal grammar of a language, and a *speaker's* 'internal' grammar used in parsing and sentence comprehension. Some clarification is also needed on the related question of how performing a derivation on a sentence in a formal grammar relates to 'parsing a sentence' by a listener in the course of language processing. We adopt with some qualification Chomsky's dictum that a formal grammar is an abstract representation of a speaker's tacit knowledge of his/her language. We accept also, and have argued previously (chapter 2) for, a degree of autonomy of syntax, which permits us to judge the grammaticality of a sentence as distinct from its meaning.

However, as will become clear from forthcoming discussion and examples, the syntactic structures that our proposed parser assigns to sentences differ in potentially important details from those of recent minimalist versions of generative grammar (GG). Even if the grammatical structures produced by our parser were identical with those assigned by a minimalist grammar, or some other linguist's grammar, 'parsing a sentence' and 'performing a derivation' are probably best regarded as operations distinct in kind, because, as we saw in chapter 4, following Chomsky and Miller (1963), linguistic performance and competence are two different things. But these are tricky matters on which writers more profound than we are apt to disagree.

## Syntactic processing and sentence comprehension

Narrowly defined, syntactic processing involves the assignment of syntactic structure to word strings that qualify as 'sentences'. There are basically two situations in which we engage in syntactic processing. First, and most relevant for our concerns, whenever we comprehend spoken or written language we inevitably undertake some level of syntactic processing. How much is a matter of debate, and may in fact vary with the context and type of communication. Secondly, we engage in syntactic processing when we make grammaticality judgements (i.e. decide whether a sentence is well-formed or not). Judging grammaticalness is not something that we normally consciously undertake, except at the behest of a linguist or a speech pathologist. But it might be something that we implicitly do whenever we process language. As pointed out in chapter 2, native speakers are quick to detect lapses in grammaticality, or grammatical features that signal style shifting, dialect variation or 'nonstandard' usage in conversation. This ability to make grammaticality judgements may be thought of as a by-product of linguistic competence or tacit knowledge of the rules of the language. Linguists rely on grammaticality judgements of native informants to formulate grammars of particular languages. Speech pathologists often use them to assess an aphasic's level of retained grammatical function.

The process of assigning syntactic structure to a string of written words or to an utterance is technically known as syntactic parsing. A device which assigns grammatical descriptions to sentences is called a parser. These terms are most often used in the context of natural language processing by computers, aimed at text understanding for various kinds of human–computer interaction, ranging from database inquiry systems to machine translation.

Syntactic parsing is a multistage operation involving word recognition, the retrieval of syntactic information from lexical entries, and the merging of this information with that of other words retrieved from the immediately surrounding context. It is precisely how this merging operation works and the nature of the syntactic representations which it constructs that are the central issues in theories of syntactic parsing.

## The grammar and the parser

A grammar is an explicit set of rules for distinguishing the well-formed sentences of a language from those that are ill-formed (ungrammatical). A generative grammar (GG) accomplishes this task by assigning structural descriptions to grammatically well-formed sentences of the language. This is known as performing a derivation. The grammar cannot assign structural descriptions to ungrammatical sentences. Such sentences will 'crash' in the course of a derivation because they violate some rule of the grammar or fail to meet some constraint on well-formedness. How then should we conceive the relationship between a GG and parser employed in a model of sentence processing?

In processing spoken language, we probably parse sentences from left to right, as words are recognized in roughly the linear order that they come to us from the speech stream. It also seems natural to assume that language comprehension operates basically in a bottom-up fashion, as lexical retrieval provides the parser with the initial information to begin the building operation and successive lexical retrievals yield further information bearing mainly on the lower levels of phrase structure, for merging local constituents such as morphemes and words into minor phrases.

By contrast, in the classical transformational model of GG, rewrite rules assign phrase structure top-down and lexical items are subsequently 'inserted' into the terminal nodes of phrase structure trees. A clear, perhaps misleadingly clear, distinction was encouraged between the operations of *parsing* from bottom up and *derivation* from top down. However, in the recent minimalist version of GG, structure assignment begins with lexical retrieval and proceeds bottom up and *right to left*, making use of operations such as 'merge', 'feature checking', 'trace formation' and 'movement'. Thus a minimalist derivation seems quite similar to our intuitive account of parsing spoken sentences in the previous paragraph, except that it proceeds right to left, and involves a good deal of trace-forming constituent movement over binary trees that appear very different from the familiar constituent structures of traditional linguistic description. Contrasting accounts of left-to-right parsing of a simple sentence and performing a derivation of the same sentence in accordance with the minimalist model of GG are shown in Figures 12.1 and 12.2.

Our informal account of parsing the simple sentence '*A cat is on the couch*' (Figure 12.1) begins with lexical retrieval of the first word *a*, which informs the parser that we are dealing with a [determiner] that agrees in [number] with a head [noun] that is to follow, but not necessarily as the next word. A 'seek' operation (like the setting of a flag) is triggered by information contained in the lexical representation of *a*. As soon as the next word *cat* is recognized and its grammatical features are retrieved, it is apparent that the conditions of the previous 'seek' operation are satisfied. Namely, a [noun] inflected for <singular> [number][1] has

---

[1] Square brackets [ ] are used for syntactic features when they have no semantic content or are simply acting to satisfy syntactic requirements. Angle brackets < > signify features that contribute materially towards semantic interpretation.

| **Trace of parse** | **Parsing Operation(s)** |
|---|---|

[DETERMINER]
<INDEFINITE>
<NUMBER>

1.  *A ...*                                                          Lexical Access and Feature Retrieval (LAFR)


[DETERMINER] ==> [NOUN, ADJ. or ...]        Seek NOUN right
<INDEFINITE>
[NUMBER]   ==> <SINGULAR>                    Seek number agreement
  *A ...*


[DET.] => [NOUN ...]        [NOUN]
<IND.>
[NUM.] => <SING.>           <SING.>           LAFR
2.  *A*                        *cat*    ...


          **NP**
[DET.]    [NOUN]
<IND.>
          <SING.>                              Merge to create NP (or DP)
3.  *A*        *cat*    ...


          NP          ==> [VERB]              Seek predicate (tensed verb) right
[DET.]    [NOUN]        [TENSE]
<IND.>
          <SING.>
4.  *A*        *cat*    ...


          NP          ==> [VERB]    [VERB]
[DET.]    [NOUN]        [TENSE]  <PRESENT>
<IND.>                          [COPULA]       LAFR
          <SING.>
5.  *A*        *cat*                  *is ...*


                    **S**
                    **VP**                     Merge to create subject and part of predicate
          NP          [VERB]
[DET.]    [NOUN]      <PRES.>
<IND.>               [COP]
          <SING.>
6.  *A*        *cat*      *is ...*


                    **S**
                    **VP**
          NP          [VERB]
[DET.]    [NOUN]      <PRES.>
<IND.>               [COP]    ==> [NP, PP, or ...]   Seek complement phrase for verb
          <SING.>
7.  *A*        *cat*      *is ...*

Figure 12.1 *Partial parsing of* A cat is on the couch

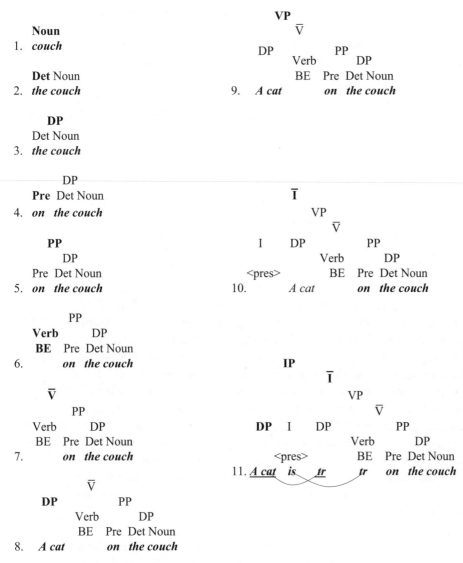

Figure 12.2 *Minimalist derivation of* A cat is on the couch

been retrieved. The 'seek' operation, being satisfied, triggers a 'merge' of the determiner and noun to form a noun phrase (NP, or 'determiner phrase' DP to use current terminology). Having built an NP in sentence initial position, the parser 'knows' from the grammar of English that this NP is likely to play the role of [subject], in which case a [predicate], most probably instantiated by a [verb] bearing [tense], is likely to follow. So a 'seek' for a tensed verb is initiated. Lexical retrieval of the next word *is* happens to satisfy the predicate seek and a partial subject–predicate construction is built with a merge operation. At the same time, the grammatical feature [copula] of the inflected verb *is* triggers a seek for a complement phrase, which could be a noun phrase, a prepositional phrase or perhaps an adjective.

This example is incomplete and somewhat oversimplified. Not all relevant features of a parse have been identified. Thematic roles need to be assigned to role-bearing constituents, like nouns. Seek operations can be established for this purpose too. A constituent may have to 'wait' or remain 'on hold' for some time until its 'seek' requirement is satisfied, as in the case of 'front shifted' wh-words in questions such as

*What did you see on the couch?*

Here, the thematic role of the wh-word must be kept 'on hold' until the lexical contents of the verb *see* can be retrieved. As we discuss later, such hold operations place a temporary memory impost upon the parser.

The minimalist derivation for the same sentence, shown in Figure 12.2, has the counterintuitive property of building its syntactic structure leftward from the last word of the sentence, perhaps implying that as a model of parsing, syntactic analysis is postponed and the preceding words are held in a temporary buffer until the end of the phrase is detected. Of course, in a competence model this awkward property of right-to-left structure building may be regarded as irrelevant. A competence grammar is not a model of sentence processing (or production for that matter). Nevertheless, it could be countered that right-to-left parsing constitutes a less than optimal interface with phonetic form (PF).[2]

Two movement operations occur in the course of deriving the sentence in 12.2: (a) the leftward movement of the copula verb to the inflection (I) node and (b) the movement of the subject NP *the cat* from its position internal to the VP (verb phrase) to an external position as specifier of the IP (inflectional phrase). From the perspective of syntactic parsing, these two movement operations seem to be quite vacuous, or a needless complication. However, both have their justification within the minimalist model. Deriving the subject DP *the cat* as specifier of the verb phrase and subsequently 'raising' it to specifier of the IP, known as 'the VP internal hypothesis', has won widespread acceptance in minimalist circles. The arguments are quite diverse (see Radford, 1997). They range from (a) providing an easy formal account of the identity of meaning between '*A cat is on the mat*' and '*There is a cat on the mat*', through (b) providing a local account of thematic role assignment and (c) a simpler account of 'stranded' quantifier expressions such as '*The cats were **both** on the couch*', to (d) an account of the behaviour of certain phrasal idioms such as '*all hell . . . breaks loose*'.

In view of the arguments, which we cannot go into here, why not simply adopt the minimalist account of phrase structure and cut the parser to suit the grammar? Our reluctance to adopt the minimalist account of phrase structure, with its binary

---

[2] An ideal or simple interface with PF and logical form (LF) is regarded as the ultimate design pressure motivating properties of UG (universal grammar). Although we do not always have a clear notion of what the perceptual or motor (input or output) constraints on a UG parser might be, the sequential ordering of the parsing operation would seem to be a reasonable candidate.

branching trees, is not simply that they represent a 'work in progress',[3] but that they depart quite radically from notions of phrase structure based upon traditional constituent structure analysis.

Ultimately, the discrepancy between the traditional notion of syntactic phrase structure adopted here and the minimalist theory of phrase structure will need to be resolved. However, nothing crucial in the following discussion of syntactic parsing in sentence comprehension hinges on this issue. So we will conceive of syntactic structure as synonymous with the 'surface' syntactic structures that most linguists would clearly recognize and justify in terms of distributional patterning in the language. That said, let us now return to the topic at hand – what role does syntactic parsing play in sentence comprehension? – and characterize the two main competing theories that have been put forward as answers to this question.

Syntactic parsing yields an intermediate representation, which serves as a platform for further inference towards a semantic interpretation of the input string. Not all computational schemes of natural language processing have adopted a two-stage model, with syntax functioning as a level of linguistic representation that mediates between word strings and sentential meanings (see Schank, 1975). But this is the model, derived from linguistics, which we shall offer as the initial default, partly for historical reasons.

## Competing models of sentence processing

How a computer parses sentences may of course be quite different from how the human parser accomplishes the task. It has been instructive and salutary to try to program a computer to parse natural language input, engendering, if nothing else, a healthy respect for the complexity and precision of the human parsing mechanism. Increasingly, psycholinguistic models of grammatical processing are cast as computer simulations and not simply as black-box diagrams, thereby imposing new levels of rigour on the formulation and testing of such models.

In this chapter, we will be concerned to choose between competing accounts of the role of syntactic processing in sentence comprehension. As a first approximation, we will pose just two alternatives: a 'traditional' modular approach to sentence comprehension which derives basically from linguistic theory of the 1960s–1980s (generative grammar in particular), and an interactive model of language processing which has gained favour over the past two decades. According to the modular theory, syntactic parsing is the responsibility of a separate component of the mental grammar. Assigning syntactic structure to sentences is based

---

[3] In recent years there has been a proliferation of abstract functional categories for which distributional evidence is lacking. In the traditional notion of constituent structure, lexical categories form the heads of phrasal categories which enter into syntagmatic relations with functional items (closed class words and inflectional clitics). Thus the number of phrasal categories is quite restricted and the contrasting distributional properties of lexical and function words provide statistical patterns of sufficient clarity in large language corpora for a stochastic analyser to be able to detect and recognize.

on a set of autonomous phrase structure building rules. Subsequently, this view came under challenge from an interactive theory of language processing, developed largely within psycholinguistics (Crain and Steedman, 1985; MacWhinney, 1987; Marslen-Wilson and Tyler, 1987; MacDonald, Pearlmutter and Seidenberg, 1994). According to the interactive theory, all the constraints which are brought to bear in assigning meaning to sentences operate simultaneously – or in parallel. There are no clearly distinct stages, with syntax assigned first and semantic interpretation afterwards, or with one syntactic hypothesis at a time being considered and accepted or rejected before an alternative analysis is considered. According to the modular theory, lexical access and syntactic structure assignment are quite distinct operations and rely upon distinct mental or brain resources. Interactionists hold an opposing view; that lexical and syntactic processing are very similar operations, governed by the same processing considerations.

## Asyntactic sentence comprehension: the case of agrammatism

Our approach to this vexed question of the role of syntactic processing in sentence comprehension will be to begin by examining some crucial cases where syntactic cues may be expected to play a key role in comprehension and to ask what consequences would be expected to follow from a selective 'blindness' or lack of access to the structural information contained in such sentences; in effect, testing a theory of agrammatism proposed in the 1970s (Caplan, 1987), based upon a notion of compensatory processing strategies that agrammatic aphasics may be expected to adopt in the face of a selective loss of grammatical competence. We shall then question the assumptions of this modular account of sentence processing, and attempt to evaluate the competing theories of syntax in sentence processing that have subsequently developed. We note at the outset that over this period (the 1970s to the present day) there have been substantial developments in the technology of on-line sentence comprehension methodologies and most recently in neural imaging. We appear to be on the threshold of being able to test architectural proposals for language processing that have hitherto eluded experimental scrutiny. However, we defer discussion of these techniques to the next chapter. Here we are content to lay out the major issues which are at stake, relying upon your linguistic intuitions and some of the classical psycholinguistic findings from off-line experiments in sentence comprehension.

### Thematic role assignment and sentence comprehension

For the kinds of sentences that grace the table at psycholinguistic dinner parties, being able to indicate 'who-did-what-to-whom', otherwise more respectably known as *thematic role assignment* (recall discussion in chapter 3), constitutes a rough working criterion or test of sentence comprehension. In the course of normal conversation, comprehension is demonstrated by an appropriate verbal response ('Is *that* so? . . . *Surely* he didn't? . . .), or in the case of testing the communicatively impaired, by pointing to an appropriate depiction of the verbalized event, or by 'acting out' the sentence meaning with toys or props.

Everyone acknowledges that *pragmatics* (world knowledge and expectations) play a crucial role in sentence comprehension. For example, in sentence (1) below, there are multiple cues, syntactic and extra-grammatical, to guide the listener in assigning thematic roles as arguments of the verb *arrest*:

(1)       *The cop arrested the teenagers.*

Pragmatic knowledge (the plausibility effect) informs us that it is *cops* who typically do the arresting and *teenagers* who are likely to be the arrestees, though it may be legally possible for a teenager to effect a citizen's arrest, as in

(2)       *The teenager arrested the cops.*

Normal listeners have no difficulty understanding implausible sentences like (2) above. Syntactic information normally overrides pragmatic expectations to derive the correct reading. Recall discussion in chapter 3 of the relation between syntax and semantic or pragmatic well-formedness. How an agrammatic aphasic would construe sentence (2) probably depends upon the severity of their language disorder.

Consider the relevant grammatical cues: (a) word order and (b) inflection. Word order in relation to the verb identifies *the teenager* as subject and *the cops* as object of the verb in (2). Inflection, in the form of the third person singular present tense subject agreement marker (3psp: -*s*), also helps identify *the teenager* as subject of *arrests*. These syntactic roles of subject and object serve as sites or 'place holders' for locating thematic roles (*agent/actor* and *patient/experiencer*) as arguments of the verb *arrest*. An agrammatic listener is more likely to overlook the agreement marker *s*, which links the singular, third person subject *the teenager* to the present tense form of the verb *arrest* than s/he would be to miss the plural marking *s* on the object NP *the cops*. All but the most severe agrammatic aphasics have been found to be sensitive to the canonical word order of their language (SVO in English), which would promote the correct reading of (2) above. But because their grasp of syntactic relations is insecure, the agrammatic may be unable to override pragmatic expectations.

## Reversible passive constructions

Sentences in which subject and object NPs can equally plausibly fill the thematic roles of agent and experiencer/recipient are known as *reversible* constructions. Such sentences, like (3) and (4) below, oblige listeners to pay attention to syntactic cues in order to successfully assign thematic roles.

(3)       *The dancer applauded the actor.*
(4)       *The actor applauded the dancers.*

Experiments with sentences like these showed that Broca's aphasics were sensitive to canonical word order, when tested on a picture matching task or an acting-out task. Schwartz *et al.* (1980) found that their aphasic group achieved a success rate of about 75 per cent for reversible active sentences. But where canonical word order was violated in a *passive construction* such as

(5)      *The actor was applauded by the dancers.*

performance was at chance level for correctly indicating who applauded whom.

In passive sentences, thematic relations do not follow canonical word order.[4] We might argue, as David Caplan (1987) has done, that agrammatic patients fail on reversible passive constructions because they rely on a heuristic, based on canonical word order, in which the NP that precedes the verb is assigned the thematic role of agent.

The notion that aphasic patients rely upon simplified parsing strategies or heuristics which work most of the time is an appealing one. It suggests that agrammatics retreat to a more primitive level of sentence processing, comparable to that of the immature language learner. This is an old idea. As we have noted previously (chapter 3), Roman Jakobson in a famous monograph 'Child language, aphasia, and phonological universals' (1941 [Eng. trans. 1968]) suggested that language breakdown in aphasia constitutes regression to an earlier stage of language acquisition. It makes sense that if some linguistic competence has been lost owing to damage to the language areas of the brain, then relearning will involve retracing steps of language acquisition. However, we have seen that crucial differences between the brain states of young first language learners and aphasics in recovery require us to be very cautious about drawing strong parallels between these two populations. Similarly, parsing heuristics based on simple, canonical, sentence patterns, which have been invoked to explain young children's processing of complex sentences, may not stand close scrutiny when applied to aphasic comprehension frailties.

For example, it has been pointed out (Grodzinsky, 1986) that if agrammatics paid attention only to canonical word order in processing reversible passive constructions such as (5) above, discarding other morpho-syntactic cues, and treating the sentence in effect as an ordered string, such as (6) below, then we would expect not a 50 per cent or chance-level correct assignment of thematic roles, but a 100 per cent error rate.

(6)        xxx **actor** xxx **applaud**xx xx xxx **dancer**x.

However, this prediction does not fit the findings. But if we assume some sensitivity to morpho-syntactic cues, in line with other studies (Friederici, 1982, 1983; Grodzinsky, 1984) which suggest differential preservation of function words and

---

[4] In a *passive* sentence, a thematic role other than the *agent* gets promoted to sentence initial position as the focused constituent, e.g.: '*A pedestrian was run down by a car.*' Here the focus is on *the pedestrian*, not *the car*, and hence the passive is the expected form to be used in reporting this type of event.

morphemes that carry significant semantic content, then we obtain a richer internal representation for (6), something like (7) below:

(7)            xxx **actor** xxx **applaud**xx *by* xxx **dancer**s.

Assuming further that the preposition *by* signals an agentive thematic role for *dancers* and that the listener also relies on the heuristic that the first NP (the subject) signals the thematic role of agent, then we have conflicting signals for thematic role assignment, and the 50 per cent correct response rate can be attributed to 'just guessing'.

You may wonder why an aphasic would cling to an unreliable heuristic when the by-phrase, which is a reliable thematic role indicator, is present in the passive sentence. A plausible answer is that the aphasic listener fails to recognize that canonical word order is suspended in the passive construction. The overt cue for this suspension of canonical word order for the assignment of thematic roles lies in the passive morphology of the verb phrase (***was** applauded*), a cue to which agrammatics are probably insensitive.

Two tentative conclusions seem to follow from the foregoing discussion. The first is that heuristics are of potential explanatory value in accounting for agrammatic comprehension performance if one is prepared to make explicit assumptions about precisely what syntactic cues the listener has access to in sentence processing. The second point to be made is that any heuristic which is postulated needs to be well motivated in terms of the language concerned. It needs to work well for the processing of simple sentences, most of the time. Sentence types which constitute exceptions to the operation of a heuristic need to be explicitly signalled by morphological or syntactic cues so that heuristics can be overridden or suspended in the course of parsing by fully competent language users.

## Canonical word order and thematic relations in complex sentences

Grammatically well-formed sentences that involve departures from canonical word order, which derail simple parsing heuristics, usually have their origin in two sources: (a) *ellipsis* in the course of complex sentence construction, and (b) the use of specific syntactic structures for special discourse effects, such as *topicalization*, as illustrated in the cleft subject and cleft object constructions, (8) and (9) below:

(8)        *It was the monkey that chased the frog.*        Cleft subject
(9)        *It was the frog that the monkey chased.*        Cleft object
(10)       *The monkey chased the frog.*                    Simple, uncleft

Both (8) and (9) above are commonly regarded by grammarians as being 'derived from' the simple declarative (10), by focusing on either the subject (*monkey*) or the object (*frog*) respectively.

Which of the two cleft constructions poses most difficulty for agrammatic aphasics in acting-out the thematic roles? Caplan and Futter (1986) found that their agrammatic subject acted out the subject cleft construction ((8) above) correctly six times out of six, but the object cleft construction only twice in six presentations. They took this as support for the thematic role heuristic based on canonical word order (*monkey-chase-frog* vs. *frog-monkey-chase*).[5]

### Strategies for processing complex sentences

Complex sentences which involve clausal co-ordination or subordination pose problems for sentence processors that use heuristics based upon the structures of simple sentences. The major reason for this difficulty is that complex sentences may involve ellipsis, the systematic omission of thematic role-bearing elements. Ellipsis produces systematic departures from canonical word order, as can be seen in the following *compound clause* and *relative clause constructions* (11–15), where the elided NPs are indicated by gaps (. . .).

| (11) | *The elephant hit the rabbit and hugged the bear.* | $NP_1$ V $NP_2$ . . . V $NP_3$ |
| (12) | *The elephant that hit the rabbit hugged the bear.* | $NP_1$ V $NP_2$ . . . V $NP_3$ |
| (13) | *The elephant hit the rabbit that hugged the bear.* | $NP_1$ V $NP_2$ . . . V $NP_3$ |
| (14) | *The elephant that the rabbit hit hugged the bear.* | $NP_1$ $NP_2$ V . . . V $NP_3$ |
| (15) | *The elephant hit the rabbit that the bear chased.* | $NP_1$ V $NP_2$ $NP_3$ V . . . |

Ellipsis serves to make linguistic expressions more economical, but it complicates their interpretation because only the thematic roles of the main clause (or the first clause in the case of co-ordinated clauses) gain full expression. Some thematic role-bearing elements in subordinated or co-ordinated clauses are elided. However, for full semantic interpretation of the sentence, all of the thematic role-bearing arguments of each verb need to be assigned.

The elided thematic role-bearing constituents do not pose difficulties for fully competent language users. The grammar of the language (quite possibly supported by universal syntactic constraints) ensures that these elided constituents are recoverable in sentence interpretation. We shall discuss the recoverability of these *trace* elements later, when dealing with on-line processing of complex sentences (see chapter 13). However, for language users who do not have access to the full syntactic processing resources of their language, and who consequently rely on heuristics based on syntactic patterns of simple sentences, the complex sentences (11–15) pose problems. When asked to act out these complex sentences, Caplan and Futter's agrammatic patient (S.P.) did not do very well at all. On the compound sentence (11), she correctly acted out the elephant first hitting the

---

[5] Note that the problem for thematic role assignment created by the cleft-object construction is different here from the case of the passive construction discussed previously, where we had two competing cues for agent role assignment, one based on canonical word order (NVN). In the case of the cleft-object construction, canonical word order does not seem to apply (NNV). So, there is some doubt as to whether both cases can be seen as support for the same parsing heuristic.

rabbit and then hugging the bear on 6/10 trials. She performed similarly poorly at chance level on the relative clause constructions in sentences (12) and (13).

Her responses were quite consistent across these three sentence types. The first NP (*elephant*) was invariably chosen as the agent of the action of the first verb. The recipient of that action was the second NP (*rabbit*) and the NP following the second verb (*bear*) was consistently selected as the recipient of the action of that verb. Where the patient's responses appeared to be random, and the source of all her errors in thematic role assignment, was in the choice of NP to fill the role of agent for the second verb (*hugged*).

Apparently, S.P. employed the same (inappropriate) heuristic for all three complex sentences that conformed to the sequential pattern N1–V1–N2–V2–N3, failing to respond to the structural cues (such as the conjunction *and* or the complementizer *that*) that would enable her to recognize the elided constituents (traces) in conjoined and relative clauses. These traces and their anaphoric links are explicitly indicated in (16–20) below:

(16)     The elephant$_1$ hit the rabbit and [t$_1$] hugged the bear.
(17)     The elephant$_1$ that [t$_1$] hit the rabbit hugged the bear.
(18)     The elephant hit the rabbit$_1$ that [t$_1$] hugged the bear.
(19)     The elephant$_1$ that the rabbit hit [t$_1$] hugged the bear.
(20)     The elephant hit the rabbit$_1$ that the bear chased [t$_1$].

For the relative clauses in (14) and (15) (19 and 20) where the sequence of nominal and verbal elements were N1–N2–V1–V2–N3 and N1–V1–N2–N3–V2 respectively, S.P.'s responses also showed evidence of a simplified thematic role assignment strategy. For sentence (14) (19, the object relative clause), the only thematic role which she consistently acted out was that of recipient of V2 (*hugged the bear*). For sentence (15) (20, another object relative), the agent and recipient roles for V1 were consistently and correctly assigned (*elephant hit rabbit*), but those for V2 indicated guessing.

## Summary: grammatical heuristics and agrammatism

These findings are quite representative of Broca's aphasics' apparently poor abilities to process complex sentences for thematic role assignment. They appear to rely on simplified heuristics based on the canonical word order of simple declarative sentences. It is tempting to conclude that there is a substantial failure in the parsing mechanism, so that agrammatics cannot construct highly articulated, multiple-clause syntactic structures that support semantic interpretation. This is substantially the picture which emerged from psycholinguistic research of the 1960s to the early 1980s, using off-line language assessment procedures. Researchers thought that they had solid evidence for a modular syntactic deficit, which they labelled with the traditional term 'agrammatism', whose consequences were a severe but selective impairment of language comprehension, under the right conditions: namely, when pragmatic inferences are controlled for by careful selection of the stimulus materials so that subjects are forced to rely on syntactic cues to work out 'who did what to whom'.

Two subsequent developments have forced a re-evaluation of this otherwise neat picture. Firstly, the off-line procedures that were used came under increasingly critical scrutiny because of their inability to speak directly to questions of what happens in on-line or real-time sentence processing. Secondly, findings of apparently intact abilities of agrammatic patients to make quite sophisticated judgements of sentence grammaticality led many researchers to conclude that their syntactic parsing capabilities were intact (Linebarger *et al.*, 1983). If this were the case then agrammatic patients would have no need of heuristics and the source of their somewhat restricted comprehension deficit would need to be sought elsewhere. We shall return to these important issues in the next chapter, when we examine the evidence from off-line and on-line experiments in aphasic language comprehension in more detail. But first we consider a class of sentences that potentially provides a great deal of insight into the syntactic parsing mechanism: sentences which support more than one parse by virtue of being syntactically ambiguous.

## Ambiguity resolution and syntactic parsing strategies

Much of the evidence on the role of grammatical processing in sentence comprehension comes from how subjects resolve *syntactic ambiguities* and how context biases or fails to bias the language processor. By context, we are referring mainly to the pragmatic context in which a test sentence is embedded. Modular theories argue that syntactic processing takes place early, before pragmatic context effects have had a chance to be brought to bear. Interactionist theories of sentence processing look for evidence that the effects of pragmatic context can be detected early in sentence processing. Consequently, questions of timing and techniques which can give us a window on *when* the linguistic processor extracts *what* from the speech signal or from the written sentence assume paramount importance. Some commonly used reaction-time-based techniques include:

- Lexical decision tasks
- speeded grammaticality judgement (ungrammaticality detection)
- eye movement and fixation studies
- time-averaged event-related potential recordings (ERP studies)

We shall first present the modular theory of syntactic processing and then show how it has had to be modified in the light of evidence which suggests that syntactic processing has much in common with lexical processing, indicating that what may be required is a single unified framework – 'a theory of everything' – which encompasses both lexical and compositional routes for mapping sound to meaning.

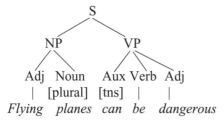

Figure 12.3  *Surface structure syntax*

## Lexical and syntactic ambiguity

Two kinds of ambiguity are usually distinguished: lexical ambiguity (e.g. *bank* <financial institution> or <side of river >) and syntactic ambiguity. Lexical ambiguity has been discussed previously (chapter 10). Syntactic or structural ambiguities have their source in how constituents are bracketed, as in

(21)     *The house on the hill by the sea*
         [house [on the hill] [by the sea]]
         <house on hill and house by sea>
         [house [on the hill [by the sea]]]
         <house on hill and hill by sea>

These are called attachment ambiguities. Alternatively, syntactic ambiguities arise from systematic ellipsis of argument structure in complex sentences so that a given surface structure may associate with more than one underlying structure (as discussed briefly in chapter 2). Thus, to use Chomsky's well-known example:

(22)     *Flying planes can be dangerous*
         <To fly planes can be dangerous>
         <Planes which are flying can be dangerous>

The underlying representations that disambiguate the two readings of sentence (22) (see Figure 12.4) will need to indicate that *flying* in one case is to be understood as a transitive verb with an unspecified or implied subject and *planes* as its object. In the other reading, *flying* is an adjective, derived from an intransitive form of the verb *fly*, pre-modifying the head noun *planes*.

   Note that no ambiguity arises in the case of the simple copula verb construction, as (23) and (24) below illustrate:

(23)     *Flying planes is dangerous.*     [The gerundive construction]
(24)     *Flying planes are dangerous.*    [The adjectival construction]

The English copula *be* inflects to agree in number with its subject, and this is sufficient to prevent ambiguity arising between the gerundive and adjectival readings of '*flying planes*'. Modal auxiliaries like *can* are not constrained to agree in number with their subject and hence support more than one reading of the subject NP. We see here another example of the indirect and somewhat arbitrary way that (surface) syntax constrains (or fails to constrain) meaning.

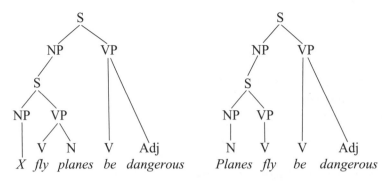

Figure 12.4 *Contrasting 'underlying' structures for sentence*

Many cases of attachment ambiguity may be resolved in spoken language by prosody. Thus, contrastive accent may be used to elicit the otherwise less accessible reading of

*house on the **hill** by the sea*. (Bold marks pitch prominence on *hill*.)
<house on hill and hill by sea>

But not all syntactic ambiguities can be resolved by prosody. Local attachment ambiguities are much more frequent than language users realize, partly because they are usually resolved by some upcoming word before the end of the utterance, or because one reading pre-empts all others.

## Why ambiguity is important for theories of language processing

It is scarcely an exaggeration to say that how ambiguities arise and how they are resolved in the course of sentence processing has been the central empirical issue in debates over competing theories of lexical access and syntactic structure assignment. While the early research on lexical and syntactic ambiguity resolution took quite separate paths, in recent years it has become clear that both are influenced by similar factors and should perhaps be modelled by a common processing mechanism (MacDonald *et al.*, 1994).

Recall from chapter 10 David Swinney's (1979) important discovery about the effects of linguistic context on lexical retrieval. Using the semantic priming paradigm, he reported that in the early stages of lexical retrieval for ambiguous words like '*bank*', *both* meanings are initially activated, even where the discourse context favours one meaning of the word over the other. However, if the probe word is delayed for several hundred milliseconds, then lexical priming occurs only for the contextually appropriate meaning. Swinney and others took this to indicate that there is an initial phase of lexical retrieval during which all meanings of a word are activated, later followed by a phase in which context exerts a winnowing effect on lexical selection.

These findings apparently favour a theory of lexical access which is modular to the extent of positing an initial context-free retrieval of lexical meaning. Subsequent attempts to replicate Swinney's findings have met with mixed results (see MacDonald *et al.*, 1994). Context effects of the kind found by Swinney apparently depend on the token frequencies of the competing lexical meanings being relatively evenly balanced. In retrospect, it is no surprise that word frequency should influence context effects in lexical retrieval. But if token frequency effects interact with context in a similar manner in syntactic ambiguity resolution, then it may be time to re-evaluate a modular theory of syntactic processing.

Let us now consider a case of syntactic (attachment) ambiguity, illustrated by the following sentence:

(25)      *John told the girl that Bill liked the story.*

What meanings do you get from the above sentence? Write a paraphrase for each separate meaning that you come up with. The first meaning that most people extract will be

(26)      *John told the girl something – namely, that Bill liked the story.*

Let us call this the *sentential complement* reading. But there is another perfectly acceptable reading:

(27)      *John told the story to the girl that Bill liked.*

Let us call (27) the *relative clause* reading. Most readers do not perceive sentence (25) as ambiguous until they are asked to reflect upon it. However, any self-respecting computational parser should yield two syntactic readings for this sentence, because both are perfectly well-formed English sentences. Human parsers show decided preferences for one structural reading over another, though on analysis and reflection all allowable readings may become apparent. Why is this so? Is it because as language users, we do not have the luxury of time to systematically compute all options and must quickly 'go with' one reading, until such time as we have evidence that we made the wrong choice and then have to back-track? What is it that makes one syntactic reading preferable to another (the sentential complement reading over the relative clause reading in this case)?

## Minimal attachment

Lyn Frazier and Janet Dean Fodor (1978) proposed a strategy known as *minimal attachment*, which is a kind of Occam's razor principle of parsing that in effect minimizes the number of levels of embedding required to parse a candidate sentence.[6] The syntactic structure assignments for the two readings of sentence (25) are given below:

---

[6] Minimal attachment is the best known of a number of parsing strategies that have been proposed. We consider it here as representative of a family of structure-based constraints that can be contrasted with other factors – lexical, pragmatic, etc. – that may influence sentence interpretation.

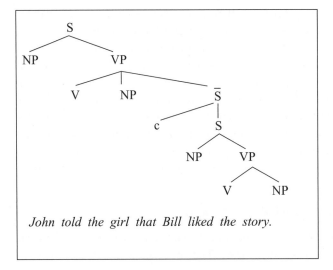

*John told the girl that Bill liked the story.*

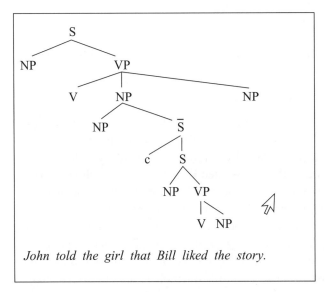

*John told the girl that Bill liked the story.*

The crucial structural difference between the sentential complement and the relative clause readings is that the latter requires an extra level of embedding (clause structure).[7] The minimal attachment principle states, in effect, 'avoid

---

[7] We have not attempted to specify exactly how minimal attachment might be implemented in parsing. However, note that *tell* will be lexically sub-categorized to take either a sentential complement (*that S*) or a noun phrase complement (*NP*). The fragment *that Bill liked* can be parsed as a relative clause, post-modifying *the girl*. Consequently, the noun phrase complement reading '*I told the girl . . . the story*' can be assigned to the main clause, but at the cost of an additional level of embedding.

unnecessary embedding'. Minimal attachment was conceived as a parsing strategy that applies without reference to pragmatic context or other factors. Triggered by configurational properties of trees constructed in the course of parsing, minimal attachment was intended as a hypothesis about the operation of a modular syntactic parser.

## Testing minimal attachment

You probably found that your mental parser preferred the sentential complement reading over the relative clause reading in the previous example. Many cases of syntactic ambiguity in which the preferred reading conforms with the minimal attachment principle could be cited ('*The house on the hill by the sea*' is one such). But by no means all parsing preferences in cases of syntactic ambiguity can be satisfactorily explained by minimal attachment or some other purely structure-based parsing principle. Compare parsing preferences for sentences (28) and (29) below (from Bresnan, 1982). They have identical syntactic structures and both are syntactically ambiguous in terms of attachment possibilities for the preposition phrase '*for Susan*'. Yet most judges agree that (28) has a preferred reading which conforms to minimal attachment while the preferred meaning of (29) violates it.[8]

(28)      *Joe carried the package for Susan.*
(29)      *Joe included the package for Susan.*

Apparently, the identity of the verb constrains the choice of syntactic complement.

## Local ambiguities and garden path sentences

Only a minority of sentences that people process may turn out to be syntactically ambiguous. However, local ambiguities are probably very common in the course of syntactic parsing. A local ambiguity arises where more than one parse is possible at a given point in sentence processing, but the ambiguity is subsequently resolved at a later point in the sentence. *Garden path* sentences constitute an especially interesting class of local ambiguities. A garden path sentence is one where the language processor is induced (by whatever factor[s]) to take what turns out to be the *wrong* reading of a locally ambiguous structure, and subsequently experiences some difficulty recovering from the initial mis-parse. The best example of a garden path sentence is also the most famous:

---

[8]  The difference in parsing preferences for the two verbs can be illustrated using the cleft construction, a focusing device. Sentence (28) has a preferred reading which can be paraphrased as '*It was the package that Joe carried for Susan*'. The reading '*It was the package for Susan that Joe carried*' is non-preferred. On the other hand, the attachment preferences are reversed in sentence (29): '*It was the package for Susan that Joe included*' is the preferred reading, and '*It was the package that Joe included for Susan*' is the non-preferred reading.

(30)        *The horse raced past the barn fell.*[9]

Most people initially think that this sentence is ungrammatical. But it turns out on re-analysis to be perfectly well-formed. Compare (30) with (31):

(31)        *The horse ridden past the barn fell.*

You can now see that a past-participle reading of *raced* as in (32) below was quite possible and legitimate.

(32)        *The horse which was raced past the barn fell.*

It just happens that *race*, like the majority of English verbs, has the same form for its past tense as for its past participle. Sentence (33) is simply ungrammatical:

(33)        * *The horse rode past the barn fell.*

For some reason you were 'led up the garden path', to analyse (30) as the past tense *intransitive* reading of *raced*. How come? Minimal attachment provides an explanation. The first six words of (30) constitute a simple main clause, whereas the reduced relative clause reading which is identical in meaning to the full relative clause in (32) requires a level of embedding, contrary to the minimal attachment criterion. However, good examples of garden path sentences are rare, and your intuitions about the example we have been considering have probably caused you to suspect that additional factors conspired to lead you up the garden path in this particular case. We now turn to consider these non-configurational factors.

**Animacy of the subject NP:** A passive reading of the verb *raced* is required to obtain the relative clause reading of '*raced through committee*' and thereby avoid being garden-pathed by *died*, the tensed verb in the main clause of (34).

(34)        *The legislation raced through committee died in the House.*

To my intuition (and yours?) (34) is perhaps a little strange, but not a garden path. It seems an inanimate subject (*legislation*), which has no power of agency, promotes the passive (past participle) reading of *raced*.

**Pragmatic context:** Another way of avoiding the garden path is to place the sentence in an appropriate discourse context, as in (35):

(35)        *There were several horses in the cross country race. They headed off in various directions.* **The horse raced past the barn fell.**

---

[9] Here are some more examples of garden path sentences, from Pinker (1994):

*The man who hunts ducks out on weekends.*
*Fat people eat accumulates.*
*The prime number few.*
*The cotton clothing is usually made of grows in Mississippi.*

The two context sentences have established several potential referents for the singular definite noun phrase *the horse*, so the listener is primed for the relative clause reading of '*raced past the barn*'. Context here has established what Crain and Steedman (1985) refer to as *pragmatic felicity conditions* for the use of the reduced relative clause. Is this context effect sufficiently strong to suppress the garden path effect? For the moment, we leave this question for your linguistic intuition to adjudicate. If pragmatic context effects can influence syntactic parsing to the extent of eliminating garden paths, then do we not have *prima facie* evidence against a modular syntactic parser operating in sentence comprehension?

How much 'context' is required to establish pragmatic felicity conditions that may override garden path effects? As Ni, Crain and Shankweiler (1996) point out, a single word adjunct, the restrictive quantifier *only*, may suffice:

(36)     ***Only*** *those horses raced past the barn fell.*

Sentences are arguably always construed in discourse context, even when presented in isolation in psycholinguistic experiments. In the absence of explicit contextual cues, listeners will strive to invoke a context in which the sentence makes sense. This may induce additional processing load, when relative clauses or other structures that make implicit discourse presuppositions are presented out of context. The critical question which remains unanswered is: at what point in the sentence comprehension process are such 'top-down' considerations invoked? We require sensitive on-line measures of sentence processing to approach this question.

*Lexical frequency effects:*  A third, now widely acknowledged, source of non-configurational influences upon garden path effects operates not under the 'top-down' guidance of an emerging contextual understanding but, rather, from statistical contingencies of lexical usage (MacDonald *et al.*, 1994). For example, many verbs may be used transitively or intransitively, and which usage is more common varies with the particular verb. Similarly, verbs vary in their frequency of usage in the past tense or the past-participle forms, which distinguish the main clause (minimal attachment) reading from the reduced relative clause (non-minimal attachment) reading in garden path sentences such as (30) above. Thus, *race* is a verb that is frequently used intransitively, where the *-ed* can only signal past tense (and minimal attachment):

(37)     *The horse raced well.*

On the other hand, *carry* is a verb that is always used transitively, except with a highly restricted class of subjects: acoustic entities, where its meaning is something like *travel*, as in

(38)     *The sound carried to the back of the room.*

So, when *carry* is substituted for *race*, in (39) the resulting sentence is less likely to produce a garden path:

(39)      *The horse carried past the barn died.*

Why is the reader less likely to be garden-pathed by (39)? The answer seems to be that with no intransitive reading of *carry* available to support a garden path interpretation, the non-garden path reading, involving *carried* as a non-tensed passive verb in a dependent clause, has a greater chance to win through as the dominant interpretation. The active transitive reading of *carry* remains available to support the garden path interpretation. But it seems the less salient of the two transitive readings, possibly because a prepositional phrase is less likely to separate a verb from its object as in (40) or – better – (41):

(40)      *The horse carried past the barn several children.*
(41)      *Santa carried in his bag several large toys.*

Hence, competition among alternative readings, governed by the statistics of word usage, may influence the strength of garden path effects. Frequency effects, as we saw in chapter 7, are a major determinant of lexical access speed in retrieving word meanings. Here we see that they may also play a role in deciding alternative syntactic parses.

## Summary

We have relied upon your intuitions to establish that the strength of the garden path effect depends on a number of factors other than configurational properties of syntactic trees: factors such as the frequency of usage of particular verb forms and their preferred complements, and discourse considerations (pragmatic felicity effects). But this is not sufficient evidence to rule against a modular theory of syntactic processing in favour of the interactionist view. We have in fact relied upon your informal *off-line* judgements as to how individual sentences should be interpreted, with or without the benefit of an explicit discourse context.

Similarly, in our earlier discussion of the role of syntactic cues, parsing strategies, and the consequences of impaired access to the full syntactic resources of the language in sentence comprehension, we appealed to off-line behavioural measures and your 'meta-linguistic' judgements as native speakers. However, what is needed for a scientific model of sentence processing is a window on what transpires in the first few tenths of a second that it takes to process a sentence *on-line* or in real time; or to pose the question in 'Watergate' fashion mentioned earlier: 'What does the language processor know and when does s/he know it?' It is not only the outcome which is of interest for a model of language comprehension, but also how the outcome was arrived at.

Much depends on the time-course of sentence processing. It may be possible to save the modular account if solid evidence can be found that different types of processing take place at different times in the course of assigning an interpretation to a sentence. For example, pragmatic influences, because they rely on encyclopaedic world knowledge and complex chains of inference, may be expected to manifest themselves later than syntactic effects in the course of sentence comprehension. Ni *et al.* (1996) refer to this as 'modularity by default'. Some types of processing simply take longer than others. Indeed, their speed of operation was postulated to be at the basis of the adaptive advantage of modular processes (Fodor, 1983). But their empirical justification must rest on evidence from time sensitive on-line measures of sentence processing. We consider the evidence from on-line studies of syntactic processing in the next chapter.

Another shortcoming of our discussion of syntactic processing thus far is that we have not yet provided solid motivation for the parsing strategy of minimal attachment, except to argue that it is a heuristic that guides the parser to avoid constructing unnecessarily complex syntactic structures. We need to state more precisely why some syntactic structures are more difficult to parse than others. To do this, we need an explicit theory of syntactic parsing. It is here that computational models have most to contribute, generating predictions about syntactic complexity which can be tested against results from on-line processing studies. To anticipate the findings, from the pioneering papers of Yngve (1960) and Miller and Chomsky (1963), to the recent cross-linguistic studies of syntactic complexity (Babyonyshev and Gibson, 1999): the major contributing factor to syntactic complexity is the transient memory load created by having to defer processing of some constituents whilst pursuing the analysis of others. This occurs whenever the syntax of the target utterance dictates a departure from incremental left-to-right processing favoured by the linear temporal nature of the speech signal.

# 13  On-line processing, working memory and modularity

## Introduction

In the previous chapter we outlined two opposing theories of the role that syntactic processing plays in sentence comprehension. According to one view – the modular theory, inspired by early psycholinguistic attempts to apply Chomsky's generative grammar – a specialized syntactic parser assigns grammatical structure to an input sentence, yielding an intermediate representation which strongly constrains the assignment of meaning, but which needs to be further operated upon by interpretive (semantic and pragmatic) processes to yield the full meaning of the utterance. According to the opposing view, dubbed the interactive model, sentence meanings are assigned incrementally to word sequences as soon as they are identified, making maximal use of whatever constraints can be applied from the speakers' tacit knowledge of the grammar of their language, pragmatic knowledge and expectations, or even collocational restrictions on word usage (such as habitual phrases or idioms). Sometimes these cues will conflict, in which case constraints may compete to produce local ambiguities which are usually resolved by further input.

In principle, it should be possible to decide between these opposing models (or some intermediate theory between the two) if we had some means of observing changes in state of the language processor as it steps through the input sentence in real time. We may never fully achieve this privileged perspective, but over the past two or three decades a variety of 'on-line' techniques, based initially upon behavioural reaction time measurements and latterly upon functional neural imaging techniques, have been devised, which arguably enable us to observe local fluctuations in 'processing load', as sentences are judged or comprehended in real time.

## Working memory, parsing and syntactic complexity

However, before we tackle the on-line processing literature in an attempt to choose between competing models of syntax in sentence comprehension, we need to explore the range of answers that have been given to the question raised at the end of the previous chapter: what makes for syntactic complexity and how is it related to notions of working memory capacity? As we shall see, the way that cognitive scientists have answered these questions has led to very different conceptions of language processing and mechanisms of comprehension deficit in aphasia.

Within the class of language processing models which we shall consider in this chapter,[1] there are two conceptions of working memory, not necessarily incompatible with one another, that have claimed the allegiance of competing schools of theory. On the one hand, cognitive neuropsychologists (Baddeley, 1986) have postulated a general-purpose working memory, which is invoked whenever mental calculations, symbolic manipulations, or simply the temporary holding of perceptual objects in conscious awareness is required to solve some problem confronting the organism. Retaining the digits while dialling a phone number is a prototypical example of general-purpose working memory in action. Normal individuals are known to differ measurably on this type of memory, commonly known as attention span, which is routinely assessed by the number of digits that can be recalled on the 'Digit Span' sub-test of a standard intelligence test, such as the Wechsler Adult Intelligence Scale (WAIS). Attention span is often impaired by traumatic brain injury.

General-purpose working memory is often likened to a 'scratch pad', a 'temporary work space' or a 'buffer', depending on the writer's preferred level of technology. The contents of working memory comprise visual, auditory, motoric or mental 'images': things that can be held in consciousness, kept 'alive' through rehearsal or simply occupy attention. Working memory needs to be distinguished from the specialized, modality-specific, sensory storage systems that have been posited to serve perceptual processing and which have an operational time base ranging from tenths of a second to an upper limit of two or three seconds. There can be little doubt of the need for some such device as general working memory, which neuropsychology has tentatively located in the prefrontal cortex, to support strategic thinking and symbol manipulation of various kinds.

But quite apart from general-purpose working memory, virtually all theorists who have attempted to offer a computationally explicit symbolic account of natural language processing (Yngve, 1960; Chomsky and Miller, 1963; Marcus, 1980, etc.) have posited the need for a more specialized device, to store interim results or partial parse traces obtained in the course of sentence processing. The precise nature and content of this specialized sentence processing memory and its relationship to general working memory has been a source of ongoing debate, much of it revolving around the role of individual differences in working memory

---

[1] The models considered in this chapter all regard language processing as a constructive and deterministic process of symbol manipulation. The problem of how such models relate to (or may be recast as) 'connectionist' models of language processing, founded on probabilistic stochastic processing, network activation and a radically different notion of 'linguistic representation', is deferred until the final chapter's discussion of 'frontier' issues, about which there is no clear consensus at the present time.

capacity and their implications for sentence processing strategies (Just and Carpenter, 1992; Caplan and Waters, 1999).

Most of the controversy has centred on the processing of complex sentences which challenge automatic parsing, using experimental paradigms that encourage the intervention of conscious attentional strategies, such as the self-paced reading task, in which a sentence is presented as a sequence of words on a screen, one word at a time, with the subject pressing a keyboard for each successive word. Under these somewhat unnatural conditions, subjects with 'high' and 'low' verbal working memory capacities, as determined by their performance on the Reading Span task (Daneman and Carpenter, 1980), may adopt different strategies for processing awkward sentences. Some of these involve garden paths, such as

(1)        *The soldiers warned about the dangers conducted the midnight raid.*

The self-paced reading task, and its auditory analogue, the Auditory Moving Windows task, in which a listener elicits successive words or fragments of a spoken sentence by self-paced pressing of a keypad (Ferreira *et al.*, 1996) are both regarded as 'on-line' measures of sentence processing. However, the relationship between these experimental tasks and understanding spoken sentences under normal listening conditions is clearly problematic.

Sentence comprehension in real time requires a memory resource that operates over a time-frame comparable to that of sensory storage (i.e. tenths of a second, not several seconds). Also, the nature of the storage system, specialized for manipulating linguistic information, is probably quite different from that which is required for general working memory. It is clearly not parsimonious to proliferate working memories, unless there are good reasons for doing so. One persuasive argument (Caplan and Waters, 1999) in favour of distinguishing between a general purpose and a specialized language processing working memory is that some patients who show severe deficits of general purpose working memory as assessed by attention span tests may nevertheless retain the ability to comprehend complex spoken utterances (Vallar and Shallice, 1990).

Advocates of a specialized working memory for language processing argue that individual differences in general working memory are usually not implicated in on-line language comprehension. However, it is readily conceded that individual differences in general working memory capacity may well influence performance in the 'off-line' tasks that are typically used in clinical language assessment (such as thematic role assignment in a picture matching task) and which were used in the earlier psycholinguistic experiments discussed in the previous chapter.

On the other hand, advocates of general-purpose working memory have claimed (Just and Carpenter, 1992) that individual differences in working memory capacity do indeed impact upon the language processing strategies that listeners employ when required to comprehend complex sentences. At the present time, this debate remains to be resolved to the satisfaction of opposing parties.

If there is a specialized working memory for language processing, then it will need to operate not within a time frame of seconds, like general working memory, but within *tenths* of a second. Also, unlike general working memory or attention span, specialized language-processing memory serves automated processes that occur too quickly to be accessible by introspection or conscious awareness. These are persuasive arguments for *not* reducing a specialized (fast-acting) and a general-purpose (slow-acting) working memory to a single mechanism on misconceived grounds of parsimony.

## Individual differences in working memory capacity and sentence processing

While attention span is typically assessed clinically by Digit Span (the number of digits that an individual can hold in working memory and successfully recall in normal or reverse sequence to which they were presented), Verbal working memory capacity (VWMC) is typically experimentally assessed by a rather different task: the Reading Span test (Daneman and Carpenter, 1980). The reading span test requires subjects to divide their attention between sentence processing and short-term verbal recall. Subjects are presented with blocks of two, three or more sentences. Each sentence is required to be processed for meaning – typically using a self-paced word-by-word reading task. Following each block of sentences, the subject is required to recall the last word of each sentence in the block. A reading span score is calculated on the average number of words or the block size that an individual can successfully recall, while simultaneously processing individual sentences for meaning. College students' reading span scores typically range from 2 (low) to 5.5 (high). Reading span scores have been found to correlate highly with Verbal Scholastic Aptitude tests (VSAT), and reading comprehension test scores. In this respect, the reading span test differs from the digit span task or word list recall measures, which typically do not correlate highly with measures of language processing skill.

A Listening Span test for spoken sentences presented in auditory mode apparently behaves in a similar way to the reading span test (Daneman and Carpenter, 1980). Both tests are regarded by their authors as alternative measures of VWMC. But what is perhaps most significant for the issue at hand (individual differences in VWMC and sentence processing) is that both forms of the test require subjects to split their attention between two distinct tasks: sentence comprehension and the recall of extraneous verbal material. Is this an appropriate task with which to assess working memory requirements for sentence processing?

Just and Carpenter (1992) argue the affirmative, and rest their case on results obtained from an experimental task 'that had previously provided the strongest support for the modularity of syntax (Ferreira and Clifton, 1986)'. Their argument is that if individual differences in VWMC can be shown to affect readers' or listeners' language processing strategies on a task that taps into on-line syntactic processing, then reading span (or its aural equivalent listening span) is indeed an appropriate measure of on-line verbal working memory capacity.

Furthermore, Just and Carpenter argue that what appear to be modularity effects in syntactic processing, when examined more carefully in the light of individual differences in VWMC, turn out to be by-products of capacity effects. That is to say, differences in VWMC induce different on-line processing strategies, and apparent modularity effects manifest themselves in sentence processing when working memory capacity is stretched. Individuals with larger VWMCs can simultaneously entertain multiple syntactic hypotheses at points of local ambiguity, or permit both syntactic and pragmatic constraints to interact. A basic question of the architecture of the language processor, it is argued, turns out to be a cognitive capacity effect. These are clearly important theoretical claims that merit close empirical scrutiny. They have far-reaching implications for models of normal language processing, agrammatism, and language comprehension disorders in general. Just and Carpenter buttress their case with simulation experiments using a computational model that they dub CCREADER: a hybrid symbolic-connectionist parser, which we discuss in chapter 14. But the central arguments for their capacity theory of language processing rest on how high and low VWMC subjects deal with complex sentences, such as subject and object relative clauses, with or without the support of pragmatic cues, presented under the self-paced reading paradigm.

Let us first weigh the evidence that modularity of processing is a by-product of capacity; an effect which emerges under conditions of high working memory load. We shall then consider Just and Carpenter's claim that parallel vs. serial processing (or entertaining more that one syntactic parse simultaneously) is also a by-product of capacity effects. To anticipate the conclusions, so that you may evaluate *our* argument more critically, we find that Just and Carpenter's evidence is largely irrelevant for language processing under normal operating conditions, but possibly quite apposite for language processing in aphasia. This then prompts us to inquire more specifically into the specialized nature of the computational memory required to parse complex syntactic structures and also to seek better behavioural and neurological measures of working memory load in on-line sentence processing.

## Modularity and VWMC

In the first instance, Just and Carpenter's case for modularity as a by-product of working memory capacity rests on experimental evidence that was regarded at the time as strong support for the modularity hypothesis: that initial sentence processing is 'informationally encapsulated' to a syntactic parse in which pragmatic expectations play no role. Ferreira and Clifton (1986) presented subjects with potential garden path sentences consisting of full (unreduced) or reduced relative clauses such as

|     | SENTENCE | TYPE OF RELATIVE | TYPE OF SUBJECT |
|-----|----------|------------------|-----------------|
| (2) | *The evidence examined by the lawyer shocked the jury.* | reduced | inanimate |
| (3) | *The evidence that was examined by the lawyer shocked the jury.* | full | inanimate |
| (4) | *The defendant examined by the lawyer shocked the jury.* | reduced | animate |
| (5) | *The defendant that was examined by the lawyer shocked the jury.* | full | animate |

Sentences were presented in the self-paced reading paradigm, in which local increases of processing load or the relative difficulty of integrating a new word into the subject's evolving interpretation of the sentence are measured by the time it takes to press a button calling for the next word. Thus, in sentence (4), at the point when a subject has seen

> *The defendant examined . . .*

syntactic parsing considerations (such as minimal attachment) and pragmatic considerations (animate nouns are more likely to be agents – cf. (2) *evidence*) might be expected to reinforce one another, directing the reader to treat *examined* as the main clause verb;[2] in which case, readers will be momentarily garden-pathed when the next word that appears is *by* and they are forced to re-analyse *examined* as a passive construction in a post-modifying relative clause. Re-analysis should cause a momentary increase in processing load, reflected in increased time to call for the word that immediately follows *by*.

Modular and interactive theories of sentence processing make different predictions about how long readers will take to assimilate the *by* phrase in sentences with animate and inanimate subjects (4 vs. 2). By the modular account, where there is a first-pass assignment of syntactic structure before pragmatic considerations come into play, there should be no additional effect of pragmatic fit attributable to the animacy of the subject NP. Ferreira and Clifton's findings supported the modular theory, showing no difference in gaze time on the *by* phrase between animate and inanimate subject reduced relative clauses.

The *by* phrase in the unreduced relative clause (3 and 5 above) was processed more quickly than its counterpart in the reduced relative clause, regardless of animacy of the subject NP, because the presence of explicit markers of subordination (the relative pronoun *who* or *that* and the tensed auxiliary *was*) causes the parser to expect a *by* phrase. A 'main clause' analysis of *examined* is excluded at this point of sentence processing in the case of the full relative constructions. The lack of an animacy effect on the full relatives may also be taken as additional support for the modular hypothesis. If we make the assumption, as most

---

[2] At least this is the prediction of the interactive model. The modular theory predicts that only syntactic considerations play a role in the initial parse of the sentence.

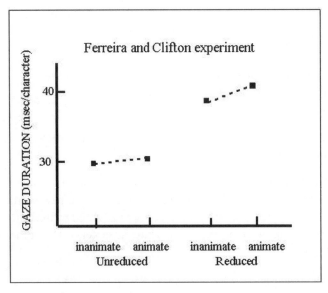

Figure 13.1  *Reading times for relative clauses: Ferreira & Clifton (1986)*

interactive models do, that syntactic and pragmatic constraints compete with one another on equal terms in the determination of sentence meaning, then the fact that a main clause reading of *examined* has been excluded by the syntactic markers of subordination already encountered should not prevent pragmatic factors from competing and thus slowing down the processing of the *by* phrase. However, contrary to pragmatic expectations, the *by* phrase in full relatives with animate subject NPs was processed no more slowly than in those with inanimate subject NPs.

Just and Carpenter (1992) conducted a near replication of Ferreira and Clifton's study, except that they included an additional factor in the experiment: subjects of low and high reading span scores. Their results indicated that the low reading span group showed the same modular pattern of performance as Ferreira and Clifton's subjects, but the high reading span group indicated an interactive processing strategy, as can be seen from Figure 13.2.

It is evident from Figure 13.2 that the high reading span subjects' gaze fixation times on the critical *by* phrase were shorter than those of the low reading span group, consistent with the expectation that the high span group are better readers. But more importantly, the high span readers show the operation of pragmatic expectations for both the full (unreduced) and the reduced relative clause constructions, which can only indicate an interactive style of processing. Just and Carpenter's explanation for this phenomenon is that the high span group have sufficient reserve processing capacity to simultaneously 'take on board' both syntactic and pragmatic constraints in on-line processing. The low span subjects, on the other hand, have no excess capacity to do more than employ the syntactic cues available. Thus, reserve capacity determines the style – modular or interactive – of on-line sentence processing that subjects adopt.

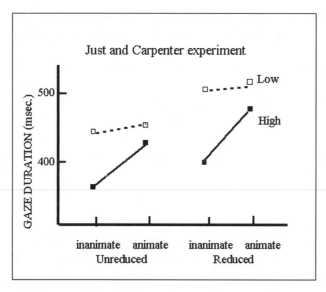

Figure 13.2 *Interaction of verbal working memory capacity with syntactic and pragmatic cues*

At face value, these results raise interesting questions which suggest some residual role for modularity, even as an expression of a 'capacity overload' effect. What determines selective attention to 'syntactic' cues over pragmatic cues when overload conditions are approached? Presumably, syntactic cues require less 'processing load' or are 'activated' more readily than pragmatic cues. Does not the preferential use of one type of cue indicate a degree of modularity in the architecture of the processing model anyway?

### Sequential or parallel processing as a capacity effect

MacDonald, Just and Carpenter (1992) presented further evidence of the impact of individual differences in VWMC upon parsing strategies in processing complex sentences, purporting to show that high capacity subjects simultaneously entertain competing syntactic analyses whereas low capacity subjects pursue only the simplest parse, which is less taxing on resources but places them at greater risk of being garden-pathed, should the simpler analysis turn out to be incorrect. MacDonald *et al.* (1992) constructed pairs of potentially syntactically ambiguous and unambiguous sentence strings which rely for their ambiguity on whether the first verb may be interpreted as a simple past tense, yielding a simpler 'main clause' reading, or as a past participle, yielding an embedded relative clause reading – such as discussed previously in the celebrated garden path '*The horse **raced** past the barn . . .*'

Two sample sentences from MacDonald *et al.* (1992) appear below. Note that (6) admits a possible continuation if *warned* is read as a past participle in a relative clause post-modifying *soldiers* (as in sentence (1) above), whereas *spoke* is unambiguously the past-tense form of *speak* (past participle form: *spoken*) and therefore *raid* signals the end of the sentence in (7). The brackets indicate where reading time measurements were taken under the self-paced reading paradigm.

Substantial differences in reading times for ambiguous and unambiguous sentence strings were found at the end position of the string (position 3) for the high span readers, but no difference in reading times at the end position for low span readers.

(6)     *The soldiers [**warned** about the dangers] [before the midnight] [raid . . .]*     Ambiguous
(7)     *The soldiers [**spoke** about the dangers] [before the midnight] [raid.]*     Unambiguous
        1                  2              3

Surprisingly perhaps in view of the high correlation between reading ability and the word span test, high span readers took longer to read the ambiguous sentences than low span readers. Both the longer overall reading times and the additional gaze time on the final word of the ambiguous sentences by the high span group may be explained if one assumes that the non-preferred parsing option is active for the high-span readers, but simply not entertained by the low span readers. But then it needs to be asked, why would high span readers entertain non-preferred parsing options in the first place? Presumably, there was something in the experimental conditions – quite possibly in the distribution of sentence types used in the experiment – that alerted readers to the possibility of the non-preferred relative clause reading. Consequently, the high reading span group adopted a comprehension strategy which kept alternative readings (parsings) open, despite the additional processing or memory costs incurred.

Other investigators (Caplan and Walters, 1999) have failed to replicate MacDonald *et al.*'s (1992) finding of longer reading times in the high span group, further suggesting that we may be dealing with a 'strategic effect', where subjects adopt response strategies that maximize their performance on the task relative to their capabilities, and where they prefer to locate their performance on the inevitable trade-off between speed and accuracy. On reflection, it is perhaps not surprising that reading span scores may effectively differentiate subjects by the strategies that they adopt in the self-paced reading paradigm. But are such strategic differences relevant for on-line spoken language comprehension, and is the kind of verbal working memory load that both tasks appear to tap relevant for on-line syntactic parsing of speech?

While these questions remain unresolved at present, we can make progress on the two questions taken separately: (a) the nature of the specialized memory resource required for syntactic parsing, and (b) results from other behavioural and neuroimaging paradigms with stronger claims as measures of on-line processing. There is a long tradition of computational and psycholinguistic research on syntactic complexity metrics, which enables us to sharpen our notions of the working memory requirements of a syntactic parser.

## Syntactic complexity

It has long been recognized that syntactic structures involving centre embedding become extremely difficult, if not impossible, to process on-line beyond a single level of embedding (Chomsky and Miller, 1963). Consider the following simple sentences, chosen for their stereotyped thematic roles to be easily processed:

(8a)        *The dog chased the cat.*
(8b)        *The cat hunted the rat.*
(8c)        *The rat nibbled the cheese.*

The following sentence with a single level of centre embedding is awkward but not too hard for normal listeners[3] to understand:

(9)         *The rat the cat hunted nibbled the cheese.*

But at two levels of centre embedding, the sentence becomes virtually impossible for most people to process on-line:

(10)        *The rat the cat the dog chased hunted nibbled the cheese.*[4]

However, a right branching construction with the same level of relative clause embedding is quite processable:

(11)        *The dog chased the cat that hunted the rat that nibbled the cheese.*

What makes centre-embedded structures such as (10) difficult to parse? Detailed explanations differ, but essentially all who have investigated this matter agree that centre-embedded constructions impose heavy demands on the parser's specialized working memory and the cause of this difficulty may be attributed to the need to suspend processing of a constituent, to temporarily place it 'on hold' while having to deal with some new constituent, before returning to the suspended constituent. The computational mechanism first proposed by Yngve (1960) for accomplishing this, and repeatedly used since, is known as a 'push down stack'.

Consider what happens when the parser encounters three NPs in succession in the highly awkward sentence (10) above. We shall assume a simple parser that seeks to associate noun phrases (thematic role suppliers) with verbal predicates (thematic role seekers). The first NP *the rat* causes the parser to seek to fill a thematic role slot in a predicate. But this operation must be placed 'on hold'

---

[3] Agrammatics, you will recall, find these embedded object relative clauses difficult, as do young children.

[4] But compare the relative ease with which you can process '*The game those boys I met invented resembles chess.*' (Smith, 1989). For a dissenting view from the conventional wisdom that the difficulty caused by these 'so called' multiply embedded structures is syntactic, see Hudson (1996), who argues that the problem is semantic.

when the next constituent encountered turns out to be not a predicate but another predicate-seeking NP, *the cat*. This second NP must in turn have its predicate seeking temporarily suspended by the third NP in the sequence, *the dog*. The appearance of the verb *chased* enables *the dog* to be linked to a predicate, but by now the parser's limited capacity for recovering unlinked constituents seems to have been exceeded and comprehension breaks down.

Edward Gibson (1998) has formulated a model of specialized working memory for syntactic parsing which seeks to explain why certain syntactic structures are consistently judged more complex or difficult than others, and how transient working memory load may vary at different points in a sentence in the course of on-line processing. Gibson's theory is one of a long tradition of models of syntactic complexity, but by general consensus one of the most comprehensive in its coverage of known complexity effects. We will therefore focus upon it to the exclusion of earlier competitors.

## Gibson's model of parsing complexity

Sentence comprehension is a constructive process that involves building syntactic and semantic relations between words and sentence fragments that are passed to the language processor by the speech perception apparatus. Specialized memory or computational resources are needed to keep activated currently unintegrated words or sentence fragments, until the syntactic and semantic relations – Gibson uses the term 'predictions' – that are evoked by the recognition of these fragments are satisfied by finding some other complementary fragment in the input. The longer a fragment has to remain unintegrated in working memory, the greater the computational cost. We can represent this integration process symbolically, using the notation of trace binding introduced in chapter 2. Thus, the *object relative* clause in (12) consumes more processing resources than the similar *subject relative* clause in (13) because the referring word *cat* as a potential thematic role bearer has to remain active and unassigned a little longer in sentence fragment (12) than it does in (13).

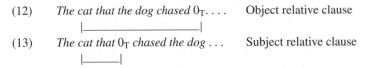

(12)    *The cat that the dog chased* $0_T$. . . .    Object relative clause
        |—————————————|
(13)    *The cat that* $0_T$ *chased the dog* . . .    Subject relative clause
        |———|

Returning to our doubly centre-embedded relative clause (sentence 10), we note that at the point just before the first verbal predicate *chased* is encountered, we have no fewer than three referring expressions (*rat*, *cat* and *dog*) awaiting thematic role assignment (see Figure 13.3). This is apparently one too many in the rather short customer queue that is preferred by the human sentence parser.

From these examples, the reader can readily appreciate how important it is to specify precisely (a) the nature of the sentence fragments which generate

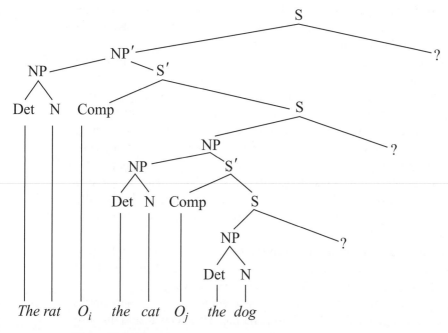

Figure 13.3  *Three NPs awaiting case assignment*

predictions or seek unification with other sentence fragments, and (b) the way that distance is measured between fragments to be unified. Rather different predictions of local processing load may result depending on how these parameters are defined.

The sentence fragments to be unified in Gibson's model are referring expressions, which may be operationally identified as nominal and predicative expressions headed by open-class lexical items.[5] Thus, '*the old man*' would qualify as a single referring expression, headed by the noun *man*. Pronouns (relative pronouns such as *who, which* . . . or central pronouns *he, her, they* . . .) are referring expressions also, but they do not contribute to Gibson's complexity metric, because they make reference to already established or 'old' discourse referents, and what counts in Gibson's metric is the number of newly encountered and not yet integrated discourse referents that the parser must hold active at any one time.[6]

The 'length of time' or, more precisely, the distance metric for measuring how long a sentence fragment must remain active depends in Gibson's model on the number of intervening referring expressions between the two fragments involved

---

[5] Reference is clearly a semantic property, but referring expressions may be identified by their syntactic form. Hence the critical importance of syntax, at some level, for semantic interpretation. Whether the notion of syntactic form should be extended to null constituents, or 'traces', is perhaps debatable, though something equivalent to 'trace recovery' is part of what we would regard as syntax-driven semantic interpretation.

[6] Some simplifying assumptions are being made here for purposes of exposition. Also, we have earlier presented evidence that the presence of explicit (but optional) syntactic cues like relative pronouns as markers of subordination do impact upon ease of processing.

in the unification (the integration operation). Thus, the distance between the noun *cat* and its thematic trace slot $= 1$ in sentence (12), owing to the intervening referring expression *dog*, but in sentence (13), the distance $= 0$.

The available computational resource for these integration operations in on-line parsing may be thought of as a quantum of energy expenditure. Energy requirements for unification operations will vary with fluctuations in local processing load across the sentence. Thus, if we have a way of measuring these fluctuations in energy expenditure, we will be able to observe on-line sentence processing. But there are also limitations on energy expenditure. Energy can only be consumed at a certain maximum rate. Thus, if an integration operation requires a larger quantum of energy, it may take longer to perform and sentence processing may slow down. However, if it slows too much, an additional processing penalty may be incurred as the processing mechanism fails to keep pace with the rate of language input.

The structural distance between sentence fragments involved in a unification operation is one factor affecting local processing load. Clearly there are others, such as ease of lexical retrieval (which as we have seen is strongly subject to frequency effects). Pragmatics or plausibility considerations may also exert strong influences over certain semantic unification operations. These considerations raise important architectural questions for Gibson's model of language processing. On the one hand, the theory has a modular character in postulating a specialized resource management system linked to a unification parser for language processing. On the other hand, Gibson clearly subscribes to a version of the competing constraints activation model discussed earlier, which allows multiple constraints to interact co-operatively and competitively in on-line processing. In order to observe the effects of structural syntactic properties of sentences in parsing, it is clearly necessary in Gibson's model to tightly control the operation of lexical, pragmatic factors, as we have done in the 'dog-chase-cat-hunt-mouse' examples that we have chosen to illustrate his theory.

## Properties of Gibson's parser

Gibson's parser is a parallel processor with limited storage capacity for holding locally possible competing readings of the input string. The processing load will vary as the parser traverses the input string, constructing a syntactic parse. If transient memory load created by all the currently active parses should exceed storage capacity at any point in sentence processing then the most memory-expensive alternative will be abandoned. Certain local ambiguities which arise all the time in sentence processing can be resolved within the working storage capacity of the parser. These are 'easy' ambiguities. They create small, virtually imperceptible interruptions to the parser. Certain other ambiguities, which are illustrated by classical garden path sentences, are more disruptive. These cause conscious difficulty and normal language users have to resort to all kinds of mental gymnastics to resolve them. Gibson's model is intended to account for both types of processing difficulty: for minor, transient increases in processing load, detectable by suitably sensitive on-line indices of sentence processing, and for garden path effects, which derail the sentence processor and provoke conscious back-tracking or failures of syntactic comprehension.

Gibson's model is similar in design to the deterministic computational parser of Mich Marcus (1980) known as PARSIFAL. PARSIFAL did not allow back-tracking. It managed to resolve local syntactic ambiguities by a limited look-ahead, provided by a three-element buffer that held constituents which were currently being worked upon. Unlike PARSIFAL, Gibson's model has not been implemented as a program for parsing text. Nor is it entirely deterministic and rule-based. In its latest form, Gibson's model is cast within a constraint-satisfaction framework.

The cost function, or what drives working memory load in Gibson's model, is *theta-role assignment*. The cost of a representation is a function of the number of elements that require θ-roles but cannot yet be assigned them and the number of elements that have θ-roles that need to be assigned but cannot yet assign them. In terms of the cost, an element with an unassigned θ-role (say, a verb) costs as much as an element that requires a θ-role assignment (say, the lexical head of an NP). Unassigned θ-role units Gibson calls 'local θ-criterion violations'. One simply adds up the number of such units over all the structural fragments that have been constructed up to the present point of the syntactic parse in order to calculate the memory processing load.

Our introduction to Gibson's theory of syntactic complexity is somewhat simplified and we have not adequately demonstrated its breadth of coverage in accounting for a wide range of processing overload phenomena across numerous constructions in a number of languages. The reader is referred to Gibson (1998) for detailed discussion.

### Summary and recapitulation

In Gibson's theory and other currently influential models of sentence processing, the predictions that drive unification operations in parsing are lexically generated. Gibson's model is agnostic on the question of whether individual differences in working memory capacity impact upon on-line processing. The strong and apparently universal restrictions that are implied by the constraint that not more than a single level of centre embedding is tolerated suggest that individual differences in specialized working memory capacity play only a marginal role in parsing. On the other hand, when non-structural factors which may affect on-line processing more generally are taken into account, there appears to be scope for individual differences to play a significant role.

We have also seen that psycholinguists have specifically chosen to study sentences which test the limits of the sentence processing mechanism with garden path sentences, structurally disfavoured constructions such as centre embeddings, and complex cases of syntactic ambiguity. Syntactic structures such as relative clauses, which entail specific pragmatic felicity conditions on their usage (Crain and Steedman, 1985), have often been presented, without a discourse context, in experimental paradigms such as the self-paced reading task that disrupt as much as they permit observations of incremental automatic processes of sentence interpretation. Also, the weight of empirical evidence has been gathered from reading rather than from spoken language comprehension. All these considerations would seem to ensure that psycholinguistic experiments will tend to maximize the influences of attentional processing and bring into play general working memory resources that are known to vary across individuals. While it may be argued that these methodological practices risk distorting the picture of language comprehension under normal conditions, by magnifying the operation of volitional and strategic factors, they may paradoxically apply more appropriately to language processing in aphasia, where a rapid and normally highly accurate automatism is replaced by a slow, faltering, strategy-prone and pragmatically saturated process that has the hallmarks of conscious problem solving.

## Syntactic trace reactivation

We have previously argued (chapter 2) that part of the operating requirements on the syntactic parser is the ability to construct the grammatical relationships that pertain not only between overt constituents that are explicitly present in sentences, but also between constituents that are there only by inference: constituents which are subject to ellipsis in complex sentences, or which appear to have been 'moved' from their canonical sentence positions. Thus, 'which book' must be recognized by the parser as the object of the verb *buy* in (14) below, but 'which student' must be construed as the indirect object of *ask* in (15):

(14)     *Which book$_i$ did John buy t$_i$ for Mary?*
(15)     *Which student$_i$ did John ask Mary about t$_i$?*

Variously described as 'filler–gap dependencies', as 'syntactic anaphora' or – within a movement or transformation-based theory of grammar – as 'traces', these syntactic inferences, and how difficult or easy they are for the listener to establish, lie at the heart of accounts of syntactic complexity, such as Gibson's theory. The occurrence of a filler (a thematic role supplier) triggers a search for a gap (a thematic role recipient), creating – while the search goes on – a temporary increase in processing load. Precisely how this gap-filling mechanism operates is still very much an on-going source of controversy. However, of equal importance for psycholinguistics is the question of how we measure the fluctuations in processing load that occur in on-line sentence processing.

We have seen that word response latencies in the self-paced reading task constitute one such measure, but have argued that the paradigm is susceptible to strategic processing effects. Eye movement tracking during sentence reading arguably provides a better measure of on-line load fluctuations because it is less disruptive of highly automated scanning behaviour in the normal reading process. But what we seek are measures that may be applied to spoken language processing.[7] One of the best-known techniques for observing filler–gap processing online involves the so-called *trace reactivation* effect using (cross-modal) semantic priming.

Subjects are presented with a spoken sentence containing a filler–gap construction, such as a relative clause or the wh-questions (14–15) above. While listening to the sentence for meaning, subjects are required to make a lexical decision about a visually presented 'probe' (word or non-word) that is synchronized to the occurrence of the 'gap' or to a 'control' position in the spoken sentence. Sentence (16) below illustrates three possible timing points for the insertion of a probe. The first 'control' position (T1) occurs just after subjects have heard the prime word, in this case *book*. The second control position (T2) occurs just before subjects hear the verb *purchase* and the critical gap position (T3) occurs just after the verb.

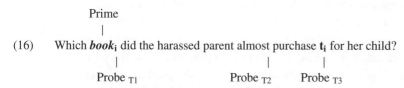

As the cross-modal priming paradigm leads us to expect, presenting a semantically related visual probe (such as *library*) at T1 elicits a faster lexical decision than a semantically unrelated probe (such as *vehicle*). However, if presented at probe position T2, the lexical decision time advantage for a related over an unrelated probe may be expected to have weakened or disappeared owing to temporal decay of the semantic priming effect. This is precisely what studies have observed (Nicol and Swinney, 1989; Swinney and Osterhout, 1990; Fodor, 1993, 1995). But the key finding upon which the 'trace reactivation effect' depends is that when tested at T3, the reaction time advantage for related probes 're-emerges'.

Why is this so? The standard explanation, inspired by transformational/generative grammar, is that the parser has succeeded in locating an attachment site for a temporarily unattached and resource-taxing constituent. As a consequence of this 'binding operation', the lexical item *book* is reactivated downstream from its initial site in the sentence and becomes available to prime a semantically related probe with renewed vigour. Trace reactivation, as detected by cross-modal semantic priming, has been considered a landmark demonstration of the psychological reality of transformational movement operations (Fodor, 1995). Also, this online paradigm provides a natural experimental vehicle for testing one of the most influential linguistic theories of agrammatic comprehension deficit in aphasia: the trace deletion hypothesis (Grodzinsky, 2000 – discussed in chapter 14). However,

---

[7] The eye movement paradigm may be adapted for spoken language processing, if we apply it to how subjects scan a visual scene as they listen to spoken sentences.

we must be wary of the dangers of over-interpreting experimental results from the trace reactivation paradigm and appreciate the stringent conditions which apply if its effects are to be replicated (Love and Swinney, 1996). Both of these points are illustrated in a notable pair of experiments that sought to disconfirm the trace reactivation effect (McKoon, Ratcliff and Ward, 1994; McKoon and Ratcliff, 1994). Swinney and colleagues typically use complex multi-clause sentences as experimental stimuli, such as

(17)     *The professor insisted that the exam be completed in ink, so Jimmy used the new* **pen**$_i$[1] *that his mother-in-law recently*[2] *purchased*[3] **T**$_i$ *because the multiple colours allowed for more creativity.*

Sentence (17) above is actually a self-contained mini-discourse. The first clause sets up a context for the target relative clause '*the pen that his mother in law recently purchased . . .*' and is intended to promote contextual understanding and the retrieval of discourse referents. The final clause '*because . . .*' is intended to remove the target construction from the domain of possibly confounding 'sentence wrap-up effects' (Swinney *et al.*, 1996). The adverb 'recently' within the target clause is there simply to provide additional temporal separation between control positions 1. and 2. (indicated as superscripts in (17)) for presentation of the probe, so as to allow a little more time for decay in activation of the prime word (*pen*), before the site of its 'reactivation' is reached (the trace position, following the verb *purchased*).

But what is the minimal context required to demonstrate the priming effect, which Nicol and Swinney (1989) interpreted as 'trace reactivation'? McKoon *et al.* suggested that it may simply be

(18)     *. . . his mother-in-law recently*[2] *purchased*[3]

and that the observed facilitation of lexical decisions for 'related' compared with 'unrelated' probe words at position 3 may be attributed to the fact that the related words provided, on average, better or more plausible continuations of a simple 'Subject–verb ____' sentence fragment, as suggested by the examples:

(19) (a)     *his mother-in-law recently purchased*
             'related' probe:                          *pencil*
     (b)     *his mother-in-law recently purchased*
             'unrelated' probe:                        *branch*

Any facilitation of lexical decisions for 'related' probe words by the simplified contexts such as (18–19) obviously could not be attributed to trace reactivation, because the [context + probe] makes up a simple sentence with no syntactic anaphora. McKoon *et al.* duly obtained facilitation effects with their simplified stimuli and suggested that such 'sentence continuation' effects may underlie syntactic 'trace reactivation' findings in general.

Love and Swinney (1996), in an elaborate experiment establishing a standard of methodological rigour for all subsequent studies in the paradigm, disposed of most but not all of the questions raised about the standard interpretation of trace reactivation. They criticized McKoon *et al.* for presenting the context sentences as well as the probe words *visually*; one word at a time, at a rate which encouraged strategic processing, and subjects responding to probes as continuations of the context sentence fragments.[8] In the cross-modal paradigm where sentences are presented aurally, it was argued, a visual probe does not intrude upon auditory comprehension of the target sentence and hence 'continuation effects' do not apply. This point was reinforced by subsidiary experiments showing that the related and unrelated probe words did not differ as plausible continuations of the target sentences at the points where probes were introduced in the priming study.[9]

Love and Swinney readily acknowledge that trace reactivation within the cross-modal priming paradigm is a fragile effect for which meticulous control of the stimulus materials is required, chiefly involving careful selection of probe words for their associative relationship with primes, and matching of lexical decision times (on a separate lexical naming task) for pairs of related and unrelated probe words to be used in the priming experiment. But matters of stimulus control aside, and acknowledging the flaws of McKoon *et al.*'s supposed 'replication' study, serious questions remain about the source of the trace reactivation effect, and how the task relates to on-line syntactic processing.

The domain over which 'trace reactivation' effects operate has yet to be determined. Love and Swinney's experiment fails to exclude the possibility that 'trace reactivation' in cross-modal semantic priming may be a strictly local effect: a consequence of lexical access of a verb, with the possible additional proviso (this requirement remains to be tested) that there is a suitable candidate residually active to fill the role of verb complement. The difference between the account just given and the 'anaphora retrieval' interpretation of the priming effect may be highlighted by quoting Love and Swinney's summary of their experiment:

> It is concluded that an underlying (deep; non-surface-level) memorial representation of the sentence is examined during the process of linking an antecedent to a structural position requiring a referent, and that the CMLP [cross modal lexical priming] task provides an unbiased measure of this reactivation.    (1996: 5)

Love and Swinney view CMLP as conditional upon reference retrieval in the course of complex sentence construal, whereas the alternative hypothesis sees CMLP as a by-product of associative connections triggered by lexical activation and not necessarily indicative of complex sentence parsing or higher-level

---

[8] Probe words were displaced on the screen and marked by asterisks.

[9] However, the goodness of fit ratings averaged close to 1.0 on a five-point scale (1 = 'bad', 5 = 'good') for each probe presentation point (1, 2, 3) and probe type (related, unrelated). In other words, none of the probe-supplemented sentence fragments provided good continuations. The reason for these uniformly 'bad' continuation ratings appears to stem from an unfortunate decision to begin all fragments from the start of the sentence (e.g. from '*The professor* . . .' as in (17) above, rather than '*his mother* . . .' (18)), which is the starting point of interest for determining minimal context requirements for the priming effect.

processes of reference assignment. Which of these interpretations of CMLP turns out to be correct obviously has important implications for how we view results obtained from applying this paradigm to the study of aphasic comprehension deficit and agrammatism in particular.

Another source of interpretive difficulty for CMLP concerns the timing of the visual probe in relation to the aurally presented target sentences and the time-course of lexical activation and retrieval. In elderly subjects and those with brain pathology, the speed of lexical access is slowed and susceptibility to associative priming (hypo- or hyper-priming) may vary with the type of aphasic syndrome (Milberg *et al.*, 1987, 1988a, 1995). The strength of the facilitation of lexical decision to a probe word presented in the temporal vicinity of the gap in the target sentence probably depends upon (a) how residually active the prime word remains at the gap site, (b) how long it takes to activate the verb which provides the gap site and (c) how both of these processes synchronize with lexical access to the visual probe. The degree of synchrony between these parallel but modality-independent processes of lexical activation is probably critical for the strength of 'trace reactivation' observed at the gap site, but the operating characteristics of these two channels are generally not known to the investigator.

## Load/capacity effects and the cross-modal lexical priming paradigm

But contemplating these imponderables leads us to consider the CMLP in a different light, emphasizing its dual-task characteristics, and the possible operation of load/capacity considerations that are quite independent of semantic priming effects. Performing a (visual) lexical decision task while engaging in spoken sentence comprehension constitutes a dual processing task that divides the subject's attention, particularly if the sentences are as complex as (17) above. Viewed from the perspective of processing the target sentence, and following Gibson's model, we expect an increased load on the parser, from the time that the prime word is first identified, until the gap site for its attachment is detected, at which time a quantum of on-line processing capacity should be released, at least until some subsequent call on resource allocation is made. The consequences of uptake and release of processing capacity by the sentence processing task should be reflected in slowed or speeded lexical decision times to probe stimuli.[10]

For object relative clause constructions, Gibson's model predicts an increased load with the processing of the second NP, for object relatives such as (17) above, followed by a drop in load following the verb:

(17′)     *Jimmy used the new* **pen**$_i$[1] *that his mother-in-law*[2] *purchased* [3] **T**$_i$
          *because* . . .

---

[10] This would be expected to occur regardless of the lexical status of the probe. However, reaction times to non-word probes are generally not reported in CMLP studies, though they are relevant for capacity/load accounts of the data.

Thus, load/capacity considerations predict facilitation for lexical decisions at the gap site (position $^3$ in (17′) above) regardless of whether the probe is semantically related to the prime, though lexical priming effects may of course provide additional facilitation for related probes.

What evidence do we have that load/capacity considerations, in addition to priming effects, apply to 'trace reactivation' in CMLP? Evidence comes from studies where 'trace reactivation effects' are predicted to occur, but have not been found in psycholinguistic experiments. Recall sentence (15). The gap site occurs at the end of the sentence where the NP 'which student' is bound as the indirect object of 'ask . . . about $t_i$'. However, at the point where the listener has just processed the verb *ask*, but before *Mary* has been recognized, it is predicted that the parser should detect a possible gap site, resulting in a 'trace reactivation' effect that should prime a semantically related probe at this potential gap. However, such priming effects are not observed. In all likelihood, the appearance of *Mary* gazumps binding of 'which student' to direct object position after the verb. Load/capacity considerations indicate that there should in fact be slower lexical decision times to a visual probe presented at the direct object gap which would tend to cancel any priming effect at this position. Thus, load/capacity considerations do seem to be needed to account for the absence of predicted priming effects at gap sites where there is competition to fill the slot between a previously encountered filler candidate and an upcoming lexical item.

Direct evidence for the operation of load/capacity effects at positions of competition for verb–object binding comes not from the CMLP paradigm but from the self-paced reading paradigm considered earlier. Stowe (1986) found slower reading times for the object pronoun *us* in sentences like (20c), compared with those like (20a) or (20b) where there is no competition between a previously activated filler (*who* in this case) and an upcoming lexical candidate (*Ruth* in these examples).

(20) (a)   *My brother wanted to know if **Ruth** will bring us home to Mom at Christmas.*

(b)   *My brother wanted to know **who** will bring us home to Mom at Christmas.*

(c)   *My brother wanted to know **who Ruth** will bring us home to t $_i$ at Christmas.*

### Recapitulation and summary: trace reactivation and the CMLP paradigm

The cross-modal lexical priming task has been extensively used as a measure of on-line processing of filler–gap dependencies, which is taken to be a critical component of the sentence comprehension process, whether or not one subscribes to a modular or an interactive theory of sentence comprehension. The paradigm better meets criteria for a behavioural measure of on-line processing than other paradigms which cannot in any case be applied to spoken language processing. However, it has yet to be convincingly demonstrated that the 'trace reactivation' effect in CMLP is specifically linked to anaphora retrieval, and is more than simply a strictly local effect, triggered by lexical access to the verb interacting with temporally contiguous lexical retrieval operations and not specifically diagnostic of complex sentence parsing operations.

We have also seen that 'trace reactivation' in CMLP can be seen as a dual-processing task, and as such appears to be sensitive to transient load/capacity effects which require for their understanding an explicit model of parsing and a metric of sentence complexity. The presence of transient load effects is both good news and bad news – good news in that it demonstrates sensitivity of the paradigm to local fluctuations in syntactic processing load, and bad news in that such effects may only be demonstrable when the combined effect of performing both tasks simultaneously (lexical decision and sentence comprehension) challenges working memory capacity and invokes strategic processing.

Partly as a result of difficulties associated with the interpretation of behavioural measures of on-line processing, psycholinguistics has turned in recent years to physiological techniques of imaging the brain's response while subjects are engaged in spoken or written language processing. The findings in this new and exciting area of research are fluid and the potential pitfalls many. This area, where angels fear to tread, shall be the locale for our next expedition.

## Neural imaging techniques and on-line sentence processing

In recent years, ERPs (event-related brain potentials) have assumed a leading role in efforts to find an empirical grounding for modular or interactive theories of on-line sentence processing. Broadly speaking, as discussed in chapter 2, three temporally distinct components of the brain's ERP responses to spoken or visually presented sentences have been identified, though their precise inter-relationships to one another and their respective functions in on-line sentence processing have yet to be firmly established. The first to be discovered, the N400 (Kutas and Hillyard, 1980a, 1980b, 1980c), has been identified with semantic anomaly detection, or with an expectancy violation ('surprise' reaction) when a word is encountered which is not anticipated in current context. A variety of unusual word collocations may provoke an N400 response, including but by no means confined to thematic role violations (e.g. '. . . eat the *home* . . . *the plane can walk faster* . . .'). The time window of the N400, which typically begins about 300 ms post-stimulus and peaks at around half a second, suggests that it may be open to control by attentional factors or strategic processing effects. This indeed appears to be the case. The magnitude of the N400 response has been found to be directly related to strength of the expectancy associated with a target noun in context, as measured by its cloze frequency (Gunter, Friederici and Schriefers, 2000).[11]

---

[11] The cloze frequency is an empirically derived measure of a word's predictability, given some pre-specified amount of verbal context.

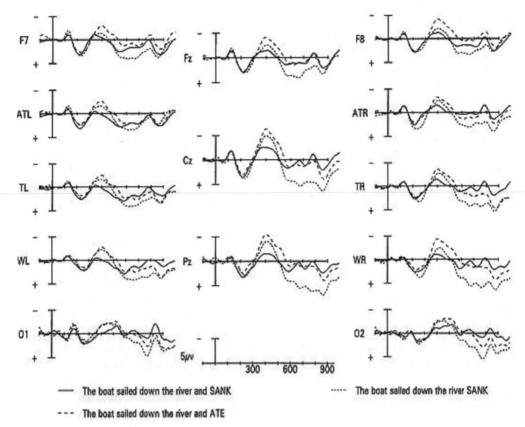

F7
Fz
F8
ATL
ATR
TL
Cz
TR
WL
Pz
WR
01
5μν
02

300    600    900

——— The boat sailed down the river and SANK            ⋯⋯ The boat sailed down the river SANK

- - - The boat sailed down the river and ATE

Figure 13.4  *ERPs to well-formed, semantically anomalous and syntactically anomalous verbs*

In addition to the N400, two primarily syntactic components of the ERP have been identified, an early, predominantly left-hemisphere, anterior, negative-signed electrical potential, peaking at around 150–200 ms post-stimulus, dubbed the ELAN by Friederici, Hahne and Mecklinger (1996), and a late, positive-signed electrical potential, with an ill-defined peak at around 600 ms post-stimulus and a long tapering tail, known as the P600. Just as in the case of the N400, these additional ERP components are observed as departures from a baseline response obtained when a sentence containing a syntactic/semantic anomaly is compared with a non-anomalous control sentence. Figure 13.4 illustrates the presence of N400 and P600 components in a 13-channel ERP recording from electrodes placed left, right and midline from front (frontal) to back (occipital) across the skull. The three central electrodes (Fz, Cz and Pz) most clearly illustrate the presence of the N400 and P600 components.

Figure 13.4 shows that the verb *ate*, which is semantically anomalous in the context of the sentence '*The boat sailed down the river and **ate** in the storm.*', elicited a typical N400 response. But the verb *sank*, when placed in the context '*The boat sailed down the river **sank** in the storm.*', yielded, in addition to the temporally more discrete N400, a sustained, accumulating P600 voltage positivity. The functional significance of the polarity (sign) of these voltage shifts is not known, but the magnitude of the ERP trace excursion from the control comparison is thought to reflect additional neural processing activity concomitant upon processing the (anomalous) target sentence. We might speculate that the sustained P600 represents an ongoing effort to reinterpret or re-parse the garden path sentence, whereas the N400 results in a temporally localized increase in processing load caused by lexical semantic discrepancy (which must remain unresolved) between a word and its sentential context.

Both the N400 and the P600 represent late or long-latency effects that are unlikely to be components of a fast-operating modular (syntactic or lexical) processing capability. However, such a component does seem to have been identified in the ELAN (N150), which is observed when the target sentence is ungrammatical owing to an error of phrase structure, such as (hypothetically) '*The boat sailed down the **sank** river.*'[12] Phrase structure errors represent violations of surface structure syntax, which require no analysis beyond the ability to track the order of word classes and inflectional morphemes in an input sentence: errors that could be detected by a syntactic pattern recognizer that pays no heed to semantic well-formedness or argument structure in the input. Does the ELAN represent the physiological signature of such a modular structural filter? That is the contention of Friederici and her colleagues (Friederici *et al.*, 1996; Hahne and Friederici, 1999).

More evidence is clearly needed, but a coherent operational picture of syntactic and semantic processing in on-line sentence interpretation is beginning to emerge from ERP investigations involving the presentation of control and experimental sentences that contain various combinations of semantic and syntactic anomaly. Some 'syntactic' errors may be visible to the parser mainly through their semantic consequences (e.g. an error of pronoun gender: '*The careless bride dropped **his** bouquet.*'). Phrase structure errors, on the other hand, may pre-empt further in-depth syntactic or semantic processing. Hence the need to consider the differential impact that certain anomalies may have upon the course of subsequent sentence processing, and how different error types may interact with one another. Also, as always, careful attention needs to be paid to particular task requirements and the response strategies that subjects may adopt to meet them. We illustrate this point by considering two recent case studies.

### Phrase structure and argument structure violations and ERPs

Frisch, Hahne and Friederici (2004) investigated components of the ERP for evidence of modularity in the way that phrase structure errors interact with verb argument structure violations. Verb argument structure violations are

---

[12] Significantly, the ELAN component of the ERP is only consistently elicited with auditory presentation of the stimulus sentences and is not observed when test sentences are presented visually, usually at a fixed interval, word by word, from a central fixation point on the computer screen.

Table 13.1 *ERP effects of phrase structure and argument structure violations*

| English example (see Frisch *et al.*, 2004 for German) | | PSV | ASV | N150 | N400 | P600 |
|---|---|---|---|---|---|---|
| *The old cat **slept** in the garden and* ... | CONTROL | no | no | – | – | – |
| *The cat **slept** old the garden and* ... | PSV | yes | no | yes | no | yes |
| *The old cat **slept** the garden and* ... | ASV | no | yes | no | yes | yes |
| *The in cat **slept** the garden and* ... | PSV + ASV | yes | yes | yes | **no** | yes |

PSV = phrase structure violation    ASV = argument structure violation

lexically specified. They arise when a verb fails to obtain its lexically specified complement, such as when a transitive verb finds itself infelicitously paired with an 'object' noun phrase, as in '*The old cat slept the garden*'. These syntactic anomalies depend for their detection on lexical access to the verb and how it is marked for transitivity. How will such lexical-access-dependent errors interact with phrase structure violations in general (such as '*The in cat slept old the garden*'), which may be detected by a fast-acting phrase structure filter?

An interactive theory of language processing might predict that errors of phrase structure and verb argument structure would be additive and qualitatively indistinguishable in terms of ERP response components. On the other hand, the modular theory of parsing would predict that phrase structure errors would be detected early and that sentences containing them may not be subjected to further processing. Phrase structure errors were known to yield an ELAN but not an N400 response. Verb argument structure violations were known to yield an N400 response. Both types of error usually produce a P600 component. The question was: what would be the effect of joint violations of phrase structure and verb argument structure?

The findings for the two error types and their combination are summarized in Table 13.1. Please note that we have used different English examples from those of Frisch *et al.* (2004), because of difficulties of translation from the German originals. Clearly there is a need to replicate the findings in English. The phrase final *and* in the examples indicates that the target structure appeared in non-sentence final position, in order to avoid possible 'sentence wrap up effects'.

Phrase structure violations (PSVs) elicited distinctly different patterns of ERP activity from argument structure violations (ASRs), with only the former eliciting the early left anterior negativity ELAN (N150), and only the latter eliciting an N400 component. However, the key finding insofar as the syntactic modularity hypothesis is concerned is the absence of an N400 effect under the condition of combined phrasal and argument structure violations. This indicates that the effects of combined phrase and argument structure violations are not additive and supports the modularity hypothesis that early detection of phrase structure violations acts as a filter on further lexically mediated syntactic and semantic processing.

Apart from the support they lend to the modularity hypothesis, these results raise a number of interesting questions. Under what conditions does detection of a phrase structure anomaly block further lexical-semantic and syntactic processing? Evidence suggests that the sanction is not absolute, but can be overridden by experimental instructions to focus on the semantic well-formedness (or plausibility) of the target sentence (Hahne and Friederici, 2002). The nature of the late positivity (P600) is also an issue of current debate. Its prolonged time course suggests an active process of repair or revision, which is likely because of its late onset to be affected by strategic processing. Research suggests that the late positivity component of the ERP (P600) is not a unitary phenomenon. It is elicited by a range of syntactic and semantic anomalies. Its strength and topographic distribution vary depending on the nature of the difficulties presented to the listener. Friederici, Hahne and Saddy (2002) conducted a study, trading off syntactic complexity of target sentences against syntactic violations. Results from their reading experiment demonstrated that although both processing aspects elicited a late positivity (P600), they were different in distribution. The repair-related positivity preceded by a negativity displayed a centro-parietal distribution, whereas the complexity-related positivity showed a fronto-central scalp distribution.

## Jabberwocky sentence processing and ERPs

Jabberwocky sentences are a long-standing source of fascination for psycholinguists.[13] They potentially constitute an elegant way of investigating the processing of morpho-syntactic structure in the (almost) controlled absence of lexical semantic content. However, Jabberwocks must be handled with care. They can bite the careless hand that feeds. An occasional Jabberwocky sentence will certainly stand out in a crowd of non-Jabberwocky sentences, syntactically well formed or not. The brain's ERP response to a Jabberwocky sentence in this mixed company is probably not very meaningful. However, Hahne and Jescheniak (2001) presented their Jabberwocky sentences composed of pseudo-words, and a matched group of 'regular' sentences composed of real words, in separate blocks of trials at least one week apart so that listeners made their judgements of grammaticality about sentences that were homogeneous as to their Jabberwocky or non-Jabberwocky status. All grammatical errors involved phrase structure violations. The Jabberwocky sentences were created from non-Jabberwocky sentences, as indicated in Table 13.2 (again, English analogues have been substituted for the German).

Both the Jabberwocky and the regular sentences which contained a phrase structure violation provoked an ELAN (N150) response, which was followed by a parietally distributed late positivity (P600). Thus it seems phrase structure errors were detected early in the Jabberwocky sentences as well as their counterparts in the regular (non-Jabberwocky) ones. This finding is consistent with a syntactic pattern recognizer, sensitive to word class inflectional morphology and word

---

[13] No respectable text on psycholinguistics can avoid acknowledging Lewis Carroll's Jabberwocky poem. We take the opportunity to remind you here: ''Twas brillig, and the slithy toves / Did gyre and gimble in the wabe; / All mimsy were the Borogoves, / And the mome raths outgrabe.'

Table 13.2 *ERP effects of Jabberwocky sentences*

| English example<br>(see Hahne and Jescheniak, 2001) | 'Dialect' | Error | N150 | N400 | P600 |
|---|---|---|---|---|---|
| *The old cat **slept** in the garden.* | nonJabb.[a] | none | no | yes[b] | no |
| *The lon garp **frept** in the kayton* | Jabb. | none | no | no | yes |
| *The old cat **slept** the in garden.* | nonJabb. | PSV | yes | no | yes |
| *The lon garp **frept** the in kayton* | Jabb. | PSV | yes | no | yes |

[a] Jabb. = Jabberwocky
[b] The comparison here was in relation to well-formed Jabberwocky sentences.

order. The persisting late positivity (P600) is more difficult to explain, particularly in the case of Jabberwocky sentences, where the absence of an N400 indicated – as expected – an absence of lexical processing. Why should the parser persevere with syntactic processing or repair in 'sentences' that are clearly non-meaningful?

Consistent with the previously mentioned study (Frisch, Hahne and Friederici, 2004), no N400 was observed in regular sentences that contained a phrase structure violation. However, there was clear evidence of an N400 response in well-formed regular sentences, when compared with their well-formed Jabberwocky counterparts. We can read this as independent support for a modular, fast-acting morpho-syntactic filter.

### Deep and surface anaphora

The foregoing studies indicating differences in components of ERP responses by the language areas to phrase structure versus argument structure violations provide support for a two-stage model of sentence processing, whereby automatic syntactic operations precede semantic binding operations. Consistent with this model, we might also expect to find evidence that syntactically controlled aspects of anaphora resolution yield a distinct signature in the ERP signal, from (semantic) processes of reference assignment. This distinction is critical for theories of agrammatism, as we shall see in the next chapter. Recall from chapter 3 that linguists distinguish between (a) the retrieval of elided constituents in structures of clause coordination or subordination and (b) the interpretive operation of assigning reference to pronouns or other referential expressions. Elided expressions (or traces) are indicated in square brackets in the examples below and their respective fillers are shown in bold.

> **John**, the rotten cad, **gave** a ring to Mary and [. . .] a necklace to Lisa.
> **The ring** that he gave [. . .] to her was made of gold.

Traces can always be filled by expressions (known as their antecedents), which have already make an explicit appearance in the sentence, prior to the gap. The rules of gap filling are part of the syntax of the language. The assignment of reference to anaphoric expressions is a matter of semantic interpretation, often said to be under pragmatic control, where there may or may not be an explicit referring expression mentioned in previous discourse, as in the following (anaphoric expressions in bold):

> *He* gave *her* a ring.

Can these two operations, which Hankamer and Sag (1976) and Sag and Hankamer (1984) (hereafter H&S) distinguished as cases of 'surface' (syntactically controlled) and 'deep' (pragmatically controlled) anaphora, be distinguished in the time signature or the topography of on-line neural processing? There are indications from recent ERP studies that they can (Kluender and Kutas, 1993; Felser, Clahsen and Münte, 2003; Streb, Hennighausen and Rosler, 2004).

Streb *et al.* (2004), working in German, presented their subjects, in a fixed-pace word-by-word reading task, with sentences such as the following (in literal English translation):

(21) (a)    *Werner gave <u>Lisa</u> a ring of shining gold and Joseph gave **Lisa** a necklace.*
   (b)    *Werner, a generous banker, gave <u>Lisa</u> a ring and Joseph gave **Lisa** a necklace.*
(22) (a)    *Werner <u>gave</u> Lisa a ring of shining gold and Joseph [. . .] Lisa a necklace.*[14]
   (b)    *Werner, a generous banker, <u>gave</u> Lisa a ring and Joseph [. . .] Lisa a necklace.*
(23) (a)    *Werner gave Lisa a ring of shining gold and Joseph gave **Anna** a necklace.*
   (b)    *Werner, a generous banker, gave Lisa a ring and Joseph gave **Anna** a necklace.*

The sentence pairs (a–b, above) were constructed so as to control for overall length and to systematically vary the distance between the antecedent expression (<u>underlined</u>) and its anaphor (given in **bold**: a null anaphor in 22a–b). A behavioural measure (reading time) and the magnitude of the averaged ERP signal indicated that sentence processing was facilitated under the 'near' condition where the anaphor was closer to its antecedent (condition a).

However, the main interest of the experimenters lay in how the ERP responses reflected differences in the way that the two kinds of anaphoric relationship, so-called 'surface anaphora' illustrated in (22a–b) and 'deep' or discourse model-interpretive (MI) anaphora (21a–b), are processed. Of course, we have no precise notion of how anaphoric relations are resolved in language processing, but H&S's linguistic investigations tell us that it is the morpho-syntactic form of expression of the antecedent which is critical in cases of 'surface' anaphora, such as ellipsis under conjunction, but that it is the conceptual entities or mental representations that make up the objects of discourse which provide the relevant antecedents for 'deep' or MI anaphora.

In order to contrast the ERP responses of these two kinds of anaphora, a subtraction was performed on the averaged ERP signals, taking the difference between the more difficult (far) and the easier (near) anaphora resolution (a–b) within each type of anaphora condition. Note that in the 'control' condition (23a–b), the anaphor (*Anna*) strictly speaking has no antecedent, either in previous

---

[14] This elided verb in the conjoined sentence is grammatically acceptable in German.

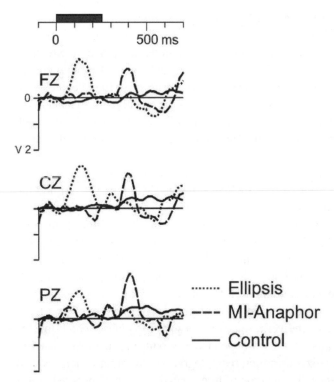

Figure 13.5 *Differences in ERPs under ellipsis and discourse model interpretive (MI) anaphora*

text, or in terms of discourse referents. The results of this subtraction operation are shown in the average residual ERP signals for frontal (Fz), central (Cz) and parietal (Pz) electrodes over the left perisylvian language area (Figure 13.5).

Figure 13.5 shows two distinct ERP response components, an early left-anterior negativity (LAN) (N150) associated with the ellipsis or 'surface' anaphora condition, and a typical N400 component associated with the MI or 'deep' anaphora condition. The topology of the two components of the ERP response differed. As its name suggests, the earlier LAN had its focus of activity over the left anterior language regions, whereas the later N400 component had its focus over the parietal language area. Thus, we have converging evidence in the temporal signature of on-line neural activity for a distinction between fast-acting and possibly syntax-driven processes in anaphora resolution and slower processes that fall within the typical time frame and (negative) polarity associated with semantic processing load. It is tempting, though possibly premature, to interpret these findings as a neural processing reflex of the distinction between syntactic binding operations and the integration of anaphoric expressions into the discourse model at a higher level of meaning construal.

It is natural to extend the investigation of syntactic anaphora to filler–gap dependencies in general, involving sentences where constituents have for all intents and purposes been 'front shifted' from their positions in canonical sentence structure such as wh-questions or topicalized NPs. As argued previously, full construal of such sentences demands the satisfaction of filler–gap dependencies very similar in kind to those required for processing of ellipsis under conjunction. Kluender and Kutas (1993) were among the first to report ERP correlates of filler–gap dependencies in non-canonical sentence structures. They also found evidence of an early LAN, which they tentatively interpreted as the neural reflex of detecting a filler and placing it 'on hold'. A later N400 component was also identified, which they hypothesized might represent the 'integration cost' of inserting a filler at its gap site.

Recently, Felser, Clahsen and Münte (2003) have sought to use the early (LAN) and late (P600) components of the ERP to separate factors that determine the cost of 'filler' detection and temporary working-memory storage, from those that determine the cost of 'integration' at the trace site. Recall that temporary storage of fillers and their integration at trace sites represent separate cost functions in Gibson's sentence processing complexity metric. Felser *et al.* (2003) recorded event-related brain potentials (ERPs) during the processing of unambiguous German sentences containing different types of filler–gap dependency. Both topicalization constructions and wh-questions were found to elicit a LAN prior to the processing of the verb, relative to a gap-free control condition. At the verb, sentences containing a wh-dependency produced a parietal positivity (P600) relative to topicalization structures. Integration cost but not memory cost was found to be influenced by the type of filler–gap dependency involved.

In summary, we have some support, mainly from ERP responses to different kinds of filler–gap dependencies, for fractionation of anaphor retrieval into distinct stages: an early and more anteriorly distributed stage, and a later and more posteriorly distributed stage of processing. These stages appear to correspond to what H&S initially identified as two linguistic classes of anaphora (Hankamer and Sag, 1976), but subsequently reinterpreted as two levels of anaphoric processing (Sag and Hankamer, 1984), corresponding to 'syntactically controlled' processing of structures of ellipsis and conceptual or 'pragmatically' controlled referent interpretation. We have also tentatively identified these two components of the ERP trace with the 'memory cost' of filler detection-and-hold, and the subsequent 'integration cost' of incorporating the filler at the gap site into the evolving sentence meaning. Future work will reveal how well these distinctions can be retained or refined.

## General summary and conclusions

We began this chapter by asking whether developments of on-line behavioural and functional neuroimaging techniques could offer empirical grounds for choosing between modular and interactive theories of sentence processing. We acknowledged that before such a question can be posed it was necessary to explore the concept of working memory in sentence processing, and considered two competing concepts of working memory capacity: (1) a strategy-sensitive, general-purpose, limited-capacity resource, which varies across individuals and is invoked when task demands are high or subjects' attention is divided between language processing and some other mental task, and (2) a dedicated storage buffer, specialized for syntactic parsing and with relatively 'hard' capacity limitations that do not vary significantly across individuals, which rarely manifests itself under normal conditions of language use, but can be induced to overload (or produce 'garden path' behaviour) by particular syntactic structures or infelicitous constructions. Although these two conceptions of working memory have vied for allegiance in the literature, they are not necessarily incompatible. Each would likely operate over a different time window (seconds in one case, and a few tenths of a second, at most, in the other). Support for both concepts may be gleaned from the literature, depending upon the experimental paradigm employed and the modality of language processing used. It would probably be fair to say that the earlier experimental results based largely on visual presentation of sentence materials under conditions that favoured strategic processing yielded evidence that tended to favour general-purpose working memory capacity accounts.

But real-life on-line language processing is usually more rapid and automated than the kind which takes place in psycholinguistics experiments. Also, the reaction-time-based behavioural techniques used to observe on-line processing that still comprise the bulk of the literature are probably overly affected by strategic processing. We examined in some detail the most celebrated of these, the so-called trace reactivation effect, based on the cross-modal semantic paradigm. We found that not only is the effect quite fragile, but its interpretation is problematical. We could not decide, on the evidence considered, whether enhanced priming at trace sites represents a behavioural index of symbolic syntactic processing in the form of anaphoric binding, as predicted by generative syntactic theory, or whether it constitutes a strictly local effect whereby identification of a verb differentially activates its likely complements.[15] Another difficulty of interpretation with the 'trace reactivation' effect stems from the dual nature of the task. Sentence processing in the auditory modality is interrupted by a visual word recognition or lexical decision task. Lexical decision response times to the visual probe may be seen as a function of the residual working memory capacity (assuming both tasks draw from the same resource). While these considerations do not constitute an argument against the mechanism of trace reactivation, they reveal an additional source of complexity in the interpretation of the reaction time data yielded by the paradigm.

Consequently experimenters have turned increasingly to functional neuroimaging techniques, of which ERP has been the most thoroughly studied. Here we

---

[15] Recent studies of long-distance dependencies in a language such as Japanese which permits 'scrambling' of constituent structure are pertinent to this point. See Nakano, Felser and Clahsen (2002).

found suggestive, though hardly conclusive evidence for the operation of a modular phrase structure filter for detecting gross anomalies of phrase structure (the LAN), and where such filtering applies, evidence that further lexical semantic processing is suspended, as evidenced by the lack of an N400 effect. These findings are relatively new and untested. Although they favour a version of the modularity hypothesis, it is not, as we shall argue later, necessarily the kind of modularity postulated by a previous generation of psycholinguistic models (Frazier and Fodor, 1978; Fodor, 1983), but quite possibly a pre-symbolic level of processing that orients or guides the parser towards a fuller syntactic and semantic analysis of the input utterance. One of the major aims of this chapter has been to set the stage for a discussion of on-line studies of sentence processing in aphasia, to which we return in the next chapter.

# 14  Agrammatism revisited

## Introduction

We suspended discussion of the nature of agrammatic comprehension impairment in chapter 12, in order to consider the role of working memory in sentence processing and to review the methodology of on-line language assessment. With a clearer picture of the alternative (but not necessarily irreconcilable) concepts of working memory resources utilized in volitional and automated language processing,[1] together with an appreciation of the current state-of-the-art in behavioural and neural techniques for monitoring moment-by-moment fluctuations in processing load, we are better equipped to critically evaluate competing theories of receptive agrammatism. But to avoid needless confusion that often attends discussion of this topic, let us be clear what we mean by 'receptive agrammatism', how it relates to the clinical classification of aphasia (Broca's, Wernicke's, anomic, conduction and transcortical aphasia), and why this particular language syndrome has preoccupied neurolinguistic research more than any other over the last quarter century or so.

Receptive agrammatism refers to a pattern of comprehension impairment that is revealed by psycholinguistic investigations of the kind described in detail in chapter 12. Subjects manifest an inability to use syntactic cues for sentence comprehension in tests of thematic role assignment, where pragmatic and lexical cues to meaning are rigorously controlled by selection of sentence materials and other aspects of the testing situation. A pattern of comprehension impairment that can be identified as receptive agrammatism has the following attributes: (1) not better than chance performance for agent identification on reversible passive constructions, (2) poor performance on object relative clauses and other structures involving departures from canonical word order, and (3) selective 'blindness' to the presence of semantically opaque function words or grammatical affixes.

Receptive agrammatism is a frequent accompaniment of expressive agrammatism, one of the defining characteristics of Broca's aphasia. But receptive

---

[1] A general-purpose working memory that is capacity-limited but variable across individuals (Just and Carpenter, 1992), used for volitional language and other symbolic processing, versus a dedicated special-purpose buffer to support automated syntactic-semantic parsing, also capacity-limited, but essentially invariable across individuals (Caplan and Waters, 1999), as discussed in the previous chapter.

agrammatism is not only found in Broca's aphasia. It can also occur in other varieties of aphasia such as anomia or even Wernicke's aphasia. Nor is receptive agrammatism confined to adult aphasia. It can be observed in the developmental language disorder known as specific language impairment (SLI). A form of receptive agrammatism may also present itself in cases of acquired or developmental reading disorder (Smith, Macaruso, Shankweiler and Crain, 1989). Lesion studies and the burgeoning neuroimaging literature most frequently implicate Broca's area in receptive agrammatism, but as often as not, other regions of the perisylvian language area[2] are also involved. No single, circumscribed lesion site has been identified as producing receptive agrammatism. Quite possibly the syndrome could arise from multiple forms of pathological interaction among regionally distributed cell assemblies.

Because receptive agrammatism can only be reliably identified by formal psycholinguistic testing and not through clinical observation or self report, its status as a clinical category remains somewhat problematical. Even more so is its status and characterization as a modular disability, as we shall presently see. However, the theoretical significance of receptive agrammatism will by now be abundantly clear to you, the discerning reader, as a potential test case for modularity of syntactic parsing in a model of language processing.

Progress in understanding language processing was impeded in the mid 1980s by doubts about the validity of the 'off-line' methods of comprehension assessment which were available to researchers at the time. Careful attention to the control of structural, pragmatic and lexical influences on sentence construal and the causes of temporary or sustained parsing ambiguities yielded a greater appreciation of the difficulties of deciding between modular or interactive architectures of language processing (Crain and Steedman, 1985). In the two decades following the original formulation of the competing modular (Frazier, 1978) and interactive (Marslen-Wilson, 1975) theories of sentence processing, there was still no empirical resolution of the fundamental architectural question. One major reason for the continued impasse was again primarily methodological. Even the best of the behavioural measures of on-line sentence processing, such as the 'trace reactivation' adaptation of the cross-modal semantic priming paradigm, were not sufficiently robust or accurate in their temporal resolution to yield conclusive evidence for or against modular sequential processing.

However, improvements in the spatial and temporal resolution of functional neural imaging has recently tipped the weight of evidence in favour of a modular and localist account of sentence processing that is broadly compatible with the classical Broca-Wernicke-Lichtheim model (BWL), which we outlined in chapter 3. Physiological measures of early post-stimulus automatic processing, based upon sensitivity to morpho-syntactic regularities, with a locus in Broca's area have been demonstrated with ERP and fMRI imaging. The case for Broca's area

---

[2] The perisylvian language area refers to the central language areas that surround the sylvian fissure: Broca's area anteriorly, and parts of the parietal and temporal lobes posteriorly – the angular gyrus and the superior temporal gyrus (Wernicke's area).

being homologous with the 'mirror neuron' gestural imitation system in area A5 of the macaque monkey brain (discussed in chapter 7) has established a plausible evolutionary basis for a syntactic pattern recognition system that provides a 'first-pass' parse of language input. Also consistent with the classical BWL model, the involvement of the posterior parieto-temporal language area in lexical retrieval and lexical-semantic analysis has been upheld by neuroimaging studies of normal individuals. Of course, many controversies and unanswered questions remain. More specifically, it has not yet been established whether the syntactic and lexical semantic automata that underpin normal, unreflective, language processing are best modelled sub-symbolically by some kind of 'neural network' or by 'symbol processing' algorithms of the kind invoked in the previous generation of pycholinguistic theories and classical AI. We shall investigate these unresolved problems in the final chapter.

## Agrammatism revisited

In the meantime, it is appropriate to revisit the question of the nature of agrammatism in Broca's aphasia, in the light of recent advances in the neurolinguistics of on-line language processing in normal individuals. Please recall the state of play where we left the game at the end of chapter 12.

Off-line investigations with a range of grammatical constructions had established a typical performance profile of impaired sentence comprehension in Broca's aphasia, which involved above-chance performance on simple canonical sentence structures and chance level performance on structures (such as fully reversible passives and object relative clauses and cleft constructions) that involve 'scrambling' or departures from unmarked constituent ordering. A fractious league of competing research teams vied for the agrammatism trophy. They divided over the competence–performance question: whether agrammatic comprehension deficit involves damage to the linguistic knowledge-base underlying grammatical performance, or whether task requirements of certain off-line language comprehension tests exceeded aphasic working memory capacities. The performance limitation view gained credibility with an influential paper by Linebarger, Schwartz and Saffran (1983), showing that Broca's aphasics often retained an ability to detect errors of grammatical well-formedness that seemed far in excess of their ability to successfully process the same structures in off-line tests of language comprehension. Faced with the seeming paradox of impaired receptive syntactic processing for language comprehension, but only mild or minimal impairment for grammatical anomaly detection, most theorists of aphasia felt obliged to retreat from the position that agrammatic language comprehension involves a global receptive parsing deficit, such as is implied in the notion of simplified parsing strategies or 'heuristic processing' described in chapter 12.

Most researchers concluded either (a) that parsing abilities are substantially spared in Broca's aphasia, but that there is a specific difficulty of thematic role assignment associated with certain complex sentence structures, or (b) that performance on certain complex sentence structures in off-line tests of thematic role assignment imposes processing load requirements that are largely absent in grammaticality judgement tasks. In the case of (a), we postulate a specific impairment of linguistic competence. In the case of (b), we postulate a task-specific computational load or working memory requirement in off-line tests of thematic role assignment, a load that Broca's aphasics find unsupportable.[3]

## Off-line methods of language comprehension assessment

Current clinical assessment techniques of language performance and the first generation of experimental psycholinguistic protocols that preceded them constitute what are known as **off-line** measures because they involve, even require, subjects to consciously reflect upon the task that they are performing. The two most commonly used off-line experimental tasks involve acting-out of verbal instructions and picture-matching.[4] Both techniques enable one to test sentence comprehension without the subject having to engage in language production. But both also engage substantial extra-linguistic (cognitive, perceptual and motor) capacities to formulate a response, task demands which are difficult to disentangle from the language processing. For example, some 'directional motion' verbs (*lead, follow*) are much more difficult to interpret from pictures than 'non-directional motion' verbs (*kick, hug*), but there is no way to distinguish the effect of picture interpretation from that of verb semantic processing. Off-line tasks clearly engage more than the largely unconscious and rapid processes which we know must underpin on-line language comprehension. As such, it is often impossible to disentangle the influences of 'primary' language processing (phonetic processing, lexical retrieval, syntactic parsing, semantic interpretation, etc.) from 'post-linguistic' processes (working memory effects, strategy formulation, etc.) required by off-line language tasks.

To illustrate the difficulties posed by off-line tasks let us consider two examples: an early study of aphasics' ability to judge word relations in sentences, widely taken at the time as a convincing demonstration of profound syntactic deficits on the part of agrammatic aphasics; and a second, involving grammaticality judgements, which appeared a decade or so later, and was equally influential in persuading the research community that syntactic abilities of agrammatic aphasics remain *intact*.

---

[3] If the reader feels uneasy about the dichotomy posed here, as to whether there is a substantive, empirically testable consequence at issue, s/he can take comfort in the reassurance that we share your misgivings. More on this point later.
[4] selection from a set of alternatives of the picture that best depicts the situation described in the test sentence.

Table 14.1 *Sentence types used in Zurif et al.'s (1972) study*

| Sentence type | Example |
|---|---|
| 1. Declarative intransitive | *The baby cries.* |
| 2. Declarative transitive | *The dog chases a cat.* |
| 3. Passive (truncated) | *The man was hurt.* |
| 4. wh-question | *Where are my shoes?* |

## A case for syntactic deficit in Broca's aphasia

In what is now something of a classical study using off-line techniques, Zurif, Caramazza and Myerson (1972) attempted to interrogate the internal representations that Broca's aphasics form of simple sentences. Word relatedness judgements were elicited from agrammatic subjects and a group of matched controls, using the method of 'triadic comparisons'. The relatedness judgements were then scaled and graphed by a procedure which produced tree diagrams or *dendrograms* that could then be compared with syntactic phrase structure diagrams yielded by a phrase structure grammar of English for the sentences in question. Two goals could be simultaneously achieved by such an investigation: (a) a demonstration of the psychological reality of phrase structure grammar (in normal language users), and (b) detection of any abnormalities that may exist in agrammatic aphasics' representations of structural relations of words in sentences.

Zurif *et al.* (1972) found that the relatedness-judgement dendrograms of the control subjects corresponded quite closely with the phrase structure trees that would be assigned by a conventional phrase structure grammar of English. But the dendrograms produced from the agrammatics' relatedness judgements indicated that they were unable to perceive grammatical relations between function words and their lexical heads. The agrammatic patients seemed to be effectively *blind* to the information carried by closed-class words and grammatical inflections.

It is worth while considering Zurif *et al.*'s method in some detail. Subjects were asked to read a simple sentence, such as one of those from Table 14.1, all of which were within the capabilities of the Broca's aphasics tested. The words that made up the sentence were then presented in pairs for subjects to make relatedness judgements according to the method of 'triadic comparisons', as illustrated below:

Which pair of words (A or B) *go best together*?

|  | A |  | B |
|---|---|---|---|
| i. | *the – baby* | versus | *the – cries* |
| ii. | *the – baby* | versus | *baby – cries* |
| iii. | *the – cries* | versus | *baby – cries* |

In the method of triadic comparisons, the relatedness of items in a set (in this case words in a sentence) is assessed from a set of pair-wise discrimination judgements (A versus B), each of which contains a triad of items: a pivot (the word *the* in

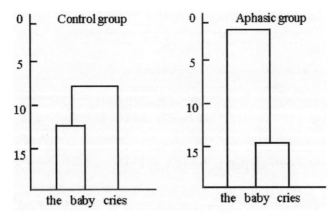

Figure 14.1  *Dendrograms for* The baby cries

comparison (i) above) plus two other items for comparison. The number of triadic comparisons required to map the relations among the items depends on the size of the item set (or the number of words in the sentence in this case). A three-word sentence requires just three triadic comparisons. The pair-wise relatedness judgements are aggregated to produce a measure of the relative relatedness of every word with every other word in the sentence. These relatedness scores may then be input to a *hierarchical clustering* algorithm to produce dendrograms, two-dimensional graphs that capture relations of similarity in terms of how the items cluster with one another in a tree, where the branching structure of the tree reflects relationships of similarity, analogous to the way that syntactic relatedness is captured in a conventional syntactic phrase structure tree.

Figure 14.1 shows the dendrograms obtained for the aphasic and control subjects for 'The baby cries'.

The dendrogram shows relatedness in two ways: (a) in the clusters that are formed, and (b) in the height of the horizontal lines linking members of a cluster. The closer to the base-line, the stronger the linkage.

It is apparent from Figure 14.1 that the similarity measures derived from the control subjects yield dendrograms that quite closely resemble constituent structure relations which would be assigned by a conventional (surface) syntactic parsing of the sentence. On the other hand, the Broca aphasics' dendrogram clusters the two open-class lexical items and leaves the closed-class item (the article) essentially unattached. Compare also the aphasic and control group dendrograms for sentences 2 and 3, shown in Figure 14.2.

Whereas syntactic properties (constituent structure relations) appeared to govern the word relatedness judgements of the control subjects,[5] the Broca's aphasics grouped the content words together, apparently failing to see how the function

---

[5] The dendrograms of the normal control subjects did not always perfectly match the grouping that would be predicted by surface structure phrase markers: e.g. the grouping of the subject noun phrase with the verb ((*The dog*) *chases*) ( *a cat*), rather than the verb with its object noun phrase (*The dog*) (*chases (a cat)*).

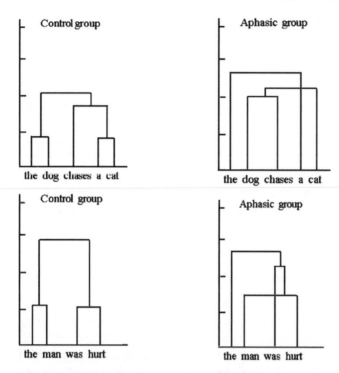

Figure 14.2  *Dendrograms for sentences 2–3*

words were related to their respective lexical heads. Here was graphical evidence, admittedly from a meta-linguistic task, that agrammatic aphasics either failed to perceive, or were much less sensitive to, syntactic relations among open- and closed-class words in simple sentences, just as might be predicted from their telegraphic distortions in sentence production.

Further tests were conducted using triadic comparisons and hierarchical clustering of word relatedness judgements of a wider range of sentence types, varying the types of function words appearing in particular syntactic slots (e.g. *The dog chased a cat* vs. *My dog chased his cat*). To contrast the performance of a narrowly defined group of agrammatic aphasics, a group of *mixed anterior* aphasics was also introduced, who combined symptoms of agrammatism with a more generalized comprehension deficit, as assessed by the Boston Diagnostic Aphasia Test. The results (Zurif and Caramazza, 1976) broadly confirmed the findings of the earlier study. However, additional insights were gained. The agrammatic group showed some sensitivity to *pronouns* as *determiners* of a head noun (*my dog*), but no apparent awareness of an *article* in the same syntactic relationship (*the dog*), whereas the mixed anterior aphasic group were equally insensitive to both, and the controls, as expected, highly sensitive to all *head–dependency* relationships. The agrammatics also showed awareness of the prepositional attachment of *by* or *to* to the head noun in the passive constructions '*Gifts were given by/to John*'. In other words, sensitivity to closed-class items was not uniformly lacking in the relatedness judgements of the agrammatic group, a finding which corresponded with the differential preservation of closed-class items that had been independently observed in studies of Broca's aphasics speech *production* (Goodglass, 1976).

On the evidence of these studies, Zurif and Caramazza (1976) concluded that agrammatic aphasics are unable to grammatically process sentences; that they 'might be capable of processing contentives and certain functors in terms of the semantic roles they establish in a sentence, but probably only to the extent that these roles and relations can be made out on independent grounds – that is, on the grounds of word meaning and semantic plausibility' (1976: 282). Their performance on the relatedness judgement task was attributed to a specific deficit or loss of syntactic competence, which expressed itself ubiquitously in language production, but selectively in comprehension, when syntactic cues were specifically required to process the sentence.

## A case against syntactic deficit in Broca's aphasia

In a highly influential experiment, Linebarger, Schwartz and Saffran (1983) examined agrammatic aphasics' sensitivity to grammatical structure by asking them to judge spoken sentences as 'good' (well-formed) or 'bad' (ill-formed). Only four subjects were used in the study, but each met narrowly defined criteria of agrammatism, i.e. a clinical diagnosis of Broca's aphasia, with severely agrammatic production, and performance at chance level on thematic role assignment in the comprehension of reversible passive constructions. Over two test sessions, each subject was exposed to some 400 sentences, carefully selected to illustrate a range of syntactic phenomena captured in the Government and Binding (GB) model of generative grammar (Chomsky, 1981).

There were equal numbers of grammatical and ungrammatical sentences, with each ungrammatical token having a well-formed counterpart. The sentences were randomized. Subjects heard each sentence spoken twice on a careful, natural reading,[6] then judged its well-formedness by pressing a button labelled 'good' with a smiling face, or pressing a button labelled 'bad' with a frowning face.

The subjects performed remarkably well in judging grammatically well-formed sentences as 'good' and the ill-formed utterances as 'bad'. A representative selection of the sentences is shown in Table 14.2, grouped by error type, according to the terminology of generative grammar. The 'per cent correct' for each type of error shows the range of correct responses across the four subjects. It is a composite measure, based on correct 'hits' and 'false alarms', where chance performance ('just guessing') would yield a score of 50 per cent.

[6] Care was taken to read both well-formed and ill-formed sentences with a natural intonation. The intonation of its well-formed counterpart was used as a model for the pronunciation of an ungrammatical token. This was an important control. Clearly, one would not wish to inadvertently signal the grammatical status of a sentence by how it was pronounced. But it is open to some doubt that prosody can be controlled to the extent that all the ungrammatical sentences could be spoken completely 'normally'.

Table 14.2 *Sentences from Linebarger* et al. *(1983)*

| | Per cent correct[a] |
|---|---|
| (1) *Subcategorization* | |
| (a) *He came my house at six o'clock. | |
| (b) He came to my house at six o'clock. | |
| (c) I hope you will go to the store now. | |
| (d) *I want you will go to the store now. | 88–98 |
| (2) *Particle movement* | |
| (a) *She went the stairs up in a hurry. | |
| (b) She went up the stairs in a hurry. | |
| (c) She rolled the carpet up in a hurry. | 88–98 |
| (3) *Subject–auxiliary* inversion | |
| (a) *Is the boy is having a good time? | |
| (b) Is the boy having a good time? | |
| (c) *Did the old man enjoying the view? | |
| (d) Did the old man enjoy the view? | 88–99 |
| (4) *Empty elements* | |
| (a) Frank$_1$ was expected [t$_1$] to get the job. | |
| (b) *This job$_1$ was expected Frank to get [t$_1$]. | |
| (c) Who$_1$ thought he$_{[1,2]}$ was going to get the job? | |
| (d) *Who$_1$ thought [t$_{1,2}$] was going to get the job? | 89–98 |
| (5) *Tag questions: subject copying* | |
| (a) *The little boy[1] fell down, didn't it[1]? | |
| (b) The little boy[1] fell down, didn't he[1]? | 76–86 |
| (6) *Incomplete extraction* | |
| (a) *How many[1] did you see birds[1] in the park? | |
| (b) How many birds[1] did you see [t$_1$] in the park? | |
| (c) *Which old[1] did you invite men[1] to your party? | |
| (d) Which old men[1] did you invite [t$_1$] to your party? | 86–99 |
| (7) *Gapless relative clauses* | |
| (a) *Mary ate the bread[1] that I baked a cake. | |
| (b) Mary ate the bread[1] that I baked [t$_1$]. | 84–98 |
| (8) *Phrase structure rules* | |
| (a) *The gift my mother is very nice. | |
| (b) The gift for my mother is very nice. | |
| (c) The gift my mother got is very nice. | |
| (d) *Do you like the gift my mother? | 91–100 |
| (9) *Reflexives* | |
| (a) *I helped themselves to the birthday cake. | |
| (b) I helped myself to the birthday cake. | |
| (c) *The famous man itself attended the ceremony. | |
| (d) The famous man himself attended the ceremony. | 77–96 |
| (10) *Tag questions: auxiliary copying* | |
| (a) *John is very tall, doesn't he? | |
| (b) John is very tall, isn't he? | 55–96 |

[a] These 'percentage correct' scores are A′ estimates, derived from signal detection theory (Pollack and Norman, 1964), which correct for the rate of false positive responses (response bias).

The key question in evaluating these results is: how much parsing of the input is required of subjects to perform at the level indicated? Is it necessary to build a complete syntactic representation in order to determine that a sentence is well-formed? How much analysis is required to decide that a given utterance is ill-formed? One conservative way to address the issue is to ask: what is the *minimal* syntactic analysis required of a given sentence in order to detect ungrammaticality? We need not assume a complete parsing for the well-formed sentences, but simply that they will be judged 'good' if no anomaly is detected when they are scanned by the listener.

It is an instructive exercise to work through the ill-formed examples in Table 14.2, trying to identify the point where parsing breaks down, and what causes it to fail. Native speakers are very consistent in their responses to these kinds of ill-formed utterances. Second language learners of English, on the other hand, find it quite difficult to identify some of the syntactic anomalies illustrated below. Let us consider how the parser may be derailed in the course of parsing the starred sentences in (1) (involving subcategorization errors). Assume that the parser attempts to build as much structure as can be inferred as each successive word is encountered.

The first word '*He . . .*' carries a lot of syntactic information. Being a pronoun, its *case inflection* sets up a fragment of phrase structure traditionally labelled 'subject of S', or in terms of GB syntax, 'specifier of an inflectional phrase'. As 'subject of S', *He* anticipates a tensed verb, an expectation which is duly met when *came* is encountered. This intransitive verb does not expect to be followed by an object noun phrase. It is this violation of the verb's syntactic subcategorization frame that the parser detects when *my* is encountered. Similarly, '*\*I want you will . . .*' violates the subcategorization frame for the verb *want*, because if *want* takes a verbal complement clause, it requires that such a clause be non-tensed: '*I want [you] to leave.*' The verb *hope*, on the other hand, requires a tensed verbal complement: '*I hope you leave/left.*' vs. '*\*I hope you to leave.*'

Violations of *subcategorization* frames (such as those in 1) tend to be quite *local* in their effects upon phrase structure, and because they involve information which is directly specified in lexical entries they tend *not* to pose great analytical burdens on the parser. Such syntactic anomalies can, for the most part, be detected from fragments of structure or short word combinations. However, agrammatics also perform quite well in detecting errors in *interrogative structures* (such as 3, 4 and 6 above) and others which involve discontinuous dependencies, indicating awareness of elaborated grammatical relations and details of phrase structure of precisely the kind which seem to be inaccessible to them when they are attempting to assign thematic roles or to engage in semantic processing. For example, to detect the mismatch between the auxiliary verb and the main-verb suffix in

(11)      *\* **Did** the old man enjoy**ing** the view?*

the parser must be sensitive to the dependency between the auxiliary verb and the inflectional suffix on the main verb *across* an intervening subject NP.

However, there were some rather simple-looking structures that most of the agrammatic subjects did not judge well – specifically, those involving pronoun–NP and auxiliary–VP linkages in tag questions (5 and 10), and the selection of an appropriate reflexive pronoun to agree with its licensing NP (9 above). In each of these cases, there is a failure of anaphoric linkage[7] within the sentence: the pronoun to its antecedent noun phrase, or the tag auxiliary to its preceding verb in the main clause. The same difficulty can be seen at work in agrammatics' poor grammaticality judgements of the following sentence types (12–14), discovered subsequent to the Linebarger *et al.* (1983) study (see Linebarger, 1995):

(12)    *Wh-head agreement*
        (a) *The pencil who you bought is nice.
        (b) The pencil which you bought is nice.          <65%

(13)    *VP ellipsis*
        (a) John is here and so is Bill.
        (b) *John is here and so does Bill.          69%

(14)    *Negative polarity*
        (a) No one who we met knew any French.
        (b) *The people who we met knew any French.     <65%

In (12) above, the structure of the relative clause is intact, but the relative pronoun is inappropriate for the NP to which it refers. In (13), *do* is an inappropriate anaphor for the copula *is*, though it serves as the anaphor for many other verbs in the ellipsis of conjoined verb phrases. The negative polarity case (Linebarger, 1987) also involves an anaphoric failure: the lack of an appropriate (e.g. negative) licensor to which *any* may be linked.

In summary, studies of Broca's aphasics with receptive agrammatism (Linebarger *et al.*, 1983; Shankweiler, Crain, Gorrell and Tuller, 1987; Lukatela, Crain and Shankweiler, 1988; Linebarger, 1995) found that subjects' performance on tasks of grammaticality judgement – and what that implied for the preservation of syntactic parsing – was much in excess of their level of performance on syntactically cued off-line sentence comprehension tests. This seemingly paradoxical finding forced a re-think of the nature of receptive agrammatism.

Nevertheless, their grammaticality judgements are not those of normal language users, who would be expected to spot close to 100 per cent of all errors in (1–14) above. Agrammatics appear to have particular difficulty with anaphoric expressions that establish a link between an anaphor and its antecedent within the sentence. This difficulty with anaphoric expressions appears to be confined to anaphoric relations that are under grammatical control, which Mauner, Fromkin and Cornell (1993) refer to as 'syntactic referential dependencies'. There is no

---

[7] We use the term 'anaphor' broadly here and not in the specialized usage of generative grammar, for any short form that refers (back) or stands in for a specific lexical item in text. Thus, not only pronouns but also relative pronouns, demonstratives, and *do* when it stands in for some specific activity verb in tag constructions, as well as cases of 'zero anaphor' (Sag and Hankamer, 1984), are included in the category.

suggestion that agrammatics have particular difficulty comprehending anaphoric expressions whose reference is determined by speaker knowledge or pragmatic constraints, or based on inferences drawn from the speaker-listener's discourse model (see chapter 15).

Re-evaluation of agrammatics' parsing capabilities in the light of Linebarger *et al.*'s (1983) finding that their grammaticality judgements are relatively intact has had basically two consequences. First, it has heightened awareness of the importance of looking closely at task parameters in assessing the linguistic performance of aphasics. Thus, it has been argued that agrammatics may revert to using immature parsing strategies for thematic role assignment whenever the complexity of the off-line comprehension task overloads working memory. Grammaticality judgement, it is claimed, is a simpler task than sentence comprehension, leaving more work space available for parsing. Hence, the discrepancy in the agrammatics' performance on these two tasks is attributed to a performance factor.

Secondly, and in competition with the above-mentioned view, more restrictive theories of the nature of agrammatic syntactic deficit have been formulated (Grodzinsky, 1984, 1990, 1995; Hickok, 1992; Mauner *et al.*, 1993). These theories are intended to simultaneously account for (a) their typical pattern of grammaticality judgements and (b) their differential impairment for various sentence types (e.g. actives vs. passives; subject vs. object relative clauses) in sentence comprehension tasks involving thematic role assignment. These restrictive models of agrammatic syntactic deficit are closely tied to the GB theory of syntax, with its machinery of underlying place holders for elided elements and movement operations. Breakdown of a single module for the assignment of syntactic referential dependencies is held responsible for agrammatic performance in sentence comprehension and grammaticality judgement. We cannot discuss the finer points that distinguish among the members of this restricted class of theories here. However, all assume that normal syntactic representations are phrase structures which are enriched with the mental equivalent of *traces* (null anaphors) co-indexed to their *antecedents*, as shown in sentences 4–7. Agrammatics have, according to this model, lost the ability to co-index traces and their antecedents. This failure of co-indexing applies not only to traces (null anaphors) and their antecedents, but to other anaphoric elements which are under syntactic control as well, such as reflexive pronouns, relative pronouns in wh-questions and relative clauses.

As we discussed earlier (chapter 13), there is suggestive evidence for the psychological reality of traces and co-indexing in normal language users from reactivation of primes in syntactic priming studies (Nicol and Swinney, 1989; Love and Swinney, 1996). Agrammatic aphasics presumably construct phrase markers that are deficient in traces and co-indexing. If this theory of restrictive syntactic impairment is correct, one would predict that agrammatic aphasics will fail to show reactivation of primes at points in a sentence where the theory dictates that traces should occur. But this is only one of three competing theories of agrammatism, which we now turn to consider.

## Three theories of agrammatism

In a review of the literature, Linebarger (1995) identified three major contending theories of agrammatism, which make contrasting assumptions about the role of competence deficits and performance constraints in agrammatic sentence comprehension and grammaticality judgement.

1.       The trade-off hypothesis (TOH: Frazier and Friederici, 1991). Agrammatics are highly sensitive to task conceptual load requirements. In off-line comprehension tests which impose significant task demands, parsing breaks down and agrammatics are obliged to resort to 'primitive' heuristics to identify thematic roles, and extract basic propositional meanings from sentences. But on tasks of low conceptual load (such as grammaticality judgement), they reveal substantially preserved syntactic parsing capabilities.

2.       The mapping hypothesis (MH: Linebarger, 1995). Agrammatics have intact syntactic parsing capabilities, hence they perform quite well on grammaticality judgements. But they are unable to make use of syntactic information in assigning meaning (interpreting the syntax). They perform poorly on tasks that require them to map (surface structure) syntax onto semantic representations. The mapping hypothesis assumes that task demands are specifically associated with semantic interpretation.

3.       The trace deletion hypothesis (TDH: Grodzinsky, 1995; Hickok, 1992; Mauner *et al.*, 1993). Agrammatics suffer from a specific linguistic impairment involving the assignment of syntactic referential dependencies of various kinds.[8] This deficit expresses itself in patterns of intact and impaired thematic role assignment, and also in specific strengths and weaknesses of grammaticality judgement. Agrammatism is thus seen as a modular deficit of syntactic competence, involving the assignment of traces in syntactic constituents that have moved from their respective sites in canonical clause structure. Agrammatics' linguistic behaviour is subject to performance constraints, but not more so than normal language users'.

The above three-way classification does not accommodate all theories of agrammatism that have been influential in recent years. Some still hold to the view, dominant in the early 1980s, that agrammatism involves a breakdown in automatic first-pass[9] syntactic parsing (Friederici and Mecklinger, 1996). Of the

---

[8] such as hold between front-shifted relative pronouns and their place holders in clause structure in wh-questions (***Which book*** did Paul buy *T* ?) and relative clauses ('*Paul bought the last copy* ***that*** *was offered T for sale.*'), or between subject noun phrases and their place holders in object position in passive constructions (***The book*** *was sold T to Paul.*).

[9] A reference to Frazier's influential two-stage model of parsing (Frazier and Fodor, 1978).

three views, the trace deletion hypothesis (TDH, also known as the (anaphoric) 'chain disruption hypothesis') makes the strongest and most restrictive claims about the linguistic abilities of agrammatic patients and should therefore be the one most amenable to testing (open to falsification) on the evidence of comprehension testing and grammaticality judgements. The TDH predicts that agrammatic aphasics will evince a distinctive pattern of syntactic comprehension and grammaticality judgement impairment that distinguishes them from other aphasics as well as non-aphasic individuals. We shall assess the evidence for these claims presently. The TDH and its variants represent a competence impairment model of agrammatism.

The trade-off hypothesis, which might better be labelled the 'reduced capacity model', predicts that there is no distinctive pattern of comprehension or grammaticality judgement disorder that sets agrammatism apart from the disruptions to language processing which may occur whenever the system is placed under stress or is operating under conditions of reduced working capacity. In view of our discussion in the previous chapter, it is germane to ask: what kind of working memory impairment? – an impaired general purpose, attention-directed working memory, or impairment to some dedicated and fleeting register that supports the specialized operations of on-line syntactic parsing? How one answers this question provides grounds for distinguishing between the two performance-based theories, which Linebarger and others dubbed the 'trade-off hypothesis' and the 'mapping hypothesis' respectively. The mapping hypothesis – or some variant thereof – sites agrammatic comprehension deficit squarely within the specialized cognitive domain of on-line language processing, claiming impaired operation of dedicated routines that map grammatical forms onto propositional meanings. It shares with the trade-off hypothesis the contention that grammaticality judgement is less demanding of cognitive resources for language processing than the full task of meaning extraction, but it parts company with the 'trade-off hypothesis' in locating the capacity reduction not in a general-purpose working memory deficit but in a dedicated language register to support specialized language processing (thematic role assignment).

The mapping hypothesis thus represents a 'third way' between two radical alternative theories of agrammatism: a competence deficit model (the trace deletion hypothesis), and a 'pure' performance deficit model (the trade-off hypothesis). As with any 'middle-of-the-road' perspective, the challenge for 'the mapping hypothesis' is to project some distinctive empirical consequences which will enable the investigator to choose between it and both of its competitors. We invite you to pause for a moment and reflect on what evidence you might look for, in terms of behavioural or brain activity, that might enable you to choose among these three alternatives. (A good idea at this point will place you at the 'cutting edge' of neurolinguistic research!) To aid you in this search, let us make some additional comparisons that may help to differentiate among the three models more clearly.

The three models differ in the extent to which they make explicit assumptions about the number and modularity of the stages of processing involved and the

Table 14.3 *Theories of receptive agrammatism*

| Theory | Type of deficit | Locus of deficit | | Principal references |
|---|---|---|---|---|
| | | Functional | Anatomical | |
| Primary agrammatism | Competence | First-pass parsing | Broca's area | Zurif et al., 1976 |
| Trace deletion hypothesis (TDH) | Competence | Second-pass syntactic anaphora assignment | Broca's area | Grodzinsky, 2000 Hickok, 1992 Mauner et al., 1993 |
| Mapping hypothesis (MH) | Competence/ Performance | Semantic thematic role assignment | Perisylvian area | Linebarger, 1995 |
| Trade-off/Reduced capacity hypothesis (RCH) | Performance | Non-specific capacity or efficiency reduction | Distributed non–localized | Frazier and Friederici, 1991 |

locus of the processing difficulty. The TDH is the most explicit and restrictive, assuming two distinct stages of *syntactic* processing: a first-pass syntactic parse that yields the equivalent of an anaphora-free 'surface' structure phrase marker, and a second level of structure-building or interpretation associated with filler–gap dependency assignment, yielding an enriched syntactic representation, the equivalent of 'logical form' in Chomsky's GB model. It is specifically at this second level of syntactic parsing that agrammatic comprehension disorder occurs, according to Grodzinsky's TDH and its variants. First-pass parsing is intact. So too are semantic and pragmatic interpretive processes, insofar as they do not depend on trace assignment.

In contrast, the MH commits itself to only a two-stage model that distinguishes between syntactic parsing and semantic interpretation. Syntactic parsing is 'essentially' intact, though working memory requirements for certain complex structures may exceed reduced agrammatic working memory resources. It is the additional resource load of thematic role assignment, an interpretive semantic process added as a second stage, which is the principal source of agrammatic comprehension difficulties, according to the MH.

The trade-off hypothesis (TOH), which postulates reduction to a single general-purpose working memory capacity, makes no particular assumptions about separate stages of language processing. Nor are 'task demands' that may be imposed by experimental conditions (such as picture interpretation) systematically distinguished from those imposed by on-line syntactic parsing or sentence comprehension, as argued for by Caplan and Waters (1999, 2003). The trade-off hypothesis of agrammatic comprehension deficit favours an interactive or 'constraint satisfaction' model of language processing discussed in chapters 11 and 12. With these comparisons in mind, let us weigh some of the evidence that bears upon the question of choosing between these three theories, plus one or two others of current interest which have not yet been mentioned. The competing theories of receptive agrammatism, with their key characteristics and references, are summarized in Table 14.3.

## Weighing the evidence

### Grammaticality judgement and sentence comprehension

Several researchers (Blackwell and Bates, 1995; Crain, Ni and Shankweiler, 2001) have advanced the argument, alluded to in the introduction to this chapter, that the pattern of agrammatic comprehension impairment is no different from that which can be elicited by subjecting a normal language processor to conditions of stress or cognitive load. This being so, the argument goes, there is nothing particularly distinctive about receptive agrammatism that cannot be straightforwardly accounted for by the reduced capacity hypothesis (RCH), with no need to invoke a specialized impairment of grammatical competence or processing. But the force of this argument is blunted if it is acknowledged that other distinctive patterns of aphasic impairment, such as phonological and semantic errors in word recognition (so-called phonological and semantic paraphasias), which are typical of Wernicke's aphasia, are also observed as occasional 'slips of the ear' that we are all wont to make under stress (Blumstein, 1973). Hence, if these parallels between aphasic and 'normal' behaviour are indicative of 'performance' lapses rather than 'competence' deficits, it also needs to be acknowledged that rather different performance factors are operative in each case, and the two cannot be encompassed by a generalized notion of 'reduced working capacity'. This appeal to the principle of double dissociation, that two clinically dissociable patterns of grammatical and lexical impairment require distinct mechanisms of impairment to account for them, may not be accepted by *all* researchers.[10] But most would probably be persuaded that receptive agrammatism requires us to posit *some* distinctive mechanism of processing disorder.

The TDH makes the strong claim that a common set of operations concerning syntactic anaphora underlie both comprehension and grammaticality judgement difficulties in receptive agrammatism (Grodzinsky and Finkel, 1998; Grodzinsky, 2000). However, the overwhelming majority of commentators on Grodzinsky's (2000) seminal *Behavioural and Brain Sciences* paper rejected this claim. The sentences which cause difficulties of grammaticality judgement for receptive agrammatics are not confined to those that contain filler–gap dependencies. Insensitivity to errors of inflectional morphology are common, particularly in experiments where test items contain a mix of semantically and syntactically anomalous sentences.

In a recent grammaticality judgement experiment, Wilson and Saygin (2004) independently varied the type of grammatical error and its ease of detection, assessed empirically from native speaker ratings. They sought to test a restrictive version of the TDH, that agrammatic aphasics are selectively impaired in their ability to process structures involving traces of maximal projections (Grodzinsky and Finkel, 1998).[11] Pairs of well-formed and ill-formed sentences involving crossed categories of 'easy' versus 'hard-to-detect' and trace versus other syntactic violations were used (see Table 14.4). If failure to detect trace relations is the sole source of impaired grammaticality judgement in receptive agrammatics, then we may expect their performance to be particularly poor on this sentence type in relation to other aphasics and age-matched controls. However, although they differed in overall level of performance, all patient groups and age-matched controls had remarkably similar performance profiles across sentence types, regardless of whether the patients were grouped according to clinical classification by the

---

[10] Recall the debate over single- vs. dual-route accounts of regular and irregular morphological errors in chapter 9. Connectionist models typically claim that a single processing mechanism accommodates two distinctive patterns of symptomatic disorder.

[11] 'Maximal constituents' are phrasal projections of lexical categories (e.g. NP = maximum projection of a noun). Trace movement of a maximal constituent involves movement of a whole phrase, as distinct from, say, 'head movement', which involves movement of the head element of a phrase (e.g. *Was he coming?*: movement of head element of a VP).

Table 14.4 *Trace violations and ease of detectability*

|  | Ungrammatical | Grammatical controls |
|---|---|---|
| TRACE/HARD | * *John seems that it is likely to win.* | *David seems likely to win.* |
|  | * *Which woman did John think that saw Tony?* | *Which woman did David think saw Pete?* |
| TRACE/EASY | * *Me the dog which bit was black.* | *The dog which bit me was black.* |
|  | * *What did Bill buy oranges and?* | *What did Bill buy besides apples?* |
| OTHER/HARD | * *Could have they left without us?* | *Could they have left without me?* |
|  | * *She donated the library the books.* | *She gave the library the books.* |
| OTHER/EASY | * *The children sang the ball over the fence.* | *The children threw the ball over the fence.* |
|  | * *Have they could left the city?* | *Could they have left without us?* |

Western Aphasia Battery or by site of lesion. The results of this study clearly support the consensual conclusion alluded to earlier, that levels of agrammatic impairment can be identified, as can a pattern of performance which might be labelled 'receptive agrammatism'. But this performance pattern is not specifically associated with trace assignment, or at least not with the specific kind of filler–gap dependencies identified in Grodzinsky and Finkel (1998).

It is time to pose the question of what grammaticality judgement tasks signify in terms of comprehension assessment. One fairly direct and simple method of assessing sentence comprehension is to elicit judgements of sentence plausibility.[12] But it is easy to confound the effects of grammaticality judgement and meaning construal when testing sentences for their 'acceptability' by fully competent native speakers, let alone language-impaired individuals. Garden path sentences remain 'ungrammatical' for people who cannot 'see' the grammatical reading. Sentences that violate putative universal constraints on movement rules tend to yield expressions that are very hard to interpret and are patently 'ill-formed', whereas other grammatical errors, such as subject–verb agreement, may have negligible impact on the meaning or likely truth value of the utterance. On the other hand, a 'syntactic' transposition of lexical word order can yield an obvious 'semantic' anomaly.

Even if the experimenters take great pains to train subjects as to the type of judgements that they seek to elicit (are these sentences (non) meaningful/(im)plausible, or (un)grammatical? see Grodzinsky and Finkel, 1998), the likelihood remains that subjects' acceptability ratings will reflect some unknown mix of grammatical constraints and constraints on meaning construal or plausibility. Linguists themselves often disagree where to draw the distinction. As language

---

[12] Provided that appropriate checks or controls are applied, so that incomplete or defective processing strategies are taken into account. Consider, for example, the effect of applying the agent-first parsing strategy to the non-reversible passive: '*The cops were arrested by the teenagers*' (chapter 12). Would the application of this immature parsing strategy bias the outcome of a plausibility judgement on this item? Indeed it would.

researchers, we just have to learn to live with this ambiguity. However, it is well to be aware that acceptability judgements will be affected by the range and type of anomalies that are incorporated into a set of test items, that subjects will cali-brate their responses accordingly, and that semantic or pragmatic anomalies are typically more salient than purely morpho-syntactic violations. Hence, the rate of detection for 'harmless' errors of inflectional morphology and agreement is expected to fall when well-formedness judgements (WFJs) depend more heavily on semantic processing, particularly so in cases of agrammatism. This is in fact what studies have found, where semantic and syntactic error types are included in the item pool (Shankweiler *et al.*, 1986; Cardell, 2006).

We have argued that Grodzinky's restrictive version of the TDH (that only trace violations involving the movement of heads of functional constituents are relevant for agrammatic comprehension deficit) cannot be sustained. On a broader reading, the TDH is difficult to distinguish empirically from a general inability to deploy function words and inflections in parsing (a version of the first-pass parsing deficit that was perhaps prematurely abandoned following the publication of Linebarger *et al.*, 1983). We now offer new evidence from grammaticality judgements to support the original view that receptive agrammatism represents a deficiency in first-order syntactic parsing.[13] The sentences involve the usually infelicitous insertion of *that* as a complementizer/relativizer in D-linked wh-questions[14] such as

(15) (a)     *Which boy did Paul think saw the movie?*
     (b)     **Which boy did Paul think **that** saw the movie?*

The language-normal control subjects had no difficulty accepting sentence (15a) as grammatical and rejecting (15b) as ungrammatical. But they experienced dif-ficulty arriving at a firm judgement on sentences such as

(16) (a)     ? *Which prisoner did the guards know hid the gun?*
     (b)     ? *Which prisoner did the guards know **that** hid the gun?*

Both (16a) and (b) are grammatical, but subtly different in meaning, deriving from the fact that the verb *know* can take either a sentential complement ([*Guards know that* [*prisoner hid gun*]] or a noun phrase [*Guards know* [*Prisoner* [*that hid gun*]]]). As a consequence, there is ambiguity over the scope of the questioned element '*which prisoner*'. Does it refer to the '*prisoner the guards know hid the gun*' (the restrictive reading) or to the '*prisoner the guards know*' (the less restrictive reading, in which case '*that hid the gun*' is a relative clause adjunct, adding additional information about the prisoner)? (A pause break or juncture between *know* and *that* naturally accompanies this latter reading.) In the alternative, narrow-scope reading, required in the case of (16a), '*which prisoner*' has scope over '*prisoner*

---

[13] See Cardell (2006) for details.
[14] D-linked or *discourse*-linked wh-questions come with the assumption that the listener can retrieve a referent from the current discourse model, as compared to plain wh-questions, which make no such assumptions that a prior referent exists (see chapter 15).

*the guards know hid the gun*', where '*hid the gun*' is a restrictive relative clause, further narrowing the scope of reference of *prisoners*.

We hypothesize that it is the ambiguity between these two readings of the pre-posed wh-constituent which causes difficulty for the listener in the case of (16a–b). In the case of (15a–b), the verb *think* requires a sentential complement. The question *'*Which boy did Paul think?*' is ill-formed and the less restrictive reading is consequently ruled out. Hence no scope ambiguity arises.

How did the agrammatic aphasics judge the grammaticality of these questions? They consistently rejected D-linked wh-questions augmented with *that* as ungrammatical, regardless of whether the controlling verb allowed an NP complement (*know*, *assume*, *feel*) or did not (*think*). Similarly, they accepted as grammatical all D-linked questions which were not *that*-augmented, regardless of the controlling verb. Hence, though they were not insensitive to the presence or absence of the function word *that*, they seemed unaware of its role with respect to the controlling verb. Thus, we have evidence that receptive agrammatism involves a loss of delicacy or precision of parsing; not a catastrophic failure of automatic procedures of structure building, but not a complete exploitation of the available syntactic cues. The decrement in performance of the parser is more apparent when grammaticality judgements are elicited under time pressure, as in the speeded anomaly detection (SAD) paradigm (Shankweiler *et al.*, 1986; Cardell, 2006).

In summary, grammaticality judgements, whether elicited 'off-line' as in the WFJ paradigm or in a more 'on-line' fashion under time pressure (SAD paradigm), yield only indirect measures of sentence processing. However, it seems clear from subsequent studies that Linebarger *et al.* (1983) underestimated the extent of syntactic impairment in receptive agrammatism. The pattern of syntactic impairment may not be qualitatively different from errors of grammatical judgement that can be elicited by placing the normal language processor under abnormal stress, and is characterized by a degradation of precision and accuracy of analysis that is typical of other domains of language, cognitive and perceptual impairment in brain damage, but is nevertheless specifically syntactic in its expression and therefore justifies the label 'receptive agrammatism'. The range and frequency of error types exposed by the WFJs of agrammatic patients expose a broader error pattern than would be predicted by a restrictive version of Grodzinsky's TDH. A broader interpretation of the TDH that encompasses phenomena of syntactic anaphora and ellipsis in the recovery of grammatical roles and relations in complex sentence processing is consistent with findings from WFJ studies. But so too is a performance deficit in first-pass parsing routines.

There is no particular evidence one way or the other for the mapping hypothesis (MH) from WFJ studies. Certainly, agrammatic patients remain sensitive to anomalies of thematic role assignment (e.g. *The baby picked up the crying mother.*), but this only shows that they are sensitive to gross violations of lexical word order. The MH was intended to explain the performance gap between (good) WFJs and (poor) comprehension of thematic roles. Insofar as we call this gap into question, the MH is weakened. It would obviously be premature to do so at this point, but we will argue in the light of the evidence overall that the MH turns out to be rather vacuous, and, insofar as it makes any proposal about the nature of agrammatic deficit, locates it in the wrong place, in the semantics of sentence processing rather than the syntax.

It is difficult to assess the role of general working memory or specialized working memory load requirements via the WFJ or SAD paradigms. For this, we require behavioural or neural on-line measurement techniques applied to agrammatic comprehension deficit, which we now turn to consider.

## Trace reactivation and on-line measures of sentence processing

The trace reactivation paradigm based on cross-modal lexical priming (CMLP), which we analysed in some detail in chapter 13, is clearly the 'prime candidate' for evaluating the TDH, notwithstanding the reservations expressed earlier. Recall the set-up. A visual *probe* word, related or unrelated to an auditory *prime* word in a spoken sentence, is flashed on the computer screen, just after the prime word has been heard, at some control position sufficiently downstream from the probe, or at a *trace position* (usually just after the verb):

(17)        Prime
*The young **actor** whom the columnist usually  despised _ gave an outstanding              performance.*
        ^                                          ^           ^                              ^
Probe position: 1. priming position         2. control   3. trace reactivation position      4. EOS
Probe word:    related = *drama*
               unrelated = *border*

First, we seek evidence of a semantic priming effect, in the form of a faster lexical decision time to the related probe (over the unrelated probe word) at position 1. Assuming this effect is observed, we then look for a residual priming effect at the control position, which we expect *not* to find, as semantic priming effects rapidly decay. But we do expect to obtain a priming effect at position 3 if trace reactivation of the prime word occurs at the gap site. This is what the majority of studies with the trace reactivation paradigm have found with language normal subjects. Position 4, at the end of the sentence, may be included to test for end-of-sentence (EOS) 'wrap up' effects, an operation postulated to occur as the meaning of the sentence is integrated into the discourse model (see below).

But in the case of receptive agrammatism, the TDH predicts that trace reactivation will not occur. The prediction of a negative result is usually not regarded as strong confirmation for a theory. But consistent with the theory, this is what Swinney and Zurif (1995) found in two experiments, with Broca's aphasics with agrammatic comprehension deficit and Wernicke's aphasics. The first experiment tested for trace reactivation priming with OS relatives (a relative clause acting as object in the main clause and subject in the dependent clause, e.g. *The man liked the tailor with the British accent, who claimed _ to know the queen.*), on which agrammatic aphasics perform above chance in off-line comprehension testing. No trace reactivation was found for the Broca's aphasics, but perhaps surprisingly, in view of their low comprehension scores, a statistically significant reactivation priming effect (p<.03) was observed in the Wernicke's group at the trace site. The same pattern of results was obtained for OO relative clauses (e.g. *The priest enjoyed the drink that the caterer was serving to the guests.*), on which agrammatic subjects perform poorly in off-line comprehension tests.

What are we to make of this apparent breakdown of automatic trace reactivation in Broca's patients, combined with relatively intact off-line comprehension (at least for the simpler OS relative clauses), and its *opposite* pattern of preserved automatic filler–gap priming combined with poor off-line comprehension by Wernicke's aphasics? It is tempting to conclude that we have evidence here of a double dissociation between automatic aspects of syntactic parsing (in agrammatic Broca's aphasics) and volitional or non-automatic aspects of meaning construal (in Wernicke's aphasia). But it would probably be wiser to first seek further corroborative evidence.

Blumstein, Byma, Kurowski, Hourihan, Brown and Hutchinson (1998) investigated trace reactivation effects in Broca's and Wernicke's aphasics, using a somewhat different priming method (not cross-modal but wholly auditory, with male and female voices to separate prime and probe stimuli), testing for a wider range of filler–gap dependencies (including wh-questions like (15a) and subject embedded relative clauses like (17) above), and of course using different subject groups. Blumstein *et al.* obtained precisely the *opposite* pattern of performance to Swinney *et al.* (1995, 1996). Broca's aphasics showed reactivation of the filler at the gap site, like the normal controls, whereas Wernicke's aphasics did not. A possibly confounding factor in Blumstein *et al.*'s experiment was that the gap site occurred at or close to the end of the sentence in the majority of items. Filler–gap effects could therefore be confounded with 'sentence wrap up effects' (Balough, Zurif, Prather, Swinney and Finkel, 1998). Swinney *et al.*'s (1995, 1996) trace reactivation experiments were free of this possible confound. The trace position always occurred several words from the end of the sentence.

Sentence wrap up effects refer to a process of meaning consolidation or information re-packaging, possibly associated with recoding of the input utterance from a 'surface structure representation' into a more economical form for longer-term memory retention, or with discourse-integrative operations whereby the language processor merges information from a sentential unit into the evolving mental discourse model. Sentence wrap up is thus thought to reflect a higher order of construal than syntactic parsing operations (Rayner, Sereno, Morris, Schmauder and Clifton, 1989). Overt evidence for sentence wrap up effects has come mainly from eye tracking studies of reading, where a static visual representation of the stimulus sentence is available for scanning and backtracking, and where its effects can be experimentally manipulated by punctuation placement. Wrap up effects in spoken language processing remain more of a hypothetical construct, with scant experimental substantiation. Balough *et al.* (1998) attribute, by a process of elimination, the re-emergence of a priming effect at the end-of-sentence position (EOS, position 4, in sentence (17) above) to a sentence wrap up effect. The absence of a priming effect for *actor* at the control position (position 2) indicates that the observed EOS priming (at position 4) could not have been caused by persistence of the original semantic priming effect at position 1. They also argue, on grounds of decay latency, that the EOS priming is unlikely to be due to the residual effects of trace reactivation priming (at position 3).

If syntactic and discourse levels of processing are confounded in Blumstein *et al.*'s trace reactivation experiment, then their findings may be reconciled with those of Swinney and Zurif (1995) and the interpretation given earlier. There is abundant support from off-line comprehension testing to suggest that agrammatic aphasics' discourse level comprehension processes remain intact, whereas Wernicke's aphasics, insofar as it is possible to judge, do not seem to construct a coherent discourse representation from what is spoken to them. Thus, the priming observed in the agrammatic patients and the failure to prime by the Wernicke's group in Blumstein *et al.*'s study could be attributed to the operation (or non-operation) of discourse-integrating, end-of-sentence, wrap up effects. However, another cautionary word is in order. Notice how the same behavioural phenomenon – save for a rather small difference in latency or timing with respect to the auditory stimulus – is being used to draw inferences about the integrity (or impairment) of two distinct, theory-dependent, levels of language processing. If this is not skating on thin ice, then penguins may fly in a strong wind. Such is the nature of on-line behavioural indices of psycholinguistic processes.

## Slow retrieval or under-activation of lexical items

As if the problem of choosing among alternatives were not hard enough with the limited on-line observational techniques at our disposal, another theory of agrammatic comprehension impairment has gained currency in recent years, which sees the underlying deficit as a by-product of delayed access or diminished activation of lexical items (Prather, Shapiro, Zurif and Swinney, 1991; Utman, Blumstein and Sullivan, 2001). If retrieval of lexical information is delayed, so the argument goes, critical time-dependent syntactic reflexes such as the resolution of filler–gap dependencies will be disrupted. Delayed or diminished semantic activation in paired associate, triplet priming and list priming in Broca's aphasics has been reported, though the evidence is mixed (Prather, Zurif, Love and Brownell, 1997). When linked to previously reported studies of impaired temporal order judgement in Broca's aphasia (Efron, 1963) and the well-known clinical observation that slowed speech improves comprehension in Broca's aphasia (see chapter 8), the delayed lexical activation hypothesis gains credibility. Burkhardt, Piñango and Wong (2003) have recently reported evidence that can be interpreted as delayed trace reactivation in Broca's aphasics using the CMLP paradigm. However, these chronometric considerations also serve to further complicate the problem of inference and to increase the chances of confounding processes operating at different levels of language processing.

## Self-paced listening and transient processing load

A recent study by Caplan and Waters (2003) using the auditory moving window paradigm (Ferreira *et al.*, 1996) to measure fluctuations in on-line processing load, and timed plausibility ratings to simultaneously assess sentence comprehension, has shed new light on the old conundrum of how agrammatism can be both a distinctive receptive deficit of Broca's aphasia and an incipient response to working memory overload which, given the right conditions, can derail the normal language parser (Blackwell and Bates, 1995). To achieve this perspective, systematic comparisons were made across diagnostic groups (Broca's aphasics, Wernicke's aphasics and an age-matched control group) and across a range of off-line agrammatic comprehension impairment (moderate, mild, or no comprehension impairment).

The auditory moving window paradigm (AMW, mentioned in chapter 13) is a self-paced listening task in which subjects press a button to hear successive phrasal fragments of a test utterance. Like its predecessor, the visual moving windows task, which has been extensively used in reading research, the AMW has been shown to be sensitive to peaks in syntactic processing load[15] such as occur following the second NP in an object relative construction:

(18)    ... *the dancer ... (that) the actor ... applauded ...*

The increased processing load on hearing *the actor* results in a measurable delay in calling for the subsequent sentence fragment, the verb *applauded*. Processing load fluctuations occur at various points in a sentence. This enables profiles of working load fluctuations over the whole sentence to be compared across subjects or subject groups, to characterize on-line processing styles.

Timed plausibility judgements were obtained following the presentation of every test sentence. Pairs of pragmatically acceptable and anomalous utterances were constructed and systematically randomized for presentation (see Table 14.5). Possibly because of the somewhat shop-worn nature of the sentence materials or the context-free manner in which their comprehensibility was tested (failing to meet felicity conditions for the use of cleft and relative clause constructions – see Crain and Steedman, 1985), the findings of this experiment do not appear to have received the attention that they merit.

Recall the double dissociation between on-line processing and off-line comprehension in Broca's and Wernicke's aphasics that we inferred might be responsible

---

[15] Caplan *et al.* (2002), using event-related fMRI in conjunction with the visual moving window paradigm, found increases in blood oxygenation level dependent (BOLD) haemodynamic responses that corresponded to regions of working memory load in the course of sentence processing in self-paced reading.

Table 14.5 *Sentence types used in Caplan and Waters (2003)*

| Sentence | Type | Syntactic complexity | Pragmatic acceptability |
|---|---|---|---|
| *The father read the book that terrified the child.* | OS | low | good |
| *The girl drank the boy that entered the hospital.* | OS | low | bad |
| *The man that the fire injured called the doctor.* | SO | high | good |
| *The secretary that the camera met drove the car.* | SO | high | bad |
| *It was the food that nourished the child.* | SC | low | good |
| *It was the car that drove the woman.* | SC | low | bad |
| *It was the boy that the woman amazed.* | OC | high | good |
| *It was the coffee that the secretary disappointed.* | OC | high | bad |

for the seemingly contradictory findings of Swinney *et al.* (1996) and Blumstein *et al.*'s (1998) trace reactivation experiments. The same effect can also be seen at work in the Caplan and Waters (2003) study, but with an additional methodological buttress to the findings. The same items and trials on which fluctuations in on-line processing load were estimated were also those on which off-line comprehension scores were obtained. It was thus possible in this study to interrogate the relationship between on-line processing load and sentence comprehension more sharply than in previous studies.

Comparing the aphasics with their age-matched controls, both groups showed the expected local increase in on-line processing load, reflected in longer listening times, following the second NP for object relative clause constructions (SO) and object clefts (OC).[16] The increased processing load attending these two sentence types was not apparent in the accuracy of the control subjects' plausibility judgements, which was close to ceiling, but there was a significant decrement in comprehension scores for the more difficult constructions by the aphasic group. Hence, the aphasics' comprehension scores were more vulnerable to the effects of syntactic complexity than were the controls'.

Despite clear differences in their comprehension scores and slower overall listening times, the on-line processing profiles of the aphasic and control groups, as reflected in their listening times for successive sentence fragments, did not differ except for the sentence-final fragment (where the aphasics had longer listening times). The authors take this as evidence that a common on-line processing mechanism was operating in the control subjects and at least the majority of the aphasic patients. To examine this question more closely, the aphasic group was partitioned into 'mild' and 'moderately' comprehension impaired groups, on the basis of an independent off-line test,[17] and their listening time profiles were then compared with one another and with that of the controls. The listening time profile of the

---

[16] The finding is more significant in the case of SO sentences. Increased processing times in the case of OC sentences could be attributed to EOS wrap-up effects.

[17] Of thematic role assignment in reversible passive sentences.

mildly impaired sub-group did not differ from that of the normal controls, but that of the low-comprehension aphasic group did, in ways that suggested more than one strategic response style induced by difficulties with on-line processing. (See Caplan and Waters, 2003, for further discussion.)

Partitioning the aphasic group into fluent (Wernicke's) and non-fluent (Broca's) sub-groups on the basis of standard clinical and site of lesion criteria did not show any significant group differences in level of sentence comprehension, but did reveal suggestive differences in their on-line listening time profiles. Broca's aphasics took longer to make plausibility judgements but did not differ from the Wernicke's group in their accuracy of judgement. Wernicke's patients showed a greater effect of syntactic complexity upon their on-line performance, suggesting by their more 'normal' reading-time profiles that initial (automatic) syntactic processing may be more intact in Wernicke's aphasia than in Broca's aphasia. This being so, the comprehension difficulties of the Wernicke's group would appear to be caused at a post-syntactic level of processing, where semantic information associated with lexical entries is integrated with structural information generated by an initial syntactic parse. Or possibly the fluent aphasics' comprehension difficulties arise at an even higher level of meaning construal, the discourse level, where the propositional content of a linguistic expression is assessed for plausibility or compatibility with real-world knowledge and the listener's discourse model.

To summarize, the Caplan and Waters (2003) study is significant for the way that it reveals the interplay between on-line processing load fluctuations and their differential impact upon agrammatic (Broca's) and non-agrammatic (Wernicke's) types of comprehension disorder, using an 'off-line' measure of sentence comprehension that is relatively free of extrinsic task demands. As we argue below, in attempting to summarize the current state of play in this highly contentious field of research, the Caplan and Waters (2003) findings help to reconcile some apparently competing but actually compatible theories of agrammatic comprehension deficit, and cast doubt upon some other views. To anticipate, their findings argue for a staged model of language processing, where it makes no sense to draw a principled distinction between 'competence' and 'performance' deficits, but where a degree of modularity of syntactic processing is upheld.

In a follow-up companion paper to the one just discussed, using the same on-line processing load and off-line comprehension measures, but with normal language users, partitioned into high and low verbal working memory capacity (VWMC) groups, Waters and Caplan (2004) found no differences between the two groups with respect to the listening time profiles induced by local fluctuations in processing load for parsing, in either syntactically more complex or syntactically simpler sentences. Taken together with the previous study (Caplan and Waters, 2003), a good case can be made that the 'working memory' impairment found in agrammatic comprehension deficit represents a functionally specific loss of dedicated computational capacity used in syntactic parsing, not simply a generalized deficit of attention-mediated symbol manipulation (which, of course, does commonly occur in brain injury, particularly in damage to the frontal lobes).

## ERP imaging of on-line sentence processing in aphasia

Understandably, there have been, as yet, few brain imaging studies of aphasic language processing, as particular care is required in interpreting patterns of electrical activity from a damaged brain, especially where the damaged region is believed to be directly implicated in the function that is being assessed. However, if the appropriate experimental controls are applied, useful insights may be obtained, as we hope to demonstrate with a recent report from the Dutch investigators Wassenaar, Brown and Hagoort (2004). Interest was focused on the P600 component of the ERP, as subjects listened to spoken sentences, a proportion of which contained errors of subject–verb agreement.[18]

Broca's aphasics and two control groups were employed: an elderly non-brain damaged group, and a group of right hemisphere damaged but non-aphasic subjects, matched in age with the aphasic group. Following a previous study, which had found that Broca's aphasics were able to detect subject–verb agreement errors across conjoined clauses (e.g. *The baker greets the customers and **ask** the boy to not make so much noise.) but were unable to do so in more complex structures of embedding (e.g. *The baker that greets the customers **ask** the boy not to make so much noise.), interest was focused on whether the P600 would register on-line sensitivity for violations of subject–verb agreement in conjoined and embedded sentences in the Broca's aphasics as well as in the two control groups.

Recall (chapter 12) that a bilateral late positive-valenced ERP voltage (the P600), peaking at around 600 ms post-stimulus and usually focused over the central-parietal region, has been found to be associated with a variety of grammatical anomalies and garden path sentences. The P600 has been tentatively identified with the detection and attempted repair of syntactic anomalies, as well as a response to increased processing load (Kaan, Harris, Gibson and Holcomb, 2000). The authors made several predictions as to the strength and timing of P600 response, in the light of previous work and hypotheses about agrammatic comprehension disorder which we have previously discussed.

For agrammatic subjects, a weaker P600 response might be expected for agreement anomalies in sentences where the processing load is higher. Similarly, the strength of the P600 should be inversely related to the severity of agrammatic comprehension impairment. If the P600 represents a specific reaction to fluctuations in language processing load or a response to the detection of grammatical anomalies, then its presence should be observed in non-aphasic brain damaged as well as normal control subjects. If it were *not* observed in this clinical control group, and the P600 were only found in non-brain damaged controls, then

---

[18] To ensure the subjects were kept engaged in active sentence processing, intermittent questions were posed about the meaning of a sentence just heard.

doubt would be cast on its specificity as a measure of language processing and the presence of the P600 could possibly be attributed simply to the absence of brain pathology.

In a further effort to ensure that any observed differences in the P600 between the aphasic and control groups were attributable to language processing and not to the non-specific effects of brain pathology, the experimenters also ran, as a control condition, a check for the presence of a non-language auditory ERP component (the P300), using tonal stimuli in an **odd-ball detection** paradigm. If the aphasics and the two control groups yielded the same P300 response in the auditory odd-ball detection test, then any differences obtained in their P600 responses could be more securely attributed to differences in on-line language processing. Normal P300 effects were observed with no significant differences between groups.

Wassenaar *et al.*'s (2004) findings with the P600, an on-line neural processing measure, converge nicely with those of Waters and Caplan (2004), who used a behavioural measure, the auditory moving window paradigm, to investigate the relationship between working memory load and grammaticality detection in aphasics. As in the Waters and Caplan study, the Broca's aphasic subjects were partitioned into mildly and more severely impaired groups on the basis of off-line tests that expose agrammatic comprehension impairment. The elderly control and right hemisphere damaged groups' performances on off-line comprehension measures were not statistically different, but the Broca's group scored progressively lower on five sentence types graded in terms of comprehension difficulty (non-reversible actives, reversible actives, reversible passives, subject embedded relative clauses, and subject embedded relatives in passive form).

The elderly normal and right hemisphere damaged controls both manifested P600 responses, which emerged approximately 500 ms following verbs that disagreed in number marking with their subject. The distributions of the P600s were statistically indistinguishable for the two groups and had the expected central-parietal focus. Both control subjects showed sensitivity to subject–verb agreement violations irrespective of whether the sentences were conjoined or embedded. In contrast to the control groups, the overall group of Broca's patients did not show clear P600 effects in response to the subject–verb agreement violations. The effects were absent for both the conjoined and the embedded sentences. The more severely agrammatic group of Broca's patients yielded no evidence of a P600 response but those with less severe syntactic comprehension impairment did yield a P600 component, for agreement violations in less complex constructions, and reduced in size but with the same time course as that of the controls.

## Summary and conclusion

If there is a moral to this tortured tale of agrammatism research, it is probably simply that insights into the nature of language processing are hard won.

We began the present chapter by questioning the most substantial achievement of the first generation of psycholinguistic research – that agrammatism was not simply a disorder of production, an inability to construct linguistic expressions, but also a loss of the facility to assign syntactic structures in the course of language comprehension; a disability that can be masked or successfully compensated for under conditions of everyday communication, because complete syntactic forms are usually neither necessary nor sufficient to glean a speaker's meaning from utterances in context.

Basically two species of termite sought to undermine the edifice of experimental evidence so cleverly and laboriously constructed by the first generation of researchers. One species gnawed away at the methodology of off-line comprehension assessment. What is being tested here is really *meta-linguistic* knowledge, not language processing in action. The other nibbled away to expose an apparently striking discrepancy between Broca's aphasics' preserved ability to judge grammaticality and their inability to use grammatical cues for meaning.

Theory renovators responded to the twin threats in a variety of ways. Some attempted to quarantine agrammatism to a module of the grammar, to a restricted kind of syntactic impairment (competence deficit); thereby also claiming independent neurological support for a theory of 'the language faculty', the holy grail of psycholinguistics and the apostles' creed of generative grammar. The trace deletion hypothesis (TDH) and its variants represent this view. Others drew attention to the extra-linguistic task requirements, intrinsic to the methods of 'off-line' comprehension testing, claiming that the limited working memory capacity of Broca's aphasics subjected them to 'performance' constraints. The trade-off hypothesis (TOH) exemplifies this view. Still others, advocates of the mapping hypothesis (MH), applied a combination of these prophylactic measures. Yes, there is impairment to the deeper levels of sentence processing, where syntax interfaces with semantics, and that is also precisely where conceptual load requirements weigh in.

Amidst all the renovation, as the original edifice disappeared behind a network of scaffolding, the introduction of new termite-proof building materials in the form of on-line behavioural and neural processing measures placed new technical demands on theory builders and presented constructional material problems of their own. Exactly what is the relationship of a semantic priming effect to the process of lexical retrieval? What is the precise mechanism of 'reactivation priming' at a gap site, and what relationship does it bear to on-line syntactic parsing or to the process of semantic interpretation of a sentence? How sensitive and robust are behavioural on-line measures? What does an increase (or decrease) in the amplitude of an ERP component signify? Is it an index of 'effort expended' in reaction to some anomaly detected in the course of processing? If so, how specific is the class of anomaly or how task-dependent is a particular ERP component? These are all key methodological questions for on-line measures, for which there are no definitive answers at the present time. Nevertheless, it is our contention that substantial progress has been made on clarifying the nature of comprehension deficit in agrammatism and in reconciling the findings from off-line and on-line measures, as we argue forthwith. But this is a highly provisional assessment of the current state of play and we invite you to conclude differently.

Recent evidence from behavioural (auditory moving window, Caplan and Waters, 2003) and neural imaging (ERP, Wassenaar *et al.*, 2004) converges on a coherent interpretation of agrammatic comprehension disorder, which also helps to reconcile apparent discrepancies between the earlier off-line and more recent on-line findings. But before we draw out the lesson from recent on-line studies, a brief caveat on off-line testing is in order.

When asked to perform a mental task that requires some conscious reflection or manipulation of symbolic objects in 'the mind's eye', the problem-solver is highly dependent, in whatever strategy s/he adopts, upon output that is delivered to consciousness, by whatever automatic perceptual, linguistic or conceptual processes are relevant to the problem. For example, if asked to judge 'which chair is largest', the problem-solver must have access to at least three things: (1) a conceptual notion of relative size, (2) an integrated visual array of objects – namely chairs, and (3) an interpreted linguistic expression referentially linking *chairs* to objects in the visual field. Each of these three elements of the problem is delivered by automated processes beyond the subject's volitional control. If any one of them fails to be delivered, the consequences will probably be catastrophic.

Theories that invoke 'limitations of working memory' make the assumption that subjects differ in terms of the number of objects that may be simultaneously attended to, or held in attention for a short period of time. People certainly differ in the size of their working memory span. But in measuring these individual differences it is assumed that all individuals in the cohort construct equivalent mental representations of the task. It is this assumption that is called into question with brain damaged subjects. To therefore attribute impairments of 'working memory capacity' to aphasic performance in off-line language tasks is quite a dangerous undertaking.

The on-line behavioural and neural indices that have recently been found to correlate with language comprehension (in the form of plausibility judgements – Caplan and Waters, 2003) and with grammaticality judgements (Wassenaar *et al.*, 2004) have been associated with local fluctuations in on-line processing load of a quite specific kind associated with syntactic parsing. The same structures that cause increased effort for normal parsers, and vary over a time base usually measured in milliseconds, not seconds, can derail agrammatic subjects' plausibility and grammaticality judgements. When subjects are partitioned by the severity of their agrammatic impairment, the mildly impaired respond with on-line processing indices that resemble those of normal language users, whereas the same indices are absent or disrupted in the more severely agrammatic subjects.

What do these findings tell us in general about the nature of agrammatic comprehension impairment? That it is a graded, not a categorical deficit. That it is not different in kind from the agrammatic errors that may be induced under certain conditions in normal language users. We can link the likelihood of comprehension difficulties to a metric of syntactic complexity, but our on-line processing techniques do not enable us to isolate the precise level of linguistic processing that is involved. Nor has a more precise brain locus of agrammatic impairment been identified than to say that it occurs within the left perisylvian field.

# PART V

# Discourse: language comprehension in context

# 15    Discourse processing

## Introduction

Discourse constitutes the highest and most complex level of linguistic representation, and is the one which interfaces directly with non-linguistic or conceptual structure. Discourse may be defined as linguistic organization above the level of the sentence, where sentences or their conceptual counterparts, propositions, are organized into larger units of information structure that in written form are commonly described as 'texts' (Johnstone, 2002). The historical antecedents of modern discourse analysis lie in rhetoric, the study of techniques of argument and persuasion. However, it is also true that a host of sentence-level syntactic phenomena, which chiefly involve departures of sentence structure from canonical word order, or optional transformational movement in the terminology of generative grammar (such as 'focusing phenomena', 'scrambling', etc.), are functionally motivated by discourse considerations. As we have seen, these discourse-motivated departures from canonical or unmarked sentence structure often pose particular difficulties for aphasic speakers and listeners.

However, it is also the case that the core elements of discourse structure, such as given versus new information and topic-comment structure, can be illustrated in the simplest of verbal exchanges:

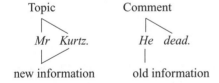

Topic-comment structure is one of the earliest identifiable structures in infant language (Hornby, 1971) and the most resistant to loss even in severe cases of agrammatism (Wulfeck *et al.*, 1989). Topics (things talked about) universally precede comments, or if they do not, the language usually provides a special topic-marking morpheme, such as the post-nominal clitic *wa* in Japanese. Furthermore, the structures of discourse analysis seem to be more changeable, to reflect the communicational requirements of a particular conversational exchange or discourse type. For example, telling a story places rather different information management demands on the narrator and the listener than the negotiation of a commercial transaction between purchaser and vendor. Discourse construction may be seen as a co-operative endeavour, conducted in accordance with Gricean principles:[1] 'be informative, be economical, be candid'. When conversational maxims are not adhered to by the speaker, the 'thread of discourse' is likely to be lost. Referents become difficult for the listener to retrieve. Communication breaks down, and, in extreme cases, the speaker's verbal production may be said to manifest signs of 'formal thought disorder'. We explore the phenomena of discourse breakdown in the next chapter.

## Discourse modelling

Unlike lower levels of linguistic processing that we have discussed in previous chapters, the planning and management of discourse structure by speakers and its decoding by listeners are largely under the control of attentional mechanisms and are accessible to conscious awareness. A corollary of this is that discourse control mechanisms in production and perception engage 'whole of brain' processing and cognitive resources, such as general-purpose (verbal) working memory. Two important implications follow. Discourse-level processes are available to introspective investigation in a way that lower-level language automata are not. This has implications for psychological model building. Secondly, disorders of discourse processing are not unambiguous language disorders. They may also be regarded as 'thought disorders' and reflect the integrity of mechanisms which enable us to consciously plan, attend to and self-monitor performance, in tasks that are substantially under volitional control.

In any given conversational exchange, both speaker and listener build a discourse model; a 'scene' or mental depiction of the topic(s) under discussion, which may be viewed from the perspective of each interlocutor (Johnson-Laird and Garnham, 1980). However, the roles of speaker and listener are not entirely symmetrical in discourse model construction. From the perspective of the speaker, it is a matter of drawing the listener's attention to salient aspects of the scene, establishing and maintaining relationships of reference, and constructing a web of propositional relationships among the objects of the discourse, some of which are explicitly asserted or foregrounded, others of which are merely implied or kept in the background.

To hold a listener's attention and guide them in the construction of a discourse model that is compatible with his/her communicative intentions, a speaker must be able to anticipate the listener's understanding of the topic and to respond rapidly by way of redirection and repair when signs that the listener's evolving discourse model is diverging from the speaker's own are detected. The listener's task, on the other hand, is usually not quite so demanding as the double act of constructing a discourse model and simultaneously monitoring another's discourse apprehension – unless, perhaps, the listener is planning to take the floor themselves.

---

[1] For his theory of conversational implicature, see Grice (1975).

Referents enter discourse as 'new' information and subsequently make their reappearance as 'old' information. Successful establishment and maintenance of a discourse model is probably the most resource-demanding component of spoken language processing and occupies the bulk of the speaker's and the listener's attention. Hence discourse control is more vulnerable to attentional lapses, and to episodic, semantic or working memory breakdown than other more automatic components of the communication act. For this reason, some of the best examples of discourse disintegration may be drawn from clinical populations where the primary cognitive deficits lie not so much in the automatic functions of language production and perception, but in generalized working memory and higher cognitive functioning, as found in the dementias and in cases of 'thought disorder' observed in acute bouts of schizophrenia or in the manic phase of bipolar mental illness. In dementia we can observe the consequences of restricted cognitive resources on discourse production or comprehension. In thought disorder, the primary deficit seems to derive from a failure of the monitoring function to take account of the listener (Rochester, Martin and Thurstone, 1977).

## Discourse construction: an example

We distinguish two kinds of discourse control devices: those to do with *reference maintenance* and management (so-called 'deep anaphora' or discourse anaphora (Hankamer and Sag, 1976)), and those pertaining to *cohesion* or the establishment and maintenance of logical, causal and temporal relationships between events, states of affairs and participants in the discourse (Halliday and Hasan, 1976). Anaphoric relations are typically linguistically marked by pronouns, specifiers of noun phrases and deictic expressions. Relations of coherence are typically overtly indicated by connectives such as *and*, *because*, *so* . . . , etc. which may link subordinate clauses to main clauses or sentences to one another in the information structure of a discourse.

For purposes of exposition, a discourse can be visualized as a theatre production where events unfold on the stage of the interlocutors' imagination. The stage, initially empty at the start of the discourse, is soon populated with one, two or several objects – things to which reference can be made. Consider two initiating discourses:

(1)       *John telephoned Bill* . . .
(2)       *Paula envied Mary* . . .

In each case, two referring expressions, proper nouns, have introduced two players (referents) on stage, both possessing the status of new information and capable of becoming objects of subsequent reference. The discourse continues:

(1)       *John telephoned Bill (because) he* . . .      [**John**/Bill?]
(2)       *Paula envied Mary (because) she* . . .       [Paula/**Mary**?]

The introduction of the pronoun does not bring on any new players (referents), but signals to the audience that reference is being made to one of the two no-longer-new actors already on stage. But which one commands the audience's attention? The two referents, which may be referred to as $NP_1$ or $NP_2$ (the subject NP in the previous clause, or the object NP) are not equally accessible in the two mini-discourses. In the case of mini-discourse (1) our attention is drawn towards *John*, but in the case of discourse (2) *Mary* seems to be the more natural referent of the pronoun *she*. What causes this bias in reference assignment towards $NP_1$ or $NP_2$ for the anaphor *he/she*?

It seems that the verb and its semantics must be responsible for biasing reference assignment of the pronoun towards the subject or the object NP. Nothing else varies between the two mini-discourses. But what of the role of the subordinating conjunction *'because'*? Does the bias still persist if *'because'* is removed? Most listeners would probably agree that the original bias remains, though it is possibly weakened by removal of the connective expression. However, substitution of a different connective expression may shift reference bias in the opposite direction:

2'.        *Paula envied Mary (so) she ...*        [**Paula**/Mary?]

It is now *'Paula'* who seems to be the more likely referent of the pronoun. Notice also, that completion of the second clause does not necessarily resolve the reference ambiguity between one or the other referent:

1'.        *John telephoned Bill (because) he was unhappy.*        [John/Bill?]
1''.        *John telephoned Bill (because) he wanted information.*        [John/Bill?]

Example 1'' suggests that how we assign reference to a pronoun depends on the interpretation of the whole structure of subordination, i.e.: *'John wanting information'* is a sound reason for *'John phoning Bill'*, whereas *'Bill wanting information'* seems a lot less plausible, though possible. On the other hand, in the case of 1'' the alternative referential reading of *'he'* as referring to *'Bill'* is more of an open possibility, particularly if we imagine that *'John'* is a beneficent kind of guy.

These examples demonstrate that reference assignment in discourse depends, at least in part, upon a complex interaction between two factors: (a) verb semantics, which focus the listener's attention, by means that we have not yet specified, on one or the other of the arguments of the verb, so as to bias reference assignment in a subsequent anaphor, and (b) the nature of the connective expression that links main and subordinate clauses or points to a coherence relation between sentences in discourse. Other factors are also relevant. Recall from chapter 2 that syntax plays a filtering role with respect to pronoun reference, by preventing co-reference between a full noun phrase and a pronoun within the same sentence which it does not c-command (recall the example *He_i thought Bill_i was a goner. He* cannot be co-referential with *Bill*: see chapter 2, p. 32 above). Thus, syntactic structure may rule out certain relationships of co-reference between a pronoun and a full noun phrase within a complex sentence. While structural relations such as 'c-command' may have a limited filtering role to play in reference assignment in discourse, the question of how and when syntactic constraints are applied in relation to semantic and pragmatic constraints on anaphora are of central interest to models of language processing. These matters have only recently been taken up by psycholinguists (Long and De Ley, 2000; Sturt, 2003; Wolf, Gibson and Desmet, 2004).

## Reference management and pragmatic knowledge

As a discourse develops, new topics enter and old topics fade from the scene. A new topic is typically introduced as a comment to an existing topic, using a full but indefinitely specified NP, except when the new topic has unique reference, in which case a proper name or a definite NP is used. When a referent attains topic status it is usually next referenced by a pronoun and while it remains 'alive' as a potential discourse referent it is marked by a definite reference. For a discourse referent to remain accessible, it must be kept 'alive' by frequent mention. However, once commented upon, a topic's accessibility as an object of reference rapidly declines, particularly with the appearance of a new topic. And comments themselves typically introduce potential new discourse referents.

Definiteness is a syntactic feature that signals unique reference. But what makes a referent unique depends upon the current state of the discourse model as well as the *pragmatic knowledge* of the interlocutors. Names for people usually have unique reference within a given discourse. Definite expressions, when appropriately framed within a discourse, also usually have unique reference which they would not otherwise possess outside that context. A skilful narrator can facilitate the listener's task of tracking discourse reference by topic sequencing which exploits shared pragmatic knowledge of whole–part relationships. Consider the following fragment from V. S. Naipaul (definite expressions have been set in bold italics):

> *Islamabad*, '*the city of Islam*', ***the capital*** *of Pakistan, was new . . .* ***Rawalpindi*** *was* ***the older city****. In one direction* ***it*** *sprawled towards* ***Islamabad****; but in* ***the centre*** *little had changed. In* ***the bazaar*** *there were still* ***the high, the dark timbered, verandahed and latticed houses*** *of* ***the Sikhs and Hindus*** *who had predominated in* ***the little town*** *before partition and had then been displaced.* ***The old British Rawalpindi club*** *was still in business –* ***the ceiling lights*** *a little dimmer,* ***the walls*** *a more muddy yellow,* ***the uniforms*** *of* ***the waiters*** *a little grubbier,* ***the atmosphere*** *at meal times more highly spiced.*          (V. S. Naipaul, *Among the believers*)

Place names (*Islamabad, Rawalpindi*, . . .) have unique reference by virtue of pragmatic (geographic) knowledge. Similarly, the unique reference of *the capital* rests on the pragmatic knowledge that a nation state can have only one capital. *The older city* has unique reference because of its mutual anaphoric link with the current topic (*Rawalpindi*) and the recently active topic *Islamabad*. Every town has a *centre*, and *houses*, and every far-eastern town has a *bazaar*. The writer exploits this pragmatic knowledge of whole–part relationships to ensure unique reference to each of these sub-topics as they are introduced for comment. Similarly, pragmatic knowledge of part–whole relationships is appealed to in providing uniqueness of reference to the various aspects of *the Rawalpindi club*. Old colonial clubs all have *ceiling lights*, *walls*, *waiters* who have *uniforms*, and *atmosphere*.

This example illustrates the critical role of (a) shared pragmatic knowledge in successfully tracking discourse reference, and (b) the speaker's skill in selecting and sequencing anaphoric expressions in such a way as to meet the Gricean maxims or conversational felicity conditions mentioned earlier: 'be informative, be economical, be candid'.

## Relevance

Grice's conversational maxims constitute a kind of pact between speaker and listener (writer and reader), guaranteeing that utterances will be readily interpretable in context, provided that the interlocutors adhere to the 'conditions of speaking', and, we might add in parentheses, provided that their current discourse models are compatible. Wilson and Sperber (2004) have suggested that of the Gricean maxims, *relevance* is of overarching significance. Relevance constrains the speaker to make explicit in each successive utterance only what can be readily inferred from the immediately preceding context.[2] In this way the listener's inferential load can be minimized in extracting the speaker's communicative intentions under constraints of real-time sentence processing. Of course, what can be readily inferred depends upon (a) what has previously been established in the discourse model up to the point when the new sentence/utterance is introduced, and (b) the shared pragmatic knowledge base of the interlocutors. Consider the following example of a conversational exchange based on discussion from Wilson and Sperber (2004).

(3)        Peter: *Did John pay back the money he owed you?*
           Mary: *He forgot to go to the bank.*

The principle of relevance dictates that Mary's answer must be construed as a reply to the question. Peter's construal process will be satisfied because Mary's reply can be interpreted as an explanation for the implied negative answer to the question, thereby satisfying the requirement of relevance.[3] In arriving at the construal, there are a host of supporting inferences that must be drawn before an explicature (an explication of the meaning of the sentence in reply) can be

---

[2] Notice the implicit assumption here: the most relevant inference to be drawn about the speaker's intended meaning is the one which is most accessible or easiest to infer in context.

[3] Though Peter may well be left wondering why Mary was not quite so direct in her answer.

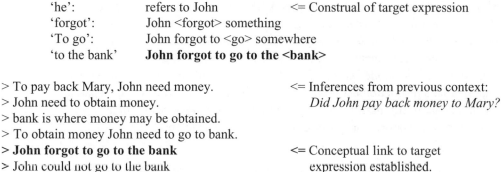

| 'he': | refers to John | <= Construal of target expression |
| 'forgot': | John <forgot> something | |
| 'To go': | John forgot to <go> somewhere | |
| 'to the bank' | **John forgot to go to the <bank>** | |

> To pay back Mary, John need money.          <= Inferences from previous context:
> John need to obtain money.                          *Did John pay back money to Mary?*
> bank is where money may be obtained.
> To obtain money John need to go to bank.
> **John forgot to go to the bank**                 <= Conceptual link to target
> John could not go to the bank                          expression established.
> John could not obtain the money.
> John could not pay back the money to Mary.
> **John did not pay back the money to Mary.**     <= Relevance satisfied
                                                                                  Construal process terminates.

Figure 15.1 *Hypothetical process of construal of mini-discourse 3*

constructed which satisfies the requirement of relevance. We might represent this as a chain of inferences, which begin with processing the sentence in reply (the target expression), followed by establishing an inferential linkage between the previous expression (the immediate context) and the target expression, and proceeding until the relevance of the response to the previous question has been established (or abandoned as too difficult to compute). A rough outline of this hypothetical process is given in Figure 15.1. Not all of the inferences that the listener/reader may compute (indicated by '>') are shown. The propositional meanings of the target and context sentences are constructed mainly on the basis of syntactic and lexical-semantic information. But many of the inferences are driven by encylopaedic pragmatic knowledge. There is no assumption that these inferences are carried out in a strictly sequential order, though many of them appear to be intrinsically ordered.[4] Some inferences (expressed as propositions) are clearly more important than others in terms of satisfying relevance.

### Strong and weak implicature and relevance

Wilson and Sperber (2004) argue that

A proposition may be more or less strongly implicated. It is strongly impli-cated if its recovery is essential in order to arrive at an interpretation that satisfies the addressee's expectations of relevance. It is weakly implicated if its recovery helps with the construction of such an interpretation but it is not essential because the utterance suggests a range of other possible implica-tures, any one of which would do.        (Wilson and Sperber, 2004: 620)

---

[4] The nature of the inferences is not strictly deductive, but inductive and adductive, or what might be called 'conventional' reasoning or implicature.

Thus, the inference (expressed as a proposition) that *<John could not pay back the money to Mary>* (because he forgot to go to the bank) strongly implicates the proposition that *<John did not pay back the money to Mary.>*, which satisfies the relevance requirement set up by the previous context, the question *<Did John pay back the money he owed to Mary?>*. The full significance of Wilson and Sperber's distinction between strong and weak implicature is only apparent when accounting for metaphorical, hyperbolic, ironic and poetic uses of language, topics which are outside the scope of our immediate concerns.

## Refining a model of discourse

But what exactly does a discourse model comprise? Our relevance theoretic account characterizes a discourse as a network of inferentially connected propositions, but one that is continuously evolving over the life of the discourse. How such an object may be modelled computationally or in terms of its neural representation in the brain is, of course, a moot question.

Earlier in this chapter we resorted to the metaphor of a stage play to characterize a discourse model, where events are enacted, and a story unfolds or is projected before the mind's eye. The stage metaphor captures some key properties of a discourse model: that it is a temporary and dynamic mental representation of a scenario, an event or state of affairs, which is continually extended by new inferences constructed 'on the fly', congruent, but at any time potentially incompatible with current presuppositions. Stage lighting, with its shifting spotlight on one or two salient objects at any one time, expresses the shifting focus of attention and the selective nature of discourse representations. But the stage play is only a metaphor and not a model of discourse. This metaphor depicts a central property required of any discourse model, that it makes reference to a situation or state of affairs made up of objects or symbols that have reference to a world beyond the discourse, knowledge of which is stored in the semantic and episodic memory of the interlocutors.

In the previously quoted passage from Naipaul, we illustrated one way that reference assignment to definite noun phrases in discourse may by achieved. A noun phrase marked [+definite] tells the listener 'I am an object of discourse with specific reference'. In this case, reference assignment was ensured by the narrator's skilful management of the listener's access to common encyclopaedic knowledge. By reference assignment, we mean the establishment of a linkage between an object of discourse and the listener/reader's pragmatic knowledge base. Such referential connections permit further inferences (conversational implicatures) to be drawn, which further enrich the discourse model. There is no requirement of any one-to-one match between discourse objects and objects in the encyclopaedic knowledge base. Objects of discourse are cognitive constructions inferred from the evidence provided by linguistic expressions (sentences in text) and things known to us from encyclopaedic knowledge. Also, novel objects of discourse can be created, which may subsequently, through memory consolidation, become part of and modify the pragmatic knowledge base. It seems that we are almost entirely ignorant of the computational medium and mechanism whereby these transactions between the discourse model and the pragmatic knowledge base take place. Perhaps they require a meta-language of 'thought'. Perhaps natural language in some mysterious way constitutes its own meta-language. One thing we can be certain of, however, is that natural language expressions are *under-specified* with respect to the meanings that they convey or permit language users to construct.

## Under-specification

We have seen under-specification in operation at the sentential level in the ellipsis of functional constituents (subjects and objects) in subordinate clauses and structures of conjunction (see chapter 2). Ellipsis is also apparent where the speaker produces a single phrase that stands in for a complete proposition, as often occurs in question–answer routines:

(4)          A: *What are you doing?*
             B: *Nothing.*

At the level of discourse (beyond the sentence), under-specification is evident in the use and also in the *absence* of usage of connective words that express inferential relations between propositions in discourse. For example:

(5)          *John was tired.*
             *He closed the book.*

The discourse model that the listener/reader builds contains not only the two expressed propositions but also the implication that John's closing of the book was a consequence of his being tired;[5] something that could have been more explicitly indicated by use of a discourse connective:

(6)          *So he closed the book.*

One has to work harder to make a discourse of

(7)          *John was tired.*
             *He opened the book.*

And harder still to construct a plausible inferential linkage for

(8)          *John was tired.*
             *So he opened the book.*

## Sentence-level discourse devices

We have previously introduced (chapter 2) the principal discourse devices that operate at the sentential level and will only briefly recapitulate them

---

[5] Based on the pragmatic knowledge that reading requires some mental effort.

Table 15.1 *Sentence-level discourse (focusing) devices*

|  | Word order | Syntactic type | Intonation |
|---|---|---|---|
| *It was* **cookie monster** *who ate the doughnut.* | non-canonical | pseudo-cleft | contrastive accent |
| *The doughnut was eaten by cookie monster.* | non-canonical | passive | |
| *The* **doughnut***, cookie monster ate.* | non-canonical | left dislocated | intonation break |

here. They involve (1) departures from canonical word order, (2) the use of special syntactic constructions that sanction such departures, and (3) intonation, frequently acting in concert with (1) and (2). As we also previously noted in chapter 2, the additional meaning introduced by the use of these sentence-level discourse focusing devices does not affect the truth-conditional status of the proposition that the sentence encodes. Rather, these devices instruct the listener/reader where to direct their attention, or to a change of the focus of interest. Similarly, the use of discourse connectives, like '*so . . .*', have no impact upon the truth-conditional status of the sentence to which they attach, but direct the reader/listener to draw certain inferences as to how the proposition encoded by the sentence is to be construed in immediate context (usually provided by the preceding sentence).

The set of discourse connectives is quite varied. The previous paragraph employed no less than four: '*As . . .*', '*Rather, . . .*', '*Similarly, . . .*', '*but . . .*'. They are typically adverbials or adjuncts, with no syntactically mandated connection to the sentence, from which they are often separated by a prosodic boundary. A little reflection on the following examples in Table 15.2 (based on Blakemore, 1987) should convince you that their principal function is to indicate a logical, causal, comparative or some such connection with previous context. Discourse connectives such as *and, but, therefore* in natural language establish implicatures that are both wider and less precise than their respective roles as logical conjunctions. For example, *and* in discourse often carries the implication of temporal sequence, even causality. The connectives *because* and *so* direct the listener's attention to one proposition as the <cause> or the <consequence> of another proposition in the discourse. The nature of the causal connection indicated is often highly 'conventional' and not a logical implicature in any strictly logical sense. Hence, the strong stereotypical implicature carried by *because*:

(9)      *He's sport crazy because he's Australian.*

Alternatively, the same stereotypical implication may be carried, but in a weaker form by 'after all':

(10)      *He's sport crazy. After all, he's Australian.*

Table 15.2 *Examples of discourse connectives*

| and . . . | *John picked up the guitar **and** he started to play.* | <temporal sequence>(Event$_1$, Event$_2$) |
|---|---|---|
| but . . . | *Nigel is at home **but** he is busy.* | <denial of expectation>(State$_1$, State$_2$) |
| because . . . | *He's sport crazy **because** he's Australian.* | <explanation P$_1$>(Proposition$_1$, Proposition$_2$) |
| so . . . | *He's Australian, **so** he's sport crazy.* | <explanation P$_2$>(Proposition$_1$, Proposition$_2$) |
| after all . . . | *He's sport crazy. **After all**, he's Australian.* | <further evidence P$_1$>(Proposition$_1$, Proposition$_2$) |
| though . . . | *Nigel is at home **though** he is busy.* | <qualification of expectation>(State$_1$, State$_2$) |

Compare the meaning of *but* and *though* (in Table 15.2), both of which appear to carry a denial of expectation created on the basis of one proposition (the context), but differ in terms of the strength of the denial, so that *though* simply carries a qualification of expectation. Notice also that the nature of the expectation is not explicitly stated. That is for the listener to infer. The use of the discourse connective directs the listener towards the type of inference to be drawn. The principle of relevance guarantees (or at least is intended to ensure) that the inference can be drawn.

We now turn to the problem of how one goes about studying discourse processing. Unless we happen to be mind readers, we do not have direct access to the kinds of inferences that listeners construct in the course of discourse processing, but one can infer quite a bit from how they deal with reference assignment of clearly anaphoric expressions.

## Studies of discourse anaphora resolution

A combination of off-line and on-line methods has been used to study discourse anaphora resolution. We will begin by illustrating investigations of the roles of verb focusing and clausal/sentential connectives in assigning reference to pronouns, which were introduced in the previous section.

The tendency of some transitive verbs to bias pronominal reference towards the object NP and others to do so towards the subject NP can be easily established by off-line sentence completion studies, where readers or listeners are asked to supply continuations to sentence fragments such as

(11)(a)     *John congratulated Mary (because) . . .*
    (b)     *Mary congratulated John (because) . . .*

Switching the gender of subject and object NPs in the stimulus sentences enables the experimenter to determine from subjects' completion responses which of the two NPs is more accessible or likely to become the object of subsequent reference. The following verbs were found to strongly focus subsequent reference on either the first (subject) or the second (object) NP in a recent study (Stewart, Pickering and Sanford, 2000):

| *Subject NP focused* | *Object NP focused* |
| --- | --- |
| fascinated | admired |
| disappointed | praised |
| concerned | despised |
| inspired | noticed |
| amused | congratulated |
| called | thanked |

What common factor(s) in the meanings of these verbs are responsible for biasing the likelihood of subsequent discourse reference to the subject or object NP? All the object-focusing verbs convey the implication that the person referred to in the object NP either did something or possesses some property which caused the state of affairs or the action referred to by the verb in the main clause. (Note that all the object-focusing verbs readily take a *for* . . . prepositional phrase.) On the other hand, subject-focusing verbs evoke scenarios in which it is some action or attribute of the subject NP that has caused the state of affairs or action referred to by the verb. When we further note that the obvious function of a connective expression like *because* serves to direct attention to a <cause>, then we can see how information contained in the verb predisposes the listener to look in the direction of one or the other of the players currently on stage: the 'subject' or the 'object' NP. Hence, in this case the type of cohesive link indicated by the clausal connective reinforces the semantic focus conveyed by the verb. But other connectives may behave quite differently.

A clausal connective like *so* directs the listener's attention to the consequences or the <result> of the action or state of affairs just stated. But because consequences are not represented in the thematic templates of verbs, no specific reference bias is activated by the verb. In cases like this, other influences are at work. In particular, there is a strong predisposition for subject NPs to serve as topics of discourse. Topic focus may be regarded as the default case for continued discourse reference.

We have seen that there are a number of influences at work shaping listeners' expectations about the likely direction that referential focus may take as discourse develops (lexical verb causality bias, the type of clausal connective, subject-as-topic bias) and how such influences may be demonstrated using 'off-line' fragment completion tests, making use of pronoun gender agreement to observe how reference is directed towards one or another of the currently active discourse referents. But we would like to know: at what *stage* in on-line processing do the various factors which influence discourse reference become operative? Does referential processing occur concurrently with lexical and syntactic processing, or is there some logical and/or temporal sequencing to the language processing and inferential operations that underlie assignment of discourse reference?

## On-line studies of discourse anaphora

Several measures of referential behaviour in on-line language processing have been studied. One well-investigated measure, reading time, exploits the effect that a pronoun whose gender forces a reference assignment which is incongruent with the reader's expectation will take a little longer to read, as a result of increased processing load, than one which is consistent with expectations:

(12) (a)    *John congratulated Mary because **he** ...*    incongruent: longer reading time for *he*
     (b)    *John congratulated Mary because **she** ...*    congruent: shorter reading time for *she*

Stewart *et al.* (2000) used on-line reading time measures in an attempt to choose between an early-lexical-inference versus a late-discourse-integrative theory of pronoun reference assignment, or a theory which represents a mixture of the two processing levels. To generate the required predictions to test the competing theories, the experimenters manipulated two critical variables: (a) the amount of discourse material containing the congruent or incongruent pronoun, and (b) the 'depth' of processing required of the stimulus materials.

We suppress some complexities of the experiment design in the following account of the findings. Using the self-paced reading paradigm, subjects were presented with the stimulus sentences in two fragments: from the start of the sentence up to and including the critical pronoun as in (12) above (the first fragment); and all the material following the pronoun to the end of the sentence (the second fragment):

(13) (a)    *John congratulated Mary because he / was very impressed.*
     (b)    *John congratulated Mary because she / won the championship.*
                    First fragment              Second fragment

Stewart *et al.* reasoned that if referential expectations are guided by early lexical inference (verb focus, amplified by the appropriate clausal connective) then reading time differences between sentences containing congruent versus incongruent pronouns should be apparent from presentation of the first fragment. If, on the other hand, discourse anaphora is assigned at the stage when sentential propositions are integrated into discourse structure, then congruity effects will be most apparent on processing of the second fragment.

Stewart *et al.* also pointed out that the integrative model of discourse anaphora requires a deeper level of processing for meaning than the lexical inference model. They sought to manipulate depth of processing through comprehension questions that subjects were posed about the test sentences they were exposed to in the course of the experiment. Under the 'deep' processing condition, subjects were required to answer a reference-related question after each experimental item (e.g. '*Who won the championship?*'). Under the 'shallow' processing condition, subjects responded only on one third of the items to a question that did not require anaphoric inference (e.g. '*Did John congratulate Mary?*').

On both counts, the depth of processing manipulation, and the first and second fragment reading times, Stewart *et al.* concluded that the results favoured the integrative model of discourse anaphora resolution. Congruity effects were greater under the 'deep' processing instructions, where subjects were obliged to fully process the sentences for anaphora retrieval. This can only be accomplished by comprehending the meaning of the dependent clause and its causal relation to the main clause.

Also, congruity effects were only consistently found on reading times for the *second* fragment, at the point of construal when the inferential connection between the two propositions contained in the main and subordinate clause is established, thus favouring the discourse integration theory of anaphora resolution. Why is it, you may ask, that lexical causality biases are found in 'off-line' sentence completion tasks, using initial sentence fragments such as (10a) and (10b) above, but are not reliably detected in on-line processing such as reading times in a self-paced reading task? The answer probably lies in the response strategy required by the 'off-line' sentence completion task. Subjects probably complete the sentence construal process before responding, invoking some imagined reading for the missing dependent clause. Indeed, that is what the 'sentence completion' ostensibly requires them to do. But in a self-paced reading or listening task, at the point when only the main clause and the subordinating conjunction have been presented, pronoun reference cannot yet be assigned, except in cases such as (11) where it is syntactically mandated by gender agreement.[6]

In a recent study, Wolf, Gibson and Desmet (2004), provided confirmation for Stewart *et al.*'s (2000) findings, and attribute the original insight that 'pronoun resolution is a byproduct of establishing coherence' to Hobbs (1979), extended in Kehler (2002). We would only add to this, by way of conclusion, the following observation: that what we have, in these cases of verb causality-biased pronominal reference, is a variant on the now familiar garden path scenario, where an initial parse of the sentence, driven by lexical biases of one kind or another, is ultimately abandoned in favour of a reading that manages to preserve 'surface structure' syntactic constraints. In other words, syntactic constraints, unlike lexical-semantic constraints, are inviolable. The implications of this observation will be taken up in the final chapter. But in the meantime, we turn in the next chapter to a discussion of language disorders that are characterized primarily by breakdown at the discourse

---

[6] Interestingly, this was the only case where there was a significant effect upon reading time of the first fragment. Initial fragments containing 'unambiguous' pronominal reference, mandated by gender agreement, were read faster than fragments where pronoun gender did not disambiguate subject or object reference. This is another example of the 'pre-emptive' role of syntax on meaning construal, which we noted in chapter 3, in connection with the celebrated ambiguity of '*flying planes can be . . .*' vs. '*flying planes is/are dangerous*'.

level, where the principal consequence or manifestation for the listener, if not the speaker as well, is a loss of coherence or 'the thread of discourse'.

## Summary

Discourse, the highest level of language processing, involves the co-operative construction of compatible conceptual representations for the speaker and the listener pertaining to the 'objects of discourse', the things-talked-about. Discourse construction is an inference-driven process that makes use of information about the meaning and use of words stored in the mental lexicon and a vast store of encyclopaedic pragmatic knowledge. We can distinguish broadly between the language-specific knowledge base contained in lexical entries of nouns, verbs, conjunctions and the like, which is used for sentence-level processing, and the language-independent encyclopaedic knowledge base that is required for discourse processing. But there is a seamless transition between these levels of processing in real-time language comprehension, which has been the cause of much debate over the architecture of the language processor.

Given the under-specified nature of linguistic expressions, perhaps the most surprising thing is that construal does not fail more often in everyday discourse than it apparently does. Relevance theory offers a programmatic explanation for the high success rate in discourse processing. Speakers adhere to conversational maxims and encode their communicational intentions in expressions that satisfy the requirement of relevance. A speaker is constrained to produce a linguistic expression whose relevance to current context can be readily inferred. This explanation is programmatic at the present time, because relevance theory has hardly begun to identify the inferences which direct discourse construction; assumptions about agency, intention, cause and effect, pertaining to our preconceptions as to how the world works.

In spite of the theoretical challenge that a theory of discourse processing poses, progress has been made with 'on-line' experiments into the determinants of reference assignment of anaphoric expressions in mini-discourses, two of which were briefly reviewed in this chapter (Stewart, Pickering and Sanford, 2000; Wolf, Gibson and Desmet, 2004). The provisional evidence we reviewed suggests that reference resolution of anaphoric expressions is deferred until propositions encoded in clause and sentence structures are integrated into a coherent discourse structure.

# 16 Breakdown of discourse

## Introduction

As we indicated in the previous chapter, a breakdown at the discourse level of language comprehension would be expected to reveal itself in difficulties of reference retrieval and failure to successfully construct and maintain a mental model that serves the interlocutors engaged in a particular discourse. Discourse construction, insofar as it involves formulating communicative intentions, reference management and taking account of the listener's perspective, places high demands on working memory and attentional resources. Deficits in these higher cognitive abilities are likely to result in violations of the Gricean pragmatic felicity conditions mentioned in the previous chapter. The spoken language which results from poor discourse model construction or management may manifest itself in incoherent or bizarre speech that is likely to be characterized as 'thought disordered' in the psychiatric literature (Andreasen, 1982).

Thought disorder is traditionally clinically characterized in terms of either 'looseness or bizarreness of association' between ideas, or as an *absence* of appropriate expressions which enable the listener to construct a coherent model of what the speaker is talking about.[1] The term *formal thought disorder* is often used specifically to indicate that what is being referred to is the 'form' of thought or its overt expression, and not necessarily a pathology of an underlying cognitive process or condition, which might nevertheless be responsible for the production of thought disordered speech.

There has been much debate about the underlying cognitive pathology of thought disordered speech. The symptom is most closely identified with schizophrenia in its acute phase. However, it is recognized that formal thought disorder may also occur in bipolar mental illness (Andreasen, 1982). In addition, the speech of Alzheimer's patients may evince signs of 'thought disorder'. Although the underlying brain pathology is quite different and the cognitive impairments are more severe in Alzheimer's disease, both conditions may share cognitive deficits that are suggested by the term 'dementia praecox', which Kraepelin (1919) originally coined for schizophrenia. The language production of some fluent aphasics

---

[1] Hence the controversial distinction which is often drawn between 'negative' and 'positive' symptoms of thought disorder, and the question of whether they represent two sides of the same coin or underlying differences in cognitive pathology (Andreasen, 1982).

may also sometimes be difficult to distinguish from thought disordered speech (Gerson, Benson and Frazier, 1977). What is common to these speech varieties, and may obscure differences in their respective aetiologies, is that in every case the discourse is hard to follow. However, it should be borne in mind that ratings of 'thought disorder' reflect a listener's failure to comprehend, as much as they do the content of what the speaker has said.

Rochester *et al.* (1977) are usually credited with drawing attention to the critical importance of indices of reference and discourse cohesion[2] for characterizing thought disordered speech. These two characteristics they attributed to a failure to take account of the listener's perspective; signs of communicative incompetence in face-to-face encounters, or symptomatic of a withdrawn and dissociated mind-set. We might dub this the *communicative incompetence* theory of thought disordered speech, caused by a partial failure of social cognition or an inability to adopt the listener's perspective, which is a prerequisite for successful discourse management. This view has gained support in recent years, through the work of Frith and colleagues (Frith and Frith, 1999).

Alternatively, a plausible explanation for discourse breakdown in thought disordered speech may be sought in a general cognitive deficit which reveals itself under the high working memory and attentional demands of discourse management. We might dub this the *cognitive deficit hypothesis* of thought disordered speech. According to this theory, discourse construction is but one of a range of complex mental tasks, that have in common a high working memory load requirement for sustained, goal-directed manipulation of symbols or visual representations. The cognitive deficit hypothesis seeks to correlate discourse breakdown with performance deficits on a variety of tests of executive 'frontal lobe' control. In contrast to the communicative incompetence model, which posits a specific disorder of social cognition that prevents the speaker from effectively self-monitoring and adopting the listener's perspective, the cognitive deficit hypothesis makes no special appeal to specific requirements of face-to-face communication.

A third and decidedly a minority position of researchers in the field also deserves mention, mainly for historical reasons: that discourse breakdown constitutes an *impairment of language competence* of one form or another; that language disorders in schizophrenia and the psychoses in general constitute attenuated forms of aphasia in one or more of its recognizable clinical varieties, though milder and possibly transient in its expression. Although this position has never enjoyed widespread support, it deserves mention because it provides one way of explaining the diverse range of language symptoms encountered in psychotic language from loose, over-productive speech similar to fluent aphasia, to poverty of speech reminiscent of Broca's aphasia.

It should be stated at the outset that these three positions, while generally in competition, are by no means completely incompatible with one another. Indeed,

---

[2] Following Halliday and Hasan's (1976) schema for discourse analysis, Rochester and Martin use the term 'cohesion' for the linguistic devices that create discourse structure in text.

a quite legitimate and productive way to view the three theories is to say that they define a range of ways in which discourse construction may be impaired, and insofar as they implicate different communicative styles and discourse behaviours, they may provide useful ways of differentiating pathologies of thought and language in clinically diverse conditions such as dementia, schizophrenia, autism, Asperger's syndrome, etc. We consider each of the three theories in turn, starting with a discussion of language performance in schizophrenia.

We shall begin our discussion by exemplifying discourse breakdown in thought disordered speech. As we did in the case of aphasia, we begin with a discussion of spoken language performance characteristics, because such data provide us with an overt expression of the relevant linguistic forms and a starting point for speculation on underlying mechanisms. However, it is the cognitive and linguistic requirements of coherent discourse construction from the perspective of the listener that motivates our inquiry into disordered discourse. What structural or anaphoric cues has the speaker failed to provide the listener? What evidence leads us to conclude that a particular discourse is 'crazy'?

We then inquire into the linguistic correlates of thought disordered speech: syntactic, lexical and semantic properties are observable from the study of language output. We find little in terms of overt linguistic signs to distinguish thought disordered speech in free narratives from that of normal language users, despite the fact that formal thought disorder can be readily detected by those trained to recognize it. The most important indices of thought disorder reside in the subjective reactions of the listener; specifically in failures of reference and discourse cohesion, aspects of language processing that we cannot as yet explicitly model, though they are readily accessible to introspective reflection.

We then turn to the question of the nature of the neurocognitive impairment underlying thought disordered speech, and schizophrenia in general, which is the diagnosis given when accompanied by 'first rank' symptoms (Schneider, 1957) of mental pathology.[3] Most empirical investigation has focused on testing the cognitive deficit hypothesis, two competing varieties of which may be distinguished. On the one hand, a breakdown of executive control is postulated over the contents of working memory and their manipulation in goal-directed problem solving, with the locus of disorder focused on the frontal lobes. Alternatively, the breakdown of executive control may be conceptualized as a disinhibition or failure to control associative semantic linkages that underpin declarative semantic memory, in which case the most probable locus of pathology is temporo-parietal. Given the variety of expression of schizophrenic cognitive disorders, it is quite

---

[3] Schneider's first-rank symptoms (1. auditory hallucinations, 2. thought withdrawal, insertion and interruption, 3. thought broadcasting, 4. somatic hallucinations, 5. delusional beliefs, 6. feelings or actions experienced as made or influenced by external agents) are viewed as primary or direct subjective manifestations of the mental pathology and 'formal thought disorder' as its linguistic expression. However, what this diagnostic framework tends to overlook is the necessary role of observer inference in detection of linguistic signs of formal thought disorder. See Ceccherini-Nelli and Crow (2003) for further discussion of linguistic disturbances and first-rank symptoms, from the psychiatric perspective.

possible that either one of these accounts my better fit the facts of individual cases of schizophrenia (Elvevag and Goldberg, 2000).

Finally, we shall turn to consider recent neural imaging studies of thought disordered and control subjects engaged in cognitive tasks requiring executive control, or the kind of 'theory of mind' mentation deemed crucial for effective discourse management according to the communicative incompetence theory of discourse breakdown. These investigations take us to the limits of present understanding of the neurological foundations of higher cognitive activities. We are dealing with mental operations not so much dependent upon the integrity of localized networks, as involving (a) spatially and temporally widely distributed patterns of activation and inhibition across cortical and sub-cortical regions in 'whole of brain' functioning, and (b) regulation by neurotransmitter delivery systems, such as the dopamine system. It may well be premature to seek to choose among competing theories of thought disorder, such as a generalized disruption of executive control versus a specific failure of social cognition or communicative competence. On the other hand, if differential spatio-temporal patterns of brain metabolic or electromagnetic activity can be reliably established for mental computations demonstrably associated with aspects of discourse processing, then it could be reasonably argued that we have at least the beginnings of a neurocognitive model of thought disorder.

## Language and psychosis

Disturbances of thought, belief (delusions), and perception (hallucinations) have remained pivotal diagnostic signs of psychosis in general and schizophrenia in particular from the early modern period of psychiatry to the present day. The overt expression of thought disorder in speech has also remained a diagnostic indicator, since it was first recognized by Bleuler who coined the term 'schizophrenia'. Pathological verbal expression in schizophrenia tends to take one of two forms, often distinguished as 'positive' or 'negative' signs of thought disordered speech. In the positive variety, there are manifest signs of incoherence in the context of fluent and abundant verbal output: odd juxtapositions of ideas that do not cohere, vague or indeterminate references, unexpected or un-flagged changes of topic, occasional neologisms, or clang associations and a rambling character, lacking direction and clarity of communicative intent – in short, 'a rave'. In the negative variety of thought disordered speech there is a poverty of verbal expression, a preponderance of simple sentence structures, incomplete expressions and a higher rate of grammatical errors. These two styles of verbal expression may have prognostic significance. Impoverished speech has been found to be associated with an early age of onset (Morice and Ingram, 1983), which is in turn associated with a high familial loading, poorer prognosis (Suvisaari et al., 1998) and lower levels of dopamine activity in the prefrontal cortex (Davis et al., 1991). Positive symptoms of thought disorder on the other hand are associated with the acute phase of schizophrenic illness, before symptoms have been stabilized by anti-psychotic medication, and with hyperactivity in sub-cortical branches of the dopamine transmitter system (Davis *et al.*, 1991).

Kleist (1970) observed the correlation that exists between the typical cognitive disturbances of schizophrenia and signs of language disorder, suggesting that both involve a common high-level pathology to the frontal and temporo-parietal cortical circuits that serve language. 'Hearing voices' is the most common form of auditory hallucination in schizophrenia – not perceptual illusions of some other sensory modality, and not auditory perceptual abnormalities of a general kind, but being spoken to by voices in one's head. Schizophrenic voices deliver linguistically interpretable messages that may form the basis of subsequently fixed delusional beliefs. They are not subjectively experienced as incoherent speech-like auditory hallucinations. Hence, they do not represent failures of language comprehension, so much as a pathological autogenic application of language interpretive processes, insufficiently constrained by any identifiable sensory input. This is strongly suggestive of a hyperactive receptive language system, but not one in which linguistic interpretive processes are damaged or compromised.

Similarly, there are obvious analogies between the impoverished linguistic expression of negatively thought disordered schizophrenics and the minimal verbal output of Broca's aphasics. But there are equally prominent differences as well. Impoverished verbal expression in schizophrenia does not occur, as in Broca's aphasia, in the context of a clearly frustrated intention to communicate, but more as an evident lack of anything to say. Hence, although Kleist is correct to draw attention to the shared neural structures involved in thought disorder and the aphasias, the underlying pathologies of the two conditions appear to be rather different. But the possibility of a mild or transient impairment of language competence should not be dismissed out of hand. An evaluation of the language competence deficit and the communicative incompetence theories of schizophrenic language and thought disordered speech was conducted by Morice and Ingram (1982, 1983) using linguistic analysis of 1000-word free narrative speech samples produced by thought disordered and non-thought disordered schizophrenics, manic (bipolar) patients, and matched non-psychiatric control subjects.

## Characteristics of thought disordered speech

Consider two typical samples of (positively) thought disordered schizophrenic speech (Ingram and Morice, 1983):

**118.**    *And er anyway further to that er we er we have to we're talking about that actually.*
*Further to it as I said is that a um we we we go on and we have to look at er this continuance of er er of upgrading upgrading the children.*

*This is the year of the child I might add and on this recording.*
*I must put that on the recording.*
*And is conducted by the United Nations and the United Nations and the*
*    year of the child.*
*And there must be a reason for this you know.*
*And in the communications um bracket communicating to children which*
*    you're going to have to control the communications of of future years*
*And they'll represent something quite um fa- fantastic or outstanding in the*
*    way we know it today even though its developing very very rapidly*
*    these days.*
*Is to get to get people*
*Now we're talking about the child.*
*I'll st- still try and keep it on the child and the parent and the teacher the*
*    teacher of that child whether it be the parent or the teach at school or*
*    the t-*
*The child learns from other children too.*

**129.**     *I have trouble you know wh- even where I live*
*Um – um a member of parliament wanted to*
*Er as it was a style of life thats brought this type of er thing on it just needs*
*    to be burnt out.*
*Um to have this type of doctor arrested and er and thrown in jail would be*
*    you know um*
*$$ say*
*You can say anything he likes in jail.*
*It'll only bring on enemies to me which is dangerous.*
*So it becomes a sort of style of life that has to be burnt out.*
*Um its just constant work.*
*Um I've been stopped that badly that I haven't even got enough money to*
*    buy a decent typewriter to start um writing articles fo for the A – soc –*
*    s – c The Advertiser and making a name for myself and getting the*
*    things I really need in life.*
                    $ = unintelligible syllable

Syntactically, these thought disordered language samples are unremarkable: both are of average or slightly above average syntactic complexity, with a slightly elevated rate of syntactic errors and dysfluencies. However, both are remarkable for their failure to cohere into comprehensible narrative texts; a property that can be documented by failures of discourse anaphora.

## A study of thought disordered speech

Free narrative language samples (1000 words in length) were collected from thirty-four schizophrenic, eleven manic and eighteen matched non-patient control subjects. The language samples were tape recorded, transcribed, and annotated for syntactic and semantic errors of various kinds and dysfluencies.

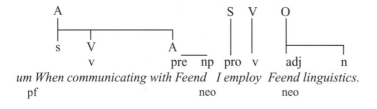

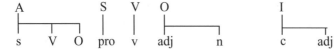

Figure 16.1 *Sample of syntactic and error coding*

Structural descriptions in the form of sentence tree diagrams after the model of Quirk, Greenbaum, Leech and Svartvik (1972) were assigned to all syntactically analysable utterances in the corpus. A sample of the syntactic and error coding is provided in Figure 16.1.

These tree diagrams provided the basis for calculating various indices of syntactic complexity. The coded language samples were stored on disk and a special-purpose program was written to compute linguistic performance profiles for each subject. Because of the large number of variables (98) in a performance profile, a principal components analysis was used to reduce the dimensionality of the variables to six factors that constituted grammatical/structural indices of the subjects' language performance. The six factors, labelled on the basis of their variable loadings, were identified as (1) syntactic complexity, (2) error-integrity factor I (loaded mainly on syntactic errors such as agreement), (3) error-integrity factor II (loaded more highly on semantic errors), (4) a verb phrase factor, (5) a (dys)fluency factor, and (6) a word-level error factor. A pragmatic analysis of anaphoric pronouns and other elliptical anaphoric expressions was also conducted, so as to provide measures of how successfully the listener/reader could resolve references in the speaker's discourse.

The essential findings from the study are summarized in Table 16.1, the results of a discriminant function analysis, which is a statistical procedure similar to regression analysis that seeks to assign subjects to diagnostic groups on the basis of performance indices from the linguistic analysis described above. Ten of the fourteen predictor variables included in discriminant function analysis were selected in the construction of three discriminant functions that assigned subjects to diagnostic groups. Overall, 78 per cent of subjects were 'correctly' assigned by the discriminant function scores to their appropriate diagnostic groups. Three non-patient controls were misallocated to the manic (2) or the non-thought disordered schizophrenic categories. No subjects were misclassified as thought disordered, though two of the schizophrenics who were diagnosed as thought disordered on the Present State Examination (the psychiatric diagnostic tool) were reallocated to the non-thought disordered schizophrenic and manic categories. The manic

Table 16.1 *Discriminant function analysis*

| Variable | Discriminant function coefficients | | |
|---|---|---|---|
| | Function 1 | Function 2 | Function 3 |
| Error-integrity II | 0.851 | 0.200 | 0.022 |
| Syntactic complexity | −0.690 | 0.501 | −0.033 |
| Self reference | 0.577 | −0.168 | 0.007 |
| Error-integrity I | 0.545 | 0.023 | 0.445 |
| Unclear reference | −0.144 | 0.745 | −0.229 |
| Word level errors | −0.014 | 0.590 | 0.034 |
| Verb phrase factor | 0.462 | −0.039 | 0.688 |
| Dysfluency | −0.123 | −0.034 | −0.623 |
| Implicit reference | −0.138 | 0.184 | 0.593 |
| Situational reference | 0.203 | 0.403 | −0.512 |

| Subject group | Group centroids | | |
|---|---|---|---|
| | Function 1 | Function 2 | Function 3 |
| TD schizophrenics | 1.530 | 2.057 | 0.331 |
| NTD schizophrenics | 0.271 | −0.667 | −0.281 |
| NTD manic | 0.695 | −0.446 | 1.341 |
| Non-patient controls | −1.629 | −0.182 | −0.109 |

group had the lowest hit rate (67 per cent) and the control group the highest (83 per cent).

The first discriminant function (and most important discriminator, accounting for 50 per cent of the common variance) separated the thought disordered (TD) schizophrenics from the non-patient controls, with the non-thought disordered schizophrenics and the manics taking mid-range values. The variables contributing most to the scores on this function were, in descending order of their standardized coefficients, as follows: grammatical/semantic errors, syntactic complexity, self reference and grammatical errors without semantic impact (e.g. errors of agreement). This function separated speakers with a higher rate of grammatical and semantic errors, lower syntactic complexity, and a higher proportion of self references, from those with a low error rate, higher syntactic complexity and relatively few self references.

Discriminant function II (37.4 per cent of variance) specifically separated the thought disordered schizophrenic group from the other subjects. Its principally contributing variables were unclear pronominal reference and word level errors. Syntactic complexity also appears to make a significant contribution to this function, but significantly, in the opposite direction. Essentially function II identifies speakers who have a higher proportion of referentially unclear anaphors, produce some neologisms or odd morphological constructions, and whose sentences tend to greater than average syntactic complexity. Function III (12.3 per cent of variance) separated the manic group from the rest. This function distinguished speakers who used a higher proportion of the implicit (recoverable, but not textually explicit) references, were more fluent, and tended to make fewer situational references. The verb phrase factor also makes a significant contribution, though its interpretation is unclear.

What do these results tell us about the nature of thought disordered speech and the two hypotheses raised earlier (the 'impairment of language competence' and the 'communicative incompetence' models)? The findings are mixed. The first and most discriminating of the three discriminant functions placed thought disordered subjects on one end, and non-patient controls on the other, of a continuum that was highly loaded with indicators of primary language impairment. This lends weight to the hypothesis that thought disorder is associated with a mild impairment of general linguistic competence. On the other hand, the second discriminant function separated the thought disordered subjects from the other patient and non-patient groups on the basis of unclear pronominal reference – a pragmatic variable – and the occasional neologism or odd word construction. The features that uniquely distinguish thought disordered speech reflect a breakdown in the listener's comprehension as much as they do properties that could be said to be overtly present in the patient's language production. Such features have inherent problems of observer bias, because they critically depend for their recognition on the violation of expectations formed, not on the basis of linguistic rules, but on the construal of meaning in a particular context of discourse.

We are led therefore to the conclusion that language production in thought disorder involves both a degree of primary linguistic impairment (not as severe as aphasia) and a pragmatic impairment resulting from the listener's inability to keep track of discourse anaphora. The uniquely distinctive 'linguistic' features of thought disorder may arise from a threshold effect which comes into play when the processes which disrupt linguistic performance reach a level that is sufficient to produce a breakdown in the listener's active construal of the patient's discourse. It is at such a point of inferential breakdown that the listener abandons all attempts to follow the speaker and concludes that s/he is 'talking rubbish'.

However, the source of the performance disruption cannot be identified by linguistic analysis alone, though there are clues in the language output which suggest that the locus of the breakdown lies at levels of the production process which are under volitional rather than automatic control and therefore point to a disruption of working memory or attentional focusing. We discuss the neuropsychological evidence for this in the next section.

## Cognitive impairment and thought disordered language

Recent studies have corroborated and extended the characterization of thought disordered speech offered above. Docherty *et al.* (1996) developed a

Table 16.2 *Categories of communication failure (Docherty et al., 1996)*

| Category | Definition | Example |
|---|---|---|
| Vague references | Overinclusive words or phrases that obscure the meaning because of their lack of specificity | 'Being sick is not bad. You can do *things* and plus you can make people afraid of you.' |
| Confused references | Words or phrases that refer ambiguously to one of at least two clear-cut alternative referents | 'Take the clock, for instance. You got ten, twelve on it, you got other numbers on it, you got a volume button on it, *it* go up and down.' |
| Missing information references | References to information not previously presented and not known to the listener | 'I like to work alright, some of those shops were filthy. I like the bakeries, some of the shops are clean.' (No prior mention of any shops or bakeries.) |
| Ambiguous word meanings | Instances in which a word or phrase could have a number of different meanings, and the intended meaning is not obvious from the context | 'I had a chance to *grow* with him but I got a divorce because I couldn't' |
| Wrong word references | Use of the wrong or apparently inappropriate word or an expression in an otherwise clear utterance | 'I was trying to *predict* them people that I need, I need to get out of there' |
| Structural unclarities | Failures of meaning due to a breakdown or inadequacy of grammatical structure | 'I was socializing with friends. Girlfriends and friends of the same as male' |

'Communication Disturbances Index', a discourse reference classification scheme not specifically linked to the behaviour of any grammatical word category, but quite similar from the listener's perspective to the analysis of pronominal reference discussed above (see Table 16.2). The speech of schizophrenic and manic subjects was found to contain much higher frequencies of each of the six types of communication failure than the speech of control subjects.

More recently, Docherty *et al.* (1999) extended their study to compare the speech characteristics of parents of schizophrenic patients with unrelated age-matched controls, using the Communication Disturbance Index (CDI). It is known that there is a hereditary predisposition for schizophrenia. The aim of the study was to see if subclinical referential disturbances of the kind that had distinguished schizophrenics from non-patient controls in the earlier study could also be detected in the speech of first-degree relatives who were beyond the age of risk, but who quite possibly shared their children's genetic predisposition for schizophrenic illness.

Ten-minute language samples were obtained from three groups of subjects: schizophrenic patients (n = 43), those parents of the patients who had no history of psychiatric illness (n = 42), and a control group (n = 23), age- and education-matched to the parent group. The language samples were rated on the CDI scales by a trained research assistant who was blind to the subject classification and the specific aims of the study.

The parents of the schizophrenics had higher overall CDI ratings than controls and in fact did not differ significantly from their schizophrenic offspring. On one sub-scale 'vague references' the parent group actually scored higher than the schizophrenic group, though the authors point out 'that their [the parents'] speech was generally not perceived by interviewers or raters as disordered'. One possible reason why parents of schizophrenics scored just as high as their schizophrenic offspring may be due to the finding that 'within the parent and control groups, age was positively associated with CDI scores at a low but significant level' (Docherty *et al.*, 1999: 99). Parental CDI scores were also significantly correlated with severity of symptoms in their patient offsprings ($r = 0.49$, $p < .04$) as assessed by the Brief Psychiatric Rating Scale (Overall, 1962).

These results are consistent with other studies in finding elevated levels of language or communicative abnormality in relatives of schizophrenics, and consistent also with an inherited genetic vulnerability in schizophrenia. The type of language breakdown seems specifically linked to listener difficulties in reference tracking and therefore points to higher order executive or cognitive disruptions that may be expected to express themselves in non-linguistic domains of performance as well.

Discourse model building, we have argued previously, requires conscious planning (for effective argument construction), working memory resources (for keeping track of referents) and flexibility (to accommodate the listener's perspective). These abilities are all components of a general executive or volitional control mechanism for problem solving, which is traditionally identified with the frontal lobes of the brain. We might anticipate therefore that thought disordered speakers, whose communication difficulties lie mainly in discourse management, would present with executive cognitive deficits associated with 'a dysfunction of the cortical-subcortical loops that project into the pre-frontal cortex' (McGrath, 1991). A competing neurocognitive model that emphasizes symptoms of semantic impairment and the frequent accompaniment of auditory hallucinations (hearing voices) has the locus of schizophrenic thought disorder in temporal lobe dysfunction (Kleist, 1970).

There is suggestive but not conclusive neuropsychological support for the impaired executive/frontal lobe model of thought disorder. Morice and Delahunty (1996) found that schizophrenics 'demonstrated significant impairments in cognitive flexibility and forward planning' in performance on the more difficult items on the Tower of London test. The Tower of London test (TOL) was originally developed by Shallice (1982) to investigate problem solving in subjects with damage to the frontal lobes.

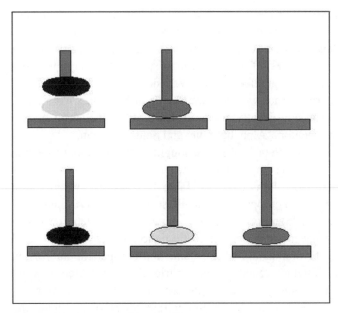

Figure 16.2 *The Tower of London Test*

A sample item from a version of the TOL is shown in Figure 16.2. Subjects are required to transform the arrangement of coloured beads in configuration A (above) until they achieve the arrangement shown below (goal configuration). They are instructed to try to achieve the goal arrangement in as few moves as possible. The TOL is generally regarded as testing planning functions of the prefrontal cortex. In Shallice's initial investigation using the TOL, patients with damage to the left anterior frontal lobe demonstrated impaired planning (i.e. greater number of moves required for solution). Patients with damage to the right anterior and left or right posterior areas of the frontal lobes were not impaired in performance on the TOL. Thus, results from this initial lesion study suggested that the left anterior frontal lobe area was involved in the planning required for solving the Tower of London test. Neuroimaging studies on normal adults lend support to this conclusion. Morris, Ahmed, Syed and Toone (1993), using single-photon emission computerized tomography (SPECT), found that the level of regional cerebral blood flow (rCBF) was significantly increased in the left prefrontal cortex during the Tower of London task. In addition, subjects who took more time planning their moves, and required fewer moves to complete a problem, had a significantly higher level of rCBF in the left prefrontal cortex. Subsequent studies using PET and fMRI have confirmed that as item difficulty is increased on the TOL test, in terms of the number of steps required to achieve the goal arrangement, both the rCBF and BOLD haemodynamic responses also increase proportionately in the left prefrontal cortex (Lazeron, Rombouts, Machielsen *et al.*, 2000; Schall, Johnston, Lagopoulos *et al.*, 2003).

Morice and Delahunty (1996) found there were no differences in performance between schizophrenics and controls for the first three levels of complexity (1–3 moves) on the TOL test, but significant, and increasing, differences emerged for the last three levels (4–6 moves). Tests of attention span and working memory were also administered. Schizophrenic patients were not found to be impaired on tests of simple short-term memory as measured by Digit Span and Word Span, but they were found to be significantly impaired compared with controls on two tests of verbal working memory, Alphabet Span and Sentence Span.

Docherty and colleagues (1996, 1999) have sought to establish more specific connections between executive capacities, working memory and communication disturbances as assessed by the CDI (see Table 16.2 above), by correlation analysis of CDI ratings with neuropsychological tests of executive/frontal functioning. Docherty *et al.* (1996) report contrasting patterns of correlation between cognitive tests of working memory and linguistic indices of reference retrieval for schizophrenics on the one hand, and for manic and non-patient controls on the other. In the schizophrenic group, reference retrieval ratings were positively associated with working memory test scores and were not related to concept formation or verbal fluency test performance. In contrast, for bipolar patients and non-psychiatric controls, reference performance was associated with concept formation and verbal fluency test scores but was unrelated to working memory test performance.

Further support for the primacy of executive impairment over semantic impairment in thought disorder in schizophrenia comes from two recent studies by Kim, Glahn, Nuechterlein and Cannon (2004) and Barrera, McKenna and Berrios (2005). Basing their research on Baddeley's model of working memory, with its distinction between verbal and spatial components and functional separation of executive (symbol manipulative) and 'maintenance' or purely retentive functions, Kim *et al.* (2004) devised parallel verbal and visual tests of working memory that independently varied symbol manipulation and retention task demands. There was a significantly greater reduction in performance on the part of the schizophrenic patients compared with demographically matched non-patient controls, when simultaneous maintenance and manipulation of symbols was required by the working memory task, in either spatial or verbal modality. But increasing the retention component of the task did not result in a differential performance loss between the two groups.

Barrera *et al.* (2005) assessed thought disordered and non-thought disordered schizophrenics and a matched non-patient group on four separate tests of 'executive' control and four tests of 'lexical semantics', summarized in Table 16.3. The patients with formal thought disorder were significantly impaired on all four executive tests compared to non-thought disordered schizophrenics, who in turn were slightly, but non-significantly, impaired on two of the four tests in relation to the non-patient control group. By contrast, the thought disordered group were significantly impaired in relation to non-thought disordered patients and normal

Table 16.3 *Tests of executive control and semantics (Barrera* et al.*, 2005)*

| Hayling Sentence Completion Test: Burgess and Shallice (1997) (executive control) | Complete a sentence with a word unconnected to the sentence in every way e.g. *The captain wanted to stay with the sinking . . .* Correct reply may be *light bulb.* |
|---|---|
| Brixton Test: Burgess and Shallice (1997) (executive control) | Subject shown series of pages with same basic array of ten circles, one of which is blue. Position of blue circle changes from page to page according to rules. Subject predicts where blue circle will move next. |
| Modified Six Elements: Wilson *et al.* (1996) (executive control) | Subject required to organize their activity in order to carry out parts of six tasks in a limited time period and without breaking certain rules. |
| Cognitive Estimates Test: Shallice and Evans (1978) (executive control) | Subject provide 'educated guesses' to a series of questions they are unlikely to know the exact answer to, e.g. *How fast do racehorses gallop?* |
| Camel and Cactus Test: Bozeat *et al.* (2000) (associative semantics) | Subject choose one of four items that has an associative relationship with target item (e.g. camel: *cactus* (the target), *tree, sunflower, rose*). |
| Word Synonym Test: Warrington *et al.* (1998) (word meanings) | Single-word comprehension that consists of 50 target words of graded difficulty, 25 concrete and 25 more abstract. |
| Graded Naming Test: McKenna and Warrington, 1983 (word meanings) | Picture naming task. |
| British Picture Vocabulary Scale: Dunn and Dunn (1997) (word meanings) | Modified Peabody picture vocabulary test. |

controls on only one of the four tests of lexical semantics: the Camel and Cactus test, which assesses associative semantics rather than word meaning through picture naming. The authors concluded that their results 'provide support for a dysexecutive hypothesis of formal thought disorder in schizophrenia, and, in line with other studies, suggest that there may be a restricted "higher-order" semantic deficit which spares naming' (Barrera *et al.*, 2005: 121). It is this preservation of naming ability which chiefly distinguishes any lexical semantic impairment discernible in formal thought disorder from that observed in aphasia.

## Summarizing the evidence on executive dysfunction in thought disorder

To summarize, there is growing evidence from a variety of neuropsychological tests pointing to an impaired executive function of working memory in patients with formal thought disorder. Aside from what they may tell us about neurocognitive impairment in schizophrenia, these findings provide neuropatho-logical support for the hypothesis that the discourse level of language processing requires the integrity of volitional control mechanisms engaged by thinking in general. The amount of symbolic manipulation required for response planning on more difficult items of the TOL test has been found to correlate positively with the activation level in the dominant lateral prefrontal lobe, the brain area consistently associated with response planning and active working memory usage in humans and primates.

But in all probability, the localized haemodynamic response decrement and its associated executive performance deficit, which is evident in active working memory tasks in schizophrenia, is only an expression of a more fundamental disruption of goal-directed mentation, caused by an underlying neurotransmit-ter system dysfunction. There are several reasons for believing that executive disruption may be a proximal (immediate) cause, but not the distal (or underly-ing) cause of schizophrenic thought disorder. First, disorders of executive control are not always accompanied by the other mental state or 'first rank' symptoms that bring a diagnosis of schizophrenia, as other recognized syndromes such as 'attention deficit disorder' attest. Secondly, working memory deficits are unre-sponsive to anti-psychotic medications, which are effective in alleviating symp-toms of thought disorder and other symptoms of schizophrenia (Goldberg, Aloia, Gourovitch et al., 1998). This strongly suggests an independent underlying aeti-ology for the two conditions. Thirdly, although the weight of evidence presented thus far favours a discourse level of impairment in thought disordered speech, Goldberg et al. (1998) argue that 'impairments in patients with thought disor-der are present even in single-word association and comprehension paradigms, neither of which involves discourse planning'. This third claim requires critical scrutiny.

We have seen that Barrera et al. (2005) found evidence of impaired judge-ment of lexical semantic associations in thought disordered patients, using the Camel and Cactus test. But this test has a large attentional component as the sub-ject judges meaning relatedness between words. Similarly, 'clang' or 'free' word associations and other irrelevant intrusions in connected speech may equally sig-nal attentional lapses as well as lexical semantic processing deficits. Studies of *automatic* semantic priming in thought disorder have yielded inconsistent results, with some studies finding evidence of hyper-priming, others of hypo-priming, and still others of levels of semantic priming that are indistinguishable from normal controls – see Minzenberg, Ober and Vinogradov (2002) for a comprehensive review. On the other hand, the findings with respect to studies of *controlled* seman-tic priming, where subjects have the opportunity to form expectations and where attentional strategies come into play, quite consistently yield *lower* than normal levels of priming in thought disordered and schizophrenic subjects, 'demonstrat-ing impairments when increasing cognitive loads are implemented, or, more gen-erally, impairments in the ability to employ cognitive strategies' (Minzenberg *et al.*, 2002: 711). In short, insofar as lexical semantic impairments have been observed in thought disorder, they are also linked with attention-demanding tasks.

## Neurological models of thought disorder

We have argued that discourse breakdown and symptoms of formal thought disorder are attributable to disruption of the executive component of working memory, which is heavily involved in discourse construction and management. But with any complex mental process that is dependent on volitional or attentional control mechanisms, there are literally innumerable possible causes of disruption – ranging from unexpected interruptions (such as loud noises or other environmental distractions) to deep pathological processes, such as disorders of brain metabolism. We suspect the latter in schizophrenia. The source of disruption (intrusive voices, hallucinatory experiences, etc.) may be quite extrinsic to the current mental task or thought processes in which the subject is engaged. Or it may be tangentially related, yet sufficiently so to trigger pathological mentation, which then derails or overwhelms the subject from their current task. How might a loss of executive control over a wide range of mental tasks, caused by any number of potential sources of disruption, be reflected in patterns of regional brain activity?

Clearly, this is a difficult problem to tackle. We review in sufficient detail a couple of notable attempts. Andreasen *et al.* (1996) used combined structural (MRI) and functional imaging (PET) to monitor brain metabolic activity, while patient and control groups performed 'practised' and 'novel' recall of short stories that they had just listened to one minute earlier. The focus was on finding patterns of co-activation among distributed neural circuits that may distinguish patient and control groups, on a task that is highly relevant for everyday functioning and for our particular interests of executive control in discourse management. The researchers were concerned to use a task that all subjects could perform successfully at a basic level, in order to demonstrate a commonly shared pattern of neural activation on the task, so as to be able to observe (pathological) patterns of departure from the base pattern as the task difficulty was increased and executive control and working memory capacity was challenged. In the 'practised' condition, subjects retold stories that they had previously practised to near perfect recall.

Under the practised story recall condition, schizophrenic and control subjects showed essentially the same pattern of activation (subtracted from a 'rest' condition, of lying quietly with eyes closed). There was heightened activation over the left prefrontal region of the cerebral cortex, the left speech motor areas, the left side of the thalamus, and bilaterally in the anterior cerebellum. Relative to the controls, the schizophrenic group had lower levels of blood flow in all of these regions. The authors conclude 'these findings can be inferred to reflect a primary neural dysfunction in the prefrontal–thalamic–cerebellar network that is used for on-line information processing' (Andreasen *et al.*, 1996: 9987).

Under the more difficult 'novel' recall condition, where subjects had heard the story for the first time, additional cortical and sub-cortical areas were activated in the control subjects, but not in the case of the schizophrenic group. One way of interpreting these findings is that the schizophrenic group failed to respond effectively to the increased memory load under novel narrative recall.

The precise functional roles of the separate components of the hypothesized distributed network for free narrative recall are a matter of speculation. The prefrontal cortex is often implicated as the site of 'executive working memory'. The roles of the thalamus and the cerebellum are less certain. Andreasen *et al.* (1996) argue that the role of the cerebellum is not confined to motor co-ordination but also co-ordinates 'mental operations', a notion that gains plausibility when one considers that a lot of thinking consists of *imagined* sequences of action and their consequences. Andreasen *et al.* (1999) go so far as to argue that disruption of the prefrontal–thalamic–cerebellar network in schizophrenia produces 'cognitive dysmetria' and that 'this poor "mental coordination" is a fundamental cognitive deficit in schizophrenia and can account for its broad diversity of symptoms' (p. 203). But this is to venture some distance beyond where the evidential trail presently permits us to go.

Fletcher *et al.* (1999) offered a new methodology for exploring functional relations between elements of distributed brain circuits and of conceptualizing the role of the cingulate cortex, which others have argued may play a significant regulatory role in schizophrenic neurocognitive disorder (Quintana, Wong, Ortiz-Portillo *et al.*, 2004). The idea is that the cingulate cortex, which lies dorsal and inferior to the prefrontal cortex, modulates neural activity levels between the prefrontal and temporal cortex and that a breakdown in this modulation, probably caused by dopamine receptor dysfunction, disrupts higher executive functions. Before we can elucidate Fletcher *et al.*'s hypothesis, it is necessary to briefly review ideas on the role of neurotransmitters and the 'dopamine hypothesis' of schizophrenia.

## The dopamine hypothesis

Dopamine is one of the principal modulatory neurotransmitters in the brain. A neurotransmitter is a substance that regulates synaptic transmission, or a nerve cell's propensity to fire (depolarize) over a given time window. Whereas a neurotransmitter in a classical synapse induces postsynaptic effects lasting up to approximately one tenth of a second, a neuromodulator's postsynaptic effects may persist from half a second or so to several hours. The neuromodulatory synapse's primary function is to transmit information that will have long-lasting effects on the postsynaptic neuron, and on its response to subsequent input. These effects are believed to be the basis of such higher functions as learning and memory. Dopamine is transmitted over one of several pathways (of which the mesocortical pathway which supplies dopamine receptors to the frontal lobes is of most relevance to schizophrenia). There are various kinds of dopamine receptors. Anti-psychotic drugs bind D2 receptors, blocking dopamine uptake in the region of the prefrontal cortex, the cingulate cortex and the limbic system. According to the 'dopamine hypothesis', developed in the 1970s (see Jones and Pilowksy, 2002), it was the degree of D2 receptor blockade which was directly responsible for the amelioration of psychotic symptoms. It was later found that psychotic symptoms could persist with high levels of D2 receptor blockade. Conversely, some patients who responded well to anti-psychotic medication showed remarkably low levels of D2 receptor blockade.

A distinction needs to be drawn between phasic (fast-) and tonic (slow-acting) dopamine neurotransmitter effects. With this distinction, it is possible to account for some of the conflicting findings associated with D2 receptor binding levels and psychotic symptoms. Moore *et al.* (1999) hypothesized that overactive phasic dopamine transmission in limbic regions could account for misinterpretation of external stimuli, resulting in delusions, and improper filtering of perceptions which could cause hallucinations. Blocking of D2 receptors in these regions would help control the positive symptoms of schizophrenia. But, on the other hand, they hypothesized that anti-psychotic blockade of D2 receptors in frontal and prefrontal cortical regions could worsen the negative symptoms of schizophrenia. They proposed that *tonic* dopamine transmission in these regions is relatively underactive in schizophrenia, and further D2 receptor blocking would result in disrupted executive functioning, poverty of thought, speech and action, and low motivation.

This parsimonious explanation neatly encapsulates the positive and negative symptoms of schizophrenia in a modified dopamine model which has stimulated the search for compounds that selectively act upon dopamine receptor subtypes concentrated in limbic or cortical regions. The model is currently under intensive investigation.

## The cingulate modulation hypothesis

Now that we have briefly reviewed changing ideas on the role of the modulatory neurotransmitter dopamine, we can state the hypothesis that Fletcher *et al.* (1999) sought to test, that

> in schizophrenia, there is an abnormality in the way in which the left prefrontal cortex influences left superior temporal cortex and, further, that this abnormality is due, at least in part, to a failure of the anterior cingulate cortex to modulate the prefronto-temporal interactions.          (Fletcher *et al.*, 1999: 338)

It had been previously found in PET studies that when normal subjects were engaged in a variety of cognitive tasks that activate the prefrontal cortex, there was deactivation in the lateral temporal regions bilaterally (Fletcher *et al.*, 1996).

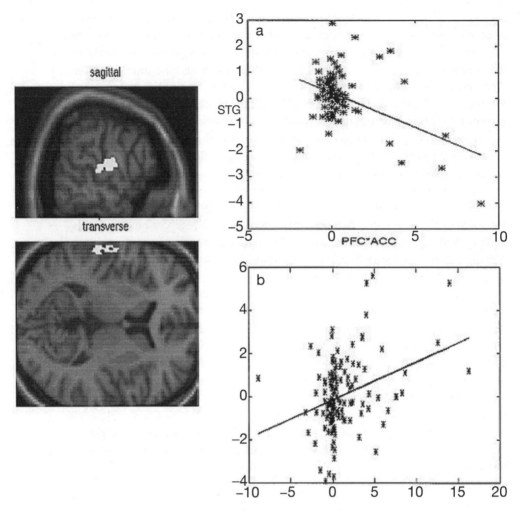

Figure 16.3 *Temporal lobe activation differences and relation to prefrontal activation in schizophrenia*

In contrast, schizophrenic subjects showed a significant failure of this deactivation, and hence, a disruption of the normal task-related reciprocal pattern of activation and deactivation. Administration of apomorphine, a dopamine antagonist, to unmedicated schizophrenic subjects raised the level of activation in the anterior cingulate cortex and showed a trend, though not statistically significant, to restore the reciprocal pattern of fronto-temporal activation found in the control subjects.

In the experiment, twelve schizophrenic subjects and seven age-matched controls were given spoken word lists of varying length (or difficulty) to attend and recall whilst undergoing PET scans. Relative to the controls, schizophrenics showed elevated levels of activity in the left temporal cortex (see Figure 16.3, left panel). Linear regression analysis on the relationship between the level of activation in the left temporal cortex and the combined activation level of the prefrontal and cingulate cortices yielded reverse sign linear relationships in the schizophrenic and control groups (see Figure 16.3, right panel), a direct relationship in the case of the schizophrenics, and a reciprocal one in the case of the control subjects.

The authors urge caution in interpreting the findings of this small study, whose significance may be more methodological than anything else, as a demonstration of how a pattern of interaction among brain regions may vary across tasks and subjects. To say that the activation of the anterior cingulate cortex induces reciprocal activation in the temporal lobe depending on the activity of the prefrontal cortex is not the only possible interpretation of the pattern of observed cortical activity levels. However, it is one which is compatible with previous experimental findings.

An alternative conception of disturbed interactivity between frontal and temporal lobes in schizophrenia is provided by Ford and Mathalon (2002) in a series of EEG and ERP functional imaging studies, aimed at understanding the mechanism underlying the characteristic auditory hallucination of hearing voices. Recall from chapter 8 the important role of connectivity between Broca's area and the auditory association cortex of the STG for speech perception and particularly the finding that activation of Broca's area has been found to raise thresholds for activation of auditory feature detectors in STG for external auditory stimuli. This may be seen as an expression of a feed-forward loop for predictive self monitoring in speech production, through selective attenuation of externally generated auditory stimuli and selective amplification of the autogenic speech signal. Alternatively, this feedback mechanism may play a facilitatory role in speech perception under noisy listening conditions, by selectively activating latent acoustic traces (stored in STG) of articulatory gestures, in accordance with analysis-by-synthesis routines as postulated by the motor theory of speech perception.

One possible consequence of disruption to this feed-forward/feedback loop, apart from interference with basic processes of speech production and perception, could be to induce confusion over the source – internal or external – of auditory stimuli perceived in the speech listening mode. If the mechanism of selective amplification or attenuation between internally and externally generated signals is disturbed, then internally generated sub-vocal speech, which often accompanies thinking, may be perceived as 'external' voices in one's head. In an elegant series of experiments, Ford and Mathalon (2002) demonstrated abnormalities in the amplitude of the N1 component of auditory ERPs in schizophrenic subjects with tendencies to evidence symptoms of auditory hallucinations. The amplitude of the N1 component of an ERP to a brief unexpected external noise is normally attenuated if it occurs when the listener happens to be talking. But no such weakening of the N1 response was observed in the schizophrenic listeners. The same failure to attenuate the N1 component while talking was also found for the schizophrenic group when instances of their own previously recorded vowel sounds were used as auditory stimuli. And, interestingly, the attenuation effect was also observed in normal listeners when they were engaged in sub-vocal or silent speech, but not so in the case of the schizophrenic listeners. Finally, an energy coherence analysis (cross-correlation of spectral components) of EEG signals across electrode pairs spanning the frontal and temporal speech areas indicated that coherence between frontal and temporal recording sites was greater during talking than passive listening for the control but not the schizophrenic subjects.

## Conclusion

It is time to reflect on the significance of the foregoing neuroimaging studies in relation to the major themes of this chapter, the nature of discourse control in a model of language processing and the nature of thought disorder in relation to a cognitive deficit model of schizophrenia. We have sought to establish a chain of reasoning, which may be broadly summarized as follows. Discourse planning and management is the highest level of language processing and involves the heaviest commitment of executive working memory. Language breakdown in schizophrenia expressed in symptoms of thought disorder primarily represents a failure of discourse management, despite its occasional presentation as an impairment of semantic memory.

The failure of discourse management is one expression of a more general breakdown of executive control over volitional symbolic processes whose locus of control, insofar as there is one, centres on the left prefrontal lobe. But the source and the mechanism of disruption in schizophrenic thought disorder remains a profound mystery. Our best neurological lead remains a version of the 'dopamine hypothesis' that has undergone considerable refinement in recent years with great advances in understanding of modulatory neurotransmitters. But, in a basic sense, these advances have only deepened the mystery of thought disorder. We know that schizophrenia profoundly disrupts our ability to plan and think effectively, but none of the recent advances in the neurochemistry or neurophysiology of thought disorder seem to have yielded new insights into the process of thinking or planning itself. That goal seems as distant as before.

# 17 Conclusion and prospectus

## Introduction

One of the small compensations afforded science writers over novelists, for the arduous obligation of eternal vigilance to potential counter-evidence whilst seeking 'the best theory', is that their stories do not require, and indeed are not expected to have, an ending, happy or otherwise. However, it is appropriate at this point to cast an eye over the broad canvas and ask where this inquiry has led us, what roadblocks stand in the way of further progress and what leading ideas appear to point the way ahead.

While it would be an exaggeration to label it a paradigm change, in recent years there has been a discernible shift in the leading metaphor employed in thinking about language in relation to brain function, away from the 'mentalese' of digital computational analogies towards what has been dubbed *embodied cognition* (Lakoff and Johnson, 1999; Garbarini and Adenzato, 2004), a conceptual shift that has been promoted by recent neurophysiological findings (such as the discovery of the mirror neuron system), by neuropsychological insights into the nature of acquired cognitive disabilities and the interconnected nature of cognitive skills and language abilities, and by attempts to re-conceptualize – in a more 'biologically friendly' or plausible manner – the nature of mental computation itself, inspired partly by connectionist modelling and partly by disillusionment with the empty rhetoric of the digital computational analogy of mind and the unfulfilled promises of high-end artificial intelligence.[1] We shall unpack this outrageously overlong sentence presently. But before attempting to do so, we need to confront a roadblock, which we have avoided dealing with at several crucial turns of the road in our previous narrative.

## Connectionist models of language processing: a case study

The roadblock, which many would interpret as *roadworks*, a temporary inconvenience for a future benefit, concerns the evaluation of computational

---

[1] By 'high-end' AI, we refer to attempts to model higher cognitive functions, including 'language understanding', as distinct from the thriving 'low-end' field of robotics, or 'ant-like' AI.

models of language processing, and connectionist computational models in particular. The role of computational modelling is problematical in all areas of scientific inquiry, from the global economy and the world's climate system on downward, to modelling the deposition of tea leaves in this cup. But in the cognitive sciences, and language processing in particular, it is not just the usual questions of how well the model captures or reflects the complexity of the natural phenomena in question. There are more profound questions raised by the modelling exercise, which have to do with the representational nature of language itself. These problems are difficult to discuss in the abstract. So let us adopt the critical case study approach.

Judging (like any good science bureaucrat) by the number of citations, one of the most influential connectionist simulations of language processing has been Jeff Elman's (1990a) paper, cleverly titled 'Finding structure in time'.[2] The problem that Elman's simulations addressed is a fundamental one for linguistic theory and natural language processing: how to extract or acquire linguistic regularities from language output, or more precisely, from a corpus of linguistic expressions (words and sentences) generated in accordance with the rules of a natural grammar – or in the case of two of the simulations, using the rules of a mini-phrase-structure grammar. The problem was, in fact, essentially one of grammar induction from exposure to linguistic data, which Zellig Harris (1970) had set himself in the late 1940s: attempting to show how the application of 'discovery procedures' could induce a language learner to acquire the grammar of their native language – a task that is accomplished naturally by young children, but one that Chomsky (1957) argued to be impossible without a specially constituted LAD (language acquisition device).

Elman used a simple recurrent neural network (SRN, sometimes referred to as an 'Elman' network, trained on the back propagation learning rule, and depicted earlier in chapter 9) which was set the task of predicting the next symbol in a partially predictable symbol sequence. His first simulation involved the induction of word boundaries from letter sequences in narrative text (the Gettysburg address); a close approximation to Harris's problem of being able to infer (bootstrap) morpheme boundaries from phoneme sequences in a transcribed corpus. The SRN network (and Zellig Harris's laborious paper-and-pencil computation) succeeded in the task, by exploiting variations in **entropy** of sound sequences, created by phonotactic constraints and the combinatorial possibilities of sound sequences at word edges.

These results are interesting because they show that a relatively simple learning algorithm supplied with an equally simple-minded teleology (*What sound is going to come next?*) can form an 'internal sense', expressible as changes in the level

---

[2] Citation rates can, of course, be misleading. The majority of the 731 citations revealed by a Web of Science search were in papers that had ostensibly nothing to do with natural language processing, but, as the title of Elman's original paper suggests, dealt with the statistical analysis of stochastic sequences of various kinds.

of uncertainty, as to where word boundaries might be located in a phoneme stream. Experimental studies with infants exposed to artificial languages offer confirmation that human brains appear to spontaneously carry out these kinds of stochastic computations (Perruchet and Peereman, 2004). The possession of such a device could go a long way to solving the word segmentation problem of speech perception discussed previously. The output of such a stochastic processor could prime phonological access to the recognition lexicon.

However, it was two higher-level language processing simulations with the SRN that posed the real challenge for psycholinguists, forming the basis of a claim that the network was capable of learning (a) semantic regularities and (b) syntactic regularities from exposure to sentence corpora. In both cases, mini-production grammars (using rewrite rules and terminal symbols representing lexical classes) were employed to generate a corpus of artificial sentences for training and testing the SRN. For the second simulation, a corpus of 10,000 two- and three-word sentences (of the ilk *Boy chase girl.*; *Woman eat cookie.*; *Dragon sleep.*) was generated by a mini-grammar that disallowed semantic selectional violations such as *\*Cookie eat woman.*; *\*Cookie sleep.* The network was trained to predict the next word in the sequence. At the end of the training period, when the error rate of prediction had stabilized, the state of the network was interrogated in the following fashion. The network's response to an input word on any given trial is determined by the pattern of activation weights across the set of hidden unit connections in the network. This pattern of weights is optimized in the course of training. Mathematically, the pattern of activation weights for a word can be expressed as a vector in n-space (where n = the number of connections among hidden units in the network). We can obtain an average activation pattern for a word in all the sentences in which it makes an appearance by calculating the average value of the vector across those sentences. Think of this average activation value as the network's representation of the meaning of the word. Calculate the average activation pattern for each word in the training vocabulary of a trained-up network. The distances in n-space among the vectors of the words in the training set may be interpreted as semantic similarities and can be subjected to standard multi-variate scaling procedures, such as *hierarchical clustering*. Figure 17.1 shows the hierarchical clustering obtained for all lexical items in the grammar, with word class labels assigned by the investigators.

As you see from Figure 17.1, the network has established quite fine-grained relationships of similarity among the lexical items, not only separating nouns and verbs into broad classes, but establishing small category clusters of 'animate' and 'inanimate' nouns (such as 'breakable' objects – i.e. nouns appearing in sentences as objects of *smash* or *break*). Verb subcategories appear to reflect transitivity – whether they take an object and if so, what type of noun. Clearly, 'this category structure reflects facts about the possible sequential ordering of inputs [words]' (Elman, 1990b: 351). The sequential constraints in this case were determined by the grammar of semantic selectional restrictions. But does this

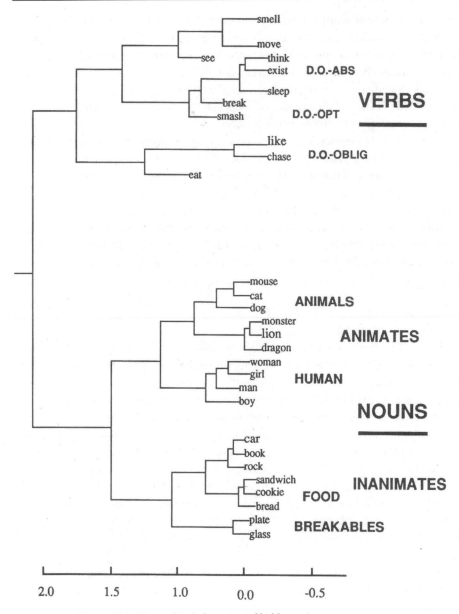

Figure 17.1 *Hierarchical clustering of hidden-unit vectors*

mean that the network 'knows' (in any psycholinguistically significant sense) anything about word meaning or the combinatorial semantics of word meaning? Recall our discussion of word meaning in chapter 10.

Elman's third and most challenging simulation used a mini-phrase-structure grammar that generated simplified sentence patterns of object and subject relative clauses, up to two levels of embedding, in order to demonstrate that an SRN is

```
S  → NP VP "."
NP → PropN | N | N RC
VP → V (NP)
RC → who NP VP | who VP (NP)
N → boy | girl | cat | dog | boys | girls | cats | dogs
PropN → John | Mary
V → chase | feed | see | hear | walk | live | chases | feeds |
      sees | hears | walks | lives

Additional restrictions:
•    number agreement between noun and verb within clause
     and between head noun and subordinate verb.
•    verb arguments: transitive verbs require an object...
```

Figure 17.2 *Relative clause mini-grammar (Elman, 1990b)*

capable of learning structures of embedding. The grammar used for this simulation is shown in Figure 17.2.

The grammar is recursive, generating an indefinite number of levels of embedding, but in practice constrained to two levels in generating the 10,000-sentence training set. Note that number agreement between verb and noun imposes significant restrictions on the structures of subordination that the grammar is allowed to generate:

(1)        *John chases Mary who chases boys.*
(2)        * *John chase Mary who chases boys.*
(3)        * *John chases Mary who chase boys.*

Noun–verb agreement can create discontinuous dependencies that hold over several intervening words, as in

(4)        * *John who Mary hits $0_T$ chase girls.*

Also note that the verb *hit* when used in a main clause requires an object NP, but when it occurs in a relative clause containing a subject, there is a null object (represented by the trace, $0_T$) which is to be found 'upstairs' in the subject NP. Hence, the syntax of NP ellipsis (discussed in chapter 2) and subject–verb agreement pose a significant learning challenge for the SRN, as they do for infant language learners.[3]

It proved necessary to put the network through a staged training procedure in order to induce it to acquire the relative clause patterns, whereby it was first of all presented with a set of exclusively simple sentences and then with successively increasing proportions of complex sentences at subsequent training stages. But the SRN eventually attained optimal performance in the task – of predicting the next word in the sequence.

---

[3] And, unlike the child language learner, the network was only exposed to *grammatical* sentence tokens during training (i.e. no negative examples).

Again, the question to be posed is: precisely what has the network learned about the structure of relative clauses in order to optimize its performance on the learning task? In this case, Elman made use of 'state space trajectories' and a dimensionality reducing technique, *principal components* analysis, to interrogate the state of the trained-up network. Recall our earlier explanation of a word's activation as a trajectory in n-space (for a fuller explanation, see Elman, 1990a). In stepping through successive words in a sentence, the trained-up network traverses a series of vectors, each of which can define a point location in an n-dimensional 'state space'. Connect up these points and you obtain a 'state space trajectory', difficult to visualize in a dimensionality greater than two or three. Principal components analysis was used for the purpose of reducing the dimensionality of the state space trajectory so that it could be plotted and visualized. Figure 17.3 shows plots of the first two principal components of the state space trajectories for sentences (a) through (d), a simple sentence and its corresponding relative clause constructions of increasing depth of embedding.

(5) (a)     Boy chases boy.
    (b)     Boy chases boy who chases boy.
    (c)     Boy who chases boy chases boy.
    (d)     Boy chases boy who chases boy who chases boy.

The respective plots of the state space trajectories shown in Figure 17.3 have a satisfying geometric coherence. The subject noun, the verb and the object noun in the simple sentence (a) occupy quite separate regions of state space. This basic configuration is preserved in the embedded relative clauses of (b), (c) and (d), where subject nouns and object nouns occupy similar regions of state space, as one might expect for words which share collocational properties. There is a suggestive graphical representation of recursion in the case of (d) where overlapping triangles are created, as similar regions of state space are revisited in successive parallel structures of embedding. But in what sense, it needs to be asked, do these diagrams constitute 'syntactic representations' of relative clause structures?

Elman is predisposed, as are connectionists in general, to confer the status of 'representations' upon these graphical depictions of state space relations, prefixing them with labels such as 'phonological', 'semantic' or 'syntactic', depending on the nature of the input data from which they were computed. But from the network's point of view, they are all the same kind of thing, stochastic patterns in the input data, as one can readily confirm with a thought experiment. What would happen if the 'semantic' constraints of simulation study (2) and the 'syntactic' constraints of simulation study (3) were to be combined into a single, very large simulation study? Assuming the network were large enough, the granularity of the connection weights fine enough, and sufficient time available for training, there is no reason to believe the SRN would not eventually settle on an optimal solution. But would such a network provide, in any significant sense, a more comprehensive, richer 'linguistic representation' in the much larger vectors of its trained-up activation weights?

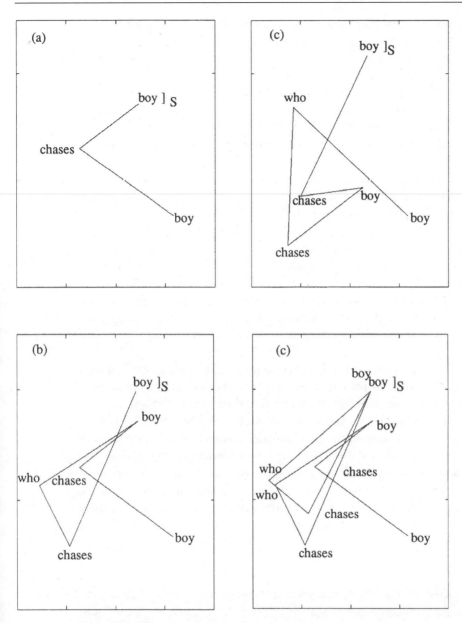

Figure 17.3 *Elman: state space trajectories*

What do we ask of a syntactic representation of a relative clause, considered as a special case of syntactic representation in general? Linguists would probably stipulate that as a minimum, we need to be able to distinguish the head noun from those of its modifying clause, to assign the correct case role to the relative pronoun (or its trace) and in some way to 'bracket' or contain the lexical elements of the dependent clause that fall within the scope of the head noun, restricting its reference. It is hard to be explicit here, but it seems doubtful that the connectionist 'representation' is capable of explicitly supporting these interpretive functions of a conventional syntactic representation. Similarly, it is difficult to see how the same 'vanilla' spatial representation can be pressed into service of the needs of lexical or sentential semantic representation, though here it must be admitted that conventional linguistic representations fare little better. (At this point, the author wishes to take the Wittgensteinian fifth amendment,[4] your honour. We think we know what information should be extracted in the course of parsing a relative clause, but we confess we have no idea how that information is represented in the brain.)

In summary, Elman's three simulations constitute an elegant demonstration of how a simple neural network can respond to relevant stochastic information in the temporal stream of language, even learn to respond to discontinuous dependencies generated by recursive rules in a simple production grammar. It is highly likely that the brain is amply equipped with such devices that may sensitize the language processor to sequential dependencies that hold at multiple levels of segmentation of the speech signal simultaneously and thereby facilitate parsing at a basic pre-conceptual level. However, the functional significance of the temporal patterns thereby extracted from language input would seem to lie quite outside the competence of such simple-minded beasts, dedicated entirely to 'finding structure in time'.

Just as a 'clever' neural network linked to an array of sensors monitoring a highly complex industrial plant may be able to predict machinery breakdowns before they occur more effectively than a team of highly skilled technicians who actually understand the intricacies of the manufacturing process, it is possible to model aspects of speech recognition or language comprehension in the absence of any real understanding of the underlying neural mechanism of language processing. Connectionists as well as their critics are quite aware of this problem. The way to address it is by building into their models constraints or conditions, both behavioural and physiological, that accord with current knowledge of human language performance and its underlying neural mechanisms. About the former we now know quite a lot, but about the latter still very little.

## Embodied cognition as a perspective on language processing

We shall now undertake a brief review of where we have come, not necessarily in the precise order that topics were discussed in earlier chapters (which was strictly a 'bottom up' progression through the stages of language processing, from speech perception, lexical retrieval and semantic processing, through to syntactic processing and higher levels of discourse analysis). Our goal here will be to highlight the problems and unresolved controversies, and to see

---

[4] 'Whereof one cannot speak, thereof one must remain silent.' Ludwig Wittgenstein, *Tractatus Logico-Philosophicus*, 1922.

if a way through them may be found by adopting the perspective of 'embodied cognition' mentioned earlier.

Smith and Gasser (2005) provide a succinct statement of the key tenet and six corollaries that define the perspective of embodied cognition:

> The central idea behind the *embodiment hypothesis* is that intelligence emerges in the interaction of an agent with an environment and as a result of sensorimotor activity.        (Smith and Gasser, 2005: 13)

As a starting point for a neurophysiological theory of intelligent behaviour this is uncontroversial and quite compatible with the classical BWL model of language representation in the brain, with its motor and sensory language centres linked both directly and indirectly through a 'conceptual processor' (recall the Wernicke-Lichtheim diagram, Figure 3.5). Brains from their most primitive evolutionary forms to their most highly evolved share the properties of a sensory-motor arc. They differ only in the complexity of the processing that goes on in between. However, what is distinctive about the embodiment perspective lies in the elaboration of this hypothesis through its corollaries, which Smith and Gasser cast as 'lessons' for those seeking to simulate intelligence, but which we simply cite as properties:

1.        Multimodality and synchronicity of sensory input
2.        Incremental development, punctuated by correlation change
3.        Priority of the physical/experiential world
4.        The ludic (playful) principle
5.        Mentorship through imitation
6.        Symbolic representation through language

*Multimodality*: Perceptual objects are overwhelmingly generated from multi-modal signals whose component sensory streams are synchronously linked. It is probably the time alignment of sensory input across different modalities which provides the brain with a computational basis for solving the binding problem. This may be why cross-modal sensory integration of speech occurs in early infancy (Kuhl and Meltzoff, 1984), long before words acquire specific meaning. Until recently, speech perception research, with its single-minded focus on decoding the acoustic signal, may have somewhat lost sight of the trans-modal nature of the speech percept, in spite of the fact that it has been known for some time that the communicatively disadvantaged (the hard of hearing, the language disordered, second language learners) benefit disproportionately, compared with normals, from perceiving speech by eye and ear rather than by ear alone (Dodd and Campbell, 1987). The importance of this point for some unresolved problems of speech perception will be discussed presently.

*Incremental development*: It is a familiar, widely accepted principle of evolution of the nervous system that higher-order cognitive functions emerge from novel syntheses of older, more 'primitive' functions. The perspective of embodied cognition adds to this the observation that the reconfiguration of functions produces new correlations between sensory and motor components that are specific to the novel function. Some concrete exemplification comes from the discovery of mirror neurons. A particular mirror neuron will fire on the performance of a particular grasping motion of the hand, or on viewing another 'beast-like-me' performing that same action, or on *hearing* that same action performed, if it normally has auditory consequences, such as the cracking of a nutshell. 'The implication is that mirror neurons can represent the meaning of an action, independently of the fact that an animal has directly executed an action or has simply heard or seen it' (Garbarini and Adenzato, 2004: 102).

*Priority of the physical/experiential world*: Again, this property is almost taken for granted by neurophysiologists or neurologists who think about how the brain may represent the world to itself. But it is perhaps more interesting if linguistic data (be they drawn from the pervasive use of 'metaphors we live by' in natural language (Lakoff and Johnson, 1980) or from comparative lexical analysis (Wierzbicka, 2004)) provide converging evidence of the penetration of the tangible experiential world into the domain of abstract thought. As we saw in chapter 12, Roger Schank (1975) was the first to systematically expound the principle that the conceptual realm may be described as a metaphorical extension of the physical world in his conceptual dependency theory of semantic representation.

*The ludic (playful) principle*: 'Evidence from human development [shows] that babies can discover both the tasks to be learned and the solution to those tasks through exploration, or non-goal-directed action.' (Smith and Gasser, 2005: 20). This principle, while arguably applicable to learning all sorts of stimulus response contingencies, including pre-speech motor control or babbling, is of less relevance than

*Mentorship through imitation*: Imitation of a mature model or mentor appears to be the primary mechanism for acquiring highly complex patterns of goal-directed behaviour, including speech. Imitation is to be distinguished from mimicry.[5] It is a highly selective, abstract and goal-directed learning mechanism, which progressively develops with maturation of the perceptual-motor system.

*Symbolic representation through language*: This is not a new principle. Recall the discussion of Deacon's co-evolution of language hypothesis and its philosophical forebears in chapter 2. Nor does it seem to be integral to the embodied cognition perspective, though Smith and Gasser (2005) align it with it.

---

[5] Our sulphur-crested cockatoo was a talented but undiscriminating mimic, who studiously ignored our attempts to teach him to say 'Hello cocky!', but spontaneously produced a very convincing rendition of the neighbour closing a car door, cranking the starter motor and revving the cold engine – but all quite softly, because, after all, the car was parked next door.

In summary, the embodied cognition hypothesis and its corollaries attempt to define a way of thinking about cognitive processes which seems more compatible with how the brain appears to represent information than the tired digital computer metaphor of a previous generation of cognitive psychology. We now turn to ask: can the embodied cognition perspective cast new light on some of the major unsolved problems of language processing that we have encountered in this book?

## Concrete or abstract perceptual representations of speech sounds

One major unresolved problem from our discussion of speech perception in chapters 5–7 concerns the concrete or abstract nature of phonological representations in the recognition lexicon. How are we to reconcile the abstract nature of phonological representations with embodied nature of the speech percept? Speech and speaker information are clearly accessible to listeners simultaneously. What implications does this have for the nature of long-term phonological information storage in the lexicon? These are questions on which there is little consensus, not only on the answers that should be given, but on how the questions themselves should be posed. We have seen that the mode of processing speech sounds and the traces registered in neuroimaging studies are quite task-dependent, suggesting perhaps that any quest for the nature of *the* underlying representation of speech sounds may be misconceived. Varying task demands shape the distribution of local regional brain metabolic activity even at the relatively fine level of granularity, such as whether listening requires close or scant attention to an internally generated articulatory model for its phonetic interpretation. The representations we construct may be manifold and varying, depending on what the brain is required to do with the speech signal.

Representations may be conceived of as interim or end-products of computational recognition processes. As end-products, they simply define the goals of the processing task and their justification as theoretical constructs is extrinsic to the recognition model. However, the status of interim representations within a more comprehensive model – such as phonemes within a model of word recognition, or syntactic structures within a model of sentence comprehension – is different. Here their status is intrinsic to any empirical evaluation of the adequacy of the model. The test of interim representations within a processing model should probably be gauged in terms of what the positing of such representations can *do*; how well do they facilitate the extraction of output or end-product representations of the recognition process? Early models of sentence processing (or production) tended to simply borrow the units of interim representation from linguistic theories (competence models). Subsequently, psycholinguists sought evidence from performance constraints for the psychological reality of these units. However, as we have indicated previously, evidence at the neural processing level for interim levels of linguistic representation is scarce at best (Phillips, 2001). The role of interim representations in a theory of language processing remains a central challenge and something of a mystery for a theory of language processing.

## Lexical retrieval mechanisms

The embodied cognition perspective, with its emphasis upon cross-modal synchronicity for object recognition, suggests that a practical way of enhancing performance for those with lexical retrieval difficulties might be to encourage 'acting out' of the relevant activity, or active imaging of a relevant context of use when automatic retrieval of the phonological form of a word fails. A patient unable to name a *'pen'* when presented with a picture of the object may spontaneously retrieve its phonological shape by pantomiming the act of signing a letter. We should be careful, however, of drawing strong conclusions regarding modularity or influence of the top-down or bottom-up processes on real-time lexical retrieval or word recognition from practical suggestions such as these.

## Discourse structure and embodiment

The central metaphor for our discussion of discourse processing (chapter 15), you will recall, was a stage or 'scenario', a projection in mental space and time, inhabited by imagined actors and objects. As the discourse develops actors move on- and off-stage and scene changes take place.

All this is even more concretely expressed in natural sign languages, where the scene is enacted not simply in 'the mind's eye' of the interlocutors but in the physical space defined by the fixed landmarks of the speaker's head and torso and bounded by the movements of the gesturing hands and facial muscles. The elements of a natural sign language – be it the sign language of the deaf (such as ASL) or one of the highly elaborated auxiliary gestural systems employed by central Australian aborigines such as the Warlpiri (Kendon, 1988) – are essentially stylized pantomime.[6]

Hence, discourse structure and sign language are expressions of 'embodied cognition'. Both are grounded in a spatio-temporal world that is a mental projection or 'representation' of the organism in its physical environment. We find it easy to talk about this meta-world, because that is what language is essentially for – a means of representing our mental representations to other people. But such descriptions as we have just indulged in, of how discourse and sign languages share common properties as embodied cognition, should not be confused with a *theory* of how language works in the brain. They are merely phenomenological

---

[6] This is not to say that natural sign languages such as ASL do not possess a fully elaborated morpho-syntax, of equal expressive power to spoken language, but rather, to assert that the phonological substance of sign languages is iconic and in this respect quite different from spoken language – a controversial issue that we cannot pursue further here.

descriptions of how the higher levels of language processing are conceptualized by language users. They may be useful 'pre-theoretical' descriptions of part of the phenomena that we wish ultimately to account for – or at least that part of language processing which is accessible to introspection – but such descriptions certainly do not provide explanations for 'how the brain does language processing'.

We argued in chapter 16 that discourse breakdown in thought disorder, which occurs episodically in schizophrenia and sometimes also in other forms of psychosis, was caused by disruption to attention-directed working memory resources. But an alternative mechanism, more consistent with the symptoms of schizophrenia and autism, was not explored: 'flattened affect', i.e. social disengagement and diminished capacity for empathy. Such a mechanism is more in the spirit of embodied cognition. The perceptual act of recognition of one's spouse, one's child, a friend, or that bastard from work is normally accompanied by feelings of one kind or another, mediated by sub-cortical mechanisms involving the amygdala that are little understood at the present time, but could also be linked to disturbances of the dopamine receptor system described previously. Suppose that, owing to brain damage, this affective component of person-recognition were absent or impaired.[7] This could induce a kind of 'disembodied' perception of other people that appears to capture the phenomenology of the schizoid reaction to people, leading to inappropriate social responses. In this case, the perspective of embodied cognition has provided us with an alternative, in some ways more specific, account of mechanisms of executive disruption (see Kohler and Brennan, 2004).

The perspective of 'embodied cognition', it may be concluded, is not entirely new, but it does seem to point towards a better synthesis of a biologically grounded account of perceptual and cognitive processes, with the structure and function of the human language faculty. However, fundamental problems to do with the nature of linguistic representations in a model of language processing remain, and whether these prove tractable to scientific investigation, in our quest to fulfil the goals of a cognitive science of language, only time, as they say, will tell.

---

[7] As occurs in Capgras's delusion (Breen, Cain and Coltheart, 2000).

# Glossary

**agnosia**  a perceptual disorder characterized by an inability to recognize the identity of perceptual objects of various kinds.

**agrammatism**  an absence or loss of syntactic features (grammatical inflections and function words) in language production (expressive agrammatism), possibly accompanied by an inability to utilize grammatical cues in language comprehension (receptive agrammatism). Part of the symptom complex of Broca's aphasia, and commonly associated, though not invariably so, with damage to Broca's area.

**ambisyllabic consonant**  a consonant that cannot make up its mind whether it belongs to the coda of the preceding syllable or to the onset of the following one, as in the '*l*' in English *balance* ['bæ.ləns] or [bæl.əns] where **.** = syllable boundary.

**amusia**  a selective impairment of the ability to identify components of musical stimuli, such as melody or rhythm, or a diminished affective response to or appreciation of music.

**anomic aphasia**  a form of aphasia characterized primarily by word finding or naming difficulties.

**apraxia**  see *dyspraxia*.

**arcs**  see *semantic network*.

**aspectual coercion**  occurs when the aspectual meaning of a verb is changed (or coerced) from its 'normal' or default reading into a different aspectual category by the nature of a verbal complement: e.g. *He jumped.* <punctual action, occurs once only> vs. *He jumped for hours.* <repeated action>, coerced by the durative reading of the prepositional phrase.

**binaural listening**  see *dichotic listening*.

**binding problem**  in perception, the problem of how the brain integrates information from property detectors in the sensory receiving areas of the brain into stable and coherent perceptual objects. Failures of perceptual binding may result in various forms of *agnosia*.

**categorical perception**  loosely speaking, the tendency of stimuli on a sensory continuum to cluster into discrete perceptual categories. More rigorously defined, categorical perception occurs on a sensory continuum where the perceiver's ability to discriminate adjacent stimuli is no better than their ability to make categorical identifications among the stimuli on the continuum. Categorical perception was once considered to be a special property of speech perception.

**coarticulation effect**  the blending or mutual assimilation of articulatory gestures which occurs when two or more speech sounds are uttered in close temporal proximity: e.g. *I'mg going* [aŋgəʊɪŋ], *asyou* [æʒ(j)u].

**cohort model** of word recognition by Marslen-Wilson, asserts that word recognition is achieved by a process of 'cohort' reduction, whereby candidates in the lexicon are eliminated as more information becomes available as successive phonemes are identified.

**conduction aphasia** a variety of aphasia, the chief symptoms of which involve an inability to repeat (parrot back) a spoken phrase that the patient has just heard. Spoken language comprehension and volitional language production remain relatively unimpaired. See *disconnection syndrome*.

**derivational morphology** the word-internal morphology of a language. Derivational affixes belong to one or the other of two broad classes, those that change the grammatical class membership of the stem to which they attach (e.g. *govern* [verb] => *government* [noun]) and those which change some aspect of meaning (e.g. ***un**happy*). Derivational morphology extends the range of use or functionality of a lexical stem. Derivational rules are typically less productive than *inflectional morphemes*.

**deterministic process** a process in which each successive step is fully determined by the previous states of the processor. As applied to syntactic parsing, a deterministic parser constructs syntactic representations without reliance on back-tracking. Contrast with probabilistic parsing.

**dichotic listening** involves the simultaneous presentation of different auditory stimulus separately to each ear over headphones, in contrast to the natural *binaural listening* situation, where the same stimulus is received by both ears. Dichotic listening is used as a behavioural test for hemispheric lateralization of speech sound perception.

**digit span** a commonly used measure of working memory capacity or attention span; the number of digits that can be retained in memory long enough to be successfully recalled following oral presentation by the examiner at a rate of about 1 digit per second.

**disconnection syndrome** a deficit of language or cognitive function that is thought to arise as a consequence of severing connecting pathways between regional cortical processing centres. *Conduction aphasia* is the classical example of a disconnection syndrome, arising from the severance of a direct pathway between the motor (Broca's) and the receptive (Wernicke's) language areas, thus disrupting the 'low level' language ability to 'parrot back' in production what has just been analysed in perception.

**discrimination function** a graph of the proportion of correct pair-wise discrimination judgements when pairs of stimuli (differing by a constant amount on a physical or perceptual scale) are judged 'same' or 'different' across a stimulus continuum. Contrast with *identification function*.

**distinctive feature** a phonetic feature or property of a sound segment which serves to carry or signal a difference in meaning. The English words *bad* and *pad* differ by a single distinctive feature (voicing) on the initial consonant.

**distributed network** used in two distinct senses: (a) a neural network whose cells are distributed over a wide region in the brain, and (b) (more technically), a network that distributes its information storage or representational states as patterns of activation over the nodes of the network as a whole, as distinct from a *localist network* in which the activation level of each node in the network represents the status of a distinct object.

**double dissociation** a methodological precept for establishing the modularity of mental abilities (A and B) through observations of patterns of impairment, such that damage to one area of the brain is found to be associated with loss of ability A and preservation of ability B and damage to another area of the brain is found to be associated with preservation of ability A and loss of ability B. A *functional modularity* may be demonstrated by showing the complementary pattern of impairment described above in two or more subjects, but without the requirement of localizing the two functions to particular brain areas.

**duplex perception**  a perceptual effect created by *dichotic* presentation and perceptual fusion of elements of synthetic speech stimulus, such as [da] or [ga]. See text for details. Used to manipulate the listening mode and to assess the speech mode hypothesis.

**dyspraxia**  a neurological motor impairment chiefly characterized by difficulties in initiating voluntary movement; a disorder of higher-level motor control. Specific types of movement control may be selectively impaired. Hence, *speech dyspraxia* is a motor impairment specifically affecting speech motor control, while initiation of non-speech oral gestures, such as blowing out a candle, remains intact. *Developmental dyspraxia* is a term widely used for delayed motor development, thought to be neurological in origin, often associated with specific learning impairment or delayed language development.

**E-language**  see *I-language*.

**entropy**  a statistical measure of uncertainty or random structure in a system.

**expert system**  a computational knowledge representation system that seeks to emulate the specialized technical knowledge of a human expert in some field: e.g. an automated system of disease diagnosis from patient supplied symptoms; typically implemented as a symbolic *semantic network*. Expert systems do not necessarily replace experts, but may be used by experts to enhance their expertise.

**factorial contrasts**  systematic contrasts or comparisons between all combinations of levels of the factors (or dependent variables) in an experiment, in their effect upon the dependent variable.

**formant**  a resonating frequency of the human vocal tract. The first two or three formant frequencies (F1, F2, F3) are the most important acoustic determinants of vowel quality.

**formant transitions**  rapidly changing formant values at the onset or offset of a syllable due to consonantal opening or closing gestures of the vocal tract at different places of articulation.

**fricative**  a consonant produced with an audibly turbulent airflow at some point of constriction in the vocal tract.

**functional modularity**  see *double dissociation*.

**Ganong effect**  a top-down lexical bias effect that operates in phoneme perception, whereby perception of an acoustically ambiguous phoneme is resolved one way or the other by being embedded in a carrier word or a non-word.

**gating paradigm**  a method employed to study incremental processing speech signals by successively removing (gating) or adding segments to the end of an auditory stimulus and observing the effects on listeners' identification judgements.

**head-turning paradigm**  an experimental procedure for testing pre-verbal infants' sound discrimination capabilities. Based on the observation that infants will turn their head towards the preferred member of a stimulus pair, or re-direct their gaze more often in the direction of a preferred sound source.

**hopfield net**  a (neural) network in which every node is connected to every other node (but itself). Hopfield networks have been used to simulate content-addressable memory systems; systems that are capable of retrieving complete stored patterns on the basis of partial or corrupted input.

**hyper-priming**  a stronger than normal *priming effect*, observed in some brain-damaged patients, often attributed to disinhibition or lowering of associative thresholds between related units in a neural network.

**I-language**  the internal representation or tacit knowledge that a native speaker possesses of their language; to be distinguished from *E-language* (external language), definable on the basis of some large or representative corpus of utterances recognized by a speech community as belonging to a given language.

**identification function**  a graph indicating the proportion of trials for which a given stimulus is identified as a member of a perceptual category. An identification function is a graphical summary of the results of an identification test. Contrast with *discrimination function*.

**image schemas**  somewhat abstract perceptual templates that enable the mind to map perceptual experience into conceptual representations, claimed to originate in Kantian epistemology; reinterpreted by cognitive linguistics to putatively explain how meanings of relational words (e.g. *in out*), or grammatical constructions more generally, represent transformations of components of image schemas, which are depicted as simple line drawings.

**inflectional morphology**  those affixes or inflections which mark a word's grammatical function in a sentence. Inflectional affixes are found in the outermost layer of morphological structure – at the right edge of a word in English. They mark gender and number in nouns and tense and aspect in verbs. They are usually highly productive and mark the transition between morphology and syntax. Contrast with *derivational morphology*.

**instance-based memory**  the theory that there is a strong episodic memory component in word recognition and that fine auditory details of speaker's voice and other non-linguistic characteristics are stored in the word recognition lexicon.

**lemma**  the semantic and syntactic properties of a word or an item in the mental lexicon, thought to constitute a separate level of representation from a lexical item's phonological properties.

**lexeme**  an abstract word; the common core of meaning underlying the various inflectional forms of a word (e.g. <dog> *dog, dogs*; <first person pronoun> *I, me*). A linguistic construct (Huddleston *et al.*, 2002), similar in meaning to the psycholinguistic term *lemma*, though perhaps without commitment on the question as to whether lexemes represent units in the mental lexicon.

**localist network**  see *distributed network*.

**localization**  in neurology, the theory that cognitive, linguistic, perceptual and motor abilities are localized to particular brain sites.

**low-pass filter**  an acoustic filter that removes the high frequency components of a (speech) signal (allowing low frequencies to 'pass'), usually employed to remove oral resonances and high frequency noise from the signal so that prosodic and voicing cues remain, but segmental information is lost to the listener.

**manner of articulation**  refers to different ways that the airstream is modulated to produce different categories of speech sound. The major manner of articulation categories are, in order of sonority or openness of the vocal tract, vowels, approximants, *fricatives* and stops (or plosives).

**morpho-phonemic**  refers to an abstract level of lexical representation in which the sound structures of words that share morphemes are given the same phonological representation, despite differences in their phonetic form (pronunciation). English spelling may be regarded as a morpho-phonemic system of phonological representation, e.g. electric – electricity [əlektrɪk] – [əlektrɪsəti]

**multidimensional scaling**  a mathematical technique for reducing the dimensionality of objects in a high dimensional space to one of lower dimensionality without unduly perturbing the distance relationships amongst the objects so scaled. One of a family of multivariate techniques (principal components analysis is another) which is useful for conceptualizing the major sources of variability in a complex multivariate domain, such as 'semantic space'.

**neighbourhood effects**  the effects upon speed of recognition or retrieval of the number of competitors or phonologically similar 'near neighbours' that a word possesses. Some words have many competitors (high neighbourhood density), e.g. *cage* (*rage*, *page*, *sage*, *save* . . .); others have few or no competitors, e.g. *corpse* ([null set]). Neighbourhood density interacts in complex ways with word frequency, and the nature of the task (e.g. word recognition or recall).

**nodes**  see *semantic network*.

**normalization of speech**  the attempt by computational means to reduce acoustic variability among speech tokens of a common type. For example, the scaling of vowel formant frequencies to compensate for variations in speaker vocal tract size, or the time normalization of speech spoken at different rates to achieve better segment time alignment.

**obstruent**  a speech sound characterized by an audible turbulence or noise burst, such as the initial consonant in the words *shoe* [ʃ], *zoo* [z], *to* [t], *cue*[k].

**odd-ball detection**  a perceptual discrimination paradigm in which a slightly different stimulus is randomly inserted into a series of identical stimuli, to see if the detection of the 'odd-ball' stimulus can be registered by the brain's response.

**off-line**  test  an indirect or non-real-time method of assessing some skill or processing capability that under normal operating circumstances takes place in real time. Thus, pointing to a particular picture among a set of distractors may be used as an off-line method of assessing auditory comprehension of lexical retrieval. Contrast with *on-line*.

**on-line**  test  a behavioural test that seeks to observe or measure some aspect of the real-time operation of some skill or processing capability, e.g. semantic priming as an on-line measure of lexical retrieval.

**pattern playback**  an early form of electronic speech synthesis whereby speech-like sounds were synthesized from stylized spectrograms.

**perceptual magnet**  a perceptual magnet effect is characterized by a warping of perceptual space near prototype or good exemplars of phoneme stimuli. Discrimination sensitivity is lower in the region of a prototype, which may be visualized as a bulge or warping of perceptual space around a prototype. The question of whether perceptual magnet effects are the complement of *categorical perception* and derive from the same basic perceptual learning mechanism is a currently unresolved issue.

**phoneme**  a sound segment (consonant or vowel) that serves to carry or signal a difference in meaning.

**phoneme restoration**  refers to a listener's ability to restore a phoneme target that has been removed from a spoken word or masked by a brief burst of noise strategically placed over a phonetic segment within a word.

**phonetic representation**  a representation of the pronunciation of a word as it is spoken (articulatory phonetic representation) or as it is heard (auditory phonetic representation).

Both senses are conflated in a conventional phonetic transcription using the symbols of the International Phonetic Alphabet (IPA).

**phonetically under-specified**  the notion that speech sounds or the sound representations of words in the recognition lexicon are comprised of only *distinctive* phonetic features and not the full set of phonetic properties that would characterize a detailed description of their pronunciation.

**phonological representation**  the form in which the sound structure of a spoken word or the gestural representation of a sign is stored in the mental lexicon. Contrast with *phonetic representation.*

**phonotactic rules**  the rules or constraints on sound sequencing of a language. Derived from the allowable syllable structures of the language, phonotactic rules are specific to the language in question, yet they are strongly constrained by language-universal considerations of syllable structure and the 'sonority hierarchy' of speech sounds. See O'Grady, Dobrovolsky and Katamba (1996), chapter 3, or other recent introductions to phonology. for elaboration.

**prelinguistic period**  period before the child produces first recognizable words, approximately 0–11 months of age.

**priming effect**  The tendency of a stimulus (usually designated as the *probe*) to be more rapidly identified, judged or activated by prior presentation of a related stimulus (usually designated the 'prime'). Priming effects are typically modelled in a neural network.

**prosodic bootstrapping**  the hypothesis that language learners employ prosodic features of spoken language to help them locate word and other kinds of linguistic boundaries in the quasi-continuous signal of speech.

**pure tone audiometry**  the assessment of hearing function by testing auditory thresholds with pure tone stimuli across the frequency range of normal hearing (20Hz–20kHz).

**pure word deafness**  see *verbal agnosia.*

**recognition lexicon**  the internal store of information that listeners use to recognize spoken words in speech perception. Also known as the 'input lexicon'. Some argue for a separate 'production lexicon' for storage of phonetic information for word production, or a 'reading lexicon' for the recognition of written words. The proliferation of lexicons is one measure of where a language processing model stands on the question of modularity.

**semantic features**  see *semantic network.*

**semantic network**  a network or graph for representing relations of meaning between lexical items or *nodes* in a conceptual space, linked by *arcs*. In a *localist network*, the nodes may be interpreted as lexical items and the arcs as semantic relations of one kind or another. In a *distributed network* the nodes and arcs do not have specific interpretations (with the exception of the output nodes, which are usually conceived as *semantic features*). Semantic similarities are coded in terms of patterns of activation over the network as a whole.

**sine wave speech**  a stimulus that has been synthesized from the spectrogram of a natural utterance, by replacing the acoustic energy in the original signal with sine waves that track the frequencies of the major spectral peaks in the original speech signal. This operation preserves information about the changing resonances of the vocal tract and the major *manner of articulation* cues, but replaces the voice source, generated by vocal fold vibration in the larynx, with a decidedly non-human source signal.

**specific language impairment (SLI)**   a childhood developmental speech/language disorder diagnosed in the absence of peripheral hearing loss, mental retardation, or (other) neurological disorder. SLI tends to run in families, suggesting a genetic predisposition to the condition. A specific chromosomal disorder has been identified in some cases of SLI. Difficulties with regular finite verb inflectional morphology (tense and aspect) constitute the principal linguistic indicators of SLI, though *verbal apraxia*, impaired temporal order judgement and other factors have been implicated.

**speech apraxia**   a speech motor disorder characterized in particular by difficulty initiating voluntary movement for speech production. A frequent accompaniment of Broca's aphasia, speech apraxia is distinguished as a disorder of executive speech motor control from aphasia (language disorder) and has been linked to damage to the precentral gyrus of the insula, a sub-cortical structure that lies just internal to Broca's area (Dronkers, 1996).

**tonotopic organization**   the mapping or projection of the frequency coding of auditory signals on the basilar membrane to higher brain regions, particularly (but not confined exclusively to) the primary receiving areas of the auditory cortex (Herschel's gyri) in the left and right temporal lobes.

**TRACE model**   of speech perception by Elman and McClelland is an activation model of word recognition implemented as a multilayer localist neural network.

**under-specification**   a pervasive property of linguistic representations. Phonological representations are underspecified in relation to their phonetic form (i.e. only selected phonetic features, those which are *distinctive*, appear in lexical representations of words – though see chapter 6 for discussion). Linguistic representations are underspecified at the sentential and discourse levels with respect to their meaning.

**velum**   soft movable tissue at the back of the mouth. Lowering the velum opens the velar-nasal port, permitting sound to excite the nasal cavity to add nasal resonance to a speech sound.

**verbal agnosia**   inability to recognize or identify spoken words.

**verbal apraxia**   see *speech apraxia*.

**voice onset time (VOT)**   the time lapse between the noise burst associated with the release of oral air pressure in the production of a stop consonant and the onset of voicing for the following vowel. VOTs reflect the timing of oral and laryngeal gestures for voicing (and aspiration) contrasts in stop consonants in word or syllable onsets.

# References

Aaltonen, O., O. Eerola, A. Hellström, E. Uusipaikka and A. H. Lang. 1997. Perceptual magnet effect in the light of behavioral and psychophysiological data. *The Journal of the Acoustical Society of America* 101 (2): 1090–1105.

Albert, M. L. and D. Bear. 1974. Time to understand: A case study of word deafness with reference to the role of time in auditory comprehension. *Brain* 97: 373–84.

Ali, L. 1971. Perception of coarticulated nasality. *Journal of the Acoustical Society of America* 49: 538–40.

Andreasen, N. 1982. Should the term 'thought disorder' be revised? *Comprehensive Psychiatry* 23 (4): 291–9.

Andreasen, N. C., D. S. O'Leary, T. Cizadlo, S. Arndt, K. Rezai, L. L. B. Ponto, G. L. Watkins and R. D. Hichwa. 1996. Schizophrenia and cognitive dysmetria: A positron-emission tomography study of dysfunctional prefrontal-thalamic-cerebellar circuitry. *Proceedings of the National Academy of Sciences of the United States of America* 93 (18): 9985–90.

Andreasen, N. C., P. Nopoulos, D. S. O'Leary, D. D. Miller, T. Wassink and L. Flaum. 1999. Defining the phenotype of schizophrenia: Cognitive dysmetria and its neural mechanisms. *Biological Psychiatry* 46 (7): 908–20.

Arbib, M. A. 2002. The mirror system, imitation, and the evolution of language. In N. Chrystopher and D. Kerstin (eds.), *Imitation in animals and artefacts*. Cambridge, MA: MIT Press.

Arbib, M. and M. Bota. 2003. Language evolution: Neural homologies and neuroinformatics. *Neural Networks* 16: 1237–60.

Archangeli, D. 1988. Aspects of underspecification theory. *Phonology* 5 (2): 183–207.

Auerbach, S. H., T. Allard, M. Naeser, M. P. Alexander and M. A. Albert. 1982. Pure word deafness: Analysis of a case with bilateral lesions and a defect at the prephonemic level. *Brain* 105: 271–300.

Avikainen, S., N. Forss and R. Hari. 2002. Modulated activation of the human SI and SII cortices during observation of hand actions. *Neuroimage* 15 (3): 640–6.

Babyonyshev, M. and E. Gibson. 1999. The complexity of nested structures in Japanese. *Language* 75 (3): 423–50.

Baddeley, A. D. 1986. *Working memory*. Oxford: Oxford University Press.

2003. Working memory and language: An overview. *Journal of Communication Disorders* 36 (3): 189–208.

Balogh J., E. Zurif, P. Prather, D. Swinney and L. Finkel. 1998. Gap-filling and end-of-sentence effects in real-time language processing: Implications for modelling sentence comprehension in aphasia. *Brain and Language* 61: 168–82.

Bamiou, D. E., F. E. Musiek and L. M. Luxon. 2003. The insula (Island of Reil) and its role in auditory processing literature review. *Brain Research News* 42 (2): 143–54.

Barrera, A., P. J. McKenna and G. E. Berrios. 2005. Formal thought disorder in schizophrenia: An executive or a semantic deficit? *Psychological Medicine* 35 (1): 121–32.

Baum, S. R. 1997. Phonological, mediated and semantic priming in aphasia. *Brain and Language* 60 (3): 347–59.

Beale, J. M. and F. C. Keil. 1993. Categorical effects in the perception of faces. *Cognition* 57 (3): 217–39.

Beckman, M. E. 1996. The parsing of prosody. *Language and Cognitive Processes* 11: 17–67.

Benson, D. F. and A. Ardila. 1996. *Aphasia: A clinical perspective*. New York: Oxford University Press.

Benton, A. L. and K. L. Hampsher. 1980. *Multilingual aphasia battery*. Iowa City, IA: University of Iowa.

Berko, J. 1958. The child's learning of English morphology. *Word* 14 (2–3): 150–77.

Best, W. and D. Howard. 1994. Word sound deafness resolved? *Aphasiology* 8: 223–56.

Bilecen, Deniz, Klaus Scheffler, Nena Schmid, Kurt Tschopp and Joachim Seelig. 1998. Tonotopic organization of the human auditory cortex as detected by BOLD-FMRI. *Hearing Research* 126 (1–2): 19–27.

Bishop, D. M. V. 1992. The underlying nature of specific language impairment. *Journal of Child Psychology & Psychiatry* 33: 3–66.

Blackwell, A. and E. Bates. 1995. Inducing agrammatic profiles in normals: Evidence for the selective vulnerability of morphology under cognitive resource limitation. *Journal of Cognitive Neuroscience* 7 (2): 228–58.

Blakemore, D. 1987. *Semantic constraints on relevance*. Oxford, New York: Blackwell.

Bleuler, E. 1911. *Dementia Praecox oder Gruppe der Schizophrenien* (*Dementia praecox; or the group of schizophrenias*, trans. J. Zinkin, 1950). New York: International Universities Press.

Blumstein, S. 1973. *A phonological investigation of aphasic speech*. The Hague: Mouton. 1994. Impairments of speech production and perception in aphasia. *Philosophical Transactions of the Royal Society of London: Series B – Biological Sciences* 346 (1315): 29–36.

Blumstein, S. E., M. Burton, S. Baum, R. Waldstein and D. Katz. 1994. The role of lexical status on the phonetic categorization of speech in aphasia. *Brain and Language* 46 (2): 181–97.

Blumstein S. E., G. Byma, K. Kurowski, J. Hourihan, T. Brown and A. Hutchinson. 1998. On-line processing of filler-gap constructions in aphasia. *Brain and Language* 61: 149–68.

Blumstein, S. E., W. E. Cooper, E. B. Zurif and A. Caramazza. 1977. The perception and production of voice-onset time in aphasia. *Neuropsychologia* 15: 371–83.

Blumstein, S. E., B. Katz, H. Goodglass and B. Dworetsky. 1985. The effects of slowed speech on auditory comprehension in aphasia. *Brain and Language* 24: 246–65.

Blumstein, S. E., W. Milberg, T. Brown, A. Hutchinson, K. Kurowski and M. W. Burton. 2000. The mapping from sound structure to the lexicon in aphasia: Evidence from rhyme and repetition priming. *Brain and Language* 72: 75–99.

Blumstein, S. E., G. W. Milberg and R. Shrier. 1982. Semantic processing in aphasia: Evidence from a lexical decision task. *Brain and Language* 17 (2): 301–15.

Boudelaa, S. and W. D. Marslen-Wilson. 2004. Abstract morphemes and lexical representation: The CV skeleton in Arabic. *Cognition* 92 (3): 271–303.

Bozeat, S., M. A. Lambon Ralph, K. Patterson, P. Garrard and J. R. Hodges. 2000. Non-verbal semantic impairment in semantic dementia. *Neuropsychologia* 38: 1207–15.

Breen, N., D. Caine and M. Coltheart. Models of face recognition and delusional misidentification: A critical review. *Cognitive Neuropsychology* 17 (1–3): 55–71.

Bregman, A. S. 1990. *Auditory scene analysis: The perceptual organization of sound.* Cambridge, MA: MIT Press.

Bresnan, J. 1982. *The mental representation of grammatical relations.* Cambridge, MA: MIT Press.

Broadbent, D. E. 1956. Successive responses to simultaneous stimuli. *Quarterly Journal of Experimental Psychology* 8: 145–52.

Broca, P. 1861. Nouvelle observation d'aphémie produite par une lésion de la moitié postérieure des deuxième et troisième circonvolutions frontales. *Bulletin Société Anatomie* 6 (ser. 2): 398–407.

Brown, R. 1973. Schizophrenia, language and reality. *American Psychologist* 28: 395–403.

Buchman, A. S., D. C. Garron, J. E. Trost-Cardamone, M. D. Wichter and M. Schwartz. 1986. Word deafness: One hundred years later. *Journal of Neurology, Neurosurgery and Psychiatry* 49: 489–99.

Burgess, P. W. and T. Shallice. 1997. *The Hayling and Brixton Tests.* Bury St Edmunds: Thames Valley Test Company.

Burkhardt P., M. M. Piñango and K. Wong. 2003. The role of the anterior left hemisphere in real-time sentence comprehension: Evidence from split intransitivity. *Brain and Language* 86 (1): 9–22.

Bussey, T. J. and L. M. Saksida. 2002. The organization of visual object representations: A connectionist model of effects of lesions in perirhinal cortex. *European Journal of Neuroscience* 15 (2): 355–64.

Bybee, J. 2001. *Phonology and language use.* Cambridge: Cambridge University Press.

Byng, S., J. Kay, A. Edmunson and C. Scott. 1990. Aphasia tests reconsidered. *Aphasiology* 4: 67–91.

Cairns, P., N. Shillcock, N. Chater and J. Levy. 1995. Bottom-up connectionist modelling of speech. In J. P. Levy, D. Bairaktaris, J. A. Bullinaria and P. Cairns (eds.), *Connectionist models of memory and language.* London: UCL Press, 289–310.

Calvin, W. H. and G. A. Ojemann. 1994. *Conversations with Neil's brain: The neural nature of thought and language.* Reading, MA: Addison-Wesley.

Capitani, E., M. Laiacona, B. Mahon and A. Caramazza. 2003. What are the facts of semantic category-specific deficits? A critical review of the clinical evidence. *Cognitive Neuropsychology* 20 (3–6): 213–61.

Caplan, D. 1987. *Neurolinguistics and linguistic aphasiology: An introduction.* Cambridge: Cambridge University Press.

1992. *Language structure, processing and disorders.* Cambridge, MA: MIT Press.

Caplan, D., N. Alpert, G. Waters and A. Olivieri. 2000. Activation of Broca's area by syntactic processing under conditions of concurrent articulation. *Human Brain Mapping* 9 (2): 65–71.

Caplan, D. and C. Futter. 1986. Assignment of thematic roles to nouns in sentence com-prehension by an aphasic patient. *Brain and Language* 27 (1): 117–34.

Caplan, D., S. Vijayan, G. Kuperburg, C. West, G. Waters, D. Greve and A. M. Dale. 2002. Vascular responses to syntactic processing: Event related fMRI study of relative clauses. *Human Brain Mapping* 15: 26–38.

Caplan, D. and G. S. Waters. 1999. Verbal working memory and sentence comprehension. *Behavioral and Brain Sciences* 22: 77–126.

    2003. On-line syntactic processing in aphasia: Studies with auditory moving window presentation. *Brain and Language* 84: 222–249.

Caramazza, A. and R. S. Berndt. 1982. The semantic deficit hypothesis – perceptual parsing and object classification by aphasic patients. *Brain and Language* 15 (1): 161–89.

Caramazza, A., A. E. Hillis, B. C. Rapp and I. C. Romani. 1990. The multiple semantics hypothesis – multiple confusions. *Cognitive Neuropsychology* 7 (3): 161–89.

Caramazza, A. and M. Miozzo. 1998. More is not always better: A response to Roelofs, Meyer, and Levelt. *Cognition* 69 (2): 231–41.

Caramazza, A. and J. R. Shelton. 1998. Domain-specific knowledge systems in the brain: The animate-inanimate distinction. *Journal of Cognitive Neuroscience* 10 (1): 1–34.

Cardell, E. 2006. Comprehension and well-formedness judgement in Broca's aphasia and anomic aphasia. Unpublished Ph.D. dissertation, University of Queensland.

Cassirer, E. 1953. *Language and myth*, trans. S. K. Langer. New York: Dover.

    1962. *An essay on man: An introduction to human culture*. New Haven, CT: Yale University Press.

Ceccherini-Nelli, A. and T. J. Crow. 2003. Disintegration of the components of language as the path to a revision of Bleuler's and Schneider's concepts of schizophrenia: Lin-guistic disturbances compared with first-rank symptoms in acute psychosis. *British Journal of Psychiatry* 182: 233–40.

Chaika, E. 1974. A linguist looks at 'schizophrenic' language. *Brain and Language* 1: 257–76.

Chenery, H. J., J. C. L. Ingram and B. L. Murdoch. 1990. Automatic and volitional semantic processing in aphasia. *Brain and Language* 38 (2): 215–32.

Cherry, C. 1978. *On human communication: A review, a survey, and a criticism*, 3rd edn. Cambridge, MA: MIT Press.

Chiarello, C. 1998. On codes of meaning and the meaning of codes: Semantic access and retrieval within and between hemispheres. In M. Beeman and C. Chiarello (eds.), *Right hemisphere language comprehension*. Mahwah, NJ: Lawrence Erlbaum Asso-ciates, 141–60.

Chocholle, R., F. Chedru, M. C. Botte, F. Chain and F. Lhermitte. 1975. Etude psychoa-coustique d'un cas de 'surdité corticale'. *Neuropsychologia* 13: 163–72.

Chomsky, N. 1955. *The logical structure of linguistic theory*. New York: Plenum Press.

    1957. *Syntactic structures*. The Hague: Mouton.

    1965. *Aspects of the theory of syntax*. Cambridge, MA: MIT Press.

    1972. *Language and mind*, enlarged edn. New York: Harcourt Brace Jovanovich.

    1981. *Lectures on Government and Binding*. Dordrecht: Foris.

    1995. *The minimalist program*. Cambridge, MA: MIT Press.

2000. *New horizons in the study of language and mind.* Cambridge: Cambridge University Press.

Chomsky, N. and G. Miller. 1963. Introduction to the formal analysis of natural language. In R. D. Luce, R. Bush and E. Galanter (eds.), *Handbook of mathematical psychology*, vol. II. New York: John Wiley.

Christiansen, M. H. 1992. The (non) necessity of recursion in natural language processing. In *Proceedings of the 14th Annual Conference of the Cognitive Science Society.* Hillsdale, NJ: Lawrence Erlbaum, 665–70.

Clare, L., P. J. McKenna, A. M. Mortimer and A. D. Baddeley. 1993. Memory in schizophrenia: What is impaired and what is preserved? *Neuropsychologia* 31: 1225–41.

Clark, H. H. 1979. Responding to indirect speech acts. *Cognitive Psychology* 11: 430–77.

Cohen, R., S. Kelter and G. Woll. 1980. Analytical competence and language impairment in aphasia. *Brain and Language* 10 (2): 331–47.

Collins, A. M. and M. R. Quillian. 1969. Retrieval from semantic memory. *Journal of Verbal Learning and Verbal Behavior* 8: 240–7.

Coltheart, M. 1983. Phonological awareness: A preschool precursor of success in reading. *Nature* 301: 370.

2002. Cognitive neuropsychology. In J. Wixted (ed.), *Steven's handbook of experimental psychology*, 3rd edn – vol. IV. New York: John Wiley & Sons, 139–74.

Coltheart, M., J. Masterson, S. Byng, M. Prior and J. Riddoch. 1983. Surface dyslexia. *Journal of Experimental Psychology* 35: 469–95.

Crain, S. and M. Steedman. 1985. On not being led up the garden path: The use of context by the psychological parser. In D. R. Dowty, L. Karttunen and A. Zwicky (eds.), *Natural Language Parsing: Psychological, computational, and theoretical perspectives.* Cambridge: Cambridge University Press, 320–58.

Crain, S. and P. Pietroski. 2001. Nature, nurture and Universal Grammar. *Linguistics and Philosophy* 24 (2): 139–86.

Crain, S., W. Ni and D. Shankweiler. 2004. Grammatism. *Brain and Language* 77 (3): 294–304.

Crutch, S. J. and E. K. Warrington. 2003. The selective impairment of fruit and vegetable knowledge: A multiple processing channels account of fine grain category specificity. *Cognitive Neuropsychology* 20 (36): 355–72.

Crystal, D. 1975. *The English tone of voice: Essays in intonation, prosody and paralanguage.* London: Edward Arnold.

Cummins, F. and R. Port 1998. Rhythmic constraints on stress timing in English. *Journal of Phonetics* 26 (2): 145–71.

Cutler, A. 1990. Exploiting prosodic probabilities in speech segmentation. In G. T. M. Altmann (ed.), *Cognitive models of speech processing: psycholinguistic and computational perspectives.* Cambridge, MA: MIT Press, 105–21.

1994. Segmentation problems, rhythmic solutions. *Lingua* 92 (1–4): 81–104.

Cutler, A. and D. M. Carter. 1987. The predominance of strong initial syllables in the English vocabulary. *Computer Speech and Language* 26: 406–18.

Cutler, A., J. Mehler, D. Norris and J. Segui. 1986. The syllables, differing role in the segmentation of French and English. *Journal of Memory and Language* 25 (4): 385–400.

1987. Phoneme identification and the lexicon. *Cognitive Psychology* 19 (2): 141–77.

Cutler, A. and T. Otake. 1994. Mora or phoneme: Further evidence for language-specific listening. *Journal of Memory and Language* 33 (6): 824–44.

Damasio, A. R. and D. Tranel. 1993. Nouns and verbs are retrieved with differently distributed neural systems. *Proceedings of the National Academy of Sciences of the United States of America* 90 (11): 4957–60.

Daneman, M. and P. A. Carpenter. 1980. Individual differences in working memory and reading. *Journal of Verbal Learning and Verbal Behavior* 19: 450–66.

Davis, K. L., R. G. Kahn, G. Ko and M. Davidson. 1991. Dopamine in schizophrenia, a review and a reconceptualization. *American Journal of Psychiatry* 148 (11): 1474–86.

de Villers, J. G. 1978. Fourteen grammatical morphemes in acquisition and aphasia. In A. Caramazza and E. B. Zurif (eds.), *Language acquisition and language breakdown: Parallels and divergencies.* Baltimore: Johns Hopkins University Press, 121–44.

de Zubicaray, G. I., K. L. McMahon, M. M. Eastburn, S. Finnigan and M. S. Humphreys. 2004. fMRI evidence of word frequency and strength effects during episodic memory encoding. *Cognitive Brain Research* 22: 439–50.

Deacon, T. W. 1997a. *The symbolic species: The co-evolution of language and the brain.* New York: W. W. Norton & Company.

1997b. What makes the human brain different? *Annual Review of Anthropology* 26: 337–57.

Dehaene-Lambertz, G., C. Pallier, W. Serniclaes, L. Sprenger-Charolles, A. Jobert and S. Dehaene. 2005. Neural correlates of switching from auditory to speech perception. *Neuroimage* 24 (1): 21–33.

Denes, G. and C. Semenza. 1975. Auditory modality-specific anomia: Evidence from a case of pure word deafness. *Cortex* 11: 401–11.

Derwing, B. L. 1976. Morpheme recognition and learning the rules for derivational morphology. *Canadian Journal of Linguistics – Revue Canadienne de Linguistique* 21 (1): 38–66.

Devlin, J. T., L. M. Gonnerman, E. S. Andersen and M. S. Seidenberg. 1998. Category-specific semantic deficits in focal and widespread brain damage: A computational account. *Journal of Cognitive Neuroscience* 10 (1): 77–94.

Dhond, R. P., K. Marinkovic, A. M. Dale, T. Witzel and E. Halgren. 2003. Spatiotemporal maps of past-tense inflection. *Neuroimage* 19: 91–100.

Divenyi, P. L. and A. J. Robinson. 1989. Nonlinguistic auditory capabilities in aphasia. *Brain and Language* 37: 290–326.

Dixon, R. M. W. 1980. *The languages of Australia.* Cambridge: Cambridge University Press.

Docherty, N. M., S. W. Gordinier, M. J. Hall and L. P. Cutting. 1999. Communication disturbances in relatives beyond the age of risk for schizophrenia and their associations with symptoms in patients. *Schizophrenia Bulletin* 25 (4): 851–62.

Docherty, N. M., E. S. Grosh and B. E. Wexler. 1996. Affective reactivity of cognitive functioning and family history in schizophrenia. *Biological Psychiatry* 39 (1): 59–64.

Dodd, B. and R. Campbell (eds.) 1987. *Hearing by eye: The psychology of lip-reading.* London and Hillsdale, NJ: Lawrence Erlbaum.

Dronkers, N. F. 1996. A new brain region for coordinating articulation. *Nature* 384: 159–61.

Dronkers, N. F., D. P. Wilkins, R. D. Van Valin, B. B. Redfern and J. J. Jaeger. 2004. Lesion analysis of the brain areas involved in language comprehension. *Cognition* 92 (1–2): 145–77.

Dunn, L. M. and L. M. Dunn. 1997. *The British picture vocabulary scale*, 2nd edn. Windsor, Berkshire: FER-Nelson.

Eccles, J. C. 1973. *The Understanding of the Brain*. New York: McGraw-Hill.

Efron, R. 1963. Temporal perception, aphasia and deja vu. *Brain* 86: 403–24.

Eimas, P. D. and J. D. Corbit. 1973. Selective adaptation of linguistic feature detectors. *Cognitive Psychology* 4: 99–109.

Eimas, P., E. R. Siqueland, P. Jusczyk and J. Vigorito. 1971. Speech perception in early infancy. *Science* 171: 304–6.

Elman, J. L. 1990a. Finding structure in time. *Cognitive Science* 14: 179–211.

1990b. Representation and structure in connectionist models. In G. Altmann (ed.), *Cognitive models of speech processing*. Cambridge, MA: Bradford.

Elman, J. L., E. A. Bates, M. H. Johnson, A. Karmiloff-Smith, D. Parisi and K. Plunkett (eds.). 1996. *Rethinking innateness: A connectionist perspective on development*. Cambridge, MA: MIT Press.

Elman, J. L. and J. L. McClelland. 1986. Exploiting the lawful variability in the speech wave. In J. S. Perkell and D. H. Klatt (eds.), *Invariance and variability of speech processes*. Hillsdale, NJ: Erlbaum, 360–81.

1988. Cognitive penetration of the mechanisms of perception: Compensation for coarticulation of lexically restored phonemes. *Journal of Memory and Language* 27 (2): 143–65.

Elvevag, B. and T. E. Goldberg. 2000. Cognitive impairment in schizophrenia is the core of the disorder. *Critical Reviews in Neurobiology* 14 (1): 1–21.

Fadiga, L., L. Craighero, G. Buccino and G. Rizzolatti. 2002. Speech listening specifically modulates the excitability of tongue muscles: A TMS study. *European Journal of Neuroscience* 15 (2): 399–402.

Fadiga, L., L. Fogassi, G. Pavesi and G. Rizzolatti. 1995. Motor facilitation during action observation: A magnetic stimulation study. *Journal of Neurophysiology* 73 (6): 2608–11.

Fellbaum, C. (ed.). 1998. *Wordnet: An electronic lexical database*. Cambridge, MA: Bradford.

Felser, C., H. Clahsen and T. F. Munte. 2003. Storage and integration in the processing of filler-gap dependencies: An ERP study of topicalization and wh-movement in German. *Brain and Language* 87 (3): 345–54.

Ferreira, F. and C. Clifton. 1986. The independence of syntactic processing. *Journal of Memory and Language* 25: 348–68.

Ferreira, F., J. M. Henderson, M. D. Anes, P. A. Weeks and D. K. McFarlane. 1996. Effects of lexical frequency and syntactic complexity in spoken language comprehension: Evidence from the auditory moving window technique. *Journal of Experimental Psychology: Learning, Memory, and Cognition* 22 (2): 324–35.

Fillmore, C. 1968. The case for case. In E. Bach and R. T. Harms (eds.), *Universals in linguistic theory*. New York: Holt, Rinehart and Winston, 1–90.

Fischler, I. 1977. Semantic facilitation without association in a lexical decision task. *Memory and Cognition* 5 (3): 335–9.

Fitch, R. H., S. Miller and P. Tallal. 1997. Neurobiology of speech perception. *Annual Review of Neuroscience* 20: 331–53.

Fletcher, P. C., C. D. Frith, P. M. Grasby, K. J. Friston and R. J. Dolan. 1996. Local and distributed effects of apomorphine on fronto-temporal function in acute unmedicated schizophrenia. *Journal of Neuroscience*. 16 (21): 7055–62.

Fletcher, P., P. J. McKenna, K. J. Friston, C. D. Frith and R. J. Dolan. 1999. Abnormal cingulate modulation of fronto-temporal connectivity in schizophrenia. *NeuroImage* 9: 337–42.

Fodor, J. A. 1975. *The language of thought*. Cambridge, MA: Harvard University Press.

    1983. *The modularity of mind: An essay on faculty psychology*. Cambridge, MA: MIT Press.

    1987. *Psychosemantics: The problem of meaning in the philosophy of mind*. Cambridge, MA: MIT Press.

Fodor, J. A. and Z. W. Pylyshyn. 1988. Connectionism and cognitive architecture: A critical analysis. In S. Pinker and J. Mehler (eds.), *Connections and symbols*. Cambridge, MA: MIT Press (A Cognition Special Issue).

Fodor, J. D. 1993. Processing empty categories: A question of visibility. In G. T. M. Altmann and R. Shillcock (eds.), *Cognitive models of speech processing*. Hillsdale, NJ: Erlbaum, 351–400.

    1995. Comprehending sentence structure. In L. Gleitman and M. Liberman (eds.), *Language: An invitation to cognitive science*, 2nd edn. Cambridge, MA: Bradford, 209–46.

Ford, J. M., D. H. Mathalon, T. Heinks, S. Kalba, W. O. Faustman and W. T. Roth. 2002. Neurophysiological evidence of corollary discharge dysfunction in schizophrenia. *American Journal of Psychiatry* 158 (12): 2069–71.

Forster, K. I. 1976. Accessing the mental lexicon. In R. J. Wales and E. Walker (eds.), *New approaches to language mechanisms*. Amsterdam: North Holland, 257–87.

    1990. Lexical processing. In D. N. Osherson and H. Lasnik (eds.), *Language: An invitation to cognitive science*, vol. I. Cambridge, MA: Bradford, 95–132.

Fowler, C. A., C. T. Best and G. W. McRoberts. 1990. Young infants' perception of liquid coarticulatory influences on following stop consonants. *Perception & Psychophysics* 48: 559–70.

Fowler, C. A., J. M. Brown and V. A. Mann. 2000. Contrast effects do not underlie effects of preceding liquids on stop-consonant identification by humans. *Journal of Experimental Psychology: Human Perception and Performance* 26: 877–88.

Franklin, S. 1989. Dissociations in auditory word comprehension: Evidence from nine fluent aphasic patients. *Aphasiology* 3: 189–207.

Franklin, S., D. Howard and K. Patterson. 1995. Abstract word anomia. *Cognitive Neuropsychology* 12: 549–66.

Franklin, S., J. Turner and A. Ellis. 1992. *ADA comprehension battery*. London: Action for Dysphasic Adults. Available from Action for Dysphasic Adults, Canterbury House, Royal Street, London, SE1 7LL.

Frazier, L. 1978. On comprehending sentences. Ph.D. dissertation, University of Connecticut.

Frazier, L. and C. C. Clifton. 1996. *Construal*. Cambridge, MA: MIT Press.

Frazier, L. and J. Fodor. 1978. The sausage machine: A new two-stage parsing model. *Cognition* 6: 291–325.

Frazier, L. and A. Friederici. 1991. On deriving the properties of agrammatic comprehension: Syntactic structures and task demands. *Brain and Language* 40: 51–66.

Freud, S. 1953. *On aphasia: A critical study*, trans. E. Stengel. New York: International Universities Press. (Original work published 1891).

Friederici, A. D. 1982. Syntactic and semantic processes in aphasic deficits – the role of prepositions. *Brain and Language* 15 (2): 249–58.

    1983. Aphasics' perception of words in sentential context: Some real-time processing evidence. *Neuropsychologia* 21 (4): 351–8.

    1995. The time-course of syntactic activation during language processing: A model based on neuropsychological and neurophysiological data. *Brain and Language* 50 (3): 259–81.

Friederici, A. D., A. Hahne and A. Mecklinger. 1996. Temporal structure of syntactic parsing: Early and late event-related brain potential effects. *Journal of Experimental Psychology – Learning, Memory and Cognition* 22 (5): 1219–48.

Friederici, A. D., A. Hahne and D. Saddy. 2002. Distinct neurophysiological patterns reflecting aspects of syntactic complexity and syntactic repair. *Journal of Psycholinguistic Research* 31 (1): 45–63.

Friederici, A. and A. Mecklinger. 1996. Syntactic parsing as revealed by brain responses: First-pass and second-pass parsing processes. *Journal of Psycholinguistic Research* 25 (1): 157–76.

Fries, C. C. 1952. *The structure of English: An introduction to the construction of English sentences*. New York: Harcourt Brace.

Frisch, S., A. Hahne and A. D. Friederici. 2004. Word category and verb argument structure information in the dynamics of parsing. *Cognition* 91 (3): 191–219.

Frith, C. D. 1992. *The Cognitive Neuropsychology of Schizophrenia*. Hove: Lawrence Erlbaum.

Frith, C. D. and U. Frith. 1999. Interacting minds – a biological basis. *Science* 286: 1692–9.

Fromkin, V. A. 1971. The non-anomalous nature of anomalous utterances. *Language* 47: 22–57.

    1975. A linguist looks at 'schizophrenic language'. *Brain and Language* 2: 498–503.

Galaburda, A. M., M. Lemay, T. L. Kemper and N. Geschwind. 1978. Right-left asymmetries in brain. *Science* 199 (4331): 852–6.

Gall, F. J. 1809. *Recherches sur le système nerveux*. Paris: J. B. Baillière.

Ganong, W. F. 1980. Phonetic categorization in auditory word perception. *Journal of Experimental Psychology: Human Perception and Performance* 6 (1): 110–25.

Garbarini, F. and M. Adenzato. 2004. At the root of embodied cognition: Cognitive science meets neurophysiology. *Brain and Cognition* 56 (1): 100–6.

Garnham, A., M. Traxler, J. Oakhill and M. A. Gernsbacher. 1996. The locus of implicit causality effects in comprehension. *Journal of Memory and Language* 35 (4): 517–43.

Gerson, S. N., D. F. Benson and S. H. Frazier. 1977. Diagnosis: schizophrenia versus posterior aphasia. *The American Journal of Psychiatry* 134: 966–9.

Geschwind, N. 1974. *Selected papers on language and the brain*. Dordrecht: D. Reidel Publishing Company.

Geschwind, N., F. A. Quadfasel and J. M. Segarra. 1968. Isolation of the speech area. *Neuropsychologia* 6: 327–40.

Gibson, E. 1998. Linguistic complexity: locality of syntactic dependencies. *Cognition* 68: 1–76.

Gielewski, E. J. 1983. Acoustic analysis and auditory retraining in the remediation of sensory aphasia. In C. Code and D. J. Muller (eds.), *Aphasia therapy*. London: Edward Arnold, 138–46.

Gokcen, J. M. and R. A. Fox. 2001. Neurological evidence in support of a specialized phonetic processing model. *Brain and Language* 78 (2): 241–53.

Goldberg, T. E., M. S. Aloia, M. L. Gourovitch, D. Missar, D. Pickar and D. R. Weinberger. 1998. Cognitive substrates of thought disorder, I: The semantic system. *American Journal of Psychiatry* 155 (12): 1671–6.

Goldinger, S. 1997. Words and voices: Perception and production in an episodic lexicon. In K. Johnson and J. W. Mullenix (eds.), *Talker variability in speech processing*. San Diego: Academic Press, 33–66.

    1998. Echos of echos? An episodic theory of lexical access. *Psychological Review* 105 (2): 251–79.

Goldstein, K. 1948. *Language and language disturbances: Aphasic symptom complexes and their significance for medicine and theory of language*. New York: Grune & Stratton.

Goodglass, H. 1976. Agrammatism. In H. Whitaker and H. A. Whitaker (eds.), *Studies in Neurolinguistics*, vol. I. New York: Academic Press, 237–60.

    1993. *Understanding aphasia*. San Diego, CA: Academic Press.

Goodglass, H. and E. Baker. 1976. Semantic field, naming, and auditory comprehension in aphasia. *Brain and Language* 3 (3): 359–74.

Gopnik, M. 1999. Familial language impairment: More English evidence. *Folia Phoniatrica Logopaedica* 51: 5–19.

Gordon, J. K. and S. R. Baum. 1994. Rhyme priming in aphasia – the role of phonology in lexical access. *Brain and Language* 47 (4): 661–83.

Gow, D. W. and D. Caplan. 1996. An examination of impaired acoustic-phonetic processing in aphasia. *Brain and Language* 52: 386–407.

Grela, B. and J. Gandour. 1999. Stress shift in aphasia: A multiple case study. *Aphasiology* 13 (2): 151–66.

Grice, P. 1975. Logic and conversation. In S. Davis (ed.), *Pragmatics*. New York: Oxford University Press, 305–15.

Grodzinsky, Y. 1984. The syntactic characterization of agrammatism. *Cognition* 16 (2): 99–120.

    1986. Language deficits and the theory of syntax. *Brain and Language* 27 (1): 135–59.

    1990. *Theoretical perspectives on language deficits*. Cambridge, MA: MIT Press.

    1995. A restrictive theory of agrammatic comprehension. *Brain and Language* 45: 396–442.

    2000. The neurology of syntax: Language use without Broca's area. *Behavioural and Brain Sciences* 23 (1): 1–21.

Grodzinsky, Y. and L. Finkel. 1998. The neurology of empty categories: Aphasics' failure to detect ungrammaticality. *Journal of Cognitive Neuroscience* 10 (2): 281–92.

Guenther, F. H., F. T. Husain, M. A. Cohen and B. G. Shinn-Cunningham. 1999. Effects of categorization and discrimination training on auditory perceptual space. *Journal of the Acoustical Society of America* 106 (5): 2900–12.

Guenther, F. H. and M. N. Gjaja. 1996. The perceptual magnet effect as an emergent property of neural map formation. *Journal of the Acoustical Society of America* 100 (2): 1111–21.

Gunter, T. C., A. D. Friederici and H. Schriefers. 2000. Syntactic gender and semantic expectancy: ERPs reveal early autonomy and late inter-action. *Journal of Cognitive Neuroscience* 12: 556–68.

Haegeman, L. 1991. *Introduction to Government & Binding Theory*. Cambridge, MA: Basil Blackwell Inc.

Hagoort, P. 1990. Tracking the time course of language understanding in aphasia. Unpublished Ph.D. dissertation, University of Nijmegen.

   1997. Semantic priming in Broca's aphasics at a short SOA: No support for an automatic access deficit. *Brain and Language* 56 (2): 287–300.

Hahne, A. and A. D. Friederici. 1999. Electrophysiological evidence for two steps in syntactic analysis: Early automatic and late controlled processes. *Journal of Cognitive Neuroscience* 11 (2): 194–205.

   2002. Differential task effects on semantic and syntactic processes as revealed by ERPs. *Cognitive Brain Research* 13 (3): 339–56.

Hahne, A. and J. D. Jescheniak. 2001. What's left if the Jabberwock gets the semantics? An ERP investigation into semantic and syntactic processes during auditory comprehension. *Cognitive Brain Research* 11 (2): 199–212.

Halliday, M. A. K. and R. Hasan. 1976. *Cohesion in English*. London: Longman.

Halperin, Y., Y. Nachson and A. Carmon. 1973. Shift in ear superiority in dichotic listening to temporally patterned non-verbal stimuli. *Journal of the Acoustical Society of America* 53 (1): 46–50.

Hankamer, J. and I. Sag. 1976. Deep and surface anaphor. *Linguistic Inquiry* 7 (3): 391–428.

Hari, R., S. Levanen and T. Raij. 2000. Timing of human cortical functions during cognition: Role of MEG. *Trends in Cognitive Sciences* 4 (12): 455–62.

Harman, H. J., M. A. Just and P. A. Carpenter. 1997. Aphasic sentence comprehension as a resource deficit: A computational approach. *Brain and Language* 59: 76–120.

Harris, Z. S. 1960. *Structural linguistics*. Chicago: University of Chicago Press.

   1970. *Papers in structural and transformational linguistics*. Dordrecht: Reidel.

Hayes, B. P. 1980. *A metrical theory of stress rules*. Bloomington, IN: Indiana University Linguistics Club.

Head, H. 1926. *Aphasia and kindred disorders of speech*. Cambridge: Cambridge University Press.

Hebb, D. 1949. *The organization of behavior: A neuropsychological theory*. New York: Wiley Science Editions, 1949.

Hellige, J. B. 1993. *Hemispheric asymmetry: What's right and what's left*. Cambridge, MA: Harvard University Press.

Hickok, G. 1992. Agrammatic comprehension and the trace deletion hypothesis. Occasional paper No. 45, MIT Center for Cognitive Science. Cambridge, MA.

Hickok, G. and D. Poeppel. 2004. Dorsal and ventral streams: A framework for understanding aspects of the functional anatomy of language. *Cognition* 92: 67–99.

Hobbs, J. R. 1979. Coherence and coreference. *Cognitive Science* 3: 67–90.

Hockett, C. F. 1960. The origin of speech. *Scientific American* 203 (3): 89–96.

Holt, L. L. and A. J. Lotto. 2002. Behavioral examinations of the level of auditory processing of speech context effects. *Hearing Research* 167: 156–69.

Hornby, P. 1971. Surface structure and the topic-comment distinction: A development
study. *Child Development* 42: 1975–88.

1974. Surface structure and presupposition. *Journal of Verbal Learning and Verbal
Behavior* 13: 530–8.

Howard, D. and S. Franklin. 1988. *Missing the meaning? A cognitive neuropsychological
study of the processing of words by an aphasic patient.* Cambridge, MA: MIT Press.

Huddleston, R. 1984. *Introduction to the grammar of English.* Cambridge: Cambridge
University Press.

Huddleston, R. and G. K. Pullum. 2002. *The Cambridge grammar of the English language.*
Cambridge: Cambridge University Press.

Hudson, R. 1996. The difficulty of 'so-called' self-embedded structures. UCL Working
Papers in Linguistics 8. http://www.phon.ucl.ac.uk/publications/WPL/uclwpl.html

2001. Review of Terrance Deacon's *The symbolic species: The co-evolution of language
and the brain. Journal of Pragmatics* 33: 129–35.

Humboldt, W. von. 1999. *Humboldt: On Language: On the diversity of human language and its influence on the mental development of the human species*, 2nd edn.
Cambridge: Cambridge University Press.

Hurford, J. 1998. Review of *The symbolic species: The co-evolution of language and the
brain. Times Literary Supplement*, 23 October, p. 34.

Ingram, J. C. L. and H. J. Chenery. 1995. The reversal of the concreteness effect in a fluent
aphasic. Paper presented at the 3rd Annual Meeting of the Aphasiology Symposium
of Australia, Brisbane, Australia.

Ingram, J. C., P. F. McCormack and M. Kennedy. 1992. Phonetic analysis of a case of
Foreign Accent Syndrome. *Journal of Phonetics* 20 (4): 457–74.

Ingram, J. C. and R. D. Morice. 1983. Reference, syntax and thought disorder in
schizophrenia. Unpublished Ms.

Ingram, J. C. and T. Mylne. 1994. Perceptual parsing of nasal vowels. In *Proceedings of
the International Congress of Spoken Language Processing ICSLP 94*, Yokohama,
Japan.

Ingram, J. C. and S. G. Park. 1997. Cross-language vowel perception and production by
Korean and Japanese learners of English. *Journal of Phonetics* 25 (3): 343–70.

1998. Language, context and speaker effects in the identification and discrimination of
English /r/ and /l/ by Japanese and Korean listeners. *Journal of the Acoustical Society
of America* 103 (2): 1161–74.

Ingram, J. C., S. G. Park and T. Mylne. 1997. Studies in cross-linguistic speech perception.
*The Asia-Pacific Journal of Speech, Language and Hearing* 2 (1): 1–23.

Iverson, P. and P. K. Kuhl. 2000. Perceptual magnet and phoneme boundary effects in
speech perception: Do they arise from a common mechanism? *Perception and Psychophysics* 62 (4): 874–86.

Jackendoff, R. 1972. *Semantic interpretation in Generative Grammar.* Cambridge, MA:
MIT Press.

1983. *Semantics and cognition.* Cambridge, MA: MIT Press.

1997. *The Architecture of the Language Faculty.* Cambridge, MA: MIT Press.

2002. *Foundations of Language: Brain, meaning, grammar, evolution.* Oxford: Oxford
University Press.

Jackson, J. H. 1866. Notes on the physiology and pathology of language. *Medical Times and Gazette* 1: 659.

Jaeger, J. J., A. H. Lockwood, D. L. Kemmerer, R. D. VanValin, B. W. Murphy and H. G. Khalak. 1996. Positron emission tomographic study of regular and irregular verb morphology in English. *Language* 72 (3): 451–97.

Jakobson, R. 1968. *Child language: Aphasia, and phonological universals*, trans. A. R. Kuler. The Hague: Mouton. (Original work published 1941).

Jerger, J., N. Weikers, F. Sharbrough and S. Jerger. 1969. Bilateral lesions of the temporal lobe: A case study. *Acta Otolarungologica, Supplement* 258: 1–51.

Jerison, H. J. 1990. Fossil evidence on the evolution of the neocortex. In E. G. Jones and A. Peters (eds.), *Cerebral Cortex*, vol. VIIIA. New York: Plenum, 285–309.

Johnson, K. 1997. Speech perception without speaker normalization: An exemplar model. In K. Johnson and J. W. Mullenix (eds.), *Talker variability in speech processing*. San Diego: Academic Press, 145–66.

Johnson-Laird, P. N. and A. Garnham. 1980. Descriptions and discourse models. *Linguistics and Philosophy* 3: 371–93.

Johnstone, B. 2002. *Discourse Analysis*. Cambridge, MA: Blackwell.

Jones, H. M. and L. S. Pilowksy. 2002. Dopamine and antipsychotic drug action revisited. *British Journal of Psychiatry* 181: 271–5.

Jusczyk, P. W., E. A. Hohne and A. Bauman. 1999. Infants' sensitivity to allophonic cues for word segmentation. *Perception & Psychophysics* 61 (8): 1465–76.

Jusczyk, P. W., P. A. Luce and J. Charles-Luce. 1994. Infants' sensitivity to phonotactic patterns in the native language. *Journal of Memory and Language* 33: 630–45.

Just, M. A. and P. A. Carpenter. 1992. A capacity theory of comprehension: Individual differences in Working Memory. *Psychological Review* 99 (1): 122–49.

Kaan, E., A. Harris, E. Gibson and P. Holcomb. 2000. The P600 as an index of syntactic integration difficulty. *Language and Cognitive Processes* 15 (2): 159–201.

Kanshepolsky, J., J. Kelley and J. Wagner. 1973. A cortical auditory disorder, clinical audiologic and pathologic aspects. *Neurology* 23: 699–705.

Katz, J. and J. A. Fodor. 1963. The structure of a semantic theory. *Language* 39: 170–210.

Kay, J., R. Lesser and M. Coltheart. 1992. *Psycholinguistic assessments of language processing in aphasia (PALPA)*. Hove: Lawrence Erlbaum Associates.

Kehler, A. 2002. *Coherence, reference, and the theory of grammar*. Stanford, CA: CSLI Publications.

Kempley, S. T. and J. Morton. 1982. The effects of priming with regularly and irregularly related words in auditory word recognition. *British Journal of Psychology* 73: 441–54.

Kendon, A. 1988. *Sign languages of Aboriginal Australia*. Cambridge: Cambridge University Press.

Kim, J. H., D. C. Glahn, K. H. Nuechterlein and T. D. Cannon. 2004. Maintenance and manipulation of information in schizophrenia: Further evidence for impairment in the central executive component of working memory. *Schizophrenia Research* 68 (2–3): 173–87.

Kimura, D. 1961. Cerebral dominance in the perception of verbal stimuli. *Canadian Journal of Psychology* 15 (3): 166–71.

Kleist, K. 1970. Schizophrenic symptoms and cerebral pathology. *Journal of Mental Science* 106: 246–55.

Kluender, R. and M. Kutas. 1993. Bridging the gap: Evidence from ERPs on the processing of unbounded dependencies. *Journal of Cognitive Neuroscience* 5 (2): 196–214.

Kohler, C. G. and A. R. Brennan. 2004. Recognition of facial emotions in schizophrenia. *Current Opinion in Psychiatry* 17 (2): 81–6.

Kohn, S. and R. Friedman. 1986. Word-meaning deafness: A phonological-semantic dissociation. *Cognitive Neuropsychology* 3: 291–308.

Kraepelin, E. 1919. *Dementia Praecox and Paraphrenia*. Ed. G. M. Robertson, trans. R. M. Barclay, 8th edn. Edinburgh.

Kripke, S. 1979. Speaker's reference and semantic reference. In S. Davis (ed.), *Pragmatics*. New York: Oxford University Press, 77–96.

Kruskal, J. B. and M. Wish. 1977. *Multidimensional scaling*. Beverly Hills, CA: Sage Publications.

Kuhl, P. K. 1991. Human adults and human infants show a 'perceptual magnet effect' for the prototypes of speech categories, monkeys do not. *Perception & Psychophysics* 50: 93–107.

Kuhl, P. K. and A. N. Meltzoff. 1984. The intermodal representation of speech in infants. *Infant Behavior and Development* 7 (3): 361–81.

Kuhl, P. K. and J. D. Miller. 1975. Speech-perception by the chinchilla – Voiced-voiceless distinction in alveolar and plosive consonants. *Science* 190: 69–72.

Kuperberg, G. and D. Caplan. 2003. Language dysfunction in schizophrenia. In R. B. Schiffer, S. M. Rao and B. S. Fogel (eds.), *Neuropsychiatry*, 2nd edn. Philadelphia: Lippincott Williams and Wilkins, 444–66.

Kutas, M. and S. A. Hillyard. 1980a. Reading senseless sentences – brain potentials reflect incongruity. *Science* 207 (4427): 203–5.

    1980b. Reading between the lines – event related brain potentials during natural sentence processing. *Brain and Language* 11 (2): 354–73.

    1980c. Event related brain potentials to semantically inappropriate and surprisingly large words. *Biological Psychology* 11 (2): 99–116.

Ladefoged, P. 2001. *A course in phonetics*, 4th edn. Fort Worth: Harcourt Brace.

Lahiri, A. and W. D. Marslen-Wilson. 1991. The mental representation of lexical form: A phonological approach to the mental lexicon. *Cognition* 38: 245–94.

Lakoff, G. 1971. On generative semantics. In D. Steinberg and L. Jakobovits (eds.), *Semantics an interdisciplinary reader*. Cambridge: Cambridge University Press.

    1987. *Women fire and dangerous things*. Chicago: University of Chicago Press.

Lakoff, G. and M. Johnson. 1980. *Metaphors we live by*. Chicago: University of Chicago Press.

    1999. *Philosophy in the flesh: The embodied mind and its challenge to western thought*. New York: Basic Books.

Lane, H. L. 1965. The motor theory of speech perception: A critical review. *Psychological Review* 72: 275–309.

Langacker, R. 1987. *Foundations of cognitive grammar*. Stanford, CA: Stanford University Press.

Laughren, M. 2002. Syntactic constraints in a free word order language. In M. Amberber and P. Collins (eds.), *Language universals and variation*. Westport, CT: Ablex Greenwood, 83–130.

Lazeron, R. H., S. A. Rombouts, W. C. Machielsen, P. Scheltens, M. P. Witter, H. B. Uylings and F. Barkhof. 2000. Visualizing brain activation during planning: The tower of London test adapted for functional MR imaging. *American Journal of Neuroradiology* 21: 1407–14.

Lecours, A. R. and M. Vanier-Clement. 1976. Schizophasia and jargonaphasia: A complete description with comments on Chaika's and Fromkin's respective looks at 'schizophrenic' language. *Brain and Language* 3: 516–65.

Lee, D. 2001. *Cognitive linguistics: An introduction.* Melbourne: Oxford University Press.

Lenneberg, E. H. 1967. *Biological foundations of language.* New York: Wiley.

Lesser, R. 1989. *Linguistic investigations of aphasia.* London: Whurr Publishers.

Levelt, W. J. M. 1989. *Speaking: From intention to articulation.* Cambridge, MA: MIT Press.

Levelt, W. J. M., P. Praamstra, A. S. Meyer, P. Helenius and R. Salmelin. 1998. An MEG study of picture naming. *Journal of Cognitive Neuroscience* 10: 553–67.

Levelt, W. J. M., A. Roelofs and A. S. Meyer. 1999. A theory of lexical access in speech production. *Behavioral and Brain Sciences* 22 (1): 1–38.

Libben, G. 1994. How is morphological decomposition achieved? *Language and Cognitive Processes* 9: 369–91.

Liberman, A. M. 1957. Some results of research on speech perception. *Journal of the Acoustical Society of America* 29: 117–33.

Liberman, A. M., F. S. Cooper, D. P. Shankweiler and M. Studdert-Kennedy. 1967. Perception of the speech code. *Psychological Review* 74: 431–61.

Liberman, A. M., D. Isenberg and B. Rakerd. 1981. Duplex perception of cues for stop consonants: Evidence for a phonetic mode. *Perception & Psychophysics* 30: 122–41.

Lichtheim, O. 1884. On aphasia. *Brain* 7: 443–84.

Lieberman, P. 1977. *Speech physiology and acoustic phonetics.* New York: Macmillan.

Linebarger, M. C. 1987. Negative polarity and grammatical representation. *Linguistics & Philosophy* 10: 325–87.

　1995. Agrammatism as evidence about grammar. *Brain and Language* 50: 52–91.

Linebarger, M. C., M. F. Schwartz and E. M. Saffran. 1983. Sensitivity to grammatical structure in so-called aphasics. *Cognition* 13: 361–92.

Lisker, L. and A. S. Abramson. 1964. A cross-language study of voicing in initial stops: Acoustical measurements. *Word* 20: 384–422.

　1971. Distinctive features and laryngeal control. *Language* 47: 767–85.

Lively, S. E. and D. B. Pisoni. 1997. On prototypes and phonetic categories: A critical assessment of the perceptual magnet effect in speech perception. *Journal of Experimental Psychology: Human Perception and Performance* 23: 1665–79.

Long, D. L. and L. De Ley. 2000. Understanding anaphors in story dialogue. *Memory and Cognition* 28 (5): 731–8.

Lotto, A. J. and K. R. Kluender. 1998. General contrast effects of speech perception: Effect of preceding liquid on stop consonant identification. *Perception and Psychophysics* 60: 602–19.

Lotto, A. J., K. R. Kluender and L. L. Holt. 1997. Perceptual compensation for coarticulation by Japanese quail (Coturnix coturnix japonica). *Journal of the Acoustical Society of America* 102 (2): 1134–40.

　1998. Depolarizing the perceptual magnet effect. *The Journal of the Acoustical Society of America* 103 (6): 3648–55.

Love, T. and D. Swinney. 1996. Co-reference processing and levels of analysis in object-relative constructions: Demonstrations of antecedent reactivation with the cross-modal priming paradigm. *Journal of Psycholinguistic Research* 25 (1): 5–24.

Lukatela, K., S. Crain and D. Shankweiler. 1988. Sensitivity to inflectional morphology in agrammatism: Investigation of a highly inflected language. *Brain and Language* 33: 1–15.

Lupker, S. J. 1984. Semantic priming without association – a 2nd look. *Journal of Verbal Learning and Verbal Behavior* 23 (6): 709–33.

Luria, A. R. 1970. *Traumatic aphasia: Its syndromes, psychology and treatment*, trans. D. Bowden. The Hague: Mouton. (Original work published in 1947).

1973. *The working brain: An introduction to neuropsychology*, trans. B. Haigh. New York: Basic Books.

1987. *The man with a shattered world*. Cambridge, MA: Harvard University Press.

Lyons, J. 1995. *Linguistic semantics: An introduction*. Cambridge: Cambridge University Press.

MacDonald, M. C., M. A. Just and P. A. Carpenter. 1992. Working memory constraints on the processing of syntactic ambiguity. *Cognitive Psychology* 24: 56–98.

MacDonald, M. C., N. J. Pearlmutter and M. S. Seidenberg. 1994. The lexical nature of syntactic ambiguity resolution. *Psychological Review* 101 (4): 676–703.

MacWhinney, B. 1987. The competition model. In B. MacWhinney (ed.), *Mechanisms of language acquisition*. Hillsdale, NJ: Lawrence Erlbaum, 249–308.

MacWhinney, B., J. Leinbach, R. Taraban and J. McDonald. 1989. Language learning: Cues or rules? *Journal of Memory and Language* 28 (3): 255–77.

MacWhinney, B. and D. Price. 1980. The development of the comprehension of Topic–Comment marking. In D. Ingram, F. Peng, and P. Dale (eds.), *Proceedings of the First International Congress of the Study of Child Language*. University Press of America.

Mann, V. A. 1986. Distinguishing language universal and language dependent levels of speech perception: Evidence from Japanese listeners' perception of English /l/ and /r/. *Cognition* 24 (3): 169–96.

Mann, V. and A. M. Liberman. 1983. Some differences between phonetic and auditory modes of perception. *Cognition* 12: 211–35.

Mann, V. A. and B. H. Repp. 1981. Influence of preceding fricative on stop consonant perception. *Journal of the Acoustical Society of America* 69 (2): 548–58.

Mannheim, B. 1991. *The language of the Inka since the European invasion*. Austin: University of Texas Press.

Marcus, M. P. 1980. *A theory of syntactic recognition for natural language*. Cambridge, MA: MIT Press.

Marshall, R. C. 1986. Treatment of auditory comprehension disorders. In R. Chapey (ed.), *Language intervention strategies in adult aphasia*, 3rd edn. Baltimore: Williams and Wilkins, 370–94.

Marslen-Wilson, W. 1975. Sentence perception as an interactive parallel process. *Science* 189 (4198): 226–8.

1984. Function and process in spoken word recognition – a tutorial review. *Attention and Performance* (10): 125–50.

1987. Functional parallelism in spoken word-recognition. *Cognition* 25 (1–2): 71–102.

Marslen-Wilson, W. and L. K. Tyler. 1980. The temporal structure of spoken language understanding. *Cognition* 8 (1): 1–71.

1987. Against modularity. In J. L. Garfield (ed.), *Modularity in knowledge representation and natural language understanding*. Cambridge, MA: MIT Press, 37–62.

1998. Rules, representations, and the English past tense. *Trends in Cognitive Sciences* 2 (11): 428–35.

Marslen-Wilson, W., L. K. Tyler, R. Waksler and L. Older. 1994. Morphology and meaning in the English mental lexicon. *Psychological Review* 101 (1): 3–33.

Marslen-Wilson, W. D. and A. Welsh. 1978. Processing interactions and lexical access during word-recognition in continuous speech. *Cognitive Psychology* 10 (1): 20–63.

Marslen-Wilson, W. M. and P. Zwitserlood. 1989. Accessing spoken words: The importance of word onsets. *Journal of Experimental Psychology – Human Perception and Performance* 15 (3): 576–85.

Martinet, André. 1957. Arbitraire linguistique et double articulation. *Cahiers Ferdinand de Saussure* 15: 105–16. Reprinted in Eric Hamp et al. (eds.). 1966. *Readings in Linguistics II*. Chicago: University of Chicago Press, 371–8.

Mattingly, I. G. and M. Studdert-Kennedy. 1991. *Modularity and the motor theory of speech perception: Proceedings of a conference to honor Alvin M. Liberman*, Hillsdale, NJ: Lawrence Erlbaum.

Mauner, G., V. Fromkin and T. Cornell. 1993. Comprehension and acceptability judgements in agrammatism: Disruptions in the syntax of referential dependency. *Brain and Language* 45: 340–70.

Mayberg, H. S. *et al*. 2002. The functional neuroanatomy of the placebo effect. *American Journal of Psychiatry* 159 (5): 728–37.

McClelland, J. L. and J. L. Elman. 1986. The TRACE model of speech perception. *Cognitive Psychology* 18: 1–86.

McClelland, J. L. and T. T. Rogers. 2003. The parallel distributed processing approach to semantic cognition. *Nature Reviews Neuroscience* 4 (4): 310–22.

McClelland, J. L. and D. E. Rumelhart. 1981. An interactive activation model of context effects in letter perception.1. An account of basic findings. *Psychological Review* 88 (5): 375–407.

1988. *Explorations in parallel distributed processing: A handbook of models, programs, and exercises*. Cambridge, MA and London: MIT Press.

McCormack, P. F. 1994. The rhythm rule in normal and ataxic speech production. Unpublished Ph.D. dissertation, University of Queensland.

McGrath, J. 1991. Ordering thoughts on thought disorder. *British Journal of Psychiatry* 158: 307–16.

McKenna, P. and E. K. Warrington. 1983. *The Graded Naming Test*. Windsor, Berkshire: NFER-Nelson.

McKoon, G. and R. Ratcliff. 1994. Sentential context and on-line lexical decision. *Journal of Experimental Psychology – Learning, Memory and Cognition* 20 (5): 1239–43.

McKoon, G., R. Ratcliff and G. Ward 1994. Testing theories of language processing – an empirical investigation of the online lexical decision task. *Journal of Experimental Psychology – Learning, Memory and Cognition* 20 (5): 1219–28.

McQueen, J. M. 1991. The influence of the lexicon on phonetic categorization: Stimulus quality in word-final ambiguity. *Journal of Experimental Psychology: Human Perception and Performance* 17: 433–43.

McRae, K. 2004. Semantic memory: Some insights from feature-based connectionist attractor networks. *Psychology of Learning and Motivation – Advances in Research and Theory* 45: 41–86.

McRae, K., V. R. de Sa, and M. S. Seidenberg. 1997. On the nature and scope of featural representations of word meaning. *Journal of Experimental Psychology: General* 126 (2): 99–130.

Mehler, J., P. Jusczyk, G. Lambretz, N. Halsted, J. Bertoncini and C. Amiel-Tison. 1988. A precursor of language acquisition in young infants. *Cognition* 29: 143–78.

Meistera, I., G. B. Boroojerdia, H. Foltysa, R. Sparinga, W. Huberb and R. Töpper. 2003. Motor cortex hand area and speech: Implications for the development of language. *Neuropsychologia* 41 (4): 401–6.

Mellars, P. 1996. *The Neanderthal legacy: An archaeological perspective from western Europe*. Princeton, NJ: Princeton University Press.

Mendez, M. F. and G. R. Geehan. 1988. Cortical auditory disorders: Clinical and psychoacoustic features. *Journal of Neurology, Neurosurgery and Psychiatry* 51: 1–9.

Mendez, M. F. and S. Rosenberg. 1991. Word deafness mistaken for Alzheimer's disease – differential characteristics. *Journal of the American Geriatrics Society* 39 (2): 209–11.

Menn, L. 1983. Development of articulatory, phonetic and phonological capabilities. In B. Butterworth (ed.), *Language production*, 2. London: Academic Press, 3–50.

Miceli, G., G. Gainotti, C. Caltagirone and C. Masullo. 1980. Some aspects of phonological impairment in aphasia. *Brain and Language* 11: 159–69.

Milberg, W. and S. E. Blumstein. 1981. Lexical decision in aphasia: Evidence for semantic processing. *Brain and Language* 14 (2): 371–85.

Milberg, W., S. E. Blumstein and B. Dworetzky. 1987. Processing of lexical ambiguities in aphasia. *Brain and Language* 31 (1): 138–50.

1988a. Phonological processing and lexical access in aphasia. *Brain and Language* 34: 279–93.

1988b. Phonological factors in semantic processing: Evidence from an auditory lexical decision task. *Bulletin of the Psychonomic Society* 26 (4): 305–8.

Milberg, W., S. E. Blumstein, D. Katz, F. Gershberg and T. Brown. 1995. Semantic facilitation in aphasia – effects of time and expectancy. *Journal of Cognitive Neuroscience* 7 (1): 33–50.

Miller, G. A. 1999. On knowing a word. *Annual Review of Psychology* 50: 1–19.

Miller, G. A. and N. Chomsky. 1963. Finitary models of language users. In D. R. Luce, R. R. Bush and E. Galanter (eds.), *Handbook of mathematical psychology*, vol. II. New York: John Wiley and Sons.

Miller, G. A. and P. N. Johnson-Laird. 1976. *Language and perception*. Cambridge: Cambridge University Press.

Milner, A. D. and M. A. Goodale. 1993. Visual pathways to perception and action. *Progress in Brain Research* 95: 317–37.

Minsky, M. 1975. A framework for representing knowledge. In P. Winston (ed.), *The psychology of computer vision*. New York: McGraw Hill.

Minzenberg, M. J., B. A. Ober and S. Vinogradov. 2002. Semantic priming in schizophrenia: A review and synthesis. *Journal of the International Neuropsychological Society* 8: 699–720.

Moore, H., A. R. West and A. A. Grace. 1999. The regulation of forebrain dopamine transmission: Relevance to the pathophysiology and psychopathology of schizophrenia. *Biological Psychiatry* 46: 40–55.

Morice, R. and A. Delahunty. 1996. Frontal executive impairments in schizophrenia. *Schizophrenia Bulletin* 22 (1): 125–37.

Morice, R. D. and J. C. L. Ingram. 1982. Language analysis in schizophrenia: Diagnostic implications. *Australian & New Zealand Journal of Psychiatry* 16: 11–21.

1983. Language complexity and age of onset of schizophrenia. *Psychiatry Research* 9 (3): 233–42.

Morris, J. and S. Franklin. 1995. Aphasia: Assessment and remediation of a speech discrimination deficit. In M. Perkins and S. Howard (eds.), *Case studies in clinical linguistics*. London: Whurr, 245–70.

Morris, R. G., S. Ahmed, G. M. Syed and B. K. Toone. 1993. Neural correlates of planning ability: Frontal lobe activation during the Tower of London test. *Neuropsychologia* 31: 1367–78.

Morton, J. 1970. A functional model of human memory. In D. A. Norman (ed.), *Models of human memory*. New York: Academic Press, 203–54.

Moss, H. E., S. F. McCormick and L. K. Tyler. 1997. The time course of activation of semantic information during spoken word recognition. *Language and Cognitive Processes* 12 (5–6): 695–731.

Moss, H. E., R. K. Ostrin, L. K. Tyler and W. M. Marslen-Wilson. 1995. Accessing different types of lexical semantic information – evidence from priming. *Journal of Experimental Psychology: Learning, Memory and Cognition* 21 (4): 863–83.

Mowrey, R. A. and I. R. A. MacKay. 1990. Phonological primitives: electromyographic speech error evidence. *Journal of the Acoustic Society of America* 88 (3): 1299–1312.

Murray, E. A. and T. J. Bussey. 1999. Perceptual-mnemonic functions of the perirhinal cortex. *Trends in Cognitive Sciences* 3 (4): 142–51.

Näätänen, R. 1999. The perception of speech sounds by the human brain as reflected by the mismatch negativity (MMN) and its magnetic equivalent (MMNm). *Psychophysiology* 38: 1–21.

Nakano, Y., C. Felser and H. Clahsen. 2002. Antecedent priming at trace positions in Japanese long-distance scrambling. *Journal of Psycholinguistic Research* 31 (5): 531–71.

Nazzi, T., J. Bertoncini and J. Mehler. 1998. Language discrimination by newborns: Toward an understanding of the role of rhythm. *Journal of Experimental Psychology: Human Perception and Performance* 24 (3): 756–66.

Ni, W. J., S. Crain and D. Shankweiler. 1996. Sidestepping garden paths: Assessing the contributions of syntax, semantics and plausibility in resolving ambiguities. *Language and Cognitive Processes* 11 (3): 283–334.

Nicol, J. and D. Swinney. 1989. The role of structure in coreference assignment during sentence comprehension. *Journal of Psycholinguistic Research* 18: 5–20.

Nishitani, N. and R. Hari. 2000. Temporal dynamics of cortical representation for action. *Proceedings of the National Academy of Sciences of the United States of America* 97 (2): 913–18.

Nolan, F. and P. E. Kerswill. 1990. The description of connected speech processes. In S. Ramsaran (ed.), *Studies in the pronunciation of English*. London: Routledge, 295–316.

Norris, D., J. M. McQueen and A. Cutler. 1999. Lexical influence in phonetic decision making: Evidence from subcategorical mismatches. *Journal of Experimental Psychology: Perception and performance* 25 (5): 1363–89.

Norris, D. and R. Wise. 2000. The study of prelexical and lexical processes in comprehension: Psycholinguistics and functional neuroimaging. In M. S. Gazzaniga (ed.), *The new cognitive neurosciences*. Cambridge, MA: MIT Press, 867–80.

Ohala, J. J. and M. Ohala. 1995. Speech perception and lexical representation: The role of vowel nasalization in Hindi and English. In B. Connell and A. Arvaniti (eds.), *Phonology and phonetic evidence*. Cambridge: Cambridge University Press, 41–60.

Oldfield, R. C. and A. Wingfield. 1965. Response latencies in naming objects. *Quarterly Journal of Experimental Psychology* 17: 273–81.

Oscar-Berman, M., E. B. Zurif and S. Blumstein. 1975. Effects of unilateral brain damage on the processing of speech sounds. *Brain and Language* 2: 345–55.

Osterhout, L. 1997. On the brain response to syntactic anomalies: Manipulations of word position and word class reveal individual differences. *Brain and Language* 59 (3): 494–522.

Ostrin, R. K. and L. K. Tyler. 1993. Automatic access to lexical semantics in aphasia – evidence from semantic and associative priming. *Brain and Language* 45 (2): 147–59.

Overall, J. E. 1962. The brief psychiatric rating scale. *Psychological Reports* 10 (3): 799–812.

Papçun, G. S., D. Krashen, R. Terbeek, R. Remington and R. Harshman. 1974. The left hemisphere is specialized for speech, language, and/or something else. *Journal of the Acoustical Society of America* 55: 319–27.

Perani, D., S. F. Cappa, T. Schnur, M. Tettamanti, S. Collina, M. M. Rosa and F. Fazio. 1999. The neural correlates of verb and noun processing – a PET study. *Brain* 122: 2337–44.

Peretz, I. and M. Coltheart. 2003. Modularity of music processing. *Nature Neuroscience* 6 (7): 688–91.

Peretz, I. and K. L. Hyde. 2003. What is specific to music processing? Insights from congenital amusia. *Trends in Cognitive Science* 7 (8): 362–7.

Perkell, J. S. and D. H. Klatt. 1986. *Invariance and variability in speech processes*. Hillsdale, NJ: Lawrence Erlbaum Associates.

Perruchet, P. and R. Peereman. 2004. The exploitation of distributional information in syllable processing. *Journal of Neurolinguistics* 17 (2–3): 97–119.

Pettigrew, C. M., B. E. Murdoch, H. J. Chenery and J. Kei. 2004. The relationship between the mismatch negativity and psycholinguistic models of spoken word processing. *Aphasiology* 18 (1): 3–28.

Phillips, C. 2001. Levels of representation in the electrophysiology of speech perception. *Cognitive Science* 25 (5): 711–31.

Pick, A. 1973. *Aphasia*, trans. and ed. Jason W. Brown. Springfield, IL: Thomas. (Original work published in 1931).

Piñango, M. M. and E. B. Zurif. 2001. Semantic operations in aphasic comprehension: Implications for the cortical organization of language. *Brain and Language* 79 (2): 297–308.

Piñango, M. M., E. Zurif and R. Jackendoff. 1999. Real time processing implications of enriched composition at the syntax–semantics interface. *Journal of Psycholinguistic Research* 28 (4): 395–414.

Pinker, S. 1994. *The language instinct*. London: Penguin.
    2000. *Words and rules: The ingredients of language*. London: Phoenix.

Pinker, S. and A. Prince. 1988. On language and connectionism – an analysis of a parallel-distributed model of language acquisition. *Cognition* 28 (1–2): 73–193.

    1994. The reality of linguistic rules: Regular and irregular morphology and the psychological status of rules of grammar. In S. D. Lima, R. L. Corrigan and G. K. Inversion (eds.), *The reality of linguistic rules*. Philadelphia: John Benjamins.

Pisoni, D. B. 1997. Word identification in noise. In F. Grosjean and H. Frauenfelder (eds.), *A guide to spoken word recognition paradigms*. Hove: Psychology Press, 681–7.

Plaut, D. C. and L. M. Gonnerman. 2000. Are non-semantic morphological effects incompatible with a distributed connectionist approach to lexical processing? *Language and Cognitive Processes* 15 (4–5): 445–85.

Plaut, D. C. and T. Shallice. 1993. Deep dyslexia: A case of connectionist neuropsychology. *Cognitive Neuropsychology* 10 (5): 337–500.

Poeppel, D. 1997. *The symbolic species: The co-evolution of language and the brain –* Deacon, T. *Nature* 388 (6644): 734.

    2001. Pure word deafness and bilateral processing of the speech code. *Cognitive Science* 25: 679–93.

Poeppel, D. and G. Hickok. 2004. Towards a functional anatomy of language. *Cognition* 92 (1–2): 1–12.

Polka, L. and O. S. Bohn. 1996. Cross-language comparison of vowel perception in English-learning and German-learning infants. *Journal of the Acoustical Society of America* 100 (1): 577–92.

Polka, L. and J. F. Werker. 1994. Developmental changes in perception of non-native vowel contrasts. *Journal of Experimental Psychology: Human Perception and Performance* 20 (2): 421–35.

Pollack, I. and D. A. Norman. 1964. A non-parametric analysis of recognition experiments. *Psychonomic Science* 1: 125–6.

Polster, M. R. and S. B. Rose. 1998. Disorders of auditory processing: Evidence for modularity in audition. *Cortex* 34 (1): 47–65.

Praamstra, P., P. Hagoort, B. Maassen and T. Crul. 1991. Word deafness and auditory cortical function. *Brain* 114: 1197–1225.

Prather, P. A., L. Shapiro, E. Zurif and D. Swinney. 1991. Real time examinations of lexical processing in aphasics. *Journal of Psycholinguistic Research* 20 (3): 271–81.

Prather, P. A., E. Zurif, T. Love and H. Brownell. 1997. Speed of lexical activation in non fluent Broca's aphasia and fluent Wernicke's aphasia. *Brain and Language* 59 (3): 391–411.

Prather, P., E. Zurif, C. Stern and T. J. Rosen. 1992. Slowed lexical access in non-fluent aphasia – a case study. *Brain and Language* 43 (2): 336–48.

Protopapas, A. 1999. Connectionist modeling of speech perception. *Psychological Bulletin* 125 (4): 410–36.

Pulvermüller, F. 2002. *The neuroscience of language: On brain circuits of words and serial order*. Cambridge and New York: Cambridge University Press.

Pustejovsky, J. 1995. *The generative lexicon*. Cambridge, MA: MIT Press.

Quillian, R. 1968. Semantic memory. In M. Minsky (ed.), *Semantic information processing*. Cambridge, MA: MIT Press, 227–70.

    1969. The teachable language comprehender: A simulation program and theory of language. *Communications of the ACM* 12 (8): 459–76.

Quintana, J., T. Wong, E. Ortiz-Portillo, S. R. Marder and J. C. Mazziotta. 2004. Anterior cingulate dysfunction during choice anticipation in schizophrenia. *Psychiatry Research Neuroimaging* 132 (2): 117–30.

Quirk, R., S. Greenbaum, G. Leech and J. Svartvik. 1985. *A comprehensive grammar of the English Language*. London: Longman.

Radford, A. 1997. *Syntax: A minimalist introduction*. Cambridge: Cambridge University Press.

Rauschecker, J. P. 1998. Cortical processing of complex sounds. *Current Opinion in Neurobiology* 8 (4): 516–21.

Rayner, K., G. Kambe and S. A. Duffy. 2000. The effect of clause wrap-up on eye movements during reading. *Quarterly Journal of Experimental Psychology* 53A: 1061–80.

Rayner, K., S. C. Sereno, R. K. Morris, A. R. Schmauder and C. J. Clifton. 1989. Eye-movements and on-line language comprehension processes. *Language and Cognitive Processes* 4: 21–49.

Richards, J. C. and J. Flamberg. 1993. Nurse Betty: The shooting script [screenplay]. New York: Newmarket Press.

Rizzolatti, G. and M. A. Arbib. 1998. Language within our grasp. *Trends in Neurosciences* 21 (5): 188–94.

Rizzolatti, G., L. Fadiga, V. Gallese and L. Fogassi. 1996. Premotor cortex and the recognition of motor actions. *Cognitive Brain Research* 3 (2): 131–41.

Rochester, S. R., J. R. Martin and S. Thurston. 1977. Thought process disorder in schizophrenia: The listener's task. *Brain and Language* 4 (1): 95–114.

Roelofs, A., A. S. Meyer and W. J. M. Levelt. 1998. A case for the lemma/lexeme distinction in models of speaking: Comment on Caramazza and Miozzo. *Cognition* 69 (2): 219–30.

Rose, P. 2002. *Forensic speaker identification*. U. K. and North America: Taylor and Francis.

Rosen, S. 2003. Auditory processing in dyslexia and specific language impairment: Is there a deficit? What is its nature? Does it explain anything? *Journal of Phonetics* 31: 509–27.

Rosenbek, J. C., M. R. McNeil and A. E. Aronson (eds.). 1984. *Apraxia of speech: Physiology, acoustics, linguistics, management*. San Diego, CA: College-Hill Press.

Rumelhart, D. E. and J. L. McClelland. 1981. Interactive processing through spreading activation. In A. M. Lesgold and C. A. Perfetti (eds.), *Interactive processes in reading*. Hillsdale, NJ: Erlbaum, 37–60.

    1986. On learning the past tenses of English verbs: Implicit rules or parallel distributed processing? In D. E. Rumelhart, J. L. McClelland and PDP Research Group (eds.), *Parallel distributed processing: Explorations in the microstructure of cognition*. Cambridge, MA: MIT Press, 216–71.

Sag, I. and J. Hankamer. 1984. Towards a theory of anaphoric processing. *Journal of Linguistics and Philosophy* 7 (3): 325–45.

Sampson, G. 1997. *Educating Eve: The 'language instinct' debate*. London: Cassell.

    1998. From grammar to science: New foundations for general linguistics. *Computational Linguistics* 24 (1): 173–6.

Sapir, E. 1933 [English translation 1947]. The psychological reality of phonemes. In D. G. Mandelbaum (ed.), *Selected writings of Edward Sapir in Language, Culture, and Personality*. Los Angeles: University of California (1949), 49–60.

Savage-Rumbaugh, E. S. and R. Levin. 1994. *Kanzi: The ape at the brink of the human mind*. New York: Wiley.

Savage-Rumbaugh, E. S., S. Shanker and T. J. Taylor. 1998. *Apes, language, and the human mind*. New York: Oxford University Press.

Schall, U., P. Johnston, J. Lagopoulos, M. Jüptner, W. Jentzen, R. Thienel, A. Dittmann-Balçar, S. Bender and P. B. Ward. 2003. Functional brain maps of Tower of London performance: A PET and fMRI study. *NeuroImage* 20: 1154–61.

Schank, R. 1975. *Conceptual information processing*. Amsterdam and New York: American Elsevier.

Schneider, K. 1957 [English translation 1974]. Primary and secondary symptoms in schizophrenia. In S. R. Hirsch and M. Shepherd (eds.), *Themes and variations in European psychiatry: An anthology*. Bristol: John Wright, 40–4.

Schnider, A., D. R. Benson, D. N. Alexander and A. Schnider-Claus. 1994. Non-verbal environmental sound recognition after unilateral hemispheric stroke. *Brain* 117: 281–7.

Schwartz, M. F., E. M. Saffran and O. S. M. Marin. 1980. The word order problem in agrammatism. 1. Comprehension. *Brain and Language* 10 (2): 249–62.

Seidenberg, M. S. and J. H. Hoeffner. 1998. Evaluating behavioral and neuroimaging data on past tense processing. *Language* 74 (1): 104–22.

Selkirk, E. O. 1984. *Phonology and syntax: The relation between sound and structure*. Cambridge: Cambridge University Press.

Seyal, M., B. Mull, N. Bhullar, T. Ahmad and B. Gage. 1999. Anticipation and execution of a simple reading task enhance corticospinal excitability. *Clinical Neurophysiology* 110: 424–9.

Shallice, T. 1982. Specific impairments of planning. *Philosophical transactions of the Royal Society of London, Series B – Biological Sciences*. 298 (1089): 199–209.

Shankweiler, D., S. Crain, P. Gorrell and B. Tuller. 1987. Reception of language in Broca's aphasia. *Language and Cognitive Processes* 4: 1–33.

Shattuck-Hufnagel, S., M. Ostendorf and K. Ross. 1994. Stress shift and early accent placement in lexical items in American English. *Journal of Phonetics* 22 (4): 357–88.

Shattuck-Hufnagel, S. and A. E. Turk. 1996. A prosody tutorial for investigators of auditory sentence processing. *Journal of Psycholinguistic Research* 25 (2): 193–247.

Shelton, J. R. and R. C. Martin. 1992. How semantic is automatic semantic priming? *Journal of Experimental Psychology: Learning, Memory, and Cognition* 18 (6): 1191–1210.

Shindo, M., K. Kaga and Y. Tanaka. 1991. Speech discrimination and lip reading in patients with word deafness or auditory agnosia. *Brain and Language* 40: 153–61.

Smith, L. and M. Gasser. 2005. The development of embodied cognition: Six lessons from babies. *Artificial Life* 11 (1–2): 13–29.

Smith, N. V. 1989. *The twitter machine: Reflections on language*. Oxford: Blackwell. 2004. *Chomsky: Ideas and ideals*. Cambridge: Cambridge University Press.

Smith, N. V., Tsimpli, I. M. and Ouhalla, J. 1993. Learning the impossible: The acquisition of possible and impossible languages by a polyglot savant. *Lingua* 91: 279–347.

Smith, S., P. Macaruso, D. Shankweiler and S. Crain. 1989. Syntactic comprehension in young poor readers. *Applied Psycholinguistics* 10: 429–54.

Sonnenstuhl, I., S. Eisenbeiss and H. Clahsen. 1999. Morphological priming in the German lexicon. *Cognition* 72: 203–36.

Spencer, H. 1977 [1876]. *The comparative psychology of man / Herbert Spencer. Last words on evolution / Ernst Haeckel. Contributions to the study of the behavior of lower organisms / Herbert S. Jennings; edited and with prefaces by Daniel N. Robinson.* Washington, DC: University Publications of America.

Spreen, O., A. L. Benton and R. W. Fincham. 1965. Auditory agnosia without aphasia. *Archives of Neurology* 13: 84–92.

Stanners, R., J. Neiser, W. Hernon and R. Hall. 1979. Memory representation for morphologically related words. *Journal of Verbal Learning and Verbal Behavior* 18: 399–412.

Steedman, M. J. 1990. Syntax and intonation structure in combinatory grammar. In G. T. M. Altman (ed.), *Cognitive models of speech processing: Psycholinguistic and computational perspectives.* Cambridge, MA: MIT Press.

Stephens, J. D. W. and L. L. Holt. 2003. Preceding phonetic context affects perception of non-speech. *The Journal of the Acoustical Society of America* 114 (6): 3036–9.

Stern, C., P. A. Prather, D. A. Swinney and E. B. Zurif. 1991. The time course of automatic lexical access and aging. *Brain and Language* 40: 359–72.

Stevens, K. N. 1972. The quantal nature of speech: Evidence from articulatory-acoustic data. In E. E. David Jr and P. B. Denes (eds.) *Human communication: A unified view.* New York: McGraw-Hill, 51–66.

1998. *Acoustic phonetics.* Cambridge, MA: MIT Press.

Stevens, K. N., A. M. Liberman, M. Studdert and S. E. G. Ohman. 1969. Cross language study of vowel perception. *Language and Speech* 12: 1–23.

Stewart, A. J., M. J. Pickering and A. J. Sanford. 2000. The time course of the influence of implicit causality information: Focussing versus integration accounts. *Journal of Memory and Language* 42: 423–43.

Stowe, L. A. 1986. Parsing wh-constructions: Evidence for on-line gap location. *Language and Cognitive Processes* 1: 227–45.

Streb, J., E. Hennighausen and F. Rosler. 2004. Different anaphoric expressions are investigated by event-related brain potentials. *Journal of Psycholinguistic Research* 33 (3): 175–201.

Studdert-Kennedy, M., D. Shankweiler and D. Pisoni. 1973. Auditory and phonetic processes in speech perception: Evidence from a dichotic study. *Cognitive Psychology* 3: 455–66.

Sturt, P. 2003. The time-course of the application of binding constraints in reference resolution. *Journal of Memory and Language* 48 (3): 542–62.

Sundara, M., A. K. Namasivayam and R. Chen. 2001. Observation-execution matching system for speech: A magnetic stimulation study. *Neuroreport* 12 (7): 1341–4.

Sussman, J. E. and V. J. Lauckner-Morano. 1995. Further tests of the 'perceptual magnet effect' in the perception of (i): Identification and change/no-change discrimination. *The Journal of the Acoustical Society of America* 97 (1): 539–52.

Suvisaari, J. M., J. Haukka, A. Tanskanen and J. K. Lonnqvist. 1998. Age at onset and outcome in schizophrenia are related to the degree of familial loading. *British Journal of Psychiatry* 173: 494–500.

Svartvik, J. and R. Quirk (eds.). 1980. *A corpus of English conversation.* Lund: Lund University Press.

Swaab, T., C. Brown and P. Hagoort. 1997. Spoken sentence comprehension in aphasia: Event-related potential evidence for a lexical integration deficit. *Journal of Cognitive Neuroscience* 9 (1): 39–66.

Swinney, D. A. 1979. Lexical access during sentence comprehension: (Re)consideration of context effects. *Journal of Verbal Learning and Verbal Behavior* 18: 645–59.

Swinney, D. and L. Osterhout. 1990. Inference generation during auditory language comprehension. In A. Graesser and G. Bower (eds.), *The psychology of learning and motivation*, vol. XXV. New York: Academic Press, 17–33.

Swinney, D. and E. Zurif. 1995. Syntactic processing in aphasia. *Brain and Language* 50: 225–39.

Swinney, D., E. Zurif and J. Nicol. 1989. The effects of focal brain damage on sentence processing: An examination of the neurological organization of a mental module. *Journal of Cognitive Neuroscience* 1: 25–37.

Swinney, D., E. Zurif, P. Prather and T. Love. 1996. Neurological distribution of processing resources underlying language comprehension. *Journal of Cognitive Neuroscience* 8 (2): 174–84.

Taft, M. 1981. Prefix stripping revisited. *Journal of Verbal Learning and Verbal Behavior* 20: 289–97.

Taft, M. and K. I. Forster. 1976. Lexical storage and retrieval of polymorphemic and polysyllabic words. *Journal of Verbal Learning and Verbal Behavior* 15: 607–20.

Tallal, P., S. L. Miller, G. Bedi, G. Byma, X. Q. Wang, S. S. Nagarajan, C. Schreiner, W. M. Jenkins and M. M. Merzenich. 1996. Language comprehension in language-learning impaired children improved with acoustically modified speech. *Science* 271 (5245): 81–4.

Tallal, P. and F. Newcombe. 1978. Impairment of auditory perception and language comprehension in dysphasia. *Brain and Language* 5: 13–24.

Tallal, P. and M. Piercy. 1973. Defects of non-verbal auditory perception in children with developmental aphasia. *Nature* 241 (5390): 468–9.

Turing, A. M. 1950. Computing machinery and intelligence. *Mind* 59 (236): 433–60.

Tyler, L. K., P. Bright, E. Dick, P. Tavares, L. Pilgrim, P. Fletcher, M. Greer and H. Moss. 2003. Do semantic categories activate distinct cortical regions? Evidence for a distributed neural semantic system. *Cognitive Neuropsychology* 20 (3–6): 541–59.

Tyler, L. K., P. Bright, P. Fletcher and E. A. Stamatakis. 2004. Neural processing of nouns and verbs: The role of inflectional morphology. *Neuropsychologia* 42 (4): 512–23.

Tyler, L. K., R. K. Ostrin, M. Cooke and H. E. Moss. 1995. Automatic access of lexical information in Broca's aphasics – against the automaticity hypothesis. *Brain and Language* 48 (2): 131–62.

Tyler, L. K., R. Russell, J. Fadili and H. E. Moss. 2001. The neural representation of nouns and verbs: PET studies. *Brain* 124: 1619–34.

Tyler, L. K., E. A. Stamatakis, P. Bright, K. Acres, S. Abdallah, J. Rodd and H. E. Moss. 2004. Processing objects at different levels of specificity. *Journal of Cognitive Neuroscience* 16 (3): 351–62.

Tyler, L. K., E. A. Stamatakis, E. Dick, P. Bright, P. Fletcher and H. Moss. 2003. Objects and their actions: Evidence for a neurally distributed semantic system. *Neuroimage* 18 (2): 542–57.

Ullman, M. T. 2001. A neurocognitive perspective on language: The declarative/procedural model. *Nature Reviews Neuroscience* 2 (10): 717–26.

Utman, J. A., S. E. Blumstein and K. Sullivan. 2001. Mapping from sound to meaning: Reduced lexical activation in Broca's aphasics. *Brain and Language* 79 (3): 444–72.

Vallar, G. and T. Shallice (eds). 1990. *Neuropsychological impairments of short term memory*. Cambridge: Cambridge University Press.

Van Essen, D. E. and H. A. Drury. 1997. Structural and functional analyses of human cerebral cortex using a surface-based atlas. *The Journal of Neuroscience* 17 (18): 7079–7102.

Varney, N. R. 1984. Phonemic imperception in aphasia. *Brain and Language* 21: 85–94.

Verspoor, K. 2005. Towards a semantic lexicon for biological language processing. *Comparative and Functional Genomics* 6 (1–2): 61–6.

Voss, S. H., T. G. Gunter, H. H. J. Kolk and G. Mulder. 2001. Working memory constraints on syntactic processing: An electro-physiological investigation. *Psychophysiology* 38: 41–63.

Warburton, E., R. J. S. Wise, C. J. Price, C. Weiller, U. Hadar, S. Ramsay and R. S. J. Frackowiak. 1996. Noun and verb retrieval by normal subjects studies with PET. *Brain* 119: 159–79.

Warrington, E. K. 1975. Selective impairment of semantic memory. *Quarterly Journal of Experimental Psychology* 27: 635–57.

Warrington, E. K. and R. McCarthy. 1983. Category specific access dysphasia. *Brain* 106: 859–78.

Warrington, E. K., P. McKenna and L. Orpwood. 1998. Single word comprehension: A concrete and abstract word synonym test. *Neuropsychological Rehabilitation* 8: 143–54.

Warrington, E. K. and T. Shallice. 1984. Category specific semantic impairments. *Brain* 107: 829–54.

Wassenaar, M., C. Brown and P. Hagoort. 2004. ERP effects of subject–verb agreement violations in patients with Broca's aphasia. *Journal of Cognitive Neuroscience* 16 (4): 553–76.

Waters, G. E. and D. Caplan. 2004. Verbal working memory and on-line syntactic processing: Evidence from self-paced listening. *The Quarterly Journal of Experimental Psychology* 57A (1): 129–63.

Watkins, K. E., A. P. Strafella and T. Paus. 2003. Seeing and hearing speech excites the motor system involved in speech production. *Neuropsychologia* 41 (8): 989–94.

Werker, J. F. and R. C. Tees. 1984. Phonemic and phonetic factors in adult cross language speech perception. *Journal of the Acoustical Society of America* 75 (6): 1866–78.

2005. Speech perception as a window for understanding plasticity and commitment in language systems of the brain. *Developmental Psychobiology* 46 (3): 233–51.

Werner, H. and B. Caplan. 1963. *Symbol formation: An organismic developmental approach to language and the expression of thought*. New York: John Wiley & Sons.

Wernicke, K. 1874 [reproduced in translation 1977]. The aphasia symptom complex: A psychological study on an anatomic basis. In G. E. Eggert (ed.), *Wernicke's works on aphasia: A sourcebook and review*. The Hague: Mouton.

Whitaker, H. A. 1971. *On the representation of language in the human brain: Problems in the neurology of language and the linguistic analysis of aphasia*. Alberta, Canada: Linguistic Research.

Wierzbicka, A. 2004. Conceptual primes in human languages and their analogues in animal communication and cognition. *Language Sciences* 26 (5): 413–41.

Willerman, R. and P. K. Kuhl. 1996. Cross-language speech perception: Swedish, English, and Spanish speakers' perception of front rounded vowels. *Proceedings of the International Congress on Spoken Language Processing ICSLP 96*, Philadelphia, PA.

Wills, C. 1993. *The runaway brain: The evolution of human uniqueness*. New York: Basic Books.

Wilson, B. A., N. Alderman, P. Burgess, H. Emslie and J. Evans. 1996. *Behavioural assessment of the dysexecutive syndrome*. Bury St Edmunds: Thames Valley Test Company.

Wilson, D. and D. Sperber. 2004. Relevance theory. In L. R. Horn and G. Ward (eds.), *The handbook of pragmatics*. Oxford: Blackwell, 607–32.

Wilson, S. M. and A. P. Saygin. 2004. Grammaticality judgment in aphasia: Deficits are not specific to syntactic structures, aphasic syndromes, or lesion sites. *Journal of Cognitive Neuroscience* 16 (2): 238–52.

Witelson, S. F., D. L. Kigar and T. Harvey. 1999. The exceptional brain of Albert Einstein. *Lancet* 353: 2149–53.

Wolf, F., E. Gibson and T. Desmet. 2004. Discourse coherence and pronoun resolution. *Language and Cognitive Processes* 19 (6): 665–75.

Wulfeck, B., E. Bates, L. Juarez, M. Opie, A. Friederici, B. MacWhinney and E. Zurif. 1989. Pragmatics in aphasia: Crosslinguistic evidence. *Language and Speech* 32: 315–36.

Wurm, L. H. and A. G. Samuel. 1997. Lexical inhibition and attentional allocation during speech perception: Evidence from phoneme monitoring. *Journal of Memory and Language* 36 (2): 165–87.

Xu, Y., A. M. Liberman and D. H. Whalen. 1997. On the immediacy of phonetic perception. *Psychological Science* 8 (5): 358–62.

Yngve, V. H. 1960. A model and an hypothesis for language structure. *Proceedings of the American Philosophical Society* 104: 444–66.

Zurif, E. B. and A. Caramazza. 1976. Psycholinguistic structures in aphasia: Studies in syntax and semantics. In H. Whitaker and H. A. Whitaker (eds.), *Studies in neuro-linguistics*, vol. I. New York: Academic Press.

Zurif, E. B., A. Caramazza and R. Myerson. 1972. Grammatical judgements of agrammatic aphasics. *Neuropsychologia* 10: 405–17.

Zurif, E. B., A. Caramazza, R. Myerson and J. Galvin. 1974. Semantic feature representations for normal and aphasic language. *Brain and Language* 1 (2): 167–87.

# Index